BIBLICAL, TALMUDIC, AND HASIDIC PORTRAITS AND LEGENDS

A TOUCHSTONE BOOK
PUBLISHED BY SIMON & SCHUSTER

NEW YORK · LONDON
TORONTO · SYDNEY
TOKYO · SINGAPORE

SAGES

AND

DREAMERS

ELIE WIESEL

TOUCHSTONE

Rockefeller Center
1230 Avenue of the Americas
New York, New York 10020

Copyright © 1991 by Elirion Associates, Inc.

All rights reserved
including the right of reproduction
in whole or in part in any form.
First Touchstone Edition 1993
TOUCHSTONE and colophon are registered
trademarks of Simon & Schuster Inc.
Designed by Edith Fowler
Manufactured in the United States of America

10 9 8 7 6 5 4 3

Library of Congress Cataloging-in-Publication
Data

Wiesel, Elie
  Sages and dreamers: Biblical, Talmudic, and
Hasidic portraits and legends / Elie Wiesel.
    p. cm.
   1. Bible. O.T.—Biography—Meditations.
2. Talmud—Biography—Meditations.
3. Hasidim—Biography—Meditations.
I. Title.
BS571.W548   1991
296'.092'2—dc20   91-26454
[B]   CIP

ISBN 0-671-74679-0
ISBN 0-671-79778-6 (pbk)

Acknowledgments

Most of these lectures were translated and all were edited by Marion Wiesel. Thanks go to my copy editor, Gerry Sachs. Special thanks to my editor and friend, Ileene Smith.

To the memory
of my mother, Sarah bat Hava-Devorah,
and my father, Shlomo ben Nissel,
whose passion for study
has sustained me to this day

Contents

Preface

THESE SAGES, these dreamers, who emerge from the incandescent light of the Bible, or heated Talmudic debates, or the joyful atmosphere of Hasidic celebrations—the more I study them, the more I love them.

I love them because they spring from ordinary life and remain profoundly human; that is, though endowed with spiritual authority, they are subject to all the flaws and weaknesses that characterize the human condition.

I love them because despite their grandeur, or thanks to it, they remain close to us everywhere and always. All we need is to call them up, and there they are. All we need is to hear a Talmudic interpretation of a Biblical verse, or to listen to a Hasidic tale, and we are surrounded by these fascinating men and women, who, seeking ancient wisdom and messianic dreams, guide us toward them through enchanted paths and obsessive melodies.

It was 1966 when I ventured, on four consecutive Thursdays in October and November at New York's most prestigious Jewish cultural center, the 92nd Street Y, to narrate the lives and destinies of these remote figures whom we think of as our Masters. Twenty-five years later, I have collected twenty-five texts, one for each of those years. Each is about a man or a woman whose inspired life story I found intriguing and demanding of investigation.

Why doesn't the name of God appear in the Book of Esther? For what reason is Ruth the Moabite overwhelmed with consideration and affection in the Talmud? How can we explain a sage like Rabbi Akiba crowning General Bar Kochba Messiah and savior of his people? Or the strange conduct of Rabbi Shimon bar Yohai's son, Rabbi Eleazar, who worked for the Romans? How can we understand a Hasidic rabbi's revolt such as the Izbitzer's against his teacher, the great Rabbi Mendel of Kotzk? Or the Grandfather of Shpole's animosity toward the celebrated Rabbi Nahman of Bratzlav? And—what can we learn from their legacy?

Again, I must stress the point that this is a collection of lectures, not essays. Lectures, by their nature, may include certain repetitions, abbreviations, and contradictions. For example, in the Talmudic section, stories about Rabbi Zeira, may in fact deal with at least three Masters, all named Zeira. The terms Academy and Sanhedrin have been used, at times, interchangeably to describe the same institution. As is often the case in the Talmud, some Masters respond to "colleagues" that lived years and years earlier.

Each of these figures stands for an epoch and its problems, conflicts, and aspirations which are often surprisingly close to our own, in this distant century. For those who care about exploring the memory of language, an introduction to these sages and dreamers of other days and another universe is a rich and enriching journey into the depths of religious history.

ELIE WIESEL
New York City
May 1991

(*Translated from the French by Stephen Becker*)

PART ONE

THE

BIBLE

From the wandering Maggidim of my childhood, I learned how to read and interpret a biblical text. Spellbound, I would listen as they juggled parables and quotations, verses and explanations, trying to extract a hidden meaning, a moral precept: a lesson. Then, after the war, in Paris, my strange teacher and master, Harav Shushani, guided me along the same path.

Noah

LET US BEGIN at the end—I mean, at what could have been the end, not of a story but of history itself. For if ever the apocalypse seemed irrevocable, if ever the universe came close to being silenced, it was then—right at the beginning. It was as though God were choosing to tell a strange tale—a tale in which the epilogue and the prologue almost touched, leaving nothing in between.

At this particular point in Scripture, Creation seems to have come to a standstill. God speaks of *Ketz kol bassar*: He mentions the end, the mystical end. The term He uses is neither *Sof* nor *Siyum* (which also mean the end), but *Ketz*: a brutal termination, a breakdown of all systems—the closing of a spectacle that has barely opened . . . to poor notices, one might say.

Thus we enter the story with unmitigated fear: the fate of mankind is at stake. Its salvation hangs in the balance. God has invented all things, created all species, and all men, and now He is about to destroy them all, in one fell swoop.

Why? We know why. We are told why, point by point. It seems that Creation has broken away from its Creator. No wonder He was disappointed. It's understandable. He had hoped to produce something unique: a work of purity and ecstasy, a colossal project with grandiose possibilities. And then came the letdown. He had been mistaken, misled, deceived.

Deceived by His favorite and most privileged creature—betrayed by man, who appeared unworthy of His trust and kindness. Their relationship could have been so gratifying: it wasn't. Why? Because man, in his foolishness, his pettiness, his selfishness, perverted and destroyed it all.

God therefore decided, Better put an end to it right then and there. Curtain, please. The author is dissatisfied with the performance. He chooses to work on another draft. And start all over. From the beginning.

Hence the tone of disillusionment reverberating throughout the story—one of the saddest and most oppressive stories in Scripture. Everything in it is threatening, hostile, implacable. Destiny has been set in motion and will not be stopped by anything or anyone except God, who clearly has no intention of stopping it. Having himself issued the order, who else could interfere with its execution?

But what about repentance? What if men everywhere suddenly opened their eyes and their hearts and decided to mend their ways? Improbable? Inconceivable. The text says so. God decided to annihilate the earth because it was beyond redemption. Its corruption was total. All men were sinners. Noah was the exception, just as Abraham would be in Sodom. Noah's world was like Sodom, only larger than a city, larger than a nation: imagine Sodom conquering the entire world, and you might conceive of society in the time of Noah. But Sodom was punished by fire, and Noah's world was punished by water.

Society was rotten, man was heinous, and life polluted, all auguring the end of the world, and there was nothing man could do about it: God had willed it that way and God's will would prevail.

Hence the peculiarly disquieting tone of the narration: it is that of a prophecy that will come to pass—at any cost, at any price. The city of Nineveh would be saved, Noah's world would not. Jonah's horror vision would remain hallucination; not so Noah's: *his* was about to turn into reality.

Read the story and you will be struck by its concrete aspects: dates, figures, measurements. One might take it for a technical report. The size of the ark, the duration of the floods, the ethnic and social composition of the survivors, their alternating moods from despair to hope, what they eat, what they think. The text is about a total event, and therefore encompasses heaven and earth in their entirety.

That is why we read the episode with the strange sensation of witnessing not the past but the future—a future as irrevocable as life. And death.

But we must ask the obvious question: Why? Why this collective punishment? Why this nearly total extinction of the human race and all species? Why those floods that swept into the abyss all that countless men and women had conceived and achieved, feared and worshiped, built and rebuilt in many lands and throughout many generations? The text offers no answer, at least none that is satisfying. All we are told is that mankind has sinned. But we are not made privy to the nature of the crime. What laws has mankind transgressed? Where? When? We do not know. We are not supposed to know. Why not? After all, if punishment is meant to fit the crime, we would like to know what crime could have caused such punishment. Shouldn't we be told, if only to prevent other catastrophes? We are informed of Cain's crime and Pharaoh's sins. But the society that saw Noah's birth and growth, what was it guilty of? Generally speaking, can an entire generation be found guilty? Can an entire generation be judged and condemned collectively? Should we not at least know why?

As I reread the story of Noah and his children, I see myself as a child in a Heder, leaning over a tattered Bible. Under the watchful eye of the teacher, I see myself and the world before . . . before the other deluge, the one my generation had to endure.

I read and reread the story of Noah and experience a joy and an anguish which are not just my own: we have repeated certain sentences so often in four thousand years that they have become immortal.

That is the profound beauty of Scripture: its characters are not mythical; their adventures are not imaginary; they vibrate with life and truth, and thus compel those of us who approach them to enter their lives and search for their meaning.

Noah—a Just Man: *The* "Just Man of his generation," or rather, "of his generations!" That is what we are told to believe, and we are happy to do so. But, as we shall see later, it is not always easy. When we analyze the man, when we observe him from different angles, he seems less appealing.

The same is true of every other protagonist in this story. As they appear before us in the text and its various commentaries, some enchanting and others disturbing, we are confronted by their duality, their ambiguity.

We shall see that the good may be less good than we—or they—think they are; and that the wicked may very well not be as bad as all that. Read and reread the sources and you shall marvel at their depth; you shall see that underneath each face there is another face, that beneath each story there is another story.

•

In the beginning, Noah is good, if not the best. His appearance on stage is greeted with applause. His name means consolation and promise. It is in the text. At the age of one hundred eighty-two, Lamech has a son whom he calls Noah "who will console us for our deeds and for the sadness in our work." Brave Lamech: he knew Hebrew well enough to make the connection between Noah and *nehama* (consolation). Melancholy Lamech: he is sad because he dislikes work. All his contemporaries are sad. Why? Possibly because of their ancestors Adam and Eve who had provoked God to curse the earth. But then, why should their descendants suffer on their account? They shouldn't, but they do. And that is why they are all depressed. Said Lamech: My son is the answer to that curse and to our sadness; he will change things; he will reconcile man with his work.

Were his task only a question of man's melancholy, Noah might have known what to do. But it wasn't. Scripture reveals with painful and striking clarity that, at that time, man's personal predicament but reflected God's cosmic sadness.

For by then men and women had multiplied; they had borne many children who must have been rather special, for sons of God fell in love with their daughters and married them. And so, in view of this mésalliance (or call it intermarriage), God, the heavenly Father of both the grooms and the brides, realized that He had made a mistake. He should not have created the world, and above all he should not have entrusted its fate to a creature as erratic as man. And so, with inscrutable divine logic He determines that drastic measures must be taken to correct the mistake: He will erase everything. All that lives will cease to live. Human beings and birds and animals and plants and flowers all must disappear. God in His disappointment and sadness leans toward radical solutions.

And then, abruptly, the story takes a sharp turn: without the slightest transition or preparation we are told that the Almighty's mood has changed: *"Ve-Noah matza khen beeinei adoshem*—And Noah found grace in the eyes of God . . ." In the previous episode, in the previous sentence, God regrets having yielded to His own illusions, He regrets having been naive with regard to all men, and suddenly He summons Noah and puts him center stage. Where was Noah until then? What had he done? What was so exceptional about him that he instantly became God's chosen? From that moment on, mankind was split in two: on the one side, despicable human beings, on the other—one man: Noah, God's comfort and joy. The text says so explicitly: *"Ele toldot Noah—Noah ish Tzaddik haya bedorotav,"* which means, "Here is the story of Noah, who was, throughout his lifetime, untouched by evil, and a just man." He is destined to come to mankind's rescue. Noah, son of Lamech, grandson of Methuselah. Noah, father of Shem, Ham, and Japheth. Noah, God's witness and spokesman. Noah—a unique human being who has witnessed a unique event, an event unequaled in the annals of human justice and inhuman punishment.

God takes him into His confidence. I have endured enough, He says. I have been patient enough, charitable enough. People are wicked and I intend to punish them. I am telling you all this so as to give you time to prepare. Build yourself an ark. Quickly. Do not waste time. Start now.

And Noah obeys. He follows the divine instructions to the letter. Whatever God wants him to do and say, he says and does. Faithful to his mission, he fulfills it to the end. Thanks to him, mankind will survive—it will survive through him. The world will drown, but Noah will have saved it nevertheless. The floods will come and go, and thanks to Noah, mankind will begin to live again: to work, to hope, to sin, to repent.

That is the subject of the story.

It reads like a play: We watch Noah make his preparations, we witness his drama, his tragedy, we see the consequences, the fallout. Step by step we follow the events from beginning to end. In fact, we follow Noah right into his ark—otherwise we wouldn't be here to tell the tale.

The setting: all the continents under the sun. The whole universe. All creation is implicated. The cast: all things and creatures in existence. And they are all about to vanish.

The cast of characters is indeed glorious—with Noah getting star billing. He is involved in every act, he dominates every scene. And what about God? God is his ally and protector. God: the supreme stage director who manipulates events and words. He decides when to raise the curtain and when to bring it down. Whatever is done must bear witness to His power and to His anger.

At first glance, the logic of the situation seems irrefutable: society is evil, hence it is doomed, Noah is not, and therefore he will be saved. As for God, He is just—He means no harm to his creatures. Quite the contrary: He wishes to help them acquire a sense of justice. How is He to rule over the universe without chastising the wicked and rewarding the good? Thus everything is simple, much like a fairy tale. Noah is all that others are not—therefore his fate must be different, better than theirs. They will die, he will live. Let it be known that good deeds bring life, and that bad deeds provoke death. Clear? Yes . . . and no. Yes in Scripture, no in its commentaries. The Talmudic interpretation of Noah's story is far more complex.

Let us look at it again. One fact seems to have been taken for granted—namely, that all men were indeed wicked and therefore deserved death. But what were they actually accused of? Lamech speaks of sadness, God of corruption. Corruption: the key word in the story—or rather, in the preparation of the story: corruption of the flesh, of the senses, of the population, corruption of the land, of the values. Corruption begets *khamass:* theft, violence, hatred—total disdain for one's fellow man. The Talmud explains: In Noah's times, people indulged themselves in every possible way, concerned only with a desire to satisfy their vilest instincts. Wealth, sexual promiscuity, and idolatry were their three principal preoccupations.

But—today we may ask, So what? Is our own society any less decadent? Can anyone convince us today that Noah's fellow men were more dominated by sex than our own? Does anyone believe that people today are less interested in money than they were in Noah's time? Or that success today commands less respect and awe than the idols of long ago?

If only the Biblical sources had been more precise in their accusations and cited individual cases to prove their point. Who did what to whom? We are not given one name, one crime, one victim: since when do we allow statistics to prevail in matters of jurisprudence? Surely, there were—there must have been—wicked people around, some more wicked than others—which means that there must have been some who were *less* wicked!

The text emphasizes people's human frailties and failures in the context of social relations. God did not resent their lack of religious faith so much as their lack of respect for one another. They were guilty of cheating, of stealing, of insulting one another—they were guilty of offending, shaming, and victimizing their fellow men. But that implies that there were both victimizers and victims. Were the victims as guilty as the victimizers? If not, why were they punished? Or, at least, why did they receive the same punishment? Granted, the world was unjust. Was God un-just as well?

On the other hand, what if Noah's contemporaries were in fact less evil than they appear in the story? Remember Rashi's commentary: *"Noah ish tzaddik haya bedorotav*—and Noah was the Just Man of his generation"—or generations—meaning, perhaps, had he lived in other times, he might not have received that title. Take Shmuel and Jephthah—both were leaders, moral leaders, as measured against their contemporaries. Yet, in Shmuel's time, Jephthah would not have attained moral leadership. Rashi offers another interpretation: "Had Noah lived in better times, in a healthier society, he would have been even greater." Whether you accept the first hypothesis or the second, one thing is clear: Noah may have been great or not so great—but his contemporaries were small; and Noah was lucky to be compared to them. But then, still another question arises: If he was not so much better than they, why was he spared? And exalted?

Since he is constantly in the limelight, let us scrutinize him further. Who is Noah? In the Biblical narrative, he appears to be pious and faithful. He submits to God's will but takes no initiative. Whatever God wants him to do, he does—but nothing more. And what if God had not chosen to talk to him? And what if God had chosen to talk to someone else? Could the others not have said to God, Listen, Master of the Universe, you are unfair; if you wanted us to behave differently, why didn't you tell us? In person, not through an emissary? Noah was obedient, of course he was. Who wouldn't be under the circumstances?

In Talmudic literature, the character of Noah is treated cau-tiously. The assessments show more nuances. Many legends are told about him—and many judgments are offered. It is clear that our sages and storytellers were intrigued by the man. Was he worthy of his destiny? The first impulsive answer is probably yes, Noah was kind and just and did indeed deserve fame, glory, and praise, not only because of what he himself must have achieved but also because of what was done to him and because of *him*. In other words: By his very existence he made a difference. During the ten generations separating Adam and Noah, Creation had become chaos. As a result of Adam's sin, animals and beasts had begun to rebel. Man was no longer their sovereign. Once he had fallen from grace, he no longer had any power over his surroundings. He recaptured it only with the advent of Noah: birds and beasts "calmed down" thanks to him whose name means "calm." Because of who he was, or what he was, they once again accepted man as their superior and master.

Legend has it that also thanks to Noah, nature recovered its regular cycle, which it had lost in the aftermath of Adam's disgrace. Before Noah, people would plant one thing and harvest another: there was no longer a relation between man's effort and its fruit. Another symptom of the universal breakdown of that time: human beings were born old—they came into the world at the age of fifty or sixty, and knew nothing of the innocence or pleasures of childhood. Whose fault was that? Adam's. And Eve's. Then, ten generations later, there were once again children and adolescents to be seen in the world. Whose doing was that? Noah's.

Noah was not only just, he was also practical. Who invented working tools? Noah. Who invented the plow? Noah. Benefactor of the working class, Noah also defended the interests of the peasant and the seaman. In short: Noah was the supreme friend of man and mankind. So much so that magicians and sorcerers feared him, according to the Midrash. When he was born, his father, Lamech, went to his father, the old Methuselah, to tell him the good news of his birth. You see, Lamech was still young: only a hundred eighty-two years old. Said Methuselah, "My son, do not name your child Noah, for the wicked ones will kill him." "What shall I call him?" asked the young father. "Call him Menahem (the comforter)," said Methuselah.

From this episode we learn several things. One: in those days parents already loved to offer unsolicited advice. Two: in those days children already could live without it. Three: nothing has changed.

The Midrash, with its flights of fancy, adds more details in praise of Noah: he was born circumcised. Precocious, intelligent, brilliant, he understood the tongues of all men and all creatures; he even understood sign language. He began to study. What? Medicine. He wrote his dissertation on medicine. But there, the truth must be told, he did get himself professional help: the angel Raphael, the same who would lend him his book on shipbuilding when Noah had to start thinking of making an ark for himself and his family. Perhaps that is why Noah stayed modest, humble, and simple. The Midrash insists on the fact that he himself took care of his father, Lamech, and his grandfather, Methuselah: instead of setting them up in an old-age home, he kept them in his own house.

A saintly man, he is ranked in the Talmud alongside Adam and Abraham. For what he achieved? No: for what he endured. Chosen to be an instrument of history, he was shaped by its omnipotent author, who engineered the scheme from beginning to end. Poor Noah: he was in fact the object of his own story rather than its subject. But then why did God choose him for this role? Because he must have been in some way different from his fellow men. Perhaps he did have qualities that God knew—that God alone knew.

At this point you may have guessed it; if not, it is time to say aloud what has only been whispered in the Talmud: Noah did not obtain the unanimous acclaim of our sages. There are those who reproach him for his lack of confidence and faith. Noah, who was the only one to show faith in God's warnings, was nevertheless later accused of complacency! One commentator maintains that Noah did not take God's words seriously. That he did not believe in the flood. The Talmud tells us: Noah went on living as before, even after the rains came; he waited for the waters to reach his ankles before he tore himself away from his home and boarded the ark. Rabbi Hanina son of Pappa may be exaggerating, but this is his version. Noah, he said flatly, did not deserve to be saved; but without him, there would have been no Moses—and God wanted Moses. So—had it not been for Moses, Noah would have been . . . a nobody.

Other commentators are angry with Noah for not having been angry enough with heaven. They accuse him of having been too obedient, too submissive, and even too selfish.

Look at the difference, says one Talmudic sage. When God intends to annihilate his people and says to Moses not to worry for He will give him another people—larger in numbers, more powerful, wealthier than the first—Moses answers: I do not wish to lead another people. I demand that You allow this Jewish people to live! *"Vayehal* Moshe," says Scripture: Moses, in fear, began to pray, to implore heaven to annul the decree. . . . Did Noah do the same? Did he ever argue with God as Abraham did? Did he ever implore Him to show mercy? Did he ever utter a single word of protest—or prayer? Did he ever try to intercede with God on behalf of the countless human beings who were already doomed but didn't know it? As soon as he learned that he himself was not in danger, he stopped asking questions, he stopped worrying altogether. Before, during, and after the catastrophe, he seems to have been at peace with himself and with God—to the point that God had to scold him and remind him of his obligations to humanity. It was God who had to incite him to respond with anger.

Let us reread a Midrashic text: When Noah finally left the ark and realized the scope and the magnitude of the universal desolation all around him, he turned toward God and asked: Master of the Universe, we call you *Rakhoum,* the merciful one, the charitable one, the compassionate one—where is Thy mercy, Thy charity, where is Thy compassion? And God put him right back in his place: You are nothing but a mindless shepherd, said the Almighty. *Now* you are asking me these questions? When it is too late—when it is over? Why didn't you speak up before? Really, Noah, when I told you to your face, *"Ki othkha raiti tzaddik lefanai,* that I considered you a Tzaddik, a Just Man," why did you think I said that? I said it for one reason only: to move you to become aware of your mission, to force you to intercede on behalf of mankind. Why else would I have called you Tzaddik? I wanted you to assume the mantle of moral leadership and speak up for my intended victims. But you kept quiet. From the moment you heard me reassuring you that you would be saved, you said nothing. You were satisfied, complacent. You chose to become my accomplice rather than humanity's friend—and only now do you begin to speak?

But another question arises. If Noah was indeed such as the Talmud viewed him, and God viewed him, why was he called Tzaddik? A man without compassion, warmth, generosity, imagination, a man without the slightest sense of involvement with society, let alone history, one who thinks only of himself, of his own pleasure and safety—what made our tradition treat him as a Tzaddik? Because he was better than most people? Why didn't he try to save them from certain death?

At the same time, let us be fair. He did change—afterward. Having witnessed destruction, he grew sensitive to its significance and had the courage to address questions to God, however belatedly. Even though he had not been a Just Man previously, he acted as one later. He was transformed by the experience of the flood. Suddenly he was no longer the same person, the same character. This true metamorphosis is illustrated in Talmudic literature as follows: Before the catastrophe he was a good son, but nothing is said of his being a good father: it's as though he thought that children were out of place in man's wicked and corrupt society. Later, he turns into a good father. He also reaches out to his neighbors. He becomes Ish adama, a landowner and a laborer, a person seeking to develop himself by working with his fellow human beings, a survivor trying desperately to rebuild a kingdom on the ruins of an adventure that had ended in blood and death.

As far as Noah is concerned, all is well that ends well—right? Wrong. The image we just gave of him—as a kind of repentant Tzaddik—is, unfortunately, misleading.

It is with sadness that we note what happens to Noah later in his life. The text reveals that on his long journey Noah loses two of his adjectives. In the beginning, before the flood, he is called "Ish Tzaddik Vetamim": he is a thorough man, just and unblemished. Later, when God speaks of him, He deprives him first of the title "Tamim" and then of the title "Tzaddik": he has taken away both titles. What remains? The name Noah, which means a quiet person who has no worries, no bad dreams, no ill feelings— perhaps not even bad memories. Noah means Noah labriot, a sociable person. Someone who gets along with people—something a Just Man rarely does.

Study the sequence of events following the Flood and you will have a clearer picture of Noah the man. What is the first thing he does after he leaves the ark? He builds an altar and offers a sacrifice to God. It's right, it's normal, it's the proper thing to do: after all, he owes God his survival—he owes Him everything.

(May I offer a personal memory? April 11, 1945: Buchenwald. Hungry, emaciated, sick and weakened by fear and terror, Jewish inmates welcome their sudden freedom in a strange manner: they do not grab the food offered by their American liberators. Instead, they gather in circles and daven: their first act as free human beings was to say Kaddish, thus glorifying and sanctifying God's name.)

But then, what does Noah do next? He listens to God, who promises him, Never again. Never again will He punish mankind that way. God concludes a covenant with Noah and gives him a solemn pledge that there will be no other flood—ever. And then? Then God suddenly begins to lecture him on the importance of life: God is celebrating life and condemning murder and suicide as never before. How absurd, or at least paradoxical: God has just condemned mankind to death, and now, almost in the same breath, He raises His voice in praise of life. How could He? At that point Noah, at last, does something touching—something unrelated to history or God, something purely personal, futile, foolish, but pleasant and voluptuous: he plants a vineyard. Not an apple tree nor a cherry tree—a vineyard. The Midrash comments: Everything occurred during the same day: the act of planting, of drinking, and of falling into debauchery. Biblical time being accelerated, Noah did everything fast. In one day he went through phases that would normally last seasons and years. Having sought an offering to God, he got drunk, fell asleep, and crawled into his tent, only to be discovered by his son Ham in his nakedness. . . . Is this characteristic of a Tzaddik? To renew history by getting drunk? Most Talmudic interpreters have judged this incident severely.

A story: On that memorable day, Satan saw Noah as he was planting his vineyard. "Would you take me as your associate?" he asked. "Yes," said Noah. "Gladly." So, using his newly acquired privileges, Satan brought a lamb, a lion, a pig, and a monkey, and buried them all under the vineyard. And so their blood mixed with wine. That is why, if you drink one glass you become sweet as a lamb; drink two and you will be strong as a lion; three, ridiculous as a monkey; four, disgusting as a pig.

Is this our hero and savior Noah? The business partner and ally of Satan? Just imagine: he had lived through a cosmic drama without equal, he had survived a catastrophe that cost the lives of practically the entire population—and all he could think of doing was to establish a wine crop, and get drunk to boot. Had the event left no mark on him, no impact on his sensibility? Had he not learned anything from it? Is it conceivable that the annihilation of mankind as a whole could find its climax in the grotesque spectacle of a drunken father humiliated by his sons?

To raise the question in a more brutal form: If Noah was not a Just Man before the Deluge, is it possible that he did not become one even afterward? Had he not repented? Had he not tried to understand what had happened to him—and to all the others?

Disappointing, Noah. As a character, he leaves much to be desired. He never acts, he only reacts. He never aspires to grandeur; he is mired in routine. To paraphrase Jean-Paul Sartre, he took great events and reduced them to small circumstances.

But then—why the uniqueness, why the title Tzaddik given to him in Scripture?

Well, there is one period in his life we have yet to explore: his activities *during* the Flood.

Tenacious, obstinate, stubborn, Noah and his sons were alone as they worked on the ark—alone against those in power, alone against power. Mocked by people, they nevertheless continued their work. Perhaps that was the major sin of his contemporaries: they humiliated Noah by laughing at him. That they were skeptics was their business; still, they had no right to ridicule him, especially in public. For the Midrash insists on the fact that Noah worked on his project in public—in order to attract attention—and to incite all neighbors and passersby to repent. The preparations lasted fifty years, according to one Talmudic source, to give the sinners plenty of time to mend their ways. Fifty years of mockery—that's a long time. To be the victim of a "moral majority," to be attacked and vilified day after day by complacent people who think they know everything, well, that's not easy. Did Noah respond? Did he show anger? Bitterness? Regret perhaps? No: he kept quiet. He made neither speeches nor demands, presented no excuses, and claimed no special privileges. All he wanted was to serve as a living example. It was enough to see him to know he had heard God's warnings, as others must have; only he decided to act. What was special about him was that he turned awareness into action.

And so, as the threat grew more serious, Noah obeyed the heavenly instructions scrupulously: the ark was ready, the skies were cloudy and dark. When would the tragedy begin? Soon. Who shall live, and who shall die? The decision was not Noah's but God's. The images are striking: all those animals and beasts and birds arriving in twos and going aboard. We see them, we hear them, we follow them: they are alive and pathetic; we feel sorry for them for becoming uprooted; we envy them for embarking on a great adventure.

An amusing anecdote from the Midrash: As the various animals marched past Noah, he suddenly noticed a weird creature, all alone. "Who are you?" he asked. "I am Falsehood," came the answer. "You came alone? Sorry," said Noah. "Singles are not admitted aboard." So Falsehood desperately tried to find a mate and finally succeeded. Another strange solitary animal named Shlimazel, or mishap, was also looking for a mate. Together they formed an ideal couple: for whatever one got through falsehood would be lost through mishap.

Anyway, Noah and his family take care of them, as they do of all their passengers. The Talmud insists on that, too: during forty days and forty nights, Noah and his children attended the wild beasts and the other animals, bringing them food and calming their anxiety. The description of the Deluge is pure literature: the rains, the rains that come relentlessly; the waves, the tempest, the darkness, the thunder—above all, the uncertainty: when will it all end? Will it ever end? It is then that Noah is at his best. Those are his finest hours. Selfless, devoted, tireless, he is everywhere, looking after every living creature. He knows whom to feed when; some eat standing, others lying down, some have to be fed in the morning, others in the evening: Noah forgets no one. . . . Well, once he forgets the lion, who leaves him a reminder of his error: Noah is bitten on the leg and will limp till the end of his life. Except for this incident, the journey is flawless. Nothing goes wrong. Noah, as captain of the ship, knows his task and performs it with vigor. He never shows signs of panic, he never manifests doubts or anxiety: he heads his small floating kingdom and brings it to a safe harbor. God is on his side: this is not always pleasant but it certainly is useful. Noah's manager, God, tells him when to board the ark, when to open the windows, when to send scouts. The language is amazingly clear, the instructions precise: *Tze, Asse,* do this, say that, count the days, count the hours. The Talmud, incidentally, criticizes Noah for having obeyed the divine orders too closely. God told Noah to leave the ark and Noah left. Rabbi Yehuda son of Rabbi Ilai commented: If I had been there, in his place, I would have been less patient, less docile; as soon as I saw the waters recede and the land dry, I would have broken the ark and jumped ashore! Not Noah. . . . A shadow of God's shadow, he follows God, and only God. With regard to other beings, he has changed; he has improved; he has become involved in their affairs, in their needs, in their lives. With regard to their common Creator, he has remained the same as before. If Noah had altered his relations with God, he would have lost his balance. Had he wept once—only once—he could not have stopped. Ever.

Yet something *did* happen to him at the end of the ordeal. Says the Zohar: Noah left the ark a different person, in a different state of mind; he was confused.

That's only natural. Imagine what he must have felt as he walked ashore and discovered the empty, devastated land. He must have looked for familiar ground, vantage points, cities of light and life, dwelling places and their sounds. He knew that they had vanished; still, he went on looking for them.

Then he was confronted by a choice: anger or gratitude. He chose gratitude. He offered thanks to heaven. For having been spared? Yes. As a survivor, the first, he chose gratitude rather than bitterness: the special gratitude of the survivor. He or she knows that every moment means grace, for he or she could have been in another's place, another who is gone.

And yet, many survivors are haunted, if not plagued, by unjust guilt feelings at one time or another. At one point Noah must have wondered, "Why me?" Surely he did not think he was chosen because he was a better person? He couldn't have been so vain as to think that. Because he had a better position in society? Others had held higher positions. Noah must have asked himself this painful question, "Why me?" over and over. Granted, he had saved his wife and their children. But what about his relatives, his neighbors, his acquaintances? Dead, all dead. Only he and his immediate family are alive. Here is Noah, master of the world— why not? There is no one left to challenge his power. Master and ruler of contemporary society, he will charter its new future. *Ele toldot Noah?* The human story will start all over again with Noah, your ancestor and mine. No one ever had his possibilities, his power, his triumph; no one ever felt such anguish.

Thus, after the first gesture of gratitude, after his first offering, he needed . . . a glass of wine!

Especially since he must have had some premonitions about the future: what had happened once could surely happen again. True, God had pledged that no flood would ever again devastate the earth. But what about all the other means of destruction? Noah must have sensed that people never learned enough from their collective memories, that they remain human, therefore vulnerable. Hardly have they left the story of the Flood than they jump into another tale of horror. They promptly begin building a gigantic tower to allow them to ascend into heaven, dethrone its Master and take His place! Remember: while the Tower of Babel is being constructed, Noah is still alive. He sees and hears it all. And he knows how it will end. Does he warn his contemporaries not to repeat past mistakes? If so, no one listens. His words are lost.

Poor Noah.

A survivor of cosmic tragedy, he is haunted by his memories, he escapes into . . . drink and sleep. Is this his response to other people's suffering? Of course not. He maintains his good relations with God. He has faith in His word, in His promise. He is glad that from now on Creation and Creator are to be linked by promises rather than threats. God speaks to him, says the Midrash, meditates with him, through him. "You are sad? So am I. You think that I enjoy winning battles? When I win, I lose; when I lose, I win. Did I not lose when I won the argument with your generation? Did I not lose a world I myself created?"

No, God will not permit another disaster. He will not provoke, nor will He be provoked. Still, what has changed? Noah is anguished. He trusts God, but he knows people: what God will not do, they very well may. God will not destroy them, but they could destroy themselves. The covenant binds Him, not them. "I will not destroy the world," said God. In other words: I will not, but what about you?

Noah is sad. His son Ham is a source of disappointment to him. Shem is better; he studies Torah. Japheth is a student. In general at least some of his children are growing up well, moving in the right direction. Bound by seven Commandments, they respect them. At home things run more or less smoothly. But outside the home the picture is far from encouraging.

During the catastrophe, Noah was a protagonist; now he has become a witness. And now, more than before, I feel sorry for him. Was he in fact a Just Man? He was a human being who, having gone to the end of night, knew that he was condemned to be free; having reached the limits of despair, he felt himself duty-bound to justify hope. I imagine him under his tent, telling his children and grandchildren stories of his own youth when he was only a hundred years old. . . . He speaks of the past in order to shape the future. *Tzaddik bedorotav,* a Just Man of his generations (in the plural), means he wants future generations to justify his existential choice.

Is it an accident? The *Parsha* of Noah—the weekly portion of the Torah that we read on Shabbat—ends with Abraham arriving onstage: his story is also part of our memory. Noah makes you sad? Abraham will make you proud. Noah is quiet, Abraham is not. Noah knows nothing of Jewishness, Abraham *is* Judaism. What do they have in common? Both experienced collective tragedy. Was Sodom something of the past? Its destruction by fire suggests the future.

Lest we remember, lest we remember.

Jephthah
and His Daughter

THIS STORY is frightening. It is so frightening that I wish it could be erased from Scripture. Its brutality is almost unsurpassed. Imagine the Akedah, the binding of Isaac, with a different ending, a brutal ending, and you will have the story of Jephthah and his daughter, a story fraught with inescapable despair.

Jephthah—a judge of the people of Israel? What kind of judge agrees to kill his only daughter? What kind of example is this for our people? What moral message does he leave to future generations?

Jephthah: a tale of cruelty and remorse; a tale of solitude and malediction. Jephthah: a chapter that brings forth darkness and is buried in the past. It has been called an accident in Jewish history. An accident? Well, a misunderstanding, perhaps, in the sense that all tragedies contain some element of misunderstanding.

Let us read the text. "And Jephthah from Gilead was a brave, courageous warrior." That is how the Book of Judges marks his appearance in the story. He was the man of the hour—the man the children of Israel needed. The chapters preceding this quotation describe their plight. They suffered for many reasons and on every level. External threats were matched by internal decline. More than one enemy attacked their borders. At home, more than one leader abused his position for personal benefits. Their conflicts seem devoid of nobility, just as their goals seem lacking in majesty; they all take on the character of petty quarrels rather than spiritual contests. Deceit and corruption were the currency of those in power and those who craved it. Abimelech killed his seventy brothers for no reason. Then he killed a thousand men and women in the tower of Shechem. Then he conquered the fortress of Tevetz and made preparations to set it on fire when a woman threw a

sword at him. Mortally wounded, he summoned his arms bearer
and said: Take your sword and kill me for I do not want people to
say that I was slain by a woman. The next ruler was his cousin
Tola, son of Puah, who in turn was succeeded by Yair: both of
them must have been insignificant, for Scripture says nothing
about them. All we learn about Yair is that he had thirty sons who
rode on thirty donkeys.

"And the children of Israel continued to do evil in the eyes of
God; and they worshiped the idols of Baal and Astarte, and the
gods of Ammon and the gods of Pelishtim; and they had abandoned God instead of serving Him. In His anger, God handed
them over to the Pelishtim and the Ammonim who oppressed and
tormented them for eighteen years. And the children of Israel
shouted to God, We have sinned in abandoning you for the
idols. . . ."

This period must have been one of the lowest of Jewish history. No doubt, there were sound reasons for its decline. The fall
was inevitable. Moses and Joshua were epoch-makers; their successors had to suffer in comparison. Under Moses, the Jewish
people had found its national identity; under Joshua, it had conquered its homeland. Is it possible that it now felt spent?

The Book of Ruth opens with the line *"Vayehi biyemei shfot
hashoftim*—It came to pass that in the days when the judged were
judging . . ." The Midrash asks: Why the repetition of *shfot* and
shoftim? To show us their degradation. Woe to a generation that is
judging its judges; woe to a generation whose judges ought to be
judged. History itself seemed exhausted. And so an age of medi-
ocrity was ushered in. Petty-minded leaders took charge of the
nation's affairs—its politics, economy, and warfare—with total disregard for any possible metaphysical implications. Idols were constantly being built and destroyed, territories were being evacuated
or retaken, there were countless border incidents with hostile
neighbors, countless intrigues, scenes of envy and jealousy; one
gets an impression of collective delinquency. Could this be the
people chosen by God to formulate His law and bring it to other
nations? Was it all a natural consequence of the terrible and terrifying bloodshed that had occurred during the conquest of the
land? Was it a punishment for the many injustices inflicted upon
its inhabitants? Whatever the reasons, the outcome was depressing. Gone was the greatness that had marked the extraordinary
moment in history when the children of Israel had their glorious

encounter with God, gone were the days when they had committed themselves to remember Him and had transformed their memory into a covenant. Everything about them had become petty and cheap. Their ambitions, their desires, their dreams seemed to be to cheat one another, and even to cheat God, who, at times, lost patience. When that happened, they repented until—the next time. . . .

As for Jephthah—

In those days, the people were ruled by judges. Some were good, others less good. Deborah, the only woman to reach that position, was better than most, not only as judge but also as military commander, strategist, and poet: her poetry occupies a page of glory in Biblical literature. In general, judges were chosen not for their ethical virtues but for their political and military skills, like Gideon or Samson, for instance. Few of them were charismatic figures. They were there because they were needed; they were there only when they were needed. Unlike kings, priests, and prophets, they operated only in the present. They were not God's messengers to his people, nor were they the people's messenger to God. They were the people's spokesmen to other people.

What is Jephthah's place among them? Was he better than most? The Talmud pays him a compliment: *"Jephthah bedoro kishmuel bedoro.* Jephthah to his generation was like Samuel to his." Strange compliment. Was it intended to downgrade Jephthah's contemporaries? What could Jephthah have been to Samuel's generation?

Let us open the Talmud:

Said Rabbi Shmuel bar Nahmani in the name of Rabbi Yonathan: Three men made improper vows; only two were answered generously. The first man was Eliezer, Abraham's servant. When he was sent by his Master to find a bride for Isaac, Eliezer said, The girl who will offer water not to me alone but also to my camels, she will become Isaac's wife. Said the Talmud, How could he gamble with Isaac's life like that? And what if he had met a young woman who was charitable but physically an invalid? Still, God sent him Rebecca.

The second was King Saul, who said, He who would defeat Goliath would be given lots of money and the kings' daughter. What? wondered the Talmud. How could a king be so frivolous and light-hearted about his own daughter? And what if the heroic warrior had been a bastard or someone unfit for marriage? Still, God sent him David to defeat Goliath.

The third one was Jephthah. His vow, too, was improper— but, in his case, God refused to interfere.

The tragic theme of Jephthah and his daughter exists in other literary traditions as well. Ancient Greek legends tell us of a river named Lupis in the barren land of Heliartus. One of its governors came to Delphi and asked a priestess for guidance. Her advice: Go home and kill the first person you meet. He met his son Lupis and struck him with his sword. Mortally wounded, Lupis attempted to escape, and wherever his blood touched the soil, a well opened in the earth, and all the wells together formed a river; it was named after Lupis, the governor's unfortunate son.

A similar legend exists about the king of Crete, who, after the destruction of Troy, killed his son, or daughter, depending on which source you believe.

Cicero says that Agamemnon had pledged to the goddess Diana that he would sacrifice to her the most beautiful creature to be born in his kingdom that year. Since no one was more beautiful than his daughter Iphigenia, he felt compelled to sacrifice her. Yet, says Cicero, he could have refused to honor his vow rather than commit such a crime. Why didn't he refuse? The honor of the king was more important to him than the life of his daughter. Also, he was afraid of losing the war, and that would mean, according to Euripides,

> *The enemy army will close in a circle of blood;*
> *There will be heads forced back, throats cut;*
> *Streets stripped, every building gutted and clashed.*

Like a Greek tragedy, Jephthah's story too, moves inexorably toward death. The moment he articulated the oath, it was binding. Sealed. True, the tale has a happy ending of sorts: the enemy was beaten. But the victory left a bitter aftertaste—a taste of mourning.

Because of Jephthah. Who was he?

He was a judge in Israel. He fought for Israel. He saved Israel. His name ought to evoke relief and gratitude—yet it resonates in the darkest recesses of our religious imagination like a warning.

A judge is supposed to be compassionate as well as fair. A judge is supposed to hold high the value, the sanctity of human life. How could such a man commit murder?

When we pray, we speak to God, we appeal to Him to be not only our judge but also our father. But a father, normally, loves his children; a father forgives his children.

And, Jephthah was, after all, a father. How could a father slay his daughter? And what about the people around them, the leaders, the elders? Why didn't they intervene? Why didn't they step in to prevent the murder of an innocent girl? And God—why didn't He make His voice heard?

A strange, disquieting story it is. It involves jurisprudence and theology, history and strategy, sin and punishment. Though the event occurred approximately eleven hundred years before the Common Era, it still weighs on us. It conjures up anguish, not hope.

Let us read: "And the leaders of Gilead, and the people too, said to one another: Who is this man who could fight the children of Ammon? He shall be the head of all the inhabitants of Gilead." Who was that man? Jephthah. Did they know him? Yes, they did. Otherwise they would not have called upon him to become *the* national leader. And since they knew him, we know him too. In fact, his personal file is thick.

Some of the facts are not too flattering. His father, Gilead, had an affair with a woman of ill repute; Jephthah was their son. Gilead also had a wife with whom he had children. From the text it is clear that all the children, including Jephthah, lived in their father's house. Later, as they grew up, the legitimate children turned against Jephthah and chased him away. They said: "You shall not inherit from our father, for you were born unto another woman." And so Jephthah fled to a land called Tob and soon gathered around him a band of outlaws and mercenaries.

He must have married in the meantime, for suddenly we hear that he has a daughter—but no sooner do we hear the news than it is already too late. She has barely appeared on-stage when she is sentenced to die. And who is responsible for her death? Her father. And who carries out this terrible sentence? Her father.

On the surface, Jephthah is a simple man, not given to doubts, to hesitations. He does what he says, and what he says he does. Unhappy at home, he runs away and somehow manages to survive. Does the nation need a fighter? He fights and wins. Did he make a mistake when he uttered a silly vow? Never mind—he will keep it, even if it hurts.

Yet as we go on scrutinizing the text, we see that Jephthah is much more complex than he at first appears. He has acquired much knowledge through suffering.

His childhood must have been miserable. We can imagine how his brothers treated him, how they humiliated the illegitimate son in their midst. And where was his mother? Had he ever seen her? Had she ever come to visit him? And what about Gilead? Had he ever been a good father to Jephthah? We know the answer. Had he been a good father, would he have allowed his other children to mistreat Jephthah? Would he have sent him to live among strangers?

As for the community at large, we see that Jephthah was not well liked by its leaders. In fact, he says so unequivocally. When they come to him to solicit his help and leadership, he snaps back at them: Why me? You hated me, you helped my brothers throw me out of my father's house—and now, when you need me, you appear at my tent, just like that? The leaders of Gilead bow their heads. We come to you, they say, because we need you. Lead us into battle. Fight for us and you will rule over all the inhabitants of Gilead. Jephthah plays hard to get; he wants a clear agreement and he lays down specific rules: If I go into battle and win, I want to remain your leader, etc. They agree. Good, says Jephthah, let us announce the terms of our pact to the entire population gathered at Mizpeh—and they did.

At that point, Jephthah makes a move which strikes us as strange. The fighter turns diplomat. Instead of attacking the enemy, he dispatches emissaries to engage in peace negotiations. He argues that there are no real differences between them. Why do you want to attack my country? he asks the Ammonite king. And the king answers, When Israel left Egypt, it took my land from the Arnon river to the Yabok to the Jordan; give me back the territories and we will live in peace. Jephthah sends more emissaries to open another round of negotiations, insisting that Israel has taken no Ammonite land. Although it could have taken the entire land, it chose to bypass it. Jephthah's message was long and well documented. It showed his excellent education: he knew geography, history, and political science. If you had claims over Arnon, he said, why did you wait three hundred years? What made you remember your claim now? He instructed his messengers to speak

to the Ammonite king as follows: Please, Sire, I did nothing
against you, whereas you plan to do something bad to me by
forcing me to do battle; may God judge between the children of
Israel and the children of Ammon. But the Ammonite king refused to heed Jephthah's words.

And suddenly, the image of Jephthah as outlaw recedes. What
we see rather is a supreme politician. Better yet: a statesman. A
warrior who hates war. A fighter who prefers peace. How can one
not feel sympathy for him? Here is a victim of society, a victim of
his own family, who nevertheless agrees to save others from humiliation and death: how can one not admire him? God Himself
likes him. The text says so. "And God's spirit rested upon Jephthah" who left Mizpch-Gilead, his dwelling place, and crossed the
river Yabok to do battle with the Ammonite army. And he made
a vow to God: If you deliver the children of Ammon into my
hands, whoever will emerge from my house to greet me will be
yours, and I shall bring him as an offering to you.

Again—what does this passage tell us? That Jephthah was not
certain of the outcome. The strong man had doubts. The commander was unsure of himself. The man of violence who sought to
avoid violence, questioning its usefulness, now turned not to his
soldiers but to God. He wanted Him on his side. But   wait a
minute: why such uncertainty? Wasn't God's spirit resting on him?
Didn't he trust God? Clearly, this is not a simple case of prophecy
and warfare. Our hero is no less mysterious than his story.

Talmudic sages describe Jephthah as an ignorant man without spiritual substance or intellectual background. The Bible is
more lenient toward him. Read his two diplomatic messages to
the king of the Ammonites as recorded in the text: they are mas-
terpieces. They combine knowledge of history, geography, theology, and . . . humor. Not only does he offer the king a summary
of events that occurred three hundred years earlier, when Moses
led his people out of Egypt, but he proves—by quoting the Bible—
that Moses had occupied territories that belonged to Sihon, king
of the Amorites—and not those that were part of Ammon or
Moab. What he cleverly omits from his quote is a line or two
saying that part of the Amorite territories had been conquered
from Moab.

What belongs to whom? Since when? Who was there first?

All these points are handled masterfully by Jephthah in his
communiqués to the Ammonite king. First, he teaches him his-

tory, not only Jewish history but also Ammonite and Moabite history. He says: We have been here three hundred years—you only two hundred. Second, do you need territory? So do we. Do what we are doing: ask God to help you. He even mentions which god could help the Ammonites. His name is K'mosh. Ask your god K'mosh, he says, let him give you territory. But isn't the Ammonite god called Milkom, not K'mosh? K'mosh is the Moabite god. In other words, admit it, says Jephthah, this territory was never yours, it was Moab's. Are you the heirs to Moab? In that case let me teach you another chapter in history: Israel and Moab had their differences long ago. This is not the first time. When? Remember Balak son of Tzipor? What did he do? He did not fight. He had his prophet—Bileam—curse us. Why don't you do the same? In any event, we will not give you our territories—for they are ours.

(It reminds us of a Sholem Aleichem story: A woman came running to her neighbor demanding that she return the huge silver pot she had borrowed. What are you talking about? answered the neighbor. First of all, the pot is not silver but copper; second, it is not really huge, it's rather small. Third, I never borrowed it from you.)

Let us turn now, not without anxiety, to the second character in the cast: his daughter. His only daughter. The text places special emphasis on this fact: *Ein lo mimeno ben o bat*—Jephthah has no other son or daughter. Like Isaac, she was meant to become *ola*—a burnt offering.

We imagine her beautiful, kind, outgoing, enchanting, innocent: the apple of her father's eye. He has no one else in his life. His father had abandoned him, his brothers had rejected him. His wife? No mention is made of her. All our attention is focused on the daughter.

We do not know her name, but her presence is felt even before she is introduced in the text. The moment Jephthah makes his vow, we *know* that his daughter is near, only a few lines away.

From the moment she appears, she dominates the scene. A radiantly happy girl, we see her singing and dancing, joyfully greeting the returning warriors. And as you read on, you feel like warning her: No, little girl, don't, don't run to your father, go back home. But it is too late. Jephthah has already seen her. He cries out, he tears his clothes; the victor has been vanquished. Overwhelmed with pain, he puts the blame on her. He is unfair but he needs to blame somebody, and she is there. Why did she have to come to greet him? What was done could not be undone. He is crushed. You sense it from the text. And she? She is marvelous. At this moment, she is stronger than he. She understands the situation even though she does not know the whole story. He tells her of a vow he has made, but not the nature of the vow. Still, she understands. She sees him tearing his clothes, she sees his pain, his agony, and she knows: She is going to die.

Her response is superb. Dignified and courageous, she does not shed a tear. Nor does she argue. She accepts the situation. She goes as far as to reassure Jephthah. You cannot go back on your word, she tells him. With extraordinary understatement, she says: *"Yeasse li hadavar haze*—Let this thing be done unto me." She doesn't say, Keep your pledge, kill me. The notion of death does not figure in her answer. It is replaced by "thing." Is she afraid of the word "death"? I choose to think that she avoids it so as not to upset her father even more. Her one request: "Give me two months so I may go, together with my girlfriends, to the mountains and weep over my youth and my innocence." Which she did. Together with her friends, she left society and went to the mountains. There she wept over the loss of her future, the loss of the joy and pleasure and love that had been in store for her. Upon her return to her father, "he did unto her the vow that he had made." Again—the word "death" is not used. Jephthah could do it but could not say it. Others did—and still do. There is a tradition in Israel that young girls go to spend four days in the mountains telling and retelling the tale of Jephthah and his daughter and their common tragedy.

This story has inspired many writers, playwrights, composers, and painters, especially during the Renaissance. Shakespeare quotes Jephthah in Hamlet. Lord Byron evokes him in a poem, as does Alfred de Vigny. Handel's last score, before he went totally blind, is about Jephthah and his daughter: it was one of a hundred musical compositions devoted to the judge and his victim.

The image of the two of them engaged in their last conversation, using simple and delicate words, fires our imagination. The scene of the young girl who refuses to weep in public but chooses to cry in the mountains is one that cannot help but move us.

Still, some questions remain. Why didn't she cry when her tears might still have influenced her father? Why didn't she resist death?

Our puzzlement grows deeper as we consider her father's actions. Why *didn't* he change his mind? Why *didn't* he run away? Why *didn't* he tell his daughter to escape, never to return? Why *didn't* he say: I sinned in making that vow, therefore let me die in her place?

Clearly, Jephthah is at the center of the mystery confronting us. Psychologists might explain to us that he did to his daughter what his father had done to him. She was innocent? So was he. In identifying thus with her, he would illustrate his own innocence. Could it have been a conscious decision on his part? Surely not. Well, after all, the subconscious existed long before Freud.

The language used in telling the story has other reverberations as well. Talmudic sages link it to an unforgettable ancient event: the Akedah. Isaac was Yakhid; Jephthah's daughter, Yekhida—the only one. Is it possible that this illegitimate off-spring of a prostitute suddenly yearned to break away from his social sphere and rise to the level of Abraham? Is it conceivable that his plan was to go beyond the Patriarch by going farther than he, whereas Abraham had stopped before it was too late? Is the whole story meant as a repudiation of the Akedah?

If this were the case, we would understand why the Talmud does not rank Jephthah among its favorite characters. One Midrash states: "Jephthah *was* a Just Man, but he lived among bad neighbors of the tribe of Ephraim; he saw them burn their sons and daughters as offerings to the gods of Baal, and so he was influenced by them." Another source calls him *Am-haaretz:* igno-rant. Had he known the law, he would have found a way to spare his daughter's life: after all, a *Neder,* a vow, can be revoked through sacrifice and prayer. "God was angry with him," says still another Midrash. Why? Because his words were irresponsible. What did Jephthah say? The first to emerge from my door to greet me will be brought as an offering to God. And what if it had been a dog or a pig or a cat? Would he have brought them as offerings? That is why God, to punish him, made his daughter go outside to welcome him.

I am not satisfied with this explanation. I can perhaps under-stand why Jephthah was to be punished—but why should his daughter have had to pay the price? Jephthah sinned and his daughter paid with her life? Is that justice?

Jephthah sinned in other ways, too, according to Talmudic sages. As I said, they don't like him. First, because they never liked military heroes. Second, they blamed him, and him alone, for the death of his only daughter. All sages agree that he could have exchanged her for . . . money. That is the opinion of Rabbi Yohanan. Certain offerings could be covered by their monetary value. Resh-Lakish maintains that Jephthah didn't even need to pay anything. He simply could have gone to the High Priest. We know his name: Pinhas son of Eleazar. The High Priest had the authority to release him from his vow. But then, why didn't he invoke his authority to help Jephthah and release him from his vow? It probably had to do with his vanity. He said to himself, After all, I am the High Priest and he needs me; why, then, doesn't he come to me? Why should I go to him? As for Jephthah, why didn't he go to see the High Priest? He probably said to himself, I am the leader and commander of Israel; it is improper for me to go to him. The Midrash comments: While this was going on between them, a poor innocent girl lost her life.

Both were punished for their vanity. The divine spirit left the High Priest. As for Jephthah, his punishment was . . . Wait: not yet. He was punished more than once, in more than one way. Having killed his daughter, something in him must have died. Moreover, his offering was not received. "You sacrificed a human being, a living soul for me?" God scolded him. "I never asked you to do that. Never have I ordered anyone to give me human beings as offerings."

And so it had all been for nothing. The anguish and the pain, the agony and the remorse—having wanted to please God, he had displeased him; having wanted to praise Him, he had offended Him. And now—he had lost both his daughter and himself.

What follows in the text is a description of Jephthah's decline. He is no longer the same man. His next battle is not with an outside enemy but with his own people, the tribe of Ephraim, whose leaders are angry at him for having gone to war with the Ammonites without them: "Why didn't you call upon us?" they ask him. "We shall burn your house down upon you." His answer is filled with anger: "For years and years I appealed for your help and received none. That is why I had to fight alone, without you."

A civil war ensued. Brother against brother. Jew against Jew. Gilead against Ephraim. Gilead was stronger and Jephthah was still in full command of his troops. Was it due to his pain? His frustrations? He fought better than ever. His victory over Ephraim was swift and decisive. The enemy soldiers ran away but Jephthah's men pursued them. Beaten and defeated, many of the Ephraim warriors hid among Jephthah's men but the refugees were quickly unmasked. The text tells us how: they were incapable of pronouncing the word *Shibolet;* on their lips it sounded like "Szibolet." So it was easy. Suspects were asked to say *Shibolet*. Forty-two thousand failed the test. Forty-two thousand perished. That was Jephthah's last victory, his last battle.

All in all he ruled over Israel six years. Nothing else is said about his reign. Did he remarry? Did he become pious? One has the impression that after the battle with Ephraim he went into seclusion. No friends, no enemies. Nothing. Only memories. Painful scars. Burning images. Silent tears.

He died and was buried somewhere in his native province of Gilead. Listen carefully to the text: it says, *"Beare Gilead.* He was buried in the cities of Gilead." Normally this would mean "in one of the cities of Gilead." The Midrash disagrees. Its interpretation is literal. If the text says "cities," plural, that means that Jephthah was buried in *many* cities. But how can one person be buried in more than one place? Says the Midrash, Jephthah became ill. That was his punishment. His body disintegrated limb by limb, and each was buried separately, one after the other, in *different* cities.

Usually there is symbolism in the punishment. For instance, take Samson. A judge, as Jephthah was, he too was punished. He was blinded by the enemy. The Midrash comments: "Samson rebelled against God with his eyes, as it is said.: 'Get the Philistine woman for me for she pleases my eyes'—therefore his eyes were put out by the Philistines."

What is the symbolism in Jephthah's punishment? Since his martial qualities were linked to his physical strength, that is what was taken away from him. His strongest point became his weakest.

Since he refused to move physically from one place to another, even though this might have saved his daughter, he was mutilated and, so to speak, disavowed by his body, which left him piece by piece. He was punished also for his vanity.

Since his vanity was the cause of his daughter's death—for he could have prevented her death by asking the High Priest to release him from his vow—he was made to die what was called in ancient Greece "a death of mice," losing one's limbs before dying.

A. A. Halevy mentions that Antiochus the wicked also died

this way. Having conquered many sites, he too was buried in many sites.

Worthy of the Akedah? Jephthah's story is more tragic than the Akedah. Abraham was rewarded, Jephthah punished. Jephthah's daughter was not saved. Her sacrifice had been willed by God. She died, and we do not even know her name.

Her pleas to her father—as recorded by the Midrash—find strange echoes in ancient Greece. Sol Liptzin saw the connection between the two sources. In Euripides's play, Iphigenia too tries to move her father, Agamemnon, to compassion:

> *Don't kill me so young! It is good to see the light!*
> *I was the first who called you father, and the first*
> *Whom you called child; the first who sat upon your knee,*
> *Caressed you lovingly, and was caressed in turn . . .*
> *Have pity on my life. . . .*

And she accuses her father of making the wrong choice, of choosing violence and murder and betrayal instead of love and justice. Too late. For victims, it is always too late.

We are now reaching the end of a tragic destiny. Jephthah, judge and hero in Israel, was punished both in his life and in his death. And another page is turned in the Book of Judges.

But I remain troubled. By Jephthah? Yes, but more so by his daughter. Why did she have to die? Her love for her father was so profound that she accepted her fate with extraordinary grace, to make it easier for him—she even went into hiding so as to spare him the sight of her weeping. Why was there no miracle, no heavenly intervention as with the Akedah? The Radak alone claims there *was:* Jephthah did not kill her; he only forced her to enter a religious community.

The Biblical text is heartbreaking enough in its crisp, poetic description, but the Midrash goes farther and moves you to tears. It is worthy of the Akedah.

The Midrash imagines the last scene, the last encounter between father and daughter. As Jephthah is about to fulfill his vow in silence, his daughter bursts into sobs and says: "Father, Father! I came to welcome you with joy and pride, and you slaughter me? Tell me, Father," she continues, "is it written in the Torah that Jews should sacrifice their children on the altar? Isn't it written that animals ought to be sacrificed, animals, not human beings?"

Jephthah lets her talk, then answers: "It is too late, my daughter. I have already made my vow." "Our ancestor Jacob," says she, "also made a vow. He pledged to God to offer Him a tenth of whatever he would have—didn't he have twelve sons? Did he sacrifice but one of them to God?" Jephthah listens but does not answer. She continues: "When Hannah promised that if she had a son, she would give him to God—did she sacrifice him?" Jephthah listens and says nothing. "You say you made a vow," she goes on. "Let me go to a tribunal, it may well release you from your vow." But it was too late.

And so it is time for us to conclude with a few lessons to be taken from this story. What are they?

First, one must be careful with words. Jephthah was not. A sentence that meant nothing when he spoke it came back to haunt him for the rest of his life. A few words cast into the wind caused tragedy, or, more precisely, a chain of tragedies.

Second, Jephthah's principle mistake was that he did not confide in his daughter. He should have told her about his vow *before* he went to battle. Why hadn't he? Probably because he considered the entire affair frivolous, unimportant, a few words that had just come to his mind. Why bother his beloved daughter? Why tell her of his uncertainty about the outcome of the battle? Better keep it to himself.

Still, as harsh as the Talmudic judgment of Jephthah may be, its judgment of Pinhas the High Priest is much more severe. That Jephthah was wrong in putting protocol before a human life is clear, but Jephthah was not a spiritual leader: Pinhas was. Jephthah didn't have to know the law: Pinhas did. That is why the onus is placed on Pinhas. *He* should have taken the first step to help Jephthah save his daughter. Because he did not, he is held responsible not only for Jephthah's daughter's death, but also for the forty-two thousand men of Ephraim who fell in battle. The *Yalkut Shimoni* links the two events as cause and effect. Had Pinhas released Jephthah from his vow, the war with Ephraim would not have taken place. The High Priest is criticized both for not having helped Jephthah with his daughter and for not having stepped into the crisis with Ephraim. When the warriors of Ephraim came to quarrel with Jephthah, according to the Midrashic scenario, Pinhas should have told them, "You did not come to free him from his vow, nor did you come to his aid when he needed you. Now you come to create problems?" But he said nothing. Therefore it is he who bears the responsibility for the forty-two thousand victims of that bitter battle.

The Midrashic language is beautiful and incisive: "Because he could have protested and chose not to, he is the one who killed the victims."

I would not go that far. But we all learn from the Midrash the essential lesson of human and social responsibility. True, we are often too weak to stop injustices; but the least we can do is to protest against them. Truc, we are too poor to eliminate hunger; but in feeding one child, we protest against hunger. True, we are too timid and powerless to take on all the guards of all the political prisons in the world; but in offering our solidarity to one prisoner we denounce all the tormentors. Truc, we are powerless against death; but as long as we help one man, one woman, one child live one hour longer in safety and dignity, we affirm man's right to live.

Ruth

ONCE UPON A TIME, in a faraway country, there lived a simple yet exceptional, poor yet exceptionally noble, woman, to whom an entire people owes not only its claim to national pride and immortality but also its redemption.

Her name—Ruth the Moabite—evokes gentleness, tenderness, and faith. A unique woman whose qualities will make her a mother of royalty.

Of course, she may resist being observed. She prefers to stay out of the limelight. That is her nature. Too shy? Let us say, unpretentious.

Ruth ha-Moavia, Ruth the Moabite: her name conjures up a past filled with doubt and pain, and a future penetrated by an irresistible light that penetrates exile, the messianic light that will put an end to suffering and injustice.

In our tradition, she is loved—oh, how she is loved. She ranks among the matriarchs. Sarah, Rebecca, Rachel, and Leah gave us the twelve tribes of Israel, but Ruth gave them—and us—a king. King David is a descendant not of Sarah but of Ruth. Without Ruth, our people might never have had a king, or else might have had another king, but not David, of whom it will be said: "*Khai vekayam*—He lives and shall go on living until the end of days."

What do we owe Ruth? King David and—our hope.

Tradition attributes the Book of Ruth to the Prophet Samuel. If this is true, Samuel had great literary gifts and a wonderful romantic imagination. This singular Book is indeed singular: it begins by describing events that are related not to national politics but to individual adventures. There are no prophetic exhortations, no miracles, no divine interventions to be found in its pages; in fact, God is surprisingly passive in this tale, which is principally about the extraordinary friendship of two ordinary women who will, in time, become exceptional. Then the plot shifts direction, and a new element—love—is added. Mysterious and delicate, full of suspense, of anxiety, too, this love story unfolds on a variety of levels, harmonizing relationships between man and woman, the individual and the community, the beginning and ultimate end of humanity. And yet, the people of Israel, a people already singed by destiny, hardly figures in it. Said Rabbi Zeira: This book contains no law related to purity or impurity, to the forbidden and the permitted, the sacred and the profane; it was written solely to teach us the rewards of generosity.

Usually the Book of Ruth is read during Shavuot, the Festival of Weeks—why? Is it because King David, Ruth's illustrious descendant, died on Shavuot? A hypothesis has been suggested by another Talmudic school: Like Ruth, our ancestors became Jewish, that is, converted to the Jewish faith, when they received the law. When was that? On Shavuot.

As we read the Book, we stumble upon bizarre passages; we come across certain written words that are not to be read aloud, and others, marginal additions, that we do read aloud, although they are not part of the text itself.

But then the very existence of the Book is strange. Just think: had Ruth's ancestors behaved differently toward our own, she may never have entered Jewish history.

Scripture tells us, "An Ammonite and a Moabite may not join the congregation—or the assembly—of God." Why not? "Because they did not offer you bread and water when you left Egypt." What? Because these two tribes had chosen to be inhospitable toward our fugitive ancestors in the desert, ought their descendants to be punished—forever? Why such harshness toward men and women who may themselves have been lacking both bread and water? Was their one-time behavior sufficient reason for us to never again be interested in their descendants' welfare? Is that fair? Should one remain *that* vindictive *that* long?

What could be the reason for such an enduring grudge? The fact that Balak, the Moabite king, once hired Bileam to curse Israel? Is that all? Bileam was hired to curse us—so what? Since when are Jews afraid of anti-Semitic curses? Anyway, didn't Bileam's curses turn into blessings? Isn't our first morning prayer—"*Ma tovu ohalekha Yaakov*—How beautiful are thy dwell-ings, Jacob"—taken from Bileam? Of course we are angry with Bileam, we are angry with the king who hired him, we are angry with his subjects, we are angry with their descendants. So much so that we may not marry their offspring. But wait a minute. Then how come a Jew could marry Ruth? Wasn't she a Moabite? Why such favoritism? Only because she was to become a celebrity as the great-grandmother of a great Jewish king? True, she converted. But—*when* did she convert? Not when she married Naomi's son. The words she pronounced, which every convert now utters—"I shall go where you go, sleep where you sleep, die where you die, your people is my people, your God is my God"—to whom did she say them? Not to her husband, but to her Jewish mother-in-law. Is this why she was accepted? Because her conversion was seen as being devoid of any ulterior motive?

Let us start from the beginning. "*Vayehi biyemei shfot hashoftim*—This is what happened at the time when the judges judged" or, according to a different version, when the judges them-selves were judged.

The country was ravaged by famine. What do we know of that land and its inhabitants, the Moabites? Quite a lot. The sources are varied: Babylonian, Egyptian, Assyrian, and—*Lehavdil*—Biblical. A major source is what is called "the Moabite stone," also known as "the inscription of Mesha, king of Moab." Much is known of their religion, their culture, their national char-acteristics. Their god, K'mosh, rewarded or punished his subjects according to their behavior. When they were good, they became conquerors; when they were bad, they were conquered by Egypt or Judea.

King David, whose great-grandmother, as we know, was a Moabite, defeated them in battle, killed two thirds of their war-riors, and enslaved the others. Hence—although no civilians were ever harmed—their lasting hatred for the children of Israel.

The Moabites figure prominently in the visions of our great prophets. Both Isaiah and Jeremiah predict Moab's downfall, but Jeremiah foresees redemption for the Moabites as part of universal deliverance. Ezekiel also believes in a Moabite "saving remnant." But Zefanyah is convinced that they will be destroyed like Sodom and Gomorrah.

The text is kind to future scholars and Biblical exegetes. Time and location are precisely indicated. We know, more or less, when our two romantic heroes, Boaz and Ruth, met and where: in the year 968 before the Common Era, in Bethlehem.

On the surface the narrative runs fast, almost breathlessly, without difficulty or obstacle. It is not written in verse? Not all holy books are. (Incidentally, this caused such distress to Paul Krauss, a famous orientalist of the thirties—who had dedicated his life to proving that the entire Bible *was* written in verse—that he committed suicide.) Still, though the Book of Ruth is not a poem, is it poetic? Based on fact, with no recourse to the supernatural, the story is defined by realism. It begins in sorrow.

There was a man named Elimelech who had a wife named Naomi. They had two sons: Mahlon and Hilion. One day, they decided to leave their home in Bethlehem, which is in Judea. Why was it necessary to mention Judea? Because villages with the same name existed in other provinces. Also, because the family decided to leave not only its home and village but its homeland. Where was the immigrant family going? To the land of the Moabites. Why did they venture into hostile territory? The motive was pragmatic in nature: it was easier to make a living there. Was it? Elimelech dies soon after they get there. His widow, Naomi, is now alone with her two sons. How will she feed her family? Her worries are short-lived: her two sons marry two Moabite girls, Orpa and Ruth. Is she unhappy that her sons married out of the faith? She doesn't say. Naomi is always quiet, withdrawn, concealing her feelings. Ten years later, her sons die. Again, she does not show her sadness. All the text tells us is that after her sons passed away, Naomi heard that the situation had improved back home in the land of Judea. It was time to go home. For Orpa and Ruth as well? Yes, for the three of them together.

They started out thinking that they would be inseparable. But halfway through their journey, something happened. Naomi had a change of heart. She looked at her daughters-in-law and decided it would be better for them to go their own way. They were young, life was still before them; why bring them into a land which was not theirs, why make them face unnecessary distress? She tried to make them see reason. She succeeded with Orpa, but not with Ruth. She made three attempts, and failed. Ruth was stubborn. Stubborn in her loyalty, solemn in her resolve. Her response was: "Your people is my people. . . . Death alone will set us apart."

What happened afterward? Afterward, Naomi and Ruth went on to Bethlehem. There lived one of Naomi's relatives who was both wealthy and a man of valor: Boaz. He was the owner of extensive cultivated fields. Ruth had the idea to go and glean among the ears of corn left behind after the harvest. Ruth didn't know it, but that particular field belonged to Boaz—who, of course, ended up noticing her. Did they fall in love right then and there? Was it love at first sight? The proverbial *coup de foudre?* We don't know. We do know that they got married, and that generations later, their descendant, David, ascended the throne of Judea. And symbolized—and will continue to symbolize—Jewish royalty till the end of time.

Now why are we so concerned with this love story? And why has it been included in the canon? It contains sensuality, but no transcendent element. It is a story about human relations, not about God and his workings. Why then is it sacred?

We shall analyze the major protagonists in the story, but first, a few words about the problem they share: that of strangeness.

In general, Jewish tradition insists on every person's right to be different. Having been a stranger in Pharaoh's Egypt, one is therefore compelled to respect all strangers for what they are. One must not seek to change their ways or views: One must not try to make them resemble oneself. Every human being reflects the image of God, who has no image: mine is neither purer nor holier than yours. Truth is one, but the paths leading to it are many. In the eyes of the Father, all His children are worthy of His love. In my eyes, the Other is the center of the universe, just as any Other ought to be in his or her eyes. Only in totalitarian regimes do all citizens look and speak and act alike.

Does the story of Ruth sound like an apology for proselytism? It is not. With rare exceptions the Jewish religion has discouraged conversion. Before a person is accepted into the fold, he or she must be forewarned of what he or she may have to endure. The candidate must be made aware of the persecutions, the sufferings, the torments, the massacres that fill Jewish memory. "Are you ready? Wouldn't you prefer a quieter life?"

Even on the personal level, efforts are made to discourage the candidate. To convert means to leave not only your present faith but also your family: you will be like a newborn child with Abraham and Sarah as parents.

To frighten the candidate, he is told that a convert may

theoretically—I insist: theoretically—marry his sister or even his mother; such marriage would no longer be considered incestuous. I wonder what Freud would say to all this. If this will not frighten the prospective convert—what will?

In Judaism, it is the freedom of the stranger—his right to self-definition—that must be respected. It is because the "Other" is other, because he or she is not I, that I am to consider him or her both sovereign and instrument used by God to act upon history and justify His faith in His creation.

When are we suspicious of the stranger? When he or she comes from our midst. There is a difference between *ger, nochri* and *zar*. All three words refer to the stranger. Scripture is kind to the *ger*, compassionate toward the *nochri*, and harsh toward the *zar*. For only the *zar* is Jewish. And a Jew who chooses to estrange himself from his people, a Jew who makes use of his Jewishness only to denigrate other Jews, a Jew of whom it may be said that "he removed himself from the community," who shares neither its sorrow nor its joy, that Jew is not our brother.

But Ruth is our sister. Why is she so loved in our tradition? Because while Jewish religion discourages conversion, it is fond of converts.

Ruth is not the only one. Other celebrated cases have been recorded, not without a certain measure of pride. The emperor's nephew Aquilas (or Onkelos), the king of Himyar of the fifth century, the Khazars of the eighth century, the learned proselyte Obadia of Normandy, some princes and bishops, Lord George Gordon, a British aristocrat, who one day decided to espouse the Jewish faith and live as a Jew, dress as a Jew, pray as a Jew even in prison, till his death. . . .

According to the Talmud, a bizarre phenomenon emerged: some of our cruelest enemies became converts. General Nevouzraddan, the murderer of hundreds of scholars and thousands of children—what did he do when there was no one left to kill? He converted. The same has been said of Nero. Then there was the descendant of Haman who allegedly established a yeshiva in Bnei-Brak. The meaning of these legends? To teach us that history is never finished. Good may emerge from bad. Evil's triumph must be temporary. Repentance is granted even to killers: One day there may be High Priests and teachers among their descendants. Or the other way around. These legends teach us modesty. Not all our ancestors have been prophets and poets; not all have, with all their scholarship, contributed to the glory of God and His law; some may even have committed sinful and criminal acts that brought dishonor to humanity.

And now let us return to the Book of Ruth which, in fairness, ought to have been called the Book of Naomi.

The principal characters are three: Naomi, Ruth, and Boaz. The secondary characters? Also three: Elimelech, Orpa, and the anonymous "redeemer" who appears, only to disappear at the end of the Book. Then, of course, as in every good drama, there are many extras: harvesters, spectators, neighbors, passersby—in short, the entire population of Bethlehem, which, like the chorus in ancient Greece, participates in the play with outcries, silent gestures, or meaningful winks and murmurs.

In the beginning, all are kind, charming, appealing.

Elimelech moves us not only by his personal tragedy, but also by his inability to overcome it. He had a wife and two sons whom he could not feed, a situation that caused him such pain that he felt compelled to leave his home and live as a stranger among strangers in the land of the Moabites. Surely he had hoped to come home one day and start all over again—but it was not to be: he died. When? We do not know. The cause? We do not know. Of misery? Of despair perhaps? Of nostalgia? It was never easy to live as a refugee. Did he die of remorse? But he had been a good father, a good husband, a good Jew. Did he regret having had to leave the Holy Land? His was a tragic destiny; it is impossible not to empathize with him.

Next, Naomi: all the tenderness and sweetness in the world are reflected in her name and mirrored in her personality. Totally selfless, she was always thinking of others, never of herself. She was happy at home in Bethlehem; that much is clear. Even in the midst of misfortune, she found ways to invent happiness— not for herself, but for those around her. One imagines her always busy—helping her husband, her children, their wives. Her sons married Moabite girls? If she was hurt—and she must have been—she did not show it. Never were Orpa and Ruth offended by Naomi's attitude toward them. Dignified in her distress, she showed exemplary courage when faced with the challenges of existence. At the end, it was she who orchestrated everything. Behind all that occurs in the Book, it is her presence that is felt. Yes, the book ought to have been named after her. Why wasn't it? My guess is that she vetoed the proposal. Naomi was *too* modest. Glory was good for others, not for her.

We are also touched by Orpa. Having lost her husband, she decided to follow Naomi to Judea. Why? Didn't she know that her life there would consist of hardship and worry? That did not matter to her. Faithful to her late husband, she wanted to stay close to his struggling people. In the end, she did yield to Naomi's persistent arguments. Why? Because she could not make the effort and go the extra mile? Because it was easier to return to her parents' home? No: she realized that it would be easier for Naomi to be on her own when she reappeared in her village. It was probably for Naomi's sake that Orpa left her.

What about Ruth? She is perfect. Humble, obedient, she accepts everything without a trace of protest or dissent. Her husband, Hilion, died? She accepted his death without complaint. Naomi wanted to go back to Judea? She would go with her. Naomi tried to dissuade her? Gently, Ruth convinced her of her desire to stay at her side. The thought that Naomi, who had been so happy and respected, so proud, would now return home alone and defeated, was intolerable to Ruth. Orpa changed her mind midway? Orpa was young, she would be happy again; not so Naomi. Naomi needed Ruth more than Orpa did. Even when Ruth remarried and had a son, it was Naomi's privilege to name him.

Now we come to Boaz: a true gentleman. Defender of the weak, protector of the poor. He noticed an unknown woman in his field, and he did all he could *not* to make her feel an intruder. Always calm, Boaz was in control of any situation. He knew what to do and what not to do. With him present, nothing bad could occur. Respected, admired, Boaz inspired a feeling of security and gratitude.

The collective image projected by Bethlehem was one of warmth and compassion. Its inhabitants were kind, never envious or bitter; strangers were always welcome. *"Hazot Naomi?"* people cried out when they saw Naomi reappear in their streets: Is this Naomi? Has she returned at last? Not only were they not angry at her for abandoning them during the famine, they were now ready to come to her aid. They felt sorry for her. Not one person said, "Is she unhappy? Good! She deserves it. She had no business leaving us." And when Ruth joined the harvesters, instead of chasing the young woman away, they allowed her to glean ears of corn in the field. Their wives did not see her as competition. When she married Boaz, there was no gossip about them. Ruth's joy was shared by Naomi—and then by the entire community.

Is that why we are so enticed by this idyllic romance? Because of its reassuring aspects? Because it has no part for a villain? Is life without villains at all conceivable? Can a story without tension and conflict be of interest to any reader?

But on second reading, we may discover some dark areas.

First of all, we realize that the narrative, from beginning to end, is bathed in unfathomable suffering. From the very first sentence we are confronted by famine and misfortune. Things are not going well. Quite the opposite. We realize that hunger, too, is a character in the drama.

In ancient times, hunger represented the ultimate malediction. Rich and poor, young and old, kings and beggars lived in fear of drought; all joined the priests in prayers for rain. Rain meant harvest, harvest meant food, food meant life, just as lack of food meant death.

It still does. And more. Hunger means humiliation. A hungry person experiences an overwhelming feeling of shame. The father who cannot feed his children. The son who witnesses his father's helplessness. All desires, aspirations, and dreams lose their lofty qualities and relate to food alone. Hence the feeling of degradation.

Shame in Hebrew is linked to one disease alone: hunger. *Kherpat-raav:* the shame of hunger. To escape it, one is ready to leave everything behind—as did Abraham. And Jacob.

And Elimelech.

With a heavy heart he and his family left for the unknown in search of survival. They expected the worst. And it came. Trials and tragedies followed one upon the other. First came the sudden death of Elimelech himself, leaving Naomi alone with her two sons. Was it because they wished to introduce some joy into the orphaned home that Mahlon and Hilion decided to get married? They found two beautiful young girls from good families. Was that the end of the tragedy? Sadly, no. After the brief period of serenity, misfortune struck again. The two young husbands collapsed and died. Of what? Did they both die from the same illness? And did both die on the very same day? The text is curiously secretive. It is as if explanations are superfluous in the face of so much suffering. One imagines the three widows under the same roof; and the silent grief that brings them closer together. One imagines their unspoken questions: Why so much sadness in one home? Why did death strike only the men? Why were the women spared?

Naomi decides to put an end to exile: she cannot go on living in a house marked by mourning. We see the three women close the door behind them and set out on the long road home. At the crossroad, a new trial is awaiting them: to stay together or not? They decide to separate. The two young widows—sisters and Moabite princesses, according to one source—part ways. Will they see each other again? Tearful, Orpa stayed in the land of Moab, whereas Naomi and Ruth headed toward Judea, their memories their only baggage.

When they reached Judea, which was no longer suffering from famine, they aroused pity. The two women were weak and poor, so poor that Ruth—the former princess—had to look for work. At the time she was forty—and in those days that was an advanced age for women. Ruth's only chance for marriage? Naomi's relative, Boaz. Guided by Naomi, Ruth will humble herself and go to meet Boaz at night in the barn. They will get married but they will not live happily ever after, for—according to one commentary—Boaz died on his wedding day.

Why so many blows directed at one person? At one family? What sins could it have committed to deserve so many afflictions? Suffering is never supposed to be gratuitous. That is part of our Jewish belief. Sin and punishment are supposed to be forever intertwined. God is just and His name is truth, and His divine truth is meant to be affirmed by human justice. So let us look more closely for possible shortcomings in the victims of our story.

The famine in Judea? It is linked to the state of moral hunger that stifles its inhabitants. Demoralization has pervaded all spheres of the population. The judicial system itself is affected. Selfishness is the accepted rule everywhere. The judges themselves are judged by those who appear before them in court. They are asked, Who are you, notorious sinners, to preach the law to us? Society has rarely been as promiscuous, as immoral. A Talmudic commentator adds: "That entire generation was bathing in exaggerated sensuality and eroticism." How could God not intervene and remind them of His presence?

Elimelech, why was he made to suffer? The Talmud declares

him guilty. He should have interceded in heaven on behalf of his contemporaries. Too selfish, Elimelech? Too egocentric. He could have prevented the national catastrophe of hunger. How? By praying. That is the least he could have done. Other commentators go further and say that Elimelech wasn't a kind person at all. He refused to give charity to the needy. The hungry beggars were sent away from his home on empty stomachs and empty-handed. Was he poor? No: he had the means to help them. He wasn't just anybody: as a descendant of the illustrious Nahshon ben Amminadab, who courageously led the crossing of the Red Sea, he was the head of his village. People looked to him for guidance. And yet, instead of sharing the tragic fate of his community, what did he do? He ran away! Where? To the Moabites, whose hostility to Israel was as old as Israel! Is that why the leader of his generation was not popular? No wonder that, after his death, the text refers constantly to him as *Elimelech ish Naomi*—Elimelech, Naomi's husband: she was the *only* one to mourn his passing.

What about his two sons? Were they not without sin? As their Hebrew names indicate, Mahlon and Hilion were almost predestined to be forgotten: *"Nimkhu vekhalu min haolam,"* says the Midrash. Obliterated from the world, erased from history. Why? They, too, were guilty on many counts. One—they, too, were wrong in deserting their fellow citizens and emigrating from Judea. Two—they adjusted too quickly to their new surroundings. They became successful and stopped being refugees almost overnight. The Midrash says so. They made money—lots of money—and became socialites to the point that King Eglon of Moab offered them his two daughters, Orpa and Ruth, as wives. And instead of responding, "We are Jewish, we are not allowed to marry Moabite girls, even be they princesses, it is against the law of Moses and Israel," they were seduced by the royal offer. Easily influenced by appearances and the trappings of power, by all that is superficial in life, they did not bring honor to their people: that is why they perished abroad.

Thus we are disappointed in the father and his sons. But what about the gentle and gracious Naomi? Wasn't she a woman of valor and impeccable virtue? Let us see. Was she good to everyone? Did she follow her husband abroad? Was she an excellent matchmaker? Yes. But what about her qualities as mother? If her children were blinded by money and power, wasn't it also *her* fault? What kind of education did she give them if at the slightest provocation they turned their backs on their people and its religious tradition? Why didn't she speak to them like a Jewish mother, warning them against marrying girls without conversion? Did she at least make an effort? Why didn't she try to persuade Orpa and Ruth to espouse the faith of their future husbands? Is there a Jewish mother who wouldn't at least cry a little under these circumstances? All the text tells us is: *"Vatishaer haisha mishne yeladeha umeisha:* Having survived the death of her husband and her two sons, she remained lonely and alone." One detects in it a note of remorse: that is natural. Rightly or wrongly, survivors feel guilty for remaining alive. What have I done to deserve life also means What have I done to deserve solitude? At times, survivors envy the departed. Naomi says to herself, If I am alone, is it because *they* have abandoned *me?* What have I done to deserve this? She almost says it, in different words: *"Ve-shadai hera li—* And God pained me, hurt me, punished me." God, not people. Is she reproaching Him? Is she reproaching herself?

Even the anonymous "redeemer" does not fare too well. He is ready to take possession of what belonged to Elimelech, but when he hears that according to law this means taking responsibility for Ruth's welfare, the coward quickly withdraws.

The good and great Boaz himself comes across as less than totally appealing. Naomi is his relative, his poor cousin; why doesn't he take care of her? Why doesn't he offer her shelter and protection? Did he at least pay her a courtesy visit? He can easily afford to subsidize her. Why doesn't he? Why doesn't he even try to find out whether she needs anything? Had Boaz been more generous, Naomi wouldn't be in such an embarrassing situation; she wouldn't have to send Ruth for food or money for the household. Whatever happened to his proverbial generosity?

In Talmudic literature, Boaz is depicted as timid, a bit frightened of everyone and everything. He wants to marry Ruth, but is unable to overcome his hesitation. He is afraid. Afraid of receiving the punishment her husband had received. Boaz says to himself, Naomi's two sons died because they married Moabite girls. What will happen to me if I now marry one of them? Is this the way a man in love speaks? Shouldn't a man in love be less calculating?

Orpa? She could have insisted a little more—made an extra effort to stay with Naomi. That she was not what she should have been is implied in the legend that she was the great-great-grandmother of . . . Goliath.

One last look at the anonymous bystanders, the chorus. Their cry *"Hazot Naomi,* Is this Naomi?" could have reflected their joy or . . . their *Schadenfreude,* their pleasure at seeing her destitute. As if to say, Ah, look at that rich snob now. Maybe they were happy to see her unhappy, all those neighbors who had been envious of her wealth and serenity . . .

Clearly, the Midrash intends to establish a pattern of its own, a system of its own, one that is aimed at "correcting" the Biblical text. In Scripture, all the protagonists are pure; in the Midrash, none is pure. In Scripture, all are generous; none is above suspicion in the Midrash. Naomi, the sweet and selfless Naomi, is angry with God who "thinks of me only to make me suffer." Boaz—the good and devoted Boaz—is actually tempted by Ruth. Listen to the Midrash: "All night, the *Yetzer Hara,* the evil spirit, tried to persuade him to move closer to Ruth, saying to him, You are free, she is free, what are you waiting for? Take her in your arms. . . ." Granted, Boaz resisted. But one version shows him caressing her hair . . . not because he desires her, God forbid. He caresses her hair to see whether she is a woman or a demon—for demons have no hair, or at least this is what Boaz thinks. Another Midrashic version tells us that when Boaz discovered Ruth so near to him in the barn in the dark, he got panicky and seized her by her legs. . . . As for Ruth—there we must stop. Ruth remains the exception. Presented in the text as pure, she remains pure and noble in all its commentaries. Ruth is untouchable, above criticism. All her thoughts are directed toward God. Nothing worldly is of interest to her. A king's daughter, she could return to the luxury of her father's palace, but she chooses poverty and stays with Naomi to save her from the ultimate pain of being alone, and a stranger in her own home. In Bethlehem, it is *her* idea to work. It is she who is ready to assure the livelihood of the small family. It is she who brings back the food. Delicately, unobtrusively, she walks *behind* the harvesters, not mingling with them in order not to disturb them, not to annoy them. She goes only where she is allowed to go by law. She picks up only what others have left behind. Naomi tells her to spend the night with a total stranger in his barn? She goes. But what will he think of her? Ruth rejects vanity. He will not think anything bad because *she* never thinks anything bad. Naomi tells her to lift up the blanket covering his feet? She does as she is told. That is the only night she spends away from Naomi. The Talmud comments: usually, a woman prefers a young

man, though poor, to an old man who is rich. Not so Ruth. Boaz
is old, but Ruth accepts him. She knows, she feels God's will.
Never does she think of anything else. God is forever present in
her deeds, in her thoughts.

But . . . how can Boaz marry her? Isn't she still a Moabite?
There the Talmud goes out of its way to invent explanations. One
sage says that she had already converted at home. Another declares
that the law forbidding acceptance of Moabites in God's assembly
pertains to men only, not to women. So, both Ruth and Boaz are
irreproachable. In fact, we suddenly discover Talmudic sages bend-
ing over backward to plead in favor of all the characters in the
story. Mahlon himself will be redeemed; his name derives from
mahal—forgiveness. God will forgive him his faults. Elimelech left
Judea? He had no choice. Had he stayed home, the story of Ruth
would never have occurred. And without Ruth, would there be a
David? Or a son of David, the Messiah?

And so we discover a new element—perhaps the most important of all—in this wondrous tale: that of coincidence. Or is it
divine design? Is the meaning of the story that there is no coincidence in Jewish history? Had there been no famine in Judea,
Elimelech and his family might have stayed home, Naomi would
not have met Ruth, who would not have married Boaz. . . . Had
Boaz not lost his wife the very day Ruth and Naomi arrived in
town . . . had it not been Boaz's custom to sleep in the barn . . .
had the anonymous redeemer not appeared on the scene at the last
moment . . . there would have been no Messiah.

In Jewish history and tradition all things and events are
linked. At the end of the Book, Boaz and Ruth reach the gates of
the city, just as the redeemer happens to pass by. Boaz seizes the
moment and sets into motion the accelerated process leading up to
his wedding. How is it that the redeemer happened to arrive at the
gates of the city at that very moment? The Midrash answers: "Had
he been at the other end of the world, God would have picked him
up and brought him to his appointment with history."

In one Midrashic source, already noted, the denouement is
sad. Boaz is eighty when he marries Ruth. He dies on the day of
his wedding. Ruth is once more a widow. Alone. And yet, at the
end, we are called upon to think not of her solitude, but of our
happiness; we must think of her descendant, David.

For—in conclusion—whenever human destiny is affected, for
better or worse, we must ask, "And where is God in all this?" The

Midrash answers: "During these events, God says, Elimelech has done his part, Naomi hers, and all the others theirs; now it is my turn to do mine."

And so—from a beautiful love story between a man and woman will be born another one: the story of a people and its eternal dream.

Solomon

THAT GOOD KING SOLOMON *is* puzzling. You never know with him: Is he strong or weak, hungry for power or for wisdom? Too pious or not pious enough? Does he overflow with joy or with sadness? As a character, he is hard to grasp. Yet, at first sight, he appears homogeneous, of one piece. The image he sends forth to us is that of a joyous and serene sovereign. So many writings, so many stories tell us about his taste for happiness. Was there anywhere a more content, more powerful, or wiser man? The mere mention of his name, and people smile. He seems blessed by God. He is an informed statesman, a master of international diplomacy, an ambitious politician, a keen psychologist. Everything he undertakes is a success. Women like him. Many important people belong to his entourage. He *is* lucky. And original, too. He is the son of a great king, but he asserts himself as a king in his own right. He does not live in the shadow of his father, the great conqueror. He shies away from the glories of war. When God—in a dream—asks him about his wishes, he knows what to answer in order to move Him: "Grant me knowledge that I might be able to distinguish right from wrong." Is that all? Is Solomon that humble? Is he satisfied with so little? God rewards him for it: "I shall give you an understanding and a wise heart: no one before will have been like you, nor will anyone ever be like you." Consequence? His life unfolds like a novel, not an epic poem. He is less colorful than his father. David wrote one book, he wrote three. Didn't he receive the unique honor of building the temple which was to be God's dwelling place on earth? And also, wasn't his reign glorified as the reign of peace, social tranquility, and happiness? Solomon, Shlomo in Hebrew: his name is derived from *shalom* and means peace, the man of peace—and therefore of inner peace as well. His name also means *shalem,* an intact being. A whole person. No cracks, no blots.

And yet, the story is more complex than it appears at first—as is the man. Then, as now, it would be impossible to care about someone who *knows* everything and *owns* anything he desires, gets anything he wants, and dominates whatever stands before him. Hence the ambiguous attitude of our sages toward him. On the one hand he is glorified. On the other he is shown as someone overcome by his weaknesses—and they are many. Some of them are so embarrassing for a son, particularly the son of David, that they are baffling: How could a great king, a great Jew, have sons who—for the most part—disgraced him?

According to the Talmud, a righteous man can be the father or the son of a righteous man—just as he can perfectly well be the son or father of a wicked man. In the Bible, too? Yes, in the Bible, too. After all, parents cannot always be held responsible for what their children become.

Let us admit it: Biblical parents were often lucky with God, but unlucky with their sons. In fact, the closer they came to God, the more removed they seemed from their children. Not so in the Talmud, where we encounter few quarrels and conflicts among the sons of famous fathers. But the Talmud does speak of *"tzaar gidul banim*—the pain of bringing up children." Was it always like that? Probably.

Since the problem seems hopeless at times, efforts have been made lately to change the problem, not the solution: today's youth are convinced that it is their right and their duty to bring up their parents.

Is Freud correct—once more? Is it possible, is it true, that often, if not always, a son's wish is to destroy or kill his father, or at least the father figure that dominates his adolescence?

Was it Oscar Wilde who said that children begin by loving their parents; then they judge them? Rarely, if ever, do they forgive them.

Let us take as a first example the first family in history: the children of Adam and Eve. Cain and Abel, as one became the murderer and the other the victim, could only make their unhappy parents more unhappy. Was that the reason for their sons' actions? Is it possible that Cain, at any rate, wanted to punish his parents for bringing him into an imperfect world?

All right, they were not Jewish—what of that? Isaac was—

and how are we to explain Jacob's cheating him? Jacob was Jewish—how are we to understand *his* sons' behavior toward *him*? One slept in his bed, another became intimate with a prostitute, and all were partners in crime, plotting to do away with their father's favorite child, Joseph. Moses's sons seem pale and uninspired, leaving scarcely a mark, whereas Aaron's sons, Nadab and Abihu, die in some obscure accident that many puzzled commentators have tried to elucidate: they went unauthorized into the sacred Tent and died in the ensuing blaze. One source accuses them of being intoxicated. Another one charges them with starting an impure fire in the purest place in the desert. A third commentator goes further: according to him, Nadab and Abihu were jealous of their famous father, Aaron the High Priest, and of their glorious uncle, Moses, whose functions they wanted to usurp. So, supposedly, they walked through the camp saying to anyone who cared to listen: "How much longer will these old men rule over us? Let them go and make room for us!" What? The very sons of the first High Priest, the founder of the line, uttering such insolent words as if they were envious politicians or disgruntled employees?

As for Samuel—the last judge and first prophet, the man who was called upon to crown and anoint two kings—his sons did not bring him much joy either. We are told that they were not too popular—mind you, that is not necessarily bad: few prophets were popular, or wanted to be. But Samuel's sons were unpopular for terrible reasons: they were judges—corrupt judges. Because of their actions justice itself was corrupted.

King Saul, too, had problems with his children Michal and Jonathan. He suspected them of liking his former protégé and rival, David, better than him: David, who was to become the most glorious of Jewish kings—and whose sons are even more of a disappointment.

He had eighteen of them. Six were born in Hebron, twelve in Jerusalem. Four brought him serious trouble. Amnon—the oldest—fell in love with his beautiful half sister, Tamar. He seduced her and then repudiated and humiliated her. The Biblical text shows him to be monstrously cunning and cruel. Look at the scenario. First, he pretends to be sick, so sick that he desperately needs company—no, he needs a nurse. Send Tamar, he tells his father. She and she alone can take care of him. Tamar, gentle and kind, falls into his trap. She is attentive and affectionate—how could she not be? He is ill, isn't he? She prepares his favorite dish, she feeds him, tries to make him feel better, and then, suddenly, Amnon, her half brother, starts to make advances to her! Naturally she retreats, but he pursues her. Courageously, she pushes him back. He is insistent, persistent—and stronger than she. Still she says no. Then, changing tactics, Amnon speaks of his love for her, you know the kind: disinterested, pure, unique, all-consuming, everlasting. He speaks like a cunning youngster trying to conquer an innocent girl. Does she believe him? Is she that naive? He ends up possessing her. Then, like the heel that he is, in a gesture of revulsion and disgust, he abandons her, throws her out. . . .

Tamar was to be avenged. By her brother Absalom—who was to kill Amnon, or have him killed, during a family celebration. A man of honor, Absalom? A man of passion—of all passions, including ambition and envy—so much so that he covets his father's throne, while the latter is still in good health. With the complicity of schemers and plotters close to the royal court, he prepares a full-fledged insurrection. On the political level, he spreads rebellion among the population; on the military level, he organizes a powerful army, more powerful than his father's.

How can one explain Absalom's success with the public? Probably one segment of the population was dissatisfied with David's economic policies. And then, Absalom was handsome. Whoever saw him was impressed with his looks, and especially his hair, which was long and braided. In the end, it got stuck in the branches of a tree, and was responsible for his fall. Unable to free himself, he remained hanging there waiting for death. Joab, the commander-in-chief of the loyal forces, David's aide-de-camp, would himself put an end to his agony.

How are we to understand Absalom's animosity—no, Absalom's hatred—of his father, which moved him to do things so unbecoming to a Jewish prince? According to the Talmud, he once entered the king's palace and seized his father's wives and concubines. For the psychologist, this demonstrates the normal or abnormal desire of a son to take his father's place in every respect. If he is unable to do so, he rejects his father and his way of life and does everything possible not to be like him. All right. But is it conceivable that one of the sons of the great King David would behave in such a despicable way? Didn't they teach him anything at home? Didn't he fear God or, at least, God's outspoken prophet,

Nathan? Didn't he consider the disastrous consequences of his actions?

Poor David. He vanquished the powerful Goliath but not the lust for power in his sons. He defeated the enemy but could not prevent Absalom from being defeated by his own foolishness. He ruled over an entire people but not his own home. And yet, David loved his sons. He easily—too easily?—forgave them all their transgressions, all their evil deeds. Actually the Talmud blames him for that. He was a great king but not a good father. He was not strict enough with his children, not assertive enough. A father should know how to affirm his authority. Love must not blind him to the point of excessive permissiveness. But then, what father would condemn David? The love of a father is not always rational. Because Absalom's opposition to his father was the most intense, his father loved him most.

The relationship between David and Absalom seems more dramatic, more engaging than that which existed between David and Solomon. Absalom's death left David dejected, bereaved, and unconsoled. "Why didn't I die instead of you, Absalom my son?" Eight times he repeated the words *"Avshalom beni, Avshalom beni*—Absalom my son." His distress and affliction were so deep and so penetrating that they almost cost him his throne once more. His aide-de-camp warned him that unless he started living again, ruling again, conducting the affairs of the kingdom again, his people would turn away from him. David was jolted back to reality and found the strength needed to stand up again and assert his power.

But his trials did not stop. The fight for the throne resumed. This time it was led by Adoniah, his fourth son, who probably thought that, as a result of his bereavement, the king would be too weak to punish him. He received help in high political and military circles, and acted as if he were already king, going nowhere without an impressive escort of horsemen and officers and preceded by fifty runners. Was David informed? If he was, he did not take offense. Did he know that Adoniah had crowned himself sovereign, that his friends and accomplices had greeted him with shouts of "Long live the King!"? If he didn't know, the prophet Nathan saw to it that he found out. First he went to see Bath-Sheba, Solomon's mother, to offer his help. He instructed her to start a quarrel with her husband. A very precise script was worked out by Nathan. Hadn't the king promised that *her* son, Solomon,

would succeed him on the throne? Was it right for him to go back
on his word? Did he realize what Adoniah was doing? Halfway
into the discussion, Nathan himself was to burst into the room
and say what was troubling *him:* that God, too, had elected Solomon, not Adoniah. Confronted by this double diplomatic offen-
sive, the king could only give in. Naturally, the prophet was right.
David ordered Solomon to be crowned king right away.

There we go again: poor David. He is still alive, and yet his
sons are already fighting over their inheritance. He is still king,
and yet his sons are already coveting his crown. How are we to
explain this lack of respect from Adoniah and from Absalom?
How are we to explain their harshness, their cynicism? What were
they doing about the divine commandment ordering children to
honor their parents? How could they even think about ruling over
the *people* of Israel when they were violating the noblest precepts
of the *tradition* of Israel?

You may argue that Solomon, at least, was a credit to his
father. But . . . why did he accept the crown while his father was
still alive? Couldn't he wait?

Still, when compared with his brothers, Solomon deserves
better grades. The text does not tell us how he conducted himself
before ascending the throne, only about his behavior afterward: he
was respectful and devoted to his father's memory.

Actually, he also demonstrated a kind of affectionate understanding of his usurping brother Adoniah. He promised to spare
his life, and in fact "did not touch a single hair on his head," did
not punish him or humiliate him in any way. Quite the opposite:
he welcomed him at the palace and sent him away loaded with
presents.

In other words, as a son, Solomon seems almost perfect. Is
that why tradition placed him on such a high pedestal? He was the
one to build the Temple. He was the one to inaugurate it. He was
the one to allow us—thanks to his parables and proverbs—to draw
from the Torah the way one draws from a living but inaccessible
fountain. He was the one to give his people a sense of security and
happiness. In the annals of Jewish history, his portrait arouses love
and reverence. He was a judge of incomparable integrity, an enlightened leader, a guide whose spiritual radiance was unprecedented. He was a perfect king, a perfect son, a perfect man. His
first name—Jedidiah—suits him: he was God's friend. God was *his*
friend. God talked to him in dreams. He asked him: "What do you

wish from me?" As he was intelligent, Solomon asked for intelligence; as he was wise, he requested wisdom. And God answered him: "You could have asked for wealth and power, but you requested wisdom and knowledge; I shall give them to you—and you will *also* have wealth and power."

His authority was unlimited. All the kings of the earth rushed forward to Jerusalem to see him and to hear him. They sent their sons to him to be his secretaries and his servants. His word became law. His will was done.

And it did not go to his head. The text says: "And God bestowed upon Solomon much wisdom and perception, and a generosity of heart as wide as the sand near the ocean.

"And Solomon's wisdom was greater than that of all the people of Kedem— and it surpassed that of the wisdom of Egypt.

"And he was wiser than all men from Eithan Ha-ezra'hi, Heman and Khalkoml and Darda—the sons of Makhol—and his name became famous among all neighboring people.

"And he told three thousand parables and sang a thousand and one songs . . . and he spoke about trees and beasts, fowl and fish . . . and from all around the people came to listen to the wisdom of Solomon. . . ."

Any other person would have succumbed to vanity—not Solomon.

Countless legends praise his wisdom as well as his humanity. The case of the two mothers arguing over who the child belonged to is well known. As a connoisseur of the human soul, he measured well the strength of a mother's love: he knew that no mother would tolerate seeing her child cut in two. He knew a son's love, too. He was the only one of all of King David's sons to respect him and to love him with all his heart and soul. In order to shelter his father's body against the sun, he ordered eagles to spread their black wings and give him shade. The eagles obeyed, for he understood all languages; he was a master of all disciplines, in all cultures. He was well acquainted with the language of the birds and that of wild beasts. All creatures submitted to him. Animals stood in line outside his kitchen to be slaughtered in his honor. The great of this world were prepared to pay anything for an invitation to dinner.

Once, after drinking some good wine, he decided to entertain his guests by ordering demons and goblins to play and dance. Thereupon a bird told him of its sorrows. "For three months, I haven't eaten, I haven't had a drink of water, I haven't slept. That's because I've just been traveling the world over in search of a place that is not under your rule, Majesty. Well, I found it. It is located in the kingdom of Sheba. There, dust is more precious than gold. Money has no value whatsoever. As for water, the inhabitants draw it from paradise itself. Another thing: that kingdom possesses numerous armies, but . . . they do not know how to fight. They are under the rule of a woman, their queen. If you will allow me, Majesty, I can go back there and bring her to you, along with her ministers and her officers."

King Solomon agrees. He ties a letter to the bird's feet with the following words, more or less: "From me, King Solomon, peace be with you and your government. . . . Surely you know that God has granted me rule over animals, birds, and demons. All kings, from the East to the West, come to pay me homage. If you will come, too, I shall cover you with honors. If you refuse, I shall send the wild animals and the small demons who are my horsemen and soldiers to strangle all of you in your beds. . . ."

The bird flies away. He arrives in the kingdom of Sheba one morning, at the very hour when the queen is leaving her palace to recite her prayers to the sun. But the sun suddenly seems to be extinguished: swarms of birds are hiding it with their wings. The frightened queen bursts into tears. Then the messenger bird descends from the sky and delivers the message to her. Intrigued and scared, the queen consults her advisers. They tell her it is safer to stay home. But she dares not turn down the invitation. For three years, she is on the road to Jerusalem. Once she arrives, she falls into a trap. The king welcomes her in a glass house. The royal visitor thinks that he is in the water, in a pool. In order to come near, she raises her skirt and involuntarily uncovers her hairy legs. "Your beauty is that of a woman," the king tells her, "but you are hairy like a man." Provoked and offended, she seeks revenge; she asks the king three riddles. He solves them easily. Dazzled, the Queen of Sheba cries out, "Now I realize that everything that has been said about your wisdom is far below the truth." From then on, a deep friendship is established between the two sovereigns, one which would provide a living for many a novelist, filmmaker, and Broadway producer.

Another virtue of King Solomon: when he sets about erecting the Temple, he avails himself of his foreign connections and his knowledge of the occult and the animal worlds. That project is dearer to him and more urgent than the building of his own palace: he puts more time and more energy into it. His whole kingdom, more than that, the whole universe, is called upon to help. One hundred and fifty thousand foreign laborers work ceaselessly under the supervision of three thousand Jewish foremen. Twenty thousand slaves are used to carry stones from the quarries to the construction yard. Everyone works night and day in an atmosphere of excitement. There are no quarrels, no strikes, no illnesses to slow down the work. Surely, now and then, there is an incident. For example: the workers that the Egyptian Pharaoh sends him are destined to die within the coming year. Astrologers have told him so. Pharaoh thinks he'll play a trick on the Jewish king. The only thing is, Solomon has a gift for prophecy. Therefore he sends back the Egyptians, and supplies them with their funeral gowns. And to Pharaoh he writes: "Apparently you are lacking in fabrics. I'm sending some to you along with your men." Miraculously, not one workman becomes ill, not one tool is broken during construction. Then comes the glorious day of inauguration. This is a unique and privileged moment: the Temple in all its splendor is about to be consecrated to God. God will have His sanctuary erected in the city of David. This is a moment of sublime union between the Creator and His Creation, of perfect harmony between the God of Israel and the people of Israel. How could one not be drunk with happiness? The king prays with his open hands reaching out toward the sky. The Midrash comments: This is—as it were—to say: Look, I have taken nothing away from the Temple, my prayer is devoid of any personal worry; I am only thinking of the welfare of the community.

Suddenly, worry sets in. The doors of the Temple won't open. It's impossible to bring in the Holy Ark. Panic-stricken, Solomon recites twenty-four songs of praise. All in vain. The doors still won't part: "Lord, do it in memory of your servant David," he cries out. This time, he meets with success. The doors open; the inauguration will take place.

At that hour, the Midrash tells us, David's enemies lost face, for the whole nation realized that God had forgiven David his illicit love for Bath-Sheba. What an admirable man Solomon was, commentators would say later. He was able to contradict tradition. While the Midrash maintains that no one can obtain pardon by proxy, David, for his part, obtained it through his son's intercession.

There is, however, one point which requires elaboration. When God informs David that not he but Solomon will be the one to build the Temple, why doesn't David protest? Why does he accept the punishment of God with so much serenity? He doesn't even argue. Could it be that he does not regard it as a punishment? Could it be that, on the contrary, he views it as a kindness? It is as if God were saying to him, "Don't worry, David. Your son will go far. You will be proud of him, as I will be. For he will build the Temple to my glory. That's right, David: You are the father of a Temple builder. . . ."

Thus, people like David's successor and heir. When he is happy, they don't envy his pride. When he is unhappy, they weep over his fate.

But in Midrashic literature our sages are not always proud of Solomon. They say he's vain, arrogant, hungry for power, grandiose, unable to stand contradiction. He imposes heavy taxes in order to finance his big projects. The beginning of his reign is a particularly bloody period. Some influential political adversaries are murdered. A High Priest is dismissed from office. The king's court is known for its pomp and is crowded with courtiers.

True, the country is enjoying an unusual period of peace but spiritually it seems to be lacking in strength, in creative energy, in faith. Foreigners, lured by material prospects, erect their own temples: to Astarte of Zidon, Milkom of Aamon, and K'mosh of Moab. Why does Solomon allow that? He doesn't intervene, doesn't forbid anything. One prophet—Ahia ha-Shiloni—takes him to task a little, but it is clear that idol worship is the last of the king's worries. Idolatry does not concern Jews; it concerns "others." Why quarrel with one's neighbors and *their* gods? Let everyone do and pray as they please. A policy of laxity? Some sages do not appreciate it.

Besides, there *are* legends told about King Solomon which one can qualify as disconcerting, so lacking are they in human warmth. In order to illustrate his proverb, "I have found one virtuous man in a thousand, but I haven't found one virtuous woman in a thousand," he took the liberty of breaking up a family. He ordered his servants to find an ideal couple, which they did. Husband and wife loved each other dearly and lived in fear of God. Solomon summoned the husband and said to him, "If you do as I tell you, I'll make you rich and powerful." The man inquired as to what he must do to please the king. "Kill your wife," said Solomon. Seduced by the king's promises, the husband overcame his shock and accepted the contract. Solomon provided him with a sword and sent him home. However, the husband could not strike his wife. As he watched her sleeping, he thought about their children and decided that nothing in the world was worth the happiness he had known with his family. Therefore he reappeared before the king and said to him, "Sorry, Sire, I cannot do it." Thereupon, Solomon had the wife summoned. And he made a similar offer to her: If she killed her husband, she would become the king's favorite concubine. She, too, declared herself ready. At night, after putting her husband to sleep with loving caresses, she seized the sword she had received from the king, and . . . the assassination attempt failed. We do not know the husband's reaction, but we do know that Solomon was happy: You see? Not one woman in a thousand is really virtuous.

I do not like that legend; nor that kind of wisdom. King Solomon should not have gone that far. Since he was so clever, he could have found some other way of illustrating his antifeminist bias. No one has the right to use human beings to prove a point. Love may be tested—but only by its own protagonists. I may try to ascertain whether someone loves me, but not whether someone loves—or betrays—someone else. Nothing justifies playing people against people. Furthermore, no one has the right to torment a family by tearing it apart, by shattering its peace—no one, surely not the king.

Of course, this legend is only a legend—but so are all the others. Some describe Solomon's powers—and others his limitations. One day he ran into the Angel of Death, who looked depressed. He wanted to know why. "Ah," answered the angel, "I am sad for I am compelled to take these two black-skinned men with me." So Solomon, wishing to outsmart him, sent the two men speedily to Loz, a special province where the Angel of Death had no jurisdiction. The next day, Solomon met the Angel of Death, who now seemed exuberant. Again, the king wanted to know why. "I am happy," said the angel, "because they came exactly where I was waiting for them." (Incidentally, this legend will reverberate in numerous stories about an encounter in Samarkand.)

Why didn't Solomon see through the angel's game? Perhaps because his wisdom was not absolute, nor was his piety. When conducting textual analysis of Talmudic tales and commentaries one will sense a growing discomfort with the king. Suddenly we learn that the population is worried—worried and discontented: the taxes are too heavy, the king has too many horses and too many luxurious carriages. In short, his life-style is too sumptuous, certainly too showy. He has too many wives. The law allows him eighteen, but he has one thousand—if one is to believe an unbelievable legend.

His passion for women does meet with serious objections in Talmudic literature. Our great sages resent his marrying an Egyptian princess, Pharaoh's daughter, the night when the construction of the Temple was completed. Couldn't the wedding have been postponed?

A sage comments: That was also the night when, far from there, Rome was founded.

Another sage adds: That night, the people of Israel experienced joy and so did Pharaoh's daughter. And her happiness was greater than that of the people of Israel. That was when, up in heaven, God decided that one day the holy city would be destroyed. This is the way one Rabbi Hillel, son of Heleni, talks about it: "It's like someone arriving in a dirty place and frowning in disgust."

There is something odd and disconcerting about sages wishing to make events coincide: on the one hand a collective climax in faith and on the other a threat of collective darkness. So—Jewish history thought it would please God by building a Temple to Him? That was a mistake: God turned away from it. That night, which was to be engraved in letters of gold and fire in God's memory and design, was also to bring grief and sorrow. Because of whom? Because of Solomon. He was too happy—that is, too happy with a woman—too happy with a foreign wife. He was wrong to mix his blessings. That night they should all have brought him closer to God. After all, that was not an ordinary night. Pharaoh's daughter should have waited. But she was impatient. The daughter of Pharaoh was cunning, too. Rav Hunia says: That night she performed eighty different dances for Solomon. Some sages go further; according to them, she hired a thousand singers who sang for him, and each time she would say to him, You see, this is how *we* worship such and such an idol. . . . Another commentator hints that Solomon had wished to stop the entertainment, to get up and open the Temple in time for the four o'clock morning service. But Pharaoh's daughter had spread out a blanket above their bed, a sort of canopy in which diamonds and other precious stones were inlaid in the shape of bright stars. Solomon would see them and say to himself, It's still nighttime, there's no need to hurry. Then, Rabbi Levi says, the people of Israel, who had gathered in front of the Temple, grew dejected. They wanted to go into the Temple and recite the appropriate prayers, but the gates were locked: the keys were kept under Solomon's pillow. And the people were afraid to wake him up. Finally, they knocked on the door of the queen mother, Bath-Sheba. And she went to wake up her son; she had harsh words for him— words only an offended mother could utter.

Was Solomon a bon vivant, a hedonist, a sinner? Was he the opposite of the wise man he was supposed to be? Was Solomon busy making love to an Egyptian wife at the very moment when his people were surrendering to God in fervor? Was Solomon sleeping even as his people were yearning to have their prayers heard? How is one to understand these shortcomings, these ethical failures in a man whose name and work remain connected to that which is most sacred in Jewish history?

Some commentators of the Talmud ascribe his lapses to his extreme intelligence: he was at its mercy. He thought he could push back *any* temptation and overcome *any* moral obstacle. For example, the Torah forbids the king to have too many horses and too many wives so he will not run the risk of being led astray. Solomon's reaction? I shall take that risk; nothing can happen to me. *That* was his mistake. Boasting is dangerous. Whoever thinks that he or she is smarter than Satan proves that someone else— Satan?—is the smarter one. The text states it explicitly: "In his old age, Solomon let his wives get the upper hand." Commented Rabbi Hiya bar Abba: "Solomon would have cleaned sewers to have this verse omitted from the Bible."

"Too late"—the expression that stamps every tragedy with its dark seal: too late to alter the past, too late to undo what has been done. At the end of his life, Solomon realized this. And so he composed *Kohelet*—Ecclesiastes—a philosophical work filled with skepticism, bitterness, and melancholy. Yet at least one Midrashic source insists that Solomon wrote *Kohelet* not when he was old, but when he was young . . . and romantic.

Perhaps. Such is the paradox of human behavior that young people love to play with death, whereas old people enjoy recalling the exuberance of their youth.

Still, the first version appears more logical, more natural. At the end of the road one has a better understanding of oneself. So many missed opportunities, so many false triumphs. Ah, there is that meeting I should not have canceled. That word I should not have written. That temptation I should have resisted. If only I could do it all over again. . . . Too late. Too late to go back, other than in your mind. Too late to try to mend the broken heart.

Having lived a long and eventful life, the author of *Kohelet* knew what all aged persons know: namely, that everything in life is ephemeral. Everything has an end.

This story, too? Yes. But . . . wait a minute, one more tale, about a bizarre "event" that almost destroyed King Solomon's self-confidence.

In some strange circumstances, an angel—some say, Ashmedai, the king of demons—succeeded in stealing King Solomon's kingdom away from him. He sat on his throne, assumed his physical appearance, his features, the expression in his eyes, the intonation of his voice. He mimicked his way of questioning, of answering, of listening, of eating, of walking, and of sleeping. The nation did not know it, but Ashmedai had become its king.

Naturally, this raises some questions. How could Solomon, the intelligent ruler, be so careless as to let a stranger, a hostile stranger, come so close? Furthermore, where were his sons? Where were they when their father was exiled from his own palace? Why didn't they protect him? Were they, too, fooled by Ashmedai?

The Midrash first portrays Ashmedai in chains, totally at Solomon's mercy. Lamenting on being a prisoner, he asks Solomon, "You already rule over the whole world, did you have to conquer me, too?" Yes. Solomon needed him, says the Midrash. Not as a prisoner but as a worker. There were certain technical tasks which only Ashmedai could perform. Solomon must have enjoyed watching Satan give his best as a construction worker.

One day, after the Temple was finished, the king and his prisoner found themselves alone somewhere, indulging in nostalgic meditations, recalling the excitement of the last days. "Tell me," said Solomon, "where does your superior strength come from?" "I will show you," answered Ashmedai. "Just free me from my chains—and lend me your ring." Succumbing to his curiosity, Solomon freed him and handed him his ring, which Ashmedai quickly swallowed only to spit it far, far away. Whereupon Solomon moaned, "What remains, then, of all that man does under the sun?" and also, "All I am left with is my cane. Before, I used to rule over Israel. Now all I rule over is my cane."

For three years, Solomon was a humbled king—punished for giving Ashmedai too many powers. He wandered from town to town, from house to house, from one place to another, knocking on people's doors and saying, *"Ani Shlomo,* I am Solomon. . . ." And the people laughed. They made fun of him and his hallucinations. They threw him out of their homes, treated him like a crazy beggar, an annoying intruder. He was unwelcome everywhere. Still, he kept repeating, "I am Solomon." "You?" people mocked. "Enough of your nonsense. While you are talking here, King Solomon is seated on his throne in Jerusalem!" One day he presented himself before the Sanhedrin—and provoked astonishment. Some judges felt that there was something odd and disturbing about the man and his unusual fixation. They opened an inquiry which uncovered the full magnitude of the scandal. With the help of the Ineffable Name, Solomon was then able to disarm Ashmedai and to imprison him once more. The king recovered his throne, his kingdom, his identity. But he was no longer the same person. Now he knew what it was like to be someone else.

In conclusion, one last question: Was he a good father? Did he learn something from his own experiences? The Bible reminds us that he had serious problems with his son Rehoboam. Let me paraphrase his words: Generations come and go, all rivers flow into the ocean—and the thirst for power is never satisfied. What then is the answer?

A legend:

Toward the end of his life, Solomon had a ring made—one that was endowed with strange powers. Whenever he was unhappy, all he had to do was put it on to find joy again. Whenever he was happy, all he had to do was to put it on to find himself unhappy as before. What was its secret? Three words: *"Gam ze yaavor*—That, too, shall pass."

What remains of a story after it is finished?

Another story.

Ezekiel

No PROPHET was endowed with such vision. No other vision was so extreme. No man has shed such light on the future—for no other light was so forceful in tearing darkness apart. But then, no one had ever seen such darkness, the total darkness that precedes the breaking of dawn.

It is enough to follow his gaze to be carried by the hope it conjures. Look when he orders you to do so and you will be rewarded by the conviction that hope is forever justified. Listen to his words, to his voice, and you will feel strong—stronger than death, more powerful than evil.

Ezekiel: Who has not heard of this intriguing and passionate speaker whose visions of horror and beauty have left an impact on innumerable generations? No messenger has hurt us more—none has offered us such balm.

When he is harsh, he seems pitiless; when he is kind, his generosity spills over. In his worst outbursts, he declares his own nation ugly and repugnant; but suddenly he recovers his compassion, and everything and everyone radiates sunshine and serenity.

He oscillates between the shame of sin and the grandeur of salvation—for him there is nothing in between. Ezekiel: the man of extremes. He goes from the ecstasy of the chariot (the *Merkava*) to the terror of dry bones in the desert. Let us read together:

> And I looked, and behold, a whirlwind came out of the north, a great cloud and a fire unfolding itself, and a brightness was about it, and out of the midst thereof as the color of amber, out of the midst of the fire.
>
> Also out of the midst thereof came the likeness of four living creatures. And this was their appearance; they

had the likeness of man. And every one had four faces,
and every one had four wings. . . .

What follows is known but rarely understood. In fact, the
entire centuries-old tradition of *Merkava* or Hekhalot literature—
the one dealing with the celestial chariot—stems from Ezekiel's
description of his first oneiric, fantastic hallucination in his book.

What are those human and animal creatures, both monstrous
and divine, that have appeared on our small orderly planet? What
do these extraterrestrial beings try to achieve in our midst? What
is the purpose of their visit?

Their feet were straight feet—and the sole of their feet
was like the sole of a calf's foot. . . . And they had the
hands of a man under their wings on their four sides—
and they too had their faces and their wings. . . . And
their wings were joined one to another. . . .

It reads like a feverish dream, if not a nightmare: all those
human and inhuman masks intertwined. Fragmented images, halt-
ing sentences, deafening shouts and soft whispers, words and
silences, are being used to describe that which defies description:
a realm where heaven and earth merge into one element combin-
ing fire and crystal, fear and joy, the first and last memory of man
facing his destiny.

"The likeness of man, the likeness of lions and eagles, the
likeness of the firmament, the likeness of the throne . . ." has
Ezekiel seen—really seen—all that? Has God really chosen to show
him all that he conceals from all others? If so, why? Why Ezekiel?
What made him so special? All the questions raised with respect to
prophets and prophecy—the element of compulsion in the divine
mission, the unpredictability of the prophet's responses—are even
more valid as they pertain to Ezekiel. What had he done to deserve
to speak in God's name? Why are his words burning with so much
anger, and then with so much deep affection?

There are, in his book and in his vocabulary, themes, subjects,
expressions that can be found nowhere else. For instance: he "eats"
his words; he mentions "heart transplants"—hearts of flesh instead
of stone; the poetic term "Ben Adam," son of man, is used with
such frequency that it almost becomes his surname. Also, he is the
prophet to speak of the synagogue as a "Mikdash-meat," a min-

iature, temporary Temple. Has he seen the real one? Only in his imagination but his description—far away from Jerusalem—is so real, so vivid, that it is a jewel in itself. Ezekiel, the prophet of imagination: more than his peer Jeremiah, he imagined both exile and redemption in ways that made them both tangible. More important, he was the first to speak of *Kiddush hashem*—of Israel's privilege and awesome obligation to sanctify the Lord's name.

No wonder, then, that his narrative seizes the reader with such force. Through turbulent years of endless wanderings, it is his voice that we follow from agony to agony and then to rebirth.

From his exile, Ezekiel speaks to all generations, and particularly to ours, for, more than his own contemporaries, we have witnessed the frailty of social structures and the irresistible power of spiritual courage and dreams.

For once upon a time some of us did indeed see a deserted land covered with dry bones.

And yes, we could testify to man's ability to transform memories of tragedy into necessary hope.

Indeed, no generation can understand Ezekiel as well—as profoundly—as ours. Just read the text and . . .

Vayehi bishloshim shana . . . And it came to pass in the thirtieth year, in the fourth month, in the fifth day of the month, I was then in exile—or among the exiled, the captives—by the river of Chebar, when suddenly the heavens were opened and I saw visions of God. . . .

Clearly, the story opens in the manner of a chronicle. The style is precise. The chronicler does not want the reader to be confused. Thus we know what happened, and where, and when, and to whom.

But just in case more information is needed, the chronicler adds that the event occurred during the fifth year of King Yehoiakin's captivity.

"*Hayo haya dvar adoshem el Yehezkel ben Buzi hakohen*. . . . The word of God came to Ezekiel son of Buzi the priest, while being in the land of the Chaldeans by the river Chebar. And the hand of God was laid upon him, and *Vaere vehine,* and I looked and behold: a whirlwind came out of the north. . . ."

But . . . do not look—not yet. We have not finished with the opening statement which presents certain problems. The story begins in the first person—*Vaani,* jumps to the third—*Vatehi Alav,* and returns to the first: *Vaere,* "and I looked."

Should we conclude from this that the prophet's knowledge of Hebrew grammar was faulty or that people even then had identity problems? Or that he wanted to illustrate his own split personality? Or that the prophet is always subject and object in his own tale? The answer probably lies elsewhere. The switch in person may indicate a certain confusion in the mind of the prophet—which would be only natural. After all, we are at the beginning of the story. The prophet has just been contacted by God—and he is still shaken by the experience. Most prophets had similar reactions: prophecy was thrust upon them. Couldn't God speak more gently to his chosen? Apparently not. Prophecy always began with a shock. Is this why Ezekiel suddenly left reality and moved into a world of fantasy? The historian has been turned into a visionary. Is this why, unlike Jeremiah or Jonah or Moses, he did not resist the call? He did not say, Why me? Leaving time and reason behind, he looked and saw chariots of fire, strange beasts, and half human, half divine creatures—he looked and saw what exists outside or above Creation.

How is one to explain the abrupt change? The man who, just one passage earlier, insists on clarity and precision, has allowed his mind to wander so much so that he forgets to tell us something that may be of essential importance. Didn't he say that "God spoke to him"? Then why doesn't he tell us what God said? No, he does not tell us what he heard because he is too busy describing what he saw!

And what he saw is so unreal that those of us who dwell in reality are forbidden to follow his gaze and look and . . . speak about it.

Listen to the Mishna in the Treatise of Hagiga: *Ein dorshin baarayot bishlosha:* One must not debate with three students questions about intimate relations between men and women, *vlo be-maase breshit bishnayim*—nor the mysteries of Creation with two students, *vlo ba-merkava beyahid*—nor the mystery of the *Merkava,* the chariot, with just one student. This last reference is, once again, to the visions that Prophet Ezekiel had in Babylon in the fifth year of King Yehoiakhin's captivity.

Merkava experiences are forbidden territory, dangerous to outsiders. One cannot approach them with impunity. Why should the mystery of Creation be considered less perilous than that of the chariot? Maimonides comments: The first is about Creation, the second about its Creator. Creation is immanent and therefore perceivable—the Creator is not.

Gershom Scholem quotes ancient texts—of the Hekhalot literature—that warn us against trespassing mystical frontiers:

"If a person was unworthy to see the King in his beauty, the angels at the gates disturbed his senses and confused him. And when they said to him, 'Come in,' he entered, and instantly they pressed him and threw him into the fiery lava stream. . . . And at the gate of the sixth of the seven palaces, it seemed as though hundreds of thousands and millions of waves of water stormed against him, and yet there was not a drop of water. . . . But he, the visitor, asked the angels, What is the meaning of these waters? And they began to stone him: 'Wretched, do you not see with your own eyes? Are you perhaps a descendant of those who kissed the Golden Calf and thus are unworthy to see the King in his beauty?' And they struck him with iron bars and wounded him. . . ."

In other words, not only are we not able to understand Ezekiel's chariot visions, but we are not even allowed to make them an object of scholarly analysis. Why? What is so special about what Ezekiel saw—and why had he, he alone, been permitted to see it?

Let us open his file. Who was he? What information is there about his life and work? We know that he was a priest, that he traveled a lot, and spoke a lot, that his command of language was both disturbing and enchanting, and . . . what else? We know his mannerisms, his style, his remarkable courage—or was it naiveté?—in using repetition. Examples? The expression "son of man" appears a hundred times; "*Adoshem, adoshem*—O Lord, O Lord"—two hundred times; "*Vayad'u ki ani adoshem*—And they shall know that I am the Lord"—fifty times; "*gilulim*—idolatry"— *only* thirty-nine times. What was his nationality? Was he a Palestinian prophet sent by God to Babylon? Was he a Babylonian immigrant from Palestine who returned to Palestine? Some sources say he was one or the other, some texts claim he was both—or neither.

From the text itself we gather that he had been exiled, together with his king and the king's court, to Babylon—we know the exact location of his dwelling: Tel-Aviv on the river Chebar.

Babylonian sources tell us that Tel-Aviv, or Tel-Abib, referred to ruins from before the Floods. In our literature the name fares somewhat better. We are told that Tel-Aviv was in ancient times the largest Jewish city in the Diaspora. Its population: ten thousand souls. They spoke Hebrew and they were prosperous and respected. We are also told that they observed Jewish law.

A Midrash tells us of a certain bird-watcher, Hananya ben Menahem, who kept two hundred and seventy-seven different species at home in Jerusalem. He was so famous that the emperor Nebuchadnezzar himself wanted to meet him—probably to offer him a job. He dispatched an emissary to Tel-Aviv but Hananya ben Menahem refused to go with him, saying, You forgot that it's Shabbat today, I don't travel on Shabbat. Instead, he traveled to Babylon one day later, and the emperor gave him a splendid apartment near or inside his palace to keep an eye on the royal birds.

As for Ezekiel, we know that he began to prophesy six or seven years before Jerusalem's final tragedy, and that he continued for another twelve to fifteen years. Was he married? Yes. His wife died of the plague, and he saw in her death a prefiguration of the destruction of Jerusalem. So affected was he that for a while he lost his power of speech, suffering from aphasia.

Did he have brothers? Friends? Allies? He had enemies—that has been established. Like most prophets, he constantly provoked anger and hostility. Some of his adversaries ridiculed him by saying, "Who is he, anyway, to talk the way he does? Isn't he a descendant of that woman of ill repute, you know, Rahab, the harlot who made Jericho famous?" Like Jeremiah, he used pantomime to promulgate his views—and fears. When he warned the people of Gilgal of the coming exile, he paraded through the streets carrying a knapsack, thus telling them that they too would become wanderers. At twilight he would dig a hole in the wall and steal out into the darkness like a fugitive, a refugee. Like Jeremiah, he must have felt that he would not die in the Holy Land. Jeremiah was buried in Egypt, Ezekiel in Babylon. Iraqi Jews thought they knew the location of his grave and came to pray there, imploring him to intercede on their behalf.

Yes—Ezekiel endured much torment and agony throughout his life. No wonder that God felt the need to repeatedly encourage and comfort him, telling him not to worry, not to heed his critics, not to be hurt by their mockery, to speak up even if his words were to fall on deaf ears—even if his mission were to bring no immediate results.

As a prophet, he was not free to choose either to speak or remain silent; he was told when to make himself visible and when to remain invisible. From the Book itself we receive the script God prepared for His emissary Ezekiel. He is ordered to stay seven days under house arrest. Alone? Yes, to illustrate loneliness. The effect on him is obvious: he becomes harsh, demanding, unyielding, misanthropic.

Occasionally he is instructed to act "dumb," or else to be provocative. He is to prepare a model of what Jerusalem would be like under siege; he is amazingly accurate, always. The halls, the gates, the light, the odors, the sounds, the mood: he describes the punishment of the sacred city, its hunger, its pain, its repulsive decline. Lying motionless, he paints the convulsions of a society at war. To symbolize the unclean food people will eat in captivity, he prepares a cake made of excrement. He shaves his head and lets the wind disperse his hair to illustrate the fate of his rebellious fellow Jews.

Naturally, Ezekiel became a perfect subject for psychoanalysts. Some experts called him "psychotic," others left it at "pathological." One analyst found that our prophet had "catatonic periods" which resulted from his "paranoiac" tendencies. Want to hear more? Here are more diagnoses: "narcissistic masochistic conflicts . . . fantasies of castration . . . unconscious sexual regression . . . schizophrenia . . . delusions of persecution, delusions of grandeur. . . ."

His sermons have the quality and the urgency of eyewitness reporting. Mindful of every detail, he tells us what is going on in God's favorite dwelling place: in short, it reminds him of Sodom, for which the key word is *Toeva*—abomination—the physical and moral prostitution, social decadence, intellectual depravation: one could produce an entire encyclopedia of sin just using Ezekiel's vocabulary. He is particularly severe with the leaders; we are informed of what they are saying, thinking, doing, plotting inside and outside the sanctuary. Are there no good people in the land? No Just Men left? He speaks of the Elders who, in exasperation, began to wonder whether God had not abandoned his people altogether . . .

I quote: "And the glory of God said unto me: son of man, look and see what they are doing in my house, to my house. . . . See the great abominations? Look well and you will notice even greater ones."

Old leaders and priests now worship idols. Listen to the language: "Son of man, have you seen what the ancients of the House of Israel do in the dark—or in the secret chambers of their imagination? They say to themselves, Anything is permitted for God cannot see us—He has forsaken this land and abandoned its inhabitants."

But that is not all, says God to the prophet. Look and you will see worse. "Then he brought me to the door of the Temple's gate and behold, there were women weeping for the idol Tammuz. . . ." Wait, says God to Ezekiel. There is even worse. And He took me inside the inner court and between the porch and the altar I saw about twenty-five men, with their backs to the Temple, worshiping the sun.

And then God uses an expression that reminded Ezekiel—and us—of Noah and the Floods: *"Ki malu et haaretz khamas.* They filled the land with violence"—and *that* was the worst. As long as people offended heaven, God, in spite of his anger, was willing to wait. But when they ceased to be human toward one another, He had to intervene—and punish them.

Few prophets have ever spoken with such despair. To the inhabitants of Jerusalem he says that they will be defeated; to those in Babylon he says that their deliverance is not near. Of course, like most prophets, he emphasizes the cycle of sin, punishment, and redemption—but according to him, redemption is far, far away. Redemption seems improbable, if not impossible. So much so that one is allowed to wonder, Why does the prophet insist with such fervor on Jewish weaknesses and transgressions? Does he enjoy shaming the Jews? One reason may be that, knowing of the catastrophe in the making, he wants the Jewish people to have an explanation; he wants to save them from absurdity. Better that they think their plight represents punishment than gratuitous cruelty. Any answer may be better than no answer.

The prophet knows the future because he observes the present. No sin will go unpunished. Collective depravation must result in collective agony. If his description is correct—if disgust, both real and spiritual, dominates the mood of the story—then tragedy is inevitable. Not immediately; later, much later. As in the case of Jeremiah, it will take two decades before Ezekiel's predictions come to pass. But then, history itself will shudder.

Now we must ask ourselves, Was Israel really that bad, that sinful?

Open the book of history and turn the pages. . . .

Though a vassal state to Babylon, Judea enjoyed internal freedom. After a short reign of some one hundred days, King Yehoiakhin and his entourage, together with skilled technicians in the thousands, had been deported to Babylon, leaving behind a newly appointed king, a weakling named Zidkiyahu (or Zedekias). Pressured by Egypt and Phoenicia to rebel against Babylon, Zedekias finally gave up his position of comfortable neutrality and allowed his militant advisers to move the nation into war. The enemy emperor, Nebuchadnezzar, dispatched his army, and thus began the military siege of Jerusalem.

Inside the country, the morale was low. The enemy was mighty and the Jews desperate. They could not comprehend God's ways: Why had He forsaken His people which, under King Josiah, had shown such force of character and faith by repudiating idolatry and sin and by undertaking one of the most impressive shows of repentance in history? Despair led to spiritual corruption. Since God seemed unjust, why should men be just?

Judea's spiritual leaders, the four prophets—Jeremiah, Uriah son of Shemaiah, Habakkuk, and Ezekiel—tried hard to change the mood; in vain. Uriah was beheaded, Jeremiah jailed, Ezekiel persecuted and humiliated.

And yet, in the gentile world, culture is flourishing. Athenians build the Acropolis and celebrate a philosopher named Thales of Miletus, Aesop's fables, Aeschylus's dramas, and the oracles at Delphi. The Chinese enjoy the wisdom of Lao-tze. The Maya build their temples in Mexico. World history is moving forward in waves of upheaval, the various emperors forever dissatisfied with what they possess, forever aspiring to enlarge their empires.

Somehow Judea is always caught in the middle of their political and strategic designs. Egypt and Babylon are enemies—and again, both need Judea. Strange: all the empires of the times seem to need Judea. And eventually all will vanish—with the exception of Judea. The Chaldeans, the Assyrians, the Phoenicians, the Persians, the Egyptians, the Romans—all had to withdraw from Judea. Judea alone remained in Judea.

Most prophets found it necessary to address themselves to other nations as well as to Judea. Just as Jeremiah was called *navi lagoyim*—a prophet to gentile nations—Ezekiel, too, could be classified as a prophet to the enemy nations. For not only did he predict the destruction of Israel, he also foretold the doom of Tyre and Egypt. That was his way of emphasizing again and again that suffering is contagious—as is evil itself. When one people is subjected to humiliation, others are bound to follow. And ultimately the destroyer will be destroyed—and the victimizer will be someone else's victim.

Is this enough to console the victim? I do not think so. That is why Ezekiel came forth with his vision of the dry bones. In the Jewish tradition, one may not rejoice over an enemy's downfall. The enemy's punishment offers no consolation to the victim. The victim's rehabilitation, and victory, and redemption must not be linked to other people's suffering. The theme, the purpose—call it the message—in Ezekiel's sermons is not victory but repentance. If the sinner repents, he will live; if he does not, he will die.

It is in Ezekiel's Book that we find the poignant verse *"Vaomar lakh bedamayikh hayi, vaomar lakh bedamayikh hayi*—And I shall tell you: you shall live in thy blood, in thy blood you shall live." In *thy* blood, not in your enemies'.

At one point, God places the sinner's fate on the prophet's shoulders: it is Ezekiel's responsibility to save him. Too heavy a burden? Perhaps. So God compromises. Your task, he says, is to try. Speak to the sinner, teach him, chastise him, warn him. If he refuses to be saved, at least you will have saved yourself.

Did Ezekiel succeed? He tried—he tired hard. Obeying God's orders to the letter, he went so far as to do supernatural things. While staying in Babylon, he "flew" back and forth to Jerusalem, he inspected the celestial chariot, described events hidden in the future, and subjected himself to humiliation and ridicule, never complaining about his own ordeal.

When he himself enters the story, we are moved. Jeremiah spoke of captives, Ezekiel referred to refugees—and he became one himself. Suspected by everyone, resented for being on God's side, for knowing too much, for protesting against false prophets and false comfort—whatever he predicted for others ultimately happened to him, too.

And yet—we sense a certain hesitation, a certain reluctance, even a coolness toward him not only from his contemporaries, but from later generations as well. Even in Talmudic literature he is treated like . . . a refugee.

His Book is the only one of those of the Prophets that almost fell victim to censorship. For a while the Book of Ezekiel was in danger of not being published. Why such discrimination? Because of his unmitigated criticism of his people? No. Others have been as frank and as daring. Then why? Some Talmudic sages maintain that there are passages in Ezekiel that are in conflict with the Torah. Others reproach him for dealing with forbidden mystical themes. For example: "It came to pass that, in the house of a teacher, a Jewish child opened the Book of Ezekiel and began studying the story of the fire and the chariot. Soon a fire came out of the fire and burnt the child down. So the sages envisaged to suppress the Book of Ezekiel altogether."

Some critics do object to Ezekiel's frankness. They would have preferred him to indulge in some kind of cover-up. About the sins of Jerusalem? No. About the heavenly secrets. He had visions? Good for him, but why reveal them to others? He saw the heavenly chariot and its strange creatures? Why did he have to boast about it? Why couldn't he have locked his impressions in his memory—for later? The fact that Ezekiel could not resist telling the story—and what a story it was!—hurt his image in certain Talmudic circles.

One commentator states, tongue in cheek: "Any maidservant saw, while crossing the Red Sea, more than what Ezekiel would see later."

A comparison between Ezekiel and a maidservant? Well, that is something he may have shrugged off. But there were other comments of a more serious nature. Said Rava: "All that Ezekiel saw, Isaiah had seen already. And yet, there is a difference between their personalities. Ezekiel could be compared to a villager who happens to come to the city where he saw the king; Isaiah is compared to a city person who is used to seeing the king frequently, even in his own palace, and therefore is not seized by such frantic desire to tell about it."

What is clear from these stories is the resentment of some toward Ezekiel for having revealed his visions. But then, isn't he a prophet? Isn't the prophet duty-bound not to keep anything to himself? Isn't he an instrument of communication between God and mankind? Clearly, nothing in his life is private. All he has, all he is, belongs to both God and His people. His fears and hopes, his joys and depressions, his moments of turmoil and his moments of ecstasy: they are not his alone. A prophet must have no ego, no individual memory. If he hears a voice, he must echo it. If he sees visions, he must share them—right? Yes and no. Yes, as far as the voices are concerned. When God speaks, the prophet becomes His vessel. But visions—that is something else. God rarely says, Tell them what you see, but rather, Tell them what you hear.

Then why did Ezekiel choose to go beyond his mission? Mind you, it was no transgression on his part. God had not told him *not* to speak of his visions. But why was his Book placed in jeopardy? Says the Talmud, "We must remember with gratitude the good

Hananya ben Hizkiya—for were it not for his intervention, the Book of Ezekiel would have been put away."

Who was this Hananya ben Hizkiya who fought so valiantly for freedom of expression? It is in his home that the sharpest conflicts were confronted and resolved. The eighteen-point program which was exceptionally adopted as the students of Shammai outvoted those of Hillel, had been discussed in his attic. He was clearly a man for impossible missions. When some of his colleagues openly complained that the Book of Ezekiel contained passages that contradicted the Torah, he ordered for his attic enough food and candles to last until all discrepancies were clarified—and they were. Characteristically, we are not told how the scholar managed to reconcile opposites.

For instance, in the Torah it is clearly stated in the name of Moses that Hashem *"poked avon avot al banim*—that God is visiting the iniquities of the father upon his children and his children's children." But, says Rav Yosse ben Hanina, Ezekiel unashamedly challenged Moses's view by flatly declaring, "Behold, all souls are mine, says the Lord: just as the soul of the father, so also that of the son of the son: only the soul that sins will die." Moses speaks of hereditary guilt, Ezekiel stresses individual responsibility. Elsewhere, with regard to another matter, we find in the Talmud—not without some exasperation—that *"Davar ze mitorat Moshe lo lamadnu,* We have learned this not from Moses"—but from Ezekiel son of Buzi the priest.

Generally speaking, one senses that Ezekiel disturbed both his contemporaries and their learned descendants. From the fact that his Book was to be subjected to quasi-censorship, we can deduce that our sages had problems with the author as well. His interpretation of Moses's laws is only one element in the equation. There must have been others. Various hints appear in Midrashic literature, all drawing distinctions between Ezekiel and his colleagues. Efforts are made to explain strange comments about him—yet some puzzles remain unsolved *"ad bo Eliyahu,"* until the time when Prophet Elijah will come and reconcile all conflicts and solve all mysteries.

Talmudic scholars had problems with Ezekiel, who apparently had problems with God. First, he was jealous. Of whom? Of his fellow prophets. At one point, he exclaimed, Master of the Universe, am I not a priest? Am I not a prophet? Why did Isaiah speak for you in Jerusalem, while I must do the same thing here, in exile?

But then, God, too, had problems with him. When God asked his prophet, *"Hatihyena haatzamot hayévéshot haelu*—Will these dry bones come back to life?" He paused for a while, obviously waiting for an answer—and when it came, it was evasive. Instead of shouting, "Yes, they will—they must—for they and we need Your miracle," Ezekiel became a politician; he adopted a noncommittal attitude. He was too skeptical.

And that is why, says the Talmud, Ezekiel was condemned to die not in the Holy Land but in Babylon.

Another legend is even more disturbing. It came to pass that King Nebuchadnezzar ordered all his subjects in all the lands under his rule to worship one of his idols, lest they all be executed. Three representatives were chosen from each nation to act on behalf of their people. Hananya, Mishael, and Azarya represented the children of Israel. They turned to their teacher, Daniel, for advice. Daniel, in his humility, sent them to Ezekiel—who urged them to reject martyrdom and choose flight instead. They disregarded his suggestion, saying that they wished to die for *Kiddush Hashem,* the sanctification of God's name. Still, Ezekiel persisted in trying to dissuade them from becoming martyrs. When they still refused to listen, he came up with yet another proposal: that they should withhold their decision until he received word from God that He would save them through a miracle. And God's answer was no. Nevertheless, the three Just Men refused to escape—or to bow to the king's will. When Ezekiel, in despair, burst into tears, God at last offered him consolation, saying, Do not worry, they will be saved—I shall save them from the burning furnace. Why couldn't He have told him so beforehand? Only to allow their faith and their martyrdom to appear more glorious?

Good for them, but what about Ezekiel? His part in the drama is less enviable than theirs. He is made to sound weak and frightened. Instead of telling the three martyrs to be strong, he wanted them to run fast.

However, Talmudic sages have their way of balancing reticence by giving praise to the prophet's wider powers. How? He became instrumental in saving the three Just Men's lives. Hananya, Mishael, and Azarya were about to die in the Babylonian furnace when Ezekiel performed the miracle of resurrecting the dry bones. The miracle encompassed more than those directly concerned. Earlier martyrs, too, were resurrected and rejoined the living community of Israel. Do you know how Nebuchadnezzar learned of Ezekiel's miracle? "He had a drinking vessel made of the bones of a slain Jew. He was about to use it, and drink from its wine, when life began to stir in the vessel, and one bone struck the king in the face, and a voice was heard proclaiming, 'A friend of this man is right now reviving the dead.' "

Did he, really? As always, Talmudic opinions are divided. Some say, Yes, he did—and some go so far as identifying the resurrected, if not by name, at least by origin and category. Those Jews, for instance, who, in their impatience, escaped from Egypt before Moses led the whole people out of bondage. Or those who—ironically—did not believe in *Tchiat-hametim*, in resurrection. Or the young Judeans taken into captivity by Nebuchadnezzar, whose beauty drove Babylonian women mad: under pressure from their husbands, the emperor ordered the young Judeans killed. Now they were brought back to life by Ezekiel.

All these possibilities were examined during a heated session of one of the academies because of some skeptics who dared to state publicly that in their opinion the entire story of the famous dry bones was nothing but a figment of biblical imagination—or to use their language, *Mashal haya*, nothing but a parable.

Actually the debate dealt with larger and more general issues: What would happen to Tzaddikim—Just Men—in the long run? After they reached paradise, would they die again? Of course, here, too, opinions were divided. Some said yes, they will die but their deaths will be painless. And they quoted the case of the dry bones: Those men whom Ezekiel brought back to life died right away—but they didn't suffer. At which point, someone got up and said, "What nonsense! The story was fiction . . ." and thus went the discussion. Said Rabbi Eliezer, The dead that were resurrected by Ezekiel stood up, praised the Lord—and died. Someone wanted to know the nature—the text—of the praise. Said Rabbi Yeoshua, They sang *"Adoshem memit umekhaye*, The Lord causes people to die and to return to life," the Lord brings them down to the abyss—and then lifts them up to the surface. Another sage then interjected a brief, sweeping remark. All this *emet mashal haya*—all this was a true parable. Rabbi Nehemia snapped, Really? How is that possible? If it was true, it was not a parable; if it was a parable, it wasn't true. The answer? *"Beemet mashal haya*, It was truly a parable." Would you say that the debate had thus exhausted its logical—or illogical—possibilities? That rarely occurs in the Talmud. Rabbi Nehemia had barely finished his linguistic contribution when Rabbi Eliezer, son of Yosse the Galilean, made his own opinion known: he opposed the view that the dead were resurrected only to die again right away. Oh, no, said he. They made aliyah to the land of Israel, they got married and had children. An audacious thought? Rabbi Yehuda ben B'teira's was more audacious: True, he stated. They made aliyah—and I am their descendant; and the tefellin—the phylacteries—that I wear are those that I inherited from my grandfather, who was one of them.

Obviously, the episode preoccupied them to an astonishing degree. They wanted to understand its meaning, with all its implications—and its place in the life of Ezekiel and in that of our people.

For, in the text, the story is forcefully and descriptively narrated; it is one of the pinnacles of prophetic literature—perhaps still unequaled in its strange mixture of poetic realism and mystical inspiration.

Remember the setting: the place where Judea's last king Zidkiyahu (Zedekias) made his last stand against Babylonian armies. The plain is now covered with the mutilated bodies of fallen Jewish warriors. And it is there, in the midst of climactic cruelty, desolation, and mourning, that Ezekiel has his most glorious and breathtaking vision:

> The hand of the Lord was upon me, and the Lord carried me out in a spirit, and set me down in the midst of the valley, and it was full of bones; and He caused me to pass by them round about, and behold, there were very many in the open valley; and, lo, they were very dry. And He said unto me: "Son of man, can these bones live?" And I answered: "O Lord God, Thou knowest." Then He said unto me: "Prophesy over these bones, and say unto them: O ye dry bones, hear the word of the Lord: Thus saith the Lord God unto these bones: Behold, I will cause breath to enter into you, and ye shall live. And I will lay sinews upon you, and will bring up flesh upon you, and cover you with skin, and put breath in you, and ye shall live; and ye shall know that I am the Lord." So I prophesied as I was commanded; and as I prophesied, there was a noise, and behold a commotion, and the bones came together, bone to its bone. And I beheld, and, lo, there were sinews upon them, and flesh came up, and skin covered them above; but there was no breath in

them. Then said He unto me: "Prophesy unto the breath, prophesy, son of man, and say to the breath: Thus saith the Lord God: Come from the four winds, O breath, and breathe upon these slain, that they may live." So I prophesied as He commanded me, and the breath came into them, and they lived, and stood up upon their feet, an exceeding great host. Then He said unto me: "Son of man, these bones are the whole house of Israel; behold, they say: Our bones are dried up, and our hope is lost; we are clean cut off. Therefore prophesy, and say unto them: Thus saith the Lord God: Behold, I will open your graves, and cause you to come up out of your graves, O my people; and I will bring you into the land of Israel and ye shall know that I am the Lord, when I have opened your graves, and caused you to come up out of your graves, O my people. And I will put my spirit in you, and ye shall live, and I will place you in your own land; and ye shall know that I the Lord have spoken, and performed it, saith the Lord."

Like all prophets, Ezekiel opened his prophecy with predictions of doom and closed it with words of consolation. The man who had been sent by God to speak unto mountains and valleys, objects and human beings, and warn them of things to come, now felt the need to reassure his people that there would be an end to suffering and to fear. The visionary who had foreseen a time when a third of Jerusalem would perish through famine, a third by the enemy's sword, and a third scattered in the wind, now took two sticks in his hand and kept them together, to show his listeners that both houses of Israel would be united again.

Yes—Ezekiel, in many respects, was a prophet like any other serving the Lord with all his heart and soul. Like all of them, he spoke truth to power, and like them his only power was truth.

And yes—he, too, dared argue with heaven for the sake of his community. Jeremiah exclaimed: *"Tzaddik ata ki ariv imakh*—I know that you are just, and yet I must take exception to some of the things that you do, or that are being done in your name." At times, when he thought the punishment was too harsh, Ezekiel would fall to his knees and shout, "Is this your will? To exterminate the last remnant of Israel?"

Remember: unlike Jeremiah, he had not seen the massacres, had not witnessed the slaughter. The torment was shown to him only in his vision, in his hallucinations. But he suffered like Jeremiah. Although he lived the tragedy from a distance, he agonized over it as if it were his own. His visions were real to him. The future was present. His exaggerations—both for good and for bad—offered proof that the impossible, in every domain, is possible. If the miracle of the resurrection was told by him as a true story—or a story of a certain immutable truth—it was because the chastisement that preceded it had also been told with the emphasis on truth. If the children of Israel could sin that much, they would be saved by miracles that great. Exaggeration of sin must be matched by exaggerated divine rescue. Here Ezekiel disagrees with Jeremiah, who believed in repentance that would generate redemption. Ezekiel believed in redemption that would come outside of repentance. Jews would be redeemed, not because they would deserve it, but because God would choose to be merciful. That is why he insisted so much on Israel's transgressions. He declared that subsequent generations ought never to give up hope. Even if their sins made them unworthy of redemption, they would be redeemed. In other words, he painted his society in such outrageous colors for a simple reason: future generations would thus be able to think, "We could never be as guilty as *his* contemporaries were; therefore hope is permitted." After Ezekiel's generation, all others could only become better.

In conclusion, let us return to our initial worry. Why the hesitation in Talmudic literature, why the reservations with regard to Ezekiel?

Was it only because of his harsh words for his people? Were they too harsh? Or was it because of his quick changes of mood? Were they too quick, too abrupt, with no transition whatsoever? Or was it really only because he was too slow to accept God's word that miracles are possible, even those related to the abolition of frontiers between life and death?

It is quite conceivable that all these elements played a role in the situation. Ezekiel *was* an extremist. He did go further than his peers in all his predictions. But what made him totally different, perhaps unique, is something else: in his case, vision and word merged and became one.

A prophet is God's spokesman. The words that he hears are those that he is duty-bound to communicate to his listeners. He repeats what God says, nothing else. If God says, "Be harsh," he must be harsh. If God says, "Be comforting," he must be comforting. It is the voice that matters: the word—the sound—complete sentences—precise thoughts—ideas—principles—ethical injunctions—memories and more memories.

Ezekiel echoed God's words. But he did something else: he used his own. To be more specific, he added his own to those he had heard from God. To put it bluntly, he said things that he should have kept to himself: things that had to do with his visions, things that are part of the *Merkava* experience.

Remember the passage *Vaere*—"and I looked"? God was kind enough to show him the chariot and its mystical creatures. But nowhere is it mentioned that God told him to tell others what he had seen. And yet Ezekiel did not hesitate to reveal *everything* he had seen. *That* was his mistake.

He did not understand that there are experiences that cannot be communicated by words. He did not understand the importance of silence—the occasional necessity for silence.

We do, and so did many Talmudic sages, particularly those who lived in the time of another *Khurban*, the second destruction of the Temple and Jerusalem.

Those were the first to elaborate on Ezekiel's *Merkava* vision. Rabbi Yohanan ben Zakkai and his close disciples taught and studied the story and the lessons of the divine celestial chariot. And we are told that whenever they did, a heavenly fire would surround them. Was it there to shield them or to isolate them from reality? To protect them from the Fire of Sinai or to remind them of it? Perhaps it was there to bring them closer to the fire that consumed the sanctuary in their time—and other living sanctuaries in later generations—or perhaps to teach them the dangers inherent in language, or to teach them that some words have the ability to burn and burn.

With such visions of fire, with such memories of fire, even prophets ought to be careful and remain silent. Then, at least, people would know that their knowledge is doomed to remain their own. What they have seen, no one would ever see. What they know, no one would understand.

Ezekiel should have been more careful. Why wasn't he? Surely he felt compelled to speak, compelled to share, to give others what he had received from God. He refused to let his visions—his memories—die with him.

Prophets are human—and therein lies their grandeur, their sacredness. The greater the person, the more human the person, and the other way around: vulnerable, weak, subject to impulses and temptations—all of these. So what? Ezekiel was too intelligent, too perceptive, too knowledgeable not to know that it is forbidden to transform one's visions into words. But he was too concerned with his fellow human beings' welfare to deprive them of their right to know. He would pay for it? So what? As messenger, he must deliver the entire message, even the parts that could be seen and not heard.

But the question is: Can the message ever be communicated in its entirety? Can we break away from the fire? Can we communicate the fire?

Finally, all the events, and all the prophetic visions in the Book, are inserted in their proper calendar. Fourteen dates are indicated to help us place the speaker and his discourse—with one notable exception: the vision of the dry bones, meaning that the resurrection is undated.

And we understand why: that vision, that promise, that hope, is not linked to either space or time.

That vision, that consolation, is offered to every generation, for every generation needs it—and ours more than any before us.

Daniel

THIS STORY, beautiful and disturbing, is about children, Jewish children. Their fate, majestic and tragic at the same time, will sound familiar to us. Exile, separation, suffering, endurance, fidelity: it has everything . . . even ferocious lions.

Right from the beginning, we sense danger. These Jewish children have been uprooted from Judea, their homeland, by a powerful, relentless enemy. Transported to Babylon, they are seen taking compulsory courses in . . . assimilation. The text says so. Let's read it. "And the king ordered Ashpenaz, chief of his eunuchs, to take a few of the children of Israel, from royal stock or nobility, young boys devoid of corporal faults, handsome, talented, and well-bred, educated and intelligent, able to serve in the royal palace, and to whom the culture and language of the Chaldeans would be taught."

Apparently, such was the custom. The victor seized illustrious children of vanquished nations. In wars, it is always the children who lose. Grown-ups fight with each other and it is the children who die. The lucky ones are deported—as were Daniel and his three friends, Hananya, Mishael, and Azarya. They became Babylonians in spite of themselves. It was in spite of themselves that they visited the royal court. It was in spite of themselves that they became heroes of Jewish history. Far from their families, far from their people, they had to confront events in which the lives of kings and their nations were at stake. Unfortunate Jewish children, tossed about by history. Innocent Jewish children, attached to their faith, their tradition. Daniel was the most celebrated among them—perhaps because he was the best student in his class. But . . . he was not a prophet.

We know this by what follows. We learn what he does, and

that he does it well. He is resourceful, but Jewish children have always managed well in the Diaspora. Aren't they to be found in the most prestigious schools? Don't they excel in the humanities as well as in diplomacy, business, law, and science? Interestingly, Daniel displays a special talent for the subject of dreams—is this surprising? So did Joseph before him, and Freud after him. Can a Jew live without dreams? Without causing others to dream?

Still, Daniel remains a special case. He is always the first in every category. He recruits his relations at the highest level. He is chief of a department here, a sector there: he knows influential people. But—he is not included among the prophets. Why not?

He knows everyone, he understands everything, he penetrates all secrets. And besides, he knows how to please, especially in high places. His title: Not "Daniel Hanavi," Daniel the prophet, but "Daniel ish-'hamudot," Daniel the beloved one. But then, since he is loved, how does he manage to find himself in a lions' den? Does he want to prove that he is loved by them, too? A good question—there is an answer that is just as good, but let us be patient. The Book of Daniel is a story—and every story has its own rhythm.

Who was Daniel? What were his real qualifications, his ambitions? To be political chief of his exiled people, like Ezra or Nehemiah? In Talmudic literature, he . . . but here too, let's not go too quickly. For the moment, let's simply say that Daniel is portrayed there as a sage, a visionary, a scholar, a psychologist, a specialist in the interpretation of dreams. But not a prophet.

We like his visions. Mystical in essence, they refer to a grand messianic denouement, and as we read them, and reread them, we feel hope, great hope: yes, all suffering has an end, all ordeals have a meaning; yes, in the end, the enemy will be brought to his knees. Yes, God will be—God is—on the side of the victim.

Often, during our exile, we read the Book of Daniel to console ourselves. Half is in Aramaic—therefore incomprehensible to the average reader? Too bad. Two thousand years ago and more, it was the only part that was accessible. At that time, Aramaic was the lingua franca of Jews and gentiles alike; it was utilized from the Middle East to the Himalayas.

But why is the book written in two languages? If the purpose was to make it popular, it could have been published entirely in Aramaic. Strange . . . But everything is strange in this work. Study it and you will realize that it presents more than a few chronological difficulties, and as many philosophical and mathematical enigmas. Sometimes we are not sure from its use of metaphors whether it is discussing Nebuchadnezzar or Nabonidus, Cyrus or Darius, Antiochus II or Antiochus IV. In the meantime, we let ourselves be swept away by the wonderful tale; so much so that we no longer try to analyze it. We leave that to the experts in Biblical criticism. Even they are not sure whether the Book of Daniel is the work of a single author or four, and whether he or they lived at the time of Nebuchadnezzar or of Antiochus Epiphanes. There are those who claim that in fact there was one pious man who was called Daniel, but he belonged to another story. . . . But then, did Daniel foresee events, or did he learn about them afterward? Daniel a historian? A visionary historian? Wouldn't the two attributes be incompatible?

The theme of Daniel has inspired many writers and artists. In the fourteenth century, Chaucer used it in "The Monk's Tale." Three centuries later, Calderón de la Barca turned it into theater, *La Cena del Rey Baltasar*. Byron and Heine were intrigued by him, as was Goethe, whose rough draft remained a rough draft. In music, it was Handel especially, who was taken by Daniel. For many painters—Delacroix, Tintoretto, Rubens, and, of course, Rembrandt—he was a favorite subject.

As we follow the text, we shall try to penetrate the mystery that surrounds our hero.

"In the third year of the reign of Yehoiakhin, king of Judea, Nebuchadnezzar, king of Babylonia, marched against Jerusalem and besieged her. . . ."

Thus begins the story, which takes on an air of historical truth. But at once difficulties arise. Some suggest that the king was called Yehoyakim, not Yehoiakhin, others that the "third year" had to be a printing error, that one had to read it as "the third month." Others insinuate that the word "revolt" should replace "reign." In short, the Biblical critics thoroughly enjoy showing that this work was not written—as the rabbinic tradition has it—during the last years of Nebuchadnezzar's reign and the first years of Cyrus's, that is to say, between 545 and 535 before the Common Era. Furthermore, they point to the anti-Jewish nature of the persecutions as corresponding to the time of Antiochus Epiphanes rather than to that of Nebuchadnezzar.

But first let's analyze the story itself. Dramatic, overwhelming, stimulating one's soul as well as one's fantasy, it revolves around two principal characters: Daniel and the king. If the king's identity is subject to controversy, Daniel's is no less so. But never mind: Both Nebuchadnezzar and Antiochus are anchored in the history of their people *and* ours. We know them, we can place them, we remember their cruel triumphs and their just defeats— whereas Daniel remains totally obscure. He comes from nowhere and goes nowhere. There is no trace of him before his appearance, no trace of him afterward. Of what family is he the illustrious son? To which lineage should he be attached? His file in Biblical literature is virtually nonexistent. Ezekiel mentions him in passing, alongside Noah and Job, as being among the great Just Men. That's all. The Talmudic sources themselves surprise us by their brevity. Read the text and you will wonder, Who was his father? How old was he when he was torn from his home and transported to Babylon? Where did he go after his adventures, his dreams, his visions?

With its taste for the imaginative, the Talmudic legend gives us a more complete portrait of the individual. He is said to be a priest and a descendant of David. We would take him for one of the Just. He lent money to the needy, gave to the poor, attended funerals, and danced for brides. The text speaks of him with respect that borders on reverence. He hasn't any faults. He turns toward Jerusalem when saying his prayers, demonstrates courage in the face of power, doesn't forget his friends when they need him. He is someone who always knows the right thing to do, the proper thing to say. He knows how to address fierce rulers, anonymous callers, he even knows how to appease starving lions. Better than anyone he knows how to disarm the anger, if not hate, which his king harbors toward Jews.

The Talmud, or the Midrash, appeals to our imagination. We *know* about Daniel only what the text reveals to us. Let's read: "The king gave the order to Ashpenaz, chief of the eunuchs, to properly feed the beautiful children of Israel. He assigned to them each day dishes from his table and the wine from which he drank, wishing to take care of them for three years, at the end of which they would be in the service of the king. . . ." In other words, the children could take pleasure in their golden exile. They were taken care of, their education was attended to and paid for; and once assimilated or integrated they would be offered important court positions.

Daniel had three friends among the children: Hananya, Mishael, and Azarya. In their dislike of Hebrew names, the Babylonians hastened to change them, to "Babylonianize" them. Daniel became Belteshazzar, Hananya became Shadrach, Mishael became Meshach, and Azarya became Abed-nego.

But they resisted assimilation: "Daniel resolved not to be tainted by the king's dishes and wine." In other words, he was determined to eat kosher. And since the royal court does not have a kosher kitchen, Daniel tries to convince his guard to let him plan his own menu, for himself and his three friends: vegetables and water. The guard is afraid: "The king will find you thin, he will punish me, he will go for my head." Daniel proposes a deal: Let us do as we wish for ten days; then you will decide what to do. Deal concluded. At the end of ten days, the diet of the four Jewish boys turns out to be a success. They are doing better than the others. You see? A Jew doesn't necessarily have to give up his faith to "make it" among gentiles. Daniel and his three friends made their way. Accepted in the service of the king, they found favor in his eyes. "In all the subjects that required wisdom and intelligence, and in which the king questioned them, he found them to be ten times superior to all the magicians and astrologers in his kingdom."

It is a repetition, if you will, of the story of Joseph in Egypt and of Mordecai in Persia. Daniel passes the test and earns respect as a Jew. He is esteemed, congratulated, his advice is sought, as is his consent. He finds himself propelled to the very center of Babylonian history—to the court of King Nebuchadnezzar.

Judging by what we have just read, King Nebuchadnezzar was a rather nasty character. He defeated Judea, burned down the Temple, took its most sacred vessels, and deported its most promising youth, thus separating them from their people, their roots, their future. It is not surprising that he didn't sleep well. "He is uneasy," says the text. "He couldn't sleep." Was he bothered by his conscience? . . . The king would summon his magicians, his astrologers, his charmers, and say, "I have had a dream. Tell me what it was." One can imagine the bewilderment of the magicians: "If the king doesn't know his own dream, how will we know? Our job is to interpret dreams, not to reveal them." But the king was stubborn: I want to be told what my dream was. If not, I will have you executed. The magicians plead, but it is useless. They are condemned, and all the sages with them—Daniel and his friends included. The king believed in radical solutions. All the sages are to be *either* honored *or* killed. The text says so. "They looked for Daniel and his three friends to make them perish like the others." Is the implication that the four Jews were considered part of the intellectual elite of the vast empire? Apprehended, Daniel asks the chief of the guards, Why this mass condemnation? The guard tells him, and Daniel expresses his desire to see the king: "I can answer his question. I can tell him his dream." He needs time, of course— to consult his friends; to pray; to receive from heaven the vision awaited during the night. The king's dream—he sees it now. And he tells the king, "You saw a huge statue of extraordinary splendor. . . . The head was of pure gold, its chest and arms were of silver; its belly and thighs were of bronze, its legs of iron, its feet part iron, part clay. As you looked on, a stone came loose, hit the feet of the statue and broke them to pieces. Then the whole statue broke, and the wind took it away without leaving a trace. . . . But the stone which had hit the statue became a large mountain, and covered the whole earth."

A strange vision, troubling, fascinating. Moreover, it corresponds to a certain logic. Daniel is intelligent, perceptive, intuitive. He guesses the king's anxiety: What will become of him tomorrow? What will be the fate of his kingdom? In other words, what is the secret of the future, how can the mystery of time be pierced? The great conqueror cannot but worry about the fate of his conquest. Thus, Daniel will speak to him of the future. The statue, Daniel tells him, represents your empire. After you, another kingdom will arise, smaller than yours; then a third and a fourth. And all will be destroyed. After that, God will create a kingdom symbolized by the stone in your dream—and that one will live forever.

Did he guess the king's dream? Or did he merely say the words the king wanted to hear? Did he assuage the king's anxiety? The fact is that the king was elated. He covered Daniel with gifts and honors and named him commander of the entire province of Babylon, and first among the sages. Naturally, Daniel obtained for his three friends high posts in the administration.

Thus all was well. Not only for the Jews—for the gentiles too. Daniel's intelligence saved all the sages from death. They should have been grateful, no? Well, gratitude was even then a rare virtue.

The Book then focuses on the ingratitude of the king, who had a huge gold statue erected, before which all his subjects were to prostrate themselves. Whoever disobeyed was to be thrown into a fiery furnace. All complied, except for Daniel's three friends. The king summoned them, questioned them, threatened them. They were not frightened. "But you will perish in the flames," he said. "And which is the God who will deliver you from my hand?" Hananya, Mishael, and Azarya replied, "Our God *can* deliver us from the fiery furnace. But even if He does not choose to do so, know that we will not serve your idols."

A dramatic confrontation between Jewish courage and pagan power. This is the first time that Jews were persecuted for their faith. Until then, persecutions had been national, political, military in character. The tyrant's goal had been to dominate Israel in order to reinforce his own power. Let Israel submit, and nothing would happen to her. That they prayed, studied, observed the law of Moses, had meant nothing to previous tyrants. This was different, without precedent. Now the tyrant required total submission, physical and spiritual, individual and collective—submission of thought, abdication of the soul. To the king's surprise, Daniel and his friends resisted. They defied the king again. The king said, "If your God is God, let *Him* save you." And they replied, "Even if He does not come to our rescue, He remains our God." How can one not see this as a prefiguration of countless ordeals to come? For Jews, persecutions do not necessarily put only God in question. Their faith can change in design, in intensity, but it does not die, even in death. Their faith survives their death. In this case, they *themselves* survived death. Thrown into a burning furnace, they were saved from the flames by an angel. A happy ending. The king recognizes the greatness of their God. The three friends are alive and leave the story forever. And Daniel? Saved forever?

Rather unstable, this King Nebuchadnezzar. He is threatening, fanatic, pitiless one moment, sweet and generous the next. Hasn't he learned anything from the preceding events? The Talmud explains: If he hasn't, his councilors were to be blamed. Jealous of Daniel, they conspired against him and succeeded in inciting the king against the Jewish people.

According to the Talmud, the three friends consulted Daniel before replying to the king. But Daniel refused to answer them. He suggested that they seek the advice of the Prophet Ezekiel (see previous chapter)—who told them to flee. Their response? If we run away, how will the name of the Lord be sanctified? *Kiddush Hashem* is an act we must perform in public, it is in public that we renounce life, if life means lies and compromise. God deserves that we live for Him, and that we die for Him. Thus it is in the Book of Daniel that the mentality of all future martyrs of the faith is revealed.

In fact, the Book can be divided into two parts: the first consists of action, the second, of vision. In the first part, the king's dreams—interpreted by Daniel—bear upon the story; in the second part, Daniel's visions imply the *end* of the story. I mean visions, not prophecies. Again: Daniel is not a prophet. But doesn't he foresee the future? He interprets the present as a function of the future. He knows how to read and decipher signs. He predicts the eschatological future. But then, how is one to describe him? As a wise man—a title conferred upon him by the Babylonian king. Even in Talmudic literature, it is the wise man who is celebrated, not the prophet.

It is true that his wisdom is praised; it is described as superior. Superior to that of the pagans? Naturally—but also to that of the Jews. The prophets Hagai, Zechariah, and Malachi, says the Talmud, did not see what he saw. But if he was so wise, so pious, if he saw more and better than the prophets, if he looked farther than they did, and deeper, why couldn't he be a prophet?

Let's continue our study. Let us explore Nebuchadnezzar's new dream. This one he remembers and tells to everyone in the first person: "I, Nebuchadnezzar, lived quietly in my house and happily in my palace. I had a dream that frightened me, the thoughts that followed me to bed filled me with terror. . . ."

No longer in need of magicians to reveal his own dream, he needs them only to elucidate its meaning. All are summoned to appear before him. And all admit their failure. Luckily there is Daniel. Daniel understands, Daniel explains. Bravo, Daniel. He explains to the king the reason for his anxiety: in fact, his future is bleak. The tree that symbolizes him will be cut down, the empire destroyed. The king himself will go through a metamorphosis à la Kafka: in "seven ages" he will cease being a man: beast among the beasts, he will dwell in the forest, will nourish himself with grass and dew. And the dream materializes. It is the king himself who tells us of his transformation. He tells the tale in the first person. Who will dare not to believe him?

But here, the reader must wonder, Why is the king being punished? Certainly he frightened quite a few Jewish citizens with his pagan decrees, but none actually died, right? For scaring people, does he deserve to undergo terror himself? And why this particular punishment? Nebuchadnezzar is presented by the Talmud on a strictly moral plane: because he sinned from pride, his punishment will touch his pride. He thought he was superior to other men, so he is shown to be inferior to the lowest, the most deprived among them. Defeated by his own vanity, vanquished, humiliated, he tells his story in a tone of penitence, and, in the end, of stunning joyousness: he had discovered faith by rediscovering his reason. It all came to pass the way Daniel had predicted it would. And yet, the well-loved sage, Daniel *Ish-hamudot,* is not considered a prophet.

Naturally, the king does not tell about his own end. No one else does either, not even Daniel. Nebuchadnezzar simply disappears at the end of Chapter IV. The next chapter opens with the baffling vision of his successor, Belshazzar, organizing a feast. Son or grandson of Nebuchadnezzar, he inherited from him a taste for the occult. He too "sees" strange things. In the middle of a state dinner, he sees mysterious fingers writing on the wall—*"Mene, mene tekel, u-parsin"*—incomprehensible words, undecipherable, which all the wise men of the court try to decode, to no avail. The king is on the threshold of despair, but it is the queen—the only feminine character in the story—who saves him. She reminds her husband of Daniel's existence, Daniel's power. They find him; here he is in the royal palace, in front of the king and the court, here he is, solving the puzzle: *"Mene, mene, tekel, u-parsin—* Count, weigh, divide." In other words, God has counted and weighed your actions; your kingdom will be divided, your reign is over. Here again the prediction is correct: forty-seven years after the fall of Jerusalem, the Babylonian empire is crushed. Now it is Belshazzar's turn to disappear—and make room for Persia. Persia rules, Persia governs the world. Cyrus is good, he rebuilds Jerusalem. Did Daniel know him? No doubt—but his greatest adventure is tied to Darius.

Darius, successor to Cyrus the Great, likes Daniel. He names him to a high position: he is appointed as one of the three prime ministers of the entire kingdom. Too much success, too much glory for a Jewish refugee? Again he is envied, especially in political circles. His rivals strive hard to undermine his influence. How to trap him? They propose a law forbidding the citizens from addressing their prayers or supplications to their gods: these may be directed only to the king himself. To transgress this law is to expose oneself to the supreme punishment, that of being thrown into the lions' den. This new decree hardly prevents Daniel from living his life as before. In his house, where the windows facing Jerusalem are open, he prays three times a day. Caught praying, he is taken to the king. He does not defend himself. He accepts the consequences of his action. But the king appears sad, sadder than the defendant. Then again, why would Daniel be afraid of lions? Didn't he have faith in God and in His kindness? A marvelous anecdote comes to mind:

In Africa, two men stand at a river which they are about to cross, when they notice crocodiles looking at them. "Are you afraid?" says one to the other. "Don't you know that God is merciful and good?" "Yes, I do," says the frightened man. "But what if God suddenly chooses right now to be good to the crocodiles?"

How could Daniel be sure tonight was not going to be the lions' night?

In Talmudic literature we embellish upon the sleepless night that Darius spends, thinking about what he is going to see in the pit: his friend and protégé cut to pieces. Some Midrashic commentators imagine the king near the pit, paralyzed by remorse and anguish. And then, miracle of miracles, in the morning, the pit is opened and Daniel emerges unscathed. The king is happy, Daniel is happy, the Jews are happy. God, too, is pleased. He should be: all citizens of Persia are ordered by the king to respect Him. "Daniel will prosper under the reign of Darius," the text tells us.

Is this the reason that Daniel is not called prophet? Because the king liked him too much? Because he was too happy? Must a prophet always be sad, pursued, cursed? Would a happy Jeremiah not have been Jeremiah?

Let us note that as soon as the word "prosper" is used, the story changes direction. Up until now, the action has turned on kings. It was they who dreamed, they who acted; Daniel only interpreted their dreams. Now, from the seventh chapter on, it is Daniel who dreams, who has strange visions; it is he who needs someone to explain what he feels, what he foresees, what he predicts. He is the bearer of a message for someone else to understand.

It is an exciting message: occasionally, Daniel speaks like Ezekiel, expressing himself in a beautiful and feverish language, a poetic, if not prophetic, mode, appealing to imagination and history alike, to the heart as much as the soul: he faces the universe, he confronts what is above, beyond man. "I was looking during my nocturnal vision," he writes, "and behold, the four winds of the heavens erupted on the great sea. And four large animals came out of the sea, each different from the other. The first resembled a lion with an eagle's wings; I looked, until the moment when its wings were torn off. The second animal resembled a bear. The third a leopard: with four wings of a bird on his back. The fourth animal, terrible and hideous, had teeth of iron, he ate and smashed and crushed all that existed. . . ."

This is an astonishing tale. A staggering vision. In his bed, Daniel is transported to the unreal. He soars through celestial spheres where nothing is ordinary. Who but Daniel is this "Ancient of Days," seated on an elevated throne. "His attire was white as snow, and the hair on his head was like pure wool; his throne was like flames of fire. . . . A river of fire flowed and gushed before him. Thousands served him." Who but Daniel is the son of the man who stepped in front of the "Ancient of Days"? "I, Daniel, I had a troubled soul. The visions in my head frightened me. . . ." Naturally. What man could see all this, absorb all this, receive all this without being afraid? He would have liked to open up to someone, but he is alone. In whom can he confide? Who will be able to reassure him? Then, stranger still, he turns toward one of the characters in his own dream for an explanation. He asks the character to give him the meaning of *his* own vision. And even stranger, the character does not push him away, does not say to him, "What do you want from me? It's your dream, not mine!" No, he responds reasonably, calmly. The animals represent kingdoms, those that will fall and those that will remain. The most arrogant will be the most chastised. Is Daniel appeased? Not at all. Even after the dream, awake, he feels troubled; he pales and remains silent.

From that moment on, his delirium overtakes him. He sees a ram with horns that no animal could oppose. The ram is hit by a he-goat; his horn is bruised. Suddenly we understand that we have been witnessing a war between East and West. Armies of the sky, stars in the heavens participate in the battle. Daniel hears one saint ask another, How long will the sanctuary and its defenders be trampled upon? How much time will pass before the fulfillment of the vision of perpetual sacrifice? And his companion replies: "Two thousand three hundred nights and mornings; then the sanctuary will be cleansed and purified."

His temperature seems to be rising from minute to minute, from dream to dream. "Someone who appeared to be a man" is in front of him. A voice says, "Gabriel, explain the vision to him." The Angel Gabriel? Daniel falls face down. Gabriel speaks, Gabriel explains; Daniel listens, Daniel understands, thinks he understands, ends up no longer knowing what he is supposed to understand. All he knows is that he must be quiet, and wait, and "keep his vision secret, as it relates to a distant time."

The end of the chapter is of particular interest: "I, Daniel was languishing and sick for several days; then I arose and took care of the king's affairs." Life had to go on. The man who had gone through so many crises, who had had so many visions, had to keep up his regular work, inspecting, disposing, ordering, speaking to people, listening to their problems, making decisions; the reality of life surpassed its turbulent unreality.

All the same, one can ask, What did he do during the days when he was sick and languishing? Who came to see him, to encourage him? A Jew of his importance, of his standing, was absent from his office for several days, and no one troubled himself to check whether he was the victim of an accident? And the angels? What were they doing?

Although recovered, Daniel continues to have visions; perhaps he now summons them. It is always a man dressed in linen, Gabriel, who "opens his mind" and talks to him. Daniel changes color, is seized with fear, falls to the ground, feels himself fainting. It is no longer animals that he sees; right now, he sees words. Gabriel, and later on, Michael, tell him the future: Persia will be conquered by Greece; the world will experience convulsions on a planetary scale. Battles between empires, violent conflicts between great powers, the humiliated will taste triumph; the proud will be humiliated.

Ish-hamudot, the beloved one: it is the angel who thus names Daniel. On more than one occasion, he pays him this compliment: Because we like you so much, we will confide in you terrifying secrets. Or perhaps we should translate *Ish-hamudot* as someone who knows how to love well? Who loves others more than himself? All his senses awakened, sharpened, inflamed, Daniel doesn't miss a nuance, doesn't let a single syllable pass him by. Of course, he doesn't always understand everything. "This king's daughter from the south" who will approach the king to reestablish harmony, who is she? Who is the contemptible man who will take her place? In the end, Daniel listens to the angel, and remembers the future as it unfolds. Four kings will follow Cyrus. Alexander the Great will extend his power everywhere, forcing back the horizon—until he, too, will be defeated. The angel announces the rise of Antiochus Epiphanes who, in a "whirlwind," will defeat Egypt and his other enemies. But at the end of all these torments, which have nothing to do with the Jewish people, the Jewish people will be saved. Daniel knows when. But the angel commands him: "Daniel, you keep these words secret. . . ." We are coming to the denouement of the story. "Seal the book," says the angel. "Many will then read it and knowledge will grow." What? If the Book is sealed, how will it be read? And whose knowledge will be increased? It's absurd, isn't it? No, not at all. At this point, the Book of Daniel teaches us a solemn and essential lesson: Mystery must remain secret in order for it to affect man's destiny. To reveal the mystery at the wrong moment is to dissipate its substance. It is only when the secret is whole—sealed—that knowledge will increase. In other words, Daniel repeats for us what the angel told him: It is forbidden to trivialize certain subjects; it is dangerous to treat them lightly. All that Daniel is authorized to tell us is: "Know that the secret exists."

Let's listen to the end of the Book. It is worthwhile. In terms of poetry and mystical lyricism, it surpasses many prophetic texts.

"And I, Daniel, was looking, and here were two other men standing up, one on this side of the river, the other on the other side of the river. One of them said to the man dressed in linen who stood above the waters of the river, When will these marvels end? And I heard the man dressed in linen who stood above the waters of the river. He raised his right hand and his left hand toward the sky and he swore, in the name of the one who lives eternally, that it would be at some time, of time and half of time, and that all these things would end when the might of the holy people would be entirely broken. I heard, but I did not understand; and I said, Lord, what will be the outcome of these things? He replied, Go, Daniel, as these words will remain secret and sealed till the end of time, or until the time of the end. Many will be purified, whitened, and purged, the wicked will do evil, and none of the wicked will understand, but the intelligent will understand. From the time when perpetual sacrifice will end, and when the devastator's abomination will be set up, there will have passed one thousand two hundred and ninety days. Happy will be the one who waits and who reaches one thousand three hundred and five days. And you, walk toward your end; you will rest, and you will stand up for your heritage at the end of days."

Let us note in passing, that the vocabulary and imagery of our prayers for the dead—the *Kel Male Rahamim*—are inspired by the last chapters. They are beautiful—that is undeniable. But what do they signify? Thousands and thousands of rabbinical and mystical scholars and commentators have attempted to pierce their secret. In every exile, in every ghetto, there were spiritual guides who, in order to console their contemporaries, tried to use Daniel's predictions. I remember, in our home too, Daniel was popular. We would spend nights and nights trying to figure out the exact combination of this "time, of time and half of time." Some were convinced they had found it. Redemption was going to arrive at dawn—Daniel said so, didn't he? But look, a time multiplied by one thousand and divided by ninety, what does that give us? Hope.

The angel will win. The secret remains secret. Daniel himself admitted his ignorance. Why would we be luckier than he?

Poor Daniel, brave Daniel: wise and famous, he wasn't at all embarrassed to say, more than once, that he didn't understand. His role was only that of messenger. To listen and repeat; to listen and transmit; to listen and to be present.

What ultimately happened to Daniel? He leaves the Book without a trace. In what circumstances did he die? Where? A Midrashic source suggests that having retired from his official duties he returned to Judea and settled in Tiberias. Proof? There is none. And here we come back to the beginning: we don't know where he came from or where he went. Having survived so many dramatic events, so many threats, so many perils, he disappeared into the night of history.

But didn't he leave children behind? No. Was he married? The absence of women in his story is striking. No mother, no wife, no daughter. A man without a family? Apparently. But isn't it man's first duty, isn't he ordered to marry, to build a home, to propagate life on earth? Yes, except . . . Daniel could not marry. Because he belonged to God? No. Because he belonged to the king who made him come to Babylon. The text doesn't state this, but the Talmudic commentary doesn't hide from us the fact that Daniel and his three friends were eunuchs. A tosaphist goes so far as to say that Daniel castrated himself to avoid having to marry a pagan princess. But most of the commentators suggest that the young Hebrews were mutilated by the king's servants. Mutilated in the flesh, was Daniel no longer qualified to serve as God's prophet? Is this the reason why he was only wise and beloved? Better loved because he was incapable of loving, of physically loving, as a man loves a woman, to celebrate life?

Now that we are aware of his physical state, we better understand his character. The humiliation to his body gave wings to his spirit. Tortured by men, he clings to angels. Feeling diminished, he soars toward the dizzying heights of the absolute.

Hence his complexity. A humble and pious Jew, he accepts to serve the court. A practitioner of politics, he dwells in mysticism. Commenting on the verse of the Song of Songs *"Bikashti et sheahava nafshi,* I searched for the being with whom my soul was in love," two Masters are in disagreement. One says, This applies to Daniel, who went to a royal meal. The other says, In fact, this applies to Daniel, but he went home to fast. A contradiction? Daniel is defined by contradiction—not entirely man, not entirely prophet, not entirely emissary, not entirely guide. A genuine Diaspora Jew, he is always torn between two forces at once.

"This whole calamity came upon us," says he, "and we did not implore the Eternal, we did not turn away from our iniquities." He is angry with the people of Israel, it's clear. But he questions the Lord, the God of Israel, as well. The Talmud says: "Moses said *Hakel hagadol haguibor vehanora*—God who is great and heroic and mighty." Along came Daniel, who declared, Heroic, He? His children are oppressed by strangers—where is His might, His bravery? Thus, in his prayers, Daniel no longer pronounced the word *haguibor.* Ah, yes, Daniel dares to rise against God when it's a question of defending tormented Jews. But didn't he say the suffering was the fault of the Jewish people? Between suffering and logic, he makes his choice; between victims and justice, he opts for victims: he conducts himself like so many of the great Masters of our people. From Abraham to Rabbi Levi-Yitzhak of Berditchev, the greatest among the great dared to take the side of Jews, even against God. All, including Daniel, agree that God was no stranger to Creation, that He acted on events. Although His responsibility does not diminish man's, He is compassionate rather than rigorous. So we understand Daniel's revolt. Moses had said, If You do not forgive Your people, erase my name from Your book. Daniel said, If You do not save Your people, I will cease to praise You. The one who had decided to pray, even at the risk of his life, was going to curtail his prayers. The one who had vowed to God his infinite love was going to breach his love on behalf of his people. A Midrashic commentary: There were two defenders of Israel before the Lord: Moses and Daniel.

He is also compared to Jacob. Jacob and Moses were the only ones to whom God revealed the mystery of the end. Jacob was going to share it with his children but forgot it. As for Daniel, he was ordered to keep it to himself.

Fascinating Daniel. In the midst of royal intrigues, he was satisfied with his power, that of the word. It is with words that he reassured the emperors, it is with words that he offered hope to generations of exiles who will evoke his name and his example while waiting for redemption.

The angel ordered him to seal the Book and not to divulge the secret of the ending. He submitted. Too bad. Couldn't he have slipped in an allusion here and there, to facilitate our task?

Maimonides and his followers consider the Book of Daniel dangerous. But I love reading and rereading it. Because it is beautiful? Because it is dangerous? Granted, we cannot decipher the secret it contains, but we know that there is a secret—and that knowledge helps us overcome banality and reject vulgarity. Yes, that knowledge enables us to endow hope with a name that preceded Creation itself.

Is this why Daniel is remembered in our sacred liturgy of the High Holidays? *"Mi sheana le-Daniel begov haarayot*—He who answered Daniel in the lions' den, may He answer our prayers!" But in the text, we find no indication of a divine response! Daniel must have prayed, that is certain—but we are not told that God answered him. We are told only that Daniel survived the danger.

Is that God's reply?

Ezra and Nehemiah

Two men, two lives, two outlooks, two temperaments, but one destiny. And one story. A story that unites them and elevates them to the rank of epoch makers in Jewish history. The exultant story of a rupture followed by a return.

Ezra, the scribe. The intellectual, the spiritual man, the student, the teacher involved with ideas, the ideologist. And, next to him stands Nehemiah, the organizer. The eternal pragmatist, the man of action. Both Ezra and Nehemiah were given powers by the king, but only Nehemiah used them. Ezra resorted to prayer, Nehemiah to reason. Ezra rejected the king's escort, for he relied on heavenly intercession; Nehemiah accepted the offer. When Ezra witnessed people sinning, he wept; when Nehemiah witnessed this, he made the sinners weep.

Together they symbolize Israel's hope, Israel's right of renewal. Together they incited their brethren to break with their familiar environment, to leave the comforts of exile, and to return home and get in touch—physically as well as spiritually—with the city of their dreams, Jerusalem. And not to fear the sight of the ruins that covered the city which God had chosen as His dwelling place among His people, the people of memory and faith.

Together, Ezra and Nehemiah brought a new hope and yet an ancient vision to their dispersed nation. Dispersed? Yes, but united, thanks to both. Without them, the history of exile would have ended differently. Without them, Jewish history might have vanished within the turbulent history of nations that have long since sunk into oblivion.

Together? Were Ezra and Nehemiah really together? Did they really participate side by side in the same efforts that culminated in the glorious reconstruction of the indestructible city of Jerusalem?

In our collective imagination, they always appear as an inseparable pair—is the image true? Does it correspond to fact and to what we like to call historical truth? Would the one have succeeded without the other? Was one more important than the other?

Theirs is a stimulating story. Filled with romanticism, patriotism, Zionism, it also contains disturbing elements. Who was at the bottom of this Jewish renewal? Ezra? Nehemiah? Not Cyrus of Persia? And once his decree was announced—what happened then? Did all the Jews pack up and go home to the land of their ancestors? No? Why not?

Let us open to the first verse of the first chapter of the first Book:

"U'vishnat achat lekoresh melekh Parass likhlot dvar adoshem mipi Yirmiyahu . . ." And it came to pass that in this year—or in this first year—of the reign of King Cyrus of Persia when God's word found its conclusion on Jeremiah's lips . . . that is when God awoke Cyrus's good will and moved him to adopt a positive, friendly attitude toward a small people that lost its kingdom and its Temple to Babylonian invaders. . . .

Thus this story begins with a precise date. We are told when these dramatic events occurred and where. And we are told why. This insistence on precision will permeate the entire Book of Ezra. Names, titles, facts: the chronicler is a man of particular thoroughness. And from the outset he wants us to know that this chapter in Jewish history will be inserted into the grand scheme of world history. It is clear from the outset that we are going to witness an important event which the text links to Cyrus on one hand and Jeremiah on the other. Jeremiah had predicted the end of exile—after seventy years—and Cyrus was going to fulfill his prophecy. Just as Babylon was chosen by God to punish Judea, Cyrus was chosen to punish Babylon. The moral of the story? Even if the Jewish people deserve to be persecuted, those who persecute them will be blamed. For they could have said to God: Choose another tool.

Let us reread the first sentence in the Book: the first word is *U'vishnat*. With a *Vav*. And in the year . . . As if the chronicler were already in the middle of the story which he was about to continue. Rashi says so explicitly in his commentary: The Book of Ezra, says he, is the continuation of the Book of Daniel. Better yet: it is a response to Daniel. Since Daniel questioned the meaning of Jeremiah's divine promise, the Book of Ezra was intended to offer

him an answer: Look, God's promise is being kept. Nahmanides—
the Ramban—prefers to locate the Book of Ezra after the Chronicles, for the last verses of the Chronicles and the first verses of
Ezra are almost identical. The *Tur* and the *Shulchan Aruch* are
convinced that Ezra's Book precedes the Chronicles, whereas the
Talmud—in the Treatise of Baba Batra—defends the idea that
between the Book of Daniel and the Book of Ezra there is room
for another Book, that of Esther, which also takes place in Persia.
Everyone is intrigued by the Book of Ezra, inventing hypotheses
upon hypotheses regarding its proper place in Scripture. And all
because of that unassuming letter *Vav*, which, after all, must mean
something. No, declares the Radak with his usual decisiveness.
The fact that the narrative begins with a *Vav* means nothing. It is
a matter of style, that's all. Of Biblical style. The Bible loves the
Vav—go argue with the Bible.

Does all this sound complicated? Wait, there's more. The
second word of the first sentence is *achat*. One? The first year of
Cyrus's reign? Chronologically impossible. We know that Cyrus
had been king and ruler for some years before he had the good
idea of becoming friend and benefactor of the Jewish people.
Another possibility: the story took place during the first year of
Cyrus's reign over Babylon. Third hypothesis: *achat* could simply
mean a year, any year. It happened one year, one day. . . . The style
of ancient fables was not necessarily limited to fables.

Thus we discover in this seemingly precise and concrete narrative much confusion. Or, at least, much room for confusion.
Jeremiah's seventy-year prophecy—from when does it date? From
the destruction of Jerusalem? Or earlier, from the day when King
Yehoiakhin and his court were deported to Babylon? Many versions have been offered—and more than one has been accepted.
Shall we then stop counting? And neglect truth for the sake of
legend? And accept the triumph of Jewish will to survive as a
beautiful story that will come to pass one day? And see in the Book
of Ezra and Nehemiah a prefiguration of what will happen to, and
in, our generation?

As always, history begins with words, and these sounded like
the fulfillment of a promise and a blessing.

Thus said King Cyrus of Persia:

"It is God, the Lord of the heavens, who gave me all the
kingdoms of the earth; it is He who ordered me to rebuild his
sanctuary in Jerusalem which is in Judea. Whoever wishes to go

there, may God be with him. . . . Whoever prefers to stay here, let him take gold and silver and other gifts and entrust them with those who are leaving as offerings for God's House in Jerusalem. . . ."

That is how it all began.

How does a nation maintain its identity in hostile surroundings? Where does it draw the strength to pursue goals ridiculed by mighty enemies? Where does it find the courage and the resolve to remain a minority instead of assimilating in Babylon, in Rome, in Yemen?

The story of Ezra and Nehemiah is astonishing in many respects. First, how is one to explain that in a relatively short time so many exiled Jews managed to do so well in Babylon? Second, since they did adjust so easily to Babylonian society, what kept them Jewish? These questions could apply to so many communities in so many lands.

But let us stay with Ezra and Nehemiah, who also fared rather well in Persia before deciding to work for their nation's renaissance.

Who was Ezra? A world-class agitator, he had no sense of public relations. He seems to have wanted to keep his private life private. If he could, he would have written his entire Book in the third person—unlike his colleague Nehemiah, who appears to have enjoyed being in the limelight. Ezra is generous; he speaks to everybody—he speaks of everybody. He alone stays in the shadow. He praises Cyrus, quotes his declaration in all its facets, draws up lists of people and their belongings, is interested in everything, attentive to everybody—except to himself.

What do we know about him? Only what he wants us to know—which is very little. His Book, as an autobiography, leaves much to be desired. Fortunately there is the Midrash and its treasures.

Born in Babylon, into a priestly family, he performs important functions in the royal palace. As a scribe? Perhaps as counselor on Jewish affairs? Is it he who prevailed upon the king to rebuild Jerusalem? The text does not say so. What the text does say is that he, Ezra, was there when the declaration was issued. Was he instrumental in obtaining it? In editing it? Or, at least, in transmitting it? Were there other agents who communicated the king's edict? There must have been, but it is Ezra who plays the principal part in acting upon it. He organizes the first Aliyah, galvanizes potential immigrants, but he himself is not part of the convoy. Why not? We do not know. Ezra the leader sends others to Eretz Israel, but he himself stays behind. Why? Because of health reasons? Because of family obligations? We do not even know whether he was married. A veil of mystery covers the latter part of his life as well. When did he die? Where? Flavius maintains that his tomb is in Jerusalem. However, the great traveler Rabbi Benjamin of Tudela, as well as Rabbi Petakhya of Regensburg and Rabbi Yehuda Elkharizi, claim that he was buried in Iraq, near Basra.

Naturally, such discretion in the Biblical text would be compensated for by Midrashic commentators and interpreters. For the Midrash, Ezra is a character so special that "had Moses not preceded him, it's through *him* that God would have given the Torah to His people." Another source states that had Aaron and he been contemporaries, Ezra would have surpassed him in greatness. When the Torah was forgotten among Jews, insists a third source, it was he, Ezra, who brought it back to them.

Like most secretive persons, Ezra intrigues the reader. And Jews are not the only ones attracted to him. Flavius, Spinoza, the Church Fathers and the Koran, all praise his powers and achievements. He is exalted by Mohammed, who claims that Jews had seen in him the son of God. A miracle maker, according to Mohammed, Ezra wrote the Torah like an acrobat: he kept five pens in his five fingers to write five different words—simultaneously.

The Midrashic version sounds even more poetic. Having gone into a retreat, Ezra dictated to five scribes the teachings of Torah. They were together forty days. After the first day, Ezra heard a heavenly voice telling him, Open thy mouth and drink. He obeyed, and a cup was handed to him filled with something that resembled both fire and water. His mouth opened to drink and remained open for the entire forty days. As for the scribes, they wrote things down in symbols they did not understand.

In the Midrash, his powers were felt both here on earth and in the heavens. Whenever the people of Israel needed an intercessor, he responded. Once he complained to God of the misfortunes of Israel, whereas pagans had it so good. An angel named Uriel tried to explain the mystery but Ezra found the answer unsatisfactory.

Strange, but neither he nor Nehemiah were prophets. No? One Talmudic source would like us to believe that actually Ezra *was* a prophet under a different name: Malachi. Yes, Ezra was the last of the prophets in Scripture. But let's not jump to conclusions: Ezra's case is not unique in this respect. Of Nehemiah, too, it has been said that he was not he—that he was someone else— Zerubbabel—which brings us to Nehemiah himself.

We already mentioned that he is different from Ezra. He does not have Ezra's inhibitions. Since he is called upon to act, he says so. Since he is destined to be at the center of crucial events, he wants it to be known. He is aware of the dangers inherent in reserve: leaders cannot afford the luxury of shyness.

Born in Shushan, or Susa, the capital of the Persian empire, he received a good Jewish education. That is implied by his name, and by that of his father. His father is called Khakhalia, which may mean *Khake-leh:* waiting for God. Or waiting for the redeemer. As for the name Nehemiah, it means "the consolation of God"; or one who will be consoled by God; or one who will console God.

Nehemiah has brothers. One of them, Hanani, lives in Jerusalem. It is he who brings a message to Nehemiah from Jerusalem and its inhabitants. Later, Nehemiah will appoint Hanani to an important position as "guardian of the gates." He is not afraid of being accused of nepotism. He is not afraid of what people may say about the way he conducts the affairs of state. Quick to make a decision, he will implement it in the best possible way.

His occupation? *Mashke-lamelekh,* the cupbearer. He is responsible for the royal bar. As such, he is also the official taster. It is he who hands drinks to the king. This is a high position in the Persian empire and in others as well. Fearing attempts on his life, the king needs someone whom he can trust, someone who will not be bought by conspirators. Certain rulers changed their cupbearers every two or three years to prevent them from being corrupted: new ministers always display greater loyalty and are more eager to please.

Close to the king, Nehemiah is in an ideal position to share with him his concerns, his fears, his plans. Let us open his book. We are at the month of Kislev of the twentieth year, which means 445 B.C.E. *"Vaani hayiti be-Shushan habirah,"* says the author. "I happened to be in the capital, Shushan. On that day I received the visit of my brother Hanani and several men from Judea; I questioned them on the fate of the saving remnant and on what was going on in Jerusalem. And they told me of the distress and shame of the survivors. Pierced are the walls around Jerusalem; her gates burned down. Then, having heard these words, I fell to the ground; as in mourning, I wept and wept for days on end; I fasted and implored God in heaven. . . ."

There is his portrait—I almost said, his self-portrait. The "I" dominates the page. It is he who is in the capital; it is he who is visited by a delegation from Judea; it is he who asks questions, it is he who takes the report to heart and weeps and fasts and implores the heavens. Today he would be called—at least superficially—egocentric. Indeed, some Talmudic passages corroborate this impression. Actually, says one source, it is he who wrote Ezra's book as well as his own. Why, then, doesn't it carry his byline? Our sages found him self-centered. "Zakhra li elokim letovah," said Nehemiah. God has remembered *me* favorably, God has rewarded *me* in helping Judea overcome its severe and tragic problems. He? He alone? And what about Ezra? And what about Zerubbabel? Nehemiah does not give them enough credit—that is why he is punished. Still, do not deduce from all this that he does not elicit esteem and affection in the Talmud. He does. Some sages lift him to dazzling heights. They compare him to the Messiah himself—or almost. How are we to reconcile these two perspectives, these two evaluations? Easily. The Talmudic tradition, as we already know, does not favor great men without shortcomings. "Nobody is perfect" could be a Talmudic dictum. The perfect sage is by definition imperfect.

But let us leave our principal heroes and return to the story that is of interest to us—a story in which they are not the only heroes. Take Sheshbazzar and Zerubbabel. These two men made Aliyah earlier than Ezra and long before Nehemiah, who was older than Ezra. To understand the significance of their return, we ought to mention, however briefly, the exile that preceded it.

The first national tragedy occurred in 595 B.C.E., when King Nebuchadnezzar of Babylon exiled King Yehoiakhin and his court to Babylon, where they remained prisoners for thirty-seven years. Constantly humbled, tormented, the royal family was subjected to the shame of hunger. The royal victor showed his royal prisoner no magnanimity, no grace, no sympathy—which was unusual for those times. Apparently Nebuchadnezzar had a special coldness in his heart for the Jewish sovereign. It was only when his son Evvil Merodach succeeded to the throne in 562 B.C.E. that

Yehoiakhin's lot improved. In the meantime, so many things had happened back home. . . . Was he aware of them, this poor imprisoned king? Did he know that his kingdom had been abolished, his city ravaged, his palace demolished, his Temple reduced to ashes? Far away, he was neither a participant in, nor a witness to, the second catastrophe, which took place in 586 B.C.E.

One must read Jeremiah's Lamentations to grasp the distress that dominated Jerusalem after its fall. Ruins everywhere. Desolation everywhere. Despair in every home, in every heart. Still, the real exile, the great mass exodus, occurred only four years later, in 582. Thus, during the intervening four years, there continued to be an organized Jewish life in occupied Jerusalem. Following a long-established policy, Babylon allowed conquered countries to go on functioning in order to finance the conqueror's military projects. Hostile or willful leaders and chieftains were deported, but the essential structure of the conquered society remained unchanged. Why then the general cruelty in 582? Because Jerusalem's Babylonian-appointed governor, G'dalya son of Ahikam, was assassinated by a group of zealots headed by a certain Yishmael ben Netanya. It is noteworthy that G'dalya was forewarned by his friend Yohanan ben Kareach, but he refused to believe him. In his naiveté, G'dalya could not believe that Jews could kill Jews. His naiveté was harshly criticized by certain Talmudic Masters who hold him responsible for the vengeance, the mass deportation, that ensued. The Babylonian enemy understood that as long as Jews remained in touch with their land, they would not be vanquished. Seven hundred forty-five persons (or families, or clans) were deported by General Nebuzaradan: they had constituted the last living community of Judea. After their departure, the land was occupied by Edomites and Ammonites. One might have concluded that Jewish history had come to an end—as was the case of so many other nations defeated by the great powers of the time.

At this point, half the Jewish population went to Babylon, the other half voluntarily sought refuge in Egypt. Jeremiah—after spending ten days and nights in prayer and meditation—pronounced himself in favor of a third alternative: to do everything possible to remain in the land of their ancestors, in spite of the enemy and his decrees. But Jeremiah was not heeded. His ideas were met with anger and indignation. He was called a liar, a false prophet.

For, let us remember, with the exception of the royal family, other Jews did not fare too poorly in their land of exile. They had taken Jeremiah's earlier advice seriously. Even before the fall of Jerusalem, he had told them in a famous letter:

"Build houses and dwell in them; plant gardens and eat their fruit; take wives and beget sons and daughters; take wives for your sons, and give your daughters to husbands, so that they may bear sons and daughters; and multiply there and be not diminished. And seek the peace of the city where you have been carried away captive, and pray for its welfare."

The Jewish community in Babylon could not complain. The local authorities were responsive to its needs. Jewish life there was truly Jewish—so much so that Ezra placed it above the semblance of Jewish life that, though miserable and debased, continued here and there in Judea. Ezra actually considered the new immigrants more Jewish than the natives. Why? First, because the elite had been taken away in captivity; second, because without spiritual leaders, Judean Jews could not flourish and remain totally faithful to their mandate. There was more tradition in Babylonian Jewry, more learning, more piety, more creativity.

Remember: a thousand years have elapsed since, under Joshua's command, the twelve tribes of Israel arrived in the land of Canaan, carried by a divine vision that made their progress irresistible and their triumph irrevocable. The Judges, the Prophets, the Kings, the generals, the Levites, the priests, the dreamers: all that history to what end? Were all the ambitions, all the battles, all the victories meant to be reduced to abdication before the foe? Of the twelve tribes, ten had been dispersed throughout the planet; of the two that remained, what had become of their grandeur? Where was the sublimation of their glory to be found?

In Babylon, under the Chaldean rule, Jews underwent different regimes. They suffered under Nebuchadnezzar, breathed the air of liberation under Evvil Merodach, and sighed again under Nabonidus. For history is never stagnant; it moves at its own pace, affecting the destinies of nations and kingdoms. Even absolute power is not eternal. Yesterday's victor is today's victim. Nabonidus adopted a new policy of repression, thinking that cruelty could elevate man to the status of god; he was wrong. Immortality can be attained neither by bloodshed nor by fire. Nabonidus was still reigning through fear and terror when a new empire was already rising on the horizon; its leader, Cyrus, defeated Babylon and established the Persian empire that was to last two centuries. Nabonidus's defeat caused the Jews to rejoice; for them it meant the closing of a circle. Another was to open, one that brought joy and consolation, and above all, a renewed sense of freedom . . .

Why was Cyrus so good to the Jews? Midrashic legends mention some heavenly intervention. One day—or one night—Babylon's king, Belshazzar, had the poor idea of giving a dinner at which the guests were served with vessels and utensils stolen from the Temple in Jerusalem. That is when God decided that enough was enough: Babylon would lose its power. To whom? To Persia. Recognizing the importance of Jerusalem, Cyrus decided to rebuild it. Other legends have Daniel playing a role in the story. But all of them stress the idea that Cyrus's pro-Jewish sentiments resulted from God's benevolence toward him. Historically, Cyrus was kind toward all the nations he had conquered. With him, it was a matter of policy. He was generous even toward Babylon. Why? Because he had conquered it without meeting any resistance. While Nabonidus and his advisers took part in orgies, the Persian army occupied the entire capital city without a single casualty. In gratitude, Cyrus ordered his soldiers to treat the inhabitants with kindness, and especially to leave the foreigners in peace. He also decreed that all idols and religious treasures taken from defeated nations and their sanctuaries be returned—those from Judea included.

Then came his historic declaration offering the Jews the possibility of going home and rebuilding their sanctuary. He ordered that an expedition be organized. To be headed by whom? Not by Ezra nor by Nehemiah, but by a Prince Sheshbazzar—fourth son of Yeoyachim—and later by Zerubbabel: both men have played an important role in the Babylonian Diaspora . . .

Sheshbazzar vanishes from the narration quickly. Zerubbabel does, too, although he stays a while longer. After all, Zerubbabel is somebody.

He is as legendary as Ezra. Like most Just Men, he was born circumcised. He obtained the post of expedition leader during the reign of King Darius, and this is how it happened. After a good meal, Darius fell asleep. To kill time, his three bodyguards played at solving riddles. What is the mightiest thing in the world? The first answered, Wine. The second answered, The king. The third—Zerubbabel—said, Women. But he corrected himself immediately: Truth is still stronger. Now half awake, Darius followed the conversation and said, Zerubbabel's answer pleases me most. He wished to reward him, but Zerubbabel politely refused all rewards. All he wanted was permission to rebuild the Temple of Jerusalem.

Another legend holds that the Angel Matatron had a special affection for Zerubbabel. Only the angel? The *Shekhina,* too, rested on him and endowed him with prophetic powers. And occasionally Zerubbabel talked with the Messiah himself. The Apocrypha literature makes Zerubbabel into one of its favorite heroes. It claims that Zerubbabel discovered the secret of redemption but that he was not yet free to reveal it. But if he was so great, so special, why does he disappear so suddenly from the story?

Anyway, it was Zerubbabel who led the first convoy toward the Holy Land, and who began the restoration. The text describes the expedition in great detail. Were there other captives who had returned home? Soon we learn everything abut them: they numbered 42,360 persons; they took with them 736 horses, 435 camels, 6,720 donkeys; we know exactly how much gold and silver—their own and what they had received from their brethren for the Temple—they had in their possession. We also know how many servants accompanied them. To protect them throughout the six hundred-mile journey, Cyrus offered them an armed escort of one thousand soldiers.

The journey that began that spring lasted from four to five months. No incident, no obstacle, no misunderstanding, no problem marked that trip: everybody felt protected, uplifted, blessed. When they left Babylon, the Babylonian Jews looked upon them with a mixture of envy and admiration: those in the convoy were *making* history, whereas those who stayed behind remained objects of history.

The mood of the Jews upon their arrival home? Let us read from the 124th Psalm: *"Beshuv adoshem et shivat Zion, hayinu kekholmim* . . . When God allowed us to return into Zion, we thought we were dreaming. . . . Our mouths were full of laughter, our tongues were filled with song."

But in Jerusalem, Zerubbabel and his friends must have experienced sadness too. The city of God was empty. The sanctuary and the Temple: piles of stone and rubble. The city in which God and his people had celebrated their alliance was now moribund and scarred.

Assisted by the High Priest Yeoshua, Zerubbabel's company did not waste a single day. They immediately began the work of restoring the glamour and beauty of the city they had so loved and missed. Priority was accorded to the building of the altar, in order not to hinder the sacred service; then came the sanctuary. The entire population participated in the work. The dedication ceremony was solemn and magnificent. Priests and Levites, dressed in their ritual garments, led the service with musicians playing their instruments and the people responding with fervor, thanking God for manifesting His grace toward the people of Israel. And—listen to this passage: "There were priests and Levites and old men who remembered the first Temple and therefore could not withhold their tears; they wept aloud, while the younger ones shouted with joy, so that people could not distinguish the sound of weeping from the sounds of singing."

Why were the old men weeping? Because they remembered that the first Temple was larger, says Rashi. The Talmud elaborates: The second Temple did not possess the arch and the cherubim, nor the eternal flame, which, in the first Temple, miraculously maintained the fire of the altar, nor did it have the Divine Presence and the prophetic spirit. . . . These explanations sound plausible, but there is another—there must be—and here it is: those who remembered the first Temple also remembered how it ended. That is why they cried: they wondered if the second Temple would not also be destroyed.

But why is Ezra still in Babylon? Why hasn't he made Aliyah yet, he who had urged others to make theirs? As a Zionist leader, why hasn't he recognized the need to teach by example? Is it that he wanted to serve as an example for those Zionist leaders who—yesterday and today—had seen fit not to show the way? Has he taught them how to justify their recalcitrance by saying that they are more urgently needed in Diaspora? The text is not clear on this issue.

The Midrash is clearer. It offers a more human and imaginative explanation: Ezra was the disciple of the prophet Baruch ben Neriah, whom he refused to abandon—and whose teaching he refused to forsake; he preferred being a student to being a leader. But another question might be raised: Why didn't Baruch ben Neriah himself go to Jerusalem? Maybe he was too old to undertake such a taxing journey. In not wanting to leave him behind, Ezra emerges as a compassionate and selfless man. Another explanation: Ezra was afraid of embarrassing the High Priest Yeoshua ben Yehotzadak, who officiated in Jerusalem. Since Ezra was more erudite than he, and more famous, there was a risk that people would urge him to replace Yeoshua ben Yehotzadak. That is why he waited. He came to Judea only after the High Priest died.

Actually, it was Ezra who led the second Aliyah, many years later. The journey lasted three months, and the convoy was much smaller: 1,746 men. As mentioned earlier, Cyrus offered them military protection, but Ezra—unlike Nehemiah later—refused it: he had more faith in prayer. From the king he asked only an authorization, which he obtained, in five parts:

1. To grant the right to anyone to join him, if he so wished.
2. To be allowed to visit Judea and its capital and see whether their inhabitants lived according to the laws of the Torah.
3. To be able to bring financial subsidies to Jerusalem.
4. To grant tax-free status to priests, Levites, and other Temple personnel.
5. To establish a judicial network throughout the land.

The king could not refuse him anything. But no sooner had Ezra arrived in Judea with the royal appointment order in hand than he was confronted by a new problem. From local dignitaries he learned that a number of citizens, influential persons among them, had married non-Jewish women. How many? One hundred and thirteen. Names and titles were in the file that was handed to Ezra, who took it badly. He rent his garments, tore at his beard, and remained speechless the entire day until the evening service, when he rose to deliver a wrenching speech of reprimand. Why such overreaction? After all, the women had converted to the Jewish faith and had accepted Jewish laws and Jewish destiny as their own. Legally they were Jewish, as were their children. Why then should they be excluded? It was the shock, perhaps. Ezra had expected to find a different situation—mixed marriages did not exist in Babylon's Diaspora. The Jews there were very strict. Assimilation was no real threat. Ezra established a kind of tribunal, or senate, to monitor the situation in Judea. All men whose wives were not Jewish-born had to register and swear that they would leave their wives and children. Not all obeyed. Ezra wept, pleaded, warned, threatened; still, his success was limited. The fact is that when Nehemiah arrived, thirteen years later, the two leaders were compelled to renew their efforts to persuade certain recalcitrants to do as they demanded.

But during those thirteen years, Ezra's authority was, on the whole, undisputed throughout Judea. With the secular powers vested in him by the Persian king, and with the spiritual powers that he represented, he was the ruler both in theory and in practice: he had the power of life and death over Jewish citizens, it was written in the royal letter. Still, Ezra preferred to appeal not to fear but to people's intelligence and sense of solidarity. A superb teacher and social worker, he introduced ten regulations: to read the Torah on the Sabbath and also on Monday and Thursday; to strictly observe the Sabbath; to hold court sessions on Monday and Thursday; to do the laundry on Thursday, not on Friday; to eat garlic on Friday—for it is healthy; to bake bread early in the morning, so it would be ready for beggars whenever they might appear; to allow women to wear girdles; to comb one's hair before taking the ritual bath; to see in prayer and study alternatives to offerings; and finally, to permit peddlers to sell cosmetics to women. He also created an educational network, established the first group of scribes who were to become the forerunners of the Tannaim—thus of the Rabbinic period; and he changed scripture from Canaanite to Assyrian, which was easier to read. Reading was his passion, his obsession. Better than anyone in his time, he understood that without study the Jewish people would have no chance to survive. And yet, this element was not covered by the royal charter he had received. This he did on his own. And when for the first time he read the Torah to the entire people in Judea, there must have been ancient reverberations of Sinai in the air.

We know when it happened. On the first day of Tishrei, in the year 444 B.C.E., Ezra had gathered all the people near the Water Gate in Jerusalem. Standing on an elevated wooden stand, he read the Torah aloud, thus giving the multitude of listeners a sense of their place in history. They all wept. They wept as they listened to the maledictions for disobeying God's law, and they wept as they listened to the promises for good behavior. That day was marked by destiny.

Nehemiah was already there. The event was staged by both of them. They formed a perfect team. One suspects that Nehemiah functioned as stage manager, Ezra as stage director. The two possessed a flair for the dramatic, for pageantry. When they dedicated, or rededicated the new Temple—in the year 515–516 B.C.E., seventy years after the destruction of the first, the nation felt uplifted and in near-ecstasy.

One reads breathlessly the description of the dedication of the new walls surrounding Jerusalem. Two choirs of Levites sang, one headed by Ezra and the other by Nehemiah, and they came from opposite directions. When they met, the assembled people were struck by the grace and the solemnity of the scene.

The ceremony marked Nehemiah's victory over those local enemies, the Ammonites and the Shomronites, who had tried again and again—through intrigues, denunciations, and assaults, to sabotage the erection of the walls. Nehemiah had to create a kind of national guard to fight them. His own account of the matter deserves to be read:

"The foes placed themselves in the low ground behind the wall, at the breaches; but I posted the people by companies, armed with sword and spear and bow. As I saw that they were afraid, I rose and addressed the authorities and the deputies and the rest of the people: 'Have no fear of them, remember the Lord, who is great and terrible, and fight for your kinsfolk, your sons and your daughters, your wives and your homes.'

"Our foes heard that we knew of their plan, and God defeated their purpose; so we all went back to the wall, every man to his work. After that, half of my retinue went on with the work, and half wore their spears and shields and bows and coats of mail, to support all the community of Judah who were building the wall. The laborers were armed; each of them worked with one hand and held a weapon in the other. The masons were each girded with a sword as they built. And the bugler stood beside me. I told the people, 'The extent of the work is great, and we are far apart from each other on the wall; so, wherever you hear the bugle sounding, rally to us there. Our God will fight for us.' This was how I and my men did our work; half held their spears from dawn until the stars appeared. I also told the citizens, 'Let each of you, man and servant alike, keep inside Jerusalem, to provide us with guard duty at night and with labor during the day.' As for myself and my retinue and the guard who followed me, none of us took off our clothes; each kept his weapon in his hand.

"Now whem Sanballat and Tobiah and Geshem the Arabian and the rest of our enemies heard that I had built the wall and that there was no breach left in it (though I had not yet erected the doors in the gateways), Sanballat and Geshem sent to ask me, 'Come, let us meet at some village in the plain of Ono.' They meant to harm me. But I sent messengers to them saying, 'I am doing a great work, and I cannot come down. Why should the work stop while I leave it and come down to you?' They sent four times, to the same effect, and I answered them to the same effect. The fifth time Sanballat sent, his servant brought me an open letter. He wrote: 'It is reported among the nations, and Geshem says so, that you and the Jews mean to rebel, and that this is why you are building the wall; you are to be their king—so people say. Now the king will be told what people say. So come and let us talk over the matter.' Then I sent him this message: 'Nothing of what you say has taken place; you are making it up yourself!' (For they all wanted to terrify us; they thought, 'Their hands will drop the work, and it will never be done.' But now, strengthen Thou my hands!)

"When I went to the house of Shemaiah the son of Delaiah, the son of Mehetabel, who kept himself apart, he said, 'Let us meet in the house of God, in the Temple, with shut doors, for they are coming to kill you—yes, coming to kill you by night!' But I said, 'Is a man like me to run away? Besides, who would go into the Temple, simply to save his life? I will not go in!' I detected at once that he had no mission from God; he was acting as a prophet against me, for Tobiah and Sanballat had bribed him, to terrify me into this act of sin, that it might be a scandal, and that they might sneer at me. O my God, remember all this against Tobiah and Sanballat and the Prophetess Noadiah and the rest of the prophets who would have scared me!

"On the twenty-fifth day of Elul, the wall was finished, in fifty-two days."

With Ezra and Nehemiah a new era opened in Jewish history. The Second Commonwealth lasted six hundred years but knew only eighty years of total independence. A turbulent history produced international upheavals. The Persian empire was defeated by the Greek empire which was defeated by the Roman empire.

Still, Ezra and Nehemiah's endeavors proved everlasting. Together they wrote the first constitution in any people's history—it is referred to in Scripture as "Omna," the charter, the covenant.

Signed by one hundred and twenty notables—the men of the
Knesset hagdola, the Great Assembly—it spelled out the reasons,
the obligations, the principles of the relationship between the
people and the state. All one hundred and twenty names are recorded. Nehemiah's is there—and Ezra's? It seems to be missing.
It seems? Some say that the name Azarya, which does appear,
actually is another name for Ezra.

As members of the Great Assembly, Ezra and Nehemiah were
the great healers of their nation. They restored its faith in God and
in itself. Listen to a Midrashic saying: "Why were they called the
men of the Great Assembly? Because they restored the splendor to
God's crown." Moses said, *"Hakel hagadol, hagibor vehanora*—God
who is great and awesome and strong. . . ." Daniel said: Foreigners have enslaved His children, where is His strength? So he
stopped saying *hagibor*. Jeremiah said: Enemies have invaded His
sanctuary—where is His awesomeness? So he stopped saying
hanora. Then came the men of the Great Assembly and said, He is
strong for He controls His anger; He is awesome for, if He were
not, how could a small nation survive among so many hostile
nations? And they restored God's attributes to His crown.

In conclusion our generation, too, has difficulties in uttering certain words in our prayers—words of unlimited praise and
infinite faith. We say them nevertheless.

Recently I read a story about the late Rabbi of Kretchenev. I
remember him from my hometown in the Carpathian mountains.
On the train taking him and his followers, and thousands of Jews
from Sighet, to the kingdom of night, he began consoling his
disciples: It is written, he said, that when the Messiah will come,
God, blessed be He, will arrange a *makhol*, a dance, for the Just.
Makhol, said the Rabbi, may also come from the verb *limkhol*—to
forgive. There will come a time, said the Rabbi of Kretchenev,
when the Just Men, the Tzaddikim, will forgive God, blessed
be He.

Ezra's end? It is as obscure as is the death of Nehemiah. Both
men vanish silently, as if on tiptoe. Some legends lead us to believe
that both returned to Babylon to plead in favor of their brethren
in Judea. Of Nehemiah it is said that he returned because he had
given his word to the king. Was he a *Yored* with a good excuse?

In so many ways our era reminds us of theirs. The end of a
certain exile; the reestablishment of a Jewish state on its ancestral

soil; the reconquest of Jerusalem. The problems, the tensions between Israel and the Diaspora. Babylon and Jerusalem. The center
and the periphery. The relations between a small but resolute
nation and its neighbors, and beyond them with the world's great
powers. What is today's America if not yesterday's Persia? What
has changed since? We need, today also, to rediscover the secrets
and the beauty of Torah each day. Today, too, we must reaffirm
the belief that Jewish communities everywhere are united. As in
Ezra's time, our sadness and our joy reflect the sadness and the joy
that exist in Jerusalem. As in Ezra and Nehemiah's time, Jewish
destiny is everywhere the same.

Esther

ONCE UPON A TIME, in a faraway land, there lived a king and his queen. . . .

It would be impossible—and perhaps improper—to begin this story any other way. For we are dealing here with a marvelously simple yet awe-inspiring fairy tale that manages to reassure the child in each of us; for at the very end, after all the ups and downs, good *does* vanquish evil, and joy *does* succeed sadness.

The story is about miracles: for once, Jews are allowed, indeed ordered, to be happy, to shout their happiness. They are even *commanded* to get drunk—and rewarded for it: The fact of drinking is counted as a *mitzva!*

Once upon a time, in a faraway land, there was a great, flourishing Jewish community which—because of a woman and her dignity, and a man and his vanity—awoke one morning to find itself in mortal danger: all its men and women, and children too, had been condemned to death; a plan that would centuries later be called genocide.

Luckily there lived a Just Man in their midst; and luckily he had a beautiful niece at his side. Together they managed to revoke the evil decree and thus save their people from certain massacre.

And so we witness the triumph of faith and prayer over terror and cruelty. Yesterday's victims emerge as today's victors. Power and glory have shifted from the haves to the have-nots, from the majority to the liberated minority.

Everybody likes a happy ending. This explains the universal popularity of Purim: a holiday that will last as long as exile—and longer. Yes, Purim will be celebrated even *after* the coming of the Messiah—even *after* the redemption of the Jewish people and, through it, of all nations and all people. Purim is something so rare, so special, so unique, that we shall never part with it. We need Purim as much as we need Yom Kippurim (the Day of Atonement).

Only because it is a joyous occasion? There are others. Because it singles out Jews, only Jews? The Book of Esther speaks of *Mordecai hayehudi*—Mordecai the Jew—and of Esther telling him *"Lekh knos et kol hayehudim*—Go and gather all the Jews. . . ." In other words, the story deals not with Persians of Jewish faith nor with members of Jewish denomination—but with Jews who are— more than anything else—Jewish. Is that the reason for Purim's popularity? Is it that simple?

In contrast to other holidays, on Purim all we have to do is listen to a story and get drunk—and the more we listen and the more we drink the better. *Ad d'lo yada:* we are instructed to drink to the point of no longer distinguishing between Mordecai the blessed and the wicked Haman. Is this a *mitzva?* Is this Jewish? Isn't Judaism based on emphasizing the difference between light and darkness, day and twilight, exile and redemption, Israel and pagans, life and death? Why must we, even for a day, a moment, erase the differences between friend and foe, danger and security, benediction and curse?

As the story unfolds on stage with mankind as audience it is anything but simplistic. Study the characters and you will discover their complexity.

Each of them ends up sounding false—all, that is, but the principal anti-Semite. And yet, even he will confuse us more often than not. Was he, and he alone, to blame for what was scheduled to happen and almost did? In fact, the story of this great event— the most important event in the life of Jewry in Shushan—could very well not have occurred at all. An event willed by God? All events are—except that in this case He does not seem to participate in the story; He is not even mentioned.

What could be the reason for His withdrawal? Nowhere in the entire Book are any of His sacred and ineffable names mentioned. Isn't the story about miracles? Could miracles occur without Him? Isn't He central to the tale? For Him to step out of history and become spectator, there must have been a reason.

That it was voluntary on His part is clear. *Minayin she-Esther min Hatorah?* asks the Talmud. What serves as proof that there is an allusion to Esther in Scripture? The verse *"Veanokhi haster astir panai*—I shall hide my countenance, my face." Rashi comments:

In Esther's time, there will be *hester-panim,* an eclipse of God's countenance. That means, the absence has divine motivation but human consequences.

Thus the Book of Esther *is* part of the canon. To hear the tale is a command that all men, women, and children must follow. All Jews everywhere must listen to the deceptively naive story of an old king and his Jewish queen. Everybody must be present when the tale is told and retold—everybody except . . . God.

Thus we realize that there are dimensions to this story that remain hidden. Instead of soothing our fears, the Book of Esther confuses us. While it enchants us with its seeming simplicity, it awakens a certain unspeakable anguish in us.

Which Jewish child is not in love with Esther and the Book of Esther? Everything in the tale seems exciting and glorious. The good are the best, the wicked the worst. The just are rewarded, their enemies punished. I read Esther and felt reassured.

The Midrash tells us that whenever Rabbi Akiba's disciples fell asleep during his lectures, he would abruptly change the subject and speak about Queen Esther. The effect was immediate: all woke up, interested, provoked.

Later I resented the Book: everything in it seemed too artificial, *too* uplifting. By then I realized that life is far from a fairy tale. In my time, the Jews of Shushan were not spared.

Forget the superficiality of the story and it will grasp you. Just go beyond the mask and you will be dazzled by the possibilities offered you. Example: for years and years—and centuries—we lived under the impression that Purim is Purim, and Passover Passover. We were wrong. In the Talmud the events occur not in the month of Adar but one month later: the thirteenth, the fourteenth and the fifteenth of Nissan: during Passover. In other words, Purim was Passover.

Let us reread the story. Once upon a time, in the capital of an empire that numbered one hundred and twenty-seven states, there lived an old, eternally bored and boring king, Ahasuerus, who one day had the ingenious idea of organizing the largest dinner party in the world during which nothing but the best would be served to the most distinguished guests: the finest dishes, the best wines, plus the highest-quality entertainment to be provided by Queen Vashti herself. For that special occasion, she was asked by her husband to perform some striptease numbers.

Naturally, everybody was excited except Vashti, who did not appreciate the role assigned to her. In fact, she turned it down. Outraged by her refusal, the king consulted his advisers on matters of protocol, legislation, human rights, and marriage counseling. Never before had anything like this happened to him. The members of his court echoed his outrage: it was clear to them that Vashti's independence threatened not only her own husband but all other husbands in the empire. Because of her, other wives might get ideas.

Something had to be done; Vashti's punishment had to serve as a warning to others. And so she was deprived of her title, her security, and ultimately her life. The text does not say so explicitly, but after she is banished, she disappears and is presumed dead. Her husband may or may not have missed her. What is clear is that his anger kept him from forgetting her, and he needed someone at his side. Consequently a national beauty contest was arranged. The prize was nothing less than an imperial crown!

At this point in the story, we are not yet obliged to ask ourselves the usual question: Was all this royal wife trouble good for Jews or bad for Jews? Why should we care about Ahasuerus's domestic problems if they are not linked to ours? But they were.

For suddenly we are told that *"Ish yehudi haya beshushan habirah*—There was a Jew who lived in the city." His name was Mordecai, son of Yair, son of Shimi, son of Kish of the tribe of Benjamin. And this Mordecai decided that his niece—some sources say she was really his wife—Hadassah (or Esther)—should propose herself as a candidate for the title. Sure enough, the old king chose her—which, as we shall see, was good for him and good for the Jews—and bad for their enemies, especially their leader, a wicked politician named Haman.

Haman, descendant of the Amalekite king Agag—whose life had been saved by King Saul, also of the Benjamin tribe—had been appointed Prime Minister and had immediately used his power to humiliate the king's subjects, and in particular to exterminate the Jews among them. Ahasuerus couldn't have cared less, especially since Haman had pledged ten thousand silver coins—taken from Jews—for the royal permission to implement his final solution.

Everything is now set: Haman consults occult seers and astrologists to decide on an appropriate date to start the operation. The decree has been issued, the killers are on alert. If nothing gets

in their way, the massacre can begin. Luckily for the Jews, Ahasuerus is in love, and the object of his love is Esther. He doesn't
know it, but she is Jewish.

At this point, she and her uncle are the only Jews aware of the
danger threatening their people; they are alone against Haman
and his official executioners, Haman and his hate. And yet they
will win and Haman will be doomed.

Surely you remember the sequence of events: Ahasuerus cannot sleep, and instead of taking a potion, he decides to read the
Book of Chronicles. Something about an unsuccessful *putsch*
catches his attention. Yes, some people had planned to chase him
from the throne. But he was saved by a Jew named Mordecai.
Mordecai, Mordecai—whatever became of him? the king wonders. From that moment on, Mordecai's star rises and Haman's
downfall becomes inevitable. In the end, Haman and his sons are
hanged, their accomplices slain, and the Jews of Shushan rejoice.
And so do we. Such was Esther's fervent wish—and who would
dare say no to a queen, especially one who is courageous and
beautiful and Jewish to boot?

Actually, she met some resistance from certain sages. They
were against the idea of celebrating: Why draw attention to our
good fortune and arouse jealousy? Don't you know that the world
cannot stand the sight of happy Jews? But Esther had an answer
for her critics: "Why should we hide our victory, when it has
already been recorded in the history books of other peoples?" She
won the argument, naturally. Esther won all her battles.

Let us have a better look at her. In the story she is the most
famous character; after all, hers is the title role. The Book bears her
name. She appears at the right place at the right moment and does
the right thing. She is the one who inspires the king to change his
mind and thus change destiny; she is the one who leads a clandestine existence, performing dangerous missions on behalf of her
people. She is the one who, at the most critical moment of the
play, decides on a scenario and distributes the tasks among Mordecai, the Jewish community, and the enemy himself. A keen
psychologist, she seems able to predict everyone's responses and
behavior. She instinctively knows what Ahasuerus will say, what
Haman will do. Well, Ahasuerus is not the only one to fall in love
with her; we all do.

Of course, she had a mentor: Mordecai, her uncle. He had
taken her in as an orphan and cared for her as if she were his

daughter: *"Lekakha lebat"* says the text. The Talmud adds, *"Al tikre lebat ki im lebayit."* "He took her" means, he married her.

Thus when Mordecai asked her to work for the Jewish people, she could not refuse. She respected him too much, and so do we. His Jewish loyalty, his Jewish pride, his strength and determination, his sense of dignity when dealing with those in power—everything about him was quite impressive.

Though he is "guardian of the royal gate"—an important position in the ancient Persian administration—he had remained faithful to the Jewish people. When they are threatened, he makes the ultimate sacrifice of sending his beloved Esther to attend the ridiculous royal beauty contest. He is determined to infiltrate the higher circles of the royal palace.

And when Esther reacts somewhat timidly—or recalcitrantly—he lashes out at her with the poignant reminder which applies to all Jewish men and women who have attained positions in society or government: *"Ki im hakhresh tachrishi baet hazot. . . ."* Should you remain silent now, when we need you, when our people are in mortal danger, we will get help from other quarters, but you—what will happen to you? What will your name evoke in our memory? Clearly, he had a sense of history.

Even old Ahasuerus is not totally unappealing—if you stay with your first impressions of the man. The Vashti episode? He is infatuated with her, proud of her beauty, and wants to show her off. What's wrong with that? Furthermore he does not seem to hate Jews—he hardly notices them. Also, if he could be bought by Haman, he could be bought by Haman's enemies as well: a ruler that could be bought was viewed with sympathy by Jews in the Diaspora. Study the text carefully and you will see that King Ahasuerus was in fact a comparatively benevolent monarch with few prejudices. Civil rights had been granted to all his subjects, Jews included. Read Haman's report on them and you will see how lucky they are to live in Shushan. They are permitted to speak their own tongue, cultivate their own culture, worship their own God, remain faithful to their own tradition, and maintain living links of Jewish solidarity between communities and individuals: a true golden Diaspora, wouldn't you say? If Haman sees them everywhere, it's because they *are* everywhere; if he is disturbed by their power, it's because they *have* power. Who wins the most coveted of all beauty contests? A Jewish girl. Who is publicly honored by the king for services rendered to the nation? A Jew.

But if Ahasuerus was so kind to Jews, why did he allow Haman to talk him into massacring them? A moment of blindness, a lapse. A mistake which he quickly corrected. After all, not one Jew lost his life under Ahasuerus.

The villain of the story? Haman. His hatred of Mordecai and the other Jews is total, unyielding—almost visceral. He will not rest as long as Mordecai is alive—the text clearly says so. Haman is wicked—*the* wicked man in Jewish history—the symbol of enmity, ferocity, cruelty, and murder. In this he resembles Amalek, whose descendant he is.

Vashti, too, is treated as a kind of villain. Poor queen: the whole world is against her. And Scripture too. And the Talmud even more so. Nobody comes to her rescue, nobody defends her honor. We seem to condone the king's rage: Why didn't she submit to his whims? If only she had accepted his invitation to perform, there would have been no Haman.

Let us review the characters: the two heroes, Esther and Mordecai; the two villains, Haman and Vashti; one neutral, Ahasuerus. And one absent: God.

Unleashed upon one another, they weave a legend of ambition and lust, vanity and treason, unquenchable thirst for power and fame on one hand, and total loyalty, faith, love, and beauty on the other.

No wonder the Book has been such a success!

But let us examine it within the context of our tradition: Is the story true? Was there a Persian king Ahasuerus? Was his wife Jewish? Was her name Esther? To what extent do the episodes involving Mordecai and Haman reflect historical events?

As far as the characters are concerned, yes. There was a King Ahasuerus in Persia who ruled from 486 to 465 before our Common Era. Herodotus mentions him, but for Herodotus his wife's name was neither Esther nor Vashti but Amestris. Also, a tablet discovered in Borsipa refers to a royal adviser named Mardukka. Traditional Jewish sources take it for granted, naturally, that the Book of Esther is based on fact. But then, how is one to explain Herodotus's statement that Persian kings could marry women from seven noble families only? There are other discrepancies in dates and names: was Mordecai himself exiled in the time of Yehoiakhin? Was his grandfather Kish? Also, when exactly did the crisis of Purim occur? Most Talmudic sources date it back to the Babylonian exile, but it is difficult to pinpoint it exactly.

Are we therefore to conclude that the story is fiction? Some scholars think so. They claim that the Jews of Shushan did not celebrate Purim to commemorate a miracle, rather, they invented a miracle to justify the celebration. Their argument: In Persia, as in other lands, ancient tribes celebrated spring simply because it meant rebirth. As for the Jews, they conferred upon the festivity a religious meaning. That is why they invented the story of Purim which, on the surface, is shockingly naive and banal with its harem intrigues on one hand and power intrigues on the other—plus a good measure of sheer fantasy.

God's absence would thus be justified, or at least comprehensible: who would not prefer to stay away?

Fortunately there is another version of the events—one that is more poetic and perhaps more truthful. I refer to the one in the Midrash.

First of all, the Midrash, without the slightest inhibition, does introduce God into the story; and it does so in a charming, almost childish way: it makes the term "king" apply not only to Ahasuerus but also—at times—to the King of the Universe.

The Midrash then goes further and uses the characters in a more enigmatic way: they become more human, more profound.

Unlike Scripture, the Midrash plays with the characters, thus erasing the frontiers separating good from evil. Nothing is irrevocable—no plot is definitive. The creative process unfolds against the background of the reader's own dreams and concepts.

Take Ahasuerus and his metamorphosis: What the Midrash does to him is not always generous. He is shown as neither exclusively stupid nor exclusively wicked but . . . both. Some sources say, *Melekh tipesh haya*—He was a foolish king; others say, *Rasha haya*—He was a bad king. At the same time we find a third category of commentators in the Midrash—out of compassion perhaps—depict him as a kind and charitable and just man. Remember the opening sentence? *Vayehi biyemei Ahashverosh hu ahashverosh?* This repetition and emphasis occur ten times in the Bible, the Midrash finds it necessary to note. Five times it is related to Just Men, and five times to wicked men. We are given a choice: Ahasuerus may belong to either group, or both.

In one place in the text he is shown as a merciless tyrant, in another as a weak sovereign. What is virtue in Scripture becomes shortcoming in the Talmud. The text tells us of his decree to allow

his guests to live freely—*Laassot kirtzon ish vaish.* "To give freedom
to all." Is there a better philosophy of action? The Midrash disagrees: the order is too large. God says to Ahasuerus, "You wish
to please everybody. Can you? If two men wish to marry the same
woman, is it in her power to marry both? If two ships travel in
opposite directions, can both their prayers for the same wind be
fulfilled? In life, man must choose one way or another—and you,
mortal, think you can satisfy all men by offering them the same
thing?" Moreover, if we emphasize his decision to allow his guests
to eat and drink freely, surely it must mean that this was not the
rule in his palace! The Talmud tells us that in the past his guests
were *forced* to drink from special cups—they went insane but they
drank! They were going to die—but they drank!

Some sources ridicule him. Why was he called Ahasuerus?
Because whoever remembers him *"khash berosho,"* gets a headache.
So ambiguous, so ambivalent is the man that everything about
him is confusing. Some sages believe he was friend and protector
of the Jews, others maintain that he was more hostile to them than
Haman.

What a strange man! exclaims one Master. He killed his
wife—Vashti—because of his friend Haman—and his friend Haman because of his wife—Esther.

Let's take another look. No longer seeming neutral, he is
obviously quick-tempered. He decides to do one thing today,
another tomorrow. Because of Vashti (who refused to entertain
his guests), he makes all women suffer by reducing them to servitude; because of Haman, he is ready to allow all Jews to be
massacred; and because of Esther he saves them. Observe the way
he acts toward Vashti. He loves her desperately, yet he hum-
bles her in public; he desires her, yet he kills her; he kills her, and
then he misses her.

When the text says *"Vekhamato baaro bo"*—that he was
angry—it is not clear at whom the anger is directed: whether at
Vashti or at himself for having executed her.

Let us look at Vashti. A princess by birth—her father is supposed to have been Balshetzar—she fares poorly in the Midrash,
and we do not understand why. How is one to explain her bad
reputation? I, for one, would rise to her defense—as any righteous
citizen should. I happen to like Vashti. In the immortal legion of
liberated women, she occupies a place of distinction.

She knows the price of her temerity, and she is ready to pay it: she will not submit to the capricious impulses of her senile husband. He wants to entertain his guests? Fine, but not at her expense. Her argument—as recorded in the Midrash—is dignified, noble: "Why do you wish me to appear naked before your guests, Sire? If they find me beautiful, they will kill you to possess me; if they think me ugly, my ugliness will blemish you." The Midrash comments: "She talked to him in hints and he understood nothing; she scratched him and he felt nothing." Enraged, she continues: "Who and what were you when you worked in the house of my father? You worked in his stable. You are used to mingling with prostitutes; now you are king but your manners have not changed." Again, the Midrash comments, "She spoke in hints and he understood nothing; she scratched him and he felt nothing." Then she sends him a last message: "Remember: in the house of my father people *were* condemned to die—but never naked." So impressive is she that the Talmud inevitably asks why she deserved to die—not from her husband's viewpoint but from ours? What can *we* reproach her for? The Midrash comes up with several original answers. She tried to incite Jewish women to give up Judaism by making them work on the Sabbath; and she dissuaded her husband from rebuilding the Temple in Jerusalem, saying: "My grandfather, Nebuchadnezzar, destroyed Jerusalem, and you want to rebuild it?" That is why she deserved punishment—and received it. And finally: When Ahasuerus gave his dinners for men, she organized parties for women. While they were having a good time, the angels complained to God: Look, Your people are suffering and they don't care! This last argument is the weakest. Why should Vashti be blamed for also giving dinners?

But wait: Vashti was condemned to death—because of whom? Haman, acting under the assumed name of Memoukhan, advises the king to get rid of her. Why? The Midrash states three reasons. One: Vashti made the mistake of not inviting Haman's wife to the royal dinner. Two: occasionally she slapped his face with her sandals. Three: he had a daughter who needed a husband—a royal widower if possible.

In truth, says the Midrash, Ahasuerus sought the advice of Jewish sages before condemning Vashti to death: She disobeyed the king, he told them. I shall bring her to you for judgment. The sages were in a predicament: If they told him to execute her, tomorrow he might regret his decision and make them regret theirs; if they told him to leave her in peace, they might be accused of tolerating crimes of lèse-majesté. They found a way out. They said to the king, Sorry, Sire, but we can be of no assistance to you; once upon a time, in Jerusalem, we knew how to pass judgment in capital cases; now, in exile, we no longer have access to that knowledge. Only then did Ahasuerus turn to Memoukhan, or Haman.

Haman himself emerges less one-dimensional in the Midrash. Anti-Semitic? Yes, but . . . how could he help himself? Like all the other anti-Semites, he is convinced that Jews are everywhere, that they are forever involved in plots to take over the world. . . . Look: Haman is chosen and loved by the king, applauded by the nation, and cherished by his family. He has everything a man could want. He could be happy, were it not for the Jews, who appear wherever he goes, only to challenge and provoke him. Who is at the imperial palace gate? A Jew, Mordecai. Inside the palace? A Jewish woman, Esther. In the official chronicles? Again a Jew. How could he help but feel hostile toward them? Don't they do everything to fan his hatred? He is at the height of his career; the king orders all citizens to bow before him, the gods are on his side—and yet there is one Jew who decides to be different, one Jew who refuses to bow. Of course, Haman should not pay attention to him. But he cannot avoid him, for he is at the entrance. What is Haman to do? Use the side door, he, the Viceroy, the Prime Minister? Haman hates Mordecai, and through him, all the Jews, because Mordecai's presence is a constant reminder of the fleeting nature of his, Haman's, power. Why does Mordecai do this to him? Why doesn't he just go away? Why can't he be like everybody else?

Naturally the Talmud also emphasizes Haman's evil nature: he is a descendant of Israel's—and mankind's—archenemy, Amalek, thus deserving death. His ancestor Agag was spared by Saul; therefore, if King Saul had been less charitable, the Jews of Shushan would not have been in danger. Thus the persecution of Persian Jews was Saul's fault—or rather, it was not entirely Haman's fault.

Some sages feel such sympathy for Haman that they are unable to accept the tragic fate that befell his children. They claim that they were not all hanged, that some survived, and that one of his descendants even became an illustrious Talmudist at a yeshiva in Bnei-Brak!

Haman's death? It is described in shocking detail. After having been defeated, he becomes Mordecai's servant and valet: he

bows to him and attends to all his needs. Now he pleads with
Mordecai for just one thing: that he be spared the indignity of
death by hanging. He accepts death, but not the indignity. He
reminds Mordecai of the injunction *"Binfol oyivkha al tismach*—
One must not rejoice at the downfall of the enemy." But Mordecai
remains deaf to his pleas. At this point, one wonders why there
was no room for pity in the hearts of our Talmudic legend
makers—pity for Haman, who had been a tool of destiny in a story
that went beyond him—and that crushed him for all eternity.

Was Mordecai thirsty for revenge? Empty of compassion?
No. He would have resisted the temptation of power, just as he
resisted threats and persecutions from people in power. His portrait in Scripture is unambiguous. Mordecai was Jewish—*Ish
yehudi*—in the capital city of Shushan. Everybody knew that he
was Jewish. As a Jew, he believed in the law. And in justice. He
believed in punishment for the enemy. People knew that he considered himself a fugitive Judean in exile, and that he worked on
behalf of Jews: that was his passion, his raison d'être. Whether
beaten or triumphant, he proudly affirmed his Jewishness. And
when danger loomed for his brethren, he devoted his energy to
rescue work. That is the sublime picture the Bible offers of the
man and his mission.

But, once again, the Midrash portrays him in a more complex
way. Not everybody is happy with him all the time. We deduct
this from the end. Remember: after the miracles obtained by Mordecai to defeat the enemy, Mordecai *"haya ratzui lerov ekhav"*—he
was accepted—or elected—by most of his people. What? Most?
Not *all*? No, says the Talmud. Not all. Some members of the
Sanhedrin opposed his leadership—and we are not given the reasons, only the fact: Mordecai ruled by majority and not by unanimity. There was a minority against him. Why such ideological
ingratitude? Moses before him had had to face similar problems.
What he endured on the part of his people—whom he had saved
from slavery and death—constitutes the most tragic and depressing part of Scripture. Perhaps he was not perfect—neither was
Mordecai. After all, it was because of *his* lack of understanding for
Haman and those who bowed to him that Jews found themselves
threatened. Is such individual salvation—at the expense of collective reprisals—justifiable? Was his stubbornness something to be
encouraged or condescendingly explained away?

Of course, Mordecai is mostly covered with praise. He was as important to his generation as Moses had been to his, says the Midrash. He belonged to the Sanhedrin, spoke seventy languages, and knew all the secrets of Torah; he had good manners, possessed rare virtues, and was worthy of redemption—but . . .

Let us not forget: It was *he* who sent Esther to the beauty pageant, he who told her to hide her Jewishness, and that was *before* the peril. He sent his wife—or niece, no matter—a poor orphan, to the imperial palace, fully aware of the risks he exposed her to! How could he? Granted, he knew the king's weaknesses. Was that sufficient reason to use Esther the way he did? To add insult to injury, he then became critical of her behavior. He blamed her for the slow pace of government bureaucracy. He accused her of being too timid. Was it her fault that the king received his wives only once a month? At one point, he accused her of being silent— and yet there is nothing in the text to justify his accusations. On the contrary: she was at the front, not he; she exposed herself to punishment, not he. He advocates courage, but it was she who would endure the consequences.

Worse: listen to the Midrash. When Esther asks him to proclaim a three-day fast, he goes to the religious calendar, checks the dates, and answers indignantly, Impossible. It falls on Passover, it interferes with our holidays. . . . Really. Esther is on a dangerous clandestine mission. She needs help, encouragement, support. And all Mordecai can do is quote the *Shulchan Aruch*, the code of behavior.

At this point, Esther has had enough. She puts him in his place: "Listen, old man," she tells him. "Of course my request interferes with Passover—and it is true that Jewish laws forbid fasting on a holiday. But what would happen to Passover if there were no Jews left to observe it?" And Mordecai, faced with such a logical interpretation of *Halakha*, admits that she is right.

Esther is clever, even shrewd: a perfect diplomat. Jewish and proud to be Jewish? During the first part of the story she conceals her Jewishness. True, Mordecai *told* her to do so—but she must have been an accomplished actress to have pulled it off. Read the text and you will admire her sense of drama; she knew how to build suspense, how to manipulate events and people. She appears before her royal husband without revealing her true motivation. Instead of telling him straightforwardly, My wish is to save my brethren, she says, All I desire is to have Your Majesty and Haman come to my quarters for dinner. Naturally, they both accept the invitation. Ahasuerus then asks her, What is your wish *now?* She says, My most fervent desire is to have you come back again. Really, now: the Jews were fasting—and Esther was wining and dining the king and his minister! The Midrash feels the need to justify her behavior. Though the dinners are difficult to comprehend at first, they were necessary. Even more than before, she had to hide her Jewishness; had she not arranged the dinners, she might have given herself away, not only to the king and his prime minister but also to the Jews of Shushan: they all had to be left in the dark. If they had learned of her Jewishness, says the Midrash, they would have felt unduly reassured. Why worry, why fast, why pray? We have one of ours inside the palace. The argument is sound, yet I find it disturbing, for it proves that Esther fooled even her own people. Of course, she already knew that sometimes the end justifies the means—or does it? Look at what she did to poor old Ahasuerus: she turned him into a farcical character. And Haman? She trapped him into a cheap melodrama. Scripture says, It happened during the second dinner. The king had too much wine and went for a walk in the garden. Haman was left alone with Esther. He stumbled and fell on her: it was his misfortune that Ahasuerus returned precisely at that moment. Esther, cool and unfazed, told the king, See? He wanted to seduce me behind your back. Well, that was the end of Haman. But—wait a second: the accusation is false! Haman never dreamed of seducing Esther. He was a devoted husband and a good father. He was happily married. Zeresh, his wife, was also his ally, his confidante. He did nothing without consulting her—and Esther must have known that. Then why did she compromise him? Why did she . . . lie?

That Haman would never have considered seducing her is a point certain Midrashic texts make in the course of commenting on her age. In Scripture, she is described as young and beautiful. Not so in the Midrash. While Rav says she was forty, his opponent, Shmuel, who always wants to outdo him, claims she was eighty. *Rabannan amru,* the consensus, was that she was seventy-five. Which means that her impact on the king had nothing to do with her youth. She must have had other qualities. The Midrash mentions her prophetic powers, her gracefulness, her piety . . . She ate kasher, never looked at another man besides Mordecai, and while Haman plotted to exterminate the Jews, she was busy preparing her home for Passover: in short, she was a good Jewish housewife. Her marriage with Ahasuerus? Utter self-sacrifice. The Zohar offers a more extraordinary, if outlandish, hypothesis: It was not Esther who lived with the old king but a demon who looked like her.

It's clear that the Midrash exaggerates because its Masters had to explain Esther's ambiguous behavior.

Another presence that must be explained is the Jewish community. After all, the Jews of Shushan are the real protagonists of this drama. It is their fate that is at stake. Their lives are in danger, their children are being handed over to the executioner. And yet, they stay in the background: objects rather than subjects of their own history. Nobody asks their opinion, inquires about their desires, presents them with choices. They are told what to do and when: when to fast, when to celebrate, when to fight, when to defend themselves, when to take vengeance and when to triumph. That is the impression one gets from Scripture. They are passive participants. Too passive?

In the Midrash one feels a tension between them and their two leaders, Mordecai and Esther, who were more Jewish, more devout than the others. The others, for instance, attended the gigantic dinner given by Ahasuerus—the Midrash blames them for that. Says the Midrash. Who were the guests at that festivity? Jewish dignitaries who sought to establish good relations with the administration. Rabbi Hanina son of Pappa goes further and specifies that the *Gdolei Hador* were among them the Masters, the dignitaries, the leaders of their generation. Except that at one point they ran away.

This imperial dinner is harshly judged in the Midrash: to have attended it was considered sinful. Why did Haman almost succeed in his criminal plot? asks the Midrash. Because Jews went to the party. According to one source, 18,500 Jews ate, drank, and allowed themselves to be seduced by the luxury and limelight of the palace—therefore Satan could easily denounce them to God, who could not help but listen to his arguments.

From all this we learn that there was a large and flourishing Jewish community in Persia's Diaspora, with its sages and disciples, merchants and customers, rich and poor. Yet, one minor incident, one capricious desire, one frustration on the part of a king or his queen, was enough to disturb the balance, threaten the security and the very existence of all the Jews throughout the entire empire.

Remember: in the beginning of the story, the Jews were not involved. The king and his queen had a domestic quarrel; some politicians engaged in their customary intrigues—and that was all: no Jew was involved in the event. Then, suddenly Ahasuerus is angry with Vashti, and Jews are persecuted. Haman seeks power, and Jews are in danger.

That Haman knew the Jews is clear; he knew many things about them. To Ahasuerus he said, "They have no respect for you, Sire. Observe them, will you please? If a fly falls into their cup, they remove it and drink the wine; but were you to touch the cup, they would consider the wine impure."

What does that tell us? Both that the Jews of Shushan were pious and that Haman had gone to the trouble of learning Jewish laws, including the one about which wine is kasher and which is not.

Incidentally, his opinion of Jews was, in a way, quite flattering. He attributed to us an international power of infinite magnitude and was convinced that we were fully committed to help one another and the Jewish people, always. If only he were right. . . .

But whatever negative points Haman made about Jews on earth were transformed into positive ones in heaven. Example: When Haman said to King Ahasuerus, "Look at his people which is faithful only to its own traditions, its own tongue, its own laws, its own customs, its own memory," the angel Michael repeated the words after him and said to God, "See, Master of the Universe, see Your people and the way it observes Your laws, the way it affirms its faith in You." And, at the end, Michael added, "Admit it, Master of the Universe, Your people is not accused of theft or rape or idolatry but only of wanting to remain Jewish. How can You not save it from massacre?"

It was then that Haman had the idea of inspiring Ahasuerus to organize a festive dinner, to seduce some Jews and corrupt them. He knew that they would go there dressed in all their finery, thus giving Satan the perfect opportunity to say to God, "Now look at Your Jews. They are having a good time and have forgotten that their Temple and Yours is in ruins; they do not deserve Your grace." God simply *had* to submit to Satan's logic; and so He asked for a parchment to inscribe the terrifying verdict that was to doom the eternal people to banishment from time and history.

Haman's plan was perfect; the timing was excellent. But then something went wrong. Ahasuerus changed his mind. He refused to play the part assigned to him by Haman. He decided that it would be unwise for him to quarrel with Israel and the God of Israel. His argument: Whoever had provoked them in the past ended in tragedy. He even quoted examples: Pharaoh, Nebuchadnezzar, Amalek. . . . Haman tired to reassure him: Yes, that was true once upon a time, when He and His people were young, but now He is old and tired. You want proof? The Temple *has* been destroyed, Jerusalem *is* in ruins, and the Jews are dispersed. You see? There is no need to worry about Him.

Finally King Ahasuerus gave his consent. The law was promulgated, the plan made, the date chosen. Now all the killers and victims could do was wait.

And while they were waiting, the Midrash envisions some breathtaking scenes up there, in heaven, where angels and seraphim dressed in mourning, and following the Torah, began to weep: How shall we live without the children of Israel? Too late, was the answer. The decree has been signed; impossible to revoke it. And so the prophet Elijah hurried to wake up the three patriarchs, Abraham, Isaac, and Jacob, from their sleep: How can you rest in peace when our people is doomed? They asked if the decree was signed with clay or blood? Fortunately, it was only with clay. Good, exclaimed the patriarchs, let us pray.

In the meantime, down below, twenty-two thousand children gathered around their teachers to fast and study together. Their mothers brought them food but they rejected it: they wanted to share in the collective prayers of their people. Yet, suddenly they closed their books and gave them back to their teachers, saying, "You promised us, in the name of Mordecai, that thanks to Torah we shall be spared—that the Torah of Israel protects the people of Israel. Now we realize it isn't so. . . ."

For they—the children—had been selected as the first to be slain—just as centuries later, the Jewish children were the first to be marked to be murdered. But the Jewish children of Shushan *did* move God to compassion. The catastrophe was averted. A miracle occurred: God would not accept the massacre of twenty-two thousand Jewish children.

And that is why we celebrate Purim with such joy and fervor: to commemorate God's pity for His children. There seems to be a limit even to His patience; even to His silence.

•

In conclusion, one question: If indeed there was a miracle willed by God, why doesn't His name figure in the tale? That He chose to hide His face before and during the catastrophe is conceivable—and is reconciled with the traditional explanation of Hester-Panim, or the divine eclipse. But why did He keep His name from the Book after the event?

I believe that is related to the end, rather than to the beginning of the story. What is the end? The Jews are saved, Haman is humiliated and finally hanged, and so are his ten sons. And if that is not enough, the Jews obtain the king's permission—drafted by Mordecai—to take revenge and kill their enemies.

I confess I never did understand this part of the Book of Esther. After all, the catastrophe was averted; the massacre did not take place. Why then this call for bloodshed? Five hundred men were slain in Shushan in one day and three hundred the next. Seventy-five thousand persons lost their lives elsewhere.

Fact or fiction? The question remains: How could our ancestors celebrate Purim in the midst of such killing? Is this why we are told to get drunk and forget? To erase the boundaries between reality and fantasy—and think that it all happened only in a dream? Or is it a way of coping with our hidden frustrations? One day a year to imagine acts of violence—during Purim when it's but a game, a play—so as to impress upon ourselves the lesson that they are prohibited on all other days?

This must explain why God chose not to give His name to the Book of Esther: He refused to be associated with the denouement—with the bloodshed. It was His way of saying, Don't ascribe this to me; I had nothing to do with it; you wanted revenge, all right—but don't make me responsible for it.

For to be Jewish means to have earned the right to punish our enemies—who inevitably turn out to be the enemies of mankind—and to choose not to.

What does this beautiful but disturbing story leave us? An impression that it is neither myth nor fiction, but everyday reality. One must look around and wonder whether a gratuitous act somewhere does not somehow implicate our lives and those of our children.

The Talmud teaches us—orders us—to begin the story of Esther at the beginning. One is not allowed to read the Megillah in reverse, starting with the miracle instead of the danger.

Commented the Baal Shem Tov: What is the meaning of

this strange injunction? What's wrong with flashbacks? The meaning is, said the Besht, not to view the story as an event of the past alone: it will forever be projected into the present—and the future.

What is Purim? Ultimately it is not so much a tale about persecution as it is a celebration of memory.

PART TWO

THE

TALMUD

I thank my childhood friend David Weiss-Halivni, who taught P'shat and D'rash of the Talmud to a fervent generation of students. His help in charting the course of these Talmudic adventures is deeply appreciated.

The House of Shammai
and the House of Hillel

AMAR RABBI ABBA AMAR SHMUEL. And this is what Rabbi Abba said in the name of Rabbi Shmuel: *"Shalosh shanim nechleku Bet Shammai ubet Hillel."* The students of Shammai and those of Hillel were in dispute for three years, each claiming that the law was as they saw it. Finally a celestial voice was heard: *"Elu veelu divrei elokim hayim*—You are both right; both positions reflect God's word and God's truth—and yet—the law is according to the school of Hillel."

Naturally, this legend raises many questions: One—how can two contradictory views, two contradictory interpretations, be equally correct?

And if indeed they can be—and are—then—and this is difficulty number two—why are Hillel's students favored over their opponents? This question is raised in the legend itself—for which we are grateful. In fact, we are even given an answer. The students of Hillel are favored because they are more sociable, more tolerant, more modest as well: they mention the opponents' view as well as their own. (In truth, this is a compliment which the students of Hillel both deserved and . . . could afford: Why not be generous when the decision will inevitably be in your favor?)

But—and now we are at question number three—why did the celestial voice intervene in the first place? Haven't we been reminded again and again that the Torah is not in heaven, but here on earth? That the Torah was given to man to be explored, interpreted, and implemented—and that celestial voices have no say in the matter? Are we not to believe that the Torah must be approached in human terms—and that supernatural interventions would be—and should be—immediately ruled out of order?

I suppose that someone had to win the debate—but why the

school of Hillel? And if Hillel had to win, why on those grounds? Is the law really a matter of good manners and fairness—nothing else? Couldn't Shammai be intolerant and fanatic—and still be right? And Hillel flexible, friendly—and wrong nevertheless?

The text itself suggests that the problem is not as simple as it appears—for it specifies that the celestial voice waited three long years before intervening in the debate. One fails to understand why it did not make itself heard right away, thus saving the scholars' time and energy, surely they had more important, more urgent things to do in those three years? Did the celestial voice have no compassion, no consideration for the scholars—on either side?

This entire Talmudic episode, whose purpose is more or less to illustrate the Hillel school's patience, forbearance, and humility, ends with yet another legend about yet another debate.

Tanu rabanan: and this is what our Masters taught us. For two and a half years, the disciples of Shammai and Hillel were engaged in violent dispute. The school of Shammai said, It would have been better—or simpler—for man not to have been born. The school of Hillel replied, Man is better off having been born. After thirty months of discussion, the issue was to be voted on. And lo and behold—this time, the school of Shammai emerged victorious. Yes, indeed, it would have been better for man not to have been born—but having been born, he must search his conscience, his soul, he must scrutinize his actions, looking for their meaning; in other words, his actions must confer a meaning upon his existence.

What a sad perspective—even more depressing than the previous one gives. It too deserves a closer look.

Here are two schools called upon to argue over laws and systems, attitudes to adopt or discard, especially toward various categories of outsiders and foreigners—practical and urgent problems all. And yet for two and a half years these scholars seem to have had nothing better to do than discuss the philosophical issue of whether man—who, after all, has been born, like it or not—wouldn't have preferred to have been spared this silly and/or tragic adventure which is his passage on earth. What was so urgent about it? Couldn't it wait? And why did they decide to take a vote after only two and a half years? What suddenly made them so impatient? Why couldn't they wait another six months for the intervention of the reliable old celestial voice, which, in *this* case, being practical, would have made sense?

Isn't it all very strange? When the argument is over *Halakha*—jurisprudence and civil law—a vote seems in order—certainly much more so than when the debaters lose themselves in purely metaphysical speculation. We would have preferred a democratic vote to end the first discussion and a heavenly pronouncement to conclude the second. How then are we to explain the total absence of logic in these legends which, though intensely poetic, are nevertheless part of the Talmud, where everything is organically linked according to rigorous logic and design? And what is one to make of the conclusion of the second legend? We all realize that life contains more burdens than joys; but from there to deny the desirability of life . . . is this really the prevailing view of our tradition? And then, assuming it is, is the answer "to go and examine my actions"? That is what the expression *Yefashpesh bemasav* means. Is there nothing else one can or should do? And how long should this self-examination last? Forever? Are we to live our entire life with the terrible feeling that it was wrong for us to be born? Is such an attitude Jewish?

Hillel and Shammai: two great Masters who, through the power of their personalities and the scope of their vision, left a lasting imprint on the literary, legal, and philosophical masterwork that is the Talmud.

We shall try to meet them as they functioned in their own period and society, and learn why it is said in the Talmud that when the sages had gathered in Yavneh after the destruction of the Temple, they said: There will be a time when man will search for words of Torah and will not find them, search for words of scribes and will not find them—that is why we must begin with Hillel and Shammai.

They knew that with Hillel and Shammai you cannot go wrong: begin with them and their discussions and their eternal arguments, and you will be in touch with the living sources of Jewish learning.

In the *yeshivot* and houses of study, throughout the centuries, the one was feared and the other loved. We tried to imagine their faces, their expressions, we could almost guess their reactions on various points whenever they met to argue—always to argue. It was easy to love Hillel—and just as easy to fear Shammai. Too easy. But this I understood only much later.

As a child I loved to study Talmud but did not really understand it. I thought—or rather, my poor teachers thought—that it was enough to learn a certain number of pages by heart. We were led to believe that all these laws and arguments and discussions were remote from life and its everyday problems—mine and those of my friends. The issues raised and the solutions offered belonged to another land, another age—not to ours. The only possible reward for studying Talmud was that, with some luck, you could become a *melamed*. So—why bother?

Today I know that the study of a Talmudic text is an adventure not unrelated to literary endeavor: a three-sentence legend often possesses the suggestive power of a lyrical poem. A discussion on a remote subject often contains more descriptive elements than a historical narrative.

Today I also know that it would be wrong to look only for the past in the Talmud. The Talmud is eternally present. Nothing in it is ever lost. The sages continue their eternal debates and the children continue to be imbued with their fervor. The holiness of Shabbat is still celebrated and, right there, the Temple is burning. And we who read the corresponding passages burn with the Temple—and perhaps for the Temple.

In the Talmud, the school of Shammai is still opposing—and fanatically so—the school of Hillel; and we are still requesting that the celestial voice issue a ruling.

Hillel and Shammai: each a founder of a school and an interpreter of law. Both were leaders of the Sanhedrin, both pillars of the oral tradition—in fact, they are the last two spiritual leaders of Judea since the *Knesset hagdola,* the Great Assembly.

So well known are the ideas and points of view of Hillel and Shammai in so many areas, both human and social, that one feels as though one knows them personally. Yet this impression is erroneous: little is known about either man. Their biographies are inaccurate and incomplete. Only the broad outlines have been preserved—showing us not who they really were, but how they were seen and judged by others.

All that we know about them is related to their divergence, stressing over and over how very different they were one from the other. In temperament, character, psychology, human relations—it is enough for us to be told how one behaved in a given situation to deduce what the other's behavior would be. When one whispered yes, it seemed probable that the other would shout no; we were given numerous examples of this pattern. But we know little—very little—about their personal lives. Were they happy, healthy, strong, small, tall? What did they do besides the Sanhe-drin? All we know is what they did and said in public. And that they never did or said the same thing.

Of the two, Hillel seems more outgoing. There are many legends about him in the Talmud, but even those give little infor-mation. We are not even told the name of Hillel's father. But we do know he had a brother—Shebna—and that he was a successful businessman, and that one day he offered Hillel a sound business deal. They would share all they had; Shebna would share his wealth and Hillel his good deeds and his place in paradise. Hillel—no expert in deals, especially business deals—said no. And remained poor.

Born in Babylon one century or so before the destruction of the Temple, he came to Jerusalem to study. We know that he did not stay there. He went back to Babylon before returning to Jerusalem, this time for good. For forty years he held the office of president of the Sanhedrin or the Academy. When he died he had—like Moses—reached the age of one hundred and twenty.

One source claims that he belonged to the tribe of Benjamin on his father's side and to the tribe of Yehuda on his mother's side, thereby making him a descendant of David.

He had come to Jerusalem hoping to study with the illustri-ous scholars Shmaya and Avtalyon. Both were descendants of converts, and if Hillel later demonstrated great affection for converts—whom he seemed to attract—it was perhaps due to Shmaya and Avtalyon, and the effect they had on him.

However, legend makes a point of telling us of the difficulties he had in becoming their disciple.

To enter the House of Study, which was even then guarded against trespassing, Hillel had to bribe the guard. Every day he gave him half of what he earned as a woodcutter.

But one day—it was a wintry Friday—he found no work. And so he had no money. The guard refused to let him in on credit. In his despair, Hillel climbed to the roof, lay down near the opening, and listened to the class below, which went on and on for hours. In the meantime it had begun to snow, but Hillel paid no attention. The snowfall grew heavier and heavier. Still, Hillel did not budge. Suddenly Shmaya turned to his colleague and re-marked, "Avtalyon, my brother, isn't it unusually dark today? The sky must be cloudy." They looked at the window in the ceiling and noticed what appeared to be a man's shape. Students were dispatched to bring the man down. Just in time—Hillel was almost frozen to death. Breaking the restfulness of the Shabbat, they washed him, warmed him, and seated him near the stove. Whereupon the teachers declared, Whoever is so possessed by a passion for learning, deserves that the holiness of Shabbat be violated to save him. Actually, the holiness of Shabbat may be violated to save anybody—but his case may well have set a precedent, so clearly was it formulated.

Anyway, in due course, the passionate disciple became a Master on his own. It was said of him that, just like Ezra the scribe, he came from Babylon so as to prevent the Torah from being forgotten.

He had eighty disciples: thirty deserved to feel the *Shekhina,* as Moses did; thirty deserved to have the sun stand still for them, as it had done for Joshua; and only twenty were average. The best scholar was Yonathan ben Ouziel (a convert's scion?) and the poorest was Yohanan ben Zakkai—the founder of Yavneh's academy.

The caliber of the students lets us measure the greatness of the Master. Legend goes out of its way to stress Hillel's qualities. He was wise, learned, and devoted; he mastered the sciences and understood all languages—those of the hills and those of the trees, those of birds and those of people, even those of demons. His erudition covered all spheres of human knowledge. What else are we told? That he was married and that his wife shared his love for the poor. He must have had children—for we know that the presidency of the Patriarchate remained in his family for over four hundred years.

He assumed the presidency long after the death of Shmaya and Avtalyon, who were succeeded by the sons of Batyra. As mentioned earlier, Hillel returned to Babylon. Why? We don't know. His family was with him in Jerusalem; what could have attracted him to Babylon? A position? A pulpit? Did he wish to make a career for himself far away? Unlikely. Hillel was beyond this kind of ambition.

A possible answer can perhaps be found in the general situation of the country. Could he have left to avoid what was happening within the Jewish kingdom? Could he have found it easier to love it from afar?

To better understand his perspective, we ought to try to imagine, however briefly, the state of the kingdom of Judea in his time.

•

Herod is in power, and his nickname—"the wicked one"— serves as commentary on his reign. A descendant of Edomites, Herod has the collaborator's mentality. He has no love for his people, whom he exploits and oppresses to please the Roman occupant. Protected by the emperor, given great powers, he uses them against his own subjects, who hate him. He, in turn, does his utmost to make them hate one another. To that end, he revives ancestral quarrels and dissensions between Sadducees and Pharisees, scholars and plebians, rich and poor; the more he divides, the firmer his rule.

Taxes are heavy, the economic situation borders on disaster. Yet the king builds himself palaces whose vestiges, discovered only recently, testify to amazing luxury. He erects a temple for idol worshipers in Shamron. He builds theaters, circuses, and arenas for savage and cruel games. Judean cities are renamed with Roman names. Caesarea becomes a pagan Roman city. He wants to imitate Rome, so he adopts the philosophy of Rome. His court reflects the atmosphere of the emperor's court; it is run by intrigue, deceit, and corruption. As a Jew, Herod should have known that there is only one king—God—and that His ways must be followed. But he was not Jewish, meaning, there was little of the Jew left in him. What *he* most wanted was to impress Rome—so he managed to serve, with great devotion, the interests of the emperor Antonius, Octavianus, and Augustus—all of whom used him. He also managed to impress Cleopatra—she even fell in love with him—but he did not respond. As a result, she began to hate Jews, specifically the Jews in her own city, Alexandria.

The Bible commands us to choose as king one of our own— "It is among your brothers that you should choose a king to reign over you"—which also means, Though he become king, he should remain your brother. Not only was Herod not a brother to his people—he was their enemy. He knew it and they knew it. At one point he grew so suspicious that he ordered that an oath of allegiance be sworn by every Judean citizen—and only six thousand students of Shammai refused. Often he would roam the streets and marketplaces in disguise in order to spy on the people. There are charitable historians who call him an evil genius; others say he was simply insane. Why else place a golden Roman eagle over the entrance to the Temple in Jerusalem? Why else embark on a policy of bloodshed? By the end of his reign, he was killing indiscriminately, suspecting an enemy in everyone, a conspiracy everywhere.

He burned his enemies alive. He ordered the massacre of Aristobulus II, Alexander, Antigonus, Aristobulus III, Hyrcanos II—
and even of his own sons and his beloved wife, Mariamne. He
killed all those who were near the throne, which is why Emperor
Augustus commented, "I would rather be Herod's dog than his
son."

Thus, it is quite possible that Hillel, so sensitive to injustice
and so compassionate to its victims, found it unbearable to witness
day after day the bitterness and anger that weighed on his people;
he chose to get as far away as possible. Better to live in exile in
Babylon than in anguish in Jerusalem.

We don't know how long he stayed away, or what he did,
whom he met, whom he taught, during this entire period. All we
know is that suddenly he reappeared in Jerusalem, where the situation had deteriorated to the point that the Sanhedrin leaders—
the sons of Batyra—had forgotten as simple a law as the one
concerning Passover: Does the sacrifice of Passover have priority
over Shabbat or not? Just imagine—the Temple is still standing,
its priests are performing their duties, the Levites are singing, and
people are coming on pilgrimage three times a year—and nobody
knows the law! What happened to the rabbis, the scholars, the
lawmakers? The sons of Batyra had to inquire publicly. Is there
anyone who knows the law? And they were told, yes, there is a
man here from Babylon and his name is Hillel, a former disciple of
Shmaya and Avtalyon; he knows. Bring him to us, the leaders
exclaimed. And so, Hillel was brought before the two leaders who
asked, "Do you know the law?" "Yes," he said, "I do." Actually, he
should have stopped there, but he did not. Instead he burst out in
anger—he who was never angry. He accused them of intellectual
laxity—he who never accused anybody. He was angry at them
because he knew more than they. Because he had to tell them how
ignorant they were. What, you don't know the law related to
Pesach when it falls on a Saturday? There are two hundred categories of holiday offerings that take precedence over Shabbat—
why should this one be different?

For his anger, he was punished on the spot: he suddenly
forgot all that he knew. For when he was asked another question,
he said, "I did know the answer but I have forgotten it . . . but
don't worry, the people will give us the answer, trust them. Let us
watch and see what they will do instinctively—and that will be the

answer." And he offered this comment: "Let the children of Israel show the way; even though they are not prophets, they are blessed with prophetic intuition." So much faith in his people had to result in an act of grace: his knowledge was restored to him. And from then on he was careful. Whenever he answered further questions, he attributed the decisions not to his own erudition but to that of his teachers. This is what I heard from Shmaya and Avtalyon, he would say. So much wisdom, so much modesty, and common sense had an immediate effect: the sons of Batyra handed the presidency over to him.

Here again, there are puzzling elements. For instance, the appointment needed the king's approval. How is one to explain that it was granted? And how is one to explain that Herod, cruel Herod, who had massacred all the sages of the Sanhedrin but two, Shmaya and Avtalyon—who had appointed a foreigner to the position of High Priest—confirmed Hillel's nomination? Because he was an unknown, and Herod chose this way to humiliate all the others who were known? Or was it because Hillel's reputation as a pacifist had already been publicly recognized? The circumstances of the nomination and the confirmation remain obscure—as does the fate of Hillel's first "number two" man.

Remember: the leadership of the Sanhedrin consisted of the president, the Av-bet-din (the chairman of the tribunal), and the Chacham—the sage. When Hillel became president, the Av-bet-din was an Essene named Menachem. Some sources indicate that this Menachem was favored by the king because the Essenes never gave him any trouble: they lived in their communes, away from the cities, away from politics, totally absorbed by their mystical way of life. When Menachem decided to return to his commune—the event is described in a brief cryptic phrase: *Yatza Menachem Nichnas Shammai*—Menachem left the Sanhedrin, and Shammai replaced him. Why did Herod let Menachem go? And why did he confirm the nomination of Shammai?

At this point, it seems only fair to turn our attention to Hillel's friend and rival, Shammai, about whom we know even less than we do about Hillel.

This withdrawn, enigmatic figure seems to live exclusively in relationship to Hillel: he is evoked only in opposition to him. *Shammai kapdan haya*—this brief sentence is supposed to cover his person and personality: he was severe. But—who was he? Where did he come from? Who were his parents? What about his family? There is a hint that he may have been a mason, because he used a mason's ruler to chase away bores. But who were his teachers? How did he manage to ascend the ladder of leadership? Where did he live? When did he die, and where? And in what circumstances?

We are told only that he was terribly strict, legalistic, and intransigent. Such an attitude is called *"Yikov hadin et hahar*—Let the law pierce the mountain": nothing must be allowed to stand in its way. Not sentiments, not pity.

When his daughter-in-law gave birth to a son on Succoth he made a hole in the roof and covered it with branches so that the son could observe the commandment of sitting and eating in the succah.

When his own son was still very young, he tried to make him fast on Yom Kippur. And when his colleagues protested, he agreed to feed him—but only with one hand.

All legends tend to depict him as a self-centered man, moody, unpleasant, almost antisocial. Only rarely is he seen with people, including even his disciples and his friend and opponent, Hillel. Whoever approaches him is sent away. He discourages all personal contact. He is particularly harsh with would-be converts: he shouts at them, scolds them, displaying shocking ill manners. . . .

And yet, he was the one who offered this advice: "Be sure always to receive any man with kindliness and good humor." What are we to make of this contradiction? Was the man different from his legend? Was he a victim of injustice? Did the Talmud diminish him so as to make his rival appear more human?

Like most children, I favored Hillel: so tolerant, so good, so friendly—I was sure that he must have looked like my grandfather. He never got angry, never made you feel ashamed for not having studied well enough or prayed long enough. Hillel never made you feel inferior or guilty—unlike Shammai, who preferred difficulties, obstacles, confrontations. Nothing could move Shammai or make him give in—neither the tears of a schoolboy nor the anguish of a student who, woe to him, was too weak to resist temptation. To think of Shammai was enough to experience terror. I was convinced that he had loved nobody and that nobody had loved him. I imagined him as a kind of *Misnaged,* an opponent of Hasidism, forever buried in books, isolated from the outside world, angry at the world for coming between him and the Torah.

And on the other side, there was Hillel—the friend of the

poor, the oppressed, and the unhappy, the big brother to their children. Hillel: I pictured him smiling, outgoing, with the right word for everyone, to make him feel welcome and wanted—even if he were not a strict adherent to the law.

Today I know that these images were false. Hillel was not always the more moderate of the two. Of the three hundred and sixteen disputations opposing the two schools, fifty-five stress the more indulgent position of the House of Shammai. Nor can one claim that the one favored the poor more than the other. Or that one was more conservative than the other. True, certain scholars do make such distinctions. Did Shammai represent the wealthy and Hillel the poor? Some claim the opposite. Though Shammai was a patrician and Hillel a plebeian, both were Pharisees. One theory maintains that the two schools differed only in their interpretation of the Torah: Shammai's view of it was accurate and literal, Hillel's was literary and imaginative. But the law is almost always according to Hillel—which does bring us to feel some sympathy for . . . Shammai.

As we listen to what Hillel says and does, we are suddenly disturbed. Imagine living in the shadow of a great man who is never angry, who is never annoyed, who *always* knows what to say and when and to whom—who is such a paragon that in his presence you cease to feel comfortable.

For everything he does is perfect—in line with his ideas. He does what he preaches, says what he believes. He is in perfect control of his mind and body: "My feet lead me wherever I want to go," said he. Doubts had no effect on him. Once he heard someone shouting with pain, and though at the time he was at the other side of town, far from his home, he said, "I am sure the shout did not originate in my home." He *knew*. Once he saw a head floating in the river; he immediately *knew* that it belonged to someone who had killed someone else.

His aphorisms are simple, almost simplistic: Be sociable, he says, do not separate yourself from the community. Or: If I am not concerned for myself—who shall be for me? And if not now—then when? Or: Do not go naked among people who are dressed, do not stand among people who are seated, do not laugh among people who are crying.

Does anyone really find greatness, imagination, or a challenge in these sayings? Why should I care about what other people may think of me? Why should I want to go along with the majority and do what everybody else does? In this respect I prefer Shammai, who is attracted by nonconformity and more often than not ends up in a minority.

Furthermore, even the anecdotes about Hillel's patience finally put a strain on mine.

Shanu rabotenu, our teachers have taught us: This is the story of two men who made a bet. Whoever would manage to provoke Hillel would get four hundred coins. It was Friday. Hillel was washing his hair for Shabbat, when he heard someone in the street shouting, "Which one of you is Hillel?" Hillel dressed quickly and came out into the street: "Are you looking for me, my son?" "Yes," said the man, "I have a very important question to ask you." "What is your question?" "Why are the heads of Babylonians round?" "Ah," said Hillel, "your question is indeed very important." And he gave him an answer. The man went away and came back an hour later, shouting, "Hillel, where is Hillel?" "Are you looking for me?" said Hillel, emerging again from his home. "Yes, I am, for I have a most urgent question to ask you." "Yes? What is it?" "Why are the eyes of Tadmorites sickly and soft?" "Oh, yes," said Hillel, "your question *is* urgent." And he gave him an answer. An hour later, the same man reappeared. "Hillel, Hillel, where is Hillel?" "Here I am, my son. What is it?" "I have a burning question to ask you." "What is it, my son?" "Africans have large feet. Tell me why." "Oh, yes, oh, yes," said Hillel, "it *is* a burning question." And he answered him. Finally the man remarked, " I have many more questions. But I am afraid to ask." "Afraid? Why?" "I am afraid to make you angry." "Don't be afraid," said Hillel. "You may ask all your questions." Whereupon the man shouted, "Are you Hillel, the president of the people of Israel?" "Yes." "Then I pray that there be no more like you in Israel." "Why are *you* angry?" Hillel asked. "Why? I'll tell you why. Because of you, I have just lost four hundred coins." "Well, you should be more careful, my son," said Hillel, "for you may lose twice as much. You see, Hillel will never be provoked."

Needless to say that with Shammai the poor man would have done better. Shammai would have dismissed him after the very first question!

A story: A stranger came to Shammai and asked him, "How many laws do you have?" "Two," said Shammai, "the written one and the oral one." "I accept the written one but not the other.

Please convert me to Judaism, and I shall observe the other law." Furious at the superficiality of the request, Shammai threw him out. So the man went to Hillel, who agreed to convert him, and after a while persuaded him that both laws are part of our tradition.

Another story: A stranger came to Shammai and without introduction told him that he would very much like to become . . . a High Priest. Why? He was frank about it. He had heard that the High Priest is covered with honors—and he, though a heathen, happened to love honors. You can imagine what Shammai's answer was. He threw him out. Hillel did not. You want to become Jewish so as to be a High Priest? All right. And so the heathen became Jewish and began to study the Torah, where he came upon the warning that any stranger who comes close to the sanctuary will be punished by death. "What?" exclaimed the student. "To whom does this apply?" "To any person who is not a descendant of Aaron, the first High Priest," said Hillel. "King David himself would have been punished, had he come close to the sanctuary. Yes, even he."

A third story: A stranger came to Shammai and asked to be taught the entire Torah very quickly—while he was standing on one foot. Shammai chased him away. Naturally, he went to Hillel, who received him cordially and said, "If that is what you wish, so be it. This is the substance of the law: 'Do not do unto others what you do not want them to do unto you.' All the rest is commentary—now go and study."

One day, the three converts happened to meet. And all three agreed that Shammai's rigor had almost torn them away from truth, while Hillel's tolerance had brought them closer to it. Clearly, the moral of these stories is, it is more constructive to be as tolerant as Hillel than to be as demanding as Shammai.

Here again, my sympathy goes to Shammai. For he refuses to play games. He dislikes conditional converts and proclaims it aloud. He does not believe that Judaism is something you can acquire on credit. True, Hillel is the better educator, and his views seem more ecumenical, but Shammai's anger is surely more genuine, more honest. What he says is logical and valid: one ought not divide Judaism into segments. Whoever does not accept Jewish history in its entirety is not Jewish; whoever wishes to identify only with one period, one tradition, one burden, or one privilege cannot be Jewish. To accept Judaism means to accept oneself within the totality of Judaism: each of us is but the conclusion of a story whose beginnings are in God's memory. And whoever is unwilling to accept all of it stays outside.

Perhaps it is the influence on me of Menachem-Mendl, the solitary visionary of Kotzk, but I am fascinated by Shammai: I respect his extremism, his obsession with truth, no matter what the consequences. Nothing could move him to compromise, to make deals. Of course, in the cases of the three unknown heathens, he could speak his mind with impunity; but he also proved his courage and his adherence to truth in a more dramatic setting.

The story I am about to tell you happened many years earlier—before he was the head of a school. He was not a recognized leader as yet; he was only a simple member of the Sanhedrin. One day the court was seized with an extraordinary case: Herod, ruler of Galilee, was accused of having murdered a certain freedom fighter named Khizkiyahu. Arrogant and full of defiance, he appeared before the learned members, accompanied by an armed escort, daring the Sanhedrin to pass sentence on him. Terrorized, all the judges kept quiet. Only Shammai (or was it Shmayahu? Opinions vary) rose to his feet and said, "My fellow members of the Sanhedrin, we all know that everyone who comes here to stand trial comes humbly, filled with fear and remorse and seeking mercy—not he! I warn you, if you release him, one day he may kill you—all of you." His was one of the most powerful addresses ever heard in the Sanhedrin—but it had no effect. Herod went free. And Shammai's prophecy was fulfilled: All the members, except two, Shammai and one other, were massacred. . . . Shammai's courage remains as an example.

What would Hillel have said in similar circumstances? All we know is that Hillel seems to be the more realistic, the more pragmatic. And yet—it is he, always Hillel, who has the last word. And when he doesn't, heaven intervenes and hands it to him nevertheless. Why?

One possible answer was suggested in a debate between the two schools. It concerns the case of a bride who—*s'zol zich nisht trefen,* it shouldn't happen to anyone—is neither charming nor pretty. Yet, according to the law, one is duty-bound to make her happy. We are even told how to go about it. One must sing and dance before the bride—any bride—and compliment her on her grace and beauty. That is Hillel's view. As for Shammai, he objects: What? And suppose she is blind and has a limp, how can one lie that much? He is right. His objection is valid. And yet, in this case, which serves as an example, it is Hillel we are told to follow.

Shammai is on the side of truth but Hillel is on the side of a poor girl who is neither pretty nor gracious, and knows it—who, moreover, is unhappy thinking that everybody else knows it.

Shammai defends the absolute, and we are grateful to him for it; but Hillel defends human beings, and we are even more grateful to him. Both may be right, provided the two options remain open; even though Hillel's decision prevails, both opinions must be transmitted. In the world to come, says the Talmud, Shammai's decisions will prevail.

For here is an essential truth of Jewish thought: We need both, we admire Shammai and we love Hillel. I would like to follow Shammai, as far as *I* am concerned, and to emulate Hillel where others are involved—ideally, to be intransigent with myself and understanding with others.

But then, Shammai and Hillel and their disciples tended to do just that. Both showed that in practice each was capable of adopting his opponent's view.

Example: Imagine a slave who belongs to two masters; imagine that he has been freed by only one—what is his status? The school of Hillel says, Let him divide himself between himself and the remaining master; let him work one day for the master and one day for himself. But the school of Shammai objects, and its reasoning is both keen and beautiful: such a decision would help the master but not the slave, who would not be free to marry a slave girl—for he is half-free; nor could he have a free woman—for he is half slave. . . . No: one must force the other owner to free him as well. And in this case, the disciples of Hillel espoused the opinion of Shammai.

Incidentally, the Talmud wants us to know that in spite of their totally conflicting positions, the disciples of the two schools maintained cordial and friendly relations; they ate at one another's tables and even intermarried. Only later, much later, when both schools had too many pupils, and when both had forgotten the teachings of their founders, did the dissensions become so critical and dangerous that one had the impression of a people divided—and I quote—"following two systems, two traditions, two laws."

Most of the disputations occurred between the disciples and

not the Masters. Throughout their entire lives, Shammai and Hillel had only three personal confrontations.

One—the most dramatic—took place in the attic of Hananya ben Hizkiyahu ben Garon, as part of a stormy and memorable meeting during which—and I quote again—"They drove a sword into the ground proclaiming, Whoever wishes to enter, may enter; but no one will leave before the debates are closed." We imagine these debates as having been tense, passionate, fierce sessions, both sides invoking proofs and arguments and precedents, dissecting every sentence, analyzing every word. On that day both sides were more stubborn than ever. And understandably so; for the issues at stake were grave. We know what they were and we know the outcome.

Eighteen laws were adopted there and then—all of them in favor of Shammai. And we are told that on that day Hillel, though he was officially the president, sat bowed down before Shammai—and that that particular day was as harsh and as cruel for the Jewish people as the one centuries earlier when the Golden Calf had been fashioned.

What are those eighteen laws? In the Jerusalem Talmud, we have it in the words of Rabbi Shimon ben Yohai: "On that day they decided on attitudes to adopt toward heathens' bread and cheese and wine, their language and gifts and children"—and so on. Outwardly they dealt with wine and bread and secular culture and intermarriage, but, in fact, they were defining the ties which Jews were or were not allowed to maintain with the pagans. By the way, a very curious sentence closes the entire chapter. It says that all those measures and laws were meant to prevent Jewish children from falling victim to homosexual pagans.

These eighteen laws, then, were to determine Jewish-pagan—or Jewish-Roman—relations. Hence the passionate debates. Shammai and his disciples sided with the militants, while Hillel and his followers, as true pacifists, preached patience and hope. Both sides had to take a stand publicly. The people were already preparing for the first uprisings. The scholars had to decide: Should open insurrection be encouraged or delayed? Shammai was for rebellion and Hillel opposed it, feeling that it was better to wait and pray for miracles. When Shammai won the argument, the people were on his side. We know the result: the loss of Jerusalem, the destruction of the Temple, the massacre of children, the deportation of Judean youths to Rome, the beginning of a long,

long exile. Who was right? Who are we to judge? We can but tell the tale. We can tell it, thanks to Hillel's disciple Yohanan ben Zakkai, who, having escaped from a besieged Jerusalem, founded academies, laid the foundations for the Talmud, and thus assured our people's survival.

Such were the issues debated then and there. And that is why the meeting took place in the attic of Hanaya ben Hizkiyahu—the son of the rebel killed by Herod years earlier.

Hananya is specially praised and loved in the Talmud—for one thing, because he saved the Book of Ezekiel from being excluded from the canon: certain passages were judged too daring, too open to misunderstandings. So Hanaya isolated himself in his attic for months and months and reconciled all the contradictions. And the book is now a part of the canon.

Hananya is also loved because he edited the Treatise of Taanit—of fasting—which is a kind of Jewish martyrology. Perhaps because of his father's death, he was fascinated by Jewish suffering. Rabbi Shimon ben Gamliel comments: We too are fascinated by the suffering of Israel, but we are unable to write down everything; even if we wanted to, we could not do it, there isn't enough ink.

Hanaya seems to have sided with Shammai. In fact, the majority was for Shammai—for armed resistance. The vote opened the way to rebellions ending in defeat. Shammai was right to want open insurrection and Hillel was right in fearing it.

In conclusion, let us return now to the two stories mentioned earlier. For three years, disciples of Hillel and Shammai were arguing over points of law and could not reach a consensus until a celestial voice was heard. Both attitudes were right—but at different times. Shammai was right during the Roman occupation—and Hillel was right afterward. God alone is always right. God alone knows history in its totality; only fragments are shown to man. Thus man's truth must necessarily remain limited. Hillel's decisions prevailed because exile is long and painful—what is needed then is a Hillel who soothes rather than a Shammai who chastises.

And now we understand why, many years later, following the defeat of Judea and the burning of the Temple, both schools asked themselves the obvious question: If redemption is conditioned by exile, if absolute truth is unattainable, why be born? Why live? Why suffer? Why witness suffering and be powerless to mitigate it? Here again, the Hillel school said, Life is worth living in spite of everything; one must wait, pray, hope, have faith. Shammai's disciples, more impulsive and demanding, said, No, life is not worth living; life is so difficult, so complex, so hopeless, that man would have been better off never having been born. And here again, Shammai's school had the upper hand. We understand why. Times were cruel, so cruel they justified pessimism. Yet both sides—the pessimists and the optimists—came to the same conclusion: Since man *was* born, since he does exist—let him question his actions, his ways.

But—whose actions, whose ways? God's? Man's? There are two possibilities, two interpretations: One, *His* ways—meaning God's. Since man is prisoner of his condition, let him turn to God, let him turn his question to God. Or, his *own* actions. Let him question his own ways, that is to say, Let him confer, be it retroactively, a meaning on his life, which may seem meaningless. For it is not man's privilege to choose either the time or the place of his birth, but it is his privilege to give his life a direction—and a justification.

Both schools subscribed to this conclusion. And each of us must do likewise. This applies particularly to my generation. Having seen man without his mask, having penetrated the darkest zones of his being, we only know that some questions are doomed to remain unanswered. None of my contemporaries knows why he is alive—or rather, why he has survived, why he and not someone else. For us every moment is a moment of grace and wonder—we and we alone can give it meaning.

Rabbi Hanina ben Dossa

ONCE UPON A TIME, in the land of our ancestors, there lived a great man who was known more for his miracles than his erudition—a man of fervor and passion who, throughout his life, was intensely involved with his people, its heritage, and its aspirations—a man of inner strength and beauty.

And yet . . . This man somehow surrounded himself with silence.

Let us read: One day Rabbi Hanina, son of Dossa, decided that, like all other Jewish pilgrims from Judea, he must not come to the Temple of Jerusalem empty-handed. The poorest of the poor had something to offer—if not a sheep, then a handful of flour. But Rabbi Hanina, son of Dossa, could not even bring that kind of offering. You see, he was poorer than the poorest of the poor. He possessed nothing, literally nothing, except his burning desire to give God something—anything.

In despair, he took a large stone and began to chisel it, saying to himself, Since I cannot do anything for the Master of the Universe, I shall try to help those who serve Him; I shall bring this stone to Jerusalem so that the weary pilgrims can sit on it and rest.

The trouble was that Rabbi Hanina was weak and the stone was heavy. He was unable to lift it, let alone carry it. As he pondered his problem, he suddenly noticed five men who were passing by. He asked them to help. They agreed—for the right price: a hundred *selaim*. A hundred? Rabbi Hanina didn't even have one. Too bad. The five men shrugged their shoulders and went on their way. But no sooner had they left than five other men appeared out of nowhere. Would *they* help him carry the heavy stone to Jerusalem? Certainly they would, for the right price. Rabbi Hanina panicked. "But I have no money!" All right, they said. We'll let you have our services—free. But under one condition: you must give us a hand. He did—and suddenly he found himself transported, with the stone, into the Temple courtyard in Jerusalem. His helpers? They had vanished. He could not even thank them; the five angels had returned to heaven.

From this tale we learn a number of things about this peculiar sage, who seems to have been both vulnerable and triumphant in the extreme.

First, we learn that he was desperately poor. Second, that he was totally impractical. Why would anyone choose to work on a stone so heavy that five people were needed to help carry it? Couldn't he have found a smaller one? We also learn that he had the power to perform miracles. It's not easy to enlist angels as one's private porters. And last, that when he did perform his miracles, he did so almost unwittingly, unconsciously. He had merely asked for help in carrying the stone—not for angels to come to his rescue.

The lesson to be drawn from this episode? Angels do not like to do all the work by themselves; they need your cooperation. You want miracles? With pleasure—but you must also take part in them. Do not rely on heaven alone.

This is what we learn from our hero—or anti-hero. His name has been linked to fables more often than to laws, to prayers and miracles more often than to ideas.

He could be mistaken for a Hasidic rabbi. As a matter of fact, one wonders why Hasidism has not claimed him as it has Rabbi Akiba, Rabbi Shimon bar Yohai, and Rabbi Meir Baal-hanes.

We shall try to see why not. He is most certainly a Talmudic Master, and as such, does he have a role of his own—a method attributed to him alone? Who is he, and what is the substance, the texture of his message? And in what way is his teaching relevant to our generation?

A fervent disciple, and perhaps also companion, of Rabbi Yohanan ben Zakkai, he must have been about his age, perhaps a little older. Like him, he lived both in Jerusalem and in the Galilee. He was married to a woman who was as famous for her piety as he was for his. People came to consult her about their problems, and she, too, accomplished miracles. She should be remembered in her own right, but, as in so many other instances, she is not given proper credit.

This is equally true of their children. We know that they had a son and a daughter but we know nothing about them—there are no sayings attributed to them, few anecdotes are attributed to them.

All the stories and legends center on Rabbi Hanina—yet they do not shed much light on his personality. The biographical information is astonishingly sketchy. He is mentioned only three times in the Mishna. Who were his parents? Where did he live, study, work? The legend we opened with leads us to believe that he was a stonecutter by trade, but that is the only possible clue we are given. We don't even know when he died—or where, or how, which is unusual for a historical figure. He quite simply vanished, not *from* the Talmud but *inside* it.

Why is he shown so seldom in the role of husband, father, and teacher? What kind of teacher was he anyway? He had no school of his own. What academic circles did he belong to? As a friend of Rabbi Yohanan ben Zakkai, he must have been a pacifist, but unlike him, he was never involved in political activities. We can easily follow Rabbi Yohanan ben Zakkai as he tries to influence events; but we can follow Rabbi Hanina ben Dossa only with great difficulty. Obsessed with the supernatural, he seems to have followed an invisible path. Only his voice reaches us. We listen to him but do not see him. We listen to his lovely, implausible stories, which are filled with wonder and naive beauty.

Like the story of his goats. People could not understand: Where did such a poor fellow get all those goats? And they were right to ask—but . . . let us read:

One day a stranger stopped in front of Rabbi Hanina's house and left him his chickens. Then, without saying a word, he disappeared. "Take good care of the chickens," Rabbi Hanina told his wife. "But remember: Do not eat the eggs; they are his, not ours." The result? The chickens laid eggs that became chickens which laid more eggs. Soon the entire house was full of chickens. They were everywhere—under the table and on top of the table, on the benches, on the bed. . . . So Rabbi Hanina's wife, in her wisdom, decided to sell the chickens, and with the money she bought a few goats. Her reasoning: goats are less noisy, and they do not multiply so fast. Years later, a stranger appeared outside Rabbi Hanina's house and asked, "Where are my chickens? I left them here." Without further ado, Rabbi Hanina gave him the goats.

Clearly, the wife was the businessman in the family. It was her idea to sell the chickens and buy the goats. Still, there is something important missing in this charming and amusing fable: a description of the expression on the stranger's face as he was presented with the goats.

A variation on the same theme:

When Rabbi Pinhas, son of Yair, son-in-law of the celebrated Rabbi Shimon bar Yohai, lived somewhere in the south of Palestine, two wandering beggars entrusted him with their sole possession, a small amount of wheat. They promised to return but did not. So—what could Rabbi Pinas do but take care of their savings? He planted the wheat and let it grow in his field, then harvested it and stored it in his granary. Year after year he followed this practice—until seven years later, when the beggars reappeared, asking for their wheat back. Of course, said Rabbi Pinhas, but first you must go and find some camels and donkeys, for you will need them to carry away what has become yours.

Never mind the differing details—one stranger instead of two beggars, chickens instead of wheat. The structure of the fable remains the same, as does its significance: Neither Rabbi Hanina nor Rabbi Pinhas wished to profit from what was not theirs.

But this is not the only story that has been attributed to both sages; there are others as well. In spite of the one hundred to one hundred fifty years that separated them, they seem to share many legends, many strange episodes. Even their donkeys played similar roles in similar situations—as we shall later see.

May we question the Talmud as to the reason for these similarities?

Perhaps because it's a matter of *Aggada,* not *Halakha,* that the Talmud feels free to take poetic license. In the realm of *Halakha*—which deals with the law and the law alone—the importance of faithfulness to tradition, therefore to fact, is forever being stressed: the author is usually given proper credit. *Haomer davar beshem omro,* to repeat a saying in its author's name, is to hasten redemption. In matters of *Halakha,* it is vital for the student to know whether a particular interpretation or decision comes from the school of Rabbi Akiba or from that of Rabbi Ishmael. The person behind the teaching is as important as its philosophy. Legal decisions are therefore linked to specific Masters. There, confusion is dangerous.

In the world of *Aggada,* of legends, the approach seems more lenient, and so the same fable may be attributed to more than one sage. Characters may be interchangeable but the story remains the same.

Another story:

One day the wife of Rabbi Hanina, overwhelmed by sadness, turned to her husband and said, "You are known as a man whose prayers are heard in heaven; why then don't you do something—anything—to help us overcome our misery?" "What would you like me to do?" he asked. "Pray," she said, with understandable exasperation. "Pray for some money. How long can we go on living like this?" "Don't you see," said Rabbi Hanina, "if we are poor here, it's because we shall be rich up there, in heaven." He thought his answer was one of pure logic, but so was the question that followed: "Then why don't you ask for an advance?" Rabbi Hanina had no choice but to obey. He prayed, and his wife's wish was fulfilled: a hand came down from heaven bearing a table leg made of solid gold, which even in those non-inflationary times was worth millions.

But that night the sage saw in a dream the celestial palace where the Just Men of all times dwell in the presence of the Eternal One and His eternal glory. He saw them all sitting at their own golden tables—their own golden *three-legged* tables. Suddenly he noticed himself sitting among them; but he seemed sad—more melancholy than the rest. He wondered why, until he understood: his table had only *two legs*.

At dawn he told his wife his dream. He told her everything: about his mutilated table, his sadness, and she agreed with him right away: the heavenly advance had to be returned. Rabbi Hanina recited another prayer, and once more a hand came down from heaven, this time taking back the golden table leg.

Whereupon some sages commented that the second miracle is more astonishing than the first, for the future is easier to change than the past. It is impossible to wipe out the memory of an event; impossible to start all over again as if it never happened. The Almighty gives but does not take back, says the Talmud. Only life is given and taken back. What happened to Rabbi Hanina is an exception to the rule.

Is Rabbi Hanina altogether an exception? Probably. Most of his contemporaries say so. They all stress the power of his prayer. The story we just read is but one illustration of his influence in heaven: he can make things appear and also disappear.

But there is one disturbing aspect to the story. Both Rabbi Hanina and his wife believed that they were so righteous and pious that they would be rewarded in the other world, the world of truth. But how could they be so sure? How could they be so sure of their worthiness? Were they not exposing themselves to the grave sin of vanity?

They were not. Both of them were innocent and pure enough to be immune to vanity. If they believed in some future reward, it was only because their present was too burdened with suffering. And so they clung to the belief that suffering, too, may be an advantage: the more pain you endure now, the less you will endure in heaven; and they had endured quite a lot.

But again I stress that this story is not about riches or poverty; it is about Rabbi Hanina's prayers.

Yes, he prayed well. That was his principal virtue; his distinction. Some Masters were known for their wisdom or their social position, others were praised for their erudition or their piety; Rabbi Hanina was praised for his prayers.

And they disturb me. They reflect him, but not his times. The dramatic events that shook his generation are totally absent from his supplications. From his prayers alone, one would never have guessed that the land of Israel was in the throes of violence provoked by Rome.

We read Rabbi Hanina's stories and fail to find in them the slightest concern for the victims of the Roman invaders. Yet we know from other Talmudic sources that the situation in Judea was disastrous, full of intrigues, plots, and counterplots. The royal family was influenced by the alien imperial family. The sages taught and studied, but the politicians listened to Rome, where murder was an accepted means of gaining power: Claudius was killed by his wife, who was killed by her son, Nero, who ordered Seneca to commit suicide, and ended up committing suicide, too. Still, Rome was conquering the world; its triumphs seemed irrevocable. Soon Rome would bring Jerusalem to her knees. And what was Rabbi Hanina doing? He said prayers—which was good; but he prayed for too little—which is disturbing. Since he could demand anything, and get it, why did he content himself with individual happiness? Why didn't he use his powers on behalf of his entire people? Why didn't he fast, as Rabbi Zadok did?

He would pray with such fervor and concentration that the outside world ceased to exist—that he himself ceased to exist. When he said what was in his heart when he spoke to God, he would attain total dissolution of being, absolute elevation of the soul.

Legend has it that a serpent wrapped itself around his leg while he was saying his prayers; but he did not feel it.

Another time he was bitten by a scorpion. How did it happen? There was a scorpion notorious for biting passersby. "Show me his hiding place," said Rabbi Hanina. They showed him a hole in the street, and he put his foot in it. Provoked, the scorpion bit him and . . . died. Then Rabbi Hanina took the dead scorpion and brought it to the House of Study, saying, "You see? It is not the scorpion that kills, it is the sin." Thereupon all the students exclaimed, "Woe unto the man who is bitten by the scorpion, and woe unto the scorpion who has bitten Rabbi Hanina."

Rashi comments on this episode in the name of the Yerushalmi: When a scorpion bites a human being, both must run to find water; whoever reaches the water first remains alive. This scorpion had already begun to crawl while Rabbi Hanina remained motionless: but a miracle occurred and a well sprang up under the rabbi's foot.

His supernatural powers gained him a reputation which spread throughout the provinces and affected all segments of society. People who were in seemingly hopeless situations came to Rabbi Hanina ben Dossa. They expected him to do the impossible; and often he did. Because, to him, nothing was impossible; prayers made all things attainable. If only people knew how to pray. . . . But most had never learned; others had forgotten. So they flocked to him.

The president of Yavneh himself, Rabbi Gamliel, needed his intercession. He sent two emissaries to Rabbi Hanina ben Dossa with an urgent plea to pray for his sick son. Rabbi Hanina did, and the president's son recovered.

Rabbi Yohanan ben Zakkai, too, addressed himself to his pious friend when *his* son fell gravely ill. Rabbi Hanina, his head buried in his lap, which was the customary position for prayer, implored God to cure the son of his revered teacher and friend; and—again—his intercession proved successful. "If I had tried to pray," said Rabbi Yohanan ben Zakkai, "I would have failed." His wife was offended. "What?" she exclaimed. "Could it be that he is worthier than you?" Rabbi Yohanan reassured her. "Between the two of us there is a difference of function, not of merit. Rabbi Hanina is, so to speak, God's servant, whereas I am his minister. A minister needs appointments, a servant comes and goes at any hour."

Strange: Rabbi Hanina always *knew* when he succeeded and when he failed—not in advance but during or after the prayer.

Often, after concluding his plea, he would turn to a parent and say, "Go home, your child is no longer in danger." The petitioner would say, "How do you know? Are you a prophet?" And he would answer, "I am neither prophet nor son of prophet. It is much simpler. When I feel that my prayer runs smoothly I know it is being heard; when it does not, I know there are obstacles."

But in fairness, he rarely met with failure. His pleas meant something in heaven; his wishes were fulfilled—even when they seemed odd or contradictory. Was he sometimes capricious? God didn't mind.

One day Rabbi Hanina took a walk with a basketful of salt on his head. Suddenly it began to rain. "Master of the Universe," he exclaimed. "Look: the whole universe is happy now—for it needs rain. Only your son Hanina is unhappy." So the rain stopped instantly. When he got home, he changed his mind—and his plea. "Master of the Universe," he said. "Look: your son Hanina is happy but the whole world is sad." Naturally, it began to rain again.

Was he hero or anti-hero? Normally—logically—Rabbi Hanina would be counted among the heroes in the Talmud. Isn't he admired by his peers and loved by their pupils? Isn't his voice heard in heaven and below? Doesn't he possess extraordinary gifts, divine powers? Isn't he wiser than the sages, more powerful than the wealthy? Isn't he famous, highly influential, and celebrated?

Perhaps a short analysis of the concept of the hero would be in order.

Usually the hero is someone who has achieved distinction, meaning someone whom others describe as hero—someone who rises above the crowd and impresses it with his—or her—particular qualities, virtues, or triumphs. A hero is someone who both acts on events and provokes them. His biography is history—when it is not the other way around. A hero is naturally center stage. Do people look at him? They look up to him. He is someone to be worshiped, idolized, but not necessarily emulated, someone whose human impulses and instincts have been exaggerated on purpose to *distinguish* them from the rest of us common mortals.

Not so in the Talmud. The Talmudic hero is just the opposite: he is someone who must forever lead the way and serve as an example; he is someone you and I can identify with.

The ancient Greeks did not praise modesty. To them, pride was considered a virtue—whereas our sages saw pride as a stumbling block. The Talmud extols modesty as much as justice. In its literature, the hero is above all endowed with qualities of the heart. Compassion for one's fellow man is one of the highest attributes in our tradition. We were born to help one another in our quest for perfection. Redemption is based on compassion for our people in exile, for the Redeemer himself, and for God, whose *Shekhina* dwells with us in exile. To hasten redemption is to perform the ultimate heroic act. But those who occasionally engage in this kind of mystical activity do so in secrecy. The ultimate hero remains invisible. The real hero is—unreal.

For the Bible, a person who is committed to both belief and action is heroic: Abraham rather than Isaac, Israel rather than Jacob. The Biblical hero is alone—alone for God, alone with God—as Abraham was alone.

The Talmudic approach is somewhat different. *Eize guibor? Hakovesh et yitzro.* A hero is he—or she—who overcomes temptation, seduction, desire, instinct, ambition. In other words, it is a spiritual attitude that makes someone a hero.

The hero is sovereign, independent. He displays the courage of his convictions and does not concern himself with the image he projects to the public; he does not strive to be the most beloved or the most feared person in the land. Nor does he have to win elections.

One might go a step further and state that in the Talmud a hero does nothing to be—or to appear—heroic, in the conventional sense of the word.

David's teacher, Achitofel, was called *Guibor betorah,* a hero in study. As for Samson—called *Shimshon haguibor,* the hero—he is considered by our sages to be one of the *Kalei olam:* a lightweight, a no-goodnik. Strange but true: great physical strength, military bravery are not virtues to be praised in Talmudic literature. The Talmud is not at all impressed with Bar Kochba's military operations. Quite the contrary: the Talmud reproaches him for his heroism for he relied too heavily on it. The greatest military figure of all—Judah the Maccabee—is not even mentioned in the Talmud.

A hero in the Talmud is someone who works on his own spiritual development for the sake of others. Someone who dwells in his own garden, alone, is not heroic. Had Moses stayed in heaven, he would have become our Prophet but not our teacher. Had Rabbi Shimon bar Yohai remained in the cave, he would have kept his visions to himself. Learning is important to the individual person—but to share it is more important. Why is a *Mamzer talmid chacham,* a learned bastard—sorry: a bastard with an education—to precede a High Priest who is ignorant? Because in learning, man can always go higher and higher. When it comes to learning, the more one gives, the more one receives. Hence the emphasis in the Talmud on study and good deeds. Theology matters less than human relations.

What about Rabbi Hanina? The texts do not mention his scholarship. All they mention is his ability to help those in need, be they strangers or members of his own family, which seems odd. We imagine a hero to be selfless, concerned exclusively with communal affairs, helping orphans and widows at his own expense. But Rabbi Hanina quite willingly performed miracles on behalf of his family. Was this proper? Was this ethical? Was this what our sages wished a hero to do?

The answer may very well be . . . yes. To care for one's family before turning to other responsibilities *is* human, and in our tradition heroes must express their humanity before they can fulfill other roles. Is it possible, Albert Camus asked, for man to be saint without God? Is it possible, *we* ask, for man to be hero without his fellow man? No, it is not. Whatever pulls the individual away from society is to be condemned, according to our tradition. *Kadima derekh eretz kadma latorah,* says the Yalkut—consideration for others must precede scholarship. Abstract erudition may turn into a futile game of the intellect. Words are links not only between words but also between human beings. The emphasis on the *other* is paramount in Judaism: *Achrayut,* responsibility, contains the word *Akher* (Acher), the Other. We are responsible for the other. And first of all, for those closest to us.

Take the High Priest, for instance. On Yom Kippur it was his duty and privilege to pray for the welfare of the entire community of Israel, but—before that he prayed for the welfare of his own family. Yes, his family ranked first. It would have been inhuman to require him to place strangers ahead of his parents and brothers and sisters. Only if he loved his own could he love the entire household of Israel. I do not think of this as a weakness. Quite the contrary: I see it as a matter of virtue and strength. Inner strength. Spiritual strength. Had Rabbi Hanina helped only strangers, he would appeal to me less. A person who is insensitive to those he knows and who love him will ultimately be insensitive to those he does not know.

The fact remains that Rabbi Hanina rarely makes use of his powers for his own benefit. He stops the rain *after* he is all wet. Why didn't he stop it before? He could become rich if he chose to, but he remains poor to the end of his life. For the simple reason that he needs nothing. Why? He simply doesn't know; he doesn't know that he is poor. That's the Talmudic hero for you: someone who needs nothing. And thinks he has everything. The text says it explicitly—and with humor—when it echoes God's astonishment: "The whole world," says the Almighty, "is being fed thanks to my son Hanina—and he is satisfied with one measure of carobs from one Friday to another. . . ." Translation: Rabbi Hanina—the pillar of Creation and darling of its Creator—could ask anything and obtain it; but he doesn't ask. He is satisfied with little—or even less than that. The result? His situation is so bad that his family has nothing to eat on Shabbat!

Meanwhile, his wife, in order not to arouse pity, made believe that all meals were provided for. On Fridays she would go through the motions of preparing them with care and piety. She would light the oven and place empty pots on the fire. Her neighbors would see the smoke and be unsuspecting of the truth—until an unfriendly one became suspicious. "I know they have nothing to cook for Shabbat," she thought, "why the smoke?" She decided to find out. She knocked on the door. In embarrassment, Rabbi Hanina's wife withdrew to her bedroom. But when her bad neighbor entered the kitchen, a miracle took place. The oven was suddenly filled with baking bread. The neighbor saw the bread in the oven and yelled out, "Quickly, the bread will be burned. Bring the bread shovel." "I know, I know," Rabbi Hanina's wife calmly replied. "I've just gone to get it."

It seems that the entire family was miracle-prone: something was forever happening to its members. One *baraita* maintains that Rabbi Hanina's wife really went into the bedroom to fetch a bread shovel because she was accustomed to such miracles. They occurred not only to the parents but to their daughter as well. One Shabbat eve Rabbi Hanina noticed that his daughter was unhappy. He wanted to know the reason and she replied, "I mistook the two vessels containing oil and vinegar, and I poured the vinegar into the Shabbat lamp." It was late afternoon, too late to correct the mistake. "Do not worry," said her father, using a simple but powerful argument: *"Mi sheamar lashemen sheyidlok,* He who ordered that oil should burn, can order that vinegar should also burn." And—says another *baraita*—it did. In fact, it burned until the next evening, until the *Havdala* ceremony.

What strikes us in all these tales of wonder is not only that miracles occur but that they are not accompanied by the usual outcries of surprise, excitement, and exuberance. They are welcomed quietly, with simplicity. Does Rabbi Hanina expect them to happen? I rather think that he hardly sees them happen. For him miracles are not miracles. They do not impress him because, on the level of God, miracles do not exist, whereas on the level of man all of life is a miracle. And that means not only those things we do not understand. The fact that we are able to grasp the meaning of certain events and understand a few elements of Creation—isn't that in itself a miracle?

Every creature, every object in Creation has its place and its meaning, and a part to play: it is up to man to understand this and, with some luck, to be able to articulate it.

Said Rabbi Hanina: The Biblical ram, sent by God to save Isaac as he already lay on the altar, was created before Creation for the sole purpose of saving Abraham from sacrificing his son. The ram did not just happen to be on Mount Moriah; he was sent there. And he has stayed on in history. Nothing of this special ram has been lost, said Rabbi Hanina ben Dossa. The ashes were dispersed in the sanctuary of the Temple. The sinews were used by David as strings for his harp; the skin was claimed by the Prophet Elijah to clothe himself. As for the ram's two horns—the smaller one called the people together at the foot of Mount Sinai, and the larger one will resound one day, heralding the coming of the Messiah.

From this poetic interpretation we learn of Rabbi Hanina's basic attitude toward life: all that exists contains a divine secret and a goal that transcends it. Reality and legend are intertwined: what is legend for *us* may have been reality for someone else. Memory and imagination are not necessarily incompatible; they may complement one another. Look at Rabbi Hanina's example of the ram whose life span encompasses the entire history of mankind: it begins before the beginning and will go on until after the end.

But then—in Rabbi Hanina's private gallery, the ram is not the only animal with a legendary destiny. His goats too were special. Remember the chickens that *became* goats? Those were the very goats Rabbi Hanina's neighbors accused of trespassing on their property. "My goats?" exclaimed Rabbi Hanina—

"impossible. You know what?" he went on, "I shall prove it to you. If they are guilty, let them be devoured by bears; if they are innocent, let each of them bring back a living bear in its horns." That afternoon the goats returned from the field with bears on their horns. . . .

I don't know what Rabbi Hanina did with the bears but the Talmud brought them into the story and kept them there, where they met other animals—there was even a lion among them and—a donkey.

The story of the donkey? The donkey was stolen. Why then didn't Rabbi Hanina use his powers to find it? Because the donkey knew how to take care of its own interests. It simply went on a hunger strike; it refused to eat. Why? Because the thieves tried to feed it with untithed—meaning ritually unfit—hay. The thieves got annoyed. What shall we do with this animal? they cried. It is going to die! So they let it go free. And naturally the donkey found its way back into Rabbi Hanina's courtyard.

Two centuries later, a Babylonian sage, a certain Rabbi Zeira, proclaimed, "If our forebears were like angels, then we are humans; if they were like humans, we are donkeys." And, after a brief meditation, he added, "but not like the donkey of Rabbi Hanina ben Dossa." (In other words, that would have been too great an honor.) That donkey was too special. Not even like the donkey of Rabbi Pinhas ben Yair!

Clearly, Rabbi Hanina and Rabbi Pinhas shared not only stories about miracles but also about donkeys and *their* wisdom. For a similar anecdote was told of Rabbi Pinhas ben Yair's donkey, which also refused to be fed whenever the hay was, according to law, unfit for nourishment.

Poor Rabbi Hanina: few stories are his exclusively. Even the tale about his role as rainmaker has been ascribed, with some important variations, as we shall see, to another sage—the famous Honi Hamaagal.

Once there was such a drought in Judea that the sages sent a messenger to Honi Hamaagal: Please, pray for rain. He in turn was so convinced that his intercession would be successful that he told them, Remove the ovens from the courtyard lest they will melt in the rain. Immediately they all did as they were told, except . . . that it did not rain. He prayed some more—with the same result, or rather, lack of result. So, he drew a circle around himself and spoke to God: "Master of the Universe, Your children asked me to pray for them, believing that I have influence on You. Therefore, I swear to You that I shall not move from here until You have mercy on them and give them rain." At that point the first raindrops began to fall, but very slowly. Said his students, "This kind of rain came only to appease *you*—not us." "I want real rain," exclaimed Honi Hamaagal. "Enough rain to fill caves and tunnels." Instantly the rain turned violent and so frightened the people that they pleaded with Honi Hamaagal not to allow it to destroy the world. Said he: "Master of the Universe, I asked for a rain of blessings, not of punishment." Only then did the rain become less violent. After a while, the people urged the sage to make it stop altogether. Commented Honi Hamaagal, "Your people, Master of the Universe, are unable to cope with excessive mercy or excessive punishment. You are very angry? They cannot stand it. You are very kind? They cannot stand that either." In time, the weather and the people settled down and things returned to normal.

Rabbi Hanina attributed his successes to God's mercy and justice more than to his own virtues and powers.

One day, he was told that the daughter of Rabbi Nechunya, the public well-digger, had had an accident: she had fallen into an open well and it was impossible to get her out.

Rabbi Hanina prayed for one hour and remarked, "She will be all right." He prayed for another hour and said, "She is all right." He prayed for a third hour and declared, "She is out."

Using his favorite expression, he explained, "I am neither prophet nor son of a prophet. Still, I was sure that nothing bad could happen to the child of a pious and just man like Rabbi Nechunya, who has contributed to the welfare of so many people."

However, the Talmud tells us that at a later date Rabbi Nechunya did lose one of his children. His son died . . . of thirst.

A similar story involves Rabbi Pinhas ben Yair. He was told of a pious man—a Hasid—who spent his time digging wells for the benefit of thirsty travelers and passersby. Instead of rewarding him, life punished him: his daughter—who was soon to be married—was swept away by a turbulent river, and no one ever saw her again. People came to console the father, who refused to be consoled. Rabbi Pinhas ben Yair heard of the tragedy and he too came to console the father, who still refused to be consoled. Said Rabbi Pinhas to his companions, "Is this the Hasid, the pious man you talked to me about? What kind of Hasid is he if he refuses to be comforted?" But when they explained the symbolism of the situation to him, he understood. And this is how he addressed the Almighty: "This man honored and served You and his fellow men with water—and now You choose to punish him with water?" Whereupon a voice was heard: The daughter had reappeared, alive and well. Commented one sage, "An angel came to her rescue; and he looked like Rabbi Pinhas ben Yair."

What then remains of Rabbi Hanina's life and work? What distinguishes him from his contemporaries? What will we remember of his teaching? What does the Talmud remember? A few anecdotes and aphorisms.

For example: If your fear of heaven precedes your wisdom, your wisdom will last; if it follows it, it will not. And also: If your deeds weigh more than your knowledge, then your knowledge will stay with you; if not, it will not.

Interesting, his emphasis on deeds—and confusing as well. Rabbi Hanina, a man of action? Have we missed some hidden element of his personality? Wasn't he known for his stories and prayers? The fact is that the Talmud insists on linking him to action. After he died, the Masters proclaimed: "With him gone, there are no more *anshe masse*, men of action, in our midst."

Perhaps we have different interpretations of the word "action." He could well have seen action as an extension of prayer and contemplation. Prayer leads to action—in that sense, prayer *is* action. Seen in this manner, Rabbi Hanina qualifies as a true man of action.

But at this point a gnawing question must be raised—and confronted: How is one to comprehend his failure to pray for Jerusalem? He was Rabbi Yohanan ben Zakkai's contemporary; thus he must have lived through the beginnings of the national tragedy, if not the tragedy itself. He may well have witnessed the siege of Jerusalem, and even the destruction of Jerusalem; and in that case he must have seen the Temple go up in flames, the sanctuary reduced to ashes, and the valiant princes and warriors of Judea deported as slaves to Rome and its circuses, and to distant slave markets everywhere. And yet—no echo of this gigantic upheaval is to be found in his words. There is no record of a single tear shed over the destruction of the holy and supposedly indestructible city. Incredible but true: the Event has no place in the wondrous tales and aphorisms by him or about him! How is one to explain such an omission from a Jew, a nationalist as fervent as Rabbi Hanina? Wasn't it he who proclaimed: *Ein adam ela mi'Israel,* that the Jew is closer to humanity than anyone else? That the Jew must be more human than anyone else? How is one to reconcile all this with his silence at the death of thousands and thousands of Jews during the Roman invasion of Jerusalem?

When you read the Jerusalem Talmud, the Babylonian Talmud, and other Midrashic sources, you realize that in the life and work of this great Master and sage the *Khurban Habayit*—the destruction of the Temple, and what it symbolizes—are totally absent. Understandably we react to this with surprise. What are we to make of it? Does it mean that for Rabbi Hanina the *Khurban* was a historical event like any other—a tragedy like any other? That he did not appreciate its religious and historical uniqueness? How is one to explain the silence he created in himself, and around him? Worse: how is one to explain the Talmudic silence around *his*?

All his contemporaries were distraught over the Event, over its mystical significance. Not he. All prayed for the salvation of Jerusalem. Not he. Why not? More than anyone, he should have wept and prayed for the sake of his people and the land of Israel. He who could with words, with words alone, alter events and save lives, why didn't he use them to prevent the unspeakable disaster and spare Jerusalem the ultimate humiliation? Why didn't he do anything? Why didn't he say anything? Was it because he didn't care? Is that why the Hasidic world did not claim him as forebear?

These are all pertinent and painful questions. The answer? Is there an answer? All we have to go on is a series of hypotheses, some plausible and some implausible.

The first one—which reflects Saul Lieberman's view—sets the time of Rabbi Hanina's death before the destruction of Jerusalem. This shows our teacher's characteristic preference for artistic simplicity: Rabbi Hanina showed no concern for the national tragedy of our people quite simply because he died *before* it occurred.

If we accept this possibility, the chapter can be closed right there and then, but what if he died later? or during the Event? Nothing in the sources reveals even an approximate date for Rabbi Hanina's death.

Thus it is quite conceivable that he did live through the tragic years of the *Khurban,* or just preceding it.

But let us suppose he did not—that he died much before the

destruction of Jerusalem—what then? The tragedy began much earlier, didn't it? The land was under Roman occupation and domination for quite some time before: the population was divided between pacifists and activists, Kamtza and Bar Kamtza, the zealots and their opponents, the rich and the poor. The nation was obviously heading toward catastrophe, and most scholars, teachers, and leaders seem to have reacted to the unfolding events each in his own way—whether with sorrow or anger, faith or resignation—only Rabbi Hanina said nothing. Did he fail to see the writing on the wall? Did he not experience the same fear as his friends? None could help but respond to the danger—if not the disaster. How did he alone manage to remain aloof?

How can one be sure of how he, in fact, reacted? How can one gauge the inner response of any man to such cataclysmic events?

Let us explore another hypothesis. He did witness the siege of Jerusalem and the burning of the sanctuary, but did *not* pray to prevent the defeat of Judea, or mourn the death of its children. The reason for his silence? He was struck dumb. In the face of the atrocities he felt powerless, speechless. A natural reaction: when pain becomes unbearable, we withdraw into our most private shelter, surrounded and protected by silence. In other words, Rabbi Hanina may have been so wounded by the tragedy that befell his generation that he could not cope with it in his usual manner—with words of prayer and supplication. He did not pray because he was unable to pray. In the presence of so many widows and so many orphans roaming through the ruins of Jerusalem, he lost his voice; his lips became sealed. The hero of prayer became a victim.

The difficulty with this approach lies in the fact that there is nothing in the text to support it: silence must be explained and corroborated by words—not by more silence. Had Rabbi Hanina's silence resulted from the reasons we just formulated, somewhere in the Talmud a clue would have been waiting for us. A sentence, a remark, a question mark. None is to be found in the text.

Therefore, let us examine another hypothesis: that he died during or after the destruction—and that he *did* try to prevent it through prayer.

As the enemy drew closer, as death's shadow loomed larger on the horizon, as darkness spread, Rabbi Hanina must have prayed with more vigor, more fervor than ever before; he must have tried to shake the heavens and appeal to the celestial throne itself to cancel the evil decrees and spare his people further pain and anguish. A man such as he, whose action was prayer, must have mobilized all his efforts and made use of all his powers to protect Jewish children from the invading legions, but . . . he failed. This time, his prayers were not heard; his pleas were not received. And that is why he remained silent—afterward. And that is why the Talmud kept silent about his efforts: so as not to blemish his memory, and also not to discourage his followers in subsequent generations from making their own attempts to save their contemporaries through prayer. . . .

And thus, the absence of the *Khurban* in his life and tales becomes understandable; we can empathize with a man for whom the *Khurban* was so deeply present that the only way he could react was with total silence. The miracle did not occur. Jerusalem was not spared.

Whatever hypothesis we accept, one thing is clear: the Talmud does not try to embellish its characters. It does not try to gain affection for Rabbi Hanina by describing his lonely fight for the preservation of Jerusalem and its glory. No one describes him as a leading figure. No one sings his praises, no one echoes his pain: his is the silence of silence.

For in the Talmudic universe the hero is often not the one who succeeds but the one who fails to succeed; he is not the one who undertakes—successfully or not—to perform miracles, but the one through whom miracles are accomplished—or withheld.

And so, it seems, Rabbi Hanina was simply Rabbi Hanina, a man who believed so totally in prayer that he broke through all the gates of heaven to obtain favors for his fellow man. Rabbi Hanina was a sage who, in the midst of climactic upheavals, chose to take care of his neighbors rather than get involved in politics; he was a Master who taught us the importance of everyday miracles, small gestures, chance encounters: every word may evoke wonder, every man can hasten redemption, every human being is the center of creation.

Like Rabbi Hanina, we wish we could go to Jerusalem with an offering, and like him, we are condemned to carry stones so heavy that they cannot be lifted—except that, unlike Rabbi Hanina, we carry them in our hearts.

Rabbi Eleazar ben Azaryah

"Bo BEYOM—on that memorable day," a serious incident occurred in the great and prestigious academy of Yavneh where hundreds and hundreds of students and scholars delved deep into the study of law under the presidency of Rabban Gamliel ben Shimon ben Gamliel.

Rabban Gamliel, an old and revered leader, was known for his disciplinarian authority. During his tenure, "on that day," he was dismissed and a virtually unknown young man was elected to replace him.

Many generations of Talmudic scholars tried to understand what happened. Was it simply an accident? Or the outcome of a power struggle? In what context should one view this revolt in an intellectual and spiritual world where for centuries respect for tradition and seniority was part of the very foundation of collective study and teaching?

The event provoked a shock that reverberated throughout the scholarly community in Judea and beyond. Understandably, not since Moses had there been an organized rebellion against a duly elected leader who personified the authority of the law—and what's more, for no apparent moral reason.

"Bo beyom"—it was as though an earthquake has shaken the Talmudic world. So much so that some sages—inaccurately—claimed that wherever this expression appears in the Talmud, it refers to that event—to that revolt and the events immediately following it.

On that fateful day, the participants felt free to reexamine laws that governed Jewish life in Roman-occupied Judea. Furthermore, they chose to act upon delicate problems that had remained unresolved since the famous disputations that had opposed the House of Shammai to the House of Hillel.

Thus one must consider "that day" extraordinary and significant: ancient customs and traditions were brushed aside in order to celebrate youth and rebellion. It was a time not unlike our own sixties.

Let us explore this intriguing episode, this scandal at the top. Let us examine its cast of characters, weigh their motives, and try to comprehend how such a rebellion became possible, and how it was eventually crushed.

Fortunately, the upheaval has been richly and abundantly documented. Those who witnessed it recorded everything. Scene after scene, incident after incident, we watch the plot unfold, first clandestinely, perhaps subconsciously, then overtly. We are able to listen to the questions, the outcries, the protests of the crowd which gropes for direction until it bursts into action. We are there as things happen, and . . .

But let us not go too fast. We shall narrate the event step by step.

It began with a disciple—at this point anonymous—who appeared before Rabbi Yeoshua and asked for a ruling on the following question: Is the Maariv prayer compulsory or voluntary?

Voluntary, of course, said old Rabbi Yeoshua. Strangely, the disciple was not satisfied, and he solicited the opinion of Rabban Gamliel himself, who, naturally, took the opposite position: The Maariv prayer, he said, is obligatory. At that point the disciple—still anonymous—voiced his astonishment: "How is it that Rabbi Yeoshua ruled otherwise?" "Oh?" said Rabban Gamliel. "Wait. Wait until the scholars arrive, wait for the debaters; they will enjoy this." When they all gathered at the House of Study, the president opened the session with the customary *Shaalu* and turned to the student whom he had just seen: "Any questions?" The single-minded disciple rose to his feet and asked his question for the third time: The Maariv prayer, the very last one, is it voluntary or not? In other words, may it ever be omitted? Normally, the question would have been followed by a discussion, but the president obviated any such thing by announcing his decision: The Maariv prayer is obligatory. He then gazed at the participants and asked whether anyone dissented. Only one voice was heard, that of Rabbi Yeoshua: "No," he said, "no one disagrees." Whereupon Rabban Gamliel, the president, evidently lost his temper: "What?"

he said angrily. "Didn't you tell a student here earlier that the evening prayer is voluntary? Rise to your feet, Yeoshua, and let testimony be given." And the old and venerable teacher, among the most respected of the academy, stood up and remained standing, listening to what Rabban Gamliel had to say. His defense was peculiar. He confessed right away, using an obscure aphorism: "When a living person opposes a dead person, the living person wins; but when the witness is also alive, how can the living go on denying?" The incident was closed, and Rabban Gamliel resumed his discourse as though nothing had happened, without even bothering to invite his adversary and colleague to sit down. This inevitably led to a reaction by the other members of the academy: they began to whisper, to fidget, to voice their displeasure at the public humiliation gratuitously inflicted upon Rabbi Yeoshua. It didn't take long for the whispers to become outcries: "Enough, enough!" they yelled. The president was forced to stop, and from then on the study session took a dramatic turn: a decision was taken to disavow the regime, to unseat President Rabban Gamliel, and to appoint someone to replace him.

Someone—who? As always in such situations, factions emerged supporting and/or opposing various candidates. The first name that came up, that of Rabbi Yeoshua himself, was discarded immediately. He was too directly involved in the incident; his nomination would have been too much of an affront to the outgoing president. They were ready to hurt him—but not that much. The second candidate? Rabbi Akiba, one of the great Masters of his generation. Why was his candidacy rejected? I do not like to admit this: Because of his social and economic status; he was not only poor but a descendant of converts. In truth, he was pained, and made no secret of his disappointment when the choice fell on a young but wealthy scholar, a member of an influential family: Rabbi Eleazar ben Azaryah, whose ancestor was Ezra the scribe. When the position was offered to him, Rabbi Eleazar was amazed. He was honored and flattered but his immediate response was: "Thank you, thank you, but . . . I must consult my wife." Which he did (and from this we learn that one must not accept a position without talking it over with one's spouse). And her answer was an emphatic no. And rightly so. Displaying an amazing knowledge of human relations, she advanced an argument whose logic seems irrefutable: Why should you accept this position? said she. What they have done to your predecessor they will end up doing to you!

Still, Rabbi Eleazar did not heed her advice—and from this some students deduce that while one must consult one's wife, one must not necessarily obey her. Anyway, Rabbi Eleazar's reasoning was as follows: Consider the use of a bottle; it may be broken tomorrow; is that any reason for not using it today? And so he announced to his friends that he had decided to accept the nomination.

He made his "acceptance speech"—which we will discuss later—and took the appropriate measures to inaugurate his reign. The first was to open the doors. Said the Talmud: "As soon as Rabban Gamliel was removed from office, the guard who stood at the entrance to the academy was dismissed; and thus all who wanted to study could enter freely and listen." As a result, hundreds of benches had to brought in to accommodate the newcomers. Next, the academy took up cases left unresolved since Shammai and Hillel. The emphasis was on change, exuberance, youth; enthusiasm ran high, hope even higher. All was well that ended well—or was it?

The rebellion was short-lived. It lasted one day, according to some sources, several months according to others. After making the old Rabban Gamliel suffer, his colleagues felt sorry for him and decided to reinstate him as president. Rabbi Eleazar ben Azaryah's wife's premonitions had come true. The very same people who had removed Rabban Gamliel now removed his successor— and then felt sorry for him, too.

Surely it was an embarrassing situation, one that offered no solution. How was it possible to spare the feelings of one leader without hurting those of the other? Not to worry: Talmudic scholars can do anything—and did. In the end, they managed to formulate a fair *modus vivendi*. Rabban Gamliel reassumed the presidency, whereas Rabbi Eleazar stayed on as his deputy. And thereafter, we are told, Rabban Gamliel lectured two Saturdays and Rabbi Eleazar the third. And soon, very soon, the storm subsided. Things settled down. Life continued as before, as though the first campus uprising in Jewish history had merely been a fleeting accident.

Is this the end of the story? Not at all. Having retold its outline, let us now analyze it in detail: all its heroes and protagonists deserve our attention. They are all illustrious, erudite, all had meaningful lives; all made an impact on Jewish thought and legend, and yet . . . I must admit that at first none of them really appealed to me. There is in all of them something perplexing, even troubling. It is only when we read the stories again and again, and bring them to our experiences and memories from other times and other fields that we begin to understand them. Well, let us stop here to pay a quick visit to Judea and bring back a firsthand report.

Rome is victorious and Jerusalem is in mourning. The latter part of the first century of the Common Era is drowning in violence. The Roman empire is declining, a new religion will soon claim its scepter, while in occupied Judea, in the Jewish land, all seems centered around Torah. Political structures have changed. The central authority has moved away from Jerusalem. Never mind—what matters is that Torah is alive. For those who teach it, as for those who study it, therein lies the meaning of life.

Ten years, twenty years have elapsed since the national catastrophe which culminated in the fall of Jerusalem and the destruction of its Temple—and yet Judea continues to live, to believe, to pray, to transmit words that have echoed in its heart since Sinai. Defeated Jewish warriors are dispersed throughout the empire but Jewish honor has not been blemished. Hadrian and his cruel edicts will not prevail; Jewish passion for learning, Jewish quest for truth and morality constitute an antidote to despair. Young freedom fighters are already organizing clandestine bases in the mountains; and when they finally strike at the occupying legions, their struggle will be remembered as one of the most glorious in history. In his message to the Senate in Rome, Hadrian will omit the traditional phrase, "I and your soldiers are well." They are not well.

Armies come and go, as do empires, but people's dreams never die. The law given to man in the desert in the hope of vanquishing the desert inside man will enhance his inner sovereignty and thirst for immortality. The proof? The ruins of Jewish nationhood are still visible everywhere, but Judea is already demonstrating an astonishing vitality, living its present without denying its past.

Those sages, those disciples of the law, those men drunk with God's word, how did they manage not to yield to sadness and resignation? They managed. At Yavneh, for instance, a city of ideas founded and extolled by Rabbi Yohanan ben Zakkai, one hears the heart of Judea singing its hope and clinging to its memory. Although for another ten years a Jewish king—Agrippa the second—occupies the legitimate throne, no one pays attention to him: people know of his admiration for, and his subservience to,

Rome; he may be king but for all practical purposes he remains an assimilated Jew. In times of crisis, when Israel's collective destiny is at stake, people turn not to him but to the sages and teachers and their students, the repositories of ancient and living knowledge, a knowledge both eternal and mystically urgent. In the academies of learning, the scholars transcend their differences and spread the word of Israel, the history of its relations and experiments with God from city to city.

Naturally, Rome watches the scene suspiciously. Domitianus orders his emissary Pompeius Longinus to reinforce discipline. Do Jews want to observe their religion? Let them—as long as their worship and study keep them out of politics. That is what concerns Rome: politics. The empire is still big and strong, but in the highest circles of power too many murders are being plotted. There is uncertainty everywhere. The war of the Jews against Rome proved that the imperial army is not invincible: today's victors may be defeated by tomorrow's. It also proved that the word "solidarity" has meaning for the dispersed Jewish communities: what happens to one appears to affect them all. What happens in Judea reverberates in Alexandria and Rome: Jews want to remain Jews even if it means to be persecuted. This is something Rome is unable to comprehend. If to be Jewish means to suffer, then why not stop being Jewish? Why cling to beliefs and customs that offer no reward? The less Rome understands, the more oppressive it becomes. Now it is increasingly dangerous to be a Jew—so much so that the leadership does not dare to convene all the members of the Sanhedrin. Rome would view any such meeting as a revolutionary plot. Delegations are dispatched to Rome to intercede on behalf of Judea. Some succeed, most fail. In the final analysis, Jewish destiny is determined by Jews alone. Their future lies in Yavneh more than in Rome.

And in Yavneh, much depends on the president. Chosen by his peers, he needs Rome's approval. A rebellion is virtually unheard of—except in the case before us.

Let us reopen our tale. The president, Rabban Gamliel, has an argument with his illustrious colleague, Rabbi Yeoshua— because of an anonymous student's inquisitive mind—and a new, little-known candidate, Rabbi Eleazar ben Azaryah, is proclaimed winner. But was he even a candidate? No. Then why was he chosen when so many sages were present? Rabbi Yeoshua and Rabbi Akiba were disqualified—all right, we can accept that. But there were others eminently qualified for the nomination. Among the many members of the Academy, there were certainly some who had, to say the least, seniority over young Rabbi Eleazar. In fact, wasn't he the youngest, a bit too young? His wife had told him so herself. When she mentioned his age, he had this touching answer: "I look old, I look like a man of seventy." And Talmudic legends add that, indeed, at that moment, his hair turned, some say gray, some say white. (The Yerushalmi disagrees, saying that he was almost seventy.) If nothing short of a miracle was needed to assure his election, why was he elected in the first place? Because he was rich and the son of influential parents? If the sages wanted to censure their leader, Rabban Gamliel, why didn't they replace him with one of his peers? Furthermore, even if they felt the need to blame him, why shame him? How is one to explain that because of a simple legal matter—regarding prayer, of all things—an assembly of great scholars decided unanimously to impeach their president—something that has never been done before? Something may have been wrong with them—not with him!

No? Sorry. Something was wrong with him, too—and with everyone else connected with the incident.

Let us study the case of Rabban Gamliel versus Rabbi Yeoshua. Much is known about the first: his thirst for power, his severity in matters of discipline; nobody doubts his leadership qualities; they are evident. He *is* a leader—strict, rigorous to the point of apparent insensitivity. He must be right—always; his superiority must always remain unchallenged. His word is law, and woe unto anyone trying to oppose him. Even when he stands alone, alone against everybody, he must win—and usually does. Just imagine: He says *"Shaalu*—any questions?" and the audience is paralyzed. The only student who dares to rise and ask a question is the one whom he had instructed to do so. And when he receives his answer, no one speaks up. Why? Why such fear? Granted, it is always difficult and probably costly to defy a president—but why did Rabban Gamliel rush to voice his opinion? He should have spoken last, not first. And, no matter what, he should never have shamed Rabbi Yeoshua.

Mind you, it was not their first public quarrel. Earlier they had disagreed about a delicate problem related to the calendar.

Two witnesses, as required, appeared before the tribunal and stated that they had seen the new moon on the night of the thirtieth day of the month, but not the next night. It doesn't matter, declared the president. They have seen the new moon, that's enough for me. Now we can establish the dates for this year's holidays. No, said Rabbi Dossa ben Harkinas. The witnesses' testimony sounds faulty: if they have failed to notice the new moon on the second night, that means they may not have seen it the first night, either. It is as if they claimed to have seen a woman giving birth tonight and will see her still with child tomorrow. Is this possible? Rabbi Yeoshua supported his view, whereupon the enraged president sent him the following message: "I order you to appear before me with your cane and purse on the day which, according to your calculations, would be Yom Kippur."

In his predicament, Rabbi Yeoshua turned to Rabbi Dossa for counsel. What to do? Rabbi Dossa's answer was, You must obey, my friend; if we begin to question the decisions taken by Rabban Gamliel's court, we shall end up casting a doubt upon all the decisions of all the tribunals including those of Moses. And Rabbi Yeoshua, in spite of his advanced age and of his position as sage and scholar, rose on the day that he thought was Yom Kippur, and, with his cane and purse, he humbly appeared before the president. The story must have made the rounds. Crowds must have gathered to observe the drama of the old teacher showing his obedience to their leader. As for the winner, he greeted the penitent warmly. He kissed him on his forehead and said, "Peace onto you, my teacher and my pupil. My teacher—for you are wiser than I am—and my pupil—for you have chosen to respect my wishes."

That was magnanimous. But what about the law? Who was right according to the law? Rabbi Dossa's position sounds more plausible than Rabban Gamliel's: the two witnesses could not have seen and not seen the new moon on two consecutive nights. They must have been mistaken; which means that their testimony was questionable. Rabbi Dossa was right in suspecting their reliability, and Rabbi Yeoshua was right in supporting his suspicions. Then why was the president so stubborn? And why was he angry, even after his opinion prevailed? You may say a president is entitled to his anger. But why was he angry, not with Rabbi Dossa, but with Rabbi Yeoshua? There can be no excuse, especially since both scholars immediately submitted to his will. His misplaced fury was not forgiven by the people; they remembered.

Another story involves a calf that had the misfortune of being a firstborn, a *B'khor,* and therefore destined only to be sacrificed in the Temple; it could not be used for any other purpose. The only way for the calf to be demoted was to break his leg or wound his lips or eyes; in other words, only an accident could save him. As a result, there were many accidents. And so, to prevent further "accidents," the rabbis—who were not born yesterday—issued a decree: Even a wounded *B'khor* may not be slaughtered for personal consumption or commercial use.

Then, lo and behold, a certain Rabbi Zadok, a pious man, revered in all circles for his honesty and integrity, happened to own a *B'khor* which had accidentally injured its mouth while eating. Being absolutely certain that this was a bona fide accident, Rabbi Yeoshua allowed Rabbi Zadok to treat the animal as any other, as though he were not firstborn. When Rabban Gamliel heard the story, he became enraged. "What?" he exclaimed. "You practiced favoritism? The law is the same for everybody. Everybody must abide by it." Here again, Rabbi Yeoshua displayed genuine humility; he admitted his error. But the president was not satisfied. In open session, he reprimanded Rabbi Yeoshua and said: "Yeoshua, rise to your feet, let testimony be given." And the old Master stood like a schoolboy while Rabban Gamliel delivered a long lecture. The audience reacted angrily to so much harshness. They began to grumble, and their protests grew louder and louder. At one point they yelled at Khutzpit the interpreter (whose role was simply to transmit in a loud voice the words uttered softly) to stop. And he did. And Rabban Gamliel was unable to finish his lecture.

But it was the final incident—the one about the Maariv prayer—that made Rabban Gamliel suffer the consequences. He was removed from office.

Come to think of it, wasn't his removal the proper thing to do? Could the academy permit its leader to offend his peers and punish them for their opinions? Could it tolerate his lack of tolerance? Could a prince of Torah be so insensitive, so arrogant? Did he truly believe that he was the sole possessor of truth, or at least of the interpretation of truth?

It is difficult to approach him. One may respect him, fear him, but one cannot love him. His identity is too bound up with power. He is not vulnerable enough, not accessible enough. Furthermore, he is not a friend to his friends. In fact, he is particularly harsh with them. He forgives Rabbi Zadok, he is lenient with Rabbi Dossa, but he remains inflexible, excessively demanding with Rabbi Yeoshua, his deputy, who has been for years his closest colleague. Why?

We fail to understand him. But let us admit that his "victim" is not much easier to understand. Why is Rabbi Yeoshua so passive, so submissive? A true teacher of Rabbi Akiba, a Talmudic giant, the Av-bet-din never protests, never argues, never stands up for his right to speak his mind. Why not? Is it weakness or exaggerated respect? How is one to explain his turnabouts? Doesn't he have personal convictions worth defending? First he sides with Rabbi Dossa, then he deserts him; he says yes to Rabbi Zadok, only to change his mind minutes later. As for the Maariv prayer, first he says one thing, then, after hearing the president, he reverses his opinion without giving any explanation. At the very least, he could have said, "Thank you, Mr. President, for changing my vote." We fail to comprehend how such a great personality and spiritual leader, whose mind is so clear and whose learning is so vast, could so humble himself in public. I would have preferred to see him courageously, even desperately, fighting for his ideas, even if it meant losing his title.

If Rabbi Yeoshua was motivated by weakness of character, he should not have attained such a high position in the first place. Intellectual leaders must be outspoken, especially when the honor of Torah is at stake. As a private individual, Rabbi Yeoshua had the right to bend his attitudes; as an official he was duty-bound to act without fear or ulterior motives. Yet he did the opposite: he was fearless outside the academy and resigned inside it—to such a degree that, because of him, Rabban Gamliel becomes a more appealing character. Isn't it possible, or at least conceivable, that Rabban Gamliel was harsh with him because of his weakness? Because he wanted to test him, to test his integrity, to see how far he would go in saying yes, and yes again?

An exaggerated need to be conciliatory, to please everybody, is not good for leadership. From a leader, even from a deputy leader, we expect some measure of . . . determination—to open new gates and vistas, to blaze new paths, to speak freely even at the risk of being unpopular.

Thus we find fault with the second member of our cast of characters.

What about the others? The sessions were attended by the most illustrious teachers and scholars of the time; they heard the president as he repeatedly reprimanded their colleague—yet they waited until the third incident, the one about the prayer, to intervene and cry for justice. Where were they during the first two unpleasant scenes? How can their passivity, their silence, be justified at a time when their colleague's reputation and honor were publicly assaulted? Even when a response finally did come—where did it originate? Not from the intellectual elite, not from the ranks of the academy—but from the people, the audience, the simple citizens who had come from all over the country to study; it was they who could not tolerate the sight of the humiliation inflicted on a teacher they must have admired for his gentleness and humanity. It is clearly indicated in the Talmudic text itself: *Ad sherinenou kol haam*—the session was interrupted by the people, not by the scholars. The people, not the scholars, whispered and protested against Rabban Gamliel's way of treating Rabbi Yeoshua. And as in any good narrative, the text tells us what the people actually said: "How long will he continue to torture Rabbi Yeoshua! Let us remove him from office!" And that is exactly what they did. They unseated him. Impulsively, without the slightest discussion or deliberation—which is additional proof that the move was made by the crowd rather than by the academy.

Does this mean that the crowd represents the "good guys" in the story? Is the implication that they are decent and worthy of praise? Well . . . they are not beyond reproach either. First, because they also waited too long. It may not have seemed long to them, but it surely must have seemed so to Rabbi Yeoshua. Second, why did they resort to such a radical solution? Couldn't they have sent a delegation to the president? Or sent him a message? Or signed petitions? Or published ads and letters in the *Galilee Times*? Third, why did they do to the president the very same thing he had done to their hero: that is, humiliate him in public? And why did they use the ultimate weapon—impeachment? And last, did they have the right to impeach him?

Of course, crowds act impulsively. They must have interpreted the silence of the sages as consent. Had but one scholar stated his opposition, had but one sage admonished them, they might have gone home quietly. But the scholars remained silent in the face of the crowd's anger. No wonder that in the general confusion the successor chosen was Eleazar ben Azaryah, a relatively young and unknown and surely inexperienced leader.

There, too, we may ask a question: Why did he accept? Why

didn't he answer, "Please do not use me as an instrument for settling your accounts. I will not allow you or anyone to manipulate me into shaming our leader. I respect Rabban Gamliel and I love Rabbi Yeoshua, and I shall not do anything to hurt the feelings of either!" Why did he say yes so quickly? Wasn't he just a bit too eager?

As we said earlier, most of our characters appear anything but flawless. Even the great Rabbi Akiba seems to have been negatively affected by the incident. He had sought the presidency, and when he lost it to Rabbi Eleazar ben Azaryah, he could not contain his disappointment. We may deduce, therefore, that *Bo beyom*, on that particular day of tension and stress, everyone concerned— except Rabbi Eleazar's wife—showed his least attractive side: the episode brought out the worst aspects of their tempers and characters.

That is, unless we are mistaken, Or unless we offer a different reading of the story, which in the Talmud is always possible, and even desirable. We can always say, *"U'meidakh gissa. . . ,* on the other hand. . . ."

Yes, on the other hand, we may find it possible, even commendable, to review the case and proclaim all the "defendants" innocent.

Rabbi Akiba, in voicing his pain, teaches us a lesson in frankness. He has sought high office and is not ashamed of it; he wants us to know that there is nothing wrong with seeking high office. One must not hypocritically diminish what one cannot obtain. It is human to aspire, and it is human to fail.

As for Rabbi Eleazar ben Azaryah, he became president against his own will. He neither sought the position nor particularly wanted it. When it was offered to him, he did not grab it. On the contrary, timidly, apprehensively, he answered that he would go home and ask his wife for advice. Poor man: he probably knew he was not chosen on merit and that his tenure could not last. Saul Lieberman is correct: Had Rabbi Akiba been selected, he would have remained president for life. The reason, then, for choosing young Rabbi Eleazar was that he could be easily demoted. Thus both Rabban Gamliel and Rabbi Yeoshua realized from the beginning that it was only an academic exercise, a game, so to speak. And he himself knew it—as did his intelligent and clever wife. Why then did he accept the nomination? Because he thought that to attain power for one day is better than not at all? Out of respect for the scholarly community, perhaps? Out of affection for his teacher Rabban Gamliel? Rabban Gamliel surely would have been more badly hurt had his title been handed to his opponent Rabbi Yeoshua, or even to one of his peers. Somehow it seemed less of a blow to be replaced by the younger Rabbi Eleazar.

Incidentally, Rabbi Eleazar succeeded him formally only as rosh-yeshiva, not as president. The difference between the two positions? That of rosh-yeshiva was a purely internal academic affair, whereas the candidate for president needed Rome's approval. Rabban Gamliel held both positions. Is it possible that the fact that he was Rome's "appointee" antagonized those who resisted Rome? Could that have been an added reason why none of the sages came to his defense? And why he himself did not put up a fight to retain his position? In a conflict, albeit symbolic, between Israel and Rome, he sided with Israel—even if he suffered because of it.

Let us now consider Rabbi Yeoshua's apparent weakness of character. But let us call it "flexibility" instead. And infinite respect for the high office of the presidency. Rabbi Yeoshua, who walked, weeping, with Rabbi Akiba on the ruins of the Temple, understood that, having lost its sovereignty, the people of Judea needed another institution to symbolize royalty and authority: in effect, the president had succeeded the kings and princes of Judea and Israel. Thus, for a scholar to disobey his leader would be tantamount to incite general disobedience: the office would be adversely affected and so would the Jewish people. That is why he consistently chose to avoid open conflicts with authority at the academy. What it must have cost him to disregard his views and bow to the president's! One can imagine him when, in the vital matters of the calendar—but only in those matters—he felt obligated to violate the sanctity of the day he knew was Yom Kippur, and went with his purse and cane to respond to the president's summons. It's simple: Rabbi Yeoshua would go to any length to avoid a scandal that could lead to dissidence. His primary concern: the collective destiny of his people. And that destiny demanded that he understand not only those who agreed with him but also those who disagreed. Had the president asked him for his opinion before offering his own, he would have given it; but once the president made his view publicly known, he refused to disagree with him, for the president represented Jewish continuity: to question his authority ultimately meant to doubt that of Moses. As Rabbi

Dossa put it, between Gamliel and Moses the chain had to remain intact. In that context, all decisions became irrevocable. Does this mean that the Talmudic tradition negates the possibility of debate? Quite the contrary: Talmud and debate are almost synonymous. Debates are important; they are necessary and even indispensable. But *before* the decision has been made—not afterward. Once the decision has been made, and made known, it is beyond the reach of scholars and students alike. Today one would say, it is beyond appeal.

Could that be the reason for Rabban Gamliel's intransigence? Son and grandson of martyrs and heroes, he had but one obsession: to maintain and preserve the integrity and the sovereignty of Jewish law and life. To rule, for him, meant to make decisions, at times difficult and painful ones. One day he exclaimed, "Master of the Universe, You know that whatever I have done was for the sake of Your name and glory; whatever I have done was to prevent quarrels within the community of Israel." Was he not always liked? Never mind. He looked for continuity, not popularity. And if that sometimes meant hurting his friends, he would hurt them—and himself. Did he consider himself a victim of circumstances, a victim of his obligations? The price of leadership was to accept his condition. To hurt and be hurt. That may be why he did not attempt to argue with those who removed him from office; he cited no law, quoted no precedent, made no appeal for compassion or support. Of course, he could have turned to Rome, but Rome's support was not what he wanted. He wanted to be Israel's spokesman to Rome, not the other way around.

Still, he was feared. As president, he had power and he could use it to impose sanctions going as far as imprisonment. His severity must have caused resentment. Is this why he was replaced by someone who was his very opposite? Rabban Gamliel cultivated the elite, Rabbi Eleazar broke down all social and intellectual barriers. Rabban Gamliel's principal interest was the law; Rabbi Eleazar loved poetry and legend: it was he who made the decision to incorporate the Song of Songs and the Book of Ecclesiastes into the canon. Whereas Rabban Gamliel chastised, Rabbi Eleazar comforted. Rabbi Eleazar's most ardent wish was to cleanse mankind from its sins, for, in his eyes, it had suffered enough. He believed in the innocence of the human being. Thus, to slander anyone was a grave sin not only for the slandered but also for him or her who heard the slander. It is he who declared: "A tribunal that passes even one death sentence in seventy years is to be called murderous." Compassionate with his fellow men, he once remarked that "to earn a living was a greater accomplishment than crossing the Red Sea." He emphasized the humanity of man and his vulnerability: what would Torah be without manners, thus without people's respect for one another? He is quoted in *Ethics of our Fathers:* "Celestial and earthly needs are inseparable; one needs both to survive." Also: "Someone whose knowledge exceeds his deeds is like a tree whose branches are stronger than its roots." His ideal was to attain truth through action. His most penetrating saying his biblical source for the emphasis that "Yom Kippur has been given us to obtain forgiveness; but God can forgive us only those sins committed against God. Sins committed against another human being cannot be forgiven, not even by God."

Rabbi Eleazar was generous, conciliatory, his words were healing: those were his virtues. He was not a great legislator; his name is quoted only seven times in the Mishna. What is remembered is his humanism: *"Hatorah nitna bilshon adam,* the Torah was given to human beings in their language," said he. The words of Torah are links, openings, offerings, not obstacles.

How can one not love Rabbi Eleazar ben Azaryah? We respond to him because of his life and his teaching. Power did not go to his head; he was not changed by it, or even affected by it. In fact, it brought him closer to people. Better yet, he strove to bring people closer to one another. Instead of polarizing Jewish scholars, he tried to establish bridges between them. His very first speech—his inauguration address?—was a solemn appeal for pluralism. He spoke of the uniqueness of God and of His people: yes, each of us may choose a different path, but at the end as at the beginning, we come to realize that God is one, and that He is the same for all His creatures. Those who purify things and those who declare them unclean, those who say yes and those who say no, we all put our faith in the same Creator. In other words: we may espouse opposing views and advocate conflicting principles, but we may not claim to be closer to the truth than the next person. This message of extreme tolerance was sorely needed in his time.

And yet, his reign was short-lived. His wife's premonitions were realized. How? Let us read the text:

"Bo beyom, on that very day an Ammonite who had converted to Judaism, a man named Yehuda, appeared before the scholars in the academy and inquired, 'Am I allowed to become part of the

Jewish community?' 'No,' Rabban Gamliel hastened to declare. 'Yes,' stated Rabbi Yeoshua. 'You have taken on our faith; you are now a son of the Jewish people.' 'What?' exclaimed Rabban Gamliel. 'Does Scripture not tell us that neither the Ammonite nor the Moabite shall enter the community of the Lord?' " The argument was excellent but Rabbi Yeoshua has a better one: "Have we not been told that the Ammonites and the Moabites no longer dwell on their lands? That King Sankheriv has merged all nations?' " In other words, we no longer know for sure who is an Ammonite or a Moabite. "But Rabban Gamliel still did not concede defeat. 'It is also written in Scripture,' he said, 'that the descendants of the Ammonites are destined one day to return to their homeland— that surely means that they are already an entity of their own.' 'Correct,' said Rabbi Yeoshua. 'But it is also written that God will bring back one day the children of Israel to their homeland, and yet many have not returned.' " In other words, what is true of Israel may be equally true of the Ammonites. And sure enough, Yehuda the convert was accepted as a full-fledged member of the Jewish community. "Soon after, Rabban Gamliel remarked, 'Since the law is now according to Rabbi Yeoshua, it is time for me to go and ask for his forgiveness.' Which he did. . . ."

The story continues, but we must stop once more and analyze what has been said so far: it contains the key to many of the questions we have raised in this chapter.

Try to imagine the scene: Rabban Gamliel has just been removed from office and yet, when a visitor asks a question, he answers with firmness, no doubt out of habit. It is as though he had not realized yet that he was no longer president. Second, again the dialogue unfolds between the two old adversaries, Rabban Gamliel and Rabbi Yeoshua. What happened to Rabbi Eleazar ben Azaryah? Why didn't he speak up? Wasn't he the newly elected rosh-yeshiva? He was, but he was still in shock. Third, both Rabban Gamliel and Rabbi Yeoshua offer proof that they were excellent debaters; but this time, Rabbi Yeoshua did not avoid the debate. Rather than submit, as he had done until now, he accepted the challenge and fought to win, which he did. Why? Because at that point, Rabban Gamliel had become just another colleague; now he could afford to disagree with him—which means, had he wished to do so before, he might have defeated him as well.

But the most touching and gratifying element in the story lies elsewhere: Rabban Gamliel did not go home; he remained in the

House of Study. Again, let us remember, he had just been humbled in public—and yet, instead of brooding or showing dismay, he stayed at the academy and took part—on that very day—in the scholarly discussions, thus teaching his peers and their disciples a magnificent lesson in humility.

Let us add that he pushed his humility to the limit when he later decided to travel to Pekiin and apologize to his old opponent, Rabbi Yeoshua. At this point, the Talmud picks up the story. Again:

As Rabban Gamliel arrived at the home of Rabbi Yeoshua, he noticed its black walls. "Could it be that you are a blacksmith?" he wondered. And Rabbi Yeoshua, unable to contain his anger, with unusual and uncharacteristic nastiness, replied, "Woe to the generation whose leader you are, woe to the ship who claims you as its captain, for you do not even know how students of Torah make a living, and what makes them suffer." "Forgive me," said Rabban Gamliel softly. But his plea was in vain. His host turned away from him. "Please," insisted Rabban Gamliel, "forgive me. If you cannot forgive me for my sake, do it for the sake of my father." Then, and only then, did Rabbi Yeoshua forgive him for having been too remote from his colleagues and their pupils to the point of not knowing how they fed their families. Not only that: Rabbi Yeoshua began right away to lobby on behalf of the fallen Rabban Gamliel in order to bring him back to the seat of power. First he persuaded Rabbi Akiba not to oppose his efforts. Then, drawing on his own gifts, his own credit, he went to Yavneh. In the end, he won the battle: Rabban Gamliel was reinstated. *That* problem was solved. But another remained: that of Rabbi Eleazar ben Azaryah, whose predicament had been almost forgotten in the meantime. What would he do? Where would he go? Back to the ranks? Out of the question. He did not deserve such humiliation. And so he was allowed to remain rosh-yeshiva with limited duties. He would preach one Shabbat out of three. And once more peace was established in Yavneh. With the passing of years, the entire question of internal power became academic. The Romans were constantly finding new tactics to stifle Jewish life and Jewish study, and thus the sages had more urgent, more vital tasks to perform to save their people.

Like many of his senior colleagues, Rabbi Eleazar ben Azaryah was sent on numerous official missions to Rome. Later we encounter him at Bnei Brak, at a clandestine meeting with other sages, where they spend an entire night studying and talking strategy until their disciples, on guard, arrive to warn them: "It is time to say the morning prayer," a coded message, perhaps, that means it is time to leave, for the Roman police are near.

(How strange: Rabbi Eleazar ben Azaryah's public life was shaped by what occurred to him between the morning and the evening prayers.)

In any event, one fact has been ascertained. Following the upheavals in Yavneh, Rabbi Eleazar ben Azaryah and Rabban Gamliel remained good friends; we find no trace of resentment in either. Life once more became normal, as intellectually vigorous and inspiring as before. Therein lies their human greatness: neither the old Master nor the young had wanted power for its own sake. Neither considered himself more personally deserving than the other, nor more just or worthy of greatness. Young or old, obscure or illustrious, each had the right to aspire to high office, and each knew his own limitations. Sadness, melancholy, rancor: neither indulged in any of those. Rabban Gamliel and Rabbi Eleazar respected and loved one another before, during, and after the crisis that could have turned them into rivals. Neither felt the need to change his views and beliefs as a result of what happened, eternities earlier, *"Bo beyom,"* on that day in Yavneh.

For ultimately, in the Talmudic tradition of Judaism, the significance of power is to act less upon others than on ourselves. To offer freedom instead of constraint, to become a symbol of sovereignty rather than compulsion. That is how we view the privilege of those who have been given the authority to speak, to decide, to chart a course for their fellow men. Power is conferred not to rule, but to share; it goes hand in hand with communal responsibility, with a feeling of belonging. We are all students of the same teachers, we are all children of the same Father; and if He is king, then we are all princes.

Now we must raise one final question which has till now been conveniently overlooked, a question that has to do with the one character whom we have failed to identify: the anonymous student who, after all, triggered the crisis at the academy—the one who went around asking provocative questions and thereby causing trouble.

Who was he?

We waited until now to reveal his name because this is exactly how it is handled in the Talmud.

Suddenly, at the end of the episode, when we have already almost forgotten the beginning, and the initiator of the entire series of events, the text gives us, as an afterthought, the following postscript:

"*Veoto talmid Shimon ben Yohai haya.* And that student was Shimon bar Yohai." The anonymous disciple was none other than the great and celebrated scholar, rebel, and mystic Rabbi Shimon bar Yohai.

But we already know that . . . that is another story.

Rabbi Ishmael

... AND IT CAME TO PASS that when the great and revered Rabbi Ishmael was tortured at the hands of Roman soldiers for having studied Torah, his pain was so overwhelming that he cried out. And so powerful was that outcry that it shook heaven and earth. Nevertheless, the torturer continued to punish the saintly Jewish scholar who later shouted again, so terrible was the pain he was made to endure. His second outcry was more thunderous than the first: it shook the heavenly throne itself. "Why has he been made to suffer so much?" the angels asked. "Is this the reward for his devotion to learning?" "Once a decree has been issued it cannot be revoked," was God's answer. And He hastened to add: "If Rabbi Ishmael cries out once more, I shall restore the universe to its primary chaos." And so kind and considerate was Rabbi Ishmael that he remained silent, and thus the world was saved.

This legend, however magnificent and awesome, presents some problems of plausibility. Since when is God so sensitive to Jewish complaints? Since when is He afraid of Jewish tears and outcries? Furthermore, is it conceivable that the very existence of mankind would be linked not only to the good manners but to the tolerance of physical pain—of any Jew? Was the good rabbi aware of his own powers? Were the Romans aware of them? More important is the question: Why didn't he make greater use of his powers? Why didn't he threaten his tormentor? "Listen, if you do not stop, I will shout, and this will bring destruction upon you." Or again, why didn't he address himself to God: "Master of the Universe: either You see to it that my torture comes to an end or the whole world will come to an end. Is that Your desire?" Why did Rabbi Ishmael choose to remain silent?

These are some of the questions to be explored.

Let us examine the legend of Rabbi Ishmael's martyrdom. What does it teach us? First, that the enemy was cruel. Second, that the victim was human. Third, that God cared. But cared for whom? The victim? The world?

For the moment, let us dwell on the story itself and analyze its known elements. We know the name of the martyr: Rabbi Ishmael.

But who was he? Already we run into difficulties. Even scholars seem to have confused Rabbi Ishmael the sage with Rabbi Ishmael, the High Priest who was his grandfather. According to the Makhzor, the prayer book for the High Holidays, Rabbi Ishmael the High Priest was the martyr; according to other sources the martyr was Rabbi Ishmael the Sage. Historians cannot make up their minds either. Some argue that both died tragically as martyrs; others claim that one—the sage—died a natural death. The consensus is that having been the friend of so many martyrs, Rabbi Ishmael must have shared their fate. After all, in those times it was dangerous just to *be* Jewish. But to teach and study Torah meant to expose oneself to torture and death. It is inconceivable that Rabbi Ishmael stopped teaching and studying. Whatever happened to his grandfather could also have happened to him.

In truth, it is easy to confuse them. Both were called Ishmael ben Elisha. Ishmael? What a strange name for pious leaders, scholars and priests! Can you imagine a Rabbi Esau in the Talmud? Or a Rabbi Bileam? True, many Talmudic sages bear Roman names: Tarfon, Marion, Papaius, even Titus. But not Moses, Aaron, or Abraham—too heavy a burden, probably. As for Ishmael, the name was indeed used, and this serves as proof, according to Talmudic commentators, that the first Ishmael, the son of Hagar, did repent. Esau did not, otherwise he would have found among the Talmudic sages a venerable Rabbi Esau.

What else do we know about Rabbi Ishmael, son of Elisha? He was a *Cohen,* a priest. His parents were wealthy. We learn something of his childhood from an episode narrated by the venerable Rabbi Yeoshua ben Hananya: While on an official visit to Rome, Rabbi Yeoshua heard one day about a Jewish child with beautiful hair, handsome features, and expressive eyes who was in prison—or worse, according to another source, in a place of ill repute. The good rabbi went there and, standing at the door, quoted aloud a prophetic verse: "Who handed me over to the enemy?" and, from the lips of the child, came the second half of the verse: "Because we have sinned." Deeply impressed and moved, Rabbi Yeoshua exclaimed, "I swear that I shall not leave before rescuing this child, even if it means that I will have to raise all the funds in the world." He fulfilled his promise and saved the child. And who was that child? Rabbi Ishmael.

From this legend we may deduce important facts. First, that the old Rabbi Yeoshua ben Hananya was an excellent . . . fundraiser. Second, that he was a good educator; he knew a good pupil when he saw—or heard—one. We also learn from this legend that young Ishmael was a sharp-witted child with a good memory for Torah: a stranger quotes the Prophets and he answers immediately. How could he be sure that the old man addressed himself to him? He couldn't. But he was sure of himself: he had heard a question and it was up to him to give an answer—*the* answer.

But there is one question to which we have no answer: How did the young Ishmael get to Rome? Who brought him there and why? and when?

After the defeat of Judea, following the destruction of Jerusalem and the burning of its sanctuary, innumerable Jewish families were exiled by the Roman conquerors to Rome and other places in the empire.

Rabbi Ishmael was still a child during those tragic years. Why, then, was he dragged to Rome? Why was he put in jail? Are we to believe that he was not only a Talmudic prodigy but a political activist as well?

Rome practiced collective punishment. And so it is quite plausible to assume that during the political and military upheavals in Judea Rabbi Ishmael's entire family had been deported to the imperial capital. The child, being attractive, could easily have ended up in some special jail, or worse.

Where was his father, Elisha? In fact, we know little about him, except that he owned property in the Galilee. He must have seemed pale and insignificant between his father, the High Priest, and his renowned son, the child prodigy.

Was it the High Priest who gave young Ishmael a good early education? His real teacher was Rabbi Yeoshua ben Hananya, the sage who had rescued him from the Roman jail. He also studied *Halakha* and Midrash under Rabbi Nekhunya ben ha-Kana. He lived at a place called Kfar Aziz, near Hebron, and became an influential member of the Sanhedrin. In fact, he played a role in the campus rebellion that removed Rabban Gamliel as president and replaced him with Rabbi Eleazar ben Azaryah.

What else do we know about him? He was married—no one knows to whom. He had two sons who died before him. This we learn from the sages who came to comfort him. Who were they? Rabbi Tarfon, Rabbi Yosse from the Galilee, Rabbi Eleazar ben Azaryah, and Rabbi Akiba. Said Rabbi Tarfon: "Beware, friends; he is a great scholar both in law and parable; I beseech you not to interrupt one another. "I shall speak last," said Rabbi Akiba. They all spoke in praise of the dead sons—but no clue is offered as to the reason for their deaths. They perished together, that we know. But of what disease? Or at the hands of what enemy? Did they belong to the Jewish underground? Did they fall in battle?

Later, after losing his wife, he remarried and had a daughter and a son—with problems of their own. They too were abducted to Rome and taken to live in two different homes. The two Roman masters met one day and spoke of the beauty of their slaves. "I have the most handsome boy in the world," said the first. "And I have a girl whose beauty is unequaled in the universe," said the other. They decided that their slaves ought to be mated. And so the boy and the girl were brought into a room together and left alone in darkness. But they remained huddled in opposite corners. The boy said, "I am a son of priests and High Priests—how can I marry a slave?" And she said, "I am a daughter of priests and High Priests—how can I marry a slave?" At daybreak they recognized one another, broke into tears—and died.

He had a sister whose son, Rabbi Eleazar, was his favorite nephew. Rabbi Ishmael would decipher his dreams, advise him in his studies, and guide him through possible perils.

Rabbi Ishmael was extremely popular with women. When he died, they lamented throughout the land of Judea: "Ye Daughters of Israel, weep over our Master Ishmael." Why so much affection? He deserved it. He was always on their side. There is a story in the Mishna: A man made a solemn vow never to marry his sister's daughter. The reason? He didn't like her. Why not? Because . . . she wasn't pretty enough. So she was brought to the house of Rabbi Ishmael, and he made her beautiful—so beautiful that the man didn't recognize her. And when Rabbi Ishmael asked him whether he had vowed not to marry her, he denied it. Rabbi Ishmael released him from his vow and the two married. Rabbi Ishmael commented, with tears in his voice: "They are beautiful, the daughters of Israel, they really are—and when they are not, it is because of their poverty."

He was less lenient—and less tolerant—toward those who

wished to involve themselves in secular Greek studies. When his nephew asked for his permission to do so, he refused. But then, since he himself knew the Greek language, why should others be forbidden to acquire it? He made a distinction between language and culture. He himself needed Greek to study Talmud, but he did not want his nephew to study Greek with the sole purpose of discovering Greek culture.

He was even harsher toward the miscreants, the heretics of his time—the Minim (dissident sects), the Sadducees, the Christians. His nephew, Rabbi Eleazar ben Dama, was bitten by a snake and he, the uncle, let him die rather than allow a certain Yaakov of Kfar Siknin to try to heal him by invoking the name of a man from Nazareth. "Call him!" Ben Dama cried in despair. "Call him and I will prove to you from Scripture that it is permitted!" Rabbi Ishmael refused to yield. His beloved nephew died, and Rabbi Ishmael said, "Happy art thou, Ben Dama, that thou did not transgress the words of thy colleagues."

As a descendant of a patrician priestly family, he had all the virtues, and also all the failings, of his class, according to Louis Finkelstein, the great philosopher of Jewish history. Rabbi Ishmael is described as morose, narrow, chauvinistic, almost reactionary, but also as tender, generous, candid, imaginative, romantic, and determined. In spite of his friendship with several students and followers of Hillel, he was not one of them, that is, he did not share their plebeian affinities. But he did believe in their pacifism. In this he opposed Rabbi Shimon ben Yohai and even Rabbi Akiba. According to Rabbi Ishmael, for instance, Torah is to be studied and interpreted as a document—divinely inspired and written—but without hermeneutic complexities. And when Rabbi Eliezer ben Hyrcanos, the old sage, did use hermeneutics, the young pupil Rabbi Ishmael protested, "You say to the *passuk*, to the verse, be silent until I interpret you." Offended, the old Master rebuked him: "You are as unproductive as a highland palm." He was proved wrong. Rabbi Ishmael became one of the most productive minds in Talmudic history.

He disagreed with many of his elders. What of it? Torah does not tolerate flattery. If he disagreed, he had the right to say so. In his conflicts with Rabbi Akiba we hear reverberations of all the other traditional debates between schools and Masters. Rabbi Akiba favored the people, while Rabbi Ishmael favored the priests, the patricians, and the farmers. Every camp had its champion.

Rabbi Ishmael was so identified with his class that some of his colleagues reacted by saying, "Naturally, Ishmael the priest favors the priests." Not exclusively. He fought for the rights of the well-to-do because his opponents so vigorously defended the rights of the poor.

Rabbi Ishmael believed in logic, in language. "Scripture speaks in human terms," he said. One must not play with words but seek and accept their meaning according to set rules. To simplify matters, he formulated thirteen rules which today would be described as linguistic modes and precepts. "When two verses seem to contradict one another," he said, "you cannot solve the problem by a compromise, however poetic it may be; you must discover a third verse to substantiate your view."

These are the seven things that remain hidden from man, according to Rabbi Ishmael: the day of our death, the day of consolation, the depth and the scope of the law, also, man does not comprehend what makes him worthy, what is going on in the heart of his friend, when David's kingdom will be restored, and when the sinful kingdom will be destroyed.

At the end of his life, Rabbi Ishmael changed. A nationalist, he stayed away from the rebels. Bar Kochba was supported by Rabbi Akiba, not by Rabbi Ishmael. Still, he eventually mellowed. He who had allowed his nephew to die rather than be treated by a heretic healer now permitted Jews to invoke the sanctity of life as a supreme commandment. For even greater tragedy had overtaken Jewish life. Martyrdom had become a daily phenomenon. So urgent was the problem that the sages decided to formulate a code establishing when death is an option—and when it is not. The consensus was that only three transgressions had to be avoided at any cost, even at the cost of one's own life: adultery, murder, and idolatry. But Rabbi Ishmael changed the law, saying, One must refuse idolatry and die, but only if the challenge takes place in public. Should the enemy, however, force a person to commit idolatry in private, the victim may submit rather than die. *"Vehai bahem,"* said Rabbi Ishmael: "This is the basic principle of Torah: one must live for and in Torah and its commandments. Torah means life, not death."

Said Rabbi Ishmael: Whenever the word *im*—"if"—appears in the Bible, it means something is voluntary—except in three cases involving charity and compassion; there it is compulsory. First, "If there be among you a poor man of one of thy brethren— open thy hand to him." Second, "If a man has nothing and is unwilling to be supported—give him a loan." Rabbi Ishmael is explicit: "If a man of good family appears and he is ashamed to ask for alms, you must suggest to him, 'My son, perhaps you need a loan?' " Third, "When it is said: *Im talve*—if you lend money to a brethren," says Rabbi Ishmael, "the *im* is rhetorical: if you have money and your friend does not, you *must* lend him money."

When the Romans seized Rabbi Ishmael, he was not alone. Rabbi Shimon, who was with him, sighed with pain: "Woe to us," said he, "woe to us for we are to be killed like any simple violator of the Shabbat, or idol worshiper, or incestuous person, or murderer." Rabbi Ishmael thought a while and asked, "May I speak? "Speak," said Rabbi Shimon. "Perhaps when you sat in your house, poor people would come and stand outside, and you would not let them in and give them food." "I swear to heaven," said Rabbi Shimon, "that this was never so. For I kept watchmen in front of my house with orders to bring any poor person inside and feed him or her as graciously as possible; and the poor ate and drank and blessed the name of God." But Rabbi Ishmael persisted. "Perhaps when you taught upon the Temple hill, and all the men and women of Judea were listening to you, you grew vain?" For a while they remained silent. Then Rabbi Shimon said: "My brother Ishmael, a man must be prepared to receive his fate." And each beseeched the executioner to let him die first. "I am a priest, son of a High Priest; let me not see the death of a friend," said Rabbi Ishmael. The other said, "I am a prince, son of a prince, spare me the sight of my friend's death." The executioner made them draw lots, and Rabbi Shimon died first.

His most sublime recommendation? "Do not overburden the camel; do not place on its back a burden too heavy to carry!" Even the strongest among us has his limitations.

Only knowledge and the thirst for knowledge have no limits—hence Rabbi Ishmael's love for scholars. "Have you seen a sage commit a sin during the day? Do not question his integrity; it is possible that he has repented during the night." Are scholars above the law? No one is above the law. Are they above suspicion? No one is. But scholars should be given the benefit of the doubt— and so should everyone else. In other words, repentance is possible. The future cannot correct the past, but at least it can explain and redeem it. "Why did God save the Jews at the Red Sea crossing?" Because of Abraham, say some sages. No, because of Noah, say others. Or Isaac. Or Jacob. "No," says Rabbi Ishmael. "That unique miracle was accomplished not because of the past but because of the future: because of the good things Jews were to do at the Temple."

What kind of person was he? Strong-minded and gentle. In *Ethics of our Fathers,* he is quoted as giving the following advice: "Be kind to all people, even the youngest ones; welcome them all with gladness; and be tolerant of them all."

His love for his people was absolute. "All children of Israel are princes," he said. And often he would add, "May I expiate for them."

He was a humanist advocating involvement in practical everyday activities. "And you shall choose life," according to him, also means, you must choose a trade to make a living. There is a time for all things. When you labor, labor; when you study, study. "Why is it written in Scripture, *Verape yerape,* Ye shall heal? Why the repetition?" he asked. And his disciples' answer was, One exhortation is addressed to the physician, the other to God. The repetition allows the physician to heal the sick—not relying on heaven but acting on its behalf.

Rabbi Ishmael was a young boy when the Temple was destroyed and the sanctuary burned down. What had remained of Jewish political sovereignty—which, though diminished since the year 63, was still tangible—was now totally lost. Agrippa the second—a caricature of a king—was vanishing in the abyss of humiliation. Judea was now less than a vassal state: it was a nation that was made to obey the victor's strangest whims and most cruel laws.

Had Ishmael seen the burning of the temple? Or had he lived it from afar—from Rome? He never spoke about it. Still, he must have been traumatized by the event. Has he joined the nationalist militant segment of the population? His people's catastrophe did not drive him to despair; his people's despair drove him to a philosophy of action.

But then why didn't he join Bar Kochba as Rabbi Akiba did? An intriguing question, but it may not be valid. What if Rabbi Ishmael died before the upsurge—or at least the emergence—of Bar Kochba? Some sources refute such a hypothesis, contending that he was alive and active. It is quite possible, too, that his two sons died in battle.

By then, Jewish resistance against Rome had lasted for nearly two centuries. Since Pompeius had conquered Judea in 63 before the Common Era, the land had known no peace. Granted, King Herod and his descendants enjoyed internal autonomy and maintained friendly relations with the emperors—but there were always elements who opposed them and militated for restoration of true independence.

What about Rabbi Ishmael? What was his involvement with the resistance movement? We know so much about Rabbi Akiba, and almost nothing about Rabbi Ishmael. The country went through endless upheavals and the sages were affected by them—but not Rabbi Ishmael. Somehow we have the impression that he lived in his private residence in Kfar Aziz, near Hebron, studying and teaching and taking part in academic debates, but not in public life. Unlike Rabbi Akiba, who led a public life—and even died a public death—Rabbi Ishmael did everything in private. When he died, his outcries were heard by God alone. The two scholars were truly different.

"Vekol haam roim et hakolot—And the entire people saw the voices at Sinai," said Rabbi Akiba. They literally *saw* the voices. But Rabbi Ishmael said, They only saw what was *visible* to them—and heard what was not. They saw the flames at Sinai and heard the voices at Sinai. Abraham J. Heschel is right. Rabbi Akiba spoke as a poet, Rabbi Ishmael as a rationalist.

When discussing the phenomenon of the manna in the desert, the two sages seized the opportunity to disagree again. Using a verse from Psalms as pretext, Rabbi Akiba explained that the manna was the bread angels eat in heaven. "What?" retorted Rabbi Ishmael. "Since when do angels eat bread?"

Rabbi Akiba emphasized imagination, Rabbi Ishmael realism. The first interpreted every word, every letter, every syllable in the Torah, whereas the second sought to clarify its greater meaning. For Rabbi Ishmael the spirit of the law was more important than the letter of the law. *"Breshit bara,* And in the beginning God created heaven and earth," means, according to Rabbi Ishmael, heaven and earth—and not some farfetched symbolism. His motto was: The law—given by God—was written in human language meant for human beings. And therefore *Ein Mukdam u'meukhar ba-Torah;* There is no linear logic in the biblical narrative. There is no chronology in the retelling of events. It's the total impact that counts. One must receive the Torah in its entirety.

Conscious of human frailty, he accepted it. He never boasted of his extreme adherence to his belief. In fact, he often admitted to giving in to his weakness.

Once he debated his friends and colleagues over the question, Is it permitted to move lit candles on Shabbat for reading purposes? The majority said no, he said yes. And so he wrote his confession on a piece of paper: "I, Ishmael son of Elisha, have moved the candle flame to enable me to read on Shabbat; and when the Messiah will come I shall bring an offering to the Temple to atone for my sin."

Sins, he said, are not only immoral; they are also unhealthy. Harsh and rigorous on the issue of abortion—he calls it murder— he is more lenient than Rabbi Akiba in matters of suicide. Why did God order the children of Israel to build a sanctuary after they worshiped the Golden Calf? He did so, said Rabbi Ishmael, to prove to them and to the world that He had forgiven them. God is forgiving. He rules with love, not with rigor. He never demands the impossible—not even the possible. "A person who manages to live without committing transgressions," says Rabbi Ishmael, "is rewarded as though he or she had performed good deeds." It is enough to stay away from sin, and thus recognize one's link to his Creator. The worst sin, according to Rabbi Ishmael? Idolatry. Therefore, not to commit idolatry is something that outweighs all other commandments.

I like Rabbi Ishmael also because of his insight into the story of Job. According to him, Job belonged to Pharaoh's royal council. And when Moses came to the king to plead for the release of his people, Pharaoh asked his three learned advisers for their opinions. Yethro said, Let them go. Bileam said, Don't. As for Job, he remained neutral—and silent. *That* is why he was punished. In times of need and tragedy, neutrality helps the oppressor and not his victims.

It was in his school—or in its name—that the awesome question was asked about God's silence in times of tragedy: For He watches and observes how His children are being shamed and tormented and persecuted and He keeps quiet!

Few have dared articulate a protest more powerful: a protest not against faith but on behalf of faith—not against God but for Him! God Himself cannot and must not remain silent. For our sake and His, He must intervene in history and stop the killers before it is too late!

In conclusion, let us articulate what has become apparent: Rabbi Ishmael and Rabbi Akiba differed on almost every subject and issue, whether in theory or in practice. Whatever the debate, whatever the argument, they forever found themselves in conflict.

And yet, though they differed in temperament, outlook, philosophy, ideology, methodology, and followed separate intellectual endeavors, their end was the same. Both died as martyrs of the faith.

And yet, even then they were different. There is no doubt about Rabbi Akiba's martyrdom, whereas Rabbi Ishmael's has been questioned. Rabbi Akiba died in public, Rabbi Ishmael in private. Many people watched Rabbi Akiba's torment; only God was privy to Rabbi Ishmael's. Furthermore, we are told that Rabbi Akiba smiled, seemingly near ecstasy at giving his life as an offering to God and as an expression of his love for Him. Not Rabbi Ishmael; he wept.

Here is another version of the story that we read earlier.

"Rabbi Ishmael and Rabbi Shimon ben Gamliel were on the way to their execution. Rabbi Shimon said to Rabbi Ishmael, "My teacher, I am pained. My heart is consumed for I do not know why I am to be executed."

Said Rabbi Ishmael to Rabbi Shimon, "Perhaps a man once came to hear your judgment, or to consult you about something, and you let him wait until you had emptied your goblet, or fastened your sandals, or put on your cloak? To hurt any person is a sin—and it counts the same whether you hurt that person in great things or in small."

After a silence, Rabbi Shimon said: "*Nikhamtani,* Rabbi. You have consoled me, my teacher."

Rabbi Ishmael was a man of great beauty. In a version of his death that differs from the one told earlier, a Roman matron watched him as he walked to his place of execution. "Tell him to raise his head so that I may see him," she said to the soldiers. "If he raises his head, I shall grant him his life."

But Rabbi Ishmael did not heed her request. When she repeated the same thing a second and a third time, he answered, "Shall I forfeit my life in the world to come for an hour of pleasure here?"

In anger, the matron told the soldiers, "Flay him!" They obeyed. They began at his chin and flayed the skin of his face. When they came to his forehead, to the place where the *tefillin*, the phylacteries, are fastened, Rabbi Ishmael uttered a piercing scream that shook the earth, and he cried: *"Ribono shel olam,* Master of the Universe, where is your mercy?" And a voice from heaven answered, If you accept the suffering, it is well; if not, if you utter one more cry, if you shed one more tear, I shall order the world to lapse back into chaos."

And Rabbi Ishmael remained silent.

Why? Why did he remain silent? Why did he not tell God, No, Master of the Universe, I will not be silent? If this is the way you want thy children to live, I want no part of it. Better return the world to chaos!

Rabbi Ishmael could have spoken thus. He had every right to do so. Jews were suffering and Rome did not care—no one cared. Jews were persecuted and God was responsible, or *co-responsible*. Rabbi Ishmael was entitled to be angry. And to let his anger explode. And punish the world in the process.

But he did not invoke that right. And that is the lesson we draw from his story.

What he told us—what he taught us—is as follows: Yes, I could destroy the world, and the world, ruled by cynicism and hatred, deserves to be destroyed; but to be a Jew is to have all the reasons in the world to destroy, and not to destroy. To be a Jew is to have all the reasons in the world to hate the executioners and not to hate them. To be a Jew is to have all the reasons in the world to mistrust prayer and faith and humanity and power and beauty and truth and language—and yet not to do so. To be a Jew is to continue using words when they heal, and silence when it redeems mankind.

Rabbi Akiba

SCHOLAR, HERO, devoted husband, loyal friend of governors, and mystical visionary: Rabbi Akiba is special. No other Talmudic Master has had such a stormy and exciting existence, no other teacher has had a life of such extraordinary grandeur.

A legend:

When Moses went up to heaven to receive the law, he found God, blessed be He, experimenting with various new symbols and ornaments for possible inclusion in the Torah. "Why don't you give it to us as it is?" Moses wondered aloud. "It is difficult enough, why complicate it even more? "I have to." God replied. "For after many generations there will be a man named Akiba ben Yoseph, Akiba son of Joseph, who will discover secrets within every word, in every syllable. But in order for him to find the secrets, they must first be placed there . . . by me." "Could you show him to me?" Moses asked, a bit puzzled. Unable to refuse Moses anything, God said cryptically: *"Khazor leakhorekha,* turn around, go backwards!" And Moses went back into the past and found himself thrust into the future. He found himself in a Talmudic academy, sitting in the eighth row, which meant the back, listening to a discourse on *his* teaching, on *his* work. But the discourse was incomprehensible to Moses. He did not understand a word; it all sounded obscure and alien to him. Naturally, Moses felt terrible. But then he heard a disciple ask the lecturer, "Rabbi, *minayin lekha?* What proof is there that what you say is true, that your interpretation is correct?" And the teacher—Rabbi Akiba—answered *"Halakha le-Moshe mi Sinai,* that is what Moses was told at Sinai." Having been given proper credit, Moses, the first Jewish author in history, felt better, reassured. Yet something kept bothering him: *"Ribono shel olam,"* he said, "Master of the Universe, if you have a man like him, a

224

scholar like him, why do you need *me*? Why don't you appoint him as your messenger? Why not have him give thy law to thy people? But God cut him short: "*Shtok*, keep quiet. *Kakh ala bemakhshava lefanai*, this is how I see things." Satisfied or not, Moses did not insist. But soon he became curious: "Master of the Universe, could you be so kind as to show me the rabbi's reward, just as you have shown me his learning?" Again God made him turn around and go back into the past, so as to see the future. This time he found himself in a distant marketplace in the midst of a crowd. It was Rabbi Akiba's last day of torture and martyrdom, the day of his execution at the hands of the Romans. Moses could not suppress his astonishment. "*Zu Torah vezu skhara?*" he burst out. "Is this the reward for devotion to Torah? Is this the fate of those who choose to obey your law and study mine?" Again God answered in the same harsh manner: "*Shtok, be quiet. Kakh ala bemakhshava lefanai*, this is how I see things, they are not to be questioned!"

And so Moses, in awe, like Rabbi Akiba after him, must have understood that there are moments when God wants His chosen to be silent.

This story has relevance for me for many reasons. First: Do not accuse me of immodesty, but on occasion I identify with Moses—not the great leader but the writer. It happens that I, too, read what people write about my work—and I, too, fail to understand a single word. Second: The theme of silence as part of theodicy has always fascinated me. Third: It is gratifying for us to learn that questions that trouble us today also troubled Moses. Fourth: I am mystified by Rabbi Akiba's passivity during his agony. He seems to have welcomed suffering and death. Rather than rebel and turn his pain into an existential insurrection, his punishment into an act of supreme protest, he decided to submit and pray. Rather than formulate the question of all questions—that of the role of divine justice in human anguish—he answered it. And for some time I did not like his answer.

As much as I admired and revered Rabbi Akiba, a hero of many dreamers, I could not help but see him as a martyr who was attracted by martyrdom—an image which preceded him. We are told in various Midrashic sources that from the very beginning of time he was meant to suffer—and to glorify suffering. Adam himself had been allowed to view Akiba's tragic ending—and he felt sorry for him, as we do. "*Samakh betorato*, he rejoiced in his learning, but felt sad about his death." Was there no free choice reserved for Akiba? He himself articulated the delightful paradox *"Hakol tzafui,* all things are foreseen, but *hareshut netuna,* we may still enjoy the privilege of choosing freely." Did he say that to explain his own condition? Was he saying that the prediction of Adam and Moses notwithstanding, he could have chosen to follow another path? Was he saying that his death was his own doing?

The fact that countless generations of victims and martyrs have claimed kinship with Rabbi Akiba has made the problem even more acute, more challenging. Who knows? Had he spoken up, had he revealed his anger, had he protested what was happening to him, his fate—and ours—might have taken a different course. . . .

I remember the nocturnal processions of Jewish families walking toward death—it seems that they, too, like Rabbi Akiba, were offering themselves to the altar. It seems that they, too, had given up on life—as he had, many of them with Shma Israel on their lips.

Why didn't Rabbi Akiba opt for defiance? Why didn't he proclaim his love of life up to the very moment it was taken away from him? Why didn't he weep instead of rejoice? Didn't he consider that to die willingly for one's faith could—eventually—be interpreted as an element of weakness in that faith? What kind of law is the law that brings suffering and cruelty upon those who serve it with all their might and with all their soul? Why was he so quiet—Why did he laugh? We shall point this out later. Is it that he meant to resist suffering by magnifying it, by pushing it to its limits? Did he mean to defy death by welcoming its dominion?

Seen in this light, Akiba, the hero of my childhood, the song of my adolescence, suddenly emerges as a disturbing figure, one who elicits reverence as well as compassion.

Is it because of the striking similarity between his times and ours that Rabbi Akiba seems more present—more relevant—than most other Talmudic personalities?

As a survivor of the destruction of Jerusalem, he had to find a way of conferring meaning upon it; he had to learn—and teach—how to deal with its aftermath, how to explain and articulate what cannot—should not—be explained, what to tell old men whose memories were wounds, what to tell young people who wondered why they should go on praying, or dreaming, or living as Jews in a world that seemed to have been drained of Jewishness, why they should go on affirming spiritual values rather than military ones. . . .

As one who walked amid the ruins of the Temple, he had to find a way to build—again—upon those very ruins. He who saw what Roman civilization had done to Jews felt the need to discover the words and images necessary to prevent Jews from giving up on all civilization. In a world shattered by despair, he had to show how to cope with despair.

This is why we feel close to him. And for more subjective reasons as well. He had the qualities of an artist; he was stubborn, passionate, uncompromising. He mastered the art of waiting. He waited years and years for his wife—and made her wait for him! He mastered the art of telling tales and of turning laughter into a weapon. He often laughed—even when his companions found cause to mourn. *Akiba sakhak or sikhek,* Akiba laughed, is an expression often used in the Talmud. And he always had a magnificent story to tell of enchanted times and faraway places; it was impossible to resist falling under his spell.

Who was he?

On the surface, his life may seem a glorious success story: A poor shepherd boy marries a beautiful girl, inherits her father's money, makes it in society, becomes famous, and even manages to die a hero. Everything about him seems exaggerated, almost unreal. When he is poor, he is the poorest. Before he was educated, he hated learned men so much that he wanted "to bite them like a donkey." "Why not like a dog?" asked his disciples. "Because a donkey's bite is more painful," he explained. When he became known, his fame spread from one corner of the world to the other. Like Moses, he is said to have lived one hundred and twenty years. Like Moses, he is said to have been buried with heavenly assistance.

Did a rich girl named Rachel fall in love with him? Did she make him marry her? Did she persuade him—at the age of forty—to go to school and begin studying? Were they disowned—and later readopted, taken back—by Rachel's father, Kalba Savua? Did the Roman governor, Tineus Rufus, seek Akiba's friendship? Did the governor's wife fall in love with him? Did she eventually marry him? There are legends upon legends that answer yes to all these questions.

And what was his attitude toward Bar Kochba? Did he encourage his rebellion? Why did he crown him as the Messiah? And what about the strange adventure he and his three friends had upon entering the orchard of forbidden knowledge, the *Pardes*? He alone emerged unharmed—why?

Everything about Rabbi Akiba is puzzling.

Born in Lud—Lydda—around the year 40 of the Common Era, he had a difficult childhood. His father, Yoseph—probably a convert or son of converts—did not have the means to send his son to school, even though under King Agrippa the first, the country was enjoying economic prosperity. Politically the situation wasn't too bad either. The Romans allowed the Jews to maintain a certain measure of national sovereignty and religious freedom. Jerusalem was still the spiritual and political center of the nation; the authority of the Sanhedrin was undisputed, and the splendor of the Temple unblemished.

Akiba must have been thirty when Titus and his legions brought Judea to her knees. Poverty, misery, oppression, humiliation: the defeat was total, the surrender unconditional. Young warriors were sent to Rome as slaves; children were abandoned, with no strength to cry; corpses of starved victims were stretched out in front of their charred homes, awaiting burial according to the law of Israel. Some Pharisees decided to give up marriage: Why multiply, why bring children into such a wretched world: Fortunately they were overruled by those who followed Rabbi Ishmael's advice: Israel had to survive; life had to go on.

Was Akiba married before he met Rachel? Yes—probably— he had a son from his first wife, who died. As shepherd in the service of Kalba Savua, the wealthiest Jew in town—who, according to some sources, opened his granaries during the siege and fed the entire population—Akiba noticed Kalba Savua's beautiful daughter or was noticed by her. Anyway, it was love at first sight. Theirs is one of the most innocent and moving love stories in the entire Talmudic literature. Disowned by Kalba Savua, the newlyweds lived in total poverty. Akiba collected wood, half to sell, the other half to use at home. Annoyed by the smoke, the neighbors complained: Akiba, *Ibadetanu beashan,* you are killing us with your smoke! In despair, they offered to buy his entire stock so he could afford candles and perhaps a better stove, but he refused. "I like wood," he said. "I study by its light, I am warmed by its heat, and at night, when I am tired, I use it as a pillow." Eventually, he did run out of wood, and then it was Rachel's turn to provide for the family. She sold her magnificent hair, and with the proceeds she bought bread. They must have felt close to despair.

Then—a legend: The Prophet Elijah, disguised as a beggar, appeared at their door. "Please, could you lend me a bit of straw?" he implored. "My wife is about to give birth and we have no bed in our home." Akiba turned to Rachel. "See?" he said. "There are people who are poorer than us." To which she said, "Go and study at the Beth Hamidrash." Not too logical a response? Rachel had her own logic.

Since their first meeting, she had made up her mind—and his, without his knowing it—that he would go to school. There is, in fact, a Talmudic story which views this as a condition of her marrying him. "Tell me," she said, "if I marry you, will you go away and study?" "Yes," he answered, "I will." So they eloped. And Akiba was bound to his part of the contract—he went away to study.

There is a third story as well—naturally. Akiba and his son were walking in the forest when they came upon a well. He asked someone who stood there, "Who made a hole in this stone?" "Drops," came the answer. "If enough drops fall on the stone, they will eventually pierce the stone." Said Akiba, "If a stone can receive water, my heart can receive Torah." And he and his son went to a teacher and began learning the Aleph-bet. At the time, he was forty.

He first studied with Rabbi Nakhum, a legendary figure who praised God for all that happened to him, good or bad. He was called Gam-zu, because of his favorite expression, *Gam zu letovah*, Everything is for the best. Was it his influence that made Akiba accept suffering with such equanimity?

Later he studied under Rabbi Eliezer ben Hyrcanos and Rabbi Yeoshua ben Hananya. Legend has it that he stayed away from home for twelve years. Upon returning, he overheard an argument Rachel was having with a neighbor. "Your father was right to disown you," the neighbor told her. "Akiba is unworthy of you. Look, he left you, he abandoned you for twelve years." "If he listened to me," answered Rachel, "he would go away and study for another twelve years." Having heard that, Akiba did not even bother to enter his home: he went back to the yeshiva for another twelve years.

But when he next came home, as *Rabbi* Akiba, as the local boy who made good, he was greeted by numerous admirers. Rachel could not even get close to him. Eventually he noticed her in the crowd and said, "Make room for her, let her come near me for *sheli ve'shelakhem, shela hu,* Whatever you and I have tried to obtain and accomplish, we owe to her."

Few women received such recognition, especially in public. He also brought her a present—which teaches us that when a husband goes out of town, he must bring a present to his wife. Rabbi Akiba brought Rachel something called *Yerushalaim shel zahav,* Jerusalem of gold, a kind of tiara that few people could afford in those times. The tiara was so splendid that the wife of President Rabban Gamliel became envious. She complained to her husband, asking him why he was less generous than Rabbi Akiba. Rabban Gamliel answered, "Have you suffered as much as Rachel has suffered? Have you done for me what she did for her husband? Have you supported me the way she supported him?"

Convinced that every woman was like Rachel, Rabbi Akiba in his legislative interpretations was often unfair to the average wife. For instance, he states that a man may divorce his wife not only for gossiping but also for arousing gossip. Or he may divorce her because he has found another woman more attractive. "If we were to adhere to your views," one sage exclaimed, "no woman would be safe with her husband!" But in this domain, Rabbi Akiba was overruled.

Another sage objected to his total devotion to study. Akiba performed a disservice to the poor, he complained. Because of him, the poor could no longer invoke poverty as a reason for their inability to pay tuition. True: Akiba was poorer than poor, and yet he managed to study. But another sage added, with exquisite humor, "Do not worry—the poor would still be able to claim in their defense that they did not have Rachel for a wife."

For Rachel, stubbornness was a virtue; for Akiba, too. We are told that he sat in Rabbi Eliezer's presence for twelve years without ever uttering a single word, without ever being asked by the teacher to intervene in the discussions. One day Akiba stumbled upon an unknown corpse in the road—what we call a *met mitzva.* Remembering that the High Priest, should this happen to him on Yom Kippur, must neglect all other duties and tend to the corpse, Akiba carried the man into town, arriving there exhausted, drenched in sweat—only to be reprimanded by his teacher: a *"met mitzva,"* he was told, "must be buried where he is found; with each step you took, you were guilty of shedding blood."

Akiba was not discouraged; he understood he still had much to learn. And he learned so well that one day he asked Rabbi Eliezer certain questions to which the old Master had no answer. In due time Akiba came to be treated as an equal by renowned teachers. And his opinion usually prevailed. Listen to the Talmud: "*Stam* or anonymous *Mishna* means Rabbi Meir; *Stam Tosefta,* additions to the Mishna left out by Rabbi Yehuda the prince, means Rabbi Nehemia; *stam sifra* means Rabbi Yehuda; *stam sifrei* means Rabbi Shimon—they are the authors or the editors, but all of them reflect the work of Rabbi Akiba." Called a great collector of ideas, notions, principles, he baffled his contemporaries with his ability to sort them out and organize them logically, coherently. The ignorant shepherd has risen to become a great teacher in Israel; and though lacking in ancestral nobility and official titles, he has emerged as a dominant figure in Rabbinic circles throughout the land. In due time he will have more authority than most of his colleagues and some of his Masters.

Popular with students, he sometimes had trouble getting along with his colleagues. He occasionally disagreed with Rabbi Eliezer ben Hyrcanos—whom he admired. Here is an example: The question was whether ritual slaughterers were permitted to sharpen their knives on Shabbat. Rabbi Eliezer said yes, because they needed sharp knives to sacrifice animals in the Temple, even on Shabbat. Rabbi Akiba said no, let them prepare their knives on Friday. His decision prevailed. Said Rabbi Eliezer, not without sorrow, "You defeated me in matters of *Shekhita* which involve knives, therefore I am afraid that knives will cause you to die."

It was Rabbi Akiba who allegedly organized the first campus rebellion in Jewish history—against Rabbi Gamliel—which resulted in the removal of the old Master as academy president. Characteristically, it was Rabbi Akiba who was chosen to bring Rabbi Gamliel the bad news, as he did in the case of Rabbi Eliezer. Because he was daring? No. Because he was delicate. His motives were never personal. His only loyalty was to Torah.

This is the way he describes his relationship to Rabbi Eliezer, the same man who predicted his tragic death:

"Rabbi Eliezer has said, 'If all the oceans were ink, and all the trees pens, and the heavens and the earth rolls of parchment, and all the men scribes, they would not suffice for the writing of the Torah, which I have studied; yet I have not covered more of the total body of the Torah than one can draw water by inserting a finger into the sea; nor have my pupils taken from me more than a brush dipped into a bottle.' " Upon which Rabbi Akiba commented, "I cannot even admit having taken that much from his teachings. What I received amounts to the fragrance given off by the citrus, and the light taken from one candle by another, and the water drawn from a brook. The beneficiary enjoys the fragrance, increases the light, and is refreshed by the water; but the giver has lost nothing."

Though teaching in his own yeshiva at B'nei B'rak, he would often visit the academy at Yavneh to take part in the Sanhedrin's deliberations. He once arrived late and waited outside in order not to disturb the scholars—until someone exclaimed, "The Torah is outside!" He had been invited to enter in order to help the assembly reach a decision.

His impact was felt in the fields of *Aggada* and *Halakha*. "If it were not for him," says the Talmud, "the Torah would have been forgotten." Thus his life and work have inspired numerous legends and fables. He appeals to the imagination of the learned and the unlearned alike. He is loved by mystics and rationalists. He is the perfect hero in everyone's book.

And yet, and yet—I have some difficulties with Rabbi Akiba. His attitude toward suffering disturbs me. I repeat: he seems to be attracted to it.

His disciples saw him weep on Shabbat. "Rabbi," they asked him, "isn't it written *Vekarata le-Shabbat oneg*—that one must find joy in Shabbat?" "Weeping gives me joy," he answered.

He was blessed with a sense of humor—and a deep sense of beauty.

On the Biblical Commandment *"Vehavta lereakha kamokha,* And Thou shalt love thy fellow man as thyself," Rabbi Akiba commented, "Yes, this is a great principle in the Torah—but— What is the restriction? Thou shalt not say, 'Because I was humiliated, my friend ought to share in the humiliation; because I was cursed, let part of the curse fall on my friend. . . . The principle applies to good things alone."

All Jews are princes, he said. In other words, the poor are rich . . . though without money.

He was a master of aphorisms; many of his sayings still govern our conduct and our *Weltanschauung* today. "What is life?" he once asked. "The store is open, the storekeeper gives you everything on loan, but the book is open and the hand is writing everything down." He also said, *"Hakol tzafoui,* everything is foreseen, and yet freedom *is* offered."

One day his friend, Governor Tineus Rufus, asked him, "Why does your God hate us pagans?" Rabbi Akiba said he wanted to sleep on it. Next day he told the governor, "I had a peculiar dream; I saw two dogs. One was called Rufus and the other Rufina." "Are you out of your mind?" shouted the governor. Rufina is my wife's name and Rufus is mine!" "I do not understand why you are angry," Rabbi Akiba replied calmly. "We eat and dogs eat; we drink and they drink; we live and die, and so do they; yet if I compare us to them, you are angry. Just imagine how angry God— creator of man and the universe—must be when you compare him to an idol which you worship as a god!"

On another occasion the same Tineus Rufus taunted him: "If God wanted some people to be poor, what right do rich people have to help them? Imagine a slave jailed by his king; if you smuggle the prisoner food, won't the king be angry?" "Imagine a king whose beloved son is in jail," said Rabbi Akiba; "If you smuggle food to that prisoner, won't you be rewarded by the father?" Rabbi Akiba concluded: "It is up to us to decide whether we want to be God's slaves or God's children."

He was hero of many tales, involving many themes. There were some he himself told—and he was a superb storyteller with a keen instinct for suspense—and there were some that others told about him. Many of his stories deal with his frequent journeys abroad. As a member of official missions and delegations, he visited Rome, Egypt, Cyprus—and in Georgia, in Russia, Jews told me of their ancient belief that Rabbi Akiba had come to visit their ancestors. He met Flavius, Hadrian; we find him in various places in Asia Minor, meeting simple people as well as generals and philosophers. A poor child of poor parents, he felt at ease with rulers and kings.

One personality he did not meet was Paul. Both wanted to save humankind, one from within, as a Jew, the other from without. They could not have met.

Some claim he traveled so much, so far, in an effort to establish calendar dates around the new moon. Others believe his motives were political in nature; that Rabbi Akiba acted as General Shimon bar Kochba's roving ambassador to distant Jewish communities, organizing them to open new fronts, recruit sympathizers and volunteers, raise funds, and engage in diversionary campaigns against Rome. This last hypothesis seems persuasive, but some scholars maintain that a scrupulous examination of the corresponding dates would prove it to be fantasy.

What has been ascertained beyond doubt is that Rabbi Akiba traveled widely to help Jews live as Jews in Judea. He must have mastered foreign tongues and sciences—including medicine and astronomy—for he was admired by non-Jewish personalities whose decisions he often succeeded in influencing in favor of Judea.

But most of the time he was at his yeshiva with his pupils, to whom he was both teacher and friend. When one of them fell ill, he came to see him so he would not feel left out. When the country needed rain, he prayed for rain. He simply recited the awesome yet heartbreaking prayer that dominates our High Holidays' liturgy: "*Avinu malkenu,* our Father and King, *ein lanu melekh ela ata,* we have no other King but You. *Avinu malkenu,* our Father and King, have mercy on us for Your sake . . ." And it rained. The Talmud asked: Why was his prayer received whereas Rabbi Eliezer's was not? Because Rabbi Akiba was patient, lenient, forbearing with other people.

Generally speaking, he was a humanist. As such, he opposed capital punishment. "If I were in the Sanhedrin," he proclaimed, "there would be no death sentence issued—ever." The court may have lost a good judge, but the Talmud gained a great teacher, and a daring one at that: he was among the first to free himself from the text—from the strict interpretation of the text. He opened an entirely new era in Talmud, especially in the field of legend—with him, the tale of the law became part of the law itself. For him, every word, every letter in Scripture carried special significance. Thus his lectures must have been well attended; his new approach could not but excite his listeners. Still, it happened that he did not always succeed. Once, while lecturing, he noticed his pupils falling asleep, so he quickly switched to another subject: the beauty of beautiful women. He spoke about Queen Esther. And they all jumped up—totally awake.

A teacher above all, teaching was his first love. It took the death of his son to move him to interrupt a session with his students.

A story:

Rabbi Akiba was in the middle of a class when he was informed that his son, Shimeon, was gravely ill. *Shaalu,* the Master said, using the ritual expression of teachers, Go on, ask questions, let us stay with the issues before us. Another messenger came to announce that Shimeon's condition was worsening: *Hikhbid.* The

Master went on teaching. A third emissary appeared: *Gosses*. Shimeon was in agony. *Shaalu,* murmured the anguished father. Then the last messenger arrived: *Hishlim*—it was all over. Only then did Rabbi Akibi remove his *tefillin,* tear his clothes, and only then did he begin to mourn, saying, "Until now we were bound to study Torah, now we must pay our respects to a man who has passed away."

At the funeral, he delivered one of the most moving eulogies in Talmudic literature: "Hear me, my brethren of the House of Israel, hear me. It cannot be that you have assembled here because I am a sage—for there are among you many who possess more wisdom than I; not because I am wealthy, for there are among you wealthier people than I. The men of the South know Akiba, but do the men of the North know him? The men may know him, do women and children know him? You have come to honor Torah—and in this I find comfort."

Glorious Rabbi Akiba: his son's—and any person's—death anguished him more than his own.

Again—I am troubled by his attraction to the suffering which precedes death—and therefore to death itself. When he came to visit the old Rabbi Eliezer on his deathbed, he consoled him with the words "*Khavivin yissurim*—There is something good about suffering, suffering has a redeeming aspect. . . ."

And I who believed that the Jewish tradition does not encourage suffering but the fight against suffering . . . And I who grew up thinking that Jewish history is not—or not only—a history of suffering but of responses to suffering . . .

Another episode in Rabbi Akiba's life troubles me: Again, the adventure in the *Pardes,* the orchard of forbidden knowledge. Four friends entered it. One lost his mind, another lost his faith, a third lost his life—and only Rabbi Akiba entered in peace and emerged in peace. How is that possible? Had an event that destroyed his friends no effect on him? Was he immune to their plight? Was he insensitive to what they had discovered in the garden?

Along the same lines—Rabbi Akiba and a sage named Ben P'tura argued over an interesting dilemma: Two men walk in the desert and one of them has a jug filled with water; the water would be sufficient for one to survive, not for two; what should they do? Said Ben P'tura, The two must share the water, even if it means that both would die in the desert. Rabbi Akiba disagreed. The owner of the jug should keep it for himself. His argument: It is written *"Vekhai akhikha imakh*—and your brother shall live with you," which means, Your life comes before that of your friend.

As one who celebrates friendship, I was upset by Rabbi Akiba's decision. How could he separate friend from friend? The romantic in me agreed with Ben P'tura. Friends must remain loyal until parted by death.

More evidence "against" Rabbi Akiba? His strange views on Bar Kochba. How could he—a man of his experience and erudition—place his contemporaries in such peril? Didn't he know that false Messiahs are dangerous to the Jewish people? Didn't he know that one must not give dates of the coming of the Messiah nor must one name the Messiah? A great sage, Rabbi Yohanan ben Torta, went so far as to tease him: "Akiba, Akiba," he said, *"Assabim yaalu bilekhayekha u'ben David lo ba*—Grass will grow out of your jaw and the Messiah will still not be here!"

One cannot avoid being troubled by these aspects of Rabbi Akiba's endeavor: still, he remains our teacher. Our hero.

Let us reexamine the problems we just referred to, starting with the last. I believe Rabbi Akiba felt close to Bar Kochba. Rabbi Akiba was already an old man when they met, and Bar Kochba must have impressed him with his youthful vigor and patriotism. Rabbi Akiba remembered a time when Judea was free, and he so wished to see it free again. Roman oppression grew harsher and harsher. The Roman was the supreme ruler over all Jews, and all Jews were treated as slaves. Jews were subjected to degradation and doom. Rome's objective was to deprive Jews of all possibility of hope. Then, suddenly, a brave young warrior appeared on the stage. Talmudic sources indicate that four hundred thousand youths rallied around him. The Roman historian Dio Cassius quotes a higher figure: five hundred eighty thousand. Even the Samaritans, ancestral enemies of Judea, joined the ranks of Bar Kochba's army. Every volunteer had to prove his courage by biting off one of his fingers. "Why are you making cripples out of our children?" the sages asked Bar Kochba. "How then should I test their bravery?" "Let every one of them, with his bare hands, uproot a cedar of Lebanon," they counseled him; "but he must do so while horseback riding." Two hundred thousand volunteers did just that.

Bar Kochba's battle lasted three and a half years. In the beginning, Hadrian did not take him seriously. The first reports from the front made him laugh. Then he stopped laughing. Dio Cassius relates that fifty fortifications and close to nine hundred cities and villages fell to Bar Kochba, forcing the Roman legion to evacuate Judea, Shomron, and the Galilee. For the first time in sixty years, Jews ruled their own land. Rome then sent reinforcements under the command of General Julius Severus. Eventually Bar Kochba's Jewish army was defeated. Because of Roman superiority? Because of Bar Kochba's vanity, says the Talmud. At one point he is supposed to have addressed himself to God, saying, "Since You have abandoned us, since You no longer fight on our side in our battles, we implore You not to interfere. We do not want Your help, but at least do not help our enemies. . . ."

Was it due to his blasphemy or his foolishness that he took on the great Roman Empire? The fact is that the war ended in tragedy. Rome won, Judea was punished by the victor in the cruelest way imaginable. Most of Rabbi Akiba's students, who had joined the fight, fell in the mountains of Judea. The tragedy that struck the population matched in intensity that of the fall of Jerusalem, sixty-odd years earlier.

But what about Rabbi Akiba? What was his role in that event? Together with other teachers, he was arrested. The governor's friendship could not protect him from Hadrian's vengeful edicts. But why did he crown Bar Kochba as the Messiah in the first place? Here is my hypothesis: As a mystic—and Rabbi Akiba was a mystic—this we learn from his *Pardes* experience—he was mainly concerned with problems related to ultimate redemption. When his *Pardes* adventure failed, he may have decided upon a different strategy. Instead of waiting for a Messiah sent down by heaven, he would force heaven to accept a Messiah chosen by him. *"Hatzadik gozer,"* says the Talmud, *"vehakadosh baroukh hu mekayem*—the Just orders, and God, blessed be He, implements his order." So, Rabbi Akiba may have thought, If I—and hundreds of thousands of children of Israel—proclaim this brave and valiant young general the redeemer, God will have no choice but to anoint him as His redeemer. But his scheme ended in disaster. History has taught us a bitter lesson. One does not play with eschatological matters with impunity. Rabbi Akiba knew this. He had tried to interfere with the laws of time, and he was ready to accept the punishment. That is why he welcomed suffering with equanimity, and death with serenity.

Death came after an imprisonment of three years. One legend

has it that the governor's wife, Rufina, interceded on his behalf with her husband—in vain. The legend goes on to say that she had fallen in love with the old sage—and that, after Rachel's passing, Rabbi Akiba married Rufina, who had converted to Judaism. If so, we understand why the jealous governor refused to commute his sentence.

But this is only a legend. What we know with certainty is that while in jail Rabbi Akiba kept on studying and teaching. His faithful student Rabbi Yeoshua ha-Garsi visited him there and served as liaison with the scholarly community outside. Later, when prison rules grew harsher, underground methods were devised. Disciples walked up and down the street posing as peddlers, with needles, shoelaces to sell, shouting, "What is the law regarding private *Halitza?*" And Rabbi Akiba answered from his cell: "How much are the needles? Private *Halitza* in your case is appropriate. . . ."

Rabbi Shimon bar Yohai came to see him and pleaded with him, "Teacher, teach me." Rabbi Akiba refused. The disciple insisted. Said the Master, allegorically: "More than the calf wants to suckle, the cow is eager to feed it, but it is dangerous." The disciple responded: "If suckling is dangerous, then the calf is in greater danger."

In other words, Rabbi Akiba was ready to endanger himself but not others. He was ready to advocate suffering for himself but not for others. That is why he taught clandestinely—unlike Rabbi Hananiah ben Teradyon, who persisted in teaching publicly.

There had been a time when Rabbi Akiba himself did so, too. He, too, gathered crowds in public squares and taught them the law. A sage named Papos ben Yehuda warned him. "Aren't you afraid?" And Rabbi Akiba answered with a parable: "One day the fish decided to leave the ocean, so strong was their fear of being caught by the fisherman's net. 'Where do you think you are going?' asked a fox who happened to see them from the top of a hill. Then the fish told the fox of their fear of being caught by the fisherman's net. 'I will help you,' answered the fox. 'Come with me. I will protect you.' 'Where is your head?' countered the fish. 'If we are in danger in our natural surroundings, how much greater will the danger be when we are out of our element!' " In other words, if studying Torah is perilous, not studying is far more perilous. For Jews in those times the only protection came from Torah!

The same sage, Papos ben Yehuda, was arrested shortly afterward. In his message to Rabbi Akiba he said, "You are lucky, Akiba. You were arrested for studying Torah, whereas I was arrested for more frivolous reasons."

Yet the study and teaching of Torah did not shield Rabbi Akiba. Sentenced to death by torture, he was among the Ten Martyrs of the Faith whom we remember on Yom Kippur.

When Rabbi Akiba died, his peers lamented, "His passing constitutes a warning; supreme chaos is about to descend upon the world."

Chaos—the ultimate punishment in Jewish tradition. Worse than war, worse than collective punishment, worse than famine and bloodshed. Chaos is the eschatological trauma in Judaism. Disorder on a universal scale, confusion and anarchy transcending time, space, and language. What is worse than evil? The triumph of evil—and that is chaos. For in chaos good and evil are intertwined and interchangeable. Evil triumphs when it poses as good.

Akiba's death was not only a tragedy for the Jewish nation; it signaled catastrophe for the Roman Empire as well—and ultimately for the whole world.

So here we are, back where we started: the scene of Akiba's execution which Moses had been allowed to observe even before it occurred.

There are many descriptions of what took place there—all of them powerful. We see the old Master in the middle of the crowd, we watch the Romans combing his flesh with iron combs—as was then the custom. He is laughing. "Are you a magician?" the governor wants to know. "Do you feel no pain?" The disciples ask him the same question, though somewhat more politely. They, too, are eager to understand their teacher's apparent elation in the face of death.

Actually, they should have known the answer. Rabbi Akiba was frequently seen laughing. Whenever his companions wept, he laughed. They saw Roman soldiers, strong and joyous, and that made them cry. He saw them too, but he laughed. Why? He answered, "If God is so kind to pagans, imagine how good He will be with His children who obey His will!"

This time, however, during his final hour, he answered differently. *"Kol Yamai,"* he said. "All my life I wanted to accomplish the commandment of loving the Almighty with all my heart and with all my soul and with all my life—now that the opportunity to do so has been given me, how could I not be happy?" And the text in the Talmud emphasizes that "*V eota shaa, shaat kriat-sh'ma hayta.*" He said *Sh'ma,* and that happened to be the hour for reciting the *Sh'ma.* Commented Rabbenou Saul Lieberman, "Rabbi Akiba recited the *Sh'ma* because that was the thing to do—had he died at another hour of the day, he would not have recited the *Sh'ma.*" In other words: In dying, he did not intend to offer himself up as a spectacle, he did not prepare shattering speeches, grandiloquent statements; he simply followed the law. The hero of legends remained a man of *Halakha.*

Naturally, I like Lieberman's approach. But I remember asking him the questions Rabbi Akiba's disciples asked Rabbi Akiba: Why the joy? Why the laughter? Didn't the great Master understand the risk inherent in his heroic behavior? Didn't he understand that he could set an example for generations of martyrs who would go to their death with prayers on their lips rather than with weapons in their hands?

I remember, inside the kingdom of night, Hasidim singing not only *Ani Maamin* but also *"Amar Rabbi Akiba, amar Rabbi Akiba Ashrekhem Israel*—and Rabbi Akiba said, Rabbi Akiba said, Blessed and happy are you, Israel—for you are purifying yourselves before Him who purifies you. . . ."

I remember a pilgrimage to Birkenau in 1979. We stood at the place where ten thousand Jews had perished every day and night. There was silence around us, silence in us. All words, all ideas, all desires had vanished. We felt abandoned by the dead, forgotten by creation. Then, all of a sudden, Rabbi Akiba's prayer came back to me. I began whispering, "Sh'ma Israel adoshem elokenu adoshem ekhad—Hear O Israel, God is our God, God is one. . . ." And again, louder, and again, still louder, at the end we were shouting with all our might our faith in God—the God of Moses and Akiba, the God of Israel, who, at times, orders us to go backward in order to move forward. . . .

In conclusion, I love Rabbi Akiba. I love him for his humanity, for his passion for study, I love him for his love of the Jewish people. His argument with Ben P'tura on the duties and obligations of friendship? His decision teaches us something important. When the surviving friend emerges from the desert, he is no longer alone; he will have to live two lives, his own and that of his dead friend. Isn't this applicable to the American Jewish community? Six million Jews live in this land: let every one of them choose to live his or her life and that of a victim who died in battle or in a mass grave.

Obsessed with the suffering of our people, Rabbi Akiba so wanted to curtail it. But he could not.

The Talmud tells us that at the end of his life, he seemed to have changed in a curious way. Once he sided with Rabbi Eliezer *against* Rabbi Yeoshua, although he had earlier concurred with the latter on that very same issue. Furthermore, three times, regarding three specific questions, he refused to take a stand and offer a ruling—something which he had never done before. Once he went so far as to repudiate opinions formulated in his name. His mood had changed. He who used to be kind and generous toward his pupils suddenly became strangely insensitive; he insulted one, shouted at another. Once he even cursed a disciple who had dared to ask for an explanation of a certain position. The disciple died that same year.

What changed him? The ill-fated adventure in the *Pardes*? The tragic denouement of the Bar Kochba insurrection? Was he, like Adam, shown the Book of Creation so that he could see all the generations until the last? Had he seen his descendants who, centuries and centuries later, would go to their death sanctifying God's name in their own way—some by doing battle with the foe and others by opposing him with prayers and tears? Was he the first martyr of my generation's catastrophe? Is it possible that six million Jews died in order to force heaven to accelerate time and bring redemption to a people that has been longing for redemption since Rabbi Akiba—and before?

Shimon ben Azzai and Shimon ben Zoma

TANU RABANAN: this is what our Masters taught us. *Arbaa nikh-nesu lepardes:* There were four sages who entered the orchard of secret knowledge. Gathered there were: Ben Azzai, Ben Zoma, Elisha ben Abouya, and Rabbi Akiba. Possibly because he was the oldest, or the most cautious, it was Rabbi Akiba who assumed the role of guide and leader. "When you approach the place where the white marble pillars are," he told his companions, "when you plunge into the immensity of the whiteness, do not shout, 'Water, water,' for it would be a lie. And no liar can maintain himself before God."

For not having followed his instructions, his companions were punished. "Ben Azzai looked and died. Ben Zoma looked and lost his mind. Elisha ben Abouya lost his faith. Only Rabbi Akiba entered in peace and left in peace."

This, in a few evocative words, is the gist of what happened. Four men, among the most learned in the annals of Jewish thought, had launched a mysterious adventure, probably a mystical one, and found themselves separated in the end.

This story is usually told as a warning—a warning of perils that lie ahead when one undertakes certain journeys and investigations. It says, Watch out, do not tread on forbidden ground, do not attempt to scale inaccessible heights, do not let yourself be lured by what lies beyond, or else you may regret it. It reminds us, Better to prepare yourself by study, prayer, meditation, obedience to the laws, and good deeds. God does not expect man to join Him in heaven. God wants man to remain human, to become more and more human—on earth.

An analysis of the text offers four basic responses to what today we call extreme situations: madness, heresy, death, and faith;

four possible attitudes which answer man's innate need to transcend himself; four consequences of the mystical quest for the absolute.

In other words, four men can pass the same gate at the same moment, live the same experience, but what they derive from it depends on their nature. Have they "seen" the same pillars?

There were four sages who entered the orchard of forbidden knowledge, says the Talmud. They had taken the decision together—was their motivation the same? The experience changed their lives, but for different reasons, perhaps, and surely with different results. And, in the end, the adventure that began in ecstasy and fervor came to nothing. The four friends were driven apart, defeated, except, of course, for Rabbi Akiba. He somehow got out *beshalom,* in peace, perhaps even as a man of peace. His apparent serenity leaves me perplexed, as does the rebellion of Elisha ben Abouya. We shall study them later.

What do we know about Ben Azzai and Ben Zoma? They were young, fervent, learned, enthusiastic, and passionately involved in mystical explorations—puzzling and tragic characters. That is more or less all we know about them. About their two companions—Rabbi Akiba and the son of Abouyah—there is much detailed information. Ben Azzai? Ben Zoma? Often their first names are omitted, perhaps because they were both called Shimon. Actually, in the vast Talmudic literature there are few sages about whom so little biographical data are available—as if the authors of the Talmud had been too embarrassed to let us get acquainted with them. They were almost certainly victims—but *whose?* Of the *Pardes?* Of their own curiosity? Of their thirst for danger?

Let us begin with Shimon ben Azzai. Born in the Galilee in the second century, he died at an unspecified age. Some sources suggest that he may have died a very young man, at the age of twenty. The *Baal hatossafot al ha-Torah* believes that he was in his forties when he passed away.

We do know that his parents were poor. We know that much because, according to one version, Rabbi Akiba's daughter—his fiancée?—supposedly urged him to dedicate himself to study and let her support him. Is this why he deeply respects women and their right to study Torah? "A father must teach his daughter Torah," he says, disagreeing with Rabbi Eliezer and Rabbi Yeoshua.

A disciple of Rabbi Yeoshua ben Hananya—whom he often quotes—and of Rabbi Akiba, whose friend and accomplice he becomes, Ben Azzai seems outspoken, hot-tempered. Once, having lost some arguments, he exclaimed, "It is easier to rule over the whole world than to convince hypocritical scholars." He studied Greek. At his death, the sages proclaimed, "With him, we have lost the last of the diligent scholars." Diligence was his signature. Endowed with a sharp mind, he impressed his peers. Much later, Abayy spoke of his own sharp insight, his *Harifut*, and compared it to that of Ben Azzai: "I am the Ben Azzai of my time," he said. His opponent, the famous Rava, used exactly the same expression: "I am the Ben Azzai of my time." And yet . . . Ben Azzai is not a rabbi. The president of the academy refused to ordain him. His case bears a strange resemblance to that of his friend Shimon ben Zoma, who did not receive rabbinic ordination either. Everyone sang their praises. They were among the four young scholars who interpreted before the sages—but they were not rabbis. The Talmud acknowledges that they deserved to be, but they were not. Were they any less learned than the others? Less pious? Why didn't Rabbi Akiba, Ben Azzai's close friend and prospective father-in-law besides, do anything for him? Precisely because he was his father-in-law? As you can see, the Talmud allows no nepotism.

Let us talk briefly about this family relationship between Rabbi Akiba and Ben Azzai; it is mentioned in a story that deals with Rabbi Akiba's own marriage. Rachel, the disowned daughter of the wealthy Jerusalemite Kalba Savua, saw her husband, Akiba, go off to study for twelve years. On the day of his return, Rabbi Akiba overheard a neighbor ask Rachel, "How long will you keep living like a widow, separated from your husband?" "If he listened to me," answered Rachel, "he'd leave for twelve more years." So Rabbi Akiba left, this time with her permission. The Talmud comments: "Rabbi Akiba's daughter acted the same way with Shimon ben Azzai: the daughter took after her mother."

In spite of the story, the facts are not so clear, except for one thing: there was a relationship—or the beginning of one—between Ben Azzai and Rabbi Akiba's daughter. But did they marry? One source says yes, but adds that they were also divorced. Another says that they were engaged, but that Ben Azzai broke the engagement. He had no children. "Whosoever has no child is like one who is guilty of bloodshed," says Rabbi Eliezer. Rabbi Yaakov disagrees: "Whosoever has no child," says he, is like one who diminishes the image of God, for it is written that God created man in His image." Whereupon Ben Azzai pronounces both of them right: "Whosoever has no child," he declares, "is like one who sheds the blood of man *and* diminishes the image of God." Strange, but the sages did not appreciate his role as peacemaker. They put him in his place: "Look who is talking," said Rabbi Eleazar ben Azaryah. "Look who is commenting on the First Commandment, to be fruitful and to multiply. One who has no child himself." And he went on, "Some speak well and act well; you speak well, but your deeds contradict your words." Embarrassed, Ben Azzai answered, "What can I do? My soul is in love with Torah." Poor Ben Azzai, torn between the demands of real life and the irresistible appeal of study. That answer is touching. So great is his love for Torah that it dominates his entire being. The Torah alone is his life—it gives meaning to his life. One does not argue with the soul, the soul defies argument. It is reason which loves to argue, not the soul. The soul burns. One must nourish its flame; one must become its flame.

But even as he is saying all this, he knows that he has no argument. In fact, his arguments turn against him. If he, indeed, loves the Torah so deeply, if he is so devoted to it, why does he not obey its First Commandment ordering man to found a home, a family, to pass life on? "*P'ru u'rvu,*" says the Torah. Man must be fruitful and multiply. The world is here to be inhabited, to be tended, to be reclaimed for future generations. Isn't it odd that Ben Azzai chooses to reject the First Commandment, a precondition for all the others?

Ben Azzai is well aware of this. The proof? "As for the world," he says, "it will go on, thanks to others." We can imagine his despair on acknowledging that he is incapable of obeying the First Commandment—the easiest of them all. Anyone can give life just as anyone can take it. But not Ben Azzai?

It is possible that he is afraid of women—afraid they might distract him from study. To him, they suggest promiscuity, and he is against it. Listen to the Talmud: "Nakhum of Gamzu whispered to Rabbi Akiba, who whispered to Ben Azzai, who whispered to other disciples, warning them that scholars ought not hang around their wives like roosters."

Still, I must admit that this hypothesis does not satisfy me. Ben Azzai's relationship with his fiancée, or wife, disturbs me, not on a physical but on a metaphysical level. I have the impression that the key lies in this seemingly minor discussion in the school of Rabbi Eliezer the Great. Ben Azzai is a complex character. We discern within him conflicts, tensions, pressures; we sense in him total anguish. *"Hitzitz vamet,"* says the Talmud. "He looked and he died." What did he want to see? The *Shekhina?* When did he die? How did he die? In what circumstances? One version suggests he might have been one of the first victims of Hadrian's persecutions. In the Midrash, *Eikha rabah,* he heads the list of the Ten Martyrs of the Faith.

Now let us turn our attention to Ben Azzai's partner and friend, whose destiny is no less bewildering.

We know even less of Shimon ben Zoma than we do of Shimon ben Azzai. A disciple of Rabbi Yeoshua ben Hananya and of Rabbi Akiba, he quickly gained a reputation as a scholar. "With him died the last exegetist of Scripture," says the Talmud. And further, "Whoever sees Ben Zoma in his dream will surely gain access to knowledge." Although not a rabbi, he won a debate with his teacher Rabbi Yeoshua ben Hananya regarding what sacrifice the Nazzir—the ascetic—must offer to God.

But who *was* Ben Zoma? Who was Zoma, the father? Where did Shimon spend his childhood, his adolescence? What were his aspirations, his fears? There are few laws bearing his name, few decisions attributed to him. Obsessed with prayer, he insisted on the need to incorporate the Exodus story in both the evening and morning services. Sage and moralist, he has contributed a number of simple but useful aphorisms. One teaches the importance of self-control. Commenting on a Biblical verse, he said, "Do not glimpse at another man's vineyard; if you did, do not enter it; if you entered, do not look; if you looked, do not touch the grapes; if you did, do not eat them; if you did—you are lost." Another: "Who is wise? One who learns from each and every person. Who is strong? One who can dominate his instincts and his passions. Who is rich? One who is satisfied with what he has. Who is honored? One who honors his fellow man."

Following the call of mysticism, he joined his companions in their unique adventure in the *Pardes.* How did he fare? *Hitzitz venifga.* He looked and lost his mind. And to explain his misfortune, the Talmud quotes a proverb of King Solomon's: "Have you found honey? Don't eat too much of it, or you will end up vomiting." In other words, Don't look too far, don't go beyond the fence. Ben Zoma did go too far. He looked where he should not have looked. His reason was shaken, and it abandoned him.

An intriguing character. We are told that as he read in the Book of Genesis the verse *Vayaas elokim et harakia*—and God made the firmament—Ben Zoma let out a cry that shook all the heavens: "What? God *made* the skies? Isn't it written that God used language to create the world?"

A scrupulous character, Ben Zoma. Uncompromising, un-yielding. That is why I find him so intriguing. And yet . . . There is something about him that eludes me. A sage in torment—that much we understand. A sage in revolt, that, too, we understand. But a sage who has lost his mind? A sage who is mad? Right from the start, Ben Zoma aroused my interest—no; more than that: my excitement. Madness—and particularly mystical madness—is, after all, present in all my writings: Is it possible that Ben Zoma, with-out my noticing it, managed to slip into my stories under one alias or another? Ben Zoma has always belonged to my world, but it took me a long time to become aware of it.

Now that I am aware, I try to get to know him better. I want to find out if reciprocity exists in our secret relationship: granted, he belongs to my world, but do my characters belong to his? Difficult question. Not enough clues. A few anecdotes, a few par-ables, a few words: not much more. Still, there is one story we can study—and remember—for later. It tells of an encounter between Ben Zoma and his Master. This encounter took place toward the end of his life; in fact, it foreshadows his end. The story is told in the Talmud four times, in three different versions.

The first: One day Rabbi Yeoshua ben Hananya found him-self on the steps of the Har Habayit, the Temple Mount. Ben Zoma greeted him but did not stand up. The Master addressed him in typical Talmudic style, that is, short and incisive: *"Meayin u'lean, ben Zoma?* Where do you come from and where are you going, son of Zoma?" And the disciple answered, "I was meditat-ing on the mystery of Creation. Scripture speaks of the waters above and the waters below with almost no separation. As it is written, 'And the spirit of God hovered upon the waters,' it re-minds me of the turtledove hovering above its young without touching them." Whereupon the Master said to his disciples, "The son of Zoma is still outside"—meaning outside of his senses.

The second version is slightly different. This time, Rabbi

Yeoshua ben Hananya was walking along the road and he met Ben Zoma, who did not greet him. There again, the Master asked his disciple where he was coming from and where he was going, and the disciple spoke of his meditations on the mystery of the waters at the moment of Creation. Commented the Master, "The son of Zoma is already outside," meaning, beyond reprieve.

The third version shows us Ben Zoma seated, lost in thought. It was his Master who passed by and it was he who greeted the disciple—who did not answer. He greeted him a second time, and still the disciple did not answer. Then the Master greeted him a third time, and only then did the disciple answer, looking and sounding panic-stricken. Rabbi Yeoshua ben Hananya asked him, "*Meayin ha-raglayim?* Where are your legs coming from?" meaning "Where do you come from?" or "Where are you at this moment?" Or, better yet, "Where are your thoughts coming from? From what source?" And Ben Zoma replied, "I was thinking," but without saying what about. The Master cried out, "I call heaven and earth as witnesses that I shall not budge from here until you have told me the source of your thoughts." Only then did Ben Zoma answer: "I was meditating on what separated the waters above and the waters below at the time of Creation." And Rabbi Yeoshua Ben Hananya commented, "Ben Zoma is already gone." And, in fact, Ben Zoma did die several days later.

We can imagine the disciple utterly disoriented. Pursuing a thought that carried him far away, he neither saw nor heard anybody: he followed other voices, saw other images. His revered rabbi was standing before him—he passed him by without taking notice. The rabbi addressed him—his thoughts were elsewhere. His spirit wandered through time and space. He was outside reality and life itself.

Let us go back to the adventure in the *Pardes*. His punishment seems harsher than that of his companions. Ben Azzai dies, but without suffering, without seeing himself diminished from day to day, without having to experience the decline of his mind. One could say that Ben Zoma died before his death. How could we not sympathize with his suffering?

But let us turn again to the question which has surely preoccupied us from the start: What did they see, those four companions, as they entered the orchard of "forbidden" knowledge? What did they glimpse that was so terrifying, that made them suffer consequences as extreme as death, madness, apostasy, and infallible faith?

Some scholars believe that what we have here is simply a group of esoteric studies as was commonly found in Judea in those times. The four sages had formed a study group dealing with certain lofty and perilous subjects, such as the mystery of the beginning, the mystery of the chariot—the divine action in history—or, perhaps, the mystery of the end, of the messianic denouement. But such studies may cause harm to the mind and spirit, since their object is beyond our grasp.

To students concerned with ethics, the adventure has a more concrete and also a more immediate meaning: The four friends had tried to understand the experience of Jewish suffering, which had reached heights unsurpassed at that time.

Perhaps we should repeat what we remember from our own reading of Jewish history.

The second century of our era had brought cruel measures against the Jewish population of Judea. The Temple was in ruins; the Jews who remained had difficulty arousing themselves from mourning. Jewish heroes were sold into slavery in the market-places of the Orient. In Rome, the emperors regarded the oppression of the Jewish people as a political priority. And yet, up in the mountains, Jewish warriors refused to give up. They were preparing to resume the battle for freedom under the command of Bar Kochba.

While living in anxiety, hiding in caves, they tried to invent reasons for hope. Because of Hadrian's decrees, the Jew became a target for every impulse of hatred and cruelty. Whoever taught Torah, whoever studied Torah, was condemned to death, as was anyone who observed the Shabbat or had his son circumcised. The land where life had been celebrated as in no other land had been turned into a cemetery for its Jewish citizens.

Rome forbade study? The Jewish people studied nevertheless. The teachers were put in prison? They went on teaching inside the prisons. At the risk of their lives, the Masters met with their disciples and taught them to become Masters in turn.

We have said it earlier: the four friends of the *Pardes* symbolized the various attitudes within the Jewish community toward Roman occupation. Ben Abouya represents active collaboration, Rabbi Akiba active resistance, Ben Azzai passive death, and Ben Zoma flight into meditation leading to madness.

And what about the *Pardes* in all this? It represents their common quest. The task they had taken upon themselves was the search for an answer to the question, Why had God chosen to punish his people so severely? The classic problem of theodicy was more acute than ever before. In the face of so much suffering, collective and individual, our sages could not possibly have abstained from inquiring into the roles of man and God. How to explain the coexistence of good and evil in God's scheme? How to justify the triumph of the godless conqueror and the agony of his victims with their impeccable past?

Here and there, voices were raised in protest against a heaven that permitted the martyrdom of the pious Masters. *Zu Torah vezu skhara?* Can this be the law and this its reward? One sage went so far as to hurl a cry of despair at God: *"Mi kamokha baelim adoshem? Al Tikra elim ki im ilemim:* Who is mute as you are, O God? You see your children humiliated and you remain silent!"

Our four friends wanted to understand. They turned to mystic contemplation to come to a better understanding. Or at least to reach the conclusion that they were unable to understand. Because that, too, is mysticism: to glimpse the path that opens up beyond comprehension. The mystic sees, the philosopher listens. Our four sages entered the *Pardes* to *see* the truth, since they were unable to understand. In mysticism, the eye may look forward or backward, toward the source or toward the goal, toward the beginning or toward deliverance.

As we shall realize later, Rabbi Akiba was looking for the resolution of history: redemption. He told himself that suffering was inflicted on man to prepare him for the coming of the Messiah. When the people suffered martyrdom, it was a sign that collective redemption was near.

Elisha ben Abouya, on the other hand, saw no link between suffering and redemption. That is why he decided to turn away from a history that established such a link. In choosing denial, he signaled his conclusion that suffering, on the level of history, is unnecessary.

As to the other two companions, what was it they found in the *Pardes?* What was their mental and philosophical attitude toward the punishment inflicted upon their people? Let us stay with them for a while.

Ben Azzai moves us, doesn't he? In his private life, he seems so naive, so innocent, almost defenseless. We sense that he is both timid and intimidated. In matters of law he is outspoken; but when the subject is personal, when he disagrees with a sage, he expresses himself with deference. Because he is younger? No. He is conscious of flaws in his private life. He knows that he is capable of debating ideas and principles, but as soon as his own life is mentioned, he feels at fault, vulnerable.

Let us listen to a somewhat delicate but revealing story. The Talmud tells of a debate concerning a jealous husband who, before two witnesses, warns his wife not to talk to a certain man; however, she and this man are observed entering a hiding place and remaining there long enough to commit a certain sin. The sages argue back and forth: How much time does a couple need to do what they ought not to be doing? Each one spoke up according to his own experience. Ben Azzai took part in the debate and expressed his opinion. And the Talmud asks what it considered a logical question. How could Ben Azzai know, since he was not married? There are, of course, only two possibilities: either he *was* married and got divorced, or he knew by the grace of God.

Which somehow leads me to think that Ben Azzai must have broken his engagement before marriage. He was not the marrying kind; the sometimes annoying, sometimes exasperating routine of married life was not to his liking. He was intoxicated with God and had no need of anyone else: there was no place in his life for another human being. He needed ecstasy—continuous, all-pervading, lasting ecstasy. And that he found only in God.

One legend depicts the bachelor Ben Azzai surrounded by his disciples, discoursing on the secrets of the Torah. Suddenly a flame descended from the sky and enveloped the group. Ben Azzai was asked, "Did this occur because you study the fiery mystery of the Merkavah?" That would have explained the fire, since God is in the fire too. "Not at all," answered Ben Azzai. "I pursue quite ordinary studies. I link the words of the Torah to those of the prophets, and those of the prophets to the written words—and it is the words themselves that have started to dance and to rejoice, as they did on the day when, lit by the divine flame, the law was given on Sinai. The words are the same and so are the flames."

Ah, how I would have liked to have been there, listening to Ben Azzai, watching his words dance in a circle of flames! Isn't this the dream of any writer, any teacher—to find words that will sing and dance, words that will burn?

Still, he was refused ordination. Did the scholars consider him too much of a poet? Surely they must have thought him eccentric. But above all they must have objected to his celibacy. Jewish tradition expects a Master to set an example for his students. It rejects cynicism as much as it condemns hypocrisy. Perfect harmony must be maintained between word and action. A Master who fails to follow his own precepts does not deserve the title. One cannot love humanity while disdaining the people who make it up. One cannot love the Torah while giving some laws preference over others. The Torah is one and indivisible. It is a father's duty to teach it to his son; and a man's duty to become a father. That is, he may not choose to be the last of his line, he may not deprive the people of Israel of its future. That is why neither Shimon ben Azzai nor Shimon ben Zoma became rabbis.

But Ben Azzai was not unhappy. Something of a fatalist, he accepted his situation. He said: Everything happens in due time; man is called upon to take his place, he is given what is his. Everything comes from above. We receive only our due. The same holds true for countries: none can take another's place. There is a point where everything comes back into balance.

Here is some useful advice he gave his readers: "Do not ascend the tribune of honor. On the contrary, you would do well to come down a few steps. It is better to be asked, 'Get up' than 'Get down.'"

Of course, he sometimes showed disappointment. He was human, after all. And he was aware of his qualities. One day he explained, "All those sages are no more to me than the skin on a head of garlic—except for Rabbi Akiba."

Rabbi Akiba was his Master. He loved and admired him. Once he followed him all the way to the toilet to find out how a student of Torah ought to behave in strictest privacy. Both he and Ben Zoma were truly perfect disciples—so says Rashi. When a man says to a girl, "You are my wife on the condition that I am a disciple," that's enough to make the marriage valid. The Talmud explicitly adds: "For a man to rightfully bear the title of disciple, there is no need to be as learned as Rabbi Shimon ben Azzai or Rabbi Shimon ben Zoma." Rashi comments: "These two sages were bachelors and never received their ordination. . . . Nevertheless, in matters of learning, they had no equal." As far as they are concerned, it is probably better to be a perfect disciple than an imperfect Master.

They were both especially well versed in Midrash. Their aphorisms convey profound moral wisdom. Ben Azzai says: "Do not despise anything or anyone, for each being has his hour and each thing its place." All that exists was created by God, all that exists bears witness to God.

And further: "Hurry and fulfill all the commandments, even those you consider of minor importance." They all come by the same right from God; they all lead to God. And further: "The reward for a good deed, a *mitzva,* is the *mitzva* itself. . . . One good deed leads to another, whereas a bad one is the result of another bad one." In his interpretation of the Biblical Commandment "Love thy neighbor as thyself," he disagrees—which he doesn't do often—with his Master, Rabbi Akiba, who puts this verse at the pinnacle of the Torah ethic. Ben Azzai says that he knows another verse that he places higher, namely *"Ze sefer toldot Adam*—This is the book of man's origins." Why? Suppose a human being dislikes himself, inflicts suffering and humiliation upon himself, seeks to destroy himself. Ought he to do the same to his fellow man? No, says Ben Azzai. The important thing is for all of us to know that we have the same origin, the same ancestors, that we are all children of the same father. Here is the universality of the Torah, here is the humanism that imbues the tradition of a persecuted people. To say that Ben Azzai formulated this thought, this principle, at a time when his brothers and sisters were being massacred by the Roman conquerer, is to recognize how exalted a vision he had of the Jewish condition and the human condition. In spite of suffering, in spite of persecutions, he envisioned a radiant future because he reminded men of their common past. In other words: If we were all to remember the source of our experiences, we could go with stronger faith toward the future. If only man wanted to remember. . . . But it seems they do not. The world could be beautiful and hospitable but it is not. Is this what Ben Azzai discovered in the *Pardes?* That it is too late? That man refuses to live happily under the sign of truth? Is this the discovery that killed him? Is this the despair he faced when he entered the forbidden orchard? Is it the same despair that pushed Ben Zoma into madness?

At the end of his life, Ben Azzai became melancholy. Listen to his sobering advice: "Whoever remembers these four things will be saved from sin. Where does man come from? From darkness. Where is he going? To darkness. By whom shall he be judged? By the Creator of the universe, who knows everything and owns everything, and can be neither flattered nor cheated. Where does man go: To hell and nothingness."

As for Ben Zoma, throughout his days, he often spoke of life with gratitude. He considered himself fortunate compared to Adam. Adam had to work hard to feed and clothe himself. "I," said Zoma, "I have all I need. Adam had to sow and reap, prepare the dough, bake bread; I have everything here, right at hand." Why did he refuse to get married and establish a home? For the same reasons as his friend Ben Azzai? No one put the question to him. A dreamer, reserved, secretive, he sought to lose himself in the mystical, in the blinding light of the obscure. His reward? Madness. The madness of a man who sought to understand that which escapes understanding; who aspired to knowledge that defies knowledge; who neglected the future because the past alone attracted him. Of the four companions, it is Ben Zoma who seems to me the most tragic. Did he know that he was losing his mind? Did he struggle to hold on to his sanity? Did he long for it, reach for it?

These are dangerous questions; perhaps they are out of place, but let us ask nevertheless. Can we say with absolute certainty that Shimon ben Azzai and Shimon ben Zoma did not enter the *Pardes* looking, one for madness, the other for death? Or perhaps for shelter from the victories of the enemy? Or to protest against them? Since all around them the wicked were powerful and fortunate, while the just lived in fear and trembling, why should the two friends not have chosen to rebel by rejecting life and reason?

The bond between the two friends is stronger than that between them and the other two. They are always together. Does fate in the end separate them? No. The expression *Hitzitz venifga*—"He looked and lost his mind"—is usually applied to Ben Azzai; but it also describes Ben Zoma's end. One could say that the Talmud makes a point of the two friends' common fate: they were subjected to the same punishment. Both lost what was most precious to them: reason and life. Both—and in this they differ from the other two—were interested in the esoteric science of the beginnings. Why? Perhaps to *place* injustice. Where did it start? Why was it part of Creation? But it is too dangerous to look too far back.

Let us read once more the story of the *Pardes*—and this time, to the end. Do you remember? *Arbaa nikhnesu lepardes:* They were four who entered the orchard of forbidden knowledge. Rashi comments: They pronounced a sacred name and found themselves in heaven, in the upper spheres where the *Shekhina* resides. Ben Azzai saw her and died. Ben Zoma lost his mind. Ben Abouya lost his faith. Rabbi Akiba alone entered in peace and left the orchard in peace. One possible explanation is the following: Ben Abouya was concerned with the present only, therefore he lost his faith; Rabbi Akiba was interested in the distant future, therefore he was spared; Ben Zoma and Ben Azzai were interested in the beginnings, and that is why they were punished.

Rabbi Akiba tried to save them. Before plunging into the adventure, he warned them not to shout "Water" when seeing white marbles. A baffling passage. The episode between Ben Zoma and Rabbi Yeoshua may help us understand it. Ben Zoma lost his mind because he had meditated on the "separation of the waters." He had not heeded Rabbi Akiba's warning against looking back at the mystery of Creation. It is dangerous to glimpse the first moment in time, the first separation willed by God.

In conclusion: For both Ben Azzai and Ben Zoma the glorious adventure of the *Pardes* ended in failure. They must have forgotten man's need and obligation to live in the present. Humanity is both impediment and refuge for man. Whoever violates humanity is bound to stumble and fall.

Only Rabbi Akiba saved himself. He sought peace for his people and for the world—and that is what saved him.

Did Ben Azzai wish to die? Did Ben Zoma seek madness? Did they succeed in protecting their people from further suffering? Thinking of them, do we suffer less?

These questions remain open, and that is their beauty. The *Pardes*, too, remains open, and that is the power of its spell—and its challenge, too. Yes: they were four sages who entered the orchard of forbidden knowledge. Why did they try to lure us along? And why did we choose to stay behind? Excessive prudence? Perhaps. What frightens us is not the whiteness of the white marble pillars. What frightens us is the darkness of the fire.

Elisha ben Abouya

... AND, HAVING ENTERED the *Pardes,* the orchard of forbidden knowledge, *Akher* (Elisha ben Abouya) lost his faith.

How can one not be touched by his tragedy? For his fate was tragic, after all. Here was a learned man, a great scholar who devoted his life to serve God and understand His ways; suddenly he cast aside his certainties and chose the perilous path of denial. Unlike his friends Ben Zoma and Ben Azzai, he was not punished. Heresy is considered a sin, not a punishment. When someone decides to rebel against heaven, it is he and not God who is responsible.

Elisha: the stranger who inhabits man, a faceless, nameless threat that comes from within. Elisha: the incarnation of extreme audacity and of solitude as well.

Here is a man who is anguished, constantly defying the heavens he is invoking, the people who are condemning him, his own brothers who are repudiating him. It is impossible to remain indifferent to his battles and to his plight. Of the four sages to haunt the secret recesses of the *Pardes,* it is he who from the literary, philosophical, and humanist point of view seems the most stimulating, and from the theological viewpoint the most challenging. His face is scarred, his soul wounded. One gets the impression that his adventure has never ended. He is still in danger; and in his presence, one's inner stability is still on the edge of being shaken.

Here is an instance of man rejecting death or faith, or even madness, as solutions, of man intent of pursuing his quest inexorably with open eyes and lucid mind, come what may. If the price to be paid is nothingness, well, he will pay it. Anything but easy options. Anything but self-delusion. He is not looking for an easy way out; he does not want to get out. What he wants is to remain on the battlefield. And to fight.

Elisha: the man who dares to proclaim that the end is not the end. And to question the pertinence of a beyond. Elisha: the man who knows that he is lost and nonetheless feels no regret.

We shall try to see what occurred to Elisha ben Abouya before, during, and after his crisis—and what he could have glimpsed inside the orchard, what could have made him break with the people to whom he was once teacher and leader. We shall try to discover the events that made a wise man cease being wise, a pious man cease being pious, that made a believing man—a rabbi—wish to become a renegade.

What could have happened to make a Master and close friend and associate of Rabbi Akiba choose estrangement, collaboration with the enemy, and perhaps treason? Furthermore, how is one to explain the amazing loyalty that the great Rabbi Meir, sage and miracle maker, showed him to the very end?

And conversely, if Elisha ben Abouya betrayed neither God nor his people, how is one to understand the hostility he aroused in the scholarly community? Why was he vilified? Why was he called *Akher* (the Other), the outsider, the alien, the traitor? Why was he deprived of his name, of his individuality, of his right to an identity? (David Weiss Halivni points out that in ancient manuscripts of the Talmud, he is praised for his creativeness, he is referred to first as Rabbi Elisha ben Abouya, then as Elisha ben Abouya, later as Ben Abouya, and finally, and definitively, as *Akher*.)

Who is Elisha ben Abouya? His story is familiar to students of Jewish lore, and yet, in order to evaluate his motivations, it is easiest to see him in profile, from the shadows.

We know that he was considered one of the most prominent Tannaim of the second century C.E. His father was upper-class and shrewd, with connections in the highest and most learned circles of Jerusalem. All of the elite were invited to Elisha's circumcision and all attended. While studying at the Yavneh Academy, Elisha was a disciple of Eliezer ben Hyrcanos and Yeoshua ben Hananyah. He was, by all accounts, a brilliant student—he must have been to have become Akiba's fellow traveler. After the destruction of Betar, he developed a taste for mysticism, which led him to the fateful excursion into the *Pardes*. What else do we know? He was married. We are told that he had at least one daughter, and at least one disciple, Rabbi Meir. We also know that his interests encompassed secular and lay sciences, Greek philosophy, and especially Greek poetry.

A more serious matter: he maintained relations with the Roman authorities. He was their adviser, if not their informer. Toward the end of his life he was destitute and ill, and, unlike his companion Rabbi Akiba and his disciple Rabbi Meir, he died in his home, in his bed.

But the essential is not known: the event that shattered his hopes or delusions, and distorted his relationship with his people and their common creator, remains shrouded in mystery. What provoked Elisha's fall, and who bears responsibility for it? After all, Elisha was not the only one to flirt, or even collaborate, with the Roman authorities. Yossi ben Kisma flattered them as much as he did, and Yehuda ben Gerim denounced his fellow Jews to them as he did. Nor was he the only one to violate commandments of Torah: Eliezer ben Dordaya and Resh-Lakish were not saints. Did he study Greek philosophy? So did Rabbi Gamliel, who had a thousand students: five hundred studied Torah and five hundred studied Greek poetry and philosophy. Many important Tannaim felt they needed to acquire some knowledge of Greek philosophy so as to be able to discuss it with foreign scholars. Why, then, is Elisha ben Abouya alone considered a renegade? Was it only because when he left the orchard, he opted for the most difficult, painful, and unrewarding path?

Of course, his apostasy provoked considerable emotion in the nation—and consequently in the Talmud. Elisha ben Abouya wasn't just anyone. His desertion was an act, not a gesture. It was pondered, commented upon, in all circles. His desertion had the effect of an explosion, with everybody trying to explain its roots and reasons.

A variety of theories have been offered. One places the guilt on his mother. Naturally. While Elisha's mother was still carrying him in her belly, she breathed the incense of pagan temples. She should have been more careful. Because she went where Jews must not go, her son, in the end, did the same. Being a good Jewish boy, he loved his mother a little too much.

A second hypothesis, to show no favoritism, places the burden upon the father, the honorable Abouya. He is the one to blame. Too rich, too calculating, too cynical. Too many ulterior motives in all his actions. Elisha himself says so. Let's listen to him:

"My father, Abouya, was among the notables of Jerusalem. For the ceremony of my circumcision he invited his peers and also Rabbi Eliezer and Rabbi Yeoshua. People ate and people drank, as is customary at such occasions. Carried away by the good cheer, some started to clap their hands, others to dance, still others to recite poems or acrostics. And then, at one point, Rabbi Eliezer turned toward Rabbi Yeoshua, and this is what he said: 'Here are these guests who are doing their work—but we are not doing ours.' And so they sat down and began to study. First Torah, then the Prophets. From the Prophets they moved to Scripture—and they studied with such fervor that a fire came down from heaven and surrounded them. Seized with fear, Abouya cried out: 'What are you doing, my Masters? Are you going to set my house on fire?' 'May God save us from such an intention,' they replied. 'We were simply studying Torah and then the Prophets and then Scripture, and the words were filled with joy, just as they were long ago when they were heard at Sinai, and a flame was licking them, just as it did long ago at Sinai, for at Sinai it was the divine fire that offered them their immortality.' Impressed, my father, Abouya, made this remark: 'If such is the power of Torah, I shall consecrate my son to its study.' " "And," concluded Elisha, "because his motives were not pure but selfish, because Abouya had in mind power and not Torah, all my studies were in vain; they did not save me."

This explanation did not satisfy the Talmud, just as the first did not. Man is not doomed by his era, nor is he by his parents. He is free to begin anew another tale, another task. For every individual, the book remains open, and it is he himself who will write it from the first page to the last. There is a limit to parents' responsibility. If Elisha opts for alienation, if he decides to break with his parents—it is not their fault.

But then, whose fault is it? God's? Yes, affirms Elisha, according to another Talmudic school of thought. Tormented by the difficult problem of theodicy, torn between faith and justice, Elisha rebels not against creation but against the Creator and his impossible laws.

A story: One day, when Elisha ben Abouya was in the valley of Gennesar, meditating, he noticed a man climbing a date tree—

on Shabbat—in order to dislodge a bird's nest. The man left the baby birds and took away the mother—and nothing happened to him. He went home safe and sound.

That same night, after Shabbat, Elisha saw another man climbing another date tree, where there was another bird's nest. This man freed the mother but took away the baby birds. When he touched the ground, he was bitten by a snake and died.

Well, it is written in Scripture, if you should encounter a bird's nest in a tree or on the ground, free the mother and take care of the little ones. This commandment is one of the two which specifically ensures man a precious reward. Whoever follows it will live a long time.

Thus we sympathize with Elisha's anger. The first man had violated the commandment and yet he went home carefree and happy; meanwhile the second man, who should have received the reward of life, was gravely punished. Disgusted, disillusioned, Elisha ceased to believe then and there. His complaint? God does not keep his promises. Since in God's universe, just men suffer and wicked ones are covered with glory, then Elisha has no use for it. If there is conflict between God's word and God's deed, then Elisha would rather change sides—and join the wicked. He does not say that God does not judge, but that God judges badly. He does not proclaim that the law is unjust, but that God does not abide by it.

A kind attitude at first glance, and understandable: choosing between a stranger and God, he rejects God. He prefers to be on the side of the victim—especially one whose condition results from divine injustice. How can one object to such moral courage? Here Elisha appears as a hero—a spokesman for man.

We find this same concern for immanent justice in another episode where the collective destiny of the Jewish people serves as a catalyst for Elisha.

During the extreme persecutions, the era of Harugei-Malkhut, he saw the tongue of Rabbi Yehuda ha-Nakhtom, the baker, dragged through the dust by a dog. This was too much for him. He began to howl: *"Zu Torah vezu Skhara?* Is this then Torah and this its reward?" Elisha ben Abouya, mad with pain, never recovered from this trauma: he broke with his Jewish past.

Variation on the same theme: he saw the tongue not of Rabbi Yahuda ha-Nakhtom, but that of another martyr: Khutzpit ha-Meturgeman, the interpreter, dragged through the dust not by a dog, but a pig. "This tongue that was spreading pearls of Torah, here it is desecrated," Elisha cried. He suffered so much that he turned to sin—and became "Other," a changed person, a renegade.

Here again we are forced to pay tribute to his rebellion. Aren't his outbursts those of a man of principle and courage who feels concern for his fellow man? After all, he could have opted for indifference. He could have turned his gaze away—made himself deaf and blind to avoid involvement. He could have buried himself in his book, which on this particular Shabbat he was in the midst of studying. Nothing indicates that *he* was hunted or persecuted by the Romans—that he personally felt any threat to his life or safety. Nothing indicates that his indictment of God was a consequence of personal suffering. He had not suffered. It was another man's plight that moved him, upset him, angered him. It was injustice befalling his fellow man that pushed him to undertake a revision of values, to disavow the system which until then had linked him to the world and what transcends it. His was a disinterested, authentic revolt, a pure and total refusal, which should weigh in his favor even today, especially today—when indifference, on an unprecedented scale, has become mankind's curse and punishment. Why then this irrevocable condemnation that became his lot? Why then does he remain in the memory we call Talmud a symbol of apostasy, synonymous with treason?

Let us turn the question around. Since this history book that *is* the Talmud does treat him as a renegade, perhaps it follows that Elisha's revolt, which we have described as pure and genuine and moral, was less pure and less selfless than we might have thought? We shall return to this later. Let us accept the premise for now that rebellion there was—and that it was complete, total, not limited to theology. Indeed, it reached into all existing domains. The epithet *Akher,* "Other," must be taken literally: he was no longer the same person.

In the first place, he changed his milieu. We no longer find him with scholars and students at the yeshiva, but in quarters of ill repute. One particular Shabbat, he meets a prostitute. He wants her. She recognizes him: "Aren't you Elisha ben Abouya?" she asks, astonished. He pulls a radish from the soil—which is forbidden on Shabbat—and hands it to her. "He is indeed Other," she states, "he is no longer one of our own." The anecdote illustrates two equally important points. One: long ago, even women of ill repute knew the sometimes complicated laws of Shabbat. Two: Elisha ben Abouya needed to buy their favors.

In the early phase of his rebellion, he still visited houses of study, but his heart was no longer in it. For him Torah became a stumbling block rather than an ally to lean on. Even his language changed: *"Zemer yevani lo passak mipif"*—he was forever quoting Greek poets, especially Homer. *"Sifrei minim nashru mikheko"*—his pockets were stuffed with atheistic, anti-Jewish pamphlets. Self-fulfillment within the framework of Judaism no longer sufficed.

He began to flirt with the Romans. Often seen with them, he became their collaborator, actively working for assimilation—forced assimilation. He would walk into schools where children, sitting in front of open books, were studying Torah, and shout, "What are they doing here? Let this one become a mason and this one a carpenter, and this one—let him follow a painter's trade, and this one, let him become a tailor! Let each one of you go and learn his trade elsewhere!" The pupils listened, closed their books and went away, which was precisely what the Romans wanted. Their goal was to silence, once and for all, the voice and the call of Torah—source and justification of Jewish survival since the beginning of time. Yes, unbelievable but true: having left the God of Israel, Elisha ben Abouya had joined the enemy of Israel, and had become its accomplice. Yes: Rabbi Akiba's friend, Ben Zomah and Ben Azzai's companion, thus became their enemies' ally—thus justifying their aims and tactics. He gave them legitimacy.

Certain texts do not hesitate to accuse him of treason—both ideological and political. They claim that he was an active informer, an *agent provocateur,* an accessory to police brutality and repression; that he used his *Halakhic* knowledge against his fellow Jews. He made it a practice to unmask Jews attempting to outwit their tormentors. An example: It is forbidden to carry a load on Shabbat, but under certain conditions two persons are authorized to do the work of one—then, technically, the sin is less serious. The Romans did not know this, but Elisha did—and so when he saw two Jews carrying a beam on Shabbat, he hastened to inform them. This is significant. Not only did he help the police mistreat the Jews, but he turned the Torah—his knowledge of the Torah—into a lethal weapon, a weapon of destruction. That is perhaps the worst part: to have used the Torah of Israel against the people of Israel. Could there be a more serious offense, a more vicious crime? Yes. Murder. Well, according to certain Talmudic sources, Elisha ben Abouya, in the end, was guilty of that too. He himself? Some say no—that he merely handed the *Talmidei khakhamim*—the scholars—over to the soldiers. Others say, yes, he was personally involved; as soon as he would discover that a sage was flouting any Roman law whatsoever, he would see to it that his head fell. His hatred of the Torah enveloped the disciples of the Torah; it made him an enemy more dangerous, more treacherous than the Roman enemy.

And so it is not surprising that he should have been judged so severely. He was gone. He was lost, hopelessly, irretrievably lost. And he knew it.

Another story: one of the most moving and shocking ones taken from Elisha ben Abouya's biography. Once again, it takes place on Shabbat. Rabbi Meir, his only remaining disciple, was lecturing in the house of Study in Tiberias, when somebody rather rudely interrupted him, saying that his master Elisha was promenading in the marketplace astride a horse. Without losing a minute, Rabbi Meir, hurt and embarrassed, ran outside to greet his Master.

For as far as Rabbi Meir was concerned, Elisha still was the Master to whom he owed loyalty and gratitude in spite of Elisha's behavior—almost in spite of himself. His friends and companions did not agree; certain students refused to understand how Rabbi Meir could refrain from repudiating the renegade. He surely must have been criticized for setting a poor example. But Rabbi Meir's concept of loyalty was too exalted, too personal to allow him to turn against the teacher to whom he owed so much.

Did Elisha appreciate Rabbi Meir's loyalty? Was he grateful? Apparently not. Proud, immensely vain, he would have preferred to remain alone, without friend or defender, alone against Israel, alone against God.

Rather than show a measure of appreciation, Elisha did not miss an opportunity to humiliate his disciple. And of all the transgressions he has been charged with, this one I consider the least forgivable. Anyone incapable of gratitude is unworthy of friendship.

Think about it: Here is a great Master who in the middle of his Shabbat study session closes his book, abandons his students, leaves the Beit Midrash, and runs to meet a renegade whom the entire community has rejected. How does Elisha react? He uses his own erudition, his own dialectical skill, his own teaching, to taunt him, ridicule him, humiliate him. He asks: "What have you taught your listeners today?" Rabbi Meir answers, and Elisha sneers at him. *"Akiba rabkha lo haya omer kach,* Your teacher Rabbi Akiba would have given a different interpretation." Rabbi Meir swallows hard and keeps silent. "Continue," says Elisha. "What other subjects did you discuss?" Rabbi Meir tells him, and Elisha proceeds to scold him: *"Akiba rabkha lo haya omer kach,* Your teacher Rabbi Akiba would have taken a different approach." And Rabbi Meir swallows his pain and remains silent. Allowing him no respite, Elisha pitilessly continues the conversation. He demonstrates the fallacy even of the principle of *teshuva,* repentance, so fundamental in Judaism. It is false, says he, because I, Elisha, am incapable of *teshuva.* And he tells him a story which must have pushed Rabbi Meir's tolerance and patience to its very limits.

"One day," said Elisha, "I was riding on my horse. It was Yom Kippur, which that particular year fell on Shabbat. I was roaming around the Beit Midrash when from the backyard I heard a celestial voice thundering, *'Shouvou banim shovevim,* come back to me, you lost children; *Shouvou elai veashouva elekhem,* come back to me and I shall come back to you—with the exception of *Akher, ki yada kokhi ou-marad bi,* for he, Elisha, knew my power and rejected me.' "

Rabbi Meir does not give up. He listens. He is *there.* As long as Elisha speaks to him, so he thinks, there is hope. At one point, he grabs his Master and drags him into a House of Study. As is the custom, they question a boy about the day's lesson. His answer, a verse from Isaiah, sounds like an irrevocable condemnation of Elisha. Rabbi Meir pulls him into a second synagogue, with the same result. The same sign in the third synagogue. And the fourth. Master and disciple will visit thirteen different sites, and everywhere, on the lips of innocent and prophetic children, there will be condemnation without appeal.

From this story, we sense Elisha's exasperation. Till now, he might have thought his conflict with heaven was a game. Now he realizes that it is not. The last boy interrogated infuriates Elisha. He quotes the verse in the Psalms *"Ulerasha amar elokim, ma lekha lesaper khukai.* And God tells the wicked: What is the use of your reciting my laws?" But the schoolboy stammers and the verse as heard by Elisha is not *"Ulerasha amar elokim* (God said to the wicked)," but *"L'Elisha amar elokim* (God said to Elisha)." The anonymous *Rasha* (the wicked) of these Psalms sounded like his name, Elisha. Bursting with anger, Elisha cries out, "If I had a knife in my hand, I would cut him [the schoolboy] to pieces."

But he did not repent.

Never? Here is another legend, a harrowing one: Many years later, Elisha ben Abouya fell ill. Rabbi Meir, who was immediately informed, hastened to his Master's bedside, where the following dialogue took place: *"Khazor bekha,"* said Rabbi Meir. "Come back to us, repent." To which the sick man replied, *"Vead kaan mekablim?* Is it still possible? After all I have done, all I have said, all the evil I have spread, will I still be accepted?" "As long as the soul vibrates," answered Rabbi Meir, "as long as it is sensitive to its own torment, the gates remain open."

And for the first time Elisha does not refute him. For the first time he silences his pride, his bitterness, his cruel inclinations; for the first time he submits to his disciple instead of mocking him. Quote: "In this hour, Elisha began to cry, and crying he died." Charitable to the end, loyal to the end, but also faithful to truth, Rabbi Meir makes this qualified remark: "It appears that my Master left this world repenting." He wasn't sure. Even *he* wasn't sure.

Later on, this question would provoke many a debate in academic circles. Rumors and legends and hypotheses circulated regarding Elisha's status in the other world. He was fascinating even when absent, intriguing even in death. Where is he? People wanted to know. In paradise in spite of his sins? In hell in spite of his learning?

It is said that flames were seen soaring from his tomb, and then smoke. Rabbi Meir was asked, "If, in the other world, you were to be given the chance to approach your father or your Master, what would your answer be?" "First my father, then my Master." "And if you were to have your way, would your Master be allowed to enter paradise?" "Yes," said Rabbi Meir, "for we must save not only the Torah but also the vessel that contains it; we must save Elisha because of his knowledge."

Of Rabbi Meir it will be said, in justification, that having found a precious fruit, he ate the flesh and threw away the skin. Thus Elisha will be partially retrieved. "When I die, I shall have salvation offered to him," promised Rabbi Yohanan. Once, poor, destitute, Elisha's daughter visited Rabbi Yehuda ha-Nassi asking for help. "I have nothing to eat." "Who are you?" he wanted to know. "I am the daughter of *Akher*." "What? Some of his brood remains?" "Rabbi," said the daughter, "remember his learning, not his deeds." And at that very moment a tongue of fire from heaven began to lash at Rabbi Yehuda's chair, and he understood that Elisha's daughter was right.

In spite of his misdeeds, Elisha is a part of Jewish history—and of the Jewish experience of all time. A man who left behind a disciple such as Rabbi Meir could not be entirely evil and could not remain outside indefinitely. In the end, Rabbi Meir *will* have saved his former teacher.

What can *we* learn from Elisha's story? In the Talmud, nothing subsists of his *Halakhic* teachings. Just a few legends, a few commentaries remain. And a few sayings dating back to his youth.

One aphorism: "Whoever studies in his youth is writing in ink on new paper. Whoever studies in old age is writing in ink on paper that has been worn."

Another: "Whosoever learns Torah in his youth will succeed in absorbing it into his blood, and the words he will pronounce will come out clear and distinct; whosoever waits until adulthood to study it must expect the contrary to occur."

Most of his parables and aphorisms, which relate to early education, seem to have been intended as barbs against Rabbi Akiba, of whom Elisha had been jealous. (Rabbi Akiba was forty when he began to study.) He resented the fact that Rabbi Meir, to the very end, considered himself the disciple of both. That was why Elisha needled him: Your teacher, Akiba, did not say that!

From all this we can draw a first lesson: You want to rebel? Go right ahead, but do it out of knowledge, not ignorance. It is not enough to want to be a rebel. One must learn and suffer, and learn even more before becoming one. To reject a heritage, you must first possess it.

Second lesson: We are responsible not only for our children, but also for our disciples. And the other way around. It is in their power to condemn us or save us.

Third lesson: Elisha had been wrong to listen "to the celestial voice." When it comes to *teshuvah*, we must listen to our own heart, to our own conscience. Repentance belongs to man alone. Repentance does not come from Heaven, and Elisha should have known this—he who knew so much about Judaism.

And yet, is this sufficient reason to condemn him forever? Certainly not. But then, should he be rehabilitated? *That* is the question.

And here I must make a confession: At first I was drawn to this tormented Master, drawn to his extraordinary lucidity and honesty. I had hoped to demonstrate the injustices perpetrated upon him in our traditional literature. At the outset, I said that I found him the most stimulating of his group, more humane than Rabbi Akiba. I'd hoped to pay him a posthumous tribute by singling him out as the forerunner of all ancient and contemporary intellectual rebels, a courageous and generous hero who, in a universe dominated by absurdity, dares to take the side of mankind against heaven. In doing so, I would have continued the work undertaken in the last century by our Haskalah (enlightened) scholars who claimed more of a kinship with him than with Rabbi Akiba.

Except that, along the way, Elisha's shadow covered the light. His faults were greater than his qualities, his cruelty weightier than his human warmth. All things considered, the authors of the Talmud were right: Elisha ben Abouya *was Akher*. He did represent dark forces in Judaism, and in man. In reaching this painful conclusion, this is what I base myself upon:

In the first place, I find his attitude toward his devoted disciple Rabbi Meir unacceptable. No man has a right to humiliate another, particularly one who has been good to him. By rewarding good with evil, Elisha did exactly that which he accused God of doing. For if in some instances it may be permissible for man to substitute himself for the Creator by performing good deeds, this permission is withdrawn when it comes to doing evil.

In the second place, I dislike the fact that Elisha ben Abouya always chose the Shabbat to ride his horse in the streets and exhibit his disagreement with God. All his provocations took place on Shabbat—and in public. My argument is, even if God did wrong, why offend the Shabbat? The Shabbat was given to man. What right had Elisha to violate it?

As a result, I felt one was entitled to doubt his "humanism." Appearances are deceiving. When he saw the man fall from the tree, Elisha rebelled. Why? Because he felt sorry for him? No. He rebelled because justice—the abstract concept of justice—had been flouted before his eyes. What concerned him was not man but the idea of divine fairness. Watching the tragic end of the martyrs of our faith, he rose not against Rome but against heaven. Their agony as human beings affected him less than philosophical arguments. To him, man was not a living creature, yearning for joy and truth and happiness, but a symbol, an idea, an abstraction. This does not qualify as humanistic! Because Elisha placed the law and the idea of man above man himself, his rebellion sprang not out of love for others, but out of conceptual disillusionment.

Surely his angry questions are valid. When he cries out, "Is this Torah, is this reward?" we admire his courage. We admire his demands. His quest is ours, his thirst is ours. Yet our paths separate when he deems it necessary *to provide answers*. Had Elisha not decided to go further, much further—had he not indicated his *solution*, his drastic solution, to the problems—he would have emerged as a beacon and a guide. After all, Jewish tradition permits man to question heaven, but one cannot pronounce judgment, one cannot boast of knowing everything. Yet—what did Elisha do? Having presented the question, he hastened to answer it. Having seen evil, having witnessed the intolerable injustice inherent in the death of a man, he proclaimed the verdict: Reward does not exist, and neither does eternity. Therein lay his mistake. He wished to acquire knowledge and thought that he *did*.

He should have contented himself with the questions. What was his *answer*? "*Yatza vekhata*" says the Talmud. He went outside and sinned." Against God? If that had been all, we would have found an excuse. But he sinned against his own brothers, and that is inadmissible. If you quarrel with God, it is your concern—His concern. But why implicate your brothers? You protest against heaven? So be it. But why express such protest by turning against your own people? And by becoming the executioner's accomplice? One must be very hardened, very inhuman indeed, to think in such categories, to act so cruelly. The only cry which is justified in our tradition is that uttered on behalf of man—and not against man. The only valid rebellion is that which helps or consoles the victim. The one which encourages the enemy is vain, futile, for it is inhuman. In other words, Elisha's mistake was to have rebelled against the human condition while contributing to its decline.

Elisha ben Abouya did not realize that suffering must bring us closer to man and not move us further away. Nor did he understand that by becoming *Akher*—the ally of the enemy—he was enhancing the evil he so ardently wished to defeat, or at least correct. Whoever thinks that he can save man by opposing him, conditioning him, jailing him—will in the end betray him.

Perhaps Elisha ben Abouya had important eschatological aims. Perhaps he tried to exorcise evil by espousing it. Perhaps he hoped to compel God to reconsider his attitudes toward his people by becoming the enemy of that people. No matter. No idea justifies the infliction of suffering. No games are valid if human lives are involved. No ideal is human if it strengthens the executioner—whoever he may be. There is no justification for a Jew's turning against his people—ever!

And so I say with sorrow, Elisha *was* guilty. Besides, the episode in the *Pardes,* the story of the excursion into the orchard, shows it clearly. Let us read it again. They were four who penetrated into the secret place of forbidden knowledge. Ben Zoma looked and lost his mind, Ben Azzai looked and lost his life. Akiba entered and came out in peace. And Elisha? It is said: *Kitzetz binetiot*—he mutilated and destroyed the plants. Of the four, he alone engaged in destructive activities—to prevent others from finding fulfillment there. Of the four, he alone used against others the discovery he made inside the orchard. He alone used knowledge against man. Just because he had unveiled certain secrets, did others have to suffer?

No: his anger was not Jewish. No: his rebellion was not meant to help Jews. No: he was not an example to be followed.

All things considered—I prefer his former companions. All things considered, I prefer Rabbi Akiba.

Rabbi Hananiah
ben Teradyon

AND IT CAME TO PASS that the old and revered Master, Rabbi
Hananiah ben Teradyon, like many of his companions, was caught
by Roman soldiers and sentenced to die at the stake for teaching
Torah in public. To make their point, the soldiers wrapped the old
man in the holy scrolls. As he stood there enveloped in his beloved
Torah, he listened to his disciples who surrounded him now as
they had every day when he explained to them the beauty and
mysteries of God's law. They watched him helplessly as he endured agony, his flesh singed by fire. Suddenly, one of the students
turned to him and asked, "What do you see *now?* Tell us, Rabbi,
what do your eyes see *now?*" And the venerable teacher, a moment
before losing consciousness, answered; "*Gevilin nisrafin*—the
scrolls are burning, I see them burning, but *haotyot porkhot baavir,*
the letters are stronger than the fire; they are indestructible; untouched, unharmed, they are flying up to heaven—they are returning to heaven. . . ."

This legend is well known. It is traditionally read as part of
the Yom Kippur liturgy in every synagogue. "*Ele Ezkera*—these I
shall remember—" is the name of the particular litany which describes poetically and precisely the martyrdom of ten sages who
chose to live and die for *Kiddush Hashem,* the sanctification of
God's holy name.

As a child I used to love reading that litany. I loved the way
these teachers, our ancestors, defied and accepted death: Rabbi
Shimon ben Gamliel and Rabbi Akiba ben Yoseph, Khutzpit the
Interpreter and Rabbi Ishmael ben Elisha the High Priest, of
whom it is said that he uttered the ineffable name to ascend the
heavens and inquire whether it was possible to revoke the decree;
he was told, Too late. Permission had already been granted to the

enemy to kill the spiritual leaders of our immortal people. One after the other, in different times and different ways, they were handed over to the executioner, and on Yom Kippur we would weep over their tragedy, which filled us not only with sadness but also with pride.

I was especially moved by and proud of Rabbi Hananiah ben Teradyon. His poignant personal response to Rome's policy of violence appealed to me, to the Jew in me, to the Jewish child in me: The spirit is stronger than its enemy; the fire of Torah is stronger than fire; one can die for truth but truth never dies. This is what every Jew learned or should learn from our teacher Rabbi Hananiah ben Teradyon. His lesson is necessary, if not vital, to the understanding of our own existence and survival. That is why we repeat the story of his plight year after year, generation after generation, with increasing empathy and fervor. Thanks to him, we have accepted the fact that while the killer may kill, his victims will outlive him in our collective memory. Therefore, whenever Jews were persecuted, we consoled ourselves with the martyr's statement: "*Gvilin nisrafin*"—only the scrolls are burning, only our homes, only our lives can be destroyed—our soul and our history remain beyond the enemy's reach.

But then, as always in the course of intense study, I developed a resistance to the text. In questioning it, I stumbled upon difficulties. I loved the Master, but still the story troubled me: I felt offended by his disciples.

There stood Rabbi Hananiah—literally, physically on fire— and all they could say was What do you see?—meaning, perhaps, *How* do you see, how do you view things? Is that all they could think of? Had they become reporters all of a sudden? Was that the time—and the place—for interviews? What were they going to ask him next during that improvised press conference? His opinion of Rome's policy? Or of the latest spectacle involving the leading gladiators—or lions—of the day?

Sorry, but I was angered by such a lack of compassion from devoted disciples for their dying teacher.

What does one do when one experiences serious difficulties with an ancient text? Abandon it? Quite the opposite: one goes back to it—and so I did. I started my quest all over again, searching for more hidden layers and clues, for other possible openings. In the end, I was rewarded and found myself reconciled with the legend once more.

Let us start from the beginning. And repeat the story—this time in its entirety. We are bound to get a different picture of the event.

Let us begin with the cast of characters. Rabbi Hananiah ben Teradyon, of course. The disciples. Who else? The executioner—a Roman soldier. What do we know about them? Quite a lot.

But first, the story. It exists in several versions, with minor differences. All agree that the old Master was arrested for teaching Torah in public, but while some maintain that he was denounced, others say that he was found teaching by Roman leaders returning from a funeral.

All versions describe his agony in more or less the same manner. First, they seized him and wrapped him in the scrolls of the Torah. Then they placed dry wood around him and lit the pyre. Furthermore, to prevent him from dying too quickly, they placed woolen cloths soaked in water on his chest.

At that point, we are told in the Midrash, his daughter, who stood among his disciples, began to weep and beat her face with her fists, shouting, "Woe unto me, Father, that I see you suffering like this." And he answered, "Do not weep, my daughter. Were I alone to perish in fire, I would find it unbearable; but I die together with the Torah. He who will demand justice for the Torah will do so for me, too." In another version, he replied somewhat differently. "Why do you weep?" he asked his daughter. "The Torah is fire, and fire cannot be burned by fire." Only *then* did his disciples ask him what he saw. The reason for the question? It is offered in one source that says, *"Nassa eynav lashamayim*—He lifted his eyes to heaven." That is what prompted them to ask what he saw. In other words, what meaning do you find there for your ordeal, and possibly ours? How much suffering are we to endure before the page is turned? Why has the enemy been granted power and his victims only tears? Now, his answer also makes sense: *"Gvilin nisrafin*—the enemy has power only over the parchment scrolls." Over the visible forms of human life, but not over the soul. The letters of the Torah—the spirit of Torah—are eternal, beyond the reach of its enemies.

Perhaps the story should end here, with this climactic and unforgettable statement. But it continues. The disciples offer a suggestion: "Why don't you open your mouth and swallow the flames and thus hasten your death?" And he replies, "It is against the law; my life is not mine; it belongs to God and only God may shorten it even by a minute."

Their dialogue was interrupted by the executioner, who is identified by his rank, Constinar or Questionar, in some sources, and centurion in others. "Master," he said, "if *I* hasten your death, will you promise me eternal life?" "I do," said the old teacher. "Swear it," said the executioner. And the teacher did. The executioner quickened the flames and removed the wet cloths from his victim's chest, and Rabbi Hananiah ben Teradyon returned his soul to God. The Roman soldier then jumped into the flames. And a heavenly voice was heard, proclaiming that both Rabbi Hananiah and the executioner had been chosen for life in the world to come.

Is this the denouement, the conclusion of the story? It is the conclusion of the event but not of the story. The story concludes with a comment Rabbi Judah the prince made later: *"Bakha Rabbi,"* says the Talmud. Rabbi Judah wept and said, "Some people can win eternal life in one hour while others need many years."

Why did Rabbi Judah weep? He wept because he found it strange that the victim and his executioner endured the same fate. And because a Jewish sage was helped by his enemy rather than his friends. He wept over the event itself for it shows the crucial role the sanctification of the name *Kiddush-Hashem* plays in Jewish history.

But at this point, let us turn our attention again to our principal hero. His origins are obscure. Who was Teradyon? What was his occupation? His social standing? These questions remain unanswered. All we can ascertain is that Rabbi Hananiah was a Master, a Tanna of the third generation. His teachers? Only one name is mentioned: Rabbi Eliezer son of Hyrcanos. His friends? One is famous—Rabbi Halafta, the father of the great Rabbi Yossi—and the second is mysterious—Rabbi Eleazar ben Parta.

Of Rabbi Hananiah himself we know that his life was fraught with tragedy. His wife was beheaded; one of his two daughters was placed in a house of ill repute; one of his two sons was executed by shady accomplices. As for Rabbi Hananiah, we know how *he* died.

The school which he headed was in Sikne, in Galilee, a village known for other reasons as well: the newly founded Christian sect held meetings there. And we know that the relations between the two communities were not too peaceful.

Rabbi Hananiah seems to have consented to debate with the

dissidents at times. We learn this from a cryptic comment in the Talmud which reads: *"Mishenikhnas Rabbi Hananiah leminut. . . ."* This means, literally, "When Rabbi Hananiah entered into heresy. . . ." Usually this phrase is interpreted to suggest that the old Master entered heresy not against his own brothers and their law, but against Rome and its system. However, there is another interpretation—quoted by Harav Menashe Hakatan—which seems plausible. *"Mishenikhnas Rabbi Hananiah Leminut"* means, "When he entered into discussions with heretics"—something most sages objected to then, perhaps for altogether practical reasons. Open discussions were dangerous: Roman spies were everywhere. For them, this was an ideal place to discover learned Jews and denounce them to the authorities.

From the few legends that exist about Rabbi Hananiah, we may come to at least one conclusion: the man was intrepid. Whatever he did, he did in public. He was fearless in the way he displayed his love for learning and his devotion to teaching.

Is it possible that he found in Torah the joy he could not find in his everyday life? Was Torah a kind of shelter for him? A refuge? A compensation?

We know of his deep involvement with study. Nothing was more important to him. He is the one who said; *"Shnayim sheyoshvin veein beinehem divrei Torah*—When two persons sit together and do not engage in study, it is as if they attended a session of clowns." The meaning of this? Two persons who do not engage in study, will ultimately talk about trivial things. *"Aval shnayim sheyoshvim,* If two persons do engage in study, the Divine Presence, the *Shekhina* will appear in their midst." Later he corrected himself. Two? Must there be two to deserve the *Shekhina?* Even one person who learns receives the *Shekhina* herself as reward.

That is one of the few sayings tradition has recorded in his name. Few laws are attributed to him. One of them is rather touching. Jews are not allowed to wash their faces on Yom Kippur—but the king and queen are exceptions to the rule. They may wash. Are they above the law? No, not in Jewish tradition. But, as leaders, they must think of the people and their feelings. To see their king and queen unclean and untidy—even on Yom Kippur—could have a demoralizing effect. However, they may not wash their bodies—only their faces.

This makes us think that Rabbi Hananiah understood people. He knew them—and they knew him. They respected him. They trusted him. Said Rabbi Eleazar ben Yaakov, One must not contribute to charity unless Rabbi Hananiah ben Teradyon serves as treasurer.

We mentioned his two daughters. One was the celebrated Brurya*, Rabbi Meir's wife, whose erudition was matched only by her audacity. Scholars avoided her, fearing inevitable embarrassment: she surpassed them in knowledge, and she wanted them to know it. Her wit, her sharp tongue, inspired numerous legends. And yet, she too was engulfed by tragedy. She lost two sons. Her husband, Rabbi Meir—Rabbi Hananiah's son-in-law—fled from his home and died abroad.

One of Rabbi Hananiah's sons, Shimon, was a scholar, but the other one—whose name has faded away—apparently went astray, joining some social or political outlaws. Eventually they murdered him for revealing their secrets; his body was found mutilated. When he was brought to the cemetery for burial, local dignitaries came to the funeral and wanted to eulogize the dead boy for the sake of his father, but Rabbi Hananiah said no.

Rabbi Hananiah's entire life was filled with mourning. Many of his peers perished as martyrs. The people of Israel seemed to have been forsaken by the God of Israel.

Judea was subjected to Hadrian's persecutions. Oppression, brutality, collective and individual cruelty were everywhere. The study and teaching of Torah meant mandatory capital punishment. As did the observance of Shabbat. And circumcision. And the reciting of Sh'ma. Challenged by the spirit of the Jewish people, Rome sought to distort and humiliate it. Public executions were daily occurrences. In order to discourage learning, great teachers were systematically put to death.

And yet—the Torah was not stifled. Since ordination was forbidden—and since the inhabitants of villages permitting it were punished by death—Rabbi Yehuda ben Baba decided to ordain his disciples between two mountains. Surprised by the Romans, he told the young rabbis to run, while he remained behind, shielding those who could not escape with his body, which, hit by arrows, instantly became like a sieve.

And when our Masters realized that Jewish learning was in absolute peril, they issued a call, one of the most inspiring in history. It remains valid to this day. *"Kol shelamad*—whoever studied—*sheyavo veyelamed*—let him come and teach; and whoever did not study—let him come and study."

*See Rabbi Meir and Brurya, pages 286–298.

And that call echoed throughout the nation. Clandestine schools were created. The more brutal the oppressor, the more fervent the oppressed, the stronger their resolve. National pride became an obsession. One sage declared: If the enemy orders you to tie your sandals with green laces, better to die than to obey him.

How is one to explain Rome's obsession with Jews? Of all the enemies Rome had, the Jews bothered them most. Why? Why was it so important for Rome to bring Jews to their knees—religiously, emotionally, philosophically?

In other lands, the Romans had to face different religions, nationalities, cultures. But in Judea they faced a united religious front. The Romans could not understand: Why were the Jews so stubborn? In *Sifre,* this incomprehension is expressed in poetic terms: "Why do you cling to your God?" asked the Romans. "You are more learned than we are, more courageous, more enterprising, more imaginative. Come and join us and you will be stronger than we are. In fact, be like us and you will be more powerful." And the Jewish answer was, "Do you want to know what we think and feel about our God?" They tell them. Still, the Romans cannot understand.

Let us be honest and admit that even within the Jewish community here and there, voices were raised urging restraint, if not resignation. Elisha ben Abouya, for instance, openly preached collaboration with the occupant.

Rumor has it that another scholar, a certain Reb Yehuda ben Gerim, somehow became so involved with the Romans that—knowingly or not—he became their informer.

Even the venerable Rabbi Yossi ben Kisma adopted a strangely disturbing attitude in this respect.

Like many other nations, we had three options when we faced the enemy: active resistance, passive resistance, and collaboration. Rabbi Yossi ben Kisma believed in passive resistance: not to anger the enemy too much, not to provoke him, not to defy him in a way that would deteriorate the situation.

A story: When Rabbi Yossi ben Kisma fell ill, Rabbi Hananiah came to visit him. At that time their relations were still friendly, trusting—after all, weren't they on the same side? It was natural therefore for Rabbi Hananiah to pay his colleague a sick call. Surely, *Bikour-kholim*—visiting the sick—is an important *mitzva*. Nobody will deny that.

But when Rabbi Yossi ben Kisma died, we find no mention

of Rabbi Hananiah's going to his funeral. How come? Isn't *Halvayat hamet*—paying last respects to the deceased—as important a commandment, if not more so?

He must have had a reason for not going. And the reason must have had to do with his sick call. As a matter of fact, on that occasion they argued. Rabbi Yossi had opened the debate: "Hananiah, my brother," he said, "don't you know that this—Roman—nation has been elevated by heaven to rule over others? It has destroyed God's temple and burned its sanctuary and massacred its pious and best sons—and yet it thrives. And as for you, my brother, I hear that you sit and study and teach in public with a *Sefer-Torah* in your lap." Said Rabbi Hananiah, "Heaven will help us." "What?" exclaimed Rabbi Yossi. "I am talking sense, and you refer to heaven! I wonder," he continued, "whether they will not burn you *and* the *Sefer-Torah* at the stake."

That exchange must have left the visitor troubled. Because of the threat? No. Rabbi Hananiah was not easily frightened. More likely his sadness was caused by his colleague's rationalization of Jewish tragedy. If Jews are being humiliated and slaughtered, it is because God wills it that way, Rabbi Yossi ben Kisma had said.

God is on the side of Rome—on the side of Israel's enemy. If Rome is powerful, it is because God gave the Romans power. Therefore Jews, according to Rabbi Yossi's view, had neither reason nor right to rebel, to resist and oppose the occupant. What—a Jewish scholar, a teacher, a rabbi of his caliber siding with Rome? No, siding with those who yielded to Rome. But even that attitude was enough to displease the entire scholarly community. If the enemy is cruel, why blame God? If Hadrian's soldiers slaughter Jewish children, why place the responsibility in heaven?

Still, when Rabbi Yossi was ill, the sages came to visit him. But when he died they refrained from attending the funeral. For two possible reasons: *Bikour-kholim*, a sick call, could be made in private—not so *Halvayat-Hamet*. Funerals are, by their nature, public events—especially when the person being buried is a public figure. To attend a funeral is a *mitzva*—and perhaps some sages were afraid of fulfilling such a *mitzva* in the open. The other reason is more convincing. The sages failed to come because they chose to make their position known. Rabbi Yossi was too close to Rome— that is why they did not come. Who did come? Roman representatives, Roman officials, Roman dignitaries. *Gdolei Romi—Yakirei Romi* . . . All the VIPs from the military and civil establishment.

And when they returned from the cemetery, they encountered Rabbi Hananiah ben Teradyon teaching Torah in public. . . .

Another version tells us that Rabbi Hananiah was arrested together with a mysterious sage named Rabbi Eleazar ben Parta. Said Rabbi Hananiah to his companion, "You are lucky—you were caught and charged with five felonies—and yet you were saved. I was accused of only one transgression: the study and teaching of Torah—and I shall not be saved."

Indeed, legend has it that miracles occurred on behalf of Rabbi Eleazar ben Parta.

But not so for Rabbi Hananiah.

Rabbi Hananiah was sentenced to die by fire, his wife to be beheaded, and his daughter to be sent to a house of ill repute. The Talmud comments: when they were made to endure their cruel sentences, all three quoted Biblical sayings, thus voicing their submission to divine justice.

The Talmud, however, does not accept their doom so readily. Our sages needed some kind of answer, some kind of explanation for Rabbi Hananiah's death—for the destruction of his entire family. How could one possibly apply to his case the Talmudic saying *"Ein mita beli khet*—Death . . . is never unrelated to sin"? Well, if scholars—and those they loved—were allowed to die so tragically, it meant that at least in some respect our perception of them must have been wrong. Perfect men and women are not exposed to punishment—just men and women are not vanquished by premature death.

The Talmud says quite specifically, Rabbi Hananiah perished in the flames because of something he had done. What? He had uttered aloud the ineffable name while studying Torah. As for his wife—she was sentenced to death because she was complacent, too passive with regard to her husband; she knew what he was doing and should have stopped him. She was condemned to die by the sword because she did not stop him. And the daughter, what about her? What had she done to warrant her humiliation? There, too, the Talmud, never short on imagination, comes up with an answer: As she was walking in the street, she overheard Roman notables say to one another, Look how beautiful she is. And at that moment, she self-consciously began to walk differently—to attract more attention. That is why she was punished.

Let us hasten to add that she did not stay long in the red light district. Brurya begged her husband to save her sister, and he did.

No one saved her parents, but they will continue to be remembered. The psalmist's verse, *Velo shakakh tzakat anavim*—And he has not forgotten the outcry of the humble—is interpreted in Talmudic literature as follows: God Almighty does not forget the blood, the Jewish blood shed during the Hadrian persecutions. All victims of slaughter by the enemy are recorded by God himself, and kept in His special archives. And at the end of time, God will ask other nations, Why have you murdered my Just Men such as Rabbi Hananiah ben Teradyon? And they will deny the charges and say, No, we have not shed their blood. Then He will open His special book of martyrology and show them: See? All the names of all the victims are there. And ultimately the killers will be judged and condemned.

Still, why martyrdom? What *is* martyrdom? In ancient Greece, it meant to bear witness—and the first martyrs in history were Jews who had grown up repeating the Biblical injunction: *Edim atem laadoshem*—You are all God's witnesses. The Talmud comments in the name of God: If you are my witnesses, then I am God. If not . . .

Among the first martyrs there was a woman: Hannah. She and her seven sons refused to bow to the edicts of Antiochus Epiphanes forcing Jews to worship idols. Hannah and her sons died as Jews, as examples to their people.

In the times of Hadrian the persecution affected not only individuals but the community at large. As the decrees became harsher and harsher, our sages felt the need to codify the law related to *Kiddush hashem,* or martyrdom. The commandment *Yehareg ubal ya-avor*—rather be killed than transgress—applied to three specific sins: idol worship, adultery, and bloodshed. In other words, if the enemy tells you, worship our idols or you shall die, do not worship his idols. And better die than commit adultery. And if the enemy tells you, kill or be killed, you may not save your own life at the expense of someone else's.

Talmudic legislators also analyzed collective behavior. If the enemy were to surround a community and order it to hand over one of its members lest everybody be killed, the community must not yield to the threat. However, should the enemy ask for someone specific—someone the enemy considers guilty—someone who sought shelter within the community, thus needlessly endangering it, then the community may hand over the fugitive.

In the Midrash we are constantly reminded of ten martyrs,

but actually there were more. Many names are not included in the list, which apparently recorded only the most prestigious and exceptional scholars of the time. Upon close scrutiny, the martyrs' deaths strike us as unwarranted even in the context of their times. Not one of them stood accused of adultery, idolatry, or bloodshed. Then why did they choose to die? Nowhere is it written that one must risk one's life for Torah. Then how is one to explain the supreme sacrifice of Rabbi Akiba and Rabbi Hananiah ben Teradyon? Is it conceivable that they in fact violated the law by broadening its scope? I prefer to believe that whatever they did, they did in conformity with the law. I believe that *Limud Torah*—teaching and studying—also implies *Kiddush-hashem*. I believe that it was not specified because it was self-evident: without *Limud-Torah*, without learning, without knowledge, how would anyone even know about the other three laws never to be transgressed? The only teacher who advocated ignorance—that is, in matters of Jewish culture and tradition—soon ceased to be called teacher and became an outsider. His name was Ben Abouya.

Even Rabbi Yossi ben Kisma, who preached coexistence with Rome, did not advise Rabbi Hananiah ben Teradyon to stop studying—he didn't even ask him to stop teaching. He only suggested he stop teaching in public.

Thus, I think it may be safely stated that, though not included in the category of immutable principles, the study of Torah was viewed by all our Masters as a commandment which one must uphold, even at the cost of one's life.

So Rabbi Hananiah was right. He knew that once Torah was forgotten everything would be forgotten, for Jewish life would have lost its meaning. Yet he also knew that such a possibility had to be considered. It had happened more than once in our history: *Nishtakha ha-Torah mi or be-Israel*—the Torah was forgotten in Israel—is a sentence that appears frequently in Talmudic texts. Therefore, rather die with and within Torah—and for the sake of Torah—than live without it. Rabbi Hananiah's conduct, therefore, is natural, as is Rabbi Akiba's and Rabbi Ishmael's.

But what about the disciples? What foolish questions did they ask of their dying teacher? Why didn't they keep silent? Why didn't they look away and grant him the right to ultimate privacy?

Saul Lieberman of blessed memory taught us the difference between the Jewish and the early Christian martyrs. Jewish sages refused to turn their deaths into public demonstrations. When

Rabbi Akiba died, he said "Sh'ma Israel," and the text emphasizes that *Ota shaa shaat kriat sh'ma hayta:* It was the hour when one was *supposed* to recite the Sh'ma. Had it not been the hour, he would not have said it, or he would have said something else, as Rabbi Hananiah did.

Then why did Rabbi Hananiah's disciples engage him in a dialogue then and there? Couldn't they wait quietly, sadly, until the end? Was it proper, was it respectful to speak to him about his pain? Or about his inner feelings?

Let us look at the scene again. And at the protagonists. Who is there? Rabbi Hananiah. The disciples. The Roman executioner. Where is Hananiah's wife? Already dead—beheaded. His sons? One is dead. The other? If he is present, he is heartbroken and silent. His daughters? One is already in distress and exile. And the other, Brurya? Yes, Brurya is here. Why? Why had she been spared? Because as a married woman, she no longer belonged to Rabbi Hananiah's household? Or because she and her husband were under the so-called protection of a Romanophile named Elisha ben Abouya who, everyone knew, was her husband's pupil?

Whatever the reasons, the fact remains that Brurya is present at her father's side. And her behavior is, I would say, somewhat out of character. Those who are familiar with her story know that in times of danger she was often so strong as to appear insensitive. When her two sons died suddenly, on the same day and in the same circumstances, she hid their bodies from her husband until after Shabbat. She was known for her coolness, for her ability to undramatize events and to control her feelings.

But here, standing near her father on the public square, she allowed herself to be openly moved to pain, anguish, and possibly despair. One text describes her as pounding her head and chest with her fists: the proud woman scholar whose opinions frequently prevailed now was only a bereaved daughter. For once, she didn't care whether or not people were looking at her, or whether they approved or disapproved of her actions. At that moment, she had to express her emotions the way many human beings do: By shouting, by inflicting physical pain on themselves. And it was her father who stopped her. Now, at this supreme moment, she became his child again—she was reunited with her father, alone with him as never before.

Out of respect for her and for her father, the other disciples restrained their impulse to interfere. At such moments no outsider has the right to stand between father and child. And if the child decides to ask questions, all anyone can do is listen.

There are several versions of the event, similar but not identical.

One text gives the father the opening line: "Daughter," he says, "why do you cry?" Normally such a question would seem odd. Why wouldn't a daughter cry when witnessing her father's agony? In this case, however, it sounds right. My daughter, Rabbi Hananiah seems to say, I have never seen you shed a tear. Why are you weeping now? She has been exposed to tragedy before, and she has always responded with astonishing dignity and calm. Why was she crying now, in the presence of so many people?

And her answer demonstrates her ability quickly to regain her composure. "I weep," she said, "because of the Torah which will be burned with you." So—do not ever accuse her of sentimentality. Brurya, composed again, had an answer to everything. Let no spectator presume that she is a weakling; yes, she allowed herself to weep in public, but not because of her father—God forbid—but because of the Torah. Then—and I imagine him smiling in spite of his pain—Rabbi Hananiah answered, "Do not worry, daughter; Torah *is* fire—and fire cannot be burned by fire. And He who will demand justice for Torah, will do so for me as well." Having spoken, he lifted his eyes toward heaven. That is when his disciples asked, "What do you see? What do you read in heaven? What is the meaning of your trial and ours? What is the sense of all that is happening to our people?" And he answered: *"G'vilin nisrafin*—the scrolls are burning but the letters are not." Physical, tangible things come and go—not spiritual ones. They stay *baavir*—suspended between heaven and earth—outside time and inaccessible to human ambitious. There is something in us mortals that is immortal.

Now the dialogue has attained a sublime but human quality. The dying have vanquished death simply by removing their inner universe from its domain. Death has no power over literature—or imagination—or spiritual quest.

Logically, I repeat, the legend should end there. As a literary or poetic exercise, it cannot go much further—or higher. Rabbi Hananiah's vision, and his rendering of it, are the most striking culmination; they would close the legend perfectly. And yet, all Midrashic versions feel the need to continue—and they bring in, as an active participant, the Roman executioner, who will now undergo a metamorphosis and become to the old sage and to himself both executioner and redeemer.

The legend continues: "Having heard Rabbi Hananiah speak about the indestructible letters, his disciples turn to him with yet another question: 'Why don't you open your mouth?' they ask. 'You will swallow the flames and shorten your agony—and die faster.' "

From Saul Lieberman we have learned that in those times, and later, too, Christian martyrs *did* open their mouths and swallow the flames. That is why in many religious drawings and paintings they are shown with open mouths. That possibility of hastening their death was known to all people: it is something that is done instinctively. Then, why the advice?

The answer is that it was not meant to be advice, but a question. "Why don't you swallow the flames?" means "Why shouldn't one hasten one's own death to avoid lengthy agony?" And that could actually be translated into an inquiry into the law: "What is the *din*—what is the law pertaining to such a situation?"

And the old Master replied that it would still be considered suicide—and suicide is not an option; Jewish law and tradition oppose suicide. But his language was more poetic, and I quote: "My soul is not mine—only its owner may decide when to take it away."

Two remarks:

One: from the structural viewpoint, the legend probably should have begun with the law and concluded with the vision. Poetically, and as a work of literature, it would make more sense. It is easier to start with *Halakha* and move to *Aggada* than the reverse. You start with reality and carry it into legend, rather than the other way around.

Why then the unconventional direction of the narrative? You must look for the answer in the Talmudic saying that one must never take leave from a friend without trading views on some legal—*Halakhic*—matter.

Since Rabbi Hananiah ben Teradyon was about to say farewell to his disciples, they all felt it appropriate to evoke a question of *Halakha*; and the one that was on their mind was whether one is permitted to die before the last moment arrives—whether one may, in order to avoid unnecessary agony, open one's mouth and swallow the flames. Ruled the Master: No. Life and death are God's domain, not ours. Just as we do not choose the place or the hour of our birth, we may not choose the hour of our death.

But then, you may well ask, Was *that* the time for study? For intellectual inquiry? Was *that* the time for disciples to address questions, however important, to their teacher?

At the outset of this journey I said that at first I was disturbed by the disciples' apparent insensitivity. Having reached our destination, I feel reconciled with the entire cast of characters—even with the Roman centurion: After all, he did diminish an old Jew's pain. Granted, he did what Rabbi Hananiah refused to do: he committed suicide. But wasn't it against the law? No: he wasn't Jewish. And there is a kind of logic to his deed. Since he could not *save* Rabbi Hananiah, he would join him. Just as Rabbi Hananiah displayed readiness to perform *Kiddush-hashem,* the Roman soldier displayed kindness and nobility by helping him. That is why Rabbi Yehuda the prince wept—for both.

As for the disciples and their questions . . .

In order for us to understand their motivation, we must try to remember Jewish life and lore in those years in Palestinian academies. Strict customs and rules governed all the schools. For any study session to begin, the president, accompanied by the head of the tribunal and the speaker, had to use the magic and indispensable phrase *Shaalu*—please ask your questions. Without such permission, the lesson could not begin.

Now, try to imagine the old teacher in agony surrounded by his disciples. They see him diminished, mutilated, unable to control his tears and dominate his pain. Naturally they could weep for him—and with him. Or they could leave him alone—and cry at a distance. But that would have been unworthy of him—and them. Pity for a Master? That would have been discourteous, condescending. Had they shed tears in his presence over his tragic fate they would have embarrassed him, even offended him. That is why, in an amazing show of respect, they chose to ask him questions instead—and thus give him the feeling that he was still their teacher, and they his pupils. That is the gift they wisely offered him at that supreme moment: the statement that, in spite of the enemy and his victories, in the shadow of death and its inevitable triumph, the relationship between Master and disciples remained as fervent as before. True, he was suffering, but they could still discuss suffering. True, he was on the threshold of death, but, until the last minute, with his last breath, he could still teach them immortal lessons about life and death. Thanks to them and their questions, he could prove to them and to himself that he was in full possession of his powers, and that he could guide them—as before—in the fields of both *Halakha* and *Aggada*.

And so, we now understand that he was worthy of them—as they were worthy of him. How can we not love them and admire them?

In conclusion, it is said that when the news of Rabbi Akiba's tragic death reached Rabbi Hananiah ben Teradyon, he and his friends tore their clothes and began mourning their loss. And one sage exclaimed, The death of this sage and just man serves as a prediction of perilous times that are about to come upon us.

If the death of one man serves as an evil omen for humankind, what should one say about the death of six million men, women, and children, *children*?

Rabbi Meir and Brurya

IT HAPPENED on a Shabbat afternoon. The celebrated Rabbi Meir was delivering his regular lecture in the House of Study. But while he enchanted his many devoted listeners with his commentaries and his ingenious parables, back at home, unbeknownst to him, his two sons were stricken down at the same time, and died at sunset. The circumstances of their death? Nobody knows. Had they been taken ill? Or fallen in an accident? Were they killed by Roman soldiers? The Talmud offers no clues, no hints. All we know is that their mother, Brurya, was strong enough and pious enough not to allow her grief to affect her observance of Shabbat. She laid her sons on a bed, covered them with a white sheet, and sat down to wait for her husband's return.

When Rabbi Meir came home after services, he inquired, "Where are my sons?" "At the House of Study," Brurya answered. "At the House of Study?" said her husband with astonishment. "But I was there. I looked for them. Why didn't I see them?" To forestall further questions, she handed him a glass of wine for *Havdalah,* the ceremony that marks the end of Shabbat.

"But where are my sons?" Rabbi Meir couldn't help but ask again. "Oh, somewhere," said Brurya, barely containing her sorrow. "They must have gone to visit friends. They'll be home soon."

She set the table. They sat down and ate. After the meal, Rabbi Meir turned to her for the last time and asked, "Do tell me, where have my sons vanished?" Only then did Brurya allow herself to touch upon the subject, and she did so with unusual tact and gentleness. "I have a question for you," she said with a feigned casualness. "Some time ago, somebody entrusted a precious treasure to me and now he is claiming it back; what am I to do?"

"What a question," Rabbi Meir exclaimed. "Did you seriously consider keeping for yourself what belongs to another?"

Thereupon she took him by the hand, led him into the other room, and silently uncovered the bodies.

And the grief-stricken father began the weep: "My sons, my sons, my Masters, my Masters—the most respectful of sons, the most enlightened of Masters. . . ."

"Do not cry," Brurya whispered softly, "do not cry. Remember your own words. Didn't you tell me that we must return what does not belong to us? God has given, God has taken back; may His name be a blessing."

Was it her voice, so soft, so sad? Or her composure? Or perhaps the power of her argument that reached Rabbi Meir? All we know is that he let himself be consoled by her.

This story, one of the most heartbreaking in Talmudic literature, throws some light on Brurya's personality and on her husband's.

Rabbi Meir appears as the serene, conciliatory, good-natured scholar, at a loss when confronted with worldly affairs—and with his wife. He is more at home at the House of Study than at home. Believing in God and in His justice, he bows his head and accepts the judgment. What he feels is sadness, not rebellion. Disarmed in the face of misfortune, he lets himself go.

Not so Brurya. Of the two, she is the more independent. While her husband is at the synagogue, she stays home. At the height of the tragedy, she seems in command of the situation. She knows what to do, what to say, and when.

Rabbi Meir weeps; she does not. Rabbi Meir cannot control his emotions; she can.

So, as we explore this episode, we glimpse the relationship between the sage and his wife, between them and the outside world, between the law of Israel and the God of Israel.

Of the two, who touches and troubles us more? Rabbi Meir, because he is defenseless and innocent? Or Brurya, because of her willpower and composure?

From Rabbi Meir's behavior, and his *repeated* inquiries, one senses his impatience, his anguish. The father has premonitions; he guesses that something is wrong, that something has happened to his children. *But where are they?* Yet, when facing a question of law, his mind is distracted. The father yields to the teacher until reality hits him head-on. Then he begins to weep and mourn. Still, why doesn't he want to know more? Why doesn't he ask for details? Why doesn't he try to learn *how* they died?

As for Brurya, what disturbs us is that, in the middle of such a catastrophe, she is thinking ahead, calculating, planning a trap for her husband. She will make him say the things she needs to hear, to make her point. It seems almost inhuman. Furthermore, why did *she* accept the untimely death of her children with such serenity? Why didn't she shout with pain—as any normal mother would have done? Didn't she have anything to say about the injustice done to both her sons? Could it have been that neither parent was surprised? That their sons had *not* been sick is clear from the text; their father was expecting them in the House of Study. Could Rabbi Meir's concern with their whereabouts have derived from their involvement with some clandestine groups fighting the Roman occupant? Who were those friends they were supposed to have visited?

Anyway, this is not an attempt to indict either Rabbi Meir or Brurya. It is merely a desire to understand them. Both of them are extremely sensitive to human suffering—as we shall later see. Brurya's conduct must be considered nothing less than admirable. Her composure is proof of experience and not of indifference. She knows how to handle tragic situations because she has been through so much. More than one misfortune has befallen her, and she has lived with death more than once. People close to her have perished for many different reasons, in many different ways.

The verbal trap she set for her husband? To be fair, it was a trap not against him but *for* him—to help prepare him for the shock to come. She knew that the only way to save him from despair was to inject his grief into a larger context. She did not use her tactics to win a debate, or to score points, but to console a fellow victim. Brave Brurya: not only did she resist histrionics, but somehow she found the courage, the wisdom, and the compassion to help a man who did not have her tremendous resources and who was more than a husband to her: he was her companion, her opponent, her friend, her challenger.

Together they form an extraordinary couple—the most unusual couple in the Talmud. Let us meet them—separately.

Let us begin with Brurya.

The choice falls on Brurya because of her genuine gifts and relevance for today. Most other feminine figures are known and remembered in connection with their husbands, fathers, or brothers. Not so Brurya. She is in a category apart. Her glory is her own, her power is sovereign. Even if she had not been the daughter of Rabbi Hananiah ben Teradyon and the wife of Rabbi Meir, she would have been noticed—and talked about.

Some of her contemporaries praised her beauty, others spoke of her piety. But the only compliments she acknowledged were those that stressed her intelligence.

Well-deserved compliments, to be sure. And she knew it. She had difficulty in finding peers among women and men alike. Haughty, she stood up to her teachers who made the law of the land. Known as a brilliant debater, she often challenged famous scholars to prove her intellectual superiority; indeed, they considered her a menace. Nobody intimidated her, no subject frightened her. She welcomed public contests. Sure of her erudition, of her reasoning, and of the other side's weaknesses, she rarely stayed on the defensive. Provocative, sharp-tongued, arrogant, she used her mind as a weapon—to strike and to win.

No wonder that she was feared in academic circles. Wherever she appeared, people took flight. Leaders of *yeshivot* avoided her. She literally paralyzed her opponents. She respected no official title, no social position; she recognized no authority. The more celebrated and important her adversary, the more she humbled him.

The Talmud reveals no other Jewish woman like Brurya. Legends about her abound. They make you smile, they move you to wonder. She was so exceptional, one finds it difficult to define her role. The first Jewish liberated woman since—since whom? Other women had more power: Isabel, Shlomtzion, Esther, Athalia. Others had more virtues: Rachel, Sarah. Or more courage: Yael, Judith . . . but none possessed her intellect and presence of mind. So—should she be described as the forerunner of today's woman rabbi? Of our career-minded women professors whose ambition is matched only by their success? Brurya needs no such definition. She was what she was: the woman who always knew better than anybody else, who wanted to be, and was, lucid and daring and invincible, and who, in the end, discovered she was more feminine than she had thought. Brurya: the hero who fell victim to her own passions, her own desires, her own principles, her own pride. Brurya: a woman of brains and heart whom one admires and loves because of her greatness—and *in spite of* her aggressive brilliance.

Her husband is different but no less intriguing. Colorful, picturesque, open to justice and mystery: his, too, is a place apart in the Talmudic gallery. In popular memory he is remembered and cherished; he is called Rabbi Meir *Baal-hanes,* the miracle man: no Jewish home in Eastern Europe ever was without a charity box, a *pushke* in his name at the entrance. The poorest beggar found a way to put pennies in *his pushke.* . . .

His origins are obscure. It was said that he descended from converted ancestors. One sage guessed that the convert in question was Nero himself, who had escaped his murderers and had become a Jew.

Nothing seems to have been recorded of Rabbi Meir's childhood. Rabbi Akiba, his great teacher, who preferred him over Rabbi Shimon bar Yohai, said he had met him—characteristically—on a boat tossed about in a stormy sea, and he had felt sorry for him without knowing who he was. Yes, Rabbi Meir was forever traveling, forever shaken, forever in flight. Whom was he fleeing? The Romans? The informers? The establishment? His own past? His formidable wife, perhaps?

His death occurred in Asia, in mysterious circumstances. He asked to be buried on the shore—and Saul Lieberman, with his usual poetic sense, explained why: to be touched and caressed by the same waves that touch the shores of Israel.

Rabbi Meir was among Rabbi Akiba's best disciples, this we do know. But Rabbi Akiba was not his only teacher. He had also studied with Akiba's friendly rival, Rabbi Ishmael.

Their first meeting is memorable because of the following conversation—one that should be studied over and over by writers everywhere.

The old teacher wanted to know his new disciple's profession. "I am a scribe," Rabbi Meir replied. "Be careful, my son, very careful. Your trade is one that carries great responsibilities. By omitting or adding a single letter, you may destroy the entire world." Yes, worlds can be built and destroyed with words.

Though an excellent scribe, Rabbi Meir was poor. He earned three *selaim* per week. One he kept for food, one for clothing, and one for charity—so not much was left for Brurya's household budget, as we learn from the following episode. Asked by his pupils why he provided so little for his children, Rabbi Meir answered, "If they are righteous, God will provide for them; if they are not—why should I bother?" We can imagine what Brurya thought of all this.

Just as Rabbi Meir could not stay in one place, he could not stay with one teacher. He also studied with Yehuda ben Baba—and with the renegade Elisha ben Abouya, to whom he remained loyal to the end, and beyond. Even when Elisha ben Abouya violated the sanctity of Shabbat, Rabbi Meir continued to show him respect. And even when Elisha profaned Yom Kippur, Rabbi Meir continued to show him reverence. This loyalty is all to Rabbi Meir's credit. Others before him had taught the importance of teaching; he taught the importance of studying, of attaining perfection—as a disciple.

Yet he himself was a great teacher both in *Halakha* and *Aggada*. He was among the seven sages gathered in Ousha who had issued the dramatic appeal, "He who knows should come and teach; he who knows not should come and learn." His name is mentioned three hundred and thirty-five times in the Mishna. A forceful storyteller, he attracted large crowds, including many women. Jealous husbands often found it difficult to restrain their annoyance.

A story: One Friday evening, Rabbi Meir gave an unusually long lecture—or was it a sermon? In the audience there was a woman who was too polite—or perhaps too absorbed—to get up and leave before it was over, although she had promised to come home at a certain hour. So she came home late—later than her husband had expected. Naturally the husband received her angrily. Which is only normal: Put yourself in his place. Except that he was angry not at his wife, but at the lecturer: "I will not let you inside the house," he shouted, "unless you go and spit in his face! That will teach him to deliver long lectures."

But the woman was too shy—and too respectful. She came to the House of Study, looked at Rabbi Meir—and cried. Rabbi Meir noticed this and made inquiries among her friends. After all, his speeches were not meant to make anyone cry. When he learned what had happened, he decided to solve her problem. At his next lecture, he suddenly remarked, "I need someone to spit in my face seven times so as to divert the evil eye from me." And on that evening the woman was able to return to her husband and reassure him: "You wanted me to spit in his face once. I did—seven times." And they may have lived happily ever after.

Let us hasten to add that Rabbi Meir was less tolerant in his relationship with other rabbis with whom he often quarreled. He was no more impressed by their high positions than was his wife. In his disputes with them, he was as demanding as only his wife could be. He was intimidated by nobody—except Brurya.

How strange that both their lives ended in tragedy.

But then, the entire period was filled with tragedy and doom. Remember, we are in the middle of the second century. True, Hadrian's cruel edicts are abolished, but not forgotten. Jerusalem, renamed Aelia Capitolina, serves as a constant reminder of Israel's humiliation. Jews are not permitted to come near their former capital except once a year, on the ninth day of Av—commemorating the national catastrophe—so they can suffer more and weep harder. . . .

So great is Jewish suffering then that the New Christians reject all connections with it. Two fathers of the church—Quadratus and Aristides—petition Rome to spare them from the persecutions, for they have nothing to do with Judaism.

In spite of the enemy, against all odds, the people of Israel succeeded in turning the Torah into a living Torah. Jewish history continued; it was stronger than the foes who sought to destroy it.

On the personal level, Brurya's life was filled with tragedy, as was her husband's. Rabbi Hananiah ben Teradyon, her father, was sentenced to be burned at the stake.

As if that wasn't enough—her mother was decapitated during Roman reprisals. Her sister, famed for her beauty, was sentenced to serve as a prostitute for the Romans. Her brother was found murdered under strange circumstances. Rumor had it that he had joined the armed rebels. Others believed that he was consorting with bandits and was killed by them.

Clearly, as the sole survivor of her family, Brurya breathed catastrophe. The world had come crushing down around her. Her people, torn apart, reflected the thousand faces of desolation and misery. Her own children were taken by death. And yet, she resisted the mentality of defeat. She did not consider herself beaten. She chose to fight. The worse the ordeal, the stronger her resistance. Never did she weep or lament. Contemptuous of self-pity, she studied, debated, quarreled, took an interest in her husband's affairs and in those of the community—in other words, she *lived*—that is, she lived courageously, creatively. Seven tales about her can be found in the Babylonian Talmud and two in the Palestinian.

She was an excellent student, serious, thorough. For three years, says the Talmud, she studied three hundred laws every day. Finally, she accumulated so much knowledge, in so many domains, that she dared—and was allowed—to participate in academic deliberations, which, as we may remember, unfolded according to a strict protocol. Not just anybody could speak up. A certain standing was needed. Once, during a stormy discussion involving questions of purity and impurity, she vigorously opposed the venerable Rabbi Tarfon. And the great Rabbi Yehuda proclaimed that she was right: *Yafe amra Brurya*—yes, this woman had understood the problem and found the solution better and faster than all the learned men around her.

Another time, she took issue with her own father. And her husband's old teacher, Rabbi Yehuda ben Baba, closed the disputation with the simple but eloquent words *Halakha kemota*—the law is and will be as formulated by Brurya.

Naturally, such success left an imprint on her character and temperament. When she was in a good and generous mood, she treated other scholars as her equals. But usually she was ironic, arrogant, condescending—sometimes even insolent.

On the street, one day, she was asked by Rabbi Yosse Haglili, "What is the direction for Lod? *"Galili Shote,"* she snapped back. "Imbecile from Galilee. Your sentence is too long. You should have said, 'Lod—which way?' " And she added with biting sarcasm, "Don't you know what the sages have told us? That one ought not talk too much with women?" This was an opportunity for revenge she could not let slip. Here she was demonstrating not only that men were more talkative than women but also more anxious to talk to women than the other way around.

Once a heretic sought to provoke her. "It is written," he said, "in the name of the Prophets, *Roni akara*—Rejoice, childless woman, for not having children. Why should she rejoice?" "Idiot," Brurya retorted. "The image deals with the people of Israel who should rejoice if women do not have children like you."

Sometimes she had recourse to more direct arguments. Noticing a student silently rehearsing his lesson, she rewarded him with a good kick, accompanied by the following pedagogical advice: Study aloud, it's good for the memory.

She practiced total freedom of expression, total independence of action. Nobody could discipline her, nothing could restrain her. Her husband himself could not avoid her barbs.

And she could also be moderate. Annoyed by hoodlums in their street, Rabbi Meir decided, rather than fight, to pray for their deaths. But Brurya did not agree with such tactics: "Pray for the

sins to perish—not the sinners." And Rabbi Meir obeyed once
again. She was right once again.

But away from home Rabbi Meir was less obedient, less easy
to get along with—less inhibited, too. To compensate for his
passivity at home? He was constantly on official missions, many of
them secret. He debated heretics and philosophers—he even carried on a dialogue with Cleopatra, of all people. She had requested
his frank and expert opinion on the question of whether the dead,
in the afterlife, go around clothed or naked. People enjoyed talking to him. His views were original, his positions daring. He liked
to surprise and be surprised. In the academies one could always
count on him to oppose established views, to incite contradiction,
to jolt the mind. Being more erudite than many of his colleagues,
more sharp-witted than most of them, he naturally was not too
popular in their milieu. Rabbi Yehuda bar Ilaï told him to get out
of his sight, and he sent his servants out to beat him up for
having come to bother him in his own home with his scholarly
tricks.

Rabbi Meir could demonstrate that an object was pure *or*
impure by using one hundred and fifty arguments—either way.
He would praise two rivals for their opposing views. Said Rabbi
Aha ben Hanina: *"Galoui veyadoua,* it is clear before God and man
that Rabbi Meir is the greatest of his contemporaries. Why then
did his laws not prevail? Because his colleagues could never get to
the bottom of his thinking." In other words, knowledge became
an obstacle for him. He knew too much; he understood and could
express his opponent's views and his own with equal talent and
passion.

Rabbi Yehuda bar Ilaï, the first to speak, always, disliked him
to the point of issuing an injunction against him and his pupils,
forbidding them entrance to the academy—the reason being that
they were quarrelsome. The injunction stayed in force even after
Rabbi Meir's death. Yet one of his disciples, Somakhus, succeeded
in bypassing what we would call today the security checks. When
he was discovered, the president ordered his expulsion and vented
his anger: "Were my orders not clear enough?" But then Rabbi
Yosse remarked softly, "What will people say? That Meir is dead,
Yehuda angry, Yosse silent—and Torah, what will become of Torah?"

Rabbi Meir had his troubles with the leadership to which he
belonged even while Rabbi Shimon ben Gamliel was still presi-

dent. The other two leadership positions were held by Rabbi Nathan and Rabbi Meir.

What made Rabbi Meir unhappy? For one thing, protocol. At the opening of a session, the audience was supposed to stand to welcome the three leaders and wait until they had been escorted to their seats. But the president didn't like that. He wanted greater honors for himself than for his two associates. So he changed the rules. Everybody had to rise when he entered; but only some for the other two.

Rabbi Meir was offended, so he incited his friend Rabbi Nathan to rebel against the president. "Listen," he told him, "I have an idea. Let us take up the Tractate of Oktzin [Stalks] which *he* knows so poorly. . . ." Thus he thought to embarrass the president and thereby weaken his position. What they did not know was that a certain Rabbi Yaakov ben Karsi secretly went to warn the president and teach him that same tractate. "Were you out to humiliate me?" Rabbi Shimon ben Gamliel shouted next day. "Out with you!"

The two ousted scholars would not give up. They would write difficult questions on pieces of paper and throw them inside through the window for students to pick up and read aloud. If the president knew the answer, the two would keep quiet and prepare the next question. If *he* kept quiet, they would shout the answer through the window.

The situation could not last indefinitely. Rabbi Yosse spoke for everyone present when he remarked with his usual gentleness, "Torah is outside—and we are inside?" The two scholars were invited to come back inside and take their places. Eventually Rabbi Nathan apologized. Rabbi Meir did not.

Yet he did have a strong sense of camaraderie: he gave to his friends what he refused to give to his superiors. Once, the discussion centered on the question of whether one was allowed to mix wine and oil on Shabbat, as a medication for a sick person. All said no, he said yes. But when he himself became sick, he refused the medication, explaining, *"Miyamai lo avarti al divre haverai*—I have never transgressed decisions taken by my friends."

Though he thought he knew better than they, and that he was right, he yielded to their collective judgment. He was a wise man.

His wisdom is illustrated by certain aphorisms. He said, "Look not at the vessel but at its content." (This saying is also attributed to Rabbi Yehuda the Prince.) To stress the principle of human equality, he affirmed that God had gathered clay from all over the world to create Adam—thus, no person could claim superiority over another.

A striking image: "Man is born with his fists closed but dies with his hands open. When he arrives, he wants everything; when he leaves, it is with nothing."

Many of his sayings deal with women: "If things go well for a couple," he said, "the Divine Presence will protect them; if not, the fire of the one will devour the fire of the other."

He hated the wicked but he hated the ignorant more. "Whenever someone marries his daughter off to an ignorant man, it is as if he bound her by her hands and feet and handed her to a lion."

Another one: "The hate an ignorant man feels toward a sage is more ferocious than the hate the enemies of Israel nourish for the Jews." And this postscript: "But even more ferocious is his wife's hatred for a sage."

Every morning he recited the benediction, "Blessed be Thou for not having made me into an ignoramus."

And this extravagant statement: "A gentile who studies Torah is worth a High Priest."

He had both compassion and wit. Once he exclaimed: "Whether Jews accomplish God's will or not, they remain His children—so if You, God, refuse to liberate them . . . I shall do it myself." One day the discussion in the academy centered around the significance of the eclipse of the sun. All agreed that it was a bad omen. But—bad for whom? "For the enemies of Israel," said Rabbi Meir—for in the darkness, they would not see the Jews whom they so anxiously wished to harm.

For Rabbi Meir and Brurya the words are adventure and discovery. They live intensely, dangerously. There is never a boring moment. They stimulate, they wound, they search. In their presence everything moves, every string vibrates, sings, and breaks.

And yet in their most private moments they are haunted by melancholy. There is the memory of the dead, so many dead, in their immediate family and beyond. The chain of disasters. The death sentences, the public executions. So many teachers, so many disciples who vanished in fire. And the sister—Brurya's sister—among the prostitutes. The couple must have been inconsolable, unconsoled.

Legends maintain that Rabbi Meir undertook a cloak-and-dagger operation to kidnap and free his sister-in-law. He discovered her general whereabouts and went there disguised as a Roman horseman. On the verge of discovery, he managed to escape and mingled with the Romans. Finally, to outwit his pursuers, he seized a non-kosher dish, dipped a finger in it, and sucked another with delight. A man who doesn't eat kosher cannot be Jewish, the pursuers thought.

Some sources believe that it was this last adventure that caused him to flee Palestine for the last time. Others claim it was related to jealousy among the leadership. Still another version puts the blame on—women. The story goes that he was trapped and seduced by a married woman and that his expatriation was but an act of penance. The Midrash claims that, wishing to die, he went to a forest hoping to be devoured by lions. He waited and finally one lion came, but it ignored him. The local rabbi pleaded with Rabbi Meir to leave the forest; having been exposed to lions was sufficient atonement. "No, this means nothing," said Rabbi Meir. "Maybe the next lion will act differently." But the second lion didn't touch him either. "Maybe he isn't hungry," Rabbi Meir said. "The next one will have a better appetite." And indeed the third one tore into his flesh. And Rabbi Meir atoned for his sin.

And then there is one more theory about his escape: that he fled Palestine because of a tragic incident that happened to . . . his wife, Brurya.

It all began with a lively discussion between husband and wife. The subject? Women. Rabbi Meir had the misfortune of stating his conviction that *Nashim datan kala*—women have weak minds and no willpower. Naturally, Brurya made it her business to prove the contrary. Which prompted her husband—according to a strange Midrash quoted by Rashi—to use a radical and questionable method. To prove his point, he asked one of his pupils to try to seduce her. And lo and behold, the student succeeded. Rabbi Meir had won a debate but lost a wife. Brurya, seized by remorse, hanged herself. She must have realized that she had been humiliated not only by her husband but also by her young lover: they had both lied to her. They had manipulated her feelings. Ashamed and crushed, Rabbi Meir left Palestine for good. He died abroad, in exile. Nobody knows the location of his tomb. The mystery of his end thus is as complete as that of his beginnings.

His tragedy was of another kind as well: his decisions did not become laws. *Ein poskim halakha kemoto,* states the Talmud. In spite of his knowledge, in spite of his intellectual abilities, his propositions are not considered binding. Ironically, some of them were adopted without being attributed to him. *Aherim omrim*—others are saying—always means Rabbi Meir. His name is not mentioned when credit is given. And irony of ironies, it was he who had proclaimed that "he who gives credit to authors brings redemption into the world." What a magnificent and generous concept! Unfortunately, it was not employed on his behalf: his laws are not quoted *beshem omram*, for attribution. Rabbi Shimon, son of Rabbi Yehuda, felt he had to speak up against such discrimination: "Father," he said, "who are those people whose wine we drink but whose names are not mentioned?" "These are men," said Rabbi Yehuda, "who tried to uproot your honor and that of your father's: they are our enemies." "But that was long ago," pleaded the son. "Their loves and their jealousies vanished long ago." Nevertheless, Rabbi Yehuda—the author of the Mishna—held fast to his grudge. He could never bring himself to quote Rabbi Meir directly and say, *"Amar* Rabbi Meir (and Rabbi Meir said)." At the most, he would say, *Amru mishum* Rabbi Meir—others have said in his name. . . ."

In conclusion, we must ask ourselves the question, "Why such hostility, why such punishment? Yosse ben Halafta called him "a great man, a holy man, a modest man," and Shimon ben Lakish called him "holy mouth." Then why were his laws ignored? Solely because of his opposition to the establishment? Or his failure to recognize the danger inherent in abstract knowledge? Or was it because of his loyalty to Elisha ben Abouya? Because he personified the disciple and not the Master? Or else because of his obscure origins? Or could Brurya have been the cause? Did he pay for her arrogance—her suicide?

Whatever the reason, his punishment seems cruel. Although we know that *Stam Mishna kerebe Meir,* that whenever the Mishna is anonymous, it belongs to Rabbi Meir, his views were rejected and his statements remain anonymous. Nothing can be more unfair to a scholar.

Rabbi Pinhas of Koretz must have been disturbed by Rabbi Meir's fate for he tried to correct it. When the Messiah will come, said Rebbe Pinhas of Koretz, the *Halakha*—the law—will be according to Rabbi Meir. Good—we will wait. We have no choice.

Rabbi Shimon bar Yohai
and His Son

RABBI SHIMON BAR YOHAI and Rabbi Eleazar ben Shimon: a
heroic father and a devoted son. Both are celebrated as great Talmudic Masters. They were close—few fathers have been as close to
their sons. Few sons have followed their fathers so far. They lived
together, hid together, suffered together, studied together, together they were subjected to fear and torment. They survived
together.

But they did not die together.

Said Rabbi Abba:

"When our Master felt he was about to return to heaven, he
raised his arms in prayer; he seemed elated. His faithful disciples
were gathered around his bed: his son Rabbi Eleazar, and Rabbis
Yuda, Yosse, Khiya, and myself. To Rabbi Itzhak, who came late,
he said, 'You are blessed, for an immense joy is awaiting you
today.' Then he turned to all of us and said: 'The hour has come
and I wish to enter the world of truth without shame. Therefore,
I shall reveal to you secrets never heard by human ears, for I do not
wish to be accused of having failed my mission by keeping them
to myself.'"

Rabbi Shimon bar Yohai spoke in a whisper. "Abba will write
what I said, my son will repeat and teach it, and the rest of you will
remember."

Said Rabbi Abba:

"I put the words we heard on paper. The last one his lips
formed was—life. Then he stopped. I went on writing. I thought
there was more to come. But nothing came. I wanted to look but
couldn't, I couldn't lift my head, for there was so much light that
my eyes could not meet his eyes. There was so much splendor

enveloping the house that no one could come near it all day. As for myself, I was lying in the dust and howling with pain. But as the splendor withdrew, I saw that our Master—the Holy Lamp, the saint among saints—had left us. Covered with his *tallith,* he lay on his right side, a mysterious smile on his face.

When his disciples carried him outside, they witnessed another miracle: his coffin suddenly rose into the air, a cloud of fire preceding it, and a voice was heard proclaiming, "Enter and take part in the wedding feast of Rabbi Shimon."

This description, taken from Zohar—the Book of Splendor—is corroborated nowhere in the Talmud or in Midrashic literature. Hence it can hardly be accepted as historically accurate. Even the most enthusiastic admirers of the Zohar do not pretend that it is of real value to historians, as is the Talmud, for instance. Whether or not the Zohar was written on behalf of Rabbi Shimon bar Yohai by his close disciples—and there are still people who piously believe it *was*—one fact is beyond dispute: the Zohar does not concern itself with concrete events but with their substance and symbols. Its tales and parables strive to transcend time and memory, its realm is the world to come and not this world, its images—dazzling and penetrating—could serve as guidelines to theologians and students in quest of mystical truth, but are useless as terms of reference to chroniclers.

Yet it seems wrong, and would be misleading, to consider these two works—of extraordinary importance and beauty—as belonging to two different domains. Instead I see them as two concentric circles: their center is one and the same.

The main danger, of course, lies in confusing genres. To study Talmud as fiction—unrelated to life and human experience—is as dangerous as reading the Zohar as a textbook for applied sciences or beginners in archaeology.

The Talmud is logic, discipline, jurisprudence, philosophy, history, and literature. Does this mean that the Zohar is none of these? It simply means that, like all great works that lift man above his condition, the Zohar, with its hallucinatory powers, possesses its own logic, its own discipline, its own literary pattern. The key phrase in Talmud is *Ta shema*—Come and listen; in the Zohar, the key phrase is *Ta khazi*—Come and see. See what words conceal, see what the mind fails to comprehend, see what man does to silence in whose sharply defined spheres God's presence is felt, glorified, and liberated. *Ta shema*—for the oral tradition is language; the esoteric one is silence; *Ta khazi*—open your eyes and look, and say not what you see, for you will see it no longer.

Talmud means study, and study implies rationalism, which, in turn, implies a kind of horizontal approach to the subject; you must follow the development of ideas and arguments, one after the other, one page after the other—and if you listen well, you may solve the problem. Zohar, by contrast, means splendor, and implies an introspective attitude: what you see, you see all at once, not consecutively. Sometimes you must close your eyes in order to see. In other words: your inner *attitude* toward Talmud and Zohar is not the same. If you don't understand a Talmudic passage, you may repeat it one hundred and one times; you will still need someone to explain it to you. But—if you repeat a page of Zohar enough times, it will offer itself to you and become yours. You may still not understand its meaning, but you will sense its secret.

Let scholars and historians argue whether Rabbi Shimon bar Yohai was or was not the author of the Zohar. To the storyteller, the question seems, in a way, irrelevant. What matters to me is that, for many generations, the Zohar *has been attributed to him*—why?

Why was *he* chosen? Why is *his* name revered in Kabbala more than any other Talmudic Master? Why is his *Yahrzeit* observed in Meron with thousands and thousands of pilgrims who spend the night singing and dancing with his name on their lips and his prayer in their hearts? Why was the holy Ari his avowed follower? Why did Rabbi Haim Vital pay him such tribute? Why was the entire movement fascinated, inspired, by *his* image? In other words, what was it in his personality, in his temperament, in his life pattern that made him, in the eyes of tradition, in the fantasy of hundreds and thousands of Jews, into the mystical leader, the mystical authority, the mystical man par excellence?

True, he probably *was* a kabbalist—but certainly not the only one. There were others, some even more renowned than he. Rabbi Ishmael the High Priest, for instance, who had frightening visions in the sanctuary. Or any other of the so-called mystical interpreters, the *Dorshei reshumot,* who, while they studied, were surrounded by heavenly fire. Or Rabbi Akiba himself—the only Master who entered the orchard of mystical truth and left unharmed. Why wasn't *he* chosen?

That the Kabbala movement had to reach so far back to find a figure to identify with is understandable. Exile and redemption are basic components of mysticism, and never did they so dominate Jewish life as in the early years of the Common Era. All that occurred later had already begun to happen then.

No wonder kabbalists turn to that period for guidance and reassurance. But the question remains: Why do they turn particularly to Rabbi Shimon bar Yohai?

Because of his general ideas? They are based on Rabbi Akiba's, he said so himself. His love of Israel, of Torah, of Eretz Israel, bear Akiba's imprint. Because of his suffering? Rabbi Akiba suffered more—in fact, any one of the Ten Martyrs went through worse torture. There were, in that time, Masters more learned than he—like Rabbi Meir—and more saintly than he—like Rabbi Zadok or Rabbi Nahum—and even, let's admit it, more daring than he. He was, after all, trying to avoid martyrdom. Then why was *he* chosen?

Not that I mind. On the contrary: I am pleased, for I am prejudiced. You see, the child in me, the yeshiva student in me, the Hasid in me, feel close to Rabbi Shimon. Why? Because his imagination was boundless. His style? Simple, concise, and evocative. No grandiloquence—no useless words. For these reasons, perhaps, he had difficulty in becoming a rabbi. Later, when he had become a rabbi, he opposed the establishment. And how can we forget his taste for solitude?

Piecing together his portrait from various texts, we find that he was born into a wealthy family in Galilee. His father, Yohai, maintained excellent relations with the occupying authorities, so Shimon ran away from home: he disliked both comfort and Romans. He spent thirteen years at Rabbi Akiba's academy, he was married, had a son—Eleazar—and became a *Halakhist* of considerable reputation.

The beginning of his career is linked—and this is symbolic—to his successful efforts on behalf of the city of Tiberias, where human bones were discovered, making it unfit for residency.

Then came Rabbi Shimon and located the cemetery, thus opening up the rest of the city, which was destined to become a great center for Jewish learning.

(Why is it symbolic? Because Jewish renaissance has often sprung from the very ground where Jews have been killed. The Crusades, the Middle Ages, the pogrom periods provide a thousand and one examples. The latest one comes from Russia. Do you know where the first militant youths met to learn Hebrew and Hebrew songs? In cemeteries—at night.)

Is this why Rabbi Shimon was chosen? Perhaps. Another reason may be that little is known about his family life. We see him with his son, we imagine him with his father—but what about his wife? She is barely mentioned. Unlike the wife of Rabbi Akiba, whose love affair with Rachel is fully described by the Talmud. And kabbalists, as you may know, tend to believe that man's only love affair should be with the Principle of Feminine Presence, embodied in the *Shekhina*. Within that frame of reference, Rabbi Shimon seems more qualified than Rabbi Akiba.

Another reason for Rabbi Shimon's influence may be his extreme single-mindedness. "There are four things," he said, "which the Holy One, blessed be He, abhors—and I dislike them, too."

On another occasion he was more explicit: "My merit is great enough to save mankind from punishment from the day of my birth until now; but should my son Eleazar join me, we might redeem it—retroactively—from the day of Creation." His generosity toward his son was touching. He was always ready to let him share his dreams and powers: his son but not his father. "I have looked about," he said, "for the *Bnei Aliyah,* those destined to reach paradise, and they are few indeed. If there be thirty, my son Eleazar and I are among them. If there be three, my son Eleazar and I would be among them. If there be two, they are my son and I. If there be one—it is I."

Would you call him an egocentric? Mysticism, egocentricity, and humility can be reconciled. As for Rabbi Shimon's words, I tend to see them as wit or self-mockery; that is why he shared his pseudo-self-glorification with his son rather than with his father: to show disrespect to one's father is a grave sin.

He did have a sharp tongue, that we know. He said, "It is written that a Jew should never stop studying Torah. Actually, it is enough for him to say *shema* mornings and evenings to fulfill the commandment. However, one must not say this in the presence of an ignoramus." Also, "It is forbidden for a man to be alone with two women, except if one of them is his wife: she would keep an eye on him."

When he came to visit Rabbi Akiba in jail, he pleaded with him: "Continue to teach me." When the Master refused, invoking how dangerous it was to study Torah, Shimon inexplicably threatened him: "I'll tell my father, Yohai; he'll hand you over to the authorities." The end of the story—which belongs to the chapter about Rabbi Akiba—is beautiful. The pupil convinced his teacher that if he stopped learning, he would be in greater danger.

Rabbi Shimon was fully aware of the risk he was running. The atmosphere in Judea was so full of suspicion that he saw informers everywhere. (Was he wrong? Wasn't his son, at one time, working for the Roman authorities?)

"Had I been standing at Sinai," Rabbi Shimon once remarked, "I would have urged the Almighty to create man with two mouths, one for Torah and the other for earthly needs." He thought a moment before continuing, "No, it wouldn't work. Man has but one mouth, and what does he do with it? He does so much informing that our world is imperiled; what would happen if he had two?"

Both he and his teacher became victims of denunciation. Their relations were ambiguous, complex. Rabbi Shimon admired Rabbi Akiba, praised him, opposed him (though rarely), only later to do penance by fasting until his "teeth turned black." At times he felt somewhat bitter about him.

Listen. Said Rabbi Abba: "In the beginning, every Master nominated, or ordained, his successors. That was the custom since Rabbi Yohanan ben Zakkai. Rabbi Akiba nominated Rabbi Meir and Rabbi Shimon. But he asked Rabbi Meir to take his seat first. At that point, Rabbi Shimon's face is said to have become twisted and to have changed color."

To understand Rabbi Shimon's hurt reaction, we must remember that students listened standing, while teachers sat. In telling Rabbi Meir to sit down first—which meant, to be ordained first—Rabbi Akiba diminished Rabbi Shimon, but was quick to reassure him: Why feel rejected? "It is enough that I and your Maker know your power."

Reassured or not, Rabbi Shimon was hurt, and let it be known. "My Master Akiba," he said, "gave four interpretations with which I disagree; mine are better." After Rabbi Akiba's death, Rabbi Yehuda quoted one of his rulings, and Rabbi Shimon replied, "No, he issued no such ruling; I was there. But, of course, then he was still alive. He may have changed his mind since."

Why did Rabbi Akiba favor Rabbi Meir? Because he was older? Kinder? More learned? Rabbi Shimon's name is related to as many as three hundred and twenty-five *Halakhot* in the Mishna, yet Rabbi Meir is ahead of him with three hundred and thirty-five. Is this why he had priority? Or was it because Rabbi Akiba felt uncomfortable with Rabbi Shimon, whose son Eleazar was not without blemish?

This story in the Talmud has the ring of authenticity.

One day Rabbi Eleazar ben Shimon gave the following advice to a police official in charge of catching thieves: "Let us say you walk into a store at four o'clock. If you see a man dozing off with a glass of wine in his hand, he may be a *Talmid khaham,* a scholar who rose early to study, or a worker who rose early for work; if he is neither—then he is a thief!"

Apparently it worked—it worked so well that it came to the attention of the king, who inquired, Who gave that advice? He was told. Said the king, If this man is so good—let him do the job! And—unbelievable but true—Rabbi Eleazar, son of the illustrious Rabbi Shimon, joined the police and began catching thieves!

He must have been successful, since the revered Rabbi Yeoshua ben Korkha found it necessary to dispatch a messenger with the question, *"Khometz ben yayin*—You, vinegar, son of wine—how long will you go on handing over our people to the executioner?" Rabbi Eleazar answered, "All I do is weed the thorns from the vineyard." The explanation did not satisfy Rabbi Yeoshua, who had the last word—one of the most magnificent in Jewish ethics and lore: "Let the vineyard not worry you; let the owner come and do away with the thorns." Meaning, no man should appoint himself instrument of God—especially not of God's wrath. If God wants to punish someone, let Him do so—alone.

What made Rabbi Eleazar join the police in the first place? Is it that he wished to resemble his grandfather, Yohai? Didn't he take into consideration his father's feelings? Or is it that Rabbi Shimon was no longer alive? Probably. Otherwise he himself would have chastised his son. Anyway, within the framework of the tale, one must empathize with Rabbi Shimon, caught in the middle between his father and his son; both worked for the enemy.

Rabbi Eleazar repented. He did *teshuvah,* that much is certain; he chose extreme suffering as a form of expiation. But what about Yohai? Was there a time when Rabbi Eleazar felt closer to him than to his father, as many children do?

Let us seize the opportunity and briefly examine the problem of father-son relationships in ancient Judaism.

In the Bible, I find them discouraging. Adam and Eve's sons introduced death through murder into history. Jacob and Esau's quarrels did not make Isaac too happy. Joseph's brothers caused enough pain to their father. What about Aaron's two sons, who entered drunk—or who brought alien fire—into the sanctuary? Samuel's sons were corrupt judges. David's were overambitious and rebellious.

Fathers and sons fare better in the Talmud. They are involved in few disputes, and in no intrigues over titles or inheritance. There, children respect their parents, pupils honor their teachers. Often fathers invoke with pride their sons' fame rather than the other way around. The reason? Power and pursuit of power are not viewed kindly in Talmudic circles. What matters there are piety, moral behavior, and learning, which is the stuff nobility is made of. Knowledge cannot be inherited—power can.

What about Rabbi Shimon and his son? Were they always together? Always united? If the answer is no, what does it say about both of them? Is it possible that the great Rabbi Shimon bar Yohai was not such a great father after all? And that the son was not always such a devoted son? What was it, what could it be, that moved the son away—though temporarily—from his father's teaching? A taste for adventure? A desire to discover the other side of Judaism? Where is the answer to be found? In his own trials? In those of his father?

It is customary to think that there are *two* Rabbi Shimons— or, at least, two portraits of him: the one in Talmudic literature, the other in the Zohar. The first is human, the second quasi-divine.

In the Talmud he appears as a forceful personality, with his likes and dislikes, his passions and weaknesses, his whims and desires. We are told that during the thirteen years spent in Rabbi Akiba's yeshiva in Bnei-Brak, he, unlike his comrade Hananya ben Ahunai, wrote home regularly; participated in campus activities; and was instrumental in removing Rabban Gamliel from office as president.

Also, we are told that he was not easy to get along with. He was stubborn, unbending. When a man exclaimed to his wife, "May I perish if Rabbi Yehuda and Rabbi Shimon don't taste your food," only Rabbi Yehuda consented to taste it; Rabbi Shimon said, "Let his children be orphans; but Shimon will not budge from his place."

On another occasion he paid a sick call to a man who was complaining to God. "Pray instead," said Rabbi Shimon. "So?"

said the patient. "In that case may God take my pain and put it into you." "I had that coming," Rabbi Shimon commented angrily. "I should have known better than to take time out from study."

Oversensitive, suspicious, he had few friends. Rabbi Akiba's sentence, quoted earlier—"It is enough that I and your Maker know your power"—indicates that Rabbi Shimon was not too popular. He was too extreme, too demanding—and totally unyielding. He said, "A scholar *must* be vindictive." And, "If you see towns uprooted, know they did not pay their scholars."

Quite a different portrait is handed down in the Zohar, which depicts him as saintly and compassionate, desirous to save man and relieve his suffering—and relieve the suffering of the *Shekhina* as well. He cries frequently—unlike the Rabbi Shimon of the Talmud. He is father, friend, defender, all at once. He consoles all those who need consolation, he brings hope to the desperate. For "all the thrones, all the heavens, all the celestial hosts, and all the angels listen to his voice." One day he saw the Angel of Death dancing in front of his disciple, Rabbi Yitzhak. So he went toward Rabbi Yitzhak, took his hand, and exclaimed, "Enter those who enter always—and no one else." Thus, Rabbi Yitzhak entered the House of Study, while the Angel of Death was kept outside.

Is it possible to combine or reconcile the two portraits? Yes—for, in truth, there are two portraits of him in Talmudic literature, too.

One precedes his entrance into the cave, the other covers the period following his return to society. The thirteen years spent in hiding underground had changed him greatly. The accumulation of so much solitude and silence had to have an effect, even on a man as strong-willed as he was.

What made him go underground? Rabbi Yuda, Rabbi Yosse, and Rabbi Shimon were gathered together, with Rabbi Yehuda—the son of converts—sitting nearby. Said Rabbi Yehuda, "How marvelous these Romans are; they have built roads, constructed bridges, and opened spas." Rabbi Yosse kept silent, but Rabbi Shimon retorted on the spot, "Whatever they have done, they have done for themselves: they needed streets for prostitutes, bridges for tolls, and spas for their physical welfare." Apparently somebody informed the authorities—could it have been Yehuda, the son of converts? Could a rabbi be a provocateur? An informer? Possible and even probable, it is hinted in the various sources. The

Talmud could have censored the news, but Jewish tradition has always been against censorship of any kind. Next we learn the results of the denunciation. The Governor proclaimed: "Yehuda praised—he shall be elevated; Yosse kept silent—he shall be exiled; Shimon blamed—he shall die."

Rabbi Shimon refused to die—even as a martyr. Unlike his Master, Rabbi Akiba, who accepted martyrdom with exultation, Rabbi Shimon preferred hiding. Taking his son Eleazar with him, he hid in the House of Study. His wife brought them bread and water. When the danger grew worse, Rabbi Shimon said to his son, "Women cannot be relied upon; they would not resist torture." So they sought refuge in a cave in the mountains.

The Midrash tells some colorful stories about their experiences there. Numerous miracles happened to them. For twelves years they lived outside society until the prophet Elijah came to inform them that the ruthless emperor had died, and so they could come out. They did—and what did they see? Life was going on as usual. They hardly believed their eyes: they had come from too far—from a different world, a different reality. They had been alone so long, their inner life was so full of hallucination that they didn't know that while they were away, others remained preoccupied with routine matters. They saw a man tilling his field and exclaimed, "How can he neglect his eternal life for earthly gains?" So enraged were they that whatever they looked upon was reduced to ashes. They met the informer and wondered aloud, "What, he is still around?" He died instantly. Then a heavenly voice was heard: "Have you left your hiding place only to destroy my world? Go back to your cave." And back they went for another year. When they came out again, Rabbi Eleazar was still angry, but his father was not. "Whatever Rabbi Eleazar's eyes wounded, Rabbi Shimon's eyes healed."

Therein lay Rabbi Shimon's greatness. He had to go beyond suffering—the last year was probably the hardest—in order to rediscover compassion and understanding. Had he remained angry and bitter to the end, he would have been remembered with awe, not with love, and surely not in mystical legend. The last year made a different man out of him. It was a year beyond: beyond suffering, beyond fear, beyond solitude.

For suffering confers no privilege on anyone; it all depends on what one does with it. If it leads to resentment and revenge, it is doomed to remain weak and sterile; if it becomes an opening toward man, then it may turn into strength.

Suddenly we understand his intrinsic relationship with the universe of Kabbala, where man is required to go beyond all limits in order to attain his own liberation—and that of Creation as a whole. And he who had mocked his Master for considering the glorious general Bar Kochba as the Messiah, now, when everything seemed lost, joined the messianic movement—the movement of men and women waiting for the Messiah. Waiting actively and creatively, he turned the waiting itself into a weapon.

His attitude toward individuals changed, too. He helped a childless couple salvage their marriage—and performed miracles so they could have children. He, the former fugitive, agreed to go to Rome on a political mission. He understood the ambiguity of suffering; it pushes man to extremes, and does not necessarily make him better. That is the meaning of his saying that the *Shekhina* accompanies Israel into exile—and from exile. Israel needs the *Shekhina* in order not to succumb to suffering, to the evil in suffering.

Somehow, in Rabbi Shimon's later period, we come across most themes that haunt the kabbalistic universe. The importance of the self: any person can save the world or destroy it. The ability, nay, the necessity, to transform curses into blessings, darkness into light. The link between human saintliness and God's—and, finally, the liberation of man as part of cosmic liberation. He quotes a parable: Imagine a ship with many passengers; suddenly one of them begins making a hole in the floor. The others protest, naturally. But he says, "Why do you object? I am only digging under *my* seat!" The same applies—the other way around—to the Just Man.

No other Talmudic sage has assigned such powers to man—or, in his words—to Israel, symbol and epitome of man. According to Rabbi Shimon, God told Israel of a covenant binding both sides: "My Torah is in your hands, while your life is in mine; if you keep what is mine, I shall keep what is yours."

But that, too, works both ways. And Rabbi Shimon, with unusual candor and courage, said so. It is written *Ki edim atem laadoshem*—And you are my witnesses, said the Lord, meaning, If you are my witnesses, I am the Lord—if you are not my witnesses, I am not the Lord.

God-*kavyachol* needs man, just as man needs God: isn't that what Kabbala is about? Is that why the Zohar was ascribed to Rabbi Shimon? Perhaps. What is certain is that the changes he underwent bring him closer to us—to our generation and its experiences.

True, Rabbi Akiba suffered more than he. But Rabbi Akiba was not alone. And he was not condemned to live underground, outside society, outside history, as was his disciple. Rabbi Shimon had to endure far more than his Master, for he survived his own ordeal. When he left his prison-cave for the first time, he felt what our generation's survivors felt when they saw what happened—or that nothing happened—while they were away. Only then were they confronted with the real problem: what to do with their anger, their pain, and their despair. Like Rabbi Shimon, they could have destroyed Creation—and like him, they chose not to.

Rabbi Eleazar was the angriest of the two, insists the Talmud. Could it be that Rabbi Eleazar was so disappointed in Judea's inhabitants that in his outrage he chose to chastise or accepted the task of chastising them if only to "teach them a lesson" by joining the police? Or was it a belated rebellion against his father's Judeocentrist philosophy? And to affirm his independence? Psychologically, such an explanation would sound valid. But the fact is that, within the Talmud tradition, father and son *are* reconciled. Both are not only remembered but also revered. Rabbi Eleazar's place in Talmud is not less secure than that of his illustrious father. Our admiration for his father may seem greater, but we love the son too. After all, remember, he did join his father when he had gone into hiding. Rabbi Eleazar was not sought by the police, his life and liberty were not threatened, he could have gone on living, studying, dreaming—but he chose to remain with his father. He could not tolerate the idea that his father would suffer alone, and alone endure hunger and thirst and fear. At that moment, his father's fate was to him more important than anything else in the world.

I think of him fondly because . . . I recall a time when I was with my father *there,* away from home. We were not alone, and yet we were. And because we were alone as never before, we grew close to one another as never before. Before—I rarely saw him. He was busy in the store or in the community. I saw him on Shabbat. Now I saw him all the time. We could finally talk and talk. He alone mattered to me, I alone mattered to him. I was essential to his life as he was to mine.

But unlike Rabbi Eleazar and his father, I left the cave alone.

One last tale: When Rabbi Shimon and Rabbi Eleazar left the cave, it was Friday afternoon. They encountered an old man carrying two myrtles. "What for?" they asked. "For Shabbat," he replied. "It is good to welcome it with the pleasant fragrance." "Why two?" they wondered. "Because the commandment of Shabbat is twofold," he said. "Shabbat is to be remembered *and* observed."

Thanks to that old man and his gift to Shabbat, Rabbi Shimon and his son could reconcile themselves with the world. And, why not with each other?

And thanks to this story, we are ready to go to Meron every Lag b'Omer and sing the glory of the sage whose tales made Jews dance and rejoice—and above all dream impossible dreams of man and God being united in hope for redemption, united in ecstasy when not in despair.

Rabbi Zeira

IT HAS BEEN SAID of Rabbi Zeira, the sage whose wisdom was surpassed only by his humility, that before setting out on his journey to the land of Israel, he fasted one hundred days—or three hundred days, or nine hundred days—in order to forget the teaching he had received in the prestigious Babylonian academies.

Whether or not the effort was successful we do not know; the Talmud chooses not to tell us. What is puzzling is Rabbi Zeira's strong desire to forget. Isn't education based on remembering? Aren't Jews committed to memory? Aren't we defined and sometimes shielded by it? Aren't we supposed to enrich it, to delve deeper into it at all costs, at all times? We are supposed, indeed, ordered, to remember—to remember what we endured in Egypt, and what we heard at Sinai. Why then did Rabbi Zeira aspire to erase from his memory what he learned when he was younger, in exile?

These are disturbing questions. There are more.

Having arrived in the land of Israel, Rabbi Zeira acquired a great reputation, which he surely deserved, but . . . whenever he spoke of Babylon, he referred to it with disdain. He seemed to harbor against its Jews some deep-seated grudge, totally uncharacteristic of his nature. "Ah, those stupid Babylonians," he would exclaim. (So, he did *not* forget them, after all?) He who usually expressed nothing but love for all people, including the sinners and the wicked, he who judged everybody favorably, charitably, showed himself strangely intolerant when it came to Babylonians. It seems even stranger when we consider that throughout the Talmud he is depicted as a likable man. He is praised for his piety, his modesty, and, naturally, for his learning.

As we shall later see, he is a kind of anti-hero, an innocent in the fullest sense of the term: everything happens to him, and the outcome is always sad. He is forever falling victim to bad luck, to unpleasant surprises. And yet he is never bitter (except when Babylonian Jews are mentioned). He goes on living his life as if nothing had happened; he goes on smiling, as if to say, Please, do not feel sorry for me, I am happy. I may even be happier than you. . . .

Compared to other Talmudic Masters—Rabbi Akiba and his heroic death, Rabbi Shimon bar Yohai and his mystical solitude, Rabbi Yohanan ben Zakkai, Rabbi Eliezer, Rabbi Yeoshua, and their efforts to rebuild Jewish culture during and after the destruction of Jerusalem—Rabbi Zeira and his life story may appear pale. Unlike most of these, he lived in quasi-normal times. The period lacked the drama, the tragic quality of the first-century Common Era, when Jewish destiny itself was hanging in the balance. Rabbi Yohanan ben Zakkai and his disciples were involved in war and the survival of the Jewish nation—not so Rabbi Zeira. During his lifetime, the situation was more or less quiet. The borders were open. You could go from Babylon to Palestine and back without difficulty. Granted, the land was dominated by foreign troops, but its spiritual and intellectual activity continued to grow. And Rabbi Zeira's life was not in danger.

But when we study the sources about him we are reminded of how deceptive first impressions can be. As a Master, he is equal to the greatest. As a person, he is fascinating in his complexity. As a subject, he illustrates a problem, a dilemma which preoccupies us, Jews of the Diaspora.

I am referring to the question—painful for some, joyous for others, and irrelevant for a few—of the relations that existed between Babylon, symbolizing the Diaspora, and the land of Israel: these two communities, these two notions, these two endeavors, these two modes of life and thought and allegiance, can they ultimately be reconciled or are they to remain forever incompatible? Where is the solution to be found: in harmony or in divorce?

No one in the Talmud has so vividly illustrated the gravity of the problem with his words and deeds as Rabbi Zeira. Why are most of his sayings from Babylon, whereas all his laws were enunciated in Palestine?

Let us follow him in his travels. We shall smile with him, not at him; we shall listen to his teachers in both countries. We shall witness with him, and, thanks to him, the magnificent explosion of Jewish learning. We shall follow him into the stimulating and dazzling universe of Talmudic study—two words with the same meaning: the study of study?—a place where times ceases to exist as an obstacle and emerges as a haven for those who, through the fiery vehicle of language, strive to rebuild a sacred Temple in honor of God and His children.

The Talmud has no end—I mean, no official end. Rav Ashi concluded the editing of the Babylonian Talmud but refrained from sealing it, and he did so on purpose: to allow us to continue. Every one of us may, while exploring its complex *Sugyot* and illuminating tales, link our soul to its own.

That is why we study Talmud with such passion; and that is why our enemies have, throughout generations of suspicion and bad faith, hated it and us with a similar passion. They envied us the Talmud more than the Bible. The Talmud filled them with fear: they sensed in it our most tangible reason for our survival in exile. That is why they tried to ridicule it, even burn it.

For us, the Talmud represents a possibility of transcending the present and extending its boundaries; we repeat an ancient discussion and we become participants; we study the interpretation of old laws and customs, and they commit us anew. We recall what was said two thousand years ago, and we gain the impression that every word, every sentence, every question and every answer were meant for us—particularly when they bear the imprint of Rabbi Zeira.

His passion for study; his all-consuming love for the land of Israel; his unbending principles, his stubborn curiosity; his belief that all suffering has meaning—Rabbi Zeira *is* someone special.

A story: The day Rabbi Zeira saw his dream fulfilled—the day he finally set foot in the Holy Land—he entered a butcher shop to buy a pound of meat. "How much is it?" he asked. "Fifty cents [or *Selaim*] and . . . one whiplash," answered the butcher, tongue in cheek. "I'll gladly give you sixty cents but spare me the whiplash," said Rabbi Zeira. "Impossible," said the butcher. "It is our custom that no one gets meat unless a whiplash is added to the price." Flabbergasted, Rabbi Zeira tried to bargain: "I'll give you seventy cents, eighty, ninety . . . I'll give you a hundred. . . ." In vain. The butcher would not budge. In despair, Rabbi Zeira accepted the whiplash and purchased his meat. Later that day, he went to the House of Study, where he met the local sages whom he had known by reputation and who knew him as well. "You sure have strange customs in your community," he told them. They asked him to explain. And so he did. "It seems impossible to get food here without being beaten up in the process," he said. They were shocked and they quickly dispatched messengers to fetch the butcher—but they were too late. Just as they arrived, his coffin was carried out of his house! Convinced that it was Rabbi Zeira who had cursed and punished him, they turned to him and said, "Do you think his practical joke deserved such harsh punishment?" Rabbi Zeira swore that he had nothing to do with it. "I wasn't even angry at him," he said. "I really believed this to be the local custom and therefore submitted to it without protest."

We may learn several lessons from this episode. First, we learn that Rabbi Zeira did his own shopping. Second, that Jewish butchers in Palestine loved to play practical jokes on their intellectual customers; third, that Rabbi Zeira was excessively credulous—and hungry. And fourth, that integration problems for newcomers were already serious in Rabbi Zeira's time.

Unfortunately, little is known of his earlier life in Babylon. What kind of childhood did he have? When did he emigrate to Palestine? Nothing of all this has been recorded either by him or by anyone else. Perhaps he considered himself so unimportant that he did not bother to discuss his private affairs . . . in public.

What do we know about his personal life? Born in Babylon in the third century Common Era, he was orphaned at a very young age. His father had served as tax collector for the royal Persian government but, unlike his colleagues, had enjoyed the general esteem of the community. Several Talmudic versions mention the fact that he died before he could educate his son. Some sources maintain that Rabbi Zeira lost both his parents when he was very young. One day he was heard exclaiming, "I am sorry to have neither father nor mother to cherish and honor, and thus obtain my share in paradise." But then he was told the story of Rabbi Tarfon, who was walking with his mother on Shabbat, when she fell and lost her slipper. Her son immediately went down on his knees and, placing his hands before her, insisted that she walk home on his palms. Our sages commented: Had Rabbi Tarfon done that even a thousand times, he would still not have shown half the respect a son owes his mother.

Rabbi Zeira was also told the story of Rabbi Ishmael's mother, who came to the sages to complain about her son's behavior: "He does not honor me enough," she said. They refused to believe her. She explained: "Every time he returns home from the House of Study, I want to wash his feet and drink the water—and he says no." Commented the sages, "If such is her wish and her pleasure, it is her son's duty not to interfere."

Said Rabbi Zeira: "Now I thank God that I had neither father nor mother; for I would never be able to honor them enough and do what Rabbi Tarfon did, nor endure what Rabbi Ishmael did."

Zeira means "little" and Rabbi Zeira was a small, weak, thin man of dark complexion. He was nicknamed *Patya Oukhma,* or "black pot." Another nickname given to him was *Kharikha k'tin shakya,* the man with narrow shoulders or narrow hips; also, "the singed one." Because he was physically unattractive, he got into trouble in places where he was not known: some people have always enjoyed being cruel to victims of nature's cruelty.

Why the nicknames?

One story has it that throughout his life Rabbi Zeira feared hell and its flames; he would pray not to be touched by them, and every month he would test himself in an attempt to ward them off: he would light the stove and enter it; the flames would touch his body but he would be unharmed. Then one day, certain sages— probably jealous of his immunity—gave him the evil eye, and divine protection was withdrawn from him. And he *was* singed.

What else are we told about him? He was a *Cohen,* married, and father of a son named Ahava or Akhva. The wedding took place during Succoth, inside a succah, which pleased him, for it meant he "could perform two *mitzvot* at the same time."

For a while he was engaged in the textile trade; he must not have been too good a businessman for he soon gave it up. Certainly his true passion, his only passion, was study—and study for its own sake. The date of his death was not recorded, but we do know that he was blessed with a long life. And that even when his physical strength was gone, his mind remained astonishingly clear.

An excellent educator, he would say: "Do not make promises to a child that you cannot keep, for then you teach him how to lie."

It was his custom to conclude his daily prayers in the following manner: "O God, help me not to go astray; help me not to bring shame to my parents."

As is the case of other Masters, his life mirrors life around him. Every biography contains and becomes an element of history.

From Rabbi Zeira's attitude toward the law, we learn much of the way it affected his generation. What were people's attitudes toward money, property, and politics? Read Rabbi Zeira's stories and decisions and you will know.

A man of legends himself, hero and victim of many stories, Rabbi Zeira generally disliked them: all books of tales were, in his view, works of magic and superstition. He was a rationalist with a thirst for clarity and precision.

In a debate on mystical initiation—on who ought to be allowed to study the secret knowledge of esoteric traditions—he took the hard line: one must be worthy of and ready for such initiation. Instant mysticism? He did not believe in it. Whereas Rabbi Hiya says that one may be exposed to some ideas of Kabbala, Rabbi Zeira states that that, too, is dangerous for anyone who is not learned and sensitive enough to deal with them.

His teaching inspired innumerable laws, commentaries, anecdotes and sayings in both the Palestinian Talmud and the Babylonian. For better or worse, he forever attracted attention among scholars who praised him, and among common people who made fun of him.

He was known for two passions: his precision in study and his love for the land of Israel. The first dominated his mind, the second his soul.

He would spend days and days, for weeks on end, tracing a proposition handed down in the name of Rabbi Yohanan or one of his colleagues; he would tirelessly run from Master to Master, especially the so-called *rabbanan nekhute*—those wandering scholars who traveled from Palestine to Babylon and back—to question them about the authenticity of a particular quote or even an afterthought. Sometimes he would insist that the traveler repeat the same idea ten times, forty times. There were those who got annoyed and told him so; he didn't care. He would not let go of his source until he got the words right, until he knew exactly what the sage in Tiberias or the Master in Tsiporis had meant.

Rabbi Zeira admired Rabbi Hiya son of Abba, and this is how he explained it: "Rabbi Hiya," he said, "made sure he never distorted anything he heard from Rabbi Yohanan." For Rabbi Zeira, this was the rarest of virtues, the highest praise: to faithfully transmit what one receives from one's teacher is a privilege that elevates both the teacher and the pupil.

Rabbi Zeira's singularity? He symbolizes a tradition which he himself epitomized: he was obsessed with the faithful transmission of fact. Every interpretation had to be checked and rechecked, every idea tested again and again, every formulation examined from all angles: if he didn't trust blind men's testimony, it was because they could not *see* the person whose words they nevertheless heard.

Now, why was accurate transmission so vitally important in those days? It is simple: no books in the Bible were available then, no written books, no published documents. Human beings served as *living* libraries that could be consulted, questioned, and even "annotated."

Were it not for those sages and their extraordinary recall, the oral tradition might have perished. That is why Rabbi Zeira was so careful, so analytical, so prudent when studying someone else's views: to print "corrections" or "retractions" was impossible then.

Rabbi Zeira's commitment to truth was absolute. And yet, it did not affect his humanness. Always sociable, he liked being with people.

Actually, his two passions were linked: one of the profound motivations for his wish to go to the Holy Land and reside there was that it would enable him to study under Rabbi Yohanan, for whom he proclaimed boundless admiration.

But then, why did he talk so much about going instead of actually going? Why did he keep on singing his love for the land of Israel instead of joining those sages who indeed had picked themselves up and gone there?

He had a problem. His Babylonian teacher, Rabbi Yehuda bar reb Yehezkel, was against his making Aliyah. On principle. He believed that Jewish law forbade going to the Holy Land before messianic redemption. He quoted the Biblical verse *"Bavela youvaou veshama yihyou*—They [meaning the children of Israel] will be brought to Babylon and will stay there." And he read it literally: "They will stay there" meant "They *must* stay there." In Babylon. Until when? Until God in heaven decides to put an end to that prophecy and replace it with another.

With a teacher like that, Rabbi Zeira was afraid to make Aliya (to emigrate to the land of Israel). Moreover, he enjoyed a genuine reputation among scholars in Babylon. Respected and admired, he had great prestige, and it went beyond his immediate circle.

One day when he was staying with Rav Huna, he served the

Exilarch a cup of wine and a glass of oil, holding both in one hand. Rav Huna's son scolded him: "Why don't you use your second hand? Has it been cut off?" Rabbi Zeira, forever timid, did not answer. But the Exilarch reprimanded his son. "Have you no shame? You allow a sage such as Rabbi Zeira to serve us while you sit, and that is not sufficient for you? Must you insult him, too?"

Granted, he was not fully ordained; no one received *Smikha,* or ordination, in Babylon. But in his case that was almost irrelevant. Everyone knew that Palestinian academies would immediately confer the title "Rabbi" on him. A sage of his caliber need not worry about titles. In fact, as we shall discover later, he cared little about them, even in Palestine. All that mattered to him was learning. And his learning was so great that people could not but be impressed.

Then, one day, Rabbi Zeira made his decision: He would break all ties with exile; he would go to Palestine. But . . . how would he go about informing his irascible teacher that he was leaving him? He made several fruitless attempts, but at the last moment he lacked the courage to begin. At the last moment he would find an excuse to postpone the confrontation till later, always later. Weeks went by. And months, possibly years. The student could not tear himself away from his Master. And then, it happened. Rabbi Zeira, as usual, came to announce his departure, but Rabbi Yehuda was taking a bath. He heard the Master telling the bath attendant what to hand him first. At this, Rabbi Zeira exclaimed, "Had I come here only to learn *that* [how to behave while bathing], it would have been worth my while." But . . . *that* was not the reason for his coming; he had come prepared, for the last time, to speak to Rabbi Yehuda, to tell him of his irrevocable decision. Well, once again, he lacked the courage to do so. And once again he left without unburdening himself of his secret dream, of his burning desire—and so he went away, he left Babylon, without saying farewell to—and without receiving the blessing of—his beloved teacher.

At this point, perhaps we ought to examine the situation of the Jews in Babylon and of their brethren in Palestine; thus we shall have a better understanding of what Rabbi Zeira left behind, and of what he was about to discover.

The contact between the communities had been maintained undisturbed—regularly, frequently—for centuries—to be more precise: since King Jehoiakin's exile. History has recorded the tragic events that followed. Nebuchadnezzar and his legions invaded Judea, burned the Temple, desecrated the Sanctuary, and carried off the defeated princes and warriors as prisoners, or caused them to become refugees. The exiles settled in nostalgia and hope: "By the waters of Babylon, there we sat, there we wept as we remembered Zion," sings the Psalmist. Jerusalem was a city of ashes, but its children, uprooted and humiliated, learned under the enemy yoke how to build on memories a new but temporary existence. In doing so, they followed Jeremiah's advice. In his famous letter to the exiled Jews in Babylon, the prophet told them to build homes, to arrange weddings for their sons and daughters—in other words, not to yield to resignation, not to give in to despair, not to accept the enemy's victory as definitive or just, but to transform waiting into dream, suffering into prayer. Live, Jeremiah told them, live and celebrate life even if it seems somber, wager on the future even if it beckons you from the other side of darkness.

And so the community grew in numbers and in depth. It became a diaspora. When its leaders returned home after seventy years to rebuild the Temple, many remained behind, unwilling to give up their new lives. And so the Jews of Babylon created their own centers of learning, their own spiritual fortresses that later had an impact on the people of Israel in Israel.

Generations came and vanished; empires changed rulers and systems; but Jewish life in Babylon continued. Persians succeeded Babylonians, upheavals followed upheavals, and yet the Jewish community managed to keep its social structures alive. As long as Jews refrained from getting involved in internal political affairs, they could undertake any project and bring it to fruition. They enjoyed freedom of religion and freedom of assembly. They could study Torah and teach it; as far as faith was concerned, the government was tolerant. Like the Romans, all the Persians wanted from the Jews under their jurisdiction was . . . money.

The Jews of Babylon were so comfortable there that in spite of their fidelity to the Temple of Jerusalem—which they supported with substantial donations—they did not support the Jewish revolt against Rome which began in the year 66 c.e.: the military and political activities of their brethren in Judea were deemed foreign and they preferred not to take part in them in order not to endanger their own well-being.

Simply put, they had it too good in Babylon—it was a kind of golden age. Two brothers, Anilai and Asinai, both courageous leaders, went so far as to establish their own sovereign province, and it lasted some twenty years.

In Babylon itself, the Jewish community was ruled by its own state-appointed president; he could, if he so wished, levy taxes and sit in judgment over a variety of offenses, including capital crimes. Only the rabbis—who demanded a tax-free status—could oppose him with impunity; after all, they wore the crown of Torah.

Moreover, some of the rabbis were prestigious teachers who could—and did—compete with their Palestinian colleagues, the Tannaim, who, however, were ultimately victorious. In case of conflict, Palestinian academies had the last word. And once uttered, it was never disputed in Babylon.

All this notwithstanding, a lively and fervent debate went on at all times between the two communities, and both benefited from it. Scholars studied with more vigor, students learned with heightened enthusiasm. In spite of geographical distances, they argued over hundreds of issues. We are witness to passionate confrontations: Jewish intellectual life was rarely so productive, so creative.

That Rabbi Zeira belonged to the elite in Babylon's Jewish society is clear. Just read the names of his colleagues and friends: Rabbi Ami, Rabbi Assi, Rabbi Abba bar Hiya, Rabbi Abba bar Kahana, Rabbi Avahou, Rabbi Yaakov bar Idi—all sought his company, all looked up to him. Once when he didn't feel well, they especially prayed for his recovery. Rabbi Avahou added: "Let Rabbi Zeira get well, and in gratitude I will offer a free meal to the sages." The great Rabbi Yehuda treated him as a favorite disciple. Rav Huna, the president, or Exilarch, often invited him to his official residence. We know this from Rabbi Zeira himself, who once expressed his views on how to deal with official favors: "I refuse to accept the president's presents, but not his invitations." First, because he would never insult anyone; second, because to reject an invitation would undermine the dignity of the office of the presidency.

But a question arises: If the president invited him to his home, if the rabbis liked him, and the people respected him, why did he wish to leave for occupied Palestine? Why give up security for insecurity, the known for the unknown? Because he loved Israel? Many did—and, I hope, many do. And yet, not all the sages were ready to uproot themselves and settle there. Why was he more eager than they?

Many Talmudic tales deal with his zeal. One legend tells us that when he reached the banks of the river Jordan, he was so impatient that he forgot to undress and thus swam across fully clothed. Another legend embellishes the picture: to cross the Jordan in those days, one could either take a small boat or walk over a narrow wooden bridge, which was considered unsafe. Naturally, Rabbi Zeira, in his haste, refused to wait for the boat and chose the bridge instead. A heretic noticed him and mocked him: "What a strange, impatient people you are," he said. "Already at Sinai, your lips preceded your ears, you pledged to do things before knowing what they were, and now . . . why do you put your life in jeopardy? Can't you wait for the boat?" Rabbi Zeira replied, "I am thinking of Moses and Aaron. I am wondering: What have I done to deserve something that was denied to them? They could not enter the Holy Land—why can I?" In other words: "And since I can, why wait another second?"

Another story: One day Rabbi Zeira went to the marketplace to buy food. As he watched the merchant, he remarked, "I hope the scale has been properly adjusted." Whereupon the merchant became angry. "Go away," he shouted, "go away, Babylonian; it is your parents and theirs, your ancestors who destroyed the Temple. Get out of my sight!" Deeply hurt, Rabbi Zeira answered softly, *"My* ancestors? Aren't they also your ancestors?" The merchant turned away in disgust. Later that day, the sage went to the House of Study and listened to a lecture given by Rabbi Sheila on the Song of Songs. At one point, he heard the Master express a disturbing thought: "Had all the Jews left Babylon at the end of the first exile [had they returned to Jerusalem], the second Temple would not have been destroyed." And Rabbi Zeira said to himself, "Yes, the merchant was right."

Let us stop here. With these two legends we have reached the heart of the matter. Rabbi Zeira mirrors all the feelings, ambiguities, contradictions, endless fears, and highest hopes of all Jews who consider themselves, permanently or temporarily, also citizens of the Diaspora. Our hesitations, our limitations, our burdens of guilt, our aspirations, our blindness, too, may be summed up as follows: Is there a place for the Jew in the Diaspora? If so, what is it? Rabbi Zeira asked himself these questions, and now it is up to his students to do the same.

When Cyrus granted the Jews permission to rebuild their Temple, only a minority followed Ezra and Nehemiah. Why? How is it possible that there were Jews, many Jews, who chose not to follow their leaders, especially when they were returning to their homeland? What kept them in exile? What made them like it?

Skip twenty-five centuries and look at Eastern Europe. For a thousand years its Jews had been told by every ruler, in every language, that they were unwanted—and yet they clung to their adopted countries. Most left only when they were cast out like thieves or lepers. Why did they wait so long?

Take our contemporaries. Let us be honest and carry the thought to its limits: if Babylonian Jewry was responsible for the welfare of Jerusalem, what about our responsibility today? If anyone had told me that I, Eliezer son of Shlomo, son of Eliezer the Levite, would be privileged to see Israel's renaissance as a free and sovereign state, I would not have believed it. But if anyone had told me that a Hasid of Wiznitz, an admirer of Rabbi Levi-Itzhak of Berditchev and a follower of Rabbi Nahman of Bratzlav, would not leave everything and go and dwell on its territory, I would have believed it even less. And yet . . .

Hence the problem. Is it possible for a Jew to assume his Jewishness outside the Jewish state? Is it possible for a son of Israel to seek and attain self-fulfillment elsewhere than in the land of Israel?

In other words, when was Rabbi Zeira more himself: when he was waiting to go to Eretz Israel, or when he was already there? Furthermore, did he consider the land of Israel the opposite of Babylon? In choosing the one, did he mean to repudiate the other? What is it in the Jewish mentality that moves many of us to favor nostalgic dreams over reality, prayer over realization? Are we more attracted by the quest than by its goal?

Even more intriguing than Rabbi Zeira's predicament is his teacher Rabbi Yehuda's. After all, the Palestinian academies would have welcomed him and his pupils with open arms. Theology aside, why did he choose to stay anchored in Babylon? What held him back? The Biblical injunction? What was good enough for Ezra and Nehemiah was not good enough for him? Just imagine—had he and his disciples made Aliyah, Jewish life in Palestine would have improved a thousandfold. Why didn't they?

I know: these are painful questions. Many Masters lived and worked *in* Babylon and some went back *to* Babylon: Rav (a pillar

of the Talmud), Rabbi Levi bar Sissi, and many others, later.
Maimonides's stay in Palestine was temporary. Rabbi Nahman's
too. Why such a defection? If indeed, *"Avira d'araa makhkim,* if
the air of Israel makes you wiser," as Rabbi Zeira put it, why did
they return to the less potent air abroad? Why did they go—or
return—to Babylon? Only to atone for sins they alone were aware
of? Or to taste—briefly, fleetingly—exile and servitude so as to
better appreciate the land of Israel? Or did they go to Babylon
solely for the pleasure of *returning* to the Holy Land later?

For the fanatical members of Neturei Karta, for example, the
question doesn't even arise. They believe that all things are determined in heaven. Both exile and return depend on God's will. But
for those of us who do not claim to possess such truth or such
faith, how do *we* orient ourselves at the crossroads? Rabbi Zeira
had been told in his dreams to wait in Babylon as long as his sins
were not forgiven. Does this apply to us too? Possibly. We believe
that since we have chosen to wait, we must do something with our
waiting. For a Jew everywhere, to be Jewish means to wait.

But in the meantime, who is right? Whom are we to follow?
Rabbi Zeira had reasons to leave Babylon, whereas Rabbi Yehuda
had arguments for staying there. He was needed in Babylon, and
so were his colleagues. They were needed as educators, as spiritual
guides, as vantage points.

Rabbi Yehuda never claimed that the Babylonian academies
were meant to replace those in Palestine. On the contrary: they
were to serve as their echo and extension. Just as Yavneh never
aspired to become the substitute for Jerusalem, Sura in Babylon
never sought to replace Tsiporis or Tiberias. In Jewish history
everything is connected as in concentric circles; we turn in the
same direction hoping to reach the inner point, the center itself,
which conceals what is eternal in time.

In other words, to attain fulfillment as part of humankind, a
Jew must live and grow in concert with his people; his individual
project must encompass the community rather than exclude it.
The more Jewish the Jew, the more universal he is. It is through
his Jewishness that the Jew speaks to his non-Jewish surroundings.

Now let us return to our hero, the shy and marvelous Rabbi
Zeira, whose own adjustment to Eretz Israel gave rise to so many
stories.

Is the butcher cruel to him? Is the merchant angry? Does he
suffer as a newcomer? All these incidents are quickly forgotten.

The sages welcome him into their midst with the respect due him. He stays with his beloved Rabbi Yohanan, and later his own disciples will stay with him and feel the same adoration for him. He learns and teaches, he receives much and give much of himself to friends and pupils alike. He is happy in Eretz Israel. So esteemed is he in the community that when his friend Rabbi Eleazar falls ill, people want to appoint him as Rabbi Eleazar's successor. But Rabbi Zeira has no taste for public office. Instead he undertakes a long fast—a hundred days—to pray for his friend's recovery.

Naturally, he is offered *Smikha*—the coveted ordination—but he goes into hiding. Excessive humility on his part? Eventually he accepts ordination—and the accolades that go with it—only when told that when someone is ordained all his sins are forgiven. Another reason for his reluctance: he wanted to demonstrate his disapproval of the rabbinic system in certain parts of Palestine where, regrettably, rabbinic titles could be bought from smaller institutions. If you could not get one for a small sum of money, you could get it for a larger sum. Clearly, for a man of integrity like Rabbi Zeira, this practice constituted supreme blasphemy. How could the honor of Torah be peddled for money? Torah can be neither bought nor sold; Torah offers itself only to those who devote themselves to her. As Rabbi Zeira's favorite disciple, Rabbi Yirmiyah bereb Abba, said, "Whoever consents to be a slave to the Torah in this world will enjoy freedom in the world to come."

A typical incident took place in Tiberias. Rabbi Zeira and his friends were chatting in front of the House of Study when they suddenly noticed one of those "false rabbis" passing by. "Let us pretend we are engaged in study," suggested one sage, "so we won't have to stand up and pay respect to his title." "No," said Rabbi Zeira. "I refuse to pretend. I want him to *know* why I am not standing up."

But he was harsh only with hypocrites. Generally he was known as someone strict yet compassionate, unbending yet charitable. "The Babylonian Hasid" they called him. He prayed a lot and fasted a lot. A poignant and charming aphorism is attributed to him: "The average person ought not to annoy his employer with too many demands, but with God it is the opposite—the more we turn to Him, the better He likes it." A variation on the same theme: "When one receives a guest, one offers him a bed for the night; if he comes back, he will be given a chair; if he reappears for the third time, he'll get a bench; if he still insists on returning, he'll be shown the door. With God, it's different: the more often you return to Him, the closer He draws you."

A story: The Talmud teaches us that whoever forgets to say his Maariv prayer and later remembers it in bed, may stay in bed. That is the law, touchingly lenient and understanding. However, it once happened to Rabbi Zeira. So—out of respect for the law, he stayed in bed; but out of love for prayer, he could not fall asleep all night.

Another story: When Rabbi Zeira was an old man, he would walk leaning on Rabbi Yirmiyah or Rabbi Haggai. One day they noticed a man who carried a load of firewood. "Please bring me a chip to clean my teeth," said Rabbi Zeira to Rabbi Haggai. But then he changed his mind. "Don't," he said. "If everybody took a chip, the man's load would disappear." Comments the Jerusalem Talmud: Not that Rabbi Zeira considered himself to be so exceedingly pious, but he wanted to warn people to observe the Torah's commandment not to deprive anyone of his livelihood.

In those times, whenever a public fast was proclaimed, the Holy Scrolls of the law would be brought into the street and ashes placed inside as a sign of contrition and mourning. When Rabbi Zeira would witness the scene, he would shiver with every fiber of his being. One day he attended a meeting where sages were discussing the coming of the Messiah. He said, "I beg you to stop, for because of your talking, his coming may be delayed. Haven't we learned from our teachers that the Messiah will appear inadvertently, while nobody pays any attention?"

He also said, "People who run to hear a sage will be rewarded for their running."

Once, when Rabbi Abba raised a judicial question, Rabbi Zeira turned to his disciples and said, "Whoever knows the answer will get a glass of special wine." Two pupils raised their hands. "There goes my wine," said the Master.

On another occasion he was asked to give his opinion on a matter that, as usual, opposed the House of Shammai to the House of Hillel: "If I were not afraid," he said, "to push my head between two lions in fight, I would answer you, but . . ." And he did not answer.

There is a strange story about him in the Treatise of Megilla. It was Purim and Rabbi Zeira, according to custom, got drunk.

Being Rabbi Zeira, he was zealously observant, so he got *very* drunk. He was not alone. His friend Rava was with him. Had they gone beyond the permissible stage of intoxication? Had they reached ecstasy, perhaps? Anyway, Rava seized a knife and cut his friend's throat, and Rabbi Zeira fainted. And died. It was not until the following morning that Rava realized the seriousness of the situation. He did what he could—he prayed—and miraculously brought Rabbi Zeira back to life. A year later, they were together again, celebrating Purim. Rava offered him wine but Rabbi Zeira refused. He was afraid. Said he, "Miracles do not occur every day."

He lived such a long life that his disciples inquired about his secret. "I never lost my temper," he answered. "I never envied anyone; I never walked four steps without wearing *tefillin* and learning Torah; I never reflected on divine matters in unholy places, not even accidentally; and I never ridiculed a colleague."

His respect for people in general can be illustrated by his interpretation of the law on leprosy. If a house has been contaminated, the priest must inspect it before declaring it worthy of being occupied. However, if the house is dark, one must not open the windows for inspection. In other words, one must give the house the benefit of the doubt. Said Rabbi Zeira, This applies to human beings as well; do not open the windows of their hearts to search for faults. Every individual is presumed just.

In his personal and academic activities, Rabbi Zeira avoided conflict and controversy. Once he threw himself into a burning furnace when he saw a man whom he might have embarrassed. That was his guiding principle: Better burn than shame your fellow man. Could that be still another reason for his nickname "the singed one"?

Being a *Cohen,* he was not allowed to take part in funerals, yet he attended at least two—one of them under compulsion. It happened after the second Rabbi Yehuda the prince passed away. For that occasion, the rabbis abolished all laws pertaining to priesthood to enable the priests to pay their last respects to their leader. Unconvinced, Rabbi Zeira hesitated to move close to the coffin, but Rabbi Hiya bar Abba, a *Cohen* himself, pushed him forward, and Rabbi Zeira could not avoid touching the corpse.

The second time, he was asked to deliver the eulogy for Rabbi Abin bar Hiya who had died tragically at the age of twenty-eight. Rabbi Zeira began with a parable: "Once upon a time the king hired workers to take care of his vineyard, but chose one of them to walk at his side and keep him company. Yet in the evening he paid them all the same salary. Some complained: 'We worked hard all day whereas he left after two hours to chat with you. Why such favoritism?' Said the king, 'What you have done in a whole day, he did in two hours.' And that," said Rabbi Zeira, "was true of Rabbi Abin himself: in twenty-eight years he had accumulated knowledge that old sages could not absorb in a hundred years."

But there comes a time when one can no longer digest ideas and impressions; there comes a time when the limbs are heavy and the mind is tired. What does one do then? How does one fulfill the *Mitzva* of study when one is too old to turn the pages of sacred books? Rabbi Zeira found a way. He would sit at the entrance to the House of Study and rise before those sages who could still study, as though to teach us yet another lesson: to respect those who respect Torah is but another form of showing respect to Torah.

When did he die? At what age? We do not know. We do know that he had prayed to God not to survive his friend Rabbi Yehuda ben Yehezkel. Both died within one month of each other.

At one point he felt death approaching; he prepared himself—and his friends for the event. He ordered his disciples not to mourn him so as not to interrupt their study, and especially not to organize the customary mourners' meal for the next day: he wanted them to fast.

Anyway, Rabbi Zeira died a very old man. Who attended the funeral? Was his son still alive? Did other members of his family survive? An anonymous speaker delivered the eulogy; its brief content had been recorded in our chronicles: "Babylon gave him birth, Eretz Israel educated him with love—and woe to Tiberias, which has lost its most precious jewel."

It is said that his death was mourned in the "underworld" as well. "Coarse men" or "wicked men," as the Talmud puts it, are quoted as having lamented aloud: "As long as he was alive, he would spend time with us and beseech divine mercy on our behalf; now that he is gone, who will intercede for us in heaven?"

Need we add that not all sages were pleased with his association with persons of questionable reputation? The text says so explicitly. But he did not care. God has many children; and if God loves them, why shouldn't we? And if God does not, then it is up to us to wonder, Why not?

And so we discover a new Rabbi Zeira. One who stood up for his principles. One who defended those who needed defense. A "small" teacher? His physical stature was in contrast to his spiritual grandeur.

True, I had trouble relating to him in the beginning. Too good a man, too kind, too passive, too innocent? His transparence must have been deceptive; one senses a mystery about his simplicity. I was intrigued. The unassuming sage has caught my fancy.

This eternal peacemaker who sincerely believed that no person is wicked, that evil does not exist, that one should not even look for it—what would he say about our century? Would he tell our generation to leave its windows closed?

Whether or not he went back to Babylon for a while, as some scholars contend, he died in the land of Israel. But surprisingly, his last words were not recorded. Did he look into the past? Into the future, perhaps? What distances separate us from him? Did he die too soon? Were we born too late?

Rabbi Zeira fasted a hundred days—or three hundred days, or nine hundred days—so as to forget. As for us, we should fast much longer.

So as *not* to forget.

Rav and Shmuel

Two NAMES, two men, two friends: their glorious place in Talmudic literature has been extolled throughout the vast universe of Jewish learning. Great scholars, strong leaders, sensitive educators, they transcended their own era. Their prestigious schools were in Babylon, but their pupils can be found—to this day—all over the world, from Jerusalem to Brooklyn, from Morocco to Manhattan.

Rav and Shmuel. Whoever studies Talmud is familiar with their voices, their lessons, their arguments, their different lifestyles.

Rav *and* Shmuel? Why not Rav *against* Shmuel? Their vigorous and endless debates remind us of those that were conducted between Hillel and Shammai, Rabbi Akiba and Rabbi Ishmael, Rabbi Yohanan and Resh-Lakish, Abaye and Rava: what better proof does one need to affirm our profound belief that the Jewish tradition of intellectual pluralism and social tolerance is as old as the Jewish people itself?

Ideological adversaries, Rav and Shmuel often disagreed on matters relating either to *Halakha* or to *Aggada,* yet they showed affection and respect to one another. Consequently they remain inseparable in our collective memory. When Rav offers an opinion, we are eager to hear Shmuel's too. One completes the other, one is enriched by the other. Together they belong to the enchanting and colorful universe of the Talmud.

A story: Shmuel and a friend of his named Karna were standing near the so-called King's River that flows near the city of Nehardea in Babylon. They stood talking quietly about current affairs. Suddenly the river rose and became violent, even though the day was sunny and the sky blue. There was no wind, and yet the waves rose higher and higher. Said Shmuel, "This is a sign that a great teacher is coming into town; go and see him." (Could this be the origin of the expression "to make waves"?) Anyway, he must have heard of the scholar's great erudition from learned personalities and students who had met him in Eretz Israel. Karna understood his friend's implication and went to see the man whose reputation had preceded him. Above all, he wanted to test his knowledge. He asked two questions which the visitor, Rav, answered satisfactorily. However, there was a third question that Karna did not raise, namely, Why had Rav left the Holy Land? What moved him to expatriate himself? What had made him come—or return—to Babylon?

As for Shmuel, there is a question about him, too—one that leaves us puzzled to this day. In spite of his erudition and his rabbinic authority in Babylon, he was never ordained. Why not? His disciples did receive the title; not he.

Thus we are already confronted with at least two sets of puzzles. There will be more. Any Talmudic text inspires us to seek them out. There is no religious literature that provokes the reader to be more daring in his investigations. To study Talmud also means to understand its questions.

Rav and Shmuel: both were Amoraim. As you may know, the Amoraim followed the Tannaim. The difference between them? "Tanna" means one who studies and teaches, and "Amora" one who speaks or interprets. The Tannaitic era began with Hillel and Shammai in the early period of Herod's reign. As authors of the Mishna, the Tannaim were innovators, creative thinkers, daring codifiers. In the course of generations, they were followed by "memorizers" who served as living libraries; they were appreciated not for their independent thought but for their total recall. Then came the Amoraim. At first, they would translate into Aramaic what the Tannaim would say in public. Later, they themselves were teachers. Still, protocol and seniority limited their authority: an Amora, for instance, would not dispute the views of a Tanna.

Rav and Shmuel were the first leading Amoraim in Babylon. In scrutinizing their portraits, one remembers all their predecessors and contemporaries in Babylon and in the land of Israel. One remembers those who followed them, those who remembered them. Memory is an act of generosity, of inclusion.

•

Inspired by them and under their guidance, Jewish scholarship attained new heights. The erudition invested in their academies was enough to nourish teachers and students for the next five
centuries—and probably more.

Except for their deep commitment to study and practice, the
two men differed in most areas, both personal and ideological.
Rav spent his formative years in Palestine, Shmuel spent his in
Babylon. Rav was *born* wealthy, Shmuel *became* wealthy. Rav was
moody, Shmuel was stable and controlled. But both loved poetry;
both composed prayers, many beautiful prayers.

Born in the second century, in the Babylonian village Kafri
near Sura, Rav—whose full name was Abba bar Aiwo—came from
an aristocratic family that traced its lineage to King David. He was
close to Rabbi Hiya, his uncle, who was also his teacher. Rav's
father, Aiwo, was Rabbi Hiya's half brother (from his father's
side), whereas Rav's mother was Rabbi Hiya's half sister (from his
mother's side). No wonder that uncle and nephew were so close to
one another. It was Rabbi Hiya who brought him to Palestine and
introduced him to Rabbi Yehuda, the prince who took a liking to
him and invited him to his table, once even going so far as to ask
him to say grace after the meal. Flattered, honored, Rav had to
struggle hard to regain his composure. Perhaps that was due to his
timidity. He was young and shy—and a stranger. Rabbi Hiya had
to teach him table manners, in addition to how to behave in class,
when to speak, when to keep silent, how to address the Master in
order to help the discussion rather than disrupt it: confusion of
issues or themes is dangerous to intellectual inquiry. Eventually he
came to be one of Rabbi Yehuda's favorite pupils. And in time he
became a member of Rabbi Yehuda's editorial committee in preparing the Mishna. Surely that was a great honor and a heavy
responsibility. For it was up to that group of scholars to decide
what to include and what to omit, what to preserve and what to
discard. The Mishna was to become a collective repository of
generations and generations of sages. The process of the Mishna
formation lasted three hundred years and encompassed such tragedies as the destruction of the Temple and the Bar Kochba revolt.
The Temple's destruction did not stop the editorial work of the
Mishna. Of 523 chapters of Mishna, only *six* contain no controversies. If we are grateful to Rabbi Yehuda for undertaking such
a monumental task, we are equally thankful to Rav for helping
him collect laws and remain truthful to all participants in all the
debates.

Why was he called Rav? He already had a nickname: Abba
Arikha, Abba the tall. He must have been strikingly tall, since his
disciple Rav Yehuda, who was also tall, reached only to his shoulder. Some scholars objected to the nickname, feeling it implied a
lack of respect to the teacher. Said Reb Yohanan, "You call him
Abba Arikha? I remember when we were both students at the
academy of Rabbi Yehuda the prince—even then he was recognized as a great scholar: he was allowed to sit while I stood seventeen rows behind him. He and Rabbi Yehuda were engaged in
a fiery debate. Sparks were in the air as the arguments flew back
and forth. And I heard everything and understood nothing. And
you call him by that name?"

But most called him by his title, Rav, because of the high
position he had attained among scholars. Just as Rabbi Yehuda the
prince was called Rabbi, Rabbi Abba was called Rav. However,
there is another explanation—there always is in the Talmud. Technically, he was Reb Abba, but since there was another Reb Abba,
the Aleph was dropped. Now the name was Reb 'Ba. The initials
of Resh and Beit are Rav.

Whatever the reason, Rav was Rav: a teacher, a Master, an
authoritative voice in the stormy world of learning. Though he
was not one of the Tannaim, he was their contemporary—he, and
he alone among the Amoraim, felt entitled to argue with a Tannaitic decision: *"Rav Tanna haya u'palig,"* says the Talmud: Rav
could oppose even one of the Palestinian teachers, which he did
more than once.

In a way, he was part of both the Palestinian and the Babylonian schools. He visted Palestine but then returned to Babylon.
After staying there a while, he went back again to Palestine, and
left it again, this time for good.

Why did he leave the Holy Land the first time? The reasons
are not clear. Before his departure, his uncle and protector, Rabbi
Hiya, had interceded on his behalf with Rabbi Yehuda the prince
to ordain him as rabbi. Rabbi Yehuda agreed but not entirely. The
formula *"Yore yore, yadin yadin,"* which is used for *Smikha*, for
ordination, to this day, originates in those customs. Rabbi Hiya
asked about his nephew: *"Yore?* May he teach?" And the ordaining
rabbi answered, *"Yore,* he may teach." *"Yadin? May he judge?"*
And the answer was, "Yadin, he may judge." However, Rabbi
Yehuda did not empower Rav to deal with *hatarat bekhorim*—with
purely ritual matters such as cases involving firstborn animals that
may not be consumed unless they are blemished. Why was Rav

denied full ordination? Perhaps because of the general policy in Palestine to discourage people from becoming *Yordim*— emigrants—by going to Babylon. Another hypothesis: Rav was knowledgeable in veterinary matters. Therefore Rabbi Yehuda may have feared that his decisions regarding animal slaughter and consumption would carry too much weight. Rav was hurt by his incomplete ordination. We know this from his appeal to Rabbi Yehuda's grandson, Rabbi Yehuda Nesiah, to correct the injustice and grant him full ordination. The appeal was rejected. "I cannot go beyond what my grandfather gave you," said the new religious leader of Palestinian Jewry.

But Rav should not have been too unhappy: after all, his friend and rival, Shmuel, received no ordination at all.

Shmuel was born in Nehardea—a famous city in Babylon which had a tradition of scholarship dating back to the time of King Yehoyakhin. His father, Abba bar Abba, belonged to the upper middle class. He was wealthy and influential, a trader in silk. He was also known for his piety. One day he met Rabbi Yehuda ben B'teira, who wished to purchase silk but realized that he had no money on him. Still, the merchant insisted that the rabbi take the goods. "Aren't your words worth more than money?" he said. "Because you have faith in words," answered the rabbi, "you will have a son who, like the prophet Samuel, will have faith in words." That is why Abba bar Abba named his son Samuel—or Shmuel.

There is a legend that a woman endowed with magic powers, and who understood the language of birds, tried to seduce Abba bar Abba, for she had heard—from the birds—that Shmuel would be a great man. Abba bar Abba managed to resist her charms—but her predictions proved correct: his son became a great man in Israel. So great that his father was often referred to not by his own name, Abba bar Abba, but by his son's: Avi-Shmuel, Shmuel's father.

Shmuel's father, Abba bar Abba, was known for his honesty; he was a trustee of orphans' funds. It happened that Shmuel was not at home when his father died, and so he was not told where his father had hidden the orphans' money. As a result, some people suspected Shmuel of misusing it. Shmuel used the ineffable name and turned to the dead at the cemetery: "I am looking for Abba." "There are many men called Abba," they told him. "I am looking for Abba son of Abba." "He is not here," they told him. "He is in the heavenly yeshiva, studying Torah." There he found him. Strangely, his father was both weeping and laughing. "Why are you weeping, Father?" "Because you will soon join me here." "And why are you laughing?" "Because your position here is strong." "Father," said Shmuel, "where is the money that belongs to the orphans?" "In the mill. There you will find three layers of money. The upper and lower ones are ours; the middle one is theirs. I wanted to protect the orphans' money. Were thieves to come, they would steal the upper layer, ours alone; should the soil damage the lower layer, ours alone would be damaged."

One day Abba bar Abba gave his son money to distribute among the poor. As Shmuel went into the street he saw a beggar eating meat and drinking wine, which were costly items in those times. So he ran back into the house, shouting, "Father, this poor man is rich!" "Go and give him more money," said the father, "he needs more."

Shmuel was versed not only in Torah but also in the secular sciences. In fact, he enjoyed a wide reputation as physician, ophthalmologist, mathematician, economist, and astronomer. Among other accomplishments, he prepared a calendar for Babylonian Jews for sixty years. His system was scientific and precise—as were his methods and inventions in medicine. His specialties were stomach and eye ailments. He invented unusual diets for his patients with nervous stomachs and concocted a special ointment for his patients with eye problems.

Together with Rav, he reigned over Babylon, which was, for a while, divided in two: one area was ruled by Rav, the other by Shmuel. In spite of the difference in their temperaments and views, they got along well. They even agreed on some issues.

When Rabbi Sheila died in Nehardea, it was proposed that Shmuel succeed him as head of the Sidra, as the yeshiva was then called. Shmuel refused: Rav had already been present and he, Shmuel, felt that Rav, his senior, was more qualified. But Rav, too, refused; he didn't want to risk hurting Shmuel.

Later, when both became heads of prestigious academies— Rav in Sura and Shmuel in Nehardea—the accepted principle was that in their debates Rav always prevailed in religious matters of *Issur veheter*—what is permitted and what is not—whereas Shmuel's opinions prevailed in all matters involving finances.

Shmuel was known for his extraordinary memory. He himself made no secret of the fact that he remembered many things far back, very far back. For instance, he once said casually, "I remember the midwife who brought me into this world. And the man who performed my circumcision." Indisputably precocious, he must have been an exceptionally gifted student—and there is evidence that he was.

In a discussion in the Talmud over the question of washing before meals—whether a person who is feeding another must also wash or not—the following story is told: "Shmuel's father found Shmuel crying. "Why are you crying?" his father asked. "Because my teacher hit me." "Why did he hit you?" "Because he told me that I fed his son and did not wash my hands." "Why didn't you?" "What?" asked Shmuel. "He is eating and I should wash?" And he added, "Isn't it enough that the teacher was ignorant—did he have to hit me, too?"

At that, Shmuel's father himself began teaching him, including giving him tests. But when he asked him four questions related to sacrificial slaughter, and Shmuel was wrong four times, the young man was sent to the great teachers of the time, including Reb Yehuda ben B'teira, whose school was in Netzivin.

When he was in Netzivin, Shmuel must have joined a special society—the *Hevra kadisha*—whose volunteers help out with funerals. This is an important *mitzva*, for it carries no reward, but the father was displeased. He wrote to his son: "Don't we have enough cemeteries here? Is this why I sent you to Netsivin? I sent you to study Torah, not to practice charity!" But the father did not need to worry. His son also studied with Levi ben Sissi and the Exilarch Rav Huna.

At one point, he visited Palestine, where he was admitted to the academy of Rabbi Yehuda the prince. We know this because he treated the sage's eye ailment. The Talmud tells us that Shmuel wanted to put a medication in his eye, but Rabbi Yehuda refused, fearing that it would hurt too much. Shmuel suggested applying some cream to his eyelids. Rabbi Yehuda still refused. So Shmuel put the cream under the rabbi's pillow, and the aroma was so strong that it cured the patient.

Still, when Shmuel wanted Rabbi Yehuda to ordain him—for ordination could be obtained only in Palestine—he met with a refusal. The reason is not clear. Some theorize that Shmuel was too learned in astronomy and the techniques of calendar calculations, that Rabbi Yehuda was worried that his views would carry too much weight in establishing the calendar year.

Others believe that he had acquired too much secular knowledge—too much for his own good. Which version is correct? We have no way of knowing. We do know, however, that Rabbi Yehuda himself expressed his regret. Rashi comments: "Maybe the time was not ripe or there were not enough rabbis present." Does this mean that the head of the academy lacked the authority to ordain on his own, that he needed the consent of senior faculty? The fact remains that Shmuel was not ordained—and we know that *he* tried to console his old Master. "Do not be sad," he implored him. "I read the Book of Adam which, according to tradition, contains the names of all the leaders till the end of time. When it came to my place in history, it said, 'Shmuel the astronomer will be called *Khakham*—sage—but not Rabbi.'" In other words, it was not the rabbi's fault; it was God's decision, not his. Shmuel then added, "The Book of Adam also says, 'Rabbi Yehuda will be cured by Shmuel.'"

Yet, with or without his rabbinic title, Shmuel's prestige among scholars was high in Babylon. His official position was secure, his leadership undisputed. When Rav died in Sura, no one succeeded him as long as Shmuel was alive—which means another seven years, until the year 254 of the Common Era. People loved him so deeply that they carried him on their shoulders to prevent him from getting tired.

And so, while we understand the various theories of why he was not ordained, we ask ourselves, Why did he *wish* to be called rabbi?

The time: from the middle of the second to the middle of the third centuries of the Common Era. The Sassanids rule in Persia. Neoplatonism is at its height in Greece. The Bishop of Rome becomes the first pope of Christianity whose persecuted martyrs are called saints. The whole world is in a state of constant upheaval. The Roman Empire is ravaged by the Great Plague. The year 248 has a special meaning for Rome: it marks the celebration of its one-thousandth anniversary. But there will be no more occasions for national celebrations. The empire's glory is fading, its decline irreversible. The old victors must yield their place to new victors. The conquerors of Judea will, in turn, be conquered. What remains of their victories? Statues and monuments—and a chapter or two in history books.

Some of the emperors were relatively good to the Jews; most

were not. One of the worst was Marcus Aurelius. His one regret was not to be able to impose heavy taxes on Jews for the air they were breathing. Severus was good; this unknown Syrian who at seventeen became emperor showed a measure of tolerance and understanding of the Jews and their beliefs. The Patriarch Rabbi Yehuda and he were close friends. As a result, the Jews of Judea lived in peace during the thirteen years of his reign.

As for the Jewish communities in Babylon, their lot was no worse. The Parthian king Artabanus looked upon them with favor and kindness. They enjoyed internal autonomy. The *Resh galuta*—the Prince of Captivity, or the Exilarch—was their leader in matters relating to politics and crime. His standing was high: he was ranked fourth behind the king. Consequently the Exilarch—a descendant of David—incarnated Jewish royalty in the midst of exile. He had servants and bodyguards, and musicians who played when he went to bed and when he rose. In fact, some sages criticized him for enjoying music and thus forgetting the destruction of the Temple. Some cities became famous centers of learning, others were known for their commerce. Makhuza was so exclusively Jewish that certain rabbis wondered aloud why its gates did not have *mezuzot* on them. The communities were so Jewish that in matters of *yichus*—of family status—Babylonian families were considered safer from assimilation than Judean families. There was no intermarriage in Babylon.

There was a great deal of intellectual interaction between Babylon and Palestine. The best of the students went to study with the last Tannaim in Palestinian academies. They must have felt that this was the end of an era—a golden era. The conclusion of the Mishna was a turning point in Jewish history—and the Jews in Babylon knew it. Some managed to catch a glimpse of Rabbi Yehuda; others went to Rabbi Yohanan; later, when the Babylonian academies became superior to the Palestinian ones, Palestinian scholars went to Babylon. "Talmud Torah *k'negued kulam*"—the study of Torah was more important to all of them than any other factor in life.

And so we are back to Rav and Shmuel.

Rav was born in 175 c.e. and died in 247 c.e. At the age of twenty he joined his uncle, Reb Hiya, on his first journey to Palestine, where he spent five years working for his uncle in Tiberias and studying under Rabbi Yehuda in Tsiporis. When he took leave of Reb Hiya, his uncle gave him this blessing: "I pray to God to protect you from something that is more bitter than death." Rav immediately understood what he meant: a nasty wife—for it is written that a bad woman is worse than death. Unfortunately for Rav, his uncle's blessing did not work: in Babylon, he married a woman who made his life miserable. An example? Whenever he asked her to prepare one kind of food, she prepared the opposite. This went on for years, until his son Hiya had an idea. He would tell his mother that his father wanted to eat . . . the opposite of what he really wanted. Surprised, Rav said to his son, "You know something? Your mother has changed for the better." When Hiya told him the truth, Rav was pleased that his son was so clever, but asked him not to do it again. It is not good to lie, he said, not even for a good meal.

To his son Aibou he said, "Since I cannot teach you *Halakha,* let me teach you business." Rav had a flair for economics. This is the advice he gives his son Aibou the businessman: "When you arrive in a village, do not linger, start selling right away." Also: "Whatever you have, sell immediately, and you will not regret it—except for wine; wait, but not too long, it may turn sour." More advice: "When you make a deal, first take the money; then deliver the merchandise."

Some of Rav's sayings:

"Do not humiliate a gentile in the presence of a convert until the tenth generation of his or her conversion."

"Do not marry two women—but if you do, marry a third one as well: if the first two conspire against you, the third will betray them."

"Whoever gives credit to authors or teachers when repeating their words hastens redemption." (This aphorism is also attributed to Rabbi Meir.)

"A scholar must have a little pride; exaggerated humility may stifle the inventive spirit."

He was afraid of the verse *"Vaavadtem bagoyim*—And you shall be lost among other nations." He was afraid because he thought it possible. Even then, assimilation was a temptation.

His general philosophy was that man should aspire to be independent in all things and not need welfare. To his disciple Rav Kahana he said, "Remove the skin of a carcass in the street and sell it; do not say, I cannot do it for I am a *Cohen,* a priest, or a great man. No work is undignified, no position unworthy. For there is nothing worse than needing someone else's charity."

What he taught, he practiced. When he returned to Babylon

from Palestine, he had no teaching position for some time. To earn some money, he accepted an offer to work for the Exilarch as a market inspector. As such, he went around from one business district to the next, making sure that the scales had not been tampered with. Then the Exilarch asked him also to supervise the setting of prices. He refused, claiming he was not qualified for such a task. The Exilarch reacted angrily to his refusal and sentenced him to jail so he could think it over. He did—and remained firm in his refusal to impose on poor people heavy taxes to the Parthian government and the Exilarch. Fortunately, Shmuel's friend Karna—who was a judge—interceded on his behalf and he was set free. He took another position in Nehardea; he interpreted for Rabbi Sheila, who at first didn't realize who he was. When he did, he was sure that Rav really considered this work unworthy of him, but he did not. Later, he even accepted invitations to serve as street preacher.

More about his stubbornness:

A man came to see Rav and asked him: "If a Jewish woman bears a child with a pagan or a slave, what is the child?" "Jewish," said Rav. "The mother's religion determines the child's." "If so," said the man, "give me your daughter; I wish to marry her." "Never," said Rav who then understood that the man was the son of a pagan.

A scholar named Shimi bar Hiya was probably present at the dialogue, for he used a Mediian proverb to express his astonishment: "If the law is the law, why doesn't Rav abide by it?" "Even if this man were Joshua ben Noun, I wouldn't give him my daughter for a wife," said Rav angrily. "If he were Joshua ben Noun," said Shimi bar Hiya, "he would marry someone else. But he is not Joshua. And if you reject him, others will too." The argument was sound, but Rav stuck to his position.

In another case, he showed more compassion. Rabba bar Hanna hired workers to pour wine into barrels. When they broke one, he confiscated their robes as a kind of indemnity. The workers complained to Rav, who ordered Rabba bar Hanna to give them back their clothes. Then they told Rav, "We are poor, tired, hungry, and we are going home empty-handed." Rav decided they were entitled to payment, and Rabba bar Hanna had to comply.

Among the ten cardinal virtues ascribed to him by the Gaonim is his humility. He was never arrogant or condescending. Also, he respected other people's right to privacy; he never looked at passersby in the street; he never indulged in small talk. At services, he never disturbed his fellow worshipers.

He loved prayer. In this domain, Rav's voice still reverberates, reaching us across the centuries. His prayer beginning *"Hayom harat olam*—Today is the birthday of the universe"—is still recited in our houses of prayer following the blowing of the shofar. Listen to it and you will sense its beauty and majesty:

"Hayom harat olam—Today is the birthday of the universe. On this day all creatures stand before You in judgment, some as children, some as servants. If You look upon us as children, then pity us as a father pities his children. But should You look upon us as servants, then we turn toward You with humility and hope until Your kindness will penetrate Your judgment on us, O revered and holy God." He also composed Alenou Leshabeach, the glorious hymn that concludes all the services.

Rav was mystically inclined. Rashi says that he could visit cemeteries and guess how people had died and when. But he was also practical. For instance, he paid much attention to problems related to marriage. Rav's concept of marriage was . . . a personal one. We read in the Treatise of Yoma that "whenever Rav would come to a place called Darshish, he would ask around: 'Is there a woman here ready to marry me for one night?' " Polygamy? No: he would divorce her next day.

No Talmudic scholar has demonstrated such affection, such empathy with young couples. His rulings in that area are daring, almost revolutionary. Until then, it was incredibly simple to get married. Boy met girl in the street, in a friend's house, or at a party, and that was enough for the boy; in the presence of witnesses, he said *"Haré at mekudeshet li*—You are thus consecrated unto me—and that was it. Countless tragedies were caused by such impulses. They also occurred in more normal circumstances, for young girls were not consulted as to whether they really wished to marry their husbands-to-be. In many cases, they didn't even see them beforehand—and when they did, under the *chuppa* (wedding canopy), it was late, too late. Sometimes they were given away while they were still children. To protect the young women—and also their future husbands—Rav issued several far-reaching rulings. A father is not allowed to marry off his daughter if she is still a minor. Commenting on this law, the Tosaphists of the twelfth century said as follows: "We live in times when fathers do marry off their young daughters. Why? Because exile is becoming harsher and harsher. People live in constant uncertainty. A father who has a dowry for his young child would not wait until she grows up, for he might, in the meantime, lose his dowry. Then what? His daughter might remain an old maid." Still, Rav's law stands. In order to protect minors, he also allowed the daughter to withdraw her consent. He insisted that an informal courtship had to precede the wedding, that the boy and the girl had to get acquainted, lest they live in a constant state of regret. And remember: all this took place some eighteen hundred years ago!

Rav *was* a great humanist; he tried to prevent suffering from spreading in the world. What about his own life? If he suffered, he never complained—at least, not about himself. He did make occasional comments, however, about troubles with women. "Anything is better than a bad woman," he would grumble—but never did he refer to his own situation. He projected the image of someone at peace with himself, of someone with a good family life. He had two sons and three daughters, one of whom married into the Exilarch's family. One son, Hiya, was an excellent student; the other, Aibou, was not. Rav did not hold this against him. He did not favor one over the other. He helped them both and gave practical lessons to both. To Hiya he said, "Do not reside in a town whose leaders are physicians." The reason: they are so busy with their patients that they probably neglect communal affairs or their families.

Rav placed much emphasis on the welfare of the community. At one period in his life he was a wandering teacher who sought out places known for their lack of intellectual or ethical standards. If, at the end, he chose Sura as the seat for his academy, it is because the region did not enjoy too good a reputation. But thanks to him it changed quickly. Thanks to him it grew into *the* center for advanced Jewish learning—even surpassing Nehardea, where his friend Shmuel was rising higher and higher.

Let us pay Shmuel a visit, shall we?

Shmuel was very different from Rav. More versatile, but less extroverted, he nevertheless cultivated good personal relations with the secular authorities. A close friend of King Shabur the First, he stressed the importance for Jews to abide by "the law of the land": *Dina d'malkhuta dina,* he proclaimed. One may not negate or oppose the existing legal system. What if the legal system is immoral? What if certain laws are unjust? In Shmuel's time they were still the law.

Remember the setting: Babylonian Jewry was caught between the battles and ambitions of three superpowers: the Parthians, the Romans, and the Persians. Some communities belonged to one empire, others to another. The Parthian king, Artabanus, was an admirer of Rav; they occasionally exchanged presents. King Artabanus sent Rav a precious stone as a gift; Rav, in exchange, send him a *mezuzah*. Said the king, "I do not understand; I sent you something that is invaluable, and you give me something that costs a few pennies?" "Majesty," said Rav, "you gave me something that I have to protect, I gave you something that will protect you." Shabur, the king of Persia, on the other hand, had a certain affection for Shmuel. When King Shabur attacked Capadoccia, its twelve thousand Jews defended the capital city with untold bravery; all were killed in battle. Strangely enough, Shmuel refused to mourn over their deaths. To be more precise, he did not mourn publicly. Surely he felt it unwise to antagonize Shabur. By then a number of religious decisions had been adopted by the Amoraim to ensure peaceful coexistence with the new regime, which fanatically persecuted its opponents and all those who refused to worship fire. Both Rav and Shmuel agreed that on Hanukah the lamps might be lit inside the home, but not in the windows, so as not to provoke the "Magi"—the Zoroastrian leaders.

If the Jews were left in peace, or at least were less persecuted, it was due to Shmuel's friendship with the king. He was so close to the king that some people called him *Arioukh*—the Aryan one. Others called him "King Shabur," to emphasize his identification with the Persian ruler. But in scholarly and academic circles he had only one nickname: *Shakoud*, the assiduous student, one who is constantly immersed in study.

Shmuel seemed happily married. He was a wealthy man; he did not need to work for a livelihood. Having inherited his father's silk business, he never had to worry about supporting his family. Sure of himself, he maintained relations with intellectuals, scientists, and even religious leaders outside the Jewish community. Compared to Rav, who said, "Whoever learns anything from a Persian Magi deserves death," Shmuel was extremely liberal. He learned from anyone and everyone, and managed to transform what he learned into useful material for his Jewish teachings.

Open-minded, rational, perceptive, Shmuel knew much about human foibles, showed tolerance for them, and, as a general rule, tried to emphasize the universality of Jewish ethics. "Cheating is prohibited," he would say. "That includes everyone. One may not even cheat pagans." Human beings are sacred and their life is holy. "Whoever dwells too long in fasting is a sinner," he said. One should never overdo anything. Exaggerated joy is as perilous as exaggerated melancholy. Everything human is incomplete. Perfection is divine; all humans can do is to aspire to it. Said Shmuel: "Why couldn't Saul's kingdom last? Because it was faultless." Perfect systems are dictatorships, and dictatorships cannot, must not last. Shmuel seems to have been well informed about political structures, for he declared, "When someone becomes a leader or a treasurer of his community, he inevitably gets rich."

Infinitely considerate with women and small children, he always took their side in legal debates; he felt they needed to be defended. Victims of the social structure must be helped by human beings, not referred to God. He did not look to miracles as substitutes for human kindness. In general, Shmuel was too pragmatic a man, his mind too scientific, to attach much importance to the supernatural. He stated with amazing conviction that "The only difference between this world and the messianic times will be that the Jewish people will no longer be dominated by other nations." Still, he believed in *Hashgakha pratit*—in heavenly supervision or intervention. Said he: "A heavenly voice is heard every day stating, This girl will marry that man, this field will belong to that person." Occasionally he would let his humor show. Whenever he had a bad dream, he would say, "Dreams are silly." When he had a good dream, he would say the same thing with a question mark, "Dreams are silly?"

When tragedy struck, he kept his pain to himself. He lost his sons. His two daughters were taken prisoner. One of them, Mary bar Abba, was raped and made pregnant by a pagan whom she eventually converted to Judaism. Shmuel never allowed his private sorrow to influence his public attitudes. Collective agony, communal pain may evoke collective responses; private pain must remain private.

From all we have learned until now, both Rav and Shmuel seem noble figures, forgiving and understanding, devoted to God and committed to their people. The image is correct on the whole.

However, they both had their weaknesses. They were human, after all.

Rav was hypersensitive. If hurt, he could lash out. Once, at the beginning of their friendship, Shmuel tried to cure his friend's stomach ailment and caused him pain. Was this the reason why Rav remarked, "Whoever torments me will survive his children"? We know that Shmuel lost his two sons.

How could Rav in this instance be so rigorous and so unforgiving? And so harsh in his response? Like most Talmudic masters, Rav was not a one-dimensional character. He was not always humble, not always gentle, not always careful with his words.

As for Shmuel, he was not forever avoiding honors. When Rabbi Yehuda refused to ordain him, he took it well; but deep down he was hurt. He revealed his pain much later, after Rav had passed away. How do we know? As long as Rav reigned in Sura, Reb Yohanan would write him letters which began with the words: "To our teacher in Babylon." Shmuel tried to prove his erudition by sending Reb Yohanan long-range calendars, opinions, innovations, all to no avail. Reb Yohanan did not call him teacher; when he finally addressed him as teacher, he was no longer alive.

There, too, we do not understand. Why did Shmuel, the great Shmuel, one of the most renowned Amoraim, attach such importance to titles? Because he, too, was human, and I find that appealing. Instead of diminishing them, Rav and Shmuel's humanity elevates them both.

But the death of great Masters concerns and involves the entire community. And so, as we draw nearer to our conclusion, let us accompany Rav and Shmuel on their last journey. Rav and Shmuel: two different names, outlooks, destinies. But two shared passions: the passion for Torah and the passion for Israel.

When Rav died in Sura, people wept all over Babylon. The Jews felt orphaned—all except one, a certain Bar Kasha of Pumbedita who, for some reason, refused to join in the general mourning. Nobody knows why. Maybe he simply wanted . . . publicity.

In Nehardea, Shmuel commented: "Gone is the man whom I feared until now"—in other words, whose judgment was superior to his, who forced him to study harder, to work harder on himself. With Rav gone, and with no disciple to succeed him as head or *Resh Sidra* in Sura, Nehardea for a while remained the center of Babylon. Not for long. Shortly after Shmuel's death in 254 or 257 C.E., Nehardea was destroyed by a wicked new emperor, Odenathus. As for Sura, the academy survived as a flourishing school of learning for another five or eight hundred years, depending on which source is consulted.

What do Rav and Shmuel mean to us? Continuity in Jewish learning and indestructibility of the Jewish spirit. True, there were teachers before them and after them, but these two, like their peers, remain irreplaceable. Rav and Shmuel were great teachers in Babylon, just as Rabbi Yehuda and Rabbi Yohanan were great teachers in the land of Israel. There is logic in Jewish history, there is beauty in Jewish destiny. The fact is that Jewish knowledge was passed on from Moses to Joshua, from Joshua to the Elders, from the Elders to the Judges, to the Prophets, to the Sages, to the Tannaim, to the Amoraim, to the Svoraim, to the Gaonim, to the Rishonim. There is creative beauty in the continuous movement of their ideas and stories—there is eternity in their words that refuse to die.

PART THREE

THE

HASIDIC

TRADITION

In preparing these Hasidic lectures, I received invaluable help from the renowned librarian and Maimonides scholar Dr. Jacob Dienstag.

The Shpoler Zeide

I BELIEVE I KNOW why I have neglected the "Shpoler Zeide" until now. He bitterly fought a man who has marked my life and work: Rabbi Nahman of Bratzlav. Excessive loyalty on my part? It is impossible to be too loyal to "my" Rabbi Nahman. I study his tales, I analyze his sayings, I teach his work: he is one of my favorite Masters. And I could never understand why the Shpoler Zeide kept harassing him. Why would anyone torment Rabbi Nahman? Why would anyone persecute a visionary, a thinker, a poet of his stature? But there is no denying it: for Rabbi Nahman and his disciples, the enemy was Reb Leib, the grandfather of Shpole. And that was for me reason enough to be suspicious of the Zeide.

Except for the tug-of-war with Rabbi Nahman, the Shpoler Zeide has all the characteristics that attract me. He was unquestionably one of the great of his time. He inspired awe and respect for the part he played in the Hasidic movement and for the miracles he performed. And then there was his age. Older than most of his peers, he had the advantage of having known the Baal Shem Tov personally. It was the Baal Shem Tov who had made him accept his destiny. How can we not love someone who had been singled out by the Besht himself? And besides, how can one not admire a spiritual leader who was born "old"? For his birth is linked to a miracle. And the miracle is linked to the Besht. This is what the Hasidic chronicle tells us:

Not far from Kiev, in the vicinity of Oman, in a castle that belonged to Count Potocky, there lived a certain Barukh. Barukh was a charitable man who welcomed beggars and wanderers and offered them food and shelter. Barukh took care of the men, while his wife, Rachel, received the women. Anxious to avert all danger of intimacy among their guests, they put them up in separate houses. While people were singing their praises, they nonetheless felt sorry for them, for Barukh and Rachel had no son.

But one day, among the beggars who knocked at their door was the Besht, who at that time was leading an anonymous existence. Disguised as a vagrant, he awaited the hour of his revelation. But Barukh unmasked him one night, when he saw a light from another world envelop the beggar. "Swear not to tell a soul," said the Besht, "and you will have a son. He will live. You will call him Leib. A great soul will inhabit him."

In 1725, the couple had a son. To celebrate his circumcision, they gave a meal to which they invited all the Jews of the region, rich and poor. Barukh was not really surprised when he noticed among them the Besht, who motioned to him not to divulge their secret. After the ceremony, the rabbis blessed the infant. Then the Besht stepped forward and expressed his wish to give his blessing, too. "I am only a poor ignorant beggar," he said, "but it so happens that I love Jewish children; they need every blessing they can get. I would like to offer mine to this child, since I have nothing else to give." And as the rabbis looked on, bemused, he continued, "I recall only one verse my father taught me. The Bible says, *'Ve-Avraham Zaken.'* What does *zaken* mean? *Av* means father, *zaken* means grandfather, or, in Yiddish: *Zeide*. My wish for this child is that he become the *Zeide* of the entire Jewish people." The nickname stuck. As the boy grew up, the neighbors never asked the parents, "How is your little Leibele?" but "How is your Zeidele?" In fact, he did very well.

At the age of eight, he knew the Torah by heart, as well as the prophets and the Mishna. But the parents' happiness was short-lived: Rachel died soon after his Bar Mitzva. Barukh remarried, and his son left for Koretz to study with the famous Rabbi Pinhas, the future friend and companion of the Besht. The High Holidays he spent with his father. According to custom, he established his own home at the age of eighteen.

To support himself, he took on various jobs—as *shochet*, or ritual slaughterer, as beadle, as tutor. One day, Rabbi Pinhas took him to visit the Besht, who in the meantime had emerged as the spiritual guide of countless communities from the Vistula to the Dnieper. When the young man saw the Besht, he cried out, "But this is the man with the shovel on his shoulder!" And he fainted. Years later he would tell his disciples: "Before my birth,

I wandered through the heavenly spheres among the sages and the Just, determined never to descend to earth: Why should I mix with mortals and expose myself to their petty ambitions? I preferred staying up there, where truth is without limits or flaws. But one day I met a man with a shovel over his shoulder who spoke to me thus: 'Listen here, I work in the mud to help the souls purify themselves and lift themselves up, and you—you want to remain on the sidelines, a spectator? Aren't you ashamed of yourself? Get down there, they are waiting for you.' When I saw the Besht, I immediately recognized him." And he recognized me. "I thought you would be stronger," the Besht said to him, smiling. "But you are young . . . you will have to work on yourself."

He never saw the Besht again. And for unexplained reasons, his father had forbidden him to become his disciple. Still, the Shpoler Zeide felt he belonged to the Besht; a kind of disciple *in absentia* perhaps? Often he murmured to himself, "Ah, if only my father had not forbidden me to see him once more." Could it be that his father was afraid his only son would get too attached to the Master and thus become estranged from his own family? As a matter of fact, Rabbi Leib left both at the same time: At the age of thirty, he chose exile—a Hasidic tradition continued by other Masters: Rabbi Elimelech of Lizensk and his brother, Rabbi Zusia of Onipol, who wandered together through Poland. Rabbi Leib was alone. For seven long years he traveled in a thousand disguises through towns and villages, near and far, never revealing his identity nor the purpose of his wanderings. Was it the Besht who had advised him to go into exile, or, in Yiddish: *oprichten goluss*? When bidding him farewell, the Besht seems to have told him quite the opposite: "I wish one thing for you," he said. "Wherever you are, may your foot be firmly anchored in the ground." And yet this only *seems* contradictory. One can feel at home in exile; one can taste eternity in one instant; one can fathom the depths of the earth by putting one's foot on the surface. When Rabbi Leib arrived in a place, he was able to take possession of it. For a brief moment it was his kingdom.

In mystical terms, this is the very essence of the experience of exile. Man must seek out the lost sparks, gather them, and deliver them to their sacred source. Everywhere there are souls waiting to be called. Everywhere, and especially beneath the ashes, sparks exist only for this call. What is required is for man to find these souls and save them; when all have been "restored," the divine flame will become the messianic light.

On the level of human quest, exile helps man become acquainted with simple people. A Hasidic rabbi must involve himself in their daily needs and problems. A true Hasidic rabbi must feel as much at ease with lumberjacks, merchants, workers, tailors, and shoemakers as with the most distinguished Talmudists. How can he measure a widow's grief, the pain of an orphan, the joy of a freed prisoner, if he is not their brother? That is why most of the great Masters of the movement began by leading anonymous existences as humble, often humiliated, wanderers, before rising to the honors of their rank. But for Rabbi Leib, the exile lasted longer than usual: seven years instead of four. Seven years of discovery, of flight, of hunger, of casual encounters, of shared pain. In short, seven years of adventure.

Few Hasidic leaders experienced so many turbulent events in their lifetime. A man of the eighteenth century, he must have experienced—from near or far—all its revolutions, its wars, its cultural upheavals. The three partitions of Poland, the bloody uprisings that shook France, the conquests and defeats of European powers such as England, Spain, the Netherlands, Sweden, Russia. The revolt of the colonies in America, the French Revolution, the advent of the Napoleonic era. All those borders that appeared and disappeared, all those conquerors who reigned sometimes no more than one night, all those henchmen who became the victims of their own terror. And at the same time, all those creative spirits who, in spite of the continent-wide bloodletting, in spite of lands ravaged by death, bestowed upon humanity reasons for pride—Kant and Goethe, Bach and Beethoven, Goya and Voltaire and Rousseau. . . . What did the Shpoler Zeide know of what was going on beyond his little Hasidic universe? What did he know of Napoleon's ventures in the Middle East? Of Robespierre and Wellington? Let us carry our inquiry further: to what extent was his romantic concept of the world influenced by that which shaped the fate of Europe?

Other Hasidic Masters reacted to the events, each one in his own way. Some sided with the Czar, others with his enemies. Rabbi Shneur-Zalmen of Ladi prayed for the victory of Czarist Russia, Rabbi Mendel Riminover for the Emperor of France. But all viewed emancipation as a grave danger to the Jewish community. Some proclaimed collective fasts, others convened quasi-political meetings.

And the Shpoler Zeide? Conservative, traditionalist, he had no desire to make innovations or changes in the popular Hasidic movement. He had friends among the great, but mostly he attracted the ill and the poor and the forsaken by the miracles he worked on their behalf. Few other Masters have had such a reputation for miracles. He had powers and did not deny having them. "When I look upon my Ethrog [a citrus one blesses on Succoth]," he said, "I see what is happening from one end of the world to the other." And when something was not to his liking, he changed it. Victims of injustice could count on him; he would alter their destinies. Like all the other Hasidic Masters, he was, of course, always on the side of the victim, for misfortune was something he was familiar with: he never forgot his years of wandering, the years of hunger, of yearning. Later, at Shpole, where he settled in 1770 at the age of forty-five, he had many opportunities to gather worldly goods; he chose not to. Whatever was given to him, he distributed among the needy. He would rather give than receive. His happiness was to make unhappy Jews happy. Such Ahavat Israel could not but impress the Hasidic communities and their leaders. In the course of the years, he became a kind of patriarch, a *grandfather* to all. Even the most famous ones, such as the Berditchever, the Neshkhizer, came to see him and consult with him.

I myself have always loved him as one loves a grandfather whose stories make one smile and long for more, and more.

What then, is the nature of those reservations I mentioned before? What was the quarrel between Rabbi Nahman and the Shpoler? Why was the Shpoler so harsh, so intransigent, so hostile toward the greatest—and also the most tragic—of all Hasidic storytellers? How are we to explain such antagonism between the two princes? The difference in age? In religious philosophy? Was there no one to mediate between two such leaders and pillars of the movement? No one to make peace between them?

They had not always been enemies. For a long time, Rabbi Nahman and the Zeide had had a friendly relationship. When Rabbi Nahman returned from the Holy Land, he hurried to visit the Shpoler Zeide, who, it must be said, was both pleased and touched: the young Rabbi Nahman was celebrated and exalted at Shpole. The quarrel broke out later—but why?

· For two reasons. The first: Rabbi Nahman decided to settle in Zlatopol. Now Zlatopol not only belonged to the province of the Zeide; it was only two miles from Shpole. And the Master could not tolerate this intrusion. Let us not forget that the Hasidic world, from the third generation on, was divided geographically rather than philosophically. Each Master had his kingdom, his territory. What right had Rabbi Nahman to "invade" Zlatopol? Particularly since Zlatopol held a very special place in the Grandfather's life story, having been the scene of quite a few of his adventures. It was there that he had been employed as beadle; there that he had revealed himself as a miracle worker. He was respected, admired. And yet, in those days, he had been expected to die young, for there was a kind of curse on the beadles of Zlatopol: they never lasted long. But not the Zeide. Curses had no power over him. He did his job, read the Torah, sounded the Shofar, and instead of complaining, like his predecessors, he helped those who complained to him. And so, when he moved to Shpole, he left a number of true and faithful friends behind. Then came Rabbi Nahman. A great-grandson of the Besht, he was well received. Did he wish to pray with his people in a little *Shtibel*? If not, the community offered him the big synagogue. Rabbi Nahman soon introduced his own *nussakh*, his personal style, for the solemn Neila service. Rumors quickly reached Shpole, having grown on the way. There was talk of impudence, of arrogance, of rebellion shown by the newcomer. In short, it was a declaration of war.

The second explanation is that there was a theoretical disagreement between the two Masters—not a personal but an ideological one.

Rabbi Nahman addressed the elite, the Grandfather of Shpole spoke to the crowd. The former sought substance, the latter popularity. Rabbi Nahman affected the mind, the Grandfather warmed the heart. One disturbed, the other reassured. One might look upon it as a rehearsal of the future conflict between the Rabbi of Kotzk and the Hasidic establishment of his time.

We who live at the end of this century can see that both sides had valid points. The Grandfather saw people in distress and did what he could to alleviate their plight. Rabbi Nahman had the same intention, but he conceptualized the issue. In his eyes, the idea of suffering carried as much agony as suffering itself. The Grandfather of Shpole refused to see suffering as a concept: to him, it was an evil that had to be fought.

Who is right? The Shpole Zeide resorts to strong measures.

He alters the laws of nature. He imposes his will on heaven. A man is in prison? He must be freed. A woman is ill? She must be cared for. The children are hungry? They must be fed. A community is in peril? He will save it by prayer. *"Hatzadik gozer"* says the Talmud, the Just Man commands and his will be done. He does not hesitate to issue the following warning: "If our enemies are stupid enough to kill a Christian child in order to accuse us of ritual murder, I would not use a Golem; I would go further than the Maharal of Prague, blessed be his memory; I would bring the child back to life and let the child point the finger at his murderers." The disciples of the Zeide claim that in his lifetime not a single ritual murder was committed in the land.

In other words, Shpole represents the miraculous, supernatural aspect of Hasidism. The Besht, too, had a reputation as healer and visionary. The Maggid of Mezeritch possessed divine "powers." His disciples, with rare exceptions, knew how to appeal to the imagination of the people by feats that were beyond ordinary human reason. We must acknowledge the circumstances; at that time, the Jews of Eastern and Central Europe were living on the brink of doom. The communities had been decimated at the time of the Ukrainian nationalist leader Khmelnitzki and convulsed by the activities of the Sabbateans, who believed in the false messiah, Shabtai-Tzvi. They were now having difficulties in getting reorganized. Especially in the villages and hamlets, isolated Jewish families were watching their own decline. Without schools, without Houses of Study, without rabbis and friends, the Jews felt they had been forgotten: forgotten by God and their own people. Having lived—or, rather survived—outside the Jewish law, far from Jewish customs, cut off from Jewish learning, many Jewish villagers no longer knew what it meant to be a Jew. They had to be brought back, not by lectures, but by song and deed. Had the Besht been a scholar, had he preached Zohar to his audience, he would have failed. He chose to sing, to pray, to tell stories, to listen. That is why he was so successful in reaching so deeply, so quickly, the far-flung Jewish communities, especially the small ones, to reawaken them, reinforce them, reintegrate them into the body of the Jewish people and its history.

Rabbi Nahman too, in his way, followed in the footsteps of the Besht. As a matter of fact, he claimed closer kinship with the Besht than did the Shpole Zeide, closer than any of his contemporaries. The Besht was, after all, his great-grandfather. We know that from childhood on, and certainly since his adolescence, he never made a decision without visiting the Besht's grave in Medzibozh, to commune with him in his thoughts and to receive his advice. If he clashed with his uncle, Rabbi Barukh, it was because each considered himself the only true and direct heir of the Besht.

But Rabbi Nahman contended that, all practical necessities notwithstanding, it was a mistake to reduce the Beshtiarevolution to simplistic formulas. He saw the work of the Besht as more profound, more complex, than that. For him, it had intellectual and mystical implications and applications. Was that "elitist"? So what? Where would Judaism be if not for the elite?

The result was war. War between a descendant of the Besht and a man without *yichus,* without rabbinical connections. Between a philosopher and a man of action. Between a thinker and a populist. The battle was waged with Biblical quotations, Talmudic aphorisms, Hasidic pronouncements. International conflicts seemed petty by comparison. In the Hasidic world, and especially in the towns near Shpole or Zlatopol or Bratzlav, people were eagerly following the most recent developments of the feud. Who had said what? To whom? In what tone? And what had been the reply?

Since the literature of Bratzlav is richer than that of the Zeide, the reader tends to get a one-sided picture. Often it is the Hasid of Bratzlav who informs us, who tells us what the Zeide and his disciples said about Rabbi Nahman. That the young Master had gone astray and had swept his disciples along with him. That they were drinking Slivovitz before morning prayers. That they let themselves go in their joy and ecstasy and thus came dangerously close to the Sabbatean ideas and practices taken over by the adepts of Jacob Frank, who was also a false Messiah. "They have erected a straw man in my image and they attack him," said Rabbi Nahman, who, incidentally, responded in kind. Passivity was not his way. He enjoyed fights and, at times, could be ferocious. His verbal attacks were very sharp. At one point, the Bratzlaver Hasidim saw in the Zeide an incarnation of Satan's emissary. An angry "old man" appears in at least one of Rabbi Nahman's dreams, trying to hurt him; it is the Zeide. "It happens," said Rabbi Nahman, "that Satan uses the services of an alleged Tzaddik to prevent the Just from fulfilling their mission." From that moment on, all that the Shpole Zeide was doing was evil, impure, harmful. Shpole was the other side, the enemy. Said Rabbi Nahman, "The Talmud advises us to jump into the lion's den in order to escape an enemy—but does one do that when the enemy is— the lion?"

Rabbi Levi-Yitzhak of Berditchev, the most respected leader of the movement, did his best to appease both camps. He was close to both Masters. And yet, possibly because of his respect for the Besht, he manifested a more pronounced sympathy for the young rebel Nahman. It is said that, in order to settle the matter at the highest level, he convened a gathering of the great leaders of the movement. If minutes were taken, they were not made available to Hasidic chroniclers. All we know is that the debates were stormy. In spite of the Shpoler Zeide's popularity, the Hasidic leaders present objected to his attacks on Rabbi Nahman. In their eyes, Rabbi Nahman was the victim, and they all knew what being the victim was like: they had been victimized often enough by their opponents.

It was clear that Rabbi Nahman suffered in Zlatopol. But he also suffered at Bratzlav, to which he later moved. Geographical distance did not improve matters. The harassments continued, and so did the war. It is said that during the summit meeting at Berditchev, someone proposed that the Zeide be excommunicated for having insulted a *Talmid khaham*, a scholar, in public. It seems that a majority could have been mustered in favor of such a resolution. But the wife of Rabbi Levi-Yitzhak objected. She urged her husband to reject such an attempt, which would give Berditchev a bad name. The Hasidism of Bratzlav claim that the *rebbetzin* of Berditchev intervened because she had received money from the Zeide—not for herself, but for the village poor. Still, the Zeide must have been in a rather difficult position. To have escaped a *herem*—excommunication—only due to the *rebbetzin's* objection was proof that there was a consensus in favor of his rival. We know that the Zeide sent many messages to many rabbis asking for their support; and that few of them responded favorably. I am convinced that Rabbi Nahman had the advantage of being considered the underdog. The Zeide, after all, ruled over a large territory, had been a leader for many more years, and counted many rich people among his followers. Young Rabbi Nahman, on the other hand, first in Zlatopol and later on in Bratzlav, never had a moment's respite: the Zeide's followers never ceased persecuting him and his disciples.

Well, we do love Rabbi Nahman, the spellbinding storyteller; it's impossible not to love a man who speaks to us of princes and fools, of beggars and sages, who live in faraway forests and listen to voices that hold the thousand secrets of Creation. . . .

Having said this, we love the Zeide no less. He, too, is endowed with admirable qualities as Master and friend. He dares to do what other rabbis do not allow themselves to do. He plays with children—they are his great love. He seems a child among children, so infectious is his joy. He loves to make children laugh. He stimulates, inspires, and generates enthusiasm by the way he dances. He is the greatest dancer in Hasidic history. As Rabbi Barukh watched him dance, he said, "What you achieve by dancing, others do not attain by praying." The Zeide's modest answer: "That's because I had an excellent teacher: the prophet Elijah himself." And he then told this story from his days of exile: In a Russian village, the *poritz,* the landowner, forced a Jew to get inside a bearskin and dance with one of the local notables. The one who would be judged the better dancer would be entitled to whip the other. Of course, the Jew did not know how to dance, while the notable did. And of course, the prophet Elijah asked the Zeide to come to the Jew's rescue by taking his place inside the bearskin. When the Zeide protested that he, too, did not know how to dance, the prophet said, "Don't worry, I'll teach you." And the Zeide saved the Jew, whipped the notable, and was left with a passion for dancing. It is said that people came from everywhere to see him dance, and that, watching him, one felt impelled by an invisible force and lifted all the way to heaven.

He, too, told stories. He told them mainly to show Rabbi Nahman that the latter was not the only one to kindle his followers' imaginations. But there was a difference: Rabbi Nahman invented his stories, while the Zeide drew them from his own experience, especially from the years of his exile before his accession to the rabbinical throne of Shpole. Every imaginable and unimaginable adventure had happened to him. He had been a member of a troupe of itinerant actors, minstrels, and clowns. He had performed in the circus, in taverns, had mingled with a variety of colorful people, including thieves. As a result, he himself had once ended up in prison: a fellow traveler had stolen some silver and, on hearing the police arrive, had handed the Zeide his bag, telling him that he had to follow a call of nature. The Zeide was beaten, arrested, imprisoned, and he found himself in a cell with thieves who demanded "membership dues" to join their "union." Since he had no money, they beat him. . . . As the Zeide told the story, he smiled and explained to his disciples that the ordeal had a purpose: He had recognized among the thieves one who had once been a Jew. He had started talking to him and persuaded him to return to his roots, to repent.

Once, on the day of Purim, he danced for hours with his followers; then, noticing Reb Zelig Podriatchik of Kiev, he called to him teasingly, "Well, Reb Zelig, did you see Reb Nahman of Zlatopol recently? They say he tells great stories, do you remember any?" "No, I don't remember," said Reb Zelig. "I only remember one about a princess, that's all." "All right," said the Zeide, "if you donate a nice sum of money to my poor for Pesach, I'll tell you a story which you *will* remember."

Listen:

Once upon a time, there was a king who wanted a palace, and he wanted it to be the most beautiful palace in the world. To whom should he turn? To his Jewish Podriatchik (caretaker) of course! That's what the Jews are for: to get you the impossible. The Podriatchik accepted the royal commission and left on a journey throughout the lands and capitals to look for the most magnificent wood, of the rarest kind, and almost impossible to find—but he did find it. The king sent him a thousand workmen to help gather the wood, cut it, and build the royal palace. When it was finished, it was indeed considered the most beautiful palace in the world. Every visitor who set eyes on it would stand there open-mouthed. Overwhelmed with gratitude, the king appointed the "Podriatchik" minister, or prime minister, in charge of the important affairs of the kingdom. And everybody was happy . . . until one day when the king had a new fancy: he wished the windows to be the same color as the wood. Again he called the Podriatchik, who again set out on a search. Finally he managed to find a Cossack, a glazier by trade, a true genius. Would he be able to satisfy the king's desire? No doubt. This Cossack could do anything with glass. He was as good as his word. The palace got the special windows, the king radiated happiness, and he appointed the Cossack minister of the court. Only that . . . "a Cossack always remains a Cossack" said the Shpoler Zeide. The Cossack became envious of the Podriatchik, and denounced him for some trumped-up crimes. The Jew was arrested, brought to judgment, condemned to death—and all the time the king knew perfectly well that he was not guilty. But the king could only commute the sentence to life in prison and exile him to Devil's Island. He also secretly gave him ten thousand rubles as well as an ax, matches, candles, and a rifle. Then he told him, "I know that you are innocent, and I know your innocence will help you escape." There follows an elaborate description of the island, with its birds, beasts, and skeletons. And the Jew took heart again. He managed to make a fire, to fish, and to build a small boat.

One day, he cut open a fish and discovered inside a golden ring which he recognized at once as the king's. And he remembered that one day when he had gone sailing, the king's ring had fallen into the water and had been carried off by the waves. The Podriatchik had an idea. And the Zeide described—again in every detail—the escape of the Jew. For if the Cossack had remained a Cossack, the Jew had remained a Jew. After many dramatic adventures, the Podriatchik's boat reached the river that flows through the capital. He went ashore, undressed, hid his clothes in the woods, and returned to the river stark naked. Later, when the king went for a walk along the riverbank, he noticed the naked man in the water. Believing that the man was about to drown, he sent one of his men to the rescue. How great was his surprise when he saw before him his beloved Jew, the Podriatchik, who proceeded to tell him his adventures: Over there, on Devil's Island, he had reached the end of his strength and had drowned. A giant fish had swallowed him, a fish so huge that he was able to walk about inside its belly for hours as if strolling through a palace. Finally the fish had spat him out before the king of the seas, the Leviathan. "His world is like paradise," said the Podriatchik. "I was unable to look the Leviathan in the eyes; they shine like the sun. He questioned me about my past and I told him everything: my work for you, your generosity toward me, and the beauty of your palace. As soon as the Leviathan heard my report, he got excited. 'That's wonderful,' he cried out. 'I, too, have a palace like that of your king, made of the same wood. I must have the same windows, I must have them.' And he entreated me to go and see you, Majesty, and convey to you his request; he needs the Cossack; send him the Cossack and you will earn his everlasting gratitude. In proof of which he returns to you the ring you lost and which was swallowed by one of his fish." The Podriatchik handed the ring to the king who then ordered the Cossack to be apprehended and thrown into the open sea as a present for the Leviathan. "And that's what happens to those who hate the Jews," said the Zeide, laughing. Because—who was this Cossack? Haman. And the Podriatchik? Mordecai, of course. When Mordecai remains Mordecai, any miracle is possible.

The Hasidism of Shpole must have liked this story. Other Masters liked it too. The Rabbi of Rizhin enjoyed having it told to him, especially on the night of Purim, and sometimes also on the Day of Atonement, Yom Kippur. He believed that it contained profound and sacred meanings. Besides, in those days, when Jews had to endure so much cruelty, it was a pleasure to listen to a story in which the wicked were punished and the Just rewarded. It was a relief to hear a story about a Jew who was reinstated in his rightful place and given back his rightful honors. As for me, I admit it freely: I love the Shpoler Zeide, but I prefer Rabbi Nahman's stories. I love his imagination, his warmth, his way of leading us out of ourselves, and back again by a shortcut, a detour, by a word that hides another, a thousand others. . . .

The Shpoler Zeide is a great person, a great personality. He is different from his peers. The others flatter and smile at their followers; he insults his, but . . . they know that on his lips insults change into blessings. His harshness hides great tenderness. That is why the Hasidim often implore him: Insult us, offend us. The angrier he gets, the luckier they feel. And though I don't like insults, I like to imagine the Hasidim happy and blessed.

Yes, he is a remarkable character. To be convinced, we need only reread the Hasidic chronicle that tells of the suit he brought against God. Like Reb Levi-Yitzhak of Berditchev, for the love of Israel he protested to the God of Israel.

One Passover Eve, the Zeide exclaimed: "According to custom, we begin the Seder with the word *Kaddish*—that is, as soon as the family comes home from the synagogue, the father must immediately sit down at the table. Why this hurry? So that the children should not fall asleep, since they must ask the four questions. '*Ma nishtana halaila haze*—Why is this night different from all other nights?' Well, Master of the Universe, we are Your children; and we are all tired, we are all exhausted. Make haste to say Kaddish—to sanctify us with joy. Make haste and deliver us from exile as long as we are awake, let us not fall asleep, for once we are sleeping you will not want to come and deliver us. . . ." When they heard these words, the Hasidim started to weep. But the Zeide stopped them: "No, brothers, no sadness tonight. Tonight we shall rejoice, and make our Father in heaven be part of our joy. Let us show Him that the child is capable of dancing in the dark."

One day he said, smiling, "Master of the Universe, try to understand us. You have put bad impulses into the human heart, and good things into the Book. No wonder we succumb to temptation! Had you done it the other way around—put the bad impulses into the Book and the good things into the heart, no one would wish to sin, I guarantee you."

And here is an eyewitness report by his beadle, Eizik Squirer;

"It happened in the third year of the Zeide's stay in Shpole. I, Eizik, was his servant. A terrible famine reigned in the land. The Jews suffered more than the rest of the population, since they were poorer. The Zeide was deeply unhappy. He held himself responsible for the starving Jews, and his inability to help them prevented him from sleeping. He no longer ate anything except a bit of bread with his tea. Among the thousands of letters sent to him from all over, there were some written by great Hasidic Masters, who begged him to use his powers to change the heavenly decrees and their heavy curses. So the Zeide wrote to ten great men and invited them to join him as soon as possible. They were: Rabbi Zusia of Onipol, Rabbi Leib the preacher of Polna, Rabbi Leib Cohen of Berditchev, Rabbi Israel and Rabbi Azriel, both of Politzkin, Rabbi Yaakov-Shimshon of Shepetivke, Rabbi Velvele of Zhitomir, Rabbi Gedalia of Lunitz, Rabbi Mordecai of Neskhiz, and Rabbi Nata of Razdal. They all came. The Zeide bade them sit down around a large table and said, 'I want you to know that I intend to bring suit against the Almighty God, blessed be He. I want you to be the tribunal.' Then they all started to pray and to weep: it was heartbreaking. After the service, the Zeide ordered me to read the customary proclamation to the effect that the court would be in session, and for what reason: 'In the name and upon the order of the holy community gathered here, I declare that Rabbi Leib, son of Rachel, is bringing suit against the Blessed Name before this tribunal, seeking judgment according to the law of the Torah. The tribunal will be in session three days from this date, in this very hall.'

"Isolated from the rest of the world, the eleven rabbis spent the next three days and three nights in prayer, shivering and preparing themselves. I alone was allowed to enter and see whether they needed anything. But as soon as I crossed the threshold, an unknown anguish took hold of me—so powerful I could not breathe. . . .

"On the fourth day, the ten judges took their places around the large table, wrapped in *tallith* and *tefillin*. The Zeide ordered me to proclaim that the tribunal was in session. I stayed close to the door so as to be able to bring a book in case one of the rabbis should wish to consult it. I heard the Zeide begin the indictment: 'In the name of all the feeble women and all the starving children, I lodge a complaint against Him who could and should feed them and help them but does not. He who gave us the Torah is obliged to respect its law. And the law enjoins the Master to take care of his servants, just as a father must watch over the welfare of his children. . . .' And the Zeide quoted sources and legal opinions to support his charge. He spoke for a long time, raising and lowering his voice whenever necessary. He was covered with sweat, his eyes were burning, and his body was trembling. I don't know how long he spoke, I know only that the ten judges listened to him with all their being. Then they exchanged some words among themselves—I was unable to hear anything, and neither could the Zeide, since he, as the plaintiff, had to move away at that point during the tribunal's deliberations. And then came the moment when the ten judges cried out as with a single voice: 'The tribunal sides with Rabbi Leib, son of Rachel. We decree that it behooves God blessed be He to feed the children and their mothers. Such is the opinion of this earthly tribunal, and we appeal to the heavenly tribunal to endorse it!' All this happened three times. Then the Zeide ordered me to go and bring shnaps and honey cake. They said '*L'chayim*' and their faces shone with a light I had never seen on them before. The famine was over shortly thereafter."

Another story: One Rosh Hashanah day, the Zeide received the visit of four great Masters: the preacher Rabbi Leib of Polne, Rabbi Leib Hacohen of Berditchev, Rabbi Zusia of Onipol, and Rabbi Mordecai of Neskhiz. After the meal, they talked of the Messiah who was not coming, and how the plight of the Jews was worsening from year to year. At a certain moment, the gentle Rabbi Zusia turned to Rabbi Leib of Polne and said quietly, "If the Messiah is late in coming, it is your fault rather than ours; you do not do enough to lead our people to repentance." Without giving the preacher time to answer, the Zeide got up and said, "*Ribono shel olam,* I swear to You by everything I hold sacred that

You will not succeed in returning Your people to the path of righteousness by punishing them: You who know everything, You know this too. Therefore I beg of You: try something else, try to reclaim them by way of happiness and plenty." Later the same day, he commented as if to himself, "I have seen what our great ones had to say about the mystery of the coming of the Messiah; some said this, the others wrote that. I have no doubt that they were entitled to say whatever they said. As for me, I can reveal only one thing: The palace of the Messiah is under lock and key. The lock is huge and terrifying. But in the year 1840 the propitious hour will come to open the gate—and there will be no one to open it. . . ."

I love the Grandfather of Shpole for his wisdom, for his daring, for his love of God and His children.

Why did he indicate the year 1840? Why not 1940? Why did he say that the palace of the Messiah would remain closed because there would be no one to open the gates? I don't know why. I only know that we must do as he did. We must live in expectation and make of our waiting a way of life, of hope, of creativity, and that we must keep repeating to ourselves that even if the Messiah is late, he will surely come in the end; one day, one day. . . . For the key is in our hands.

Rabbi Abraham Joshua Heschel of Apt

ONCE UPON A TIME, somewhere in Eastern Europe—near Kielce and Radom—in a place called Opatov, or in Yiddish, Apt, there lived a sage, a Master unlike any other, to whom all others had vowed obedience—a man deeply concerned with all those who suffer in anonymity, who painfully drag their lives of misery across an oppressive and hostile landscape.

He is our hero: the supreme arbiter of ideological controversies which split the turbulent movement of the Besht. His was the court of last appeal whose authority no one dared challenge or question. He was Rabbi Abraham Joshua Heschel of Apt.

Does this mean that he had no opponents? Not at all. Even Moses had opponents. The Rabbi of Apt had real enemies; a mind that asserts itself cannot help but collide with opposing forces. Any personality, any leader, any teacher, will encounter obstacles. Indeed, their absence would imply that one's impact was insignificant. This is true of all creative minds; and it is true as well of the Hasidic movement, which, God knows, did not lack internal conflicts. And yet, nothing could stop the idea, the flame, the message. Fervor cannot be stifled. And that is what Hasidism is: fervor. Humanity cannot be choked. And that is what Hasidism is: a profound outcry of humanity. For life, for hope, for love.

Love is the word that best evokes our hero. It appears on his tombstone—the only virtue he allowed his disciples to mention in their eulogy on his stone: "Ohev Israel, Lover of Israel." Yes, he loved his Jewish brethren. He loved his people. He loved every human being created by God in his image, every man and woman bound to the soil but seeking the sky and its stars.

Other Masters had practiced love for Israel, or "Ahavat Israel": Rabbi Levi-Yitzhak of Berditchev, Rabbi Moshe-Leib of

Sassov, Rabbi Israel of Rizhin. But Rabbi Abraham Joshua Heschel was alone in receiving the almost official title of "Ohev Israel." He *was* Israel's lover. Whatever he did, whatever he said, was for the love of his people. Moreover, he gave lessons in the subject: How to reconcile love of God with love of humanity, how to link love of life with love of truth, and passion with humor. Before his death, he said, "If you pay me too many compliments, I shall be embarrassed; I could not live up to it up there. What? I—one of the Just? I—a scholar? Compared to my Masters—and to theirs—I am less than nothing. There is only one title I may lay claim to: Yes, I have loved Israel, I have loved the Jews, I have tried to help them, console them, I have tried to ease the burden of their exile. Will you condemn me for that?"

Let us then try to make his acquaintance. How does he differ from his peers? How can we recognize a story as being authentically his? Wherein lies his greatness, his individuality?

Actually every Hasidic Master was great and unique, each in his own way. The shining wisdom of Rabbi Pinhas of Koretz, the dark passion of Rabbi Menahem-Mendel of Kotzk, the simplicity of Rabbi Wolfe of Zbarazh, the vision of the Seer of Lublin . . .

Who is of greater importance: the architect or the dreamer? The man everybody looks up to or the beggar forgotten in his corner by the chimney? They are all important. And that is precisely what Hasidism teaches us: Every being holds a sacred spark, every spark is drawn from the primordial fire, every gaze contains the nostalgia of exile, and every heart has the strength to endure. At a certain level, all beings are equal. All meet in Adam who was surely not a saint, who was surely not perfect. And yet: Was there a man closer to his Maker?

The Hasidic movement places its emphasis on relationships between human beings. Man is not alone. He is linked to his fellow creatures and at the same time to God who needs them all, and they all need him. The Tzaddik of Apt needs his disciples when he readies himself to appear before the heavenly tribunal. He needs them to lay title to his share of paradise, to provide him with evidence. Altruism supersedes all else; love of one's fellow man is one of the great principles of Torah.

All this is contained in the story about the rabbi's tombstone. What does it teach us? First of all, that the Rabbi of Apt prepared himself for death. That is what most Just men do. The Talmud confirms it: the Just are given advance notice—time to put their affairs in order.

Second, the Rabbi of Apt believed that life does not end with an individual's death. It goes on, as does Creation, in another, more sublime realm—if not in conscience itself.

Third, somewhere there is judgment. The human being will be judged. His deeds will be weighed. Nothing is forgotten.

Fourth, what is a virtue here on earth may be considered a flaw in heaven. Earthly virtues may well turn into vanity. It is therefore dangerous to take pride in one's virtues or to take them seriously. Or to take oneself seriously.

Fifth, Ahavat Israel, the love of one's fellow man, is the only redeeming virtue available to man. No one has the right to obstruct it. A Hasid may well say, Who am I that I should be loved? But he cannot say, Who am I that I should not love?

Finally—and this is the force that drove the Rabbi of Apt—he knew how to make himself beloved as well as how to love. Here was a man of exceptional gifts and more than a touch of mystery.

One day he watched his followers push to approach his table. "Don't," he said quietly. "It's no use. Those who know how to listen will hear from a distance; those who don't know how won't hear even from close by."

Another story: perhaps the most important one of his rabbinical career and one he himself corroborated. One day he received the visit of a woman known—too well, perhaps—for her conduct. Whatever malicious tongues like to tell about a beautiful and rich and intelligent woman, they said about her. "Rabbi," she said, "I need your help, your intervention for me in heaven: I want to repent, I want to change my ways—help me." They were not alone in the rabbi's office; there were the secretary (the *gabbe*) and the servant and also a Hasid or two, no doubt. They all listened as the Master said angrily, "You dare come to me? Shameless woman, you have the temerity to appear before me? Don't you know that I have eyes to see and that my eyes see into your innermost soul?" And to prove it to her, he proceeded to reveal certain things she had done. The woman paled and then answered gently and sadly: "I don't understand you, Master. Why must you reveal in public what God Himself prefers to keep secret?" And she went away. One version says she was thrown out. And she said, God is kinder; He allows me to stay in His house. Later, the rabbi felt deeply troubled and stirred in his very soul. "This is the only person who has gotten the better of me," he later said to his disciples. "This encounter has humbled me; it will remain a turning point in my life. It made me see suddenly that I was on the wrong path, for I chose *din*—judgment—over *rakhamim*—compassion. A dangerous path for a rabbi, a barren one for a Hasid. Man is not meant to judge his fellow human beings, and even less to condemn them; he is meant to understand them."

Let us in turn try to understand him. At first glance, his case seems clear, without a shadow of ambiguity. Born into a prominent rabbinical family, it is only logical that he should settle into this vocation. Disciple of a great Master, he becomes a great Master himself. He is admired, he is worshiped, he has followers—as is only natural. He embodies the sublimation of our aspirations. Whenever he speaks, people listen. Whenever he is silent, they listen even more closely. His authority is accepted; it is total. And everybody is happy—the rabbi, because he feels he is in a position to help his followers, and the followers because they need his help. Not a shadow hovers over his good fortune. Or does one? Let us consult the files.

He was born around 1750. Some say two years earlier, some say two years later, but everybody is in agreement as to the place of his birth: Novomiast. His father is the rabbi of the town. The son has a happy childhood, a studious adolescence. An excellent student, he learns Talmud, plunges into the Kabbala, makes a name for himself within the religious community. A splendid career is predicted for him—and the prediction comes true. He is appointed Rabbi of Kolbasov, later Rabbi of Yassi, then of Apt, and finally of Medzibozh, where he died at the age of seventy-two—or seventy-five?—years. Thus he will have reigned in Galicia, Romania, and the Ukraine, and everywhere he will be remembered as a Master endowed with great powers.

But how did he become a Hasid? He himself tells the story:

"It happened in Kolbasov. I was studying a difficult passage in the Talmud. Suddenly I heard a carriage arrive. Two men got off, one young, one old. I offered them something to eat and drink and then I stepped aside so as not to disturb them—and not to be disturbed myself in my studies. But it was not easy. They talked among themselves and I could not help listening. Worse: I did not understand a word of what they were saying. At night, all three of

us went to the House of Prayer and then we returned home together. My two guests kept talking to each other, and still I did
not understand a word. At midnight I recited my prayers and so
did they—but apart from me. The next day they left without
telling me who they were. This annoyed me all the more since,
after their departure, I felt deeply intrigued by their remarks. Without being aware of it, my two guests had dealt with questions
which had for a long time preoccupied me. I was angry at myself
for having let them leave like that, without asking whence they
came and where they were going. Two weeks later, as chance
would have it, they appeared again in their carriage. I rushed over
to them and asked whether I could be of service. 'A bagel,' they
said. 'Bring us a bagel.' They took it and rode away again. I started
running after them. They made me get into the carriage. When we
arrived in the next village, they suggested I turn back. 'We like
you,' they said, 'but you belong to another; you belong to Rabbi
Elimelech of Lizensk.' Who were the two travelers? Rabbi Moshe-
Leib of Sassov and Rabbi Levi-Yitzhak of Berditchev. It is thanks
to them that I discovered the wondrous and vibrant world of
Lizensk."

Hasidic legend tells us that the old Master, Rabbi Elimelech,
and his young disciple were united in pure friendship. It seems
that on his deathbed Rabbi Elimelech bequeathed his powers to
his closest disciples: to one he gave his piety, to the other his
erudition; the Rabbi of Apt received his wisdom. No wonder,
then, that other Masters would turn to him in times of crisis. His
common sense, his thirst for fairness, his understanding for people
and their problems, made him universally popular. This was the
reason for his many moves. Other Masters also had to move frequently, but that was because they were compelled to leave home,
often driven away by implacable opponents. With the Rabbi of
Apt it was different: he left one place because he was invited to
another. In fact, he was invited everywhere. Often when his community would not let him go, he assumed his old or new post from
afar . . . Twice a year he'd come back to his former congregation,
and the people were satisfied: better this than nothing at all. At
Jassy, they promised him everything and gave him . . . more promises. He offered the following consolation to the bereaved people
of Apt: "Don't be too sad. I shall insist on being called the Rabbi
of Apt even when I am elsewhere." He kept his word. Even in
Medzibozh, where he lived the last thirteen years of his life, he

continued to be known as Rabbi Abraham Joshua Heschel of Apt.

His two sons did not succeed him; neither did his three sons-in-law. But they remained inside the Hasidic kingdom and filled other offices in other places, far from Apt. Apt remains identified mainly with Rabbi Abraham Joshua Heschel. In this, too, he differs from his colleagues, whose sons succeeded them.

Other personal features: It was well known that he liked to exaggerate. In this he resembled the legendary Talmudic sage Rabbah Bar-Bar Hanna, whose imagination surpassed that of the greatest Oriental storytellers. In this, the Rabbi of Apt also recalled his famous contemporary Rabbi Nahman of Bratzlav—but the Rabbi of Bratzlav employed his imagination in his stories, whereas the Tzaddik of Apt employed his in his life.

For example: he loved to eat. A lot. No other Master—and few Hasidim—could match him when it came to emptying a plate. Occasionally he even grabbed the plate of a neighbor at the table. His Hasidim whispered that surely there had to be a deeper meaning to his behavior. He could not possibly suffer such hunger. Therefore, if he ate so much, there had to be another reason—perhaps a mystical one, surely a religious one. To eat is, after all, a *mitzva: Ushmartem lenafshotkhem meod.* One is duty-bound to take care of one's health. "When the Messiah will come, all days of fasting will be abolished—with the exception of two: Tisha b'Av, the ninth day of Av, which commemorates the destruction of the Temple, and Yom Kippur . . . On Tisha b'Av—who *can* eat? And on Yom Kippur—who wants to eat?

Rabbi Eleazar Hakohen of Paltusk tells of the way the Rabbi of Apt conducted his *tisch*: "In the middle of the meal, he suddenly placed his head on the table and began to sigh and shout and tremble—and all of us around him shivered too. Then he began saying Torah—one thought deeper than the next, one secret more burning than the next. His face was aflame and so were his words and so was the song that followed them—and so were we who tried to follow him. . . ."

Occasionally, he would talk a lot—and well. But that is of secondary importance. In general, a Hasidic Master owed it to himself to set an example: not to give in to hunger, to distrust talk, to cleanse himself in silence and song and prayer and study. But the Rabbi of Apt talked—and when he talked, his voice covered all sounds.

Everyone paid attention. Everyone was conscious of the fact

that the rabbi was talking—even though some people never managed to understand him or to follow what he said. It was not that his discourse was complicated or obscure; it was rather that his words appealed so much to the imagination.

An example—and I quote him:

"For my son's wedding, the cooks prepared noodles so long that they had to be hanged from the rooftop to dry, and from the roof they reached the ground. . . . So many guests came to the wedding that two full wagons of straw had to be purchased so people could clean their teeth after the meal. . . . From eggshells and onion peelings used in the kitchen it was possible to build two long bridges over the largest river in town."

He gave his son a coat whose hair was so long that a soldier on his horse—with his sword drawn—could hide in it; and yet, the coat itself was so small that it could be placed in a nutshell.

Many Hasidim heard this story. Why did he tell it? And why to none other than Rabbi Barukh of Medzibozh, the grandson of the Besht himself! Still, Rabbi Barukh, who did not like any of his peers, seemed to appreciate the depth and significance of the story. "Never have I heard anything so beautiful from the golden mouth of a man," remarked Rabbi Barukh.

To Rabbi Levi-Yitzhak of Berditchev—whose pleas in defense of his people had made him famous—the Rabbi of Apt once told of how the people of Jassy had erected a giant bridge in front of his house. A thousand times a thousand boards had to be brought, and still they were not enough. The Hasidim, used to their Master's exaggerations, listened, as always, much impressed. Suddenly one of them, a merchant from Jassy by the name of Noah, started nodding his head as a sign of approval. But the Rabbi of Apt rebuked him: "Reb Noah," he said angrily, "what *I* am allowed to do, you are not—is that understood?" Reb Noah learned his lesson. But why was the rabbi angry? Was it that he felt he had no need of corroboration? Did he perhaps wish that no one confirm what he said? That his words remain in the realm of fantasy? Did he intend to teach his followers an important and pragmatic lesson: that the rabbi is entitled to do and say things which they, the Hasidim, must refrain from doing and saying? If he was afraid of being imitated, his fears were unfounded. No one would have dared to do what he did—to transform real life into impossible and implausible myths.

The Maggid of Kozhenitz came to worship with him at his

services. One day he said, "Rabbi of Apt—what has Adam, the first man, been doing here today?" "Oh, I'll tell you," said the Rabbi of Apt. "I suddenly had an idea which explains Adam's first sin—and so he came by to say thank you."

He had two teachers: Rabbi Elimelech of Lizensk and Rabbi Yehiel-Mekhel of Zlotchov. Of the latter, he said: In every generation there lives a Just Man who owns keys to the Torah. How did I know that he was my teacher? I heard him speak and all my questions were resolved; when he stopped speaking, they all returned to me. That is how I knew.

He was convinced that this was not the first time he lived in this world. The ancient concept of Gilgul, of the transmigration of souls? On his lips, the tale took on a personal and urgent tone. "As you see me now," he said to his disciples, "I have come ten times into the world here below, and each time in a different body. I remember having been a High Priest, I remember having been a prince, a king, a president of the Diaspora, a Resh-galuta. Every time I endeavored to live up to the commandment which guides my life—the commandment to love my fellow man—I tried with all my strength, committing every fiber of my being to the effort, but there was always something, some detail, some occurrence, an omission, an error, a denial—some obstacle that arose. Then I would come down again in another guise and start again, and fail again. This is the tenth time that I am here to try. I hope I shall succeed; yes, this time I would so much like to succeed. . . ."

One day a Hasid came to confide in him. Sobbing, the man recounted his sins, but the rabbi laughed and laughed. He roared with laughter. The Hasid was shocked. He repeated his tale of woe and added details, one more terrible than the other— and the rabbi kept laughing. Then the Hasid described what measures of penance he had taken as atonement—long days of fasting, nights without sleep, the tormented dawns, years of wanderings, beatings, humiliations and tortures inflicted upon his body and upon his soul. He talked and talked of these. The rabbi still kept laughing. Later he explained to his followers: I met this man two thousand years ago in Jerusalem. He came with his offerings to atone for some inadvertent sin. He wept, poor man, and I wept with him. By now, all his sins have long been forgiven; he has no more reason to weep. He ought to laugh as I do, laugh with me. . . .

He differs from his friends in his imagination, and also in his attitude toward political realities. His contemporaries—the Seer of Lublin, Rabbi Mendel of Riminov, Rabbi Naphtali of Ropshitz, the Rabbi of Lyady, the Maggid of Kozhenitz—all involved themselves in current events. They felt that they should—and could—play a role, even an active role, in such events as the Napoleonic wars. As for Rabbi Abraham Joshua Heschel of Apt, he remained aloof, though his reign coincided with the French Revolution and the rise of Napoleon, the Revolutionary War in America, the partitions of Poland, the invasions of Russia, and the arrival of French armies in the Holy Land. The end of the eighteenth century and the beginning of the nineteenth heralded the advent of a bloody and bloodthirsty civilization, to be surpassed only by the one which succeeded it in the following century. We need only read the testimonies of the time: "We went from country to country," said René de Chateaubriand, "the sword in one hand and the message of human rights in the other." Napoleon—the liberator of enslaved peoples, the emancipator of the masses? How much blood did the Rabbi of Apt's contemporary spill in the name of great ideals! Let us read what an eyewitness tells about the conquest of Jaffa: "Napoleon, the stage manager of spectaculars, gives free rein to his soldiers to celebrate the victory. It happened on March 7, 1799. Soldiers and civilians alike are massacred by the French. The carnage lasts for thirty hours, after which 30,000 prisoners still remain. Then [so tells François Millot, Deputy Commissioner for the wars in Egypt] the prisoners of Jaffa were made to march into a huge quadrangle formed by the troops of General Bon. . . . The Turks marched helter-skelter, already guessing their fate; there were no tears; there were no outcries; they were resigned. Some of the wounded who were unable to keep up the pace were slaughtered en route. . . . When at last they arrived in the sand dunes southwest of Jaffa, they were stopped next to a pool of yellowish water. The officer divided the crowd into small groups and had them shot down. . . . The Turks calmly performed their ablutions. Then, having touched their hearts and mouths in the Moslem manner of greeting, they held hands, giving and receiving their eternal farewell. I saw an old and distinguished-looking man whose manner and tone of voice indicated his distinction . . . who calmly ordered a hole dug in front of him, deep enough for him to be buried. He wanted to die by the hand of his own people. He lay down on his back . . . and his comrades soon covered him with sand and then trampled the sand down. . . ."

Pardon this digression. I have always been fascinated by the phenomenon of parallel lives and events happening within the same time frame. How can we explain that some beings live happy innocent lives while at the same moment, somewhere far away, or simply on the other side of a border, whole communities are being wiped out? How can we explain that, while the earth trembled in Europe under the boots of fanatical soldiers, the Jews, on the fringes of history, found reasons for living and believing? Robespierre and Danton, Marat and Desmoulins, Marx and Hegel, served the gods of violence at the same time that the Besht and his disciples dreamed their great dreams of a nobler and more humane society. How can we reconcile Rabbi Abraham Joshua Heschel of Apt's lessons of generosity with the scenes of horror in the Holy Land and in war-torn Europe?

Was he even aware of what was happening so close to his kingdom? Of course. He had to be. After all, the events did affect the Jews. Shifting borders, armies in pursuit of one another, laws which are proclaimed and rescinded: they all bring suffering upon the Jews more than upon the others. Is it conceivable that the Rabbi of Apt was not aware of their plight? Or that he remained indifferent? In his writings, in his talks, in his metaphors, current events hardly figure at all. Did he live on the sidelines of war, of rebellions, killings, and of the fear that accompanies and precedes war? Hasidic chronicles mention one incident in which he was involved. Three Masters were denounced to the French occupying army and were arrested: the Seer of Lublin, Rabbi Mendel of Riminov, and Rabbi Abraham Joshua Heschel of Apt. They were accused of espionage. They were released—some say by miracle. Others say thanks to bribery. Perhaps both versions are correct: back home, in my childhood, the Hasidim used to say that an official was "charitable" when he accepted their money. So, a miracle took place: the police allowed themselves to be bought! There is another, more detailed version, told by the followers of the rabbi: the three accused men confronted the examining magistrate and it was he who backed off. Let us listen to an excerpt of the dialogue. "Who are you?" asked the judge. "We are the servants of God," answered their spokesman, Rabbi Mendel of Riminov. "And unless you show respect when talking to us, we shall not answer you!" Then Rabbi Mendel donned his *shtreimel*. The judge started trembling with fear and set them free at once.

To be sure, the Rabbi of Apt did not even do that much; he had no need of donning his *shtreimel* as a strategic deterrent because the gesture of his colleague, Rabbi Mendel of Riminov, had proven effective. And so the Rabbi of Apt extricated himself quickly from the political incident in which he had become involved. Was this the sum of his public activities outside the Hasidic world? The world was in chaos—did he think only of his followers and their usual troubles? Actually, why not? Nobody else gave them a thought; why should he not dedicate all his efforts and his talents to them? Having said this, we shall discover in Hasidic chronicles mention of another intervention on his part, and this time one of more pronounced political character. There are two versions of the incident. The first speaks of a rabbinical convention in Galicia, convoked to consider measures against the new laws of emancipation which obliged the Jews to renounce their customary way of dressing and to send their children to public school. In short, to integrate themselves—for better or for worse—into the community in which they lived. Nowadays we would call this convention a political protest meeting. No doubt there were stormy speeches, passionate debates.

The other version is more subtle. Listen: Rabbi Abraham Joshua Heschel was still staying with Rabbi Elimelech at Lizensk when a certain Reb Feivel, a pious and erudite Hasid, approached his Master one night and said to him, "Rabbi, I have a Din-Torah with the Holy One, blessed be He; I want to bring suit against Him." "Not now," said Rabbi Elimelech. "It is night and the courts are not in session at night. Come and see me tomorrow morning." Reb Feivel knocked at his door the next morning. In the room of the Master he found the Master's three great friends: the Seer of Lublin, the Maggid of Kozhenitz, and Rabbi Abraham Joshua Heschel of Apt. "Speak," said the Master. "Well, it's simple," said the plaintiff. "The Talmud says that a half-liberated slave can marry neither another slave nor a free woman. That is why there is no such thing as partial freedom as far as slaves are concerned: every man must want to be free. Now, we belong to our God, blessed be He. How can we submit to the laws of a temporal king as well?" Under the impact of these words, pronounced with sorrow and passion, the three judges lowered their eyes for a long moment. Then Rabbi Abraham Joshua Heschel said: "According to the law, the two opposing parties must retire while the court deliberates. Feivel, leave. As for You, Master of the Universe, forgive us, but we know very well that You are everywhere, and even if You were to leave, You would still be here. But . . . we vow that we shall render justice without fear or favor." And, in effect, the rabbis set about deliberating whether it was in accordance with Torah to impose laws on the Jews which prevented them from serving their eternal God. After lengthy debates intermingled with interminable quotations, the court rendered its verdict: "Yes, Reb Feivel is right. The law concerning secular education and forced emancipation is unjust." Believe it or not, it was abolished three days later.

Yes, I do prefer this version. Study and prayer were, in times past, more effective, even in politics, than the schemes of the politicians. And, besides, the concept of the trial against heaven has always fascinated me.

Let us also acknowledge that the Rabbi of Apt, like most of the Hasidic Masters, never discouraged man from entering into discussion or arguing with God. For instance, when speaking of Abraham in Sodom, he said: "Why did God agree to haggle with Abraham over the number of Just Men in the city? Fifty, forty, thirty, ten . . . God knew perfectly well, right from the start, that there were none! Why did He not say so right away? Instead, he let Abraham play the part of the peddler in the marketplace. Is that nice? Is it fair? How could He do that to His only friend? The answer, according to the Rabbi of Apt, is this: God wanted to teach Abraham a lesson. One must always ask questions, engage in dialogue, one must welcome and encourage discussion. In other words, God, knowing the future of the Jews, wished to teach them the need of arguing, even against Himself. It is no wonder that the Hasidic factions turned to the Rabbi of Apt in their search for the supreme arbiter.

One event which constituted a turning point in the history of Hasidism took place at the occasion of a wedding celebrated at Ostila. This wedding earned its place in Hasidism not because it united two illustrious families—the bride was a granddaughter of the Rabbi of Apt, and the groom the son of a prominent family of Botoshan—but because it forestalled a split in the movement.

Some explanations may be in order. At the time, the movement suffered considerable internal upheavals. At Pshiskhe, the half-blind Rabbi Bunam exhorted his followers to transcend themselves through fervor and study. Too many rabbis had too much power. The kingdom was apparently doing too well.

Complacency had supplanted anguish. It was pleasant to be a Hasid, and above all, it was easy. Too easy. One no longer came to the rabbi to cling to him while he ascended to celestial spheres. Instead one came to extract a blessing, a good position, a little advice.

Then the alarm was sounded at Pshiskhe, a call to return to study, to the basic principles of the Besht—to the flame of the beginnings. A return to the source. To disdain the easy life, superficial honors, artificial values. A scandal ensued, everyone set out to fight Pshiskhe amid cries of anger, stormy debates. This was no longer a battle between Jews and non-Jews, nor between Hasidim and Mitnagdim. This was a battle among the Hasidim themselves. Everyone had to take sides. Whoever was for Pshiskhe declared himself to be totally against the others. Rabbi Itzhak Meir Rutenberg—later known as the Rabbi of Ger—left his Master, the Maggid of Kozhenitz, to join up with Rabbi Bunam. The Maggid commented: "Poor, poor Itze-Meir, he has disturbed my Sabbath. I am afraid the same, if not worse, will happen to him." And indeed the Rabbi of Ger had thirteen children and lost them all. Every one died on Shabbat.

The war against Pshiskhe had all the Hasidic centers of Europe seething. Some wanted Pshiskhe to be excommunicated, but first, all other measures had to be exhausted. Why not a public hearing? A trial before the eyes of the whole world? A certain Reb Yosef of Yaritchov had a brilliant idea. The wedding ceremony which was to take place at Ostila would not fail to attract the greatest Masters and their disciples; why not invite Pshiskhe to come and defend their ideas? The proposal was accepted, and suddenly everyone was guessing who would be named counsel for the defense and who for the prosecution. But no one had to guess the name of the judge. Naturally it would be the venerable Rabbi Abraham Joshua Heschel of Apt.

Thousands and thousands of Hasidim converged on Ostila. Two hundred Masters clad in white were seated at the table of honor. There was the customary singing and dancing. Dressed as Cossacks, Hasidim performed for the bride and groom, but everybody anxiously awaited the moment when the debate would open. Then tension heightened when a Hasid of Pshiskhe climbed on a table, undid his shirt and bared his chest. "Rabbi of Apt," he shouted, "look, look right into my heart. There you will see my Master, the Rabbi of Pshiskhe, falsely accused!" Thereupon the spokesman for Pshiskhe and the one for his opponents presented their arguments according to the rules.

Just then a tragi-comic incident occurred. A Russian prince arrived in Ostila on business and his carriage could not move because of the crowds that filled the streets. "What is going on?" he inquired, and was told, "A Hasidic wedding." He did not understand. "What's a Hasid?" They tried to explain. The prince's reaction? To have the Rabbi of Apt arrested. The rabbi acknowledged the offense of his "Cossacks": Yes, they ought to have shown more respect for the prince. They had to be punished. Right then and there, in the prince's presence, he summoned several Hasidim prancing about as Cossacks, and, with great flourish, tore off their epaulets. "You are no longer a Cossack," he declared sternly. And from this incident dates the Yiddish expression *Oi's Kozak*.

Like this incident, the debate had a happy ending. Pshiskhe carried off a definitive victory thanks to the Rabbi of Ger, who managed to persuade the Rabbi of Apt with his Talmudic and mystical knowledge: the Master of such a disciple had to be pure and worthy of respect.

The event had one more beneficial result: the old Rabbi of Apt grew fond of the young Rabbi Israel of Rizhin, who was present at the wedding. When the latter dropped his belt, the Rabbi of Apt bent down to pick it up!

Rabbi Abraham Joshua Heschel liked his role as discoverer of young talent. It was he who discovered the first Master of Pshiskhe and quite a few others. One day he ordered one of his disciples to inaugurate his reign. "But I am not worthy," pleaded the disciple. "If I can be a rabbi," answered the Master, "so can you."

He had a marvelous sense of humor. One day he called out to God: "Master of the Universe, if you insist on sending me to hell, go ahead! But You know me. I do not have an easy temper. I would argue with the wicked until the supervising angels become exasperated. So I suggest to You the following: Clear out all the wicked from Hell, and then I'll gladly walk in."

Also: "Man is but a vessel," he said. "A pitcher. It is God who does the pouring. Into some he pours wine, into others vinegar."

A man came to him to tell him of his troubles: "The Almighty God will help you," said the rabbi. "But what should I do until then?" "He will help you wait for His help, too," said the old rabbi.

Commenting on the verse of the Psalms "*eynayim lahem velo*

yirou—those idols that have eyes but do not see, ears but do not hear"—the Rabbi of Apt explained that the reference was not to idols but to those who *make* idols. Those men and women who think only of making money, more and more money, they are the blind ones: they never appreciate what they have because they are looking for what they do not have.

One day he came to a town in which two important men vied for the honor of being his host. Both were pious, both devoted, both well off. But only one had a sterling reputation, the other was the object of gossip, innuendo. Rabbi Abraham Joshua Heschel made his choice: he stayed with the one about whom people were talking. "I don't judge anybody," he explained. "God alone knows the truth. I only know one thing: A man about whom everybody has only good things to say, nothing but good things, such a man can easily become conceited; and, with reference to the conceited man, God says, a conceited man says 'I'; therefore his 'I' and mine cannot dwell under the same roof. As to the other Jew, of whom everybody speaks unkindly—well, let us suppose that he has sinned. But since God says that He dwells among the sinners, by what right would I avoid them?" Does this mean that the rabbi *loved* sinners? Of course not. He loved their repentance. He often quoted the case of King David. Because David had sinned, and because he had repented, he was accorded the privilege of composing his Psalms.

The rabbi was asked to explain the verse "For the Lord recognizes the path of the Just, but the path of the Godless leads astray." At first sight, the sentence does not make sense. Does it mean that the Lord does not recognize the path of the wicked? The Rabbi of Apt commented: There is more than one path for all of us, wicked or just, and yet, for the Just it is always a path that leads to God, who knows it, whereas the wicked walk straight ahead, not knowing that the road does not lead *anywhere*. God alone knows that the wicked who do *not* seek Him out, come to an inaccessible mountain at the end of their days. They can no longer advance nor can they retreat. It is too late to go back. Only then do they realize that they have gone astray, that they are lost.

The only thing left is repentance.

The Rabbi of Apt often talked about repentance. But unlike the other Masters, he did not speak of sin. The chronicle testifies: He never spoke ill of anyone. Some disciples had tempted him, provoked him—to no avail. He thought only of speaking well of everybody, of pleading for his people. It is said that whenever he felt some impending danger to the people of Israel, he would retreat to his room, take off his glasses, and start polishing them, while he searched the future with his inner eye, intent on improving it, making it more agreeable.

Hasidic sources extol his prophetic gift. In his early youth, he questioned the leaves of the trees, the clouds in the sky. Later, he listened to the footsteps of people who passed in the street. Then came a time when he refused to probe the future if it looked too dark. He would lock himself in his room—to no avail: the future kept taking hold of his spirit. The limbs of his body revealed to him what the morrow had in store for him and his family and the whole family of Israel. In his anguish he would weep and plead with the heavens to take back his gift. And finally God did take it back.

Later, the Rabbi of Apt tried to persuade his friends and pupils to do the same: it is dangerous to see what is hidden, especially since it is impossible to change the course of events. It is given to the Just to see, but not always to understand.

To be sure, the Rabbi of Apt, like most of his contemporaries, interceded with heaven to prevent misfortunes from happening, or at least to limit their effect. Innumerable miracles are attributed to him, sometimes the same ones that are attributed to others—which is a miracle in itself. But the true miracle is that in a world of upheavals, at a time of bloodshed, he succeeded in acting as a wall, a powerful rampart, between his Hasidim and a hostile and alien world. At his court politics and plots were not discussed. No attention was paid at Apt to wars among kings and the mighty. Under his bemused or compassionate gaze, the Hasidim lived outside their times and found their fulfillment in song and in faith—an active, dynamic, humane, warm, and infectious faith.

He died at the age of seventy or seventy-five, in the year 1825, which others remember for other reasons: John Quincy Adams began his presidency, Pushkin wrote his *Boris Godunov,* and Beethoven's Ninth Symphony was given its premiere in England.

Toward the end of his long life, burdened by his years, and crowned with his victories over despair, Rabbi Abraham Joshua Heschel of Apt finally allowed sadness to invade his soul. Once

Rabbi Yitzhak Isak of Komarno saw him console a widow; the rabbi, too, was sobbing. Later he explained: She was the *Shekhina*—the widow of Knesset Israel—the widow of Zion. One day he commented on the Biblical verse "And it was here that Moses died, the servant of the Lord." (That is what Moses is called in the first sentence of the Book of Joshua.) How was it possible for Moses to serve God *after* his death? Rashi explains: "Before his death, Moses was allowed to see the Promised Land in order to bring the news to the patriarchs: Listen, Abraham, Isaac, and Jacob—God *has* kept the promise he made you long ago." In other words, even after his death, Moses remained the messenger of God.

During the month in which he was to pass from world to world—from the world below to the world of truth—the rabbi frequently gathered his children and his disciples around him in his room and talked to them of death. They all listened in silence, deeply affected. Sometimes he would pace the room, his face aflame, his eyes burning with a vision that was already carrying him far off to the other side, toward eternity and peace. One day he stopped his pacing and, standing in front of his table, he exclaimed, "There comes a moment when beings and objects stand up to bear witness. I therefore ask you, table of wood, to bear witness for me. You will testify that I have eaten according to the law, that I have used you to study, that I have used you to teach, that I have never put you to shame. Will you say so? Table of wood, will you testify on my behalf?"

Another day he fell into a dreamy, melancholy mood—something weighed heavily upon his heart. A disciple dared ask him the reason. "I feel," he said, "I feel that I shall soon be leaving; I shall be going to present myself before the heavenly tribunal; I shall be asked, Who are you? And I shall not know what to say." Barely had he finished uttering these words when a messenger appeared at the door. He had come from the Holy Land with a message for the rabbi: the Kolel—the saintly community of Vohlnia, residing in Tiberias—had elected him president. The rabbi was very pleased. He ordered a great feast to be prepared. He radiated happiness. He entrusted a sum of money to the messenger and said to him, "As soon as you get back to Tiberias, tell them to buy a plot for me—a grave—next to the one of Prophet Hosea."

And the legend continues: The night Rabbi Abraham Joshua Heschel of Apt died, a heavenly voice woke the members of the community of Vohlnia in Tiberias and said to them, "Get up. All of you, get up. Your Master is arriving, attend to Him! Honor him as a leader of a holy community deserves to be honored, as he returns to his resting place." The watchman of the community saw a casket whooshing through the air, accompanied to the cemetery by thousands and thousands of souls.

Another legend tells of another curious episode: On the eve of the rabbi's death, a vegetable vendor in Apt—or was it Medzibozh?—told her neighbor of a dream she had had the night before. She had seen her late husband pass by without noticing her. She ran after him and cried, First you left me with little orphans; and now you don't even recognize me! "Do not shout," whispered her husband. "I could not stop—I was not allowed to stop and talk to you; I had to purify the air for all the just souls who are preparing themselves to escort the holy Rabbi of Apt into the world of truth."

Finally, one more legend: At the moment of his death, Rabbi Abraham Joshua Heschel of Apt opened his eyes, looked at his sons and grandchildren, his disciples and their children, his devoted friends, all those invisible men and women whom he had loved with all his heart, and he started to weep. He was gripped by compassion for each one of them, and for all of them together, as he murmured, "And the Messiah, the Redeemer, who still is not coming—when will he come at last, when? We are waiting for him, we are waiting, and he is late in coming—why?" He stopped to catch his breath and then continued in an infinitely sorrowful voice, "I remember . . . when Rabbi Levi-Yitzhak of Berditchev left this world, he promised he would go to see all our saintly ancestors; he would beg them to do something; he would not leave them in peace until the Messiah would come to save his people. But the angels deceived him. They lifted him from sphere to sphere, ever higher, from sanctuary to sanctuary, revealing to him truths that were both ancient and unheard of, lights which were clear and dark at the same time; in his delirium and his ecstasy he forgot his promise. Yes, too bad for us: the Rabbi of Berditchev forgot his promise. But I, I won't forget. I swear to you: I shall not forget."

I am thinking of this last legend, and an unspeakable sadness comes over me.

There was a time when many of us—friends and anonymous, faceless, ageless Jews—declared that if, by a miracle, by the grace of the almighty God, we should be spared, we would dedicate our lives to telling the story of our agony and the agony of human multitudes engulfed by the kingdom of night. If we survive, we said to each other and to ourselves, we should make each day a monument and each night a prayer so that, upon the ruins of Creation, new hope would arise for future generations.

Now we ask ourselves: Have *we* kept our promise? In the grip of daily worries, locked into circumstances filled with temptations, with fears, with challenges, we do so many things—too many things—we find so many pretexts, so many reasons. . . .

Who among us can say that he or she has kept the pledge given to the dead?

Rabbi Avraham the Angel

THEY CALLED HIM the Angel—Rabbi Avraham the Angel. A rabbi unlike any other, a Tzaddik unlike any other, his place in Hasidic literature and legend remains unique.

Other Masters were loved and admired by their followers. But he, Rabbi Avraham the Angel, ran away from those who sought to become his followers. Other teachers elicited affection and loyalty from their disciples. But Rabbi Avraham the Angel had no Hasidim, for he chose to be alone.

Is this why they called him the Angel?

Because angels are not to be seen? It is said that people were actually afraid to look at his face. According to legend, a visiting Tzaddik once inadvertently gazed at him and was seized by such panic that he forgot to pray over the drink he held in his hands. For some time afterward, he could touch neither food nor wine. What startled him so? No clear reason was given. Maybe he was afraid to reveal the reason for his fear.

Another legend has it that a Hasidic Master was eager to meet the celebrated Rabbi Avraham. Therefore he spent weeks and weeks preparing himself for the encounter. Finally the day came when he entered Rabbi Avraham's study. But upon seeing the rebbe, the visitor felt such terror that he ran away without so much as greeting him.

It is said that the Besht's own two grandsons, Rabbi Moshe-Chaim Ephraim and Rabbi Barukh, felt uncomfortable when they first met Rabbi Avraham. The older brother, Rabbi Moshe-Chaim Ephraim, was so unnerved that he let his eternal Book of Psalms slip from his hands and fall to the ground—the first time such a thing had ever happened to him.

What was it about Rabbi Avraham that frightened whomever was in his presence? . . .

We shall try to penetrate the universe of this strange Master who refused to be a Master, and we shall try to discover his secret dreams and desires. What did he wish to achieve through his quest for solitude and silence? As we have already seen, he tends to shun visitors, so we will stop before his portrait and scrutinize it instead.

For this, we shall go to Mezeritch, the renowned capital of Hasidism, where his father, the holy Maggid Rabbi Dov-Ber was carrying forward the work and the mission of Rabbi Israel Baal Shem Tov, the Besht.

We had occasion to meet the holy Maggid years and years ago when we left Mezeritch after the passing of the Besht (see *Souls on Fire*). We had gone to Mezeritch because the whole world—in Hasidic terms, the whole Hasidic world—which was then still rather small, went to Mezeritch. Where else would they have gone? The Maggid was the Besht's worthiest successor. That was clear to anyone familiar with the scene.

Granted, the Besht's son, Reb Tzvi-Hersh, was alive and well; he could have occupied the throne but said no. Right away? Some sources say; No, not right away—after two years.

Granted, too, the Besht's learned disciple Reb Yaakov-Yoseph of Polna, the author of the *Toldot* was ready and willing to assume the mantle of leadership. Few men were as close to the Besht as he had been. Still, the choice fell on the Maggid.

Strange: few Masters had seen the Besht less frequently than the Maggid. Some sources say that they had had only three private visits with him. Yet their link was profound. When the Maggid was crowned leader of the entire movement, few voices rose in dissent.

Then why did the Maggid's son, Rabbi Avraham, not stay in Mezeritch to follow in his father's footsteps? Why did he leave the kingdom fortified and organized by his father?

We shall try to comprehend the case of this reluctant Master— later. We shall explore the relationships that existed between fathers and sons, teacher and pupils, disciple and disciple, within the turbulent Hasidic family.

Meanwhile a few preliminary remarks:

Some may argue that my attitude toward Hasidism is remarkably uncritical. This may be true. My approach to the Beshtian movement is influenced by what I have taken from it, namely, the need and obligation to love the Jewish people, and, through it, all people who need compassion in a cold and cynical society. Ahavat Israel is still to me the principle that characterizes a Hasid—and a Jew—and therefore a human being. No wonder Rabbi Akiba had such appeal for the Hasidim. His insistence on *"Vehavta lereakha kamocha—*and you shall love your fellow man" focused the humanistic tendencies of the Hasidic message and way of life.

The trouble is that some Hasidim are only willing to abide by this principle selectively. They love Hasidim but only those who belong to their particular rebbe. They love only those who are subjects of their particular Master. We have seen some of them at work. Hasidism can, like everything old, be distorted. In its name, through various disputes and quarrels, it has been divided more than once. The Hasidim seemed to have forgotten the Besht's emphasis on tolerance. Equal rights and human rights are an inherent part of the Jewish tradition. All human beings are God's children and all Jews are entitled to claim Moses as their teacher. And all Hasidim may say that they are followers of the Besht.

And now, let us move on to Mezeritch.

Of all the Hasidic Masters whose ways and words are shrouded in mystery, those of Rabbi Avraham the Angel seem most mysterious.

Is it because of the shadow cast by his father's greatness? Or because he died too young—at the age of thirty-six? There is something about him that eludes us; something about him seems alien to the spirit and message of Beshtian Hasidism.

The Besht had taught his followers to search for joy in life; there was no apparent joy in Rabbi Avraham's days and nights on this earth. The Besht urged his disciples to respect man's needs in *this* world; Rabbi Avraham devoted himself to the higher spheres alone. His goal was to attain the other world—the one below he aspired to leave behind as quickly as possible.

And yet few have been as extolled, as admired, as glorified.

A few words about Rabbi Avraham's celebrated father:

In spite of what the Hasidic tradition wants us to believe, the choice of Rabbi Dov-Ber, the Maggid of Mezeritch, was not unanimous. Unanimity in Judaism is rare, and even more so in Hasidism. Reb Yaakov-Yoseph of Polna would have liked to succeed the Besht. And he must have had some support. For instance, the great Rabbi Pinhas of Koretz was close to him. Did he endorse his candidacy? It seems that Rabbi Pinhas's first choice was Nahum of Tchernobil. Still, the Maggid prevailed. After he was crowned, no one disputed his authority.

No doubt he was endowed with what is today called charisma. Though physically disabled, his spiritual aura left no visitor unmoved. Nearsighted, limping so much that he could walk only with crutches, constantly plagued by obscure ailments, it was enough for him to appear in the House of Study for the students to flee in fear. But fear was not all he inspired. To a greater degree he inspired admiration, devotion, and loyalty. His words were taken as commands. His messengers to communities distant and near never questioned his decisions. They went wherever he sent them, always recognizing the validity of his judgments. He sent Rabbi Aharon Karliner and Rabbi Shneur-Zalmen to White Russia, where Talmudic scholars were needed—whereas Rabbi Israel of Kozhenitz and Rabbi Elimelech of Lizensk were dispatched to Galicia, where simplicity alone was needed to bear fruit. Possessing both *Nigla* and *Nistar*—the oral *and* the esoteric traditions—he knew whom to teach what—and for what purpose.

If the Besht was the founder of the movement, the Maggid was its architect. It was the Maggid who gave it its structure. It was he who was responsible for its organization and for the success of its programs.

Before him, Hasidism was impulsive, vague, fragmentary. The Besht appeared in a village, saw, was seen, was heard, and that was enough for the movement to gain another follower who had become a Hasid almost without knowing it. If anyone is to be credited with giving shape to the Hasidic commitment, it was the Maggid. It was he who introduced the notion of the Tzaddik, the Just Man, into Hasidic reality. What was a vague concept for the Besht was transformed into a cornerstone of doctrine by the Maggid. As he saw it, the Tzaddik had to combine the virtues and the gifts of teacher, sage, guide, and spiritual father. He had to be both spokesman for the Eternal One in His dealings with man, and intercessor for man in his dealings with the Eternal One. He was required to accept honors without becoming vain, to pursue knowledge but never for its own sake, to be accomplished in the art of speaking in order to know when to remain silent, and to be accomplished in the art of silence in order, when necessary, to articulate both simple and complex ideas.

By placing the emphasis on the Tzaddik, on the rabbi, and by setting almost unattainable standards for him, the Maggid focused his attention on the elite, on his close circle, rather than on the average Hasid. Few stories tell of simple Jews being directly helped by the Maggid: simple Jews were helped by those who were helped by the Maggid. His circle of intimates was exclusive. He chose his disciples personally, according to criteria known only to himself. The Master–disciple relationship, so special in every school of true learning, was indeed special in Mezeritch.

But what about the father–son relationship? What kind of father was the Maggid of Mezeritch?

Born in 1741, Avraham was ten or eleven when his father first met the Besht. Thus, in Rovno, where they lived until then, father and son had time to be together. Were they close? It seems so from the entries in various chronicles. The Maggid loved his son—so much that he once remarked that the four matriarchs—Sarah, Rivka, Rachel, and Leah—had interceded in heaven on behalf of his first wife, so that she could give birth to Avraham.

Later, after his meeting with the Besht, did he still have time for his son? Did the new disciple forget his duties as a father? Strange as it may sound, the Maggid did not spend too much time away from his home and family. Some sources believe that he and the Besht met only twice (not three times)— the second time, they remained together six months. The two men remained spiritually inseparable. And the son, Avraham? What about him? What was to be his role in the great design of Hasidic innovation or renovation? Did he as much as meet the Besht?

When the Maggid ascended to the throne, he asked two of his trusted disciples to take care of his son. Rabbi Shneur-Zalmen was to teach him Talmud, and Rabbi Zusia of Onipol was to teach him the virtues of humility.

Rabbi Shneur-Zalmen seems to have been reluctant. Avraham was not known for his Talmudic scholarship and Rabbi Shneur-Zalmen may have feared wasting his time with him. "You teach him Talmud," said the Maggid. "He will teach you Kabbala." It is worth noting that by that time, Avraham was already in his twenties; and yet, he still needed a tutor in Talmudic studies.

Though the Maggid must have had a high opinion of his son's mystical knowledge, it was rarely expressed. These are the instructions he left in his last will for "my dear and beloved son, the saintly and just Avremenyu": he should *daven* Minha and Maariv every day *betzibur*, every day with a *minyan*, he should learn one *Halakha*—one law—from Maimonides's book, *Yad Hakhazaka* a day; between wearing the *tefillin* of Rashi and Rabbenu Taam, he should eat something before going on with his learning; he should recite four Psalms every day with the same *kavvanah*—with the same intention—that accompanies the recitation on Yom Kippur Eve; he should, for heaven's sake, not isolate himself for more than one day—but on that day he ought not utter a word, not even to members of his family. What else? The entire testament deals with similar obligations: to give charity, to avoid fasting on his—the Maggid's—*Yahrzeit*, to *daven* from a Siddur, from a prayerbook without commentaries, to remain silent—even passive—if attacked by critics and adversaries. . . .

An astonishing document. One would have expected the Maggid—a giant in the field of mysticism—to leave a loftier message to his son the kabbalist. Didn't the father wish his son to inherit his role? Didn't the father wish his son to succeed him?

When the Maggid passed away, in 1772, some of his disciples turned to his son to ask him to assume the position of teacher and leader. This is a *Ktav hitkashrut*—a sort of loyalty oath—written and signed by three renowned Masters—one week after the passing of the Maggid:

"We, the undersigned, are desirous of linking our spirits and souls to Him whose name is a blessing, and for this purpose we submit to the authority of our teacher and Master Rabbi Avraham—may he live forever—the son of our Master and teacher, the head of all exiled, the Maggid of Rovno—may he rest in peace—and we shall respect and love him. . . . We pledge to fulfill every word he will say, and we shall do so immediately with true dedication. And in so doing we hope, under his guidance, to climb higher on God's ladder together with him . . . And so we ask our teacher and guide that, as soon as he will receive this first letter from our hands, to inspire us with his holy spirit and penetrate us with wisdom and understanding and good counsel and fear of heaven and love for our people. Onipol, Hanukkah 1772. Signed:

Rabbi Yehuda Leib Hakohen, Rabbi Meshulem Zusia, Rabbi Shneur-Zalmen."

If these three great men chose him to succeed his father, they must have had good reasons for doing so. For at that time it was not yet customary for sons to inherit the mantles of their fathers. Rabbi Avraham would have been the first. If the choice fell on him, it was not because of the father, but because of the son himself. Was there a resemblance between them? The Maggid accepted his role as guide; his son rejected *his*. The Maggid preached the Beshtian principle of non-asceticism; his son was infatuated with its appeal. The father was a leader with every fiber of his being; his son refused to be a leader. The Maggid was a preacher who addressed large audiences, his son sought shelter in silence and isolation.

And yet, the Maggid's greatest disciples wanted the son to become their teacher, their leader, their master.

As is the case with many Hasidic figures, Rabbi Avraham was a legend among people who had no access to him. Since the Maggid was legendary, everything about the Angel was legendary too. His garments, his prayer shawl, his prayer books, his pulpit, his table, his chair: there are stories about all of them. If that is true of the Maggid's objects, it is that much more so of his offspring. No wonder, then, that legends about his father and mother—and about his son—abound. Since the Maggid was destined to have poor health, his son would choose to become sick by punishing his body, by depriving it of food and rest and other earthly necessities. Since the Maggid wished to see only special visitors, the son would choose to see nobody. Since the father was profoundly human, the son would become an angel. Often, he would fast until he lost consciousness. Sometimes he would say the first word of a prayer and lose himself in that word for hours. His powers of concentration were such that he wouldn't even feel the presence of those around him.

It is said that when Rabbi Avraham got married, his wife fainted. She could not bear the sight of him: his face was that of an angel. That first night he could not come near her. Hasidim claim that he could not descend from the higher spheres to come into physical contact with his own wife. Still, he was eventually persuaded of the importance of the First Commandment in Scripture. Before his wife died, she gave birth to two children—a son and a daughter.

The Maggid insisted that his son remarry. His second wife was the daughter of a renowned scholar, Reb Feivish of Kremnitz—a descendant of the legendary Reb Shaul Wahl, who is said to have been crowned "king for one night" by Polish noblemen who, during a long but fruitless debate, decided that the first man they would meet in the street would become king of Poland: they happened to stumble upon Reb Shaul Wahl.

Rabbi Avraham's second wife was young—twelve or thirteen—when she was brought to Mezeritch. Was it because of her youth, or because she had a great influence on her husband, that the Maggid showed her special attention? Legend has it that she actually preserved her husband's life for twelve years.

In a dream she found herself in an immense hall facing a solemn and august group of men who looked like judges or angels or other heavenly figures. At one point, one of them said, "It is time for us to bring him into our midst." She understood the meaning of his words—to remove her husband from the world of the living—which received unanimous approval. Approaching their table, she began pleading for the life of Rabbi Avraham. Her pleas were passionate and emotional, but also rational. She did not know how long she spoke. All she knew was that one of the men turned to his peers and said, "Well, let us give him another twelve years." The next day the Maggid smiled at her and said, "Thank you for what you have done for my son."

She was always dreaming—all the stories about her involve dreams—but this part of the tale can wait. For we are still exploring the strange attitudes of her husband, who refused to be Master, just as he must have resisted his role as husband.

Actually, the Masters of the first generation rarely sought to occupy positions of leadership. None aspired to titles or honors. Power was of little interest to them. The Besht himself was compelled by heaven to reveal himself. The Maggid was elected by his peers and saw his victory as a punishment. Rabbi Pinhas of Koretz would not hear of becoming a celebrity. The same is true of Rabbi Levi-Yitzhak of Berditchev. In the School of Pshiskhe, the rabbis had to be coerced to accept the verdict of their colleagues. The Rabbi of Kotzk, the eternally angry Menahem-Mendl, preferred twenty years of solitude to one hour of glory. Many Masters had gone into exile and anonymity before emerging as leaders:

Oprikhten goluss, they called it—to be nobody before becoming somebody. The Shpoler Zeide joined a caravan of minstrels and clowns. Rabbi Nahman, on his way to the Holy Land, spent many weeks under an alias in Istanbul. Rabbi Shmelke of Nicholsburg and his brother Rabbi Pinhas, Rabbi Elimelech of Lizensk and his brother Rabbi Zusia mingled among beggars and wanderers in strange inns and marketplaces.

Why, then, should Avraham have been different? Why should he have wished to attain what others wished to reject? Was he less humble than they? From one of his sayings one may deduce the opposite.

"There exists a Tzaddik," he said, "who is unable to lead his generation because it cannot bear him. As he is head and shoulders above the people, his perception is so elevated that those below are not even touched by it. He belongs to the higher sphere of knowledge—so high is he that he cannot even bend down to lift up the generation that is walking or lying down there in the lower spheres."

To whom does this refer? To himself? That would be vanity— unbecoming a Tzaddik, and surely an angel. He must have been referring to a certain Tzaddik. In other words, Avraham is refer- ring to a man who is too great, too holy, too learned; therefore, people cannot reach him, just as he cannot reach them. Does this mean that he opposed excess in all things? This is a letter he wrote to his friend and mentor Rabbi Zusia:

"To the friend of God and mine, a living Tzaddik who em- bodies the sacredness of this generation and its grandeur, Rabbi Zusia, may his candle continue to burn . . . I am surprised at a Tzaddik such as he is. . . . He and Reb Zalmenke and I have heard from my holy father and teacher that a man must see himself as nothing—but not as something small. Quite the contrary—man must at times see himself as great in order to perceive the greatness of the Eternal One. Therefore my advice to him is not to yield. . . . And all those who fight us will fall like straw, and we shall rise and be courageous. These are the words of his friend who loves him truly and who is waiting for his people's salvation. . . . Avraham son of Reb Dov-Ber."

What provoked the writing of this letter is not clear; though it appears to be related to persecutions that Hasidim were sub- jected to by Mitnagdim, their traditional fanatic opponents. Rabbi Zusia must have maintained that suffering is not the worst calamity that could befall a Hasid—for, in Rabbi Zusia's view, suffering, too, was a gift from heaven, whereas Rabbi Avraham must have asserted the opposite, namely that suffering ought to be countered and resisted, especially when it involves other people. But the most significant part of the letter deals with man's relationship to the infinite—to his Creator. There is virtue in being vulnerable, in needing help from heaven. There is virtue in smallness, says Rabbi Avraham. To be small means to pray for small victories, for small miracles, and to see humanity as a whole composed of small fragments. To be small means to realize the greatness of the Creator and the emptiness of man when he—or she—is empty of faith in God, empty of God. To be small also helps man to confront nothingness. Who but man is aware of his own unworthiness—of his own nothingness? At this point, Rabbi Avraham gives an abrupt twist to his thoughts and proclaims: The awareness, the knowledge of one's own nothingness—or of the nothingness in the world of false perceptions and illusions—is better than the understanding of one's own smallness. Better to say that since God is God, I am nothing, than to believe that since God is great, His Creation is small. To be attracted by nothingness can be instructive, to be drawn to smallness is humiliating. The opposite of God—if there can be an opposite of God—is not smallness but nothingness; it, too, can be infinite.

In choosing his ascetic mode of existence, Rabbi Avraham's goal was not to reduce himself to smaller dimension but to confront the nothingness that is revealed to man in his loneliness.

In living a life of self-denial, Rabbi Avraham had a secret purpose in mind; he sought to prove something, to accomplish something. His asceticism was not capricious. Some mystics choose to suffer so as to prevent others from suffering; they court dangers so as to diminish danger in the world; they intensify their own sense of exile so as to abolish exile and hasten the coming of the Messiah. Could all this be applied to Rabbi Avraham as well?

A story: Once, on the eve of Tisha b'Av, the ninth day of Av, Rabbi Avraham sat with the faithful on the floor of the synagogue—as is customary—mourning over the destruction of the Temple in Jerusalem seventeen centuries earlier. With candles in their hands, they waited for the Baal T'fila to start reciting the Lamentations. After a while, he began: *"Ei'ha yashva badad*—Oh, how the city of Jerusalem was left sitting alone. . . ." *"Ei'ha"* repeated Rabbi Avraham as if to himself. With his head buried in his knees, he meditated on the meaning of the image, the implications, the destiny of the word. He remained in that position throughout the service, throughout the night, until the next morning. A Hasidic Master who was present trembled when he saw him with his head in his knees. "I never knew," he said, "I never knew that one can be here, in this synagogue, and relive from afar the destruction of our sanctuary as if he had been there, when and while it happened. . . ."

Still, this story could have been told about other Masters as well. Most of them, if not all, shared a profound longing for Jerusalem and wept over its tragic fate. Who did not—or does not—mourn on Tisha b'Av? The memory of what Titus and his legions did to our sanctuary is still burning in our conscience today. But Rabbi Avraham may have felt it on more than one day. Most mystics do. They rise at midnight to recite litanies, they weep over the exile of the *Shekhina*—and the *Shekhina* weeps with them. Is this why Rabbi Avraham deprived himself of joy and happiness? How could he be happy when the *Shekhina* was sad? How could he experience joy when the *Shekhina* was in distress? How could he dream of redemption when his entire being was open to nothingness? How could he believe in fulfillment in a world that was so twisted?

Is this why he was so beloved in the Hasidic kingdom? Because of his constant melancholy? Because of his self-inflicted wounds? Because of his voluntary rejection of anything that could bring him pleasure and satisfaction, grace and peace?

Or is it simply what we said earlier: that Rabbi Avraham was beloved because he was the son of the great Maggid? And the other way around: Wasn't his problem that he was the son of the Maggid? To be the son of a great man is to carry heavy burdens that have not been chosen.

Why do children so often rebel against their famous fathers? Ancient and modern history is full of examples. Where are the Jewish descendants of Moses Mendelssohn? Why hasn't Theodor Herzl left any heirs? Why did one of the Rizhiner's sons oppose the Hasidic community? Why did one of Rabbi Shneur-Zalmen's sons leave him? Were they all acting in anger, to punish their fathers for being known as something other than their fathers? Is it not possible to live for one's people at the same time as for one's own children? Must one make a choice? Must one make a sacrifice?

My feeling is that Rabbi Avraham found it problematic to be the son of the great Maggid. He may have felt that if people flocked to him, it was not because of who he was but because of who his father was. He could never have been sure whether his leadership was his own or a reflection of his father's. That is probably why he refused to accept it and chose to accomplish in solitude what his father had accomplished with his disciples and followers through the movement he had created with them and for them. That is why he had to follow his own path and establish his own goals. He had to free himself from his father, in order to be able to admire him later—and be faithful to him later.

That there had been rebellion in him is beyond dispute. A legend brings his dead father into his dream. "Why do you follow the path of asceticism?" the Maggid asks him. "Why don't you obey my will and implement my teaching? Am I not your father? Aren't you commanded by the Torah to honor my will? And, in his dream, Rabbi Avraham answers, "My spiritual father is God; I owe Him and Him alone obedience." One need not be a psychoanalyst to interpret this dream. The son rejected what he learned from his father and abolished his allegiance to him.

Then again, isn't it possible that it was precisely because of his infinite love for his father and his pride in him that he refused to imitate him, or even to take his place in Mezeritch?

Actually, the place was not Mezeritch but Onipol. For a bizarre thing happened to him during his father's last year. Suddenly, without any explanation, the Maggid decided to move from the Hasidic capital, Mezeritch, to the small town of Onipol. Why? No answer is given in Hasidic literature. Did he feel that his task had been accomplished? That his disciples, all reigning rabbis in Eastern and Central Europe, no longer needed him? Did he seek greater soul-searching, alone?

My suspicion is that his motive lay elsewhere. It could have been related to his son. Quite simply, the father may have wished to spend more time alone with his son. The Maggid had given so much to so many disciples and followers that he may have wondered, at the end of his life, whether he had been unfair to his own son—whether he had neglected him by not paying enough attention to his problems and concerns. That is why he may have gone to Onipol with his family. Why Onipol? Perhaps because that was the home of Rabbi Zusia, who was Rabbi Avraham's closest friend.

The father's renewed relationship with his son may also explain the letter his three great disciples wrote to Rabbi Avraham, offering him the succession to the throne. In doing so, they may have thought to please the father.

In Onipol, father and son were probably together as never before—so much so that Rabbi Avraham's second wife may have felt excluded. Did she object? Did she try to create obstacles? In the various texts about Rabbi Avraham, one senses an obscure hostility toward his widow. Is it because she was much younger than he? In other words, because she survived him? Or because she had her own identity? Or because she did not follow him to Pastov?

Rabbi Avraham did go to Pastov alone, after accepting a position there. He had refused to return to Mezeritch or to stay in Onipol. He seemed to prefer a new locality, a place where his father had not been. But his wife was against it. She wanted to stay. Later, she explained that her father-in-law came into a dream and warned her against traveling to Pastov. She did not even go there for the High Holidays. Rabbi Avraham sent messengers to persuade her to come and join him, but she refused. Rabbi Yehuda-Leib ha-Kohen, the preacher of Polna, and Rabbi Zusia—who may have been Rabbi Avraham's emissaries—did not hide their displeasure with her. Shortly after this incident Rabbi Avraham the Angel passed away.

Anyway, she was not present at her husband's death. She wasn't even informed about it. A messenger came to Onipol, went to her home—and said nothing to her. But he did confide the secret to her young son, Sholem, so that he could say the orphan's Kaddish. She still did not know. A day or two afterward, however, she noticed that Sholem rose too early for services. And unbeknownst to him, she followed him. From behind the wall, she heard him say Kaddish. Only then did she understand. According to law, she began observing the week of mourning. At its completion, she went to Pastov to receive her late husband's possessions. We are told that the whole town came to greet her. Important Hasidic leaders celebrated Shabbat in the home where she stayed. They sang and danced, but she watched them with melancholy eyes. At one point she fell asleep. In her dream, she saw her dead husband enter a large hall, followed by a group of distinguished elderly men. He asked them to take their seats. Then he turned to them and said, Here is my wife, may she live a long life; she is angry at me for having been apart from her for long periods of time, and rightly so; that is why I turn to you, and in your presence I am asking her forgiveness. She waited a moment and said, I forgive you. When she awoke, all her sadness was gone.

But her sadness must have returned for she lived in misery. Rabbi Nakhum of Tchernobil wanted to marry her—she was only twenty-four or twenty-five—but in her dreams, she was told by her late husband that he was against it. Her son, Sholem, eventually married Nakhum's daughter. In turn, they had a son who became one of the great Masters of Hasidism—Rabbi Israel of Rizhin. But Rabbi Avraham's widow did not live to see this. In her despair, she left Onipol and went to the Holy Land incognito. She made a living by doing laundry for well-to-do families. She died in poverty, and no one knows where she is buried. "Ah," the Rizhiner once exclaimed, "if only someone could tell me where her tombstone is to be found!"

A strange ending to a strange story: Why was she abandoned by Rabbi Avraham's admirers and his father's followers? Why did she choose anonymity in the Holy Land? Why didn't she reveal her identity to the Hasidim there, who surely would have given her the honors due her? Could it be that she was repentant for having interfered, in Onipol, in the relationship between her husband and his father?

In conclusion—our fondness for Rabbi Avraham the Angel remains strong. The son of a strong-willed father, he must have felt helpless, if not useless, when he realized that suffering is, for most human beings, a question, not a solution.

Of himself, he once said: "In the beginning I punished my body so that it would bear my soul; then I punished my soul so that it would bear my body."

Could this be what life is all about? An endless process of self-inflicted punishment? Is this, could this be true to the life-affirming tradition of the Jewish people? Could this be in line with the Hasidic view that joy leads to truth and to God, who is the ultimate truth?

"Master of the Universe," Rabbi Avraham the Angel once whispered, "if one could imagine this world for one second without Your intervention and presence, what good would it do us? Without You, who needs the other world, the world of eternity? Who needs redemption and the Messiah, if You are not here to see it happen? Who needs the resurrection of the dead, if You are not present in our life? Without You, Master of the Universe, how could anything else be?"

Without God, life would be without problems, without anguish, without hope. For God is not only the answer to those who suffer as a result of questions; God is also the question to those who think they have found the answer.

Kotzk and Izbitze

How is one to explain the estrangement of two friends who together had followed the same Master in his daring and demanding quest for truth, a quest which had culminated in prayer and study?

How is one to comprehend the painful fact that within the Hasidic movement, an episode could tragically separate Master from disciple, teacher from comrade, pushing each into his own refuge of melancholy solitude?

This will not be an easy task. Both men are Masters, both contributed greatly to the growth of the movement. And for a while they belonged to the same legend. Whoever met the celebrated visionary Rabbi Menahem-Mendel of Kotzk (or the Kotzker) must have glimpsed, in his shadow, the enigmatic silhouette of his favorite follower, Rabbi Mordechai-Yoseph Leiner of Izbitze (or the Izbitzer), who, suddenly and mysteriously, turned into his most powerful adversary.

Let us hasten to meet them while they are—for the last time—still together. It is the year 1839, at the end of the High Holidays. It is snowing over Kotzk and the neighboring villages. The streets are empty. Rabbi Mendel's House of Study is packed with students and followers who have come from all over Poland to spend a Shabbat under the Master's roof. To pray together. To dream impossible dreams together—only the impossible is considered worthy of interest in Kotzk.

It is Friday evening. Services are over, and have been for several hours. Now the crowd is waiting. Waiting for the rabbi to appear, say the blessing over wine and bread, and allow the Shabbat inside him to dispel their doubts and imbue with its joy all that exists, all that suffers. Yes, the crowd is already uneasy as it anxiously waits for the Master to lead it closer to Torah and truth, to God and His will. But the rabbi is late, and time is running out.

Suddenly, the rabbi bursts into the room, makes his way to the table. The crowd is breathless. Do the Hasidim sense the threat hovering over them and Kotzk? They dare not look at one another. They look only at him.

He remains silent a long time. Then he recites the Kiddush, slowly, haltingly, obviously between two impulses, two memories, and then something happens—what, exactly? We do not know nor shall we ever know (see *Souls on Fire*). All we're told is that the rebbe saw, said, or did something that no rebbe had ever seen or done before him, something so serious and frightening that he himself is crushed by the experience: he loses consciousness. Close disciples carry him into his room and there he stays, rarely venturing outside for the next twenty years.

What else do we know? We know that this incident marked the first split in the Kotzker movement: the rabbi's closest follower, adviser, and friend, Rabbi Mordechai-Yoseph Leiner, left Kotzk, slamming the door behind him.

"Mi laadoshem elai," he shouted. "Whoever belongs to God— follow me." Also, "The Torah no longer dwells in Kotzk; all that can be found here are fragments of the broken tablets." Some of the Hasidim followed him and left Kotzk, others chose to stay with their strange master. Thus ended a long, tormented friendship.

Naturally, there are other versions of this same event. Some claim that the split occurred several weeks later—others say several months earlier. Hasidic facts are known for their lack of precision. Let historians worry over that aspect of our tale. We will worry about the human facet. What happened was tragic—everyone agrees on that. Hasidic chronicles have frequently recorded tensions and conflicts between Tzaddikim, and even more frequently, tensions among their followers. But this was different because Kotzk was different. Why did the tragedy happen in Kotzk? And what exactly did happen?

Let us quickly state that there exists no proof to corroborate the allegation made in Haskala (or emancipation) circles that the rebbe in his grief had violated the Shabbat; this version was rejected unanimously by the entire Hasidic movement. Significantly, even after the incident, great scholars, pious leaders such as the

Rabbi of Ger and the Gaon of Sokhatsov remained faithful to the Rabbi of Kotzk. Had he done something reprehensible, they surely would have left with Rabbi Mordechai-Yoseph Leiner and gone to Izbitze.

But—why did Mordechai-Yoseph leave Kotzk? And why did five hundred—or was it eight hundred—Hasidim join the dissident? Because of certain words the rabbi may have uttered, certain words that sounded too harsh? Others had spoken them before him: Rabbi Levi-Yitzhak of Berditchev said things to God—about God—that only a man with his faith could have said, and no one was shocked. Why was it different with the Rabbi of Kotzk? Was there another reason?

Many years later, when older Hasidim tried to measure the grief and harm the split had caused the movement, they wondered whether at the time they had done everything in their power to avoid it.

Hasidic chroniclers have retained a short yet incisive dialogue between a certain Reb Shmuel and Reb Avrohom of Sokhatsov:

"I do not understand," said Reb Shmuel. "You were so many in Kotzk; you had in your midst the very best intellectual and spiritual exponents of Hasidism. You had the authority to intervene; you could have summoned Rabbi Mordechai-Yoseph and ordered him to behave responsibly. A slap in the face would have been enough."

"Perhaps," said Reb Avrohom of Sokhatsov. "But we were not sure."

"Sure of what?"

"Of the purity of our own intentions. We could not tell whether our opposition to the dissident was motivated by truth or by . . . vile jealousy."

First, who was this Tzaddik of Izbitze?

Mordechai-Yoseph Leiner of Izbitze was born at the beginning of the nineteenth century in the village of Tomashov. His parents were wealthy, pious, and learned Jews. He went to Heder, then to yeshiva and ended up at the court of the famous Rabbi Bunam in Pshiskhe, where the Besht's classical concepts were turned into life experiences. Mordechai-Yoseph was married by the time he went there. He had children and a comfortable income from his parents and inlaws. As a young prodigy—an *Iloui*—he was entitled to certain privileges to enable him to dedicate his days and nights to study without earthly concerns. His devotion to God was boundless.

What made him choose Pshiskhe? In Hasidic circles that was the accepted thing to do for young scholars. Pshiskhe was at the center of all conversations: one had to take sides—for or against the new school that had split away from the Seer of Lublin. Nobody could remain neutral. One had to throw oneself into the battle and find one's place in it—and in his own life. Mordechai-Yoseph was for Pshiskhe, which seemed different, new, revolutionary. As his contemporaries put it, Pshiskhe was a laboratory for souls; in Pshiskhe souls were washed, cleansed, and restored.

Mordechai-Yoseph Leiner was nineteen or twenty when he appeared before Rabbi Bunam. Hasidic chroniclers describe their first encounter with an almost childish anecdote: "Let us see who is taller," said Rabbi Bunam, who was tall, very tall, whereas his young student was small and thin. Mordechai-Yoseph said nothing, but to his surprise the rebbe rose from his armchair and came to stand next to him, as if to boast of his own height. The young visitor was taken aback, a bit embarrassed, and began wondering whether he had not wasted his time in coming to Pshiskhe. But he decided to give it a chance. After a few months, he was clinging to the rebbe with his entire soul. But what was the meaning of that first test? Neither Pshiskhe's nor Izbitze's scholars have bothered to offer any explanation. All we know is that at the end of that memorable first meeting Rabbi Bunam smiled and remarked, "Do not worry, you are young; you will grow."

It was there, in Pshiskhe, that he met his friend Reb Mendel. What attracted them to one another? They were different in many ways. Reb Mendel was moody, Reb Mordechai-Yoseph mischievous. One was solitary, the other gregarious. Legend has it that Reb Mordechai-Yoseph enjoyed playing tricks on his friends; that he was a practical joker. Once a certain Baruch, son of philanthropic parents, came to visit Rabbi Bunam and was royally received by his entourage. Reb Mordechai-Yoseph was offended by the respect that money could buy even in Pshiskhe. He waited for the right opportunity to make his ideas known. When one day Baruch and some of the students went swimming in the river, Reb Mordechai-Yoseph followed them from a distance. He waited till all were in the water, and ran off with Baruch's clothes. Baruch was angry. Worse, the rabbi's wife was angry, and sure enough, she complained to Rabbi Bunam. Listen, my dear husband, she

said, you are poor and you attract only the poor; for once God has
sent us one student who is rich, who could help us, and look what
happened! He was humiliated—for no good reason. Where is
justice? When the *rebbetsin* has a good argument, even the rabbi
must abide by it.

The master summoned Reb Mordechai-Yoseph and ordered
him to leave Pshiskhe. The student chose not to argue his case. He
merely took his belongings and left. But then, Reb Mendel came
to Rabbi Bunam and interceded in his friend's behalf. It was not
fair, he said, to chase away a man of his caliber for such a trivial
matter. Good, said the rabbi. Run after him. If he is still on this
side of the bridge, bring him back; if not, let him go his own way.
Reb Mordechai-Yoseph was already on the other side, but Reb
Mendel brought him back nevertheless. Rabbi Bunam commented: You cheated, you will live to regret it; one day he will
leave *you*—and no one will bring him back.

Still, Rabbi Bunam treated the young rebel with special
warmth and thought of him as one of his best disciples.
"Mordechai-Yoseph," he once said, "is like the waters of the river
Shiloah: they flow slowly, silently—and they are deep." Rabbi
Bunam's perception of the man was correct: Reb Mordechai-
Yoseph was patient, tireless, relentless in his search for depth—
depth in ideas, values, experiences. Like Reb Mendel Kotzker, he
rejected whatever seemed facile, obvious, superficial. That was
why he stayed in Pshiskhe: Pshiskhe meant a return to fiery beginnings, a return to authenticity.

Elsewhere in the Hasidic kingdom, from Medibozh to Lizensk, and even in Lublin, many leaders and their disciples yielded
to success. A protest against sadness, solitude, and despair, Hasidism had become an instant remedy for all woes and suffering.
The rebbe had turned into Tzaddik: healer and comforter, source
of knowledge and truth. Between the Master and his follower a
new relationship had been established: the Master had powers. In
other words, power over his followers. One was hungry? One
went to the rebbe. One's children were sick? Life was full of
hardship? Exile became intolerable? The rebbe had the answer. He
became the answer. But this was too easy for the faithful in
Pshiskhe. For them, Hasidism was more than a glass of wine, a
Shabbat meal, more than a climate of good cheer. For them,
Hasidism had to remain what it had been originally: a romantic
appeal to transcend the present, to reject all aspects of routine and

authority inherent in the movement which had become the new establishment. And Pshiskhe was against any establishment. Truth, to Pshiskhe, was not something one received; it was something to be obtained through sacrifice.

Of the two students who constituted the attraction in Pshiskhe, Reb Mendel is the more fervent, the more extreme. He is Pshiskhe at its outer limit. He wants to go farther than the others, to penetrate the ultimate meaning of words and beings, in order to confront the deepest truth, the one which either saves or crushes them. He is aptly called the dark one, the somber one.

So strong is Reb Mendel's personality that, at the passing of the Master, Rabbi Bunam, he is chosen as his successor. At first he refuses to accept the crown; only when his peers insist does he yield to their arguments—does he yield to their friendship. As the new leader of the movement, he leaves Pshiskhe and settles for a while in Tomashov—Reb Mordechai-Yoseph's hometown. From there he moves to Kotzk. And all the great minds and souls from Pshiskhe follow him there. The rabbi and his friends have become allies in the war against falsehood and complacency: together they hope to restore purity to Creation, and make it worthy of its Creator. These are Kotzk's finest hours. They remind one of the Besht and his legendary beginnings when those who became his disciples were still his companions.

Is all this Reb Mendel's influence? Reb Mordechai-Yoseph, who is wealthy, distributes all his possessions among his friends. All the Kotzker Hasidim did just that. Kotzk was a kind of commune, a kind of kibbutz. There one renounced earthly possessions to gain spiritual riches. Reb Mordechai-Yoseph follows this practice to the letter: he gives everything away. As a result, his family is penniless. Even to provide for a Shabbat meal becomes a problem. His friends, worried about his welfare, organize what we might call a fund-raising campaign on his behalf, in order to assure him of a regular subsidy. But the solution is inadequate, for he refuses to hold on to any money at all. As soon as he receives it, he gives it away to the poor. His friends come up with a practical solution: they give the money to his wife.

During that first period in Kotzk, the two friends enjoy a harmonious relationship, one that seems both inspired and inspiring. At times, they leave the village and go for long walks in the forest, especially on Fridays, not unlike the Ari Hakadosh, who, centuries earlier in Safed, had done the same thing with his disciples. They would walk and watch the world getting ready for the Queen of Shabbat, who would arrive with her retinue of beautiful angels of peace and joy.

From Hasidic chronicles we know that on these walks outside Kotzk, Reb Mendel remains silent, as does his friend: they listen to one another—to one another's silence. When they return to Kotzk, Reb Mendel often seems angry, whereas his companion appears serene—perhaps for the same reasons.

The friendship lasts for thirteen years: thirteen years of intense collaboration and camaraderie. Granted, they differ on many issues and in many ways. But in spite of their differences—or perhaps because of them—they move toward the same goal. They help one another, they complete one another, they need one another. When Reb Mendel becomes a widower and considers marrying the sister of Reb Itshe-Meir of Ger, he asks Reb Mordechai-Yoseph to serve as matchmaker. Reb Mordechai-Yoseph is also charged with the care of the best intellectual elements that descend on Kotzk. He teaches them Talmud and Kabbala and soon becomes their friend, their mentor, their older brother. He views all these functions as necessary to the mission of a Hasidic Master. Whereas Reb Mendel seeks solitude, Reb Mordechai-Yoseph emphatically rejects it. In Izbitze, where he eventually establishes his kingdom, he will be remembered as the most accessible and likable of all Hasidic Masters.

Unlike Reb Mendel Kotzker, he does not feel the need to leave his disciples and isolate himself in the forest or in his study; he never loses his temper, he never builds walls between his pupils and himself. He is there to serve them, to be present for them, to play a role in their lives and listen to their pleas, and share with them his discoveries, his memories, his dreams. For him, it is the function of a rebbe to live in the consciousness of his followers just as they live in his. That is why he does not have office hours. His door is always open. Anyone may see him anytime.

In the evening, he meets his followers for a course in Talmud. He is brilliant, erudite, generous: he speaks for hours and hours; and his disciples listen, rapt, for hours and hours.

However, if spontaneity is the rule for his personal relationships with his Hasidim, ritual is the rule for the study of Talmud. It is always the *shamash*—the secretary, the assistant—who appears first in the House of Study. He carries two candles and a volume of the Talmud in his hands. That is the signal that the rebbe is about to enter. Students and visitors rush to their seats and wait in total silence. When he appears at the door, all rise. They remain standing until he sits down.

He begins the lesson. First he treats the subject under examination. Then he moves to others, from the particular to the general. From Talmud to Torah to Midrash to *Halakha* to Zohar. He speaks until midnight, sometimes until dawn. If he is weary, he doesn't show it. But then, he, too, has a secret side to his personality. Just as he is understanding with regard to his followers, he is unbending with regard to himself. He does not favor mortification for others—only for himself. Having once accidentally put on his left shoe first—the right side of one's body symbolizes divine charity—he decided to expiate this action by fasting. He often punished his body, which was sufficiently punished already. He suffered from tuberculosis. Often the pain was unbearable but he never complained. Once he remarked with a smile, "My body takes its revenge. But what can I do? To appease it would mean to inflict punishment upon *myself.*"

In other words, as far as his own person was concerned, he was as strict and unyielding as his friend Reb Mendel Kotzker. Both remained faithful to Pshiskhe; both reflected Rabbi Bunam's dark vision of the human condition. Didn't Rabbi Bunam's own son, Reb Avroham-Moishe, complain that there was too much preoccupation with death in Pshiskhe? All my life, said Rabbi Bunam, I have done nothing but ready myself for the hour when I shall meet the Angel of Death. Reb Mendel dwells in darkest depression.

A story: It is Purim Eve and all the Jews in Izbitze celebrate the miracle that had occurred centuries earlier in Shushan—the miracle of the Jewish community that survived Haman's threat of extermination. The Hasidim are happy but their rebbe is not. Rabbi Mordechai-Yoseph is meditating on some painful subject; he seems sad, melancholy. Suddenly he begins to describe an episode from his distant past. "It was on Shabbat Eve," he said. "We were in Pshiskhe. Rabbi Bunam lifted his cup of wine to recite the *Havdalah* but stopped at the last minute. Instead, with the cup in his hand, he began to predict the future. One day, he said, before the coming of the Messiah, Jews will be so accustomed to luxury, [and] they will need so much money, that they will be living beyond their means; and thus, they will look for occupations and positions to earn money on the side. And they will run right and left to make money—and when I think what they will look like then, I feel pain at the root of my hair; and I feel my nails piercing the skin of my hands. . . . I know," said Rabbi Mordechai-Yoseph, "I know that Rabbi Bunam was right. I know that we are facing difficult times. Our Hasidim will no longer be able to feed their souls with Hasidism alone; they will look for other things—and they will find nothing; they will continue to look—and what they find will be bad. Only faith can save them. Unfortunately, they will rely too much on man, and not enough on heaven."

This vision could have been expressed, or more likely repressed, by his former friend Mendel Kotzker, with whom he continued to share more than one fear, more than one obsession. Both were learned and pious; both believed in self-sacrifice.

Both were suspicious of the written word; both were published posthumously and both of their works have been compiled by others. Both were physically vulnerable; both were prone to illness; both lived in fear and trembling. But then, if they had so much in common, why did they part? Was it *because* they resembled one another so much?

No. There were other reasons—there must have been, Reb Mendel was an individualist, Reb Mordechai-Yoseph was not. Reb Mordechai-Yoseph loved people, Reb Mendel did not. Both were repelled by money; but the Kotzker hated all money, whereas the Izbitzer hated only his own. Reb Mordechai-Yoseph accepted man's weakness. Reb Mendel repudiated it. Man must be worthy of his Creator, said the Kotzker. God must be compassionate toward His creatures, answered the Izbitzer. Kotzk rejected the world, which to him seemed condemned to eternal ugliness; Izbitze believed that ugliness is temporary and misleading: one can transform it into something else.

For Kotzk, life meant the endeavor and the failure to accept the absolute power of God; for Izbitze, life meant an invitation to God to leave heaven and enter into the mutilated world of man. For man and woman to join forces and give life, said Reb Mordechai-Yoseph, they must temporarily—for a fraction of a second—forget God; out of that forgetfulness a child will be born, and that child may one day enrich God's glory. But for the Kotzker, this possibility seemed outrageous. What? To forget God—

even for a second? The world wouldn't survive that second—nor would it deserve to!

Kotzk believed that man is limited, plagued by his instincts; Izbitze had faith in man's aspirations to overcome them. Reb Mordechai-Yoseph went so far as to suggest that man is incapable of doing anything evil—that is, without God's being a part of it. The Talmud claimed: "*Hakol biydei shamayim khoutz mi-yirat-shamayim*—that everything is from heaven except fear of heaven." Reb Mordechai-Yoseph said, "*Afilou yirat-shamayim*. Even fear of heaven is willed in heaven." Good or evil, man is too weak, too poor, too helpless to do anything without God. When the Messiah will come, said Rabbi Mordechai-Yoseph, God will dwell only in good—and man will do only good deeds. Until then, both are in exile.

That is why Rabbi Mordechai-Yoseph loved to quote the strange prophetic call: "*Et laassot ladoshem, heferou toratekha*— There are times when to best serve God, one must transgress His laws." Does that mean that one must oppose God? Never. It means that even in transgressing the law, one remains linked to the One who gave the law.

There are also practical differences between Kotzk and Izbitze. Rabbi Mendel wanted to remain at Sinai—and wanted to keep his followers there; Rabbi Mordechai-Yoseph believed that this was impossible: no one can live that intensely all the time—no one can hear God's voice twenty-four hours a day! No one can live so close to Revelation; one would be consumed.

The Kotzker's answer to this? Who cares? Better one minute of fire than a year of boredom. Better one fragment of truth than a load of empty statements. Kotzk opposed compromises, no matter what the consequences.

In Kotzk, the rebbe worked on himself and his disciples as though they were metaphysical raw material, elaborating his concept of man projected into the universe oscillating between truth and death, death and God.

Rabbi Mendel seemed drawn to, hypnotized by, the abyss. The idea that he might find an answer or even glimpse a certainty at the end of his journey only increased his anguish.

To his friend Yitzhak-Meir he said, "When He cursed the serpent, God condemned him to slither on the ground and feed on dust. What a strange malediction! The serpent will never be hungry; is that a malediction? Yes, it is, and a dreadful one at that!"

A need that could be satisfied, a thirst that could be quenched, was of no interest to him. A God whose intentions he could understand would not suit him. To Rabbi Yaakov of Radzimin, who told him that the purpose of man was to work for the perfection of his soul, he replied disdainfully, "No, no, it wouldn't be worth it. The purpose of man is to raise the sky."

Easier said than done. Stated the Kotzker, "It is easier to extract Israel from exile than exile from Israel." The problem is that men want to live in this world as much as in the other. "Since God is God, let Him come down from His throne. Let him visit the huts, the hearts in distress. There are children to be fed, to be clothed, there is the wife to take care of, the creditor to placate; there is the head that is bursting."

Confronted with worshipers who saw in him a rebbe like all the others, here to help them carry their burdens, the Kotzker cried out: "What do they want from me? Why do they harass me? How am I to make them understand that it is not my task to fill their stomachs and appease their sleep?"

"Pray for me," a Hasid begged him. "Things are going badly, I need help; intercede on my behalf." And the rebbe answered harshly, "Are you too sick to say your own prayers?" "I don't know how." "What? You don't know? *That* is your true problem!" And he dismissed him.

One night he awakened his friend Hersh Tomashover. There he stood, a candle in his hand, saying, "Look, here in my heart there is such pain, such terrible pain, and they, out there, think of nothing else but haunting me with their foolishness and foibles."

Disillusioned and bitter, the rebbe detaches himself more and more from his followers. He is burdened with disciples who are ordinary. They irritate him and he thinks they do it on purpose. He becomes impatient, intolerant, more unrelenting than ever. Their timorous servility makes him nasty. He sees their behavior as petty. "Whoever believes in miracles is an imbecile, whoever does not is an atheist," he says derisively.

One cannot win with him. He states something and promptly denies it. Not content to revel in paradox, he drives it to paroxysm. He demands erudition but rushes to mock it. He stresses the importance of preparations for services, but the services themselves are dispatched almost absentmindedly. The external signs of joy repel him, but he does not appreciate those who attempt to "buy" God with tears. He aspires to wrest man from his all too human condition, yet at the same time he declares that sanctity itself must be human. The man who addresses God in a familiar way incurs His displeasure as much as the man who treats Him as a stranger.

Of course, the more peculiar his behavior, the greater his prestige. Characteristically, this displeases him. When he is denounced in the other Hasidic courts, he rejoices. He finds his disciples' praise much more embarrassing than adversaries' censure. He feels stifled, he would like to be free, but his faithful are in his way. He is convinced of it; they are holding him back. He would give anything to see them go. But they do not. On the contrary, their numbers increase. This living knot, tense with contradictions, is clearly in touch with higher forces. They admire him, they would lift him to the clouds. Fortunately, he is on his guard. He gives free rein to his rage: "Long ago, in my youth, when I could still see inside myself, all these people did not dare approach this closely!" The more he screams, the more they crowd his doorstep. He wins men by the fear he inspires.

In Kotzk, one lives in awe and fear. And in misery as well. In Kotzk one does not speak; one roars or keeps quiet. One spends one's time fighting, cheating desire; one does the opposite of what one feels like doing. One eats when one is full, one does without water when one is thirsty. One prays either later or earlier than is customary. The rebbe says: "When one feels like shouting and doesn't, that is when one truly shouts." A convalescing Reb David is questioned by his father: "You thought you were going to die?" Yes, that was what he had thought. "And what did you feel?" "The need to recite the Sh'ma Israel to proclaim my faith in God." "And did you do it?" No, the son had checked himself. "Very good," cries the Rabbi of Kotzk, "you are a true Hasid!"

Silence in Kotzk is so heavy, so dense that it disrupts the nights. One doesn't dream, one is delirious. One doesn't walk, one runs. One walks a tightrope, and it is he, the rebbe, who holds both ends. He is present in all eyes, in all thoughts. One runs after him, but he flees. Sometimes he awakens a faithful and tells him, "Go away, I am the Master here." And the other bursts into sobs. It is enough for the rebbe to look into someone's eyes for the other to faint. "Why do you address God by calling him Father?" he scolds a young man. "Who told you He is your father? Did he? If you want Him to be, you must force Him!" Another time he stops a disciple: "Do you know where God resides?" And as the other gapes in astonishment, the rebbe continues: "I'll tell you: He resides where He is allowed to enter."

With his questions, his outbursts, he terrorizes people; as soon as he appears, they feel guilty. Guilty of weakness, of cowardice. "Faces, faces, you all have faces," he cries one night, "but is there one, just one, that could compare itself to God's?" Created in God's image, man owes it to himself to resemble Him, to be whole like Him. Says he, "I prefer a total miscreant to a Jew who is only half Jewish." And he also spoke these powerful words: "If I am You and You are You because I am myself and You are Yourself, then I am I and You are You; but if I am You because You are You, then I am not I and You are not You."

His words are repeated over and over; they are endowed with special meanings. One hesitates between the desire to understand and the fear of violating an interdiction. In the end, even his friends are at a loss. Without explanation, he will praise someone he publicly insulted the day before. When his son gets married, it takes a great deal of persuasion to make him attend the wedding.

As for Rabbi Mordechai-Yoseph, he refuses to see only anger and fear in God's Creation. He rejects solitude as a virtue—or even a vehicle for attaining truth. If God is everywhere, why shouldn't man try to be everywhere? Izbitze, therefore, comes closer to Lublin and Lizensk than to Pshiskhe: the rebbe is seen not only as guide and teacher but also as miracle maker. Rabbi Mordechai Yoseph does everything Rabbi Mendel refuses to do: he intercedes in heaven on behalf of his people: the poor, the wretched, the abandoned, the sick, the destitute. Whereas the Kotzker aspires to climb mountains, the Izbitzer wants to stay with the men and women who are too weak, too poor ever to leave their homes. "The summit is not to be found up there," he once said, "but here below—with us, inside us." The mountaintops are for the elite—and unlike the Kotzker, the Izbitzer refuses to identify with the elite. He enjoys quoting a story about Rebbe Elimelech of Lizensk, who, when he refused to receive a certain Tzaddik who had chosen to live in solitude, gave this explanation: God says, in the Book of Jeremiah, "*Im yissater ish bamistarim veani lo erenou?*—The man who hides, will I not see him?" No, said Rebbe Elimelech. When the question mark is replaced by an exclamation point, the citation reads: The man who hides from his fellow man, well, I refuse to see him too!

"*Lo taashok et reakha*—do not steal from your friend" means in Izbitze, "If you are able to help your fellow man and do not, you are a thief." The Talmud is explicit on this subject: Whoever is able to pray for his friend and refuses to do so is a sinner. And who should pray for the Hasid if not the rebbe who is also his friend?

To Kotzk's objection to closeness between the chosen and the crowd, the scholar and the ignorant, Izbitze responds with the Biblical verse: *"Hashokhen itam betokh tim'atam*—God dwells in his people, even in their impurity." What? Is it possible that God associates with the wrong people? The answer is: God associates with those who live in misery—with those who are doomed to dwell in sickness both material and spiritual. If the *Cohen,* the priest, is ordered to take care of the *mezoraim*—the men and women who, as lepers, live outside the community—why should the rebbe do otherwise?

The result of all this? Izbitze became more attractive, more popular than Kotzk: the crowds who had given up on being allowed to see Rabbi Mendel now came to be received by Rabbi Mordechai-Yoseph. All those who sought miracles and were chased away from Kotzk, now gathered in Izbitze. Does this mean that only the simplest, the most ignorant Hasidim, as it were, could be found in Izbitze? Not at all. When Rabbi Mordechai-Yoseph left Kotzk, some of its luminaries joined him, among them, the famous Reb Leibele Eiger and the great, illustrious Reb Zadok Hakohen of Lublin. Both were renowned Talmudic scholars. Reb Leibele was Reb Akiba Eiger's grandson. As for Reb Zadok: when he was still young he met Reb Yaakov Orenstein, who said to him, "I hear that you know half the Talmud by heart—is that true?" "Yes," it is possible, said the young Zadok, who refused to tell a lie. "But which half?" asked Reb Yaakov. "Any half," answered Reb Zadok Hakohen.

If Reb Leibel and Reb Zadok opted for Izbitze, it must have meant that Izbitze was not just a place for simple villagers. But, let us admit it: scholarship was not what attracted people to Izbitze. They came in search of compassión, sympathy, human warmth.

One day a group of *klezmorim*—wandering musicians—came to the rebbe and poured out their grief. The village lord, they said, had promised them a good fee for a performance, but then had canceled it, and, to make matters worse, had invited a Polish company to perform instead. "What do you want *me* to do?" asked the master. "Simple," said the chief *klezmer.* "Make him love good music." And, lo and behold: a miracle occurred. Overnight the village lord became a connoisseur of good music.

The rebbe never failed to respond to solicitations with warmth and concern. He never failed to find words of encouragement for those who needed help. One day a follower came to tell him that an astrologer had predicted that the end of the world was near. Two comets would collide and, in the process, destroy our planet. Many people gave credence to the forecast and stopped working, studying, teaching, taking care of their businesses and families: the threat of collective resignation became real. Do something, Rabbi, say something! his disciples pleaded. "Don't worry," said Rabbi Mordechai-Yoseph, "and tell others not to worry. I shall tell you why. It is written in the Book of Amos that God will do nothing without first revealing His secret to his prophetic servants. And—God has not revealed anything to me. Which means that the predictions are false."

And obviously they were.

Did he really think of himself as prophet? No. As miracle worker perhaps? Surely not. Anyone who sees himself as being capable of performing supernatural wonders will *not* perform them. Vanity is one of the pitfalls that even Tzaddikim cannot avoid. That is why all the Masters spoke of their struggle against *peniot* (unholy thoughts). *Shemetz shel gaavah* (the slightest feeling of vanity) can erase all previous good deeds and qualities. Rabbi Mordechai-Yoseph was too clearsighted, too perceptive, not to know that. Yet he felt that it would be arrogant for him to be different, not from the Kotzker, but from the other Masters. Like the others, he was always on the side of the sufferer. Like the others, he offered his Hasidim hope and joy by allowing them to believe in miracles. Like the Besht and his disciples, he even took the side of sinners. Few before him had manifested such tolerance for them. If God chooses to judge them, that is His business; no man ought to tell God what to do. No other Tzaddik was as explicit in this respect: Izbitze believed that the task of Jews is to bring sinners back to Judaism, not to expel them from it. Furthermore, Rabbi Mordechai-Yoseph maintained that sinners ought not to be seen as sinners; in other words, their sins ought not to be seen. God alone can forgive, only God knows what to forgive: no one has the right to do God's work for Him. To judge is God's prerogative, and His alone. To persecute others is wrong—but to invite persecution is equally wrong.

Sadly, Rabbi Mordechai-Yoseph *was* persecuted not by sinners but by other Hasidim. Those who stayed in Kotzk *could not* forgive their former friends who, they felt, had deserted Rabbi Mendel by moving to Izbitze.

For the split had profoundly affected all levels of the Hasidic world in and around Kotzk. It had resulted in broken families, enemy brothers, rivalries, resentment, hostility. Every Hasid had to choose between the old and the new, between the silence of the Kotzker and the warmth of the Izbitzer. Chroniclers tell of Kotzker Hasidim who did not stop at anything to torment their adversaries. Once during a harsh winter they filled the Izbitzer House of Study with snow. Another time they demolished the home of a Hasid in Levertov. They even put sand in the Rabbi's Shabbat food and destroyed a House of Study which, by sheer luck, was empty at the time. In brief, it was in the best—or the worst—tradition of violent internal Hasidic quarrels.

Rabbi Mordechai-Yoseph specifically ordered his followers not to fight back. Some obeyed, others did not; they were human, not saints. They felt compelled to answer the insults, to respond to the persecution. Can one blame them? Kotzk was never known for its tolerance.

A story: Two Hasidim were partners and friends. They trusted one another, they were ready to make sacrifices for one another—until Izbitze proclaimed its dissidence from Kotzk. Then, naturally, one remained loyal to Rabbi Mendel, the other to Rabbi Mordechai-Yoseph. But for the sake of peace—and business—they decided never to speak about their opposing loyalties. For a while, they succeeded. But one day business was bad—and when that happens, what does one do? One goes to the rebbe; only he can prevail in heaven to change one's fortunes. But the two partners were in a serious predicament; which rebbe would they consult? Actually, the answer was simple. They could not go to the Kotzker, who surely would have thrown them out; he wasn't interested in questions related to material gains or miracles. So they should go to the Izbitzer, right? The problem was that the Kotzker Hasid would not. How could he, a fervent follower of Rabbi Mendel, betray him by seeking out his rival? His partner first tried to reason with him, then became emotional: "If we don't do something soon, we'll go bankrupt!" Still, the Kotzker Hasid refused. His partner fell ill and now implored him to go see Rabbi Mordechai-Yoseph in *his* name, to at least ask him to pray for his recovery. That helped: the recalcitrant partner relented and went to see Rabbi Mordechai-Yoseph. But he warned the Izbitzer immediately: "I feel I must tell you not to misinterpret my presence here; I am not your follower but the Kotzker Rebbe's, may he live a long life. If I am here it is only as a messenger for my associate who is sick; *he* believes in you, not I." "Supposing I performed a miracle," said Rabbi Mordechai-Yoseph. "Supposing I cured your friend—and your business?" "I would call it witchcraft," replied the Hasid. "Supposing I convinced you that I was telling the truth?" "Impossible. Only the Kotzker Rebbe knows the truth," said the Hasid. He could not be shaken. He went so far as to leave Izbitze without saying goodbye to the rebbe who nevertheless was so impressed by his sincerity that he gave him his blessing in absentia . . . and it worked. The sick partner recovered—as did their business. But the Kotzker Hasid was still not convinced.

In fact, the hostility between the two camps never abated. The literature of Izbitze simply ignores the thirteen years Rabbi Mordechai-Yoseph had spent with the Kotzker. The Kotzker tradition does mention them but always scornfully. Those of Rabbi Mordechai-Yoseph's friends who had stayed behind refused to be associated with him, or even to cross his threshold; such was the case with Reb Itse-Meir of Ger. Some Kotzker loyalists said: "It is because of the dissidents that the Messiah was delayed in coming." As for the Izbitzer loyalists, they repeated their rabbi's argument: "Everything is *min-hashamayim,* everything is ordained in heaven; if I broke away from Kotzk, it is because I had to." The Rabbi of Worke refuted this argument, saying, "If you received instructions from heaven, you could have and should have . . . turned to the Kotzker Rabbi for advice; he would have told you what to do."

At this point, let us stop and examine the split itself. What happened in Kotzk that motivated the revolt against the revolutionary kingdom of the awesome Rabbi Mendel? Was it an event? An accident perhaps? Was it simply the logical outcome of a situation filled with ideological tensions and conflicts? All the sources point that way. They suggest that Rabbi Mordechai-Yoseph left because of Rabbi Mendel's decision to become a recluse. I humbly suggest another hypothesis. But first the story itself.

We are in the year 1839: Rabbi Mendel's adventure is still in its first phase. Kotzk means ambition, daring projects to bring God's truth back into man's world. Though moody, Rabbi Mendel is still accessible to his disciples and incites them to take greater risks in order to attain higher levels of ecstasy. At times he chooses to be alone—but even then he welcomes visits by Rabbi Mordechai-Yoseph, one of his intimate friends. One day, as Rabbi Mordechai-Yoseph emerges from Rabbi Mendel's room, he stumbles upon Reb Henekh of Alexander, who asks, "What is new in there?" "Nothing," replies Rabbi Mordechai-Yoseph. "I knew already then," said Reb Henekh much later, "that he no longer was one of us." But if Reb Henekh knew, he did not reveal it to anybody. At any rate, even Rabbi Mordechai-Yoseph did not know. In fact, he continued to play a dominant role in Kotzk for some time. He belonged to its intellectual elite and served as intermediary between the reclusive Master and the disciples eager to approach him. Since they could not be received by Rabbi Mendel, they had to be satisfied with his close friend Rabbi Mordechai-Yoseph; he listened to their woes, showed interest in their problems, and tried to solve them. Thus he knew better than anyone else what the average Hasid—to the extent that there could be an "average" Hasid in Kotzk—needed. At any rate, he knew more than Rabbi Mendel himself—and for good reason: the rebbe didn't want to know. Rabbi Mendel sought silence and was angry with anyone who dared to interfere with his solitary quest for seemingly unattainable victories.

More than anyone, Rabbi Mordechai-Yoseph was in a position to see the dangers threatening his friend. Helplessly he watched him sink deeper and deeper into his anger, which ultimately imprisoned him. One Friday evening, just before Kiddush, he heard him whisper as if to himself, "They do not understand me; they fail to understand that there are two ways to attain heaven: one way is to dig on the outside, and the other is to dig on the inside." Rabbi Mordechai-Yoseph found those words terrifying. Such tunnels could surely lead to the abyss.

In the meantime, Rabbi Mendel rejected all who were attracted to him, shouting and flying into fits of rage. He found it unbearable to be in the presence of those who were not entirely true and pure. One Friday evening he frightened his Hasidim by shouting, "This week we read in the Biblical portion that '*Vay-ishlach Yaakov malakhim el Esav*—And Jacob sent messengers to his brother, Esau': What do you want me to do with a Jacob who uses angels as emissaries to an Esau?"

Rabbi Mordechai-Yoseph heard everything and suffered. He knew that something had gone wrong in Kotzk: his friend had finally gone too far. In the name of abstract truth, he had turned his back on the suffering of real people. True, Pshiskhe had been a rebellion against Hasidic complacency, but there was a point beyond which the revolt itself could become complacent.

And so the rebellion against the Kotzker rebellion grew. Rabbi Mordechai-Yoseph could no longer restrain himself: "Hasidism needs a rebbe, not a saint who hates his fellow men for being human."

The crisis nearly exploded on Simhat Torah. The evening before, hundreds of Hasidim had danced with the Torah and celebrated it in joy. Rabbi Mendel was late—unusually late. "Let us go and have *hakkafot* [the seven rounds with the Torah] at my place," suggested Rabbi Mordechai-Yoseph. Some joined him, others stayed behind. Soon after, Rabbi Mendel arrived. They began the ceremony and the rabbi, as was the custom, danced at the *hakkafot* named after King David; and as was his custom, he invited his friend Rabbi Mordechai-Yoseph to the dance named after Joseph—but Mordechai-Yoseph was not there. So Reb Mendel inadvertently handed the Holy Scrolls to his own son, Reb David. Suddenly he realized his mistake and wanted to take back the *Sefer-Torah*, but strangely, Reb David refused to let go. Rabbi Mordechai-Yoseph commented much later: "He thought he had handed me the scrolls—that is why he tried to take them back; he wanted to deprive me of my powers—and that is why I was not there."

Now it was clear, inevitable: the two friends were about to break their ties. And yet they did try desperately not to reach the point of no return. When Rabbi Mordechai-Yoseph left Kotzk to go home to Tomashov, he was escorted to his carriage by the rebbe himself. When Rabbi Mendel asked him for a farewell present, Mordechai-Yoseph handed him all the *kvitlekh* (the written requests) he had received from disconsolate Hasidim.

The irrevocable split occurred several weeks later, during the fateful Friday evening when the Kotzker Rabbi did something or said something that has remained a burning scar in Hasidism. One single word may have been enough to put an end to a fervent friendship and perhaps to a unique struggle. One single word may have marked the beginning of Izbitze.

And of Rabbi Mendel's virtual isolation, which lasted some twenty years.

I believe that Reb Mordechai-Yoseph left *before* the Kotzker entered absolute seclusion. Why? Why didn't he wait a bit longer? Why didn't he remain at his friend's side when he was most needed to help overcome the growing anguish? Isn't it conceivable that we were mistaken until now? That the sequence of events was inverted? That it was not Rabbi Mordechai who reacted to the Kotzker, but the Kotzker who reacted to Rabbi Mordechai? Isn't it conceivable that Rabbi Mendel chose solitude because his close friend, companion, and associate deserted him? It is only after the defection—which must have brought great disappointment and grief—that the obstacles before him became insurmountable; that he wished to find in solitude all that he could not find in his relations with people. That friends, too, could drive man to despair was something he discovered only then.

This would explain Kotzk's extreme hostility toward Izbitze, which otherwise would seem excessive. After all, it was not the first split in Hasidism; there had been others—those between Lizensk and Lublin, Lublin and Pshiskhe—but none was so personal. Because of what Rabbi Mordechai-Yoseph had done to their Master, and, through him, to all of Kotzk, he became the enemy. If it had not been for Izbitze, Rabbi Mendel might not have run away from his followers. If it had not been for Izbitze, Kotzk would have kept its human, clement image.

Between Kotzk and Izbitze the chasm was never bridged. Some Hasidim who had left Kotzk, overcome by remorse, and even nostalgia, tried to come back to Rabbi Mendel; they were not readmitted. The Kotzker Rabbi himself sent them back to Izbitze. "Why did you come back?" he asked them. "To see me? Who do you think I am? A chimney sweep?" Of course, some refused to be discouraged. The greater the resistance they encountered, the more they wished to stay. The magic and the power of Kotzk were stronger than the kindness and the novelty of Izbitze. Still, why not admit it? Izbitze, too, kept on growing. Hundreds of Hasidim came to see the man who had dared to defy Rabbi Mendel. When the Kotzker learned of his rival's popularity, he smiled one of his rare smiles and said to his wife, "Are you surprised? Why should you be? What do you think he learned from me? To be a shoe-maker, perhaps?"

The Kotzker died in 1859. The Izbitzer died seven years later, and his dynasty flourished for five generations, ultimately merging into other Hasidic families. His fifth descendant was Rabbi Shmuel-Shlomo of Radzin (a relative of my friend Rose Stroch-litz), who, in a ghetto near Sobibor, rose against the Germans and the Judenrat, with powerful appeals to armed resistance and com-bat. The great poet Yitzhak Katznelson devoted a magnificent and heartbreaking poem describing the Radziner Rabbi's glorious bravery as he wandered through Poland trying to ransom dead Jews and bring them to Kever Israel (to consecrated ground). "Give me fifty men," he told his disciples. "I will be their leader. We shall fight. We shall set the ghetto on fire and stop the killers and the murderers: silence is dangerous, silence means consent, consent means complicity. . . ." His pleas went unheeded. When he was finally apprehended by a German officer in 1942, he spat in the German's face. He was executed. And buried in the Jewish cemetery.

And so both Kotzk and Izbitze remain two separate rivers, both flowing into the sea of Jewish history where events and stories disappear only to emerge again just as nocturnal chants vanish into the night only to be heard again by man at dawn.

The Ostrowtzer Rabbi

WE SHALL SPEAK of a strange Hasidic Master who, unlike most of his predecessors, chose suffering as a way of attaining truth, if not redemption.

But isn't Hasidism opposed to suffering? Wasn't Hasidism, as conceived by the Besht, meant to serve as a remedy against suffering? Isn't the entire Jewish tradition a protest against suffering? Then why did a great Master in Hasidism choose suffering and in doing so proclaim its necessity if not its virtue?

These are some of the questions that will accompany us, as we set out on our pilgrimage to a small city in Poland, where a great Rabbi, the Ostrowtzer Rabbi, has been waiting for us.

Let us be on our way.

Are there still Ostrowtzer Hasidim around? Yes, there are. They can be found in Israel, in the United States, in Canada. But if you wish to meet any of them, you'd better hurry. They are old. Some are old enough to have known the first Ostrowtzer Rabbi, the founder of the dynasty—the last Hasidic dynasty in modern history. Do any Ostrowtzer Masters still hold court anywhere? No. Chronicles mention only two Masters altogether, history books, none. Open Buber, Heschel, Horodetzky: nothing about Ostrowtzer rabbis. Will their dynasty be remembered not only as the most recent but also the most short-lived in Hasidism?

Of the first Ostrowtzer Rabbi, Yehiel-Meir Halevy Helsstock, it is said that he fasted for over forty years—like the legendary Talmudic scholar and sage Rabbi Zadok. Did they fast for the same reasons? Rabbi Zadok tried to prevent the destruction of the Temple in Jerusalem. At the end, we are told, he was so emaciated that his body was transparent. What did the Ostrowtzer Rabbi hope to achieve with *his* mortification? What was on *his* mind? What was *his* goal?

I confess: I was not familiar with the Ostrowtzer Rabbi's story. Perhaps I was—and still am—too involved with the earlier Masters. Between the Besht and the Kotzker, there are so many charismatic, enigmatic figures whose tales captivate my imagination. I first heard of the Ostrowtzer Rabbi from a Jewish scholar, a librarian who was my neighbor in shul, Reb Yaakov Dienstag. Was there enough material about him? I asked. Of course, he said. He even went to the trouble of finding it for me. Thanks to my friend, I discovered a modern dynasty.

Of course, I *knew* of latter-day rabbis whose sons and grandsons enlarged the territory of Hasidism in Eastern Europe. Some even conquered America. We now have a great man such as the Bostoner Rabbi in Massachusetts. I have heard of the Junctioner Rabbi in Toronto, so named because he resided at the junction of two streets.

In Eastern Europe dynasties were established when rebbes' sons were "placed" in big cities or small villages, thus adding names to the established list of Hasidic masters. New ones appeared every year.

Take the school to which I belong—the Wizsnitzer. The founder was the Rizhiner's son-in-law, Reb Mendele Hager. His son, Reb Boroukh'l, had ten sons—all destined to occupy Hasidic thrones. I knew two of them: Reb Pinkhas'l of Borshe, who lived across the street from my parents' house, and Reb Yisroel'tse Wizsnitzer, whose court was in Nagyvarad, or, in Yiddish, Grosswardein.

Reb Pinhas'l was kind, gracious, warm. I never heard him scold anyone. It wasn't necessary. It was enough for him to look at you, and you repented. On Shabbat and during the High Holidays I would *daven* in his House of Study and Prayer. There must have been tens of thousands of worshipers there—do I exaggerate? I was young, thirsty for fervor, open to ecstasy—and I could not count. . . . On Rosh Hashanah I stood behind Reb Pinkhas'l, shielded by my grandfather's heavy *tallith,* trying to follow the rebbe's prayers as well as the path of his tears. During the silent service, he would occasionally sigh, *"Riboine d'alme koule*—Master of the entire Universe": and there was so much sorrow, so much pain in his voice, that I was sure that God himself was moved to compassion.

His oldest brother, the heir to his father's throne, Reb Yis-roel'tse, used to visit our town and the neighboring villages reg-ularly. Multitudes would converge upon the house he would choose as his temporary residence. I remember his last visit, in 1935 or '36. My mother brought me to him for his blessing. He received her warmly, asked her about my grandfather—for whom he had special affection—and about my father. Then he tested me, want-ing to know what I had learned that week in Heder. After a few minutes he told my mother to leave us alone. He then sat me on his knee and we talked; we talked for hours and hours—no, for endless minutes, for minutes that I wished would never end. . . . At one point he asked me to go outside and he asked my mother to come back—alone. When she emerged from her second meet-ing with him she frightened me: she was sobbing. I had never seen her weep so desperately. I thought I must have done something wrong. "Why are you crying?" I asked. She refused to answer. I insisted: What did I do? She still refused to answer. Well, I was a *nudnik,* or could be on occasion, and so I kept on asking the same question over and over again. In vain. Soon afterward, Reb Yis-roel'tse passed away—and when she heard the news, my mother wept even more than before. So did I. I had come to love this man whose smile brought comfort to countless followers.

One day, some thirty years later, I was called by a cousin of mine, a surgeon in New York, to hurry to his hospital; another cousin, Reb Anshel Feig, needed immediate surgery but refused to submit to it unless I came. Naturally I jumped into a taxi and rushed to the hospital. I was led to the operating room. Anshel looked at me, smiling: Good that you came, I want you to give me your blessing. What? I exclaimed. You want *my* blessing? Are you out of your mind? Your prayers have a better chance of reaching their destination than mine. Well, I gave him my bless-ing, wishing him a *refua shlema,* a speedy recovery. The surgery was successful—surely not because of me. Some time later, as my cousin was recovering, I visited him and asked, Anshel, what happened to you? What was the idea of asking for my blessing? He took his time answering me, smiling to himself for a long while, as though searching for the right words. Finally he said, "Do you remember the last time the Wizsnitzer Rabbi came to our town?" "Do I remember?" I shouted. "Of course I remember: my mother cried and cried, and refused to tell me why. I still don't know why she cried." "I do," said Reb Anshel. And he told me later

. . . but let us stop here. The end of our story can wait . . . for my memoirs.

Renowned for his piety, charity, and scholarship, the Ostrowtzer Rabbi Yehiel-Meir Halevy Helstock was born . . . when? Some say in 1850, others prefer 1852. Both dates appear in Hasidic chronicles.

Such a confusion of vital statistics is not infrequent in Hasidism, particularly in its early period. Even the origins of the Besht, the best known of the Hasidic rabbis, are shrouded in mystery. Was he born in 1698 or in 1700? In those days, official records seem to have been approximative. And so, the Besht managed to elude historians, who could not even locate his place of birth: Okop? Where is Okop?

But we do know where Sobin is: it is a small town near Warsaw. The Ostrowtzer was born there; all chroniclers agree on that. His father was a simple man, a baker. He and his wife lived in a single room, in a wooden barrack. . . . People said that as he kneaded his dough, he cried and recited psalms. And so, in Sobin, people would say, "Reb Avraham Itzhak makes his cookies with Psalms. His mother, a pious and fervent woman, was told early on that her son was destined to greatness. Several legends refer to that prediction. When she was well into her pregnancy, at one point she stopped "feeling" her child. She went to see Rabbi Osher, the son of the celebrated "Jew of Pshiskhe," who advised her to go to *shul* and face the Aron Kodesh, the Holy Ark: "When a Tzaddik sees the Torah," said Rabbi Osher, "he trembles." She followed his advice. Standing in front of the Holy Ark, she felt her child move in her womb. Later, the same Rabbi Osher promised her that her son would be like a precious jewel whose light would shine throughout the world.

Similar legends circulated about other Hasidic Masters. Somehow the parents were made aware of the importance of their descendant before he was born. The reason for these stories? They are meant to teach us that a Tzaddik is a Tzaddik is a Tzaddik— from the very first moments of his life, if not earlier. His trajectory is straight, his destiny inflexible. No curves, no surprises. Sent from heaven to help enlighten his people, he is irresistibly drawn to a goal both sacred and human. The Besht was the Besht before he revealed himself. And—remember?—his parents too knew that he would be important to a great many people.

But the stories about the Ostrowtzer's childhood do not reflect the same saintliness—nor even the same interest in saintliness. Some chroniclers report that in his youth Yehiel-Meir was more interested in games than in study. He himself is quoted as saying that as an adolescent he was amazingly strong—physically.

One legend portrays him as a wild, undisciplined boy who would run away from school to play in the woods. He would climb trees and throw stones at passersby. One day he hit the Rabbi of Grodzisk, who happened to be traveling through in his carriage. The rabbi's Hasidim ran after him and caught him. They were ready to teach him a lesson, but the rabbi stopped them. He asked the boy whether he attended *heder*. Yes. Then why wasn't he there? Because he had learned enough. Had he really learned all his lessons? Yes, if the rabbi wished, he could examine him. The rabbi did. And he marveled at the young boy's erudition. It was then that he offered to become his teacher.

Another version: The Rabbi and the boy met, not in the woods but in Grodzisk. Yehiel-Meir was ten years old. On the Sabbath, after services, the Grodzisker Rabbi traditionally would lecture on Biblical, Talmudic, and Hasidic themes, and hundreds of disciples would gather to hear him. One Shabbat, the renowned scholar Reb Berl came after the lecture and asked the Hasidim whether they could tell him what the rabbi had spoken about. No one could remember accurately. Except . . . the ten-year-old Yehiel-Meir. He repeated the whole lecture word for word. That is when the boy was asked to stay and study in Grodzisk.

He surely was an exceptional child. Most stories stress his keen intelligence and his thirst for knowledge. Talmud was his favorite subject. "When I discovered the commentaries of the Maharam Schieff," he said, "I had a taste of paradise." In *heder*, he was so brilliant—asked so many questions, offered so many suggestions—that his fellow classmates had difficulty in keeping up with him. That is when his parents realized they had to get him the best teacher in town.

Everybody was astounded by the power of his memory. Whatever he read once, he retained and could repeat by heart. At eleven, he had mastered the Talmud so well that he felt ready to open a path through some of its obscure passages, but he was too timid to so do in the presence of his elders. Still, he had to share his new ideas with someone, so he would write them on the walls of the House of Study. His strength was *Pilpul*—a kind of free association of ideas, sayings, laws, and Biblical verses—and it was said of him that like Atniel, son of Knaz, he brought back thousands of laws and interpretations that had been forgotten since the time when the people of Israel mourned the passing of our teacher Moses.

The young Yehiel-Meir stayed at Rabbi Elimelech of Grodzisk's court a long time. Was it that he needed a teacher more than a father? Interestingly, the decision was not his, but his father's.

Rabbi Yehiel-Meir often spoke about his father's influence on his development. Not only had he taught him love of God and love of Torah, but the poor, hardworking baker also taught him simple yet essential lessons about human behavior. Reb Yehiel-Meir reminisced, and I quote: "When I was young I thought I could conquer the world with a machine, the machine that was in my mouth; it was enough to open it for words to flow out and get me whatever I wanted. Now that I am older and wiser, I realize that my father, the baker, was right: You want the oven to gain heat? Don't open it. The less one opens one's mouth, the deeper, the more intense, what one needs to say."

From his father he also learned the virtue of humility. But— wasn't he too successful to be humble? too famous? In Hasidism, the more celebrated the rabbi, the more modest he becomes. The greater the Master, the more he understands the futility of honors.

In the case of the Ostrowtzer Rabbi, humility came with the years.

He married at seventeen in Worke, where a group of students had gathered around him. Later he was engaged as rabbi in Skarniewicz, whose trustees were impressed by his double ordination. It is said that when he came to visit Reb Yeoshua'le Kutner, soliciting his help for his job application in Skarniewicz, he was asked by the old Master, "What do you know?" And the young man is said to have answered, "I know all the answers to all the questions in the tractate of Yevamot." And he did. Reb Yeoshua'le praised him as one of the giants of his generation, and the Gaon Rabbi Hayim-Eleazar Waks wrote, "How can I, a fly without wings, make pronouncements on an eagle who rises to the skies?" He walked with him through Nalevke street, known for its poverty. At number 7, he stopped and bade him farewell, quoting a beautiful anecdote from the Talmud: One day, a tired and hungry man wandering in the desert found an oasis with a date tree and a spring; he sat down under the tree and ate from its fruit; then he drank water from the spring. When he got up to continue on his way, he said, "Tree, tree, with what could I bless you? With fruit? You have the best. So let me wish that your fruit may grow and give birth to a tree like you." And: "Spring, spring, with what could I bless you? Let me wish that another tired and hungry traveler may enjoy your water."

One morning, the military governor of Skarniewicz entered his room. Rabbi Yehiel-Meir was so absorbed in his studies that he did not notice his presence. Awed by the rabbi's powers of concentration, the governor could not stop looking at him. Finally the rabbi raised his eyes and saw his distinguished guest. He greeted him in Russian—a language he had learned out of dictionaries—and apologized. Don't apologize, said the governor. Later he told community leaders, "You have a treasure in your midst."

Another time, while Rabbi Yehiel-Meir was still in Skarniewicz, he was informed that a traveling Yiddish theater company had arrived in town and was going to perform on Friday evening—which is forbidden, for it violates the Shabbat. There were many people in the audience when the rebbe arrived and sat down in the first row. People understood what he was doing and became embarrassed. They began to steal out of the hall one by one. Finally the rebbe remained alone. As soon as Shabbat was over, he reimbursed the company out of his own pocket.

In 1887, at the age of thirty-five or thirty-seven, he was invited to serve as Rabbi of Ostrowtze. The truth was, he had not been the community leadership's first choice. Their first choice was Reb Gershon-Henokh of Radzin, who, after lengthy consideration, refused. Why? He liked the community but was apprehensive of its leaders, who were too strong-willed, in his view. He was afraid that he would have to spend too much time fighting with them. Reb Yehiel-Meir was not afraid—and this is how he explained why not: David, in his eulogy of Saul, mentions that Saul had wanted to teach his people the art of *Keshet*—of fighting with bow and arrow. For a bow to be useful, it has to bend. Sometimes, said Rabbi Yehiel-Meir, you must bend in order to obtain the desired results.

Humility or pragmatism?

There is a world of difference between genuine and false humility. A truly humble man does not know that he is humble.

Was it the Ostrowtzer who asked: If humility is so important a commandment, why isn't it mentioned in the Torah? Maybe because if it were a biblical commandment, people would compete with each other: I am more humble than you, and the other would say: No, I am more humble . . . Yes, humility must be part of a person's subconscious. Take the best example: Moses. He wrote about himself: "And the man Moses was the humblest among all men. . . ." He wrote it without realizing that he was describing himself. Or perhaps he meant the description as a goal indicated by God: Moses, work on yourself hard, very hard, so you become the humblest among men. The Ostrowtzer Rabbi never thought that he was humble enough. Speaking about those who speak about humility, he commented: "Abraham said of himself, 'I am but dust and ashes.' Moses and Aaron said, 'What are we?' King David said, 'I am a worm, not a man.' Still," remarked the Ostrowtzer Rabbi, "it is much better—and safer—to say nothing."

We are told that it was the Ostrowtzer Rabbi's custom on Yom Kippur Eve to ask the beadle to give him the ritual thirty-nine lashes on his back as atonement for his sins. Of course, the beadle would try hard not to hurt him—while the rabbi would try hard to be hurt. . . .

On his walk to the synagogue for Kol Nidre, men, women, and children would line the streets to accompany him there. "God has forgiven you," he would whisper to every group, "God has forgiven you."

Why did he choose asceticism? Why did he inflict pain on himself? Why the prolonged fasting? We know that he began rejecting food in Skarniewicz—but he never really stated his reasons. Was it but another expression of his search for humility? Was it his desire to push himself to the limits of endurance? Did he think that by depriving his body he would enrich his soul? His peers and his disciples tried, in vain, to reason with him. Could it be that he wanted to suffer on behalf of his people—for them, in their place? Can one, should one, suffer *for* someone else?

In fact, his fasting began with humiliation. Once, in his youth, when he was hungry, a Jewish merchant refused to offer him food. Since he could not eat when he wanted to, he would stop eating altogether.

Over the years, his faithful servant, Reb Pinhas'l, who never let him out of his sight, would plead with him: Rebbe, Rebbe, eat something, *something!* It is against nature not to eat! And the rebbe would answer, Pinhas'l, you don't understand, I want to break the rules of nature. When the Gerer Rabbi, Avrohom Mord-'hai, said to him, "But food is good for you," he replied, "How do you know? How do you know that food is good for man?" In order to remain awake, he would refuse to undress at night from Sunday to Friday. Only on Shabbat did he agree to sleep.

Because he enjoyed music, he chose not to listen to it.

A strange man? Yes, and a strange Hasidic rabbi. For hadn't he learned from the Master of all Hasidic Masters, the Besht, that asceticism is *not* the way to truth and God?

Rabbi Yehiel-Meir once said to a visitor: From the School in Pshiskhe I learned that *Ahavat Israel* is linked to *Ahavat Hashem:* the love of Israel and the love of God are intertwined; if you wish to know whether you are coming closer to *Hashem,* closer to God, ask yourself whether you have come closer to your people, to your fellow human beings. One must be ready to sacrifice oneself for one's fellow man. An example? Again, Moses. When he complained to God about what was happening to him, God told him, Listen, Moses. I took an oath that either you or Israel would die. The choice is yours. If you wish to go on living, the people of Israel will have to disappear. And Moses exclaimed, Let Moses die a thousand times—for I refuse to see a single soul in Israel vanish.

Could it then be that Rabbi Yehiel-Meir wanted to suffer to prevent Jewish suffering on a large scale? If so, why did he instruct his son and heir, Rabbi Yehezkel, "not to indulge in self-inflicted suffering, not to fast except on days when one is forbidden to eat"? He was evidently harsher on himself than on others. In fact, his leniency was legendary. Even when the poorest of people needed a rabbinic decision—whether a certain chicken was kosher or not, for example—he went out of his way to help.

He asked, Why was Rabbenu Gershom called "Meor Ha-gola," the light of the Diaspora? What did he do? He decreed that bigamy is forbidden, and that a man is not allowed to divorce his wife against her will. Now, when the people of Israel sinned and God wanted to divorce it, we said to Him, You cannot do that, it is against the law of Rabbenu Gershom. . . . And should He decide to take another people, and have two—we would again tell Him: You cannot do that, bigamy is against the rule as enunciated by Rabbenu Gershom. You see? Thanks to Rabbenu Gershom, we stay with God and God stays with us—even in exile.

The Ostrowtzer Rabbi's kindness was such that the community leaders finally asked him gently not to involve himself with practical issues: let other rabbinic judges cope with them. All he, the rabbi, was asked to do was study and teach and live in the midst of the community.

His Hasidim feared him, loved him, admired him. He was the center of their universe, what the Besht and the Maggid of Mezeritch had been to their disciples: guide, friend, teacher, all in one. When they were happy, he rejoiced in their happiness. When they were sad, he brought them consolation. He gave meaning to their lives.

A merchant came to him with a complaint: When I inherited my store from my father, business was good. Now it isn't. Help me. "In the early days, did you have customers all the time?" asked the rabbi. "No, not all the time." "And what did you do while waiting for customers?" "I studied Torah or Mishnayot." "And now, what are you doing while you wait?" "I read newspapers." "See?" said the rabbi. "There is the problem. Before, when you studied, the evil spirit sent you customers to distract you from study. Now that you read papers, the evil spirit doesn't care if you go on reading."

Did he make them laugh? Occasionally. More often, he made them smile.

A man wished to marry off his daughter but needed four hundred rubles for the wedding. Where could he go? To the rabbi, naturally. Did the rabbi have money? No, but he knew people who did—in particular, one of the man's relatives. So he went to see the man with a plea for his poor cousin. "Four hundred rubles?" the wealthy cousin cried. "Impossible!" "At least, tell me that you agree that he needs the money." "I agree, but . . ." "Wait. Now, agree with me that if you could give him such a sum of money, you would." "I agree." "Then say so." "I told you, didn't I?" "Say so with words! Say that if you could help him, you would." The wealthy man was forced to repeat his statement several times, until he broke down. He could tell a lie once, but not five times. The wedding took place.

Once he heard of a rabbi who had troubles in his community. He decided to go there and help make peace. On the road leading to that community, he met two rabbis who had just come from there on a similar mission: "It is no use," they told him. "The situation is hopeless. The entire community is united in its oppo-

sition to the rabbi." "United, you said?" said the Ostrowtzer
Rabbi. "You said the community is united? Good! Where there is
unity, there is Divine Presence. Where there is Divine Presence,
justice and kindness prevail. Let us all go there and see what we
can do to help."

He once said: In our daily prayers, we repeat three times
"*Vehavta et adoshem elokekha.* You shall love thy God with all your
heart, all your soul, all your fortune." The Talmud comments:
With all your soul means, Even if it is at the price of your life. Why
isn't it said also about money? Why aren't we supposed to love
God even at the price of one's money? Because it's easy, said the
rabbi. When you lose your money, it is so easy to love God . . . too
easy.

A wealthy man asked him, Why are you fasting so much? Are
your sins so great? "Why are you rejoicing so much? Are your
good deeds so great?" the Ostrowtzer Rabbi snapped back. "You
probably want to participate in other people's joy—whereas I want
to take part in their woes."

He summoned a man to his home and said, "How dare you
violate the Sabbath?" "Rabbi," answered the visitor, "aren't you
doing the same thing? It is forbidden to fast on the Sabbath, yet
you eat so little that it is almost like fasting."

The rabbi thought for a moment, then replied, "You are
right. But there is a difference between you and me. No one will
dream of imitating me, but many may copy you."

He spent Rosh Hashanah with Reb Leibush of Uzherov,
who said, "I would gladly invite you to stay for Shabbat as well.
But since you fast even on Shabbat, your being here would be
dangerous to both of us. Either I will be influenced by you, in
which case my Hasidim will leave me, or you will be influenced by
me, in which case your Hasidim will leave you."

He once was asked to inscribe the last words of a newly
written *Sefer-Torah*. People shouted their wishes: "May you live
long enough to attend more and more such ceremonies in the
years ahead." The rabbi shook his head. "No, no," he said, "of
holy scrolls we have enough, but where are the pupils to study
them?"

Another time he was asked, Why is it that a father loves his
son more than a son loves his father? His answer? All men have
their origins in Adam, whose virtues and abilities they inherit.
Adam had sons whom he could love—but he had no father.

(I am not sure I agree with the great rabbi's interpretations—unless he meant them to be ironic. Nowhere in the Bible do we find that Adam loved his sons Cain and Abel. Had he loved them, perhaps tragedy could have been avoided.)

The Ostrowtzer Rabbi had an older brother named Hayim, who rarely left his house. A strange man, this Hayim. Shy, reserved, he would sit from morning till evening in the same corner, softly reciting psalms. Clearly, he did not wish to be noticed. When the rabbi's daughter Yentele became a widow with six orphans, it was Hayim who spent time with them. He loved children—only children. The rabbi showed him infinite respect and affection, but Hayim kept his distance. He may not have wanted to embarrass his brother. But both were absorbed with matters of faith. A chronicler recorded that Hayim often visited his niece Yentele to comfort her in her grief, and to plead with her not to rebel against the Almighty. Does this mean that the rabbi's daughter *did* rebel against God's mysterious ways? What did Hayim tell her? Did he convince her that God is always just? *Did* he convince her? Is this why the rabbi chose suffering—to atone for someone else's impatience?

A Hasidic Master knows that he must be linked to his people as it waits for redemption; and the Ostrowtzer disciples swore that he literally waited for the Messiah, watch in hand, every day. Exile, for him, was going to be temporary. When asked where he resided, he would answer, "Like all Jews, I reside in the land of Israel. I am here in Poland only on a visit." He once said: "*Vetitaenu bigvulenu*—In our prayers we implore God to settle us inside the borders of our land." But I would rather interpret *vetitaenu* differently: Almighty God, allow us to argue with you—from the root *taana* or *tiun*—from inside our borders. Let us not argue abroad, among strangers, but at home, inside our borders, and "*Vesham naase lefanecha et korbenot khovotenu,* There we shall give you back all that we owe you." Here, we can pay nothing. We possess nothing. We are not the masters of our own lives.

Yes, like all Hasidic Masters the Ostrowtzer Rabbi was waiting for the Messiah. Is that why he fasted? To hasten his coming? Who among the Masters did not dream of precipitating events, of forcing the Messiah out of seclusion?

The great Hebrew and Yiddish poet Hillel Zeitlin wrote about the Ostrowtzer: "He followed all major events in the world—without ever reading a newspaper—attempting to detect in them signs of the coming of the Messiah. . . . And when he realized that instead of the long-awaited redemption, there were more upheavals, more trials, more persecutions to come, when he understood that instead of salvation our people was about to be handed poverty and slaughter and humiliation, he ascribed all evil to come to the cardinal sin of gratuitous hatred. "That sin," he said, "is rooted in the betrayal of Joseph by his brothers, and runs through all generations. But it gains strength and scope especially in pre-messianic times. Only when the true light of the Messiah will illuminate Jewish souls will it disintegrate."

The Ostrowtzer Rabbi always returned to the same subject, said Zeitlin—the story of Joseph, a victim of his brothers' hate. "This hate is still here, with us," the rabbi said. "And it is our fault. Let us stop hating one another; let us stop claiming that we alone are right, and all others are wrong; let us stop looking for sins in the other, always in the other, just as Joseph's brothers were accusing him, only him, of all the sins in the world; only then will things change, only then will they improve; only then will redemption come."

Well, it didn't. During his seventy-six or seventy-eight years, the Ostrowtzer Tzaddik witnessed more turmoil than peace, more hate than harmony. Violence had become the answer to hunger and oppression.

His generation knew the Crimean war, the French-Austrian war, the Civil War in the United States, the bloody insurrection of the Commune in Paris, Russia's war against Turkey, Rasputin and Lenin, Garibaldi and Trotsky, the Dreyfus Affair, and then World War I. All this in one lifetime.

In 1912, during the famous Beilis trial in Kiev, Jews throughout Poland lived in fear of the pogroms. In Ostrowtze, Rabbi Meir-Yehiel summoned the community leaders to an emergency session and ordered all Jewish inhabitants to arm themselves with hatchets and knives, and to resist. The rabbi himself was the first to acquire a hatchet. Four hundred Jews occupied the synagogue and turned it into a fortress. As a result, the local "Pogromchiks" retreated.

Ostrowtzer Hasidim claim that their leader foresaw the Great War, as it was called. His custom was to deliver a sermon to the entire community, assembled in the main *shul,* on Shabbat Shuva, the Sabbath between Rosh Hashanah and Yom Kippur. Usually his sermon would last several hours—not this time. Before reading the Torah, he ascended the Bimah and faced his audience. He uttered a few words and stopped. His face wrapped in his *tallith,* he remained silent. A long minute passed. Two. Three. Five. Nothing like this had ever happened before. He could not speak. Something prevented his words from leaving his throat. Suddenly he began shouting, "Jews! I see that in heaven they do not want me to speak! Who knows what the future has in store for us. Let us repent and do penitence together. . . ." He left the Bimah and returned to his seat. Soon after, people understood the meaning of the incident: Europe plunged into the nightmare of the First World War.

Ostrowtze was first occupied, then liberated, by armies from both camps, bringing equal measures of fear and uncertainty to its Jewish inhabitants. Was the rabbi affected? He was. Jews were arrested and it was his duty to seek their liberation. Both the Russians and the Austrians tried to recruit spies among Jews. The Rabbi opposed the practice. In other words, the Rabbi was involved in daily events. He acted and reacted, giving counsel, offering warnings, standing behind all those threatened by danger.

One of his Jews was arrested for spying during the war and was sentenced to death. The rabbi interceded on his behalf and saved his life.

One Passover, the military command ordered the Jewish bakers to provide its troops with bread. The bakers refused; the military displayed their anger. Finally, it was the rabbi who saved the situation by allowing the Jewish bakers to bake bread during Passover. If it's a sin, he said, I will take it on myself.

Was he aware of what was happening outside Ostrowtze? What did Hasidim know of what was going on elsewhere in the world? What did the Rabbi want them to know? Like most Masters, all he wanted was for them to study the law and observe it. He urged them to fulfill themselves as Jews, to live according to the precepts of Moses and the vision of the prophets. Everything else could wait. Material considerations were secondary. The rabbi may well have understood that all the cultural triumphs of civilized society would not prevent the murderous onslaught on his people. Is that why he fasted? Is that why, on Friday evenings, he often sobbed uncontrollably, whispering: "I see, I see terrible days and terrible nights which Jews will be made to endure. . . .

•

Why not admit it? I am troubled by his deliberate inclination toward suffering. I was always led to believe that Judaism opposes suffering; that our tradition does not endow suffering with redemptive qualities. I was led to think that the Torah was given to man so that he could improve his life. *Vehai bahem:* Torah affirms life, it sanctifies whatever sustains life. *Ushmartem lenafshotekhem:* to take care of one's physical health is a Biblical command. If suffering is imposed on us, we must reject it. A Nazir (an ascetic) is crowned by God, but the same Nazir, for choosing suffering, must bring an offering to atone for his sin. To suffer without reason *is* a sin. The entire Hasidic approach to life was to teach Jews that the path to God is joy, not sadness; fervor, not suffering. Wasn't Rabbi Yehiel-Meir a Hasidic rebbe?

At first, he preferred *not* to be. In the early days, he saw his role as that of a teacher. Undoubtedly inspired by the Kotzker Rabbi, he refused to have followers. Students, yes. Students only. When they tried to give him *kvitlech*—written pleas—he did not want to accept them. He did not seek to be a miracle maker. There were enough wonder rabbis in the land. Still, when he was pressed by them to accept their *kvitlech,* he finally had to yield. Even so, he never performed earthshaking miracles, nor did he turn to the supernatural to solve practical problems.

His followers were poor and learned, totally without influence or ambition in the community. They came and went quietly, without attracting attention; they never engaged in traditional Hasidic quarrels over "whose Master is holier, whose is greater." When they needed an ear, he listened. When they needed a heart, his own broken heart was sensitive to their pain and anguish.

From the early days in Ostrowtze, he had made it his custom to collect funds for the poor. He would go from store to store, from house to house, asking for charity—but avoiding the store of a certain widow whom he knew to be needy. He did not want to embarrass her. But she saw him and sent her son with some money—which he accepted, so as not to shame her. He believed that the poor must never be made to feel that they have nothing to give, or are unworthy of giving.

When he scolded people for disregarding the law, he immediately asked their forgiveness. When a woman complained that six wealthy Jews refused to allow her son to study with their tutor because his clothes were torn and he walked barefoot, he forced the rich men to buy the boy shoes and clothes. A company of wandering magicians came into town to perform. The rabbi went to see them: "I order you to tell me," he said, "is what you are showing true or not?" The chief magician reassured him: "No, it is not true. It is but an illusion; ours is work of agility, not witchcraft." "Thank God," exclaimed the Ostrowtzer Rabbi. "I did not sleep all night because of you. Maimonides says that there are no sorcerers left in this world—and here I thought you were claiming that he was mistaken."

He favored philosophical inquiry—as per Maimonides—under one condition: it must be anchored in faith, not outside faith. In our liturgy, he said, we start singing *Ein kelokenu,* no one is like our God"—and then we ask "*Mi kelokenu?* Who is like our God?" The order ought to be reversed. First we ought to ask "Who is like our God?" and then the answer would follow: "No one is like Him." There is a lesson in this, said the Ostrowtzer Rabbi. Once we affirm that God is God, and there is no one like Him, we may ask: Who is our God? Faith must precede philosophical interrogation.

Eventually he was weakened from fasting, plagued with all kinds of illnesses, and had to be carried to the synagogue. He spent days and nights lying in bed, getting up only for services. He slept little and was tormented by bad dreams. So every morning he would ask three of his disciples to help him perform the ritual which is meant to remove the bad omen from the dream and transform it into a good dream. It became a daily tradition at his home. But what *were* his dreams? What did he see that frightened him so? Is it possible that, as some disciples and chroniclers believe, he had visions of the futureless future of his people in Poland and the rest of Eastern Europe? Is that why he fasted? To alter the future, to force history to change its course?

Whatever his motives, the bad dream of man and his Creator eventually turned into reality. But Rabbi Yehiel-Meir was no longer there to see it happen. He died a few days after Purim, 1928. One Shabbat morning, he felt that his end was near. "Something will happen today," he told the *rebbetsin.* A service was held in his room. When the Torah was read, he was helped up to recite the blessings. His voice was clear. He died that same afternoon and was buried the next day. Thousands and thousands of people came to pay him their last respects. Rabbi Shlomo of Radzimin said in his eulogy: "Were the earth to know what treasure it is about to receive, it would burst into song."

•

His son Reb Yehezkel was elected to succeed him. The second Ostrowtzer Rabbi was known for his weeping. When he prayed, when he delivered sermons, when he studied, people would see tears streaming down his face. He too saw the dark clouds covering Europe and he spoke about them. To an American visitor—a certain Robinson—he is quoted as saying, "I know that the enemy will be defeated, but I am afraid that for us European Jews, it will be too late. Our decree has been sealed already. I no longer pray for our sake, but for yours. I pray for our brethren in America and in the land of Israel. I pray to the Almighty to save them, since we will not be saved."

When the war broke out, he was in Warsaw, where he remained during the German siege. Later, an ambulance brought him back to Ostrowtze—back to his community, where there were harsh decrees from the occupying authorities, cruel edicts, anti-Semitic incidents, and finally the creation of the ghetto. In spite of the perils involved, the rabbi continued to hold services in his overcrowded home. Hasidim visited him at every opportunity, eager for encouragement and consolation.

Then came the night when Rabbi Yehezkel and the last of his followers went to the ancient cemetery in Ostrowtze to bury the holy scrolls that had once belonged to the various synagogues in town. The Hasidim wept as they said goodbye to the scrolls and paid their respects to the first Ostrowtzer Rabbi, Yehiel-Meir, whose dreams were surely buried with him in his tomb.

It is one of the Rabbi Yehezkel's disciples, a certain Reb Yeshayahu Zoberman, who has left a detailed account of his last months: in the summer of 1942, the Ostrowtzer ghetto was liquidated. Most of its fifteen to twenty thousand Jews were killed. Some fifteen hundred were still alive, the rabbi and his immediate family among them. "Suddenly," reported Reb Yeshayahu Zoberman, "the Gestapo appeared and searched the workshops, looking for the rebbe. The rebbe was well hidden, and the Gestapo's efforts were fruitless. Thereafter, the decision was made to move the rebbe to Sandiemierz (Tzuzmir in Yiddish). The German authorities had announced that if all those Jews who were still in hiding would come out and register, they would be granted total safety, sent to work in German factories until the end of the war. Many Jews left their hiding places in the forests and cellars and came to register in Tzuzmir. Did they really believe the Nazi murderers?

Doubtful. But they were exhausted, hungry, and cold. They no longer had the strength to continue, to undergo further torment.

"The rebbe, in hiding, was placed in a secluded, walled-in area, part of a larger room. He received food through a hole, invisible to the outside. He might have stayed there indefinitely, but one day in the latter part of the month of Kislev (December) the chief of the Gestapo, a man named Braun, appeared in the ghetto and ordered the community leaders to hand the Ostrowtzer Rabbi over to him. They answered that he was not in the ghetto. If the Rabbi was not handed over to him in one hour, threatened the Gestapo chief, he would arrest two hundred Jewish men, women, and children and burn them alive in the synagogue.

"The community leaders informed the Rabbi. His answer was that he wanted to be led to the Gestapo chief. Braun asked him various questions, but Rabbi Yehezkel Halevy Helstock, the second Ostrowtzer Rabbi, ignored them. Then the Gestapo chief had him photographed from all sides and handed him back to the community leaders, making it their responsibility to hold him until nine o'clock in the morning. Were the Rabbi to escape, two hundred hostages would be massacred.

"Throughout that night the Rabbi and several of his followers sat in the community building and recited psalms. Before dawn, the rabbi went to the mikva—the ritual bath—and purified himself.

"That night the entire ghetto remained awake.

"At dawn (it was the tenth day of Teveth—a day of fasting and penitence) the Rabbi put on his white *kittel,* his *tallith,* and *tefillin,* said his morning prayers, said the penitential litanies, the Slikhot, Al Khet—and the whole ghetto wept with him.

"At 9 A.M. precisely, the Gestapo chief appeared, accompanied by Nazi policemen. Some twenty Jews went to Braun and offered to die in the Rabbi's place. Braun laughed. Very well, your offer is accepted; you will be shot—together with your Rabbi. All were led outside. The Rabbi was ordered to stand with his back to the wall of the synagogue building. When Braun took out his gun and aimed it at the rabbi, the second and last Ostrowtzer Rabbi said aloud in a clear quiet voice: 'Sh'ma Israel, adoshem elokenu adoshem ekhad—Hear O Israel, God is our God, God is one.' Six bullets were fired. More bullets followed. The Rabbi's twenty disciples accompanied him into death."

His seven sons and one daughter perished, too. And so the

last Hasidic dynasty was also the shortest. Like Rabbi Zadok in ancient times, Rabbi Yehiel-Meir had not succeeded, despite his long fasting, in saving the Jewish kingdom. But Rabbi Zadok was saved, whereas Rabbi Yehiel-Meir and his descendants were not.

I often think of the first Ostrowtzer Rabbi's nightmares; I still don't know what they were. Maybe I do.

Glossary

AGGADA: Legend
AKHER (the Other): Nickname given to Elisha Ben Abouya
ALIYAH: Emigration to Israel
ALEPH-BET: Hebrew alphabet
AV-BET-DIN: President of a tribunal

BAAL SHEM: Master of the Name
BARAITA: Tannaitic material not included in the Mishna
BAR KOCHBA: Commander of the anti-Roman rebellion
BEIT MIDRASH: House of study
THE BESHT (ISRAEL BAAL SHEM TOV): Master of the Good Name
BIMAH: Podium

CHUPPAH: Wedding canopy
CHACHAM: Sage

DIN: Law, rigor

GAMLIEL: Head of Sanhedria
GAON OF VILNA: Talmudic genius of eighteenth century
GER: Stranger
GILGUL: Reincarnation
GOLEM: Man-made creature

HALAKHA: Legal system
HASKALAH: Emancipation; enlightenment
HAVDALAH: Prayer recited at the end of the Sabbath
HASID: Member of Hasidic community
HEDER: School for young children
HIGH HOLIDAYS: Rosh Hashana and Yom Kippur

ISH-HAMUDOT: A pleasant man

KABBALA: Mysticism
KABBALIST: Mystic
KADDISH: Prayer for the dead
KAVVANAH: Concentration
KHAMASS: Violence
KIDDUSH HASHEM: Martyrs' sanctification of the Name
K'MOSH: Name of Moabite god
KOHEN: Priest

LAG B'OMER: Thirty-third day of the counting since Passover
LIEBERMAN, SAUL: Great Talmudic scholar

MAARIV: Evening prayer
MAGGID: Preacher
MASTER: Teacher
MEZUZAH: A box with Biblical passages affixed to the doorframe
MERKAVA: Celestial chariot
MIKVAH: Ritual bath
MINHA: Afternoon service
MINYAN: Quorum of ten men
MISHNA: Collection of laws edited by R. Yehuda Hanasi
MITNAGDIM: Opponents of Hasidism

NIGLA: Revealed tradition
NISTAR: Hidden tradition
NOCHRI: Stranger

PARDES: Orchard of forbidden knowledge
PESACH: Passover
PILPUL: A pedagogical method

RABBAN, RABBI, REB, REBBE: Rabbinic titles; both rabbi and
    rebbe apply to Hasidic Masters

SANHEDRIN: Court
SEFER-TORAH: Scrolls of Torah
SHABBAT: Sabbath
SHABTAI-TZVI: False messiah
SHALOM: Peace, greeting
SHAVUOT: Holiday of Weeks, Pentecost
SHEKHINA: Divine Presence
SHOFAR: Ram's horn
SHTETL: Small village
SHTIBEL: Small oratory

SHTRIEMEL: Fur hat
SHUL: Synagogue
SHULCHAN ARUCH: Code of behavior
SIDDUR: Prayer book
SIMHAT TORAH: Celebration of the Torah

TALLITH: Prayer shawl
TANNAIM: First Talmudic masters
TEFILLIN: Phylacteries
TEN MARTYRS: Those who died for the Sanctification of the Name
TESHUVA: Repentance
TISHA B'AV: 9th day of Av, commemoration of the destruction of
    Jerusalem and its Temple
TORAH: Body of wisdom and law in Jewish Scripture
TZADDIK: Just Man

YAHRZEIT: Anniversary of a death
YAVNEH: Place where first Academy was established
YEHOIAKHIN: King of Judah
YICHUS: Genealogy
YOHANAN BEN ZAKKAI: Talmudic Master

ZOHAR: Book of Splendor, a mystical commentary on the Pen-
    tateuch

About the Author

ELIE WIESEL received the Nobel Peace Prize in Oslo, Norway, on December 10, 1986. His Nobel citation reads: "Wiesel is a messenger to mankind. His message is one of peace and atonement and human dignity. The message is in the form of a testimony, repeated and deepened through the works of a great author." He is Andrew Mellon Professor in the Humanities at Boston University and the author of more than thirty books. Mr. Wiesel lives in New York City with his family.

IN THE STILL OF THE NIGHT

Lindsay's cell phone, perched on her nightstand, rang just after midnight and jerked her awake. Accustomed to being awakened in the middle of the night, she sat up and answered it. "Hello?"

No answer.

She shoved back her hair and glanced at the clock on the bedside table. Sam had dropped her off more than three hours ago and she'd fallen into bed exhausted. "Hello?"

There was breathing on the other end. Normally, when she got late-night calls, it was a frightened woman hiding out from her abuser, too afraid to talk. Often she had to coax the woman into speaking.

But tonight, she didn't sense someone in trouble. She sensed danger. Her voice harsh, she demanded, "Who is this?"

There was a moment's pause. And then the line went dead.

Lindsay hurried past her roommate's closed door and went down the carpeted stairs to check the lock on the front door. She peered out the peephole. Nothing. Then she went to the back sliding door. Locked. She moved from window to window checking them. All locked.

She flipped on the floodlight and it shone over her backyard garden. She stared into the yard looking for any sign of movement.

Nothing moved.

And yet she had the feeling that someone was watching. . . .

Books by Mary Burton

I'M WATCHING YOU

DEAD RINGER

DYING SCREAM

SENSELESS

MERCILESS

BEFORE SHE DIES

Published by Kensington Publishing Corporation

I'm
Watching
You

MARY
BURTON

ZEBRA BOOKS
KENSINGTON PUBLISHING CORP.
http://www.kensingtonbooks.com

Chapter One

Thou shalt not kill.

The shadowed figure squatted in the darkness by Harold Turner's lifeless body, amazed that excitement, not shame, surged.

The sense of power and righteousness was nearly overwhelming. God's calling to be the Guardian had never been clearer.

Placing the .45-caliber handgun and silencer into a black duffle bag, the Guardian eyed Harold's body, propped against dented metal trashcans.

Even in death, Turner appeared pompous. Arrogant.

A neat part divided Harold's thinning black hair. Manicured nails glistened in the moonlight. His double-breasted suit and white shirt still looked crisp, and his yellow silk tie matched the handkerchief packed in his breast pocket. Gold monogrammed cuff links told anyone worth knowing that Harold had money and taste.

But beneath the expensive suit that Harold always wore were track marks on his arms and behind his knees. It was an open secret that Harold had been a drug addict for years.

The Guardian adjusted Harold's tie over the growing plume of blood staining the attorney's shirt. Countless hours had been spent planning this first murder, strategizing and worrying to near exhaustion. And in the end, luring Harold here had required only the promise of drugs. Firing the bullet from the .45 into his chest had been effortless.

"A fitting place, don't you think? I mean, a battered women's shelter. Your wife certainly would understand why I chose this place."

The shelter behind them was housed in a white Colonial, and it blended so seamlessly into the middle-class subdivision that most neighbors didn't know the home's true purpose. Soft moonlight washed over the shelter's grassy backyard. A six-foot privacy fence corralled assorted kick balls, bicycles, and rusted wagons—all donated toys used by the children staying at the shelter. There was a swing with a long yellow slide surrounded by mulch.

Thoughts of the children stirred anger in the Guardian. "There shouldn't be places like this. It's not right. Children should feel safe in their own home."

The Guardian leveled an accessing gaze on Harold. The high-and-mighty attorney had stood up in federal court this morning to defend his drug dealer client, speaking with authority, visibly comfortable with his ability to manipulate "reasonable doubt."

The Harold Turner who had appeared in the county courtroom was a far cry from the man who'd stood here just minutes ago with tears running down his face begging for his life. *That* Harold had never understood a fear so sharp it burned.

But *this* Harold had.

This Harold had dropped to his knees. He'd offered money and promised lavish favors—anything to buy back his miserable life.

"But fancy appeals don't work on me, do they Harold?" the Guardian had said. "There is no redemption for you."

A slight breeze rustled through the thick canopy of leaves above. Soon the sun would rise and with it the heat. This had been one of the hottest Julys on record and the heat was drying up yards, draining water tables, and straining tempers.

In the distance a dog barked. A cat screeched. They ran through the dark yards, their sounds vanishing in the night.

The Guardian stared up at the shelter, searching for any sign that the animals had awoken anyone. A light on the second floor came on but it just as quickly went dark. In the last hour of the night, the people in the shelter and the neighborhood slept.

This was a sacred and blessed time. Predawn's quiet and peace conjured feelings of invincibility and invulnerability.

The Guardian unfastened the gold cuff link on Harold's left wrist and carefully tucked it in the attorney's pocket before neatly pushing the shirt and jacket sleeves up to his elbow. A platinum wedding band squeezed the ring finger on Harold's left hand.

"His power is great, and He never lets the guilty go unpunished." The Bible verse had given the Guardian comfort during the darkest days after Debra's death. Sweet, sweet Debra, dead at thirty-nine, her life stolen by her own husband. Like Harold, Debra's husband had been a respected man in the community, but a violent man at home. His tyranny had trapped Debra and her daughter in hell for years.

Memories of Debra and her child brought sadness and regret. Debra had cried out for help. She'd wanted out of her marriage. She'd wanted a fresh start. But no one had come to her rescue. No one had cared what happened behind the closed doors of her house.

And then Debra's husband had killed her. He'd violently beaten her to death and then, like the coward he was, had retreated and killed himself. Debra's only child had found her mother. The violence of that day had left its mark on the girl and she'd run away.

Many a night the Guardian had dreamed about Debra and her child and prayed for their forgiveness.

Twelve years had passed. And then the sign from God came a few months ago. The sign was an article in a magazine. It was so clean and pure and it made the Guardian weep. There had been no question then that the time for revenge had come.

Debra was gone forever, as was her child's lost innocence, but those who hurt their families could be rooted out and severely punished. They could be made to pay for their sins against their families.

The Guardian removed a machete from the black duffle bag and raised the blade high overhead. The edge was razor sharp, finely honed on a whetstone until the blade could slice paper.

Moonlight glinted off the blade before it came down in one slicing blow that severed the flesh and bone of Harold's left hand.

Blood splattered onto Harold's face and shirt as well as the Guardian's jumpsuit and gloved hands. The blood looked brown in the moonlight as it oozed from the stump and pooled in the dry earth around Harold's body.

Primal energy surged through the Guardian. For a moment, life had never felt sweeter.

Retribution is mine.

After wrapping the hand in a plastic zip-top bag, the Guardian shoved it into the duffle bag along with the machete, still dripping with blood.

Satisfied that no one had seen, the Guardian zipped the duffle bag closed and then jogged across the back-yard, slipped though the privacy fence gate, and sprinted to the waiting van parked halfway down the block.

Opening the van's front door tripped the dome light. Blinking against the brightness, the Guardian quickly got in and closed the door. Darkness shrouded the cab once again. For several seconds, the Guardian sat in the darkness scanning the homes around to make sure no one had seen. The homes remained dark.

Finally, satisfied that no one would intrude, the Guardian shifted his attention to the open flower box on the passenger seat. The box was filled with purple irises. Each individual stem had been capped with a vial of water to preserve freshness.

After removing Harold's hand from the canvas duffle bag, the Guardian reverently wrapped it in green tissue and nestled it under the flowers.

The choice of irises was inspired. She would under-stand their meaning.

Friendship. Hope. Wisdom. Valor.

After replacing the lid back on the flower box, the Guardian tied the red silk ribbon around it into a pre-cise bow, removed a prewritten card from the glove box and slipped it under the knot.

The Guardian switched on the ignition. The dash-board light washed over the box and the thick, bold handwriting on the card.

It read, *"For Lindsay."*

Chapter Two

Lindsay O'Neil was late for work. Desperately late. She was running so far behind because a power outage had silenced her alarm clock and she'd overslept by almost three hours.

She glanced down at her Jeep's speedometer. It hovered just above thirty miles per hour, but she'd gladly have doubled that speed if Broad Street's four lanes of westbound traffic hadn't been so clogged with commuters.

Tension squeezed her chest. Normally, it took fifteen minutes for her to make the ten-mile trek from her apartment to the women's shelter where she worked. But normally, she didn't sleep as soundly as she had last night. Most nights dreams woke her frequently and she had no trouble rising early and leaving by five A.M.

Lindsay turned on the radio. She punched the "scan" button several times before finally settling on a song she liked. The music and lyrics calmed her and enabled her to take a few deep breaths. Some of the tension released from her body.

For the last year and a half, Lindsay had worked as the

director of Sanctuary Women's Shelter. Her schedule was always jam-packed with counseling sessions and administrative meetings, and most days she barely had time to eat.

And today's schedule was going to be busier than most. In the last two and a half hours, Lindsay had missed the seven A.M. group-counseling session that she held each Monday. The meeting was mandatory for all shelter residents. She'd also missed an eight A.M. conference call with the chairman of the shelter's board of directors, Dana Miller, who expected weekly updates.

Missing the teleconference was a problem, but she could talk her way out of it. However, sleeping through the group session with her residents was inexcusable. The women who attended that meeting were all in abusive relationships. Many hadn't worked in years, and most were more afraid of the unknown that lay ahead than they'd been when they'd lived with the threat of physical violence. Often Lindsay did little more than listen, dispense tissues, and offer hugs. What was important was that she was always there to bolster them up—*no matter what.*

And today she'd let them all down.

She flipped open her cell phone. She'd rushed out so quickly this morning, she'd not thought to call the office. However, the phone's screen was blank. The battery was dead. Hadn't she set it on the charger? "The power outage. Damn it."

Lindsay stopped for a red light and tossed the phone onto the passenger seat. Heat spiraled up from the road's black asphalt. Even though she had the air-conditioning on full blast, the heat rose up through the floorboards. The Jeep's engine fan came on and within seconds the motor hesitated and threatened to cut off.

"Damn it," she muttered.

She'd been promising herself for months to take the Jeep in for a tune-up but kept putting it off. There never seemed to be enough time. Now the engine balked in the high temperature. She shut off the air conditioner and rolled down the window. Thick, heavy July air rushed into the car.

Without the strain of the air conditioner, the engine settled down.

She started to perspire.

"God, I hate the heat."

It coiled around her. It made her temper rise. It made her remember. . . .

"Mom," she whispered, closing her eyes.

Twelve years ago a seventeen-year-old Lindsay had come home early from her lifeguard job on a hot, stormy afternoon. Usually, she worked until closing time, past nine in the evening. But on that hot day, thunderstorms had sent streaks of lightning across the cloudy sky. The manager had closed the pool around two and had sent the lifeguards home.

Her lifeguard buddy from the club, Joel, had given her a ride home. "Hey, are you sure you don't want to catch a movie?" Joel was a skinny kid with blotchy skin and braces. "It's my treat."

She knew Joel had a crush on her and she didn't want to hurt his feelings. "Thanks, but I don't get a chance to spend much time with my mom. But I promise we'll go next week?"

"It's a date." He dropped her off at the top of the circular drive in front of the green framed house built almost a hundred years ago by her great-grandparents.

Lindsay waved and with her pool bag dashed past her mother's prized flower beds filled with daylilies, begonias, and marigolds. The front screen door wasn't locked, which bothered her. She'd warned her mother about keeping the door locked.

Her mother had forced her father out two months earlier, because she could no longer endure the verbal and physical abuse. Since his departure, the house had taken on a lighter air. Her mother had begun singing again and she'd taken to wearing makeup. Now Lindsay no longer searched for excuses not to come home. In fact, she looked forward to it.

Lindsay dropped her pool bag by the front door and checked her watch. Her mother's waitress shift at the Ashland Town Restaurant wouldn't start for a few more hours so it gave them time to hang out together.

Thunder boomed and shook the windowpanes in the house. Dark clouds hovered over the corn fields and the distant trees. Gusty breezes inverted the oak tree leaves, making the tree line look more silver than green. The storm was heading east fast and soon it would be all around them.

"Mom?"

No answer.

From the kitchen, the radio crooned *California Dreamin'* by The Mamas & the Papas. It was her mother's favorite song. Lindsay smiled, recalling how the two of them had danced to the tune just a few weeks ago. Her mother dreamed of going to California, of seeing the Pacific Ocean and visiting Universal Studios in Hollywood. Lindsay had promised to drive her mother cross country next summer right after she graduated from high school. For fun, they spent their spare time mapping the route west.

"Mom!"

The song's chorus repeated the verse about churches, kneeling and pretending to pray.

Lindsay started to hum and grabbed a soda from the refrigerator, popping it open.

That's when Lindsay spotted her father's worn work gloves on the kitchen table. Suddenly, her stomach churned. What was her father doing here?

He'd called her mother once or twice in the last couple of weeks. The calls had worried Lindsay, but when she had questioned her mother about them, her mother had downplayed everything and told her not to fret.

Everything looked as it should. The linoleum floor was swept clean. Dishes drained in the strainer. White lace curtains fluttered in the window. The Formica-topped table had two place settings arranged across from each other. Her father could be charming when he wanted to be and most likely had convinced her mother to fix him lunch.

Now a stir of cold air brushed the back of Lindsay's neck. The house suddenly felt different. Wrong. Apprehension squeezed her heart.

Lindsay glanced around. "Mom!"

She crossed the kitchen, pushed the back screened door open, and glanced at the swing and glider by the toolshed in the backyard. Dark clouds covered the horizon.

"Mom, where are—"

Lindsay turned to the right side of the yard. She stopped abruptly. Her mother lay on her back near the trash cans by the fence.

She rushed toward her mother and stopped just inches from her. Her mother's face was so beaten, so swollen, it was nearly unrecognizable. Blood pooled around her head. Beside her body lay a bloody hammer that looked as if it had been hurriedly discarded.

Dropping to her mother's side, Lindsay reached out to her mother but hesitated. She was afraid to touch her.

Afraid to touch the woman who'd loved her, cared for her, and refused to abandon her no matter what.

A honking horn wrenched Lindsay from the memory

and brought her back to the present. She glanced up at the green light. Sweat beaded on her forehead. Her hands trembled. Cursing, she punched the gas.

Twelve years and her hands still trembled when she remembered that day. Twelve years and she still had nightmares. Twelve years and she felt that if she didn't have a white-knuckle grip on her life it would all slip away.

"Stop it, Lindsay," she muttered. "It's long over. *Done.*"

Purposefully, she shifted her mind from the past to her to-do list that she made certain never ended. The first thing she needed to do was call her boss Dana and apologize for missing their conference call. The second must-do job was to write the summation for the grant application, which, if they won, would pay the salary for a full-time counselor. Then there were the fund-raiser ideas, the notes for her talk to a local church group tonight, and the hospital intervention awareness seminar. . . .

A therapist had once called Lindsay's jam-packed schedule an avoidance device. He'd said it was easier for her to stay busy than to think about her losses. Lindsay hadn't argued, because she knew he was right. But she didn't know how to slow down and keep the dark thoughts at bay.

When she turned into the quiet residential neighborhood where Sanctuary was located, she slowed to the twenty-five-mile-per-hour speed limit. She was so far behind schedule today that she'd be working late into the night just to break even.

She downshifted to first gear when she spotted the two police cars and the unmarked Impala parked in front of the shelter.

Her fingers tightened on the steering wheel and tension nearly choked her breath away. "Oh, God, what's happened now?"

The last time the cops had been to the shelter's secret

location, one of the residents, Pam Rogers, had broken strict protocol and called her abusive husband. Pam had divulged the shelter's location and asked him to come get her. He'd arrived fifteen minutes later. She'd run out to him, begging him to take her back. Instead of welcoming her, he'd hit her and then ordered her into his car. When the hysterical overnight volunteer had called Lindsay at home, Lindsay had immediately contacted the one brother Pam had mentioned. He didn't know where his sister was so Lindsay had called in favors hoping to find Pam.

The woman was found dead the next day behind a convenience store. She'd been badly beaten and strangled. The cops had tracked down the husband two weeks later and arrested him. Jack Rogers had shown no remorse but had talked about his rights as a husband.

His rights. What about his wife's right to live a life free of fear?

Lindsay pulled her Jeep into the paved driveway. She jerked the parking brake up, grabbed her satchel purse, and hurried up the concrete sidewalk to the glass front door.

Sanctuary was on a corner lot and wasn't distinguished by signage but by a wide front porch furnished with weathered white rockers. A collection of planters that Lindsay had filled with red geraniums over the Fourth of July weekend added a splash of color. The yard was neatly cut and edged and the beds had been freshly mulched. It had been her experience that people in the neighborhood didn't pay much attention to those who kept their yards in good shape. And going unnoticed was vital to Sanctuary's success.

The shelter's first floor had four main rooms that were divided by a center hallway. The first room on the right didn't serve as a living room but her office. It was closed off by French doors and filled with stacks of files, manuals, and sacks of unsorted donations.

A conference room, a dining room in a conventional home, adjoined her office. In its core there was a circle of chairs that reminded her of the counseling meeting she'd missed that morning. The walls were decorated with posters that denounced domestic violence.

Across the hallway was a den furnished with a large television, a couple of secondhand couches covered with white sheets, and huge throw pillows on the floor. At the back of the house was a kitchen she'd painted yellow last month. Upstairs there were five rooms, each having two sets of twin beds. Often women moved here with their children and she tried to put the entire family in one room together. She even had a couple of cribs and a bassinet.

The house was normally teeming with the women and their children who made Sanctuary their temporary home. The chatter of women and children often mingled with the TV and ringing phone.

But now, the place was silent and it appeared deserted.

Silver bracelets jangled on Lindsay's slim wrist as she pulled the rubber band from her blond hair and released the too tight ponytail that was already giving her a headache. Blunt, straight hair fell around her shoulders.

Lindsay started toward the kitchen, unable to suppress the growing panic as she searched for last night's volunteer. "Ruby!"

A heavyset black woman rushed out of the kitchen, a phone in hand. Ruby Dillon, when she wasn't working at the nursing home as an aid, volunteered nights at the shelter. About fifty, Ruby was a big woman who wore her hair short and her pants and shirts oversized. Her dead-on honesty about her own past mistakes, including time in prison and drug use, had earned the residents' respect.

"It's about time you got here. I've been calling you for an hour," Ruby said, shaking the phone at her.

"My power went out last night. The house phones didn't work and my cell phone didn't charge. What's with the police? What's going on?"

"They came because of the body."

Images of her mother lying dead in her backyard flashed in her mind. "Body? Please tell me it wasn't one of ours."

Ruby touched Lindsay gently on the arm. "No, no, honey. It wasn't one of our residents. All our people are off to work or school."

Relieved, Lindsay closed her eyes. She had to choke back a sudden rush of tears. "Who?"

Ruby shrugged. "I don't know. But the body is male. I found him when I was taking out the garbage this morning. He was propped up against the trash cans behind the toolshed, his suit buttoned up and his hair combed as if he were headed to Sunday church."

Lindsay moved down the hallway into the kitchen and looked out the window over the sink. The backyard was filled with a half dozen cops gathered at the yellow tape. Most were uniformed but in the center stood a plainclothes detective. His back was to her.

The cops blocked Lindsay's view of the corpse. "Did you recognize him?"

Ruby folded her arms over her chest. "Who? The dead guy? No, ma'am. And I didn't look in his face either. The devil can steal your soul if you look the dead in the face."

Lindsay dropped her purse on a well-worn kitchen table that was covered with nicks and flecks of paint from a child's weekend craft project. "I've seen my share of death. Maybe the devil has stolen my soul."

"Don't even kid about that."

"Do the police know who the dead guy is?"

"If they do, they're not telling me. A detective just arrived minutes ago. I told him everything I know, but he was pretty tight-lipped when I asked questions. He's the one who said to stop what I was doing and track you down." Ruby's sharp gaze traveled over Lindsay. "Are those the clothes you wore yesterday?"

Lindsay glanced down at the faded jeans and pink cotton top. She smoothed a wrinkle from her shirt. "Yes."

Ruby cocked a dark eyebrow. "Where have you been? Lord, I hope you've been with a man."

The idea made Lindsay blush. "Nope."

"Too bad. You certainly could use a man in your bed. That no-account husband of yours hasn't paid you any attention this last year."

"We're separated, remember?"

"No man in his right mind would leave you."

Lindsay was unwilling to get into another discussion about her failed marriage or her monastic, workaholic life. "I taught a yoga class yesterday afternoon and then went home to work on this grant. I fell asleep in my clothes on the couch. The power went out sometime last night and the alarm didn't go off." If not for her roommate, Nicole, who'd been awakened by a barking dog, she could have slept a couple more hours.

Ruby grunted. "Well, if you ain't got a man, I'm glad you at least got a good night's sleep. You work too hard. You're burning the candle at both ends, if you ask me."

This last year, since she'd separated from her husband, she had stayed particularly busy, even by her own standards. "You'll be glad to know that I slept like the dead."

Ruby grimaced and glanced toward the heavens. "Don't be making fun of the dead. The devil will come and get you."

Lindsay pushed her hand through her hair. "Sorry. Morbid jokes are a holdover from having lived with a cop."

Ruby frowned. "Your husband is a cop?"

"Yeah." This was another topic she did not want to explore. "I'm going to talk to the police. I want to get those squad cars away from my house before everyone figures out we're a shelter."

Ruby's heavy feet trailed behind Lindsay. "Don't waste your breath. I tried a couple of times to talk to that 'detective.'" The word *detective* sounded like an expletive. "He said to stay out of his crime scene. He even locked the back door and pocketed the key from the deadbolt so no one would go in or out that door."

That ticked Lindsay off. Sanctuary was her creation. "This cop is on my turf now and he is going to tell *me* what's going on?"

Grinning, Ruby shook her head. "Sometimes I think you'd rather fight than eat."

She smiled. "Somebody's got to lead the charge."

Ruby snorted. "Honey, you've got too many causes. About time someone worried about you."

"I'm better off taking care of myself." She'd said those words so often in the last year that she almost believed them.

Lindsay headed out the front door and went around the side of the house to the loose slats in the privacy fence. She bent the slats back and slipped through unnoticed.

The closest cop to her was a patrolman. He stood at the lip of the yellow tape and faced the crime scene, his back to her. He was slender, a little gawky, and appeared fresh out of the academy. He couldn't have been much more than twenty-one.

A humid breeze tunneled through the backyard's still,

hot air and carried with it a host of smells. Blood. Waste. Gunpowder. Death.

From this angle she couldn't see the body beyond the circle of six cops who stood around it.

She approached the uniformed cop. She cleared her throat. "Do you know anything about the victim?"

The young cop whirled around and glared down at her. "Where'd you come from?"

"That house." She crooked her head toward Sanctuary and then nodded to the crowd of cops. "Do you know who was murdered? I hear it was a man."

The young cop started to answer, then caught himself. He puffed out his chest. "Ma'am, this is a police crime scene. You are not supposed to be here."

His attempt to intimidate her barely registered on her radar. She'd stared down far scarier people than this kid. "Look, Officer . . ." She glanced down at the bronze name badge on his chest. "Bennett. That house is Sanctuary Women's Shelter and I'm the director."

"I don't care who you are. You can't be here."

Her tone had sounded brittle and she was reminded of Ruby's frequent advice to soften her delivery. She remembered something about catching more flies with honey than vinegar.

With a conscious effort, she smiled and relaxed her stance. "I really need to know who was killed in case it involves one of the women staying here. It's my job to keep them safe."

The cop's frown deepened. "Even if I knew, I couldn't tell you."

His attitude annoyed but didn't deter her. "How'd the guy die?"

"I can't say."

"Do you know the time of death?" She edged around

the cop. If she got a little closer she might find out more about the victim.

He shifted and blocked her path. "No one gets in that crime scene."

She leaned around him. Even from this angle, most of the crime scene remained blocked by the broad shoulders of the detective, who had now removed his suit jacket, rolled up his sleeves, and donned rubber gloves and booties. She couldn't see his face but noted his military short black hair and crisp white shirt. His hands rested on his narrow hips.

He must be the bossy detective Ruby had mentioned. Lindsay summed him up in a nanosecond: an alpha male, a by-the-book tight-ass, and a bully.

She suddenly felt very weary. She'd been dealing with bullies far too long. But if he was the one she needed to talk to, then so be it.

Reading her thoughts, the officer said, "The detective in charge is going to talk to you when he's ready."

She pushed her hand through her hair. "This detective got a name?"

"Detective Kier."

She swallowed. "Zack Kier?"

A smug smile lifted the edge of the officer's lip. "That's right."

Zack Kier was her estranged husband. They'd not spoken in almost a year.

She glanced toward the plainclothes detective again. Since when had Zack moved from undercover narcotics to homicide? When had he cut his hair, shaved the beard, and taken to wearing suits? Her Zack had worn his thick, long hair tied at the nape of his neck. He had preferred faded jeans, T-shirts, worn boots and a well-worn black leather jacket.

Everything about him had changed in the last year. And nothing had changed.

She should have recognized the rigid, controlled stance, which had always announced his unwavering commitment to police work. He also still tapped his index finger against his belt buckle when his hands rested on his hips.

Raw emotions she'd struggled to bury this last year enveloped her in a rush. Love. Hate. Fear. Betrayal. All ripped through her and for a moment left her speechless.

Lindsay's knee-jerk reaction was to retreat. She'd have preferred avoiding this meeting with Zack and sidestep the messy tangle of emotions that were sure to follow.

Then she caught herself. Her therapist had pointed out that she had a habit of running from emotions that were personally painful. He had told her she had to learn to face her feelings for Zack. When she'd expressed her doubts, he'd reminded her that she'd risen above her father's brutality and her mother's death. Zack and their marriage should be no exception.

Still, Lindsay had to swallow before she could shout, "Zack!"

All the other cops turned first and stared at her while Zack's body stiffened. For a moment he seemed frozen, but then he turned slowly and stared at her from behind aviator sunglasses.

Instinct screamed *run*. She stood her ground.

The sunglasses hid Zack's sharp blue eyes, but she knew even without the shades his expression would have been unreadable. He'd always been so good at hiding his emotions. It's why he'd made a great undercover cop and a lousy husband.

"Zack, can you tell me who the body is?" Her voice sounded surprisingly controlled—a minor, but appreciated miracle.

For a moment, Zack tensed and she expected him to walk toward her. Their relationship was unconventional and damaged, but they had a history and that had to be worth something.

He drew in a breath but didn't move toward her. "I'm not ready to interview you yet, Lindsay. Go back inside and wait for me."

Zack sounded so controlled. So together. He'd anticipated seeing her.

That realization angered her. He could have given her a heads-up and called her on her cell. *Crap.* She remembered her cell was dead and so was her home phone. Maybe he had tried to call.

Still, the insight didn't soften the sharp emotions digging at her. "Well, I'd like to talk to you now, detective." She'd laced the words with attitude, knowing he'd hate it.

Zack's left hand flexed. She recognized the gesture. It signaled he was irritated. Good.

Speaking to the young cop, Zack said, "Officer Bennett, escort Ms. O'Neil away from my crime scene now."

The curt dismissal had her squaring her shoulders. "This is shelter property, Detective Kier. You can't shut me out. Whoever was killed on my property affects my residents."

Zack didn't answer. Instead, he turned back toward the body.

Honey not vinegar. Honey not vinegar.

With effort, Lindsay drew in a breath and softened her tone. "Look, Zack, my assistant found the body and it's in our backyard. Can't you give me any information?"

"Not now, Lindsay," Zack said. He crouched by the body, pulled off his sunglasses, and chewed the earpiece as he stared at the body.

Barely a few moments together and already it was clear that the emotional wall between them was as thick as it had been a year ago. It was hard now to believe that they'd ever been close.

Lindsay always felt most alone when she tried to connect with him and he shut her out. "Detective, can you at least move the marked police cars?" she asked. "Sanctuary doesn't need any more bad publicity."

He didn't respond.

Officer Bennett took Lindsay's arm. "Ma'am, you need to leave this area."

She snatched her arm free. "Yeah, yeah, yeah. I'm going."

Chapter Three

For the past two days, Detective Zack Kier had been running down leads on a suspicious murder in the county's east end. He'd pieced together enough information to prove that the woman who had fallen to her death had committed suicide, and that it was not a murder. He had been ready to clock out and start a stretch of three days off when dispatch had reported a homicide at Sanctuary Women's Shelter.

He'd taken the assignment without hesitating or clearing it with his supervisor. The action would no doubt come back to bite him in the ass but he didn't care. He'd needed to make sure Lindsay was okay.

He'd not only seen her, but he'd also managed to piss her off.

Now, it wasn't even ten o'clock and Zack was juggling what was going to be a high-profile murder and Lindsay. *Shit.*

Zack decided to focus on the lesser of the two evils— the crime scene.

The responding uniformed officer had roped off a

generous perimeter around the body and had done a good job keeping everyone out and the area secure until Zack had arrived.

A monthlong drought had left the ground bone dry, so the chances of retrieving footprints, DNA, weapons, the victim's hand, and anything else left behind by the killer were all good. But they'd have to work fast. Thick rain clouds that looked ready to burst hovered above.

"Officer Watt," Zack said, speaking to the older officer behind him. "What do you have so far?"

In his midfifties, Watt's gray crew cut emphasized a perpetual scowl. Usually, he had little to say, but when he did speak smart detectives listened. "Call came in from a Ruby Dillon. She found the body just after eight. Ms. Dillon spent the night at the shelter. She was in charge of supervising the overnight residents and getting the four female residents off to work and the two male children to summer school. The place was empty when she came outside to dump the trash and discovered the body."

Zack patted his shirt pocket in search of cigarettes. The pocket was empty. He'd quit smoking nine months ago, but cravings still plagued him. "Did she hear or see anything last night?"

"Not a word. And none of the residents mentioned anything out of the ordinary to her before they left for the day. It was an unusually quiet night."

Zack studied the corpse's bloated features. He didn't need ID to know who he was: Harold Turner.

Turner was well known at headquarters, because he wasn't particular about whom he defended as long as the case translated into cash or media attention. Turner had been in the news this past week for his defense of drug dealer Ronnie T., who, after numerous delays, was on trial for tax evasion. Now that Turner was dead, Ronnie

T.'s trial could be compromised. That worried Zack. Eighteen months ago, he had been one of the under-cover cops who'd gathered evidence against the affable Ronnie T.

Zack rose and removed a notebook from his breast pocket. He jotted notes: interview Quinton Barlow, Harold's law partner. Examine Turner's client list. Talk to Mrs. Turner.

He glanced left and right at the surrounding houses. With his partner on vacation, he would also be knocking on a lot of doors today. "Any other witnesses?"

Officer Watt shook his head. "Not yet."

Zack was careful to stay clear of the blood-caked grass and dirt around the body's mutilated arm. The scent of decaying flesh made his stomach clench. He'd been a cop for thirteen years, could look at any grisly sight with-out flinching, but the smells always got to him.

"Do you have an ETA for forensics?" Zack asked Watt.

"They've been called twice and should be arriving any minute."

"The sooner the better. We're not going to have much time with this one and I don't want any evidence com-promised by the weather, curious cops, or reporters."

"Understood."

Zack glanced at the shelter. "Also, make sure Ms. Dillon and Ms. O'Neil don't leave the shelter unless I know about it. I want to talk to them both."

"Sure."

Ms. O'Neil. Lindsay.

Zack had not seen his wife since the meeting at the lawyer's office almost a year ago when she'd served him with divorce papers. She had let the attorney do her talk-ing and had refused to acknowledge him, because he had been drinking.

Hell, who was he kidding? He'd been drunk. *Shit.*

Zack had worked undercover narcotics for three years before he met Lindsay. Drugs had been a part of that world. He'd been careful to stay clear of the drugs, knowing he got tested by the department regularly. But he had started drinking more heavily during that time. Ego had had him believing he could handle the booze. He'd been wrong.

When he'd met Lindsay, he'd cut way back on his drinking. But then he'd started working more undercover assignments. The stress of hiding his private life from the drug world grew along with the cravings for booze. Soon he was chasing beers with shots of bourbon.

Lindsay had figured out what was happening very quickly. She had begged him to stop drinking and to consider AA meetings. He'd assured her he didn't have a problem. He'd seen the hope in her eyes. She'd wanted to believe him but when he hadn't quit, she'd tossed him out. He'd felt betrayed, furious, and he'd done the dumbest thing he could have. He'd slept with another woman. Lindsay had found out and there'd been no going back after that.

That day in the lawyer's office, he'd been royally pissed because she'd not returned any of his phone calls. He'd said terrible things to Lindsay, hoping to wound her the way her throwing him out had hurt him. His words had found their mark. Unshed tears had glistened in her eyes when she'd fled the attorney's office.

Zack would like to have said he'd joined AA right after that meeting. But he hadn't. He'd stayed drunk another month before his brother, Malcolm, had threatened to expose his drinking to the department if he didn't get sober. Zack had agreed. With the help of his family, he had sobered up.

After he'd been sober sixty days, he'd known he'd have to leave narcotics. So he'd parlayed his arrest record and gotten a transfer out of narcotics to homicide. He'd been in the new job eight months.

Zack had wanted to call Lindsay after he'd gotten sober and apologize for all the crap he'd put her through. But he'd been afraid she'd reject him and he didn't fully trust his sobriety those first few weeks. Days turned into weeks. Weeks into months. He got stronger, more in control of the cravings that would never really leave him. But now, nearly a year had passed since that day in the lawyer's office, and here they were: married strangers.

He wasn't sure what he expected when he saw Lindsay, but he did know that their first meeting wouldn't be easy under the best of circumstances—nothing with his wife had ever been uncomplicated. Intruding into his crime scene was classic Lindsay.

What he hadn't anticipated was her pale skin and the veil of bravado that was as thin as her frame.

This past year had been hard on her too.

Zack's head throbbed. He shoved out a breath and buried the remorse. He had a job to do.

The snap of rubber gloves had Zack turning toward the forensics tech, Sara Martin. Tall, slim, and in her early thirties, she wore her long auburn hair in a tight ponytail at the base of her neck. She'd slid crisp blue coveralls over her clothes and booties over her shoes. In the three years he'd known her she was always immaculate, always contained no matter what the situation.

"Sorry it took me so long." Sara's sweet perfume drifted above the blood's pungent rusty smell. "When my beeper went off I was still in the shower. So what do we have?"

"Harold Turner."

She didn't look surprised. "It's a wonder he lived this long. Guy had a ton of enemies." A digital camera dangled from her neck and she switched it on, then started to snap pictures. "Jesus, his left hand is gone."

"Yeah."

"What can you tell me about the murder?" Sara said.

"I just got here myself. But from the looks of it, Harold was shot point-blank in the chest and his left hand severed. In which order, I don't know yet. The medical examiner should be able to tell me."

Sara nodded, lowered the camera. "Blood-splatter patterns suggest he was shot where he fell. The bullet to the chest would have been enough to kill him."

She squatted and studied the body. "There seem to be no bruises, no scratches, and no signs of trauma. And there'd be signs of all that if the killer tried to take the hand first."

"Harold was a street-savvy guy and didn't trust easily. But it looks like he came of his own free will with the killer. His car isn't parked on the street."

That caught her off guard. "He rode here with his killer?"

"I think so. But that only narrows the search to about a million people," Zack said.

"What would make him get into the car with a killer?"

"Look at his left arm."

She frowned. "Track marks. You think he came for drugs?"

Zack understood the power of addiction. "Wouldn't surprise me."

She snapped more pictures. "With all the blood it will be a miracle if the killer didn't get any on his feet. I'll search for footprints." Sara glanced up at the sky and frowned before she lowered her lens back to Harold's wrist. "Any sign of the hand?"

"Not yet. I've got officers walking the backyard searching for it."

"Why take the hand? Some kind of trophy?"

"Maybe."

She glanced around at the houses. "I'm guessing a silencer was used. Gunshot residue will tell me if the killer was close."

"Work fast. I don't think the weather is going to hold."

Sara nodded. "Morning news says late morning thunderstorms coming out of the west."

Not good. A scene like this could take days to process and it appeared that they might only have hours.

"I'll leave you to your work. Thanks." Zack stepped back, aware that tension had settled in his lower-back muscles. He wanted a beer but that was out of the question. He'd have to settle for a long run along the river.

"Hey, Zack."

"Yeah?"

Sara flipped her bangs out of her eyes, which were bright with anticipation. "I'm having a party this weekend to celebrate my promotion. Care to come?"

Over the last couple of months Sara had asked him out a few times. He'd made the mistake of sleeping with her a year ago. Since then, he had made a point of keeping their relationship professional and sidestepping all of her invitations. He couldn't explain why but he felt he owed fidelity to Lindsay until the divorce papers were signed. "Thanks, Sara, but I don't think I'll make it."

She didn't hide her disappointment. "You sure you can't come? Everyone at headquarters is going to be there. The party should be a real crush."

"Sorry. I'm going to have to pass, Sara." He offered a wan smile and took a step back.

Sara nodded thoughtfully and let her gaze drift from him to the shelter. "When you see Lindsay, tell her I said hello."

Chapter Four

Lindsay leaned over the sink in the shelter's kitchen, staring out the window toward the crime scene. Zack had expanded the crime scene to include the entire backyard. No doubt, he'd seal it for days, months. If anything, he was thorough.

Any hopes she'd had of preserving the shelter's anonymity had vanished when she'd spoken to Zack. He wasn't going to cut one corner on this investigation. She'd asked Ruby to call around to other shelters to find beds for her six residents.

Lindsay watched as the forensics technician brushed her bangs off her forehead as she stared up at Zack. The tech leaned toward him a fraction, her smile subtle but flirty. One hundred dollars said the chick was wearing perfume.

A familiar knot burned in the pit of her stomach. Was she the one Zack had slept with the night she'd thrown him out of their apartment? Painful memories compressed her heart. She turned from the window. It took a moment before she could breathe deeply.

Lindsay's fingers tightened into fists. "I don't care who he sleeps with now."

Ringing phones startled her from her mood. All at once three lines lit up on the phone on the kitchen wall.

Lindsay slid open the pocket door that separated the kitchen from the conference room. Ruby sat at a small desk, the phone cradled under her ear. She mouthed "line two."

"Got it." Lindsay picked up the line in the kitchen. "Sanctuary Women's Shelter."

"Lindsay?"

It was Dr. Sam Begley, chief resident in emergency medicine at Mercy Hospital. Immediately, the pressure in her shoulders relaxed. Sam and Lindsay had met six months ago when she'd given a seminar on domestic violence to the hospital staff.

"Sam, what can I do for you?" She leaned against the sink, her back to the murder scene.

"You might want to come down here," he said in a sober tone. "I've got a woman in cubical six who's been badly beaten. Her story has changed a couple of times. I think the abuse is domestic."

A protective urge welled inside her. "How bad are her injuries?"

"Cracked ribs. Bruised arms. Sprained wrist."

She rubbed her temples with her fingertips. A headache was starting to pound behind her eyes. "Did she say who did it?"

"No, but she exhibits all the signs you outlined. No bruises on her face. Whoever did this didn't want anyone to know she'd been slapped around."

"Did she say anything about what happened?"

"She said she fell down some stairs. I was hoping the shelter had a bed available."

Lindsay turned toward the window facing the cops

crowding her backyard. "I don't think we'll have a bed for a few days. But I could talk to her, try to get her in another place if she'll take it."

He sighed into the phone. "Good. She needs someone to talk sense into her."

"You sound tired. Did you pull another eighteen-hour shift?"

He chuckled. "No rest for the wicked."

Lindsay admired Sam. He was one of the hardest-working people she knew. She checked her watch. Better to stay, deal with Zack, and be done with him. "I'm stuck here at the shelter for another hour or so. Can you hold on to her?"

"She's over eighteen and can walk out of here any time she wants." He dropped his voice a notch. "But you know how slow the paperwork moves around this place. It could easily take a couple of hours before she's discharged."

Lindsay couldn't help but smile. Sam made life easy. "I'll be by as soon as I can."

"Good."

"You're one of the good guys, Dr. Sam Begley." She imagined his face turning red.

"You're the one who does the real work." He hesitated. "I had fun at the movies last week. We should do it again sometime soon."

"Sounds good." She hadn't really thought of their outing as anything more than a friendly trip to the movies until Sam had kissed her. The awkward moment underscored the fact that she'd not been out with another man since she'd left Zack.

"How about tonight?" he said quickly. "I'll buy you a slice of birthday cake."

Her birthday was in two days. She'd almost forgotten. Leave it to Sam to remember.

"I'm going to be working late tonight." She was grateful

to have a real excuse. "Rain check? Maybe next week? And make the cake carrot."

He laughed. "Consider it done."

She glanced at her phone console, noticing two other lines blinking. "Hey, look, I've got other calls. Lots of stuff going on here today."

"Everything all right?"

"It's a long story. I'll tell you when I see you."

"No problem. See you in about an hour."

"Thanks." Lindsay hung up and caught Ruby's gaze.

Ruby cupped her hand over the receiver. "Line three. Dana Miller."

Lindsay's stomach knotted with tension. "Thanks."

Dana, the shelter's board chairman, was essentially Lindsay's boss. Had Dana already heard about the murder or was the call about the missed teleconference? Neither topic boded well.

She punched line three. "Hello, Dana."

"What's going on over there? First you miss our phone meeting and then the director at Riverside Shelter calls and tells me Ruby requested bed space for some of your residents."

Lindsay sighed. No beating around the bush with Dana. "A body was found behind the shelter."

"What!"

"It wasn't one of our residents," she rushed to say.

"Who the hell was it?"

"I don't know. The police aren't telling me much right now."

"Damn it, Lindsay. This is not good."

Lindsay pictured Dana sitting in her high-rise office wearing her trademark red Brooks Brothers suit. On her desk there'd be a half-full cup of coffee and a cigarette burning in a crystal ashtray. Dana had made millions in real estate and had built a reputation as a hard-driving ball buster who distained sloppy emotions. Lindsay never could figure why she'd decided to champion battered women or Sanctuary.

"I know the victim is a man, and as soon as I know anything else I'll call you," Lindsay said.

"Do you know how the guy died?"

"No."

Dana exhaled. "We don't need bad press, Lindsay. Not after what happened before with that other woman."

"Her name was Pam Rogers." Dana may have forgotten the woman's name but Lindsay never would.

Dana blew out a lungful of smoke into the receiver. "Handle this, Lindsay. I don't want to defend the shelter again to the media. It's not good for me or you."

Handle this. "Consider it done."

The line went dead.

Ruby poked her head into the kitchen, clearly having overheard the conversation. "Sorry about that. I wanted to call Riverside first thing. If we can get Aisha Greenland and her boys transferred there, the boys won't have to switch schools."

"The children's well-being comes before politics. You did the right thing. Did they get bed space?"

"Yes. I've also put a call in to Michelle Franklin over at Hayden House." The shelter was in the east end of the county. "They've got two beds."

"We've got six people here now." Lindsay mentally went through the list of residents. "Greenlands to Riverside. Tracy and Cindy to Hayden House. Call the Y and see if they have a bed for Barbara."

"I'll take care of it."

"I'll contact the women at work and tell them what's happening. The last thing they need is to hear about this on the news."

Ruby shook her head. "What a mess."

"Yeah."

Lindsay called each of the women, did her best to downplay the situation, and promised to transfer their goods to the new shelters so they wouldn't have to return to Sanctuary. Ruby would pick the Greenland boys up at school and take them directly to Riverside.

By the time she hung up the phone, Lindsay's head was really pounding. She needed caffeine.

At the kitchen sink, she rinsed out stale coffee from the coffeemaker carafe, refilled it with tap water, and dumped it in the machine's reservoir. She tossed out the old grounds, scooped fresh into the metal filter, and switched the machine on.

A flicker of movement caught her eye. She turned in time to see Zack step through the front door, a cell phone cradled under his chin. He'd loosened his tie. Thick stubble covered his chin, as if he'd been up all night. His gun rested on his narrow hip.

He spoke into his cell. "Ayden, you and Warwick need to see this. Yeah, well, tell him his vacation is over."

The deep timber of Zack's voice swirled around Lindsay, raking over her frayed nerves. Just having him close made her nervous.

Zack had a strong profile and Lindsay found herself liking his hair short. It suited him. Unexpected desire flickered to life. A part of her still wanted Zack. Probably always would. Damn. Her fickle libido was the last thing she needed to deal with right now.

"I need to talk to the shelter director first," he added.

She turned back to the hissing coffeepot, in a sudden rush to have something to do. She pulled the half-full carafe out. Hot coffee dripped down on the machine's burner as she quickly poured a cup, then replaced the pot. Coffee spilled over the edge of the burner.

She grabbed a handful of paper towels and started to mop up the mess. "Damn."

Footsteps sounded behind her. "Patience never was your specialty," Zack said.

Lindsay ignored the greater meaning behind his words and swallowed a tart retort. "No, I guess not." *Be nice,* she thought. Turning, she held up a mug. "You want a cup?"

"That would be great."

She filled a Styrofoam cup with black coffee and handed it to him. He thanked her. The forced civility didn't fit them. Their relationship had never been lukewarm. When they fought, laughed, or made love the intensity could have shaken the rafters. And she'd been proud of that. She'd never figured that that same intensity would also rip them apart.

Lindsay nodded toward her office door. "We can talk in my office."

Tension snapping at her, she headed past him, down the center hallway to her office. Her office, like every other room in the shelter, served many purposes. The public health nurse used her desk when she visited, residents used the space for private meetings, and donations were usually left there before they were sorted.

Stacks of papers covered her desk but she could, at any given moment, find anything she needed.

Lindsay removed a donated clothes bag from a chair and set it behind her desk. She motioned for Zack to sit as she took her chair behind the desk. Here she felt safe.

Zack took a seat and flipped open his notebook. "Are you going to tell me who was murdered?"

In no rush, Zack sipped his coffee and then set it on the edge of her desk before settling his gaze on her. "You had any trouble here at the shelter lately?"

That was so Zack to answer a question with a question.

"Not lately. You know about Pam Rogers, the woman who revealed the shelter location to her husband. He picked her up and later he killed her."

"Nine months ago, right before I joined homicide. I read the file."

"Since then, we've had no trouble."

"No threatening phone calls? No messages in the mail?"

"No, nothing out of the ordinary." She sipped her coffee. It tasted bitter. "So who was murdered?"

He watched her face closely. "Harold Turner."

Stunned, Lindsay dropped open her mouth. "The attorney?"

"That's right. You know him?" He stared at her, gauging her reaction.

Yeah, she knew Harold. He liked to slap his wife around, a fact few knew. Lindsay had found out about the abuse when Jordan had cornered her in the ladies' room at the Race for the Cure fund-raiser two weeks ago. Jordan had told Lindsay everything: Harold's drug use, the beatings, and the verbal abuse. Lindsay had comforted Jordan and begged her to come to Sanctuary. But Jordan Turner had refused. She had admitted that she enjoyed Harold's wealth far too much to abandon it. She had wiped her tears away, fixed her makeup, and assured Lindsay she could handle Harold. She'd called her tears a momentary lapse and then downplayed the entire incident.

Lindsay had likened Jordan's emotional outburst to a leak in a dam. Eventually, the water would widen the dam wall, erode the foundation, and rush out with devastating force.

My God, had Jordan shot Harold? Had she lured her husband to the shelter and killed him as some kind of message to Lindsay? *I can handle Harold.*

If convicted, Jordan could spend the next thirty years in jail for ridding the earth of human slime. The need to protect Jordan overrode Lindsay's responsibility to tell Zack what she knew.

"Sure, who doesn't know Harold? He's in all the newspapers. He's defending some drug dealer."

"Have you ever met him in person?"

"Sure. We crossed paths at different fund-raisers. Two weeks ago, as a matter of fact, at the Race for the Cure gala at the Virginia Museum."

Blue eyes narrowed. "That's it? You've never spoken to him any other time?"

She didn't look away. "Nope."

His gaze held hers as if he were waiting for her to say more. When she didn't, he frowned. "You're not telling me everything."

Uncomfortable, she leaned forward. "Are you some kind of psychic?"

"I know you."

She noticed his ring finger. The absence of a wedding band wasn't a surprise. Because of his undercover work, he'd rarely worn it when they were married. "You *knew* me, Zack."

His face hardened. "I know when you're holding back information, Lindsay."

She stiffened. "As I remember, you were good at hiding things."

His jaw clenched slightly, but otherwise he looked unaffected by her comment. "Lindsay, I'm here to investigate a murder, not rehash our marriage. We'll save that gem for another day. Right now, I want to know if Harold Turner had a connection to the shelter."

"You're right. Harping on ancient history is foolish." She shifted in her seat. "He's never been here before, if that's what you're asking."

"I'm going to need to see your files."

She had started a file on Jordan. Only a few notes, but

it was enough to prove a connection. She wasn't going to make it easy for Zack to arrest Jordan. "My files are confidential. If you want to know what's in them, you're going to have to get a court order."

"Consider it done." He studied her with more intensity. "Why not just tell me all that you know?"

"You know why. The women who come through my doors or who talk to me are frightened, battered, and often humiliated. Some go on to better lives. Some go back to their husbands. Either way, they know I'll guard their privacy. They count on me. I can't betray their trust unless the court orders me to."

"Did Jordan Turner ever visit the shelter?"

"No."

"You ever meet her?"

She folded her hands in front of her. "She was at the fund-raiser two weeks ago. We spoke briefly." She sipped her coffee. "How was Harold killed?"

"Not ready to release that yet."

"Harold had a lot of enemies. He'd sell anyone out for a buck."

"Then why was he murdered behind the shelter?"

"I don't know."

"Any of your residents have a drug problem?"

"No. We test all who want to stay here. They're clean."

Always one to play his cards close to his vest, Zack simply nodded. "I think his body was positioned behind the shelter for a reason."

Jordan. "Just because Turner's body was found behind the shelter doesn't mean his death had anything to do with me."

"I've never put much stock in coincidence." He ran his hand down his tie as he leaned back in his chair. "Where were you last night and this morning?"

His proprietary tone rankled her nerves. He didn't

have any rights to her time now. "I was home asleep. And I overslept this morning."

He lifted an eyebrow, amused. "As I remember it, you rose at five every morning come hell or high water."

"A power outage knocked out all of electricity in my row of town houses. My alarm didn't go off."

"I also never remember you sleeping through the night."

"I did last night."

"Can you prove you were home last night?"

He didn't trust her and that hurt more than it should. "Do I have to?"

"It would be nice."

Very few knew Lindsay had taken on Nicole Piper as a roommate. Her former college roommate had shown up two weeks ago on Lindsay's doorstep begging for a place to stay. Nicole had left her abusive husband and was hiding from him. Lindsay had taken her in without question. If Zack knew she had a roommate, he'd start checking into Nicole's past. And that could tip off Nicole's husband as to her whereabouts.

"Sorry, I can't prove anything. I was home alone. You'll just have to take my word for it."

He studied her and then deliberately glanced around the office. "How many women does the shelter serve each year?"

She rolled with the change of topic. "We saw about a hundred women last year."

"Impressive." He scratched a few words in his notebook.

"Sadly, business is booming."

He nodded thoughtfully as if remembering that afternoon in Byrd Park when she'd confided her own horrific past to him. She'd told him of her mother's murder, of her father's suicide, and of her running away. He, better than anyone, understood her drive to protect the women and children under her care.

"I want a list of everyone who was here last night," Zack said. "I want to see records of all the women who've been through the doors since you opened."

"Only when the warrant arrives."

He looked annoyed. "You always have to be so stubborn."

With an effort, Lindsay kept her tone light. "It's what I do best."

His lips flattened as he rose. "Thanks for the coffee."

She stood. "Always happy to help."

At five ten, she stood eye to eye with most men. Zack had a good six inches on her. "Is it all right if I leave the shelter? I received a call from Mercy Hospital to counsel a battered woman. The doctor is trying to delay her, but he won't be able to hold her more than an hour, which leaves me about twenty minutes."

He seemed to gauge the truth of her words. "Keep your cell phone on this time. I want to be able to reach you easily."

"It's always on."

"Not this morning."

He had tried to call.

"As I said, there was a power outage in my town house complex. I'm sure you can verify it with maintenance. And I put my phone in the charger as soon as I arrived here."

Zack studied Lindsay again as if trying to pry into her brain.

Lindsay folded her arms over her chest, matching his glare.

"I'll be back this afternoon or tomorrow at the latest with the warrant."

Thanks to Harold's murder, she would have to deal with all the agonizing baggage she shared with Zack and had done her best to ignore this past year. "I can't wait."

Chapter Five

Monday, July 7, 11:02 A.M.

On the way to the hospital, Lindsay called Jordan Turner twice. The first time she got her voice mail. She didn't bother to leave a message. What was she going to say? Mrs. Turner, did you murder your husband?

Thanks to light midday traffic, Lindsay made good time driving downtown. Still, the Mercy Hospital parking deck was crammed with cars, forcing her to drive to the bottom level, where she found an open spot in a darkened corner.

She shut off the car engine, waited until it shuttered off, got out, and locked the car. Her sandals clicked against concrete as she moved along the line of parked cars. A horn honked, the sound echoing from the level above. A car door closed.

She'd parked on this deck a thousand times before, always cautious but never afraid. However, today, the hairs on the back of her neck prickled. She scanned the rows of parked cars around her. The air-conditioning system whirred overhead and condensation dripped from the ductwork.

The deck appeared deserted. On a deck below, a car horn honked again. There was no need to be nervous yet her nerves tightened, as if someone were close.

Watching.

She tightened her hold on her purse. "Is anyone there?"

No answer.

It wasn't like her to be so jumpy. Crossing quickly to the elevator, she punched the button, careful to keep her back to the doors. She dug in her purse fishing for her mace and cursed when she couldn't find it in all the clutter. When the elevator doors whooshed open, she rushed into the empty car. Her heart pounded in her chest.

As the doors closed, a nearby car door slammed shut, the sound echoing from an unseen corner.

Lindsay punched level four, the lobby level. She dragged a shaking hand through her hair. "Get a grip."

Within seconds the elevator doors opened to the muted sounds of gurneys rolling past, carts clattering, and telephones ringing. The smell of antiseptic cleaner blended with the bright hospital lights. Her nerves settled and the parking garage was forgotten.

She walked up to the nurses station and smiled at the familiar face behind the counter. "Hey, Jennifer."

Jennifer Watkins glanced up from a chart and grinned. Red hair scraped back in a tight bun accentuated green eyes that sparked behind wire-rimmed glasses. "What's shaking, Lindsay?"

"I missed you at yoga on Friday night." She didn't want to talk about the murder. It would be headlines soon enough.

"I know. I'm sorry I missed your class. It had been a long day and I was beat."

Lindsay taught yoga at a small studio near her town

house. She'd gained a reputation as a patient but exacting instructor. "You'll be better for it if you make the time."

"I know, I know. If anyone needs yoga, baby, it's me. I'm about as flexible as a piece of plywood."

Lindsay smiled. "You carry too much stress in your shoulders, but if you keep at it, your body will open."

Jennifer held up her hands in mock surrender. "Okay, okay, I promise to be there Wednesday night."

"Good. Hey, I'm here to see Sam."

"He's just finishing up rounds. He should be passing by in just a second."

"Great."

Jennifer leaned forward. "I hear you and Sam had a date last week."

Color rose in Lindsay's face. Jennifer knew everyone and their business. Hospital staff jokingly called her "Jenni-dot-net." "I wouldn't call it a date at all." The idea that Jennifer and likely now everyone else was calling her evening with Sam a date didn't sit well.

Jennifer wagged thin eyebrows. "What would you call it?"

Lindsay shoved fingers through her hair. "A friendly night out."

"Friendly?" A smile twitched the edges of Jennifer's full lips, made her eyes spark. "I've seen the way Sam looks at you."

Since Lindsay was a child, she'd been careful to keep her private life private. Her home life shamed her and she didn't want anyone to know about it. But the days of hiding a violent home life had long passed and there was no need to keep secrets. Yet the habit of hiding persisted.

Her evening out with Sam wasn't shameful or dark, just fun, and it had been exactly as she'd described it—

friendly. "Movies. Dinner at a burger joint. Home by nine. Very pleasant."

Jennifer looked disappointed. "That can't be it."

"It is."

"Ah, come on, there must be more details," Jennifer said.

"Nope. Sorry."

Sam's voice drifted down the hallway as he gave orders to a nurse.

Lindsay sighed her relief.

Jennifer laughed. "The cavalry has arrived."

"See you around. I've got to run." Lindsay tossed Jennifer a grin and hurried down the hallway toward Sam.

Sam stood in front of a curtained cubicle wearing his green scrubs, a patient's chart in hand. An inch taller than her, Sam was trim but not muscular. He looked like a tennis player who belonged at a country club. Blond hair curled at the edges above his ears. Horn-rimmed glasses accentuated intelligent brown eyes.

"Sam."

He peered over his glasses and smiled warmly as he closed the chart. "I was beginning to think you'd forgotten me."

Her smile came easily. "Sorry, we had some trouble at the shelter."

Worry creased his forehead. "What?"

She lowered her voice and leaned close to him. "This is not for anyone else to hear right now, but Harold Turner's body was found in the shelter's alley this morning."

"What?!" His voice raised in shock.

Lindsay glanced around and noticed several nurses staring at them. "I don't have many more details than that. The cops were at the shelter this morning interviewing me. In fact, they'll be there for days."

"No one else was hurt?"

"We're all fine."

He let out a long breath. "Damn. Harold Turner. His wife came through here two months ago with a sprained arm and bruised ribs."

"I know. She cornered me at a charity party two weeks ago and told me about her marriage. I offered her a bed at Sanctuary but she refused."

Sam shook his head. "Sanctuary is a big step down from a mansion on River Road."

"Yeah." *I can handle Harold.* Jordan's words replayed in Lindsay's head. "I can't imagine her sleeping in a bunk bed or sharing kitchen duties."

"I'd say your morning ranks high on the stress meter."

"You've no idea."

Sam laid his hand on her shoulder. "You look like hell."

Lindsay couldn't help but smile as she leaned into him. "You know how to make a girl feel good."

He grinned. "It's a talent."

She rubbed the back of her neck.

Sam studied her closely. "What gives with your neck?"

"I fell asleep on my couch last night. I must have slept crooked."

Sam captured her elbow in his hand. "Exam room three is open."

"I don't need to be checked out. And I need to see that woman you called me about."

"You've got a minute or two to spare."

Aware Jennifer hadn't missed a second of their exchange, she hesitated. "Sam, we are quickly becoming grist for the rumor mill."

He didn't look worried. "Since when do you care what people think?"

She glanced at the nurses. Their eyes gleamed with laughter. "Let's just say I've been gossiped about enough in my life. I don't like it."

"It's harmless." He pushed her toward the exam room and nodded toward the table. "Sit."

She stood stock straight. "I just need to talk to that woman and get back to the office. I've got cops crawling all over the shelter."

"For a moment, take the advice you give your yoga students and the women you counsel. Sit. Take a deep breath."

He was right. She'd been running on adrenaline since she'd been startled awake. She climbed up on the table as he closed the curtains behind them.

He moved behind her and began to massage the muscles around her neck. "My God, you're tense. It's a wonder you haven't collapsed yet. Your schedule is more insane than an intern's."

"I'm fine." His gentle touch soothed but didn't excite, like Zack's, which was a good thing. Excitement was overrated.

"So you're the doctor now?"

"I know my own body." She took several deep breaths.

His fingers worked up the back of her neck. God, it felt good. She closed her eyes. She could let her defenses down, if only for just a moment. "I'm so tired of holding it together all the time."

"You want to talk about it?" He leaned a little closer. His breath felt warm on her cheek. "I've been told I'm easy to talk to."

"Maybe another time."

Sam's fingers stilled and she feared this would turn into a tug-of-war. When she'd first met Zack, he hadn't been content until he'd known everything about her present and past. To her surprise, Sam leaned forward and kissed her lightly on the side of her neck. "Have dinner with me tonight."

Awkwardness replaced worry. Nearly thirty and she still turned knock-kneed when a man got romantic. "Uh, Sam, we've been through this. I'll be working late tonight."

"So we'll have breakfast at the diner. We'll grab coffee." When she hesitated, he added, "It wouldn't kill you to live a little."

Something she'd done very little of since she and Zack had separated. "I suppose not."

"That's a yes?"

She nodded. "Yes to dinner *tomorrow* night."

"What time?"

"Six."

"Done. I'll pick you up at the shelter."

"Better make that my town house. The cops sealed the area off."

"Will do."

Sam's cell phone vibrated on his hip. Groaning, he yanked it off and flipped it open. "Dr. Begley."

Immediately, his light expression darkened. He glanced at Lindsay and cupped his hand over the phone. "I've got to take this, Lindsay. See you tomorrow night?"

"Right." Lindsay slid off the table, thankful for the interruption.

He managed a strained smile.

"Where is that woman you told me about?" she whispered.

"Number six." Already he was turning from her.

"Thanks." She scooted around the curtain.

"Yes, damn it, I'm still here." Sam's angry whisper caught her attention and made her stop.

In the few months she'd known Sam, he'd never uttered a harsh word. He seemed to be the nicest guy on the planet.

"I told you I'd do it and I will," Sam said. "I've got to go."

Lindsay hurried down the hallway toward room six, surprised that there was something more to Dr. Sam Begley than just his quick smile and great bedside manner.

Chapter Six

Lindsay checked the name on the chart. She scanned Sam's notes. Cracked ribs. Contusions on the arms. A sprained right wrist. The injuries were classic. Her stomach knotted. She closed the chart and shoved aside the curtain to cubical six.

She found a petite woman sitting on the exam table wearing neatly pressed jeans, tennis shoes with double-knotted laces, and a white long-sleeved shirt. Small manicured fingers were clenched into tight fists.

Over the years, Lindsay had seen hundreds of battered women like this, but the sight always enraged her. Careful to keep her face neutral, she managed a smile. "Gail Saunders?"

The woman's tired gaze held a hint of anger. "Yes. Do you have my discharge papers?"

Irritation was a good sign. It meant spirit. She hadn't given up.

Lindsay closed the curtain behind her. "No, I'm not with the hospital. Dr. Begley asked me to talk to you for a few minutes."

Understanding dawned in Gail's gray eyes. "You're a social worker, aren't you?"

Lindsay dug a Sanctuary business card out of her purse and handed it to Gail. "My name is Lindsay O'Neil. I'm the director of a women's shelter."

Gail snatched the card, studied it. "Sanctuary. A haven for battered women." She tossed the card on the floor. "I don't need this."

Lindsay picked it up and laid it beside Gail. "That's right. We shelter women who've been abused. The number on the card is the hotline." She pulled out a pen and wrote her cell number on the back. "You can always reach me at this other number, day or night."

Gail slid off the exam table, wincing when her feet hit the ground. "I'm not abused. I told that stupid doctor that I fell down the stairs. What's the big deal?"

"He was concerned."

Her lips flattened as if she were barely holding on to her control. "Well, I'm fine."

Lindsay remained by the curtain so Gail wouldn't feel crowded. If she didn't tread carefully, the woman would bolt. "There are old bruises on your neck and they look like they were made by fingers."

Color flooded Gail's face. "I hit my neck on the banister as I fell down the stairs."

"Why the long sleeves and pants in July?"

"I'm cold natured."

Lindsay's voice remained soft and calm, but sadness and anger welled inside her. "Gail, I think you've been bullied enough already. So I'm not going to debate the issue with you. Experience has taught me that victims can be excellent liars."

Gail bristled. "I'm not a liar. My husband is a good man. He loves me. He works hard and would never hurt me on purpose."

"But he did hurt you," Lindsay said quietly.

Gail crushed the card in her hand. "I didn't say that!"

"Honey, the bruises did."

Tears welled in Gail's eyes, and for a moment Lindsay thought she would open up. She looked so small, so beaten down by life. Instead, the woman straightened her shoulders and grabbed her purse off the exam table. "I don't have to listen to this."

Lindsay pressed her card deeper into Gail's hand. "No, you don't. Just know you can reach me twenty-four/seven."

A tear rolled down Gail's face and she angrily brushed it away. She moved toward the curtain and shoved it open. "I won't be calling."

"I hope you do." She laid her hand on Gail's shoulder. "If things do get bad, remember to run to a room with soft furniture. Stay away from the kitchen and the bathrooms. They can be dangerous."

Gail hesitated, then left the room.

Lindsay listened to Gail's footsteps meld into the confusion of the hospital. For a moment her knees felt weak and she had to sit in the metal chair by the exam table. How many times had her mother made excuses for the bruises that had marked her body? How many times had she forgiven her father and stayed when she should have fled?

Like Gail's, her mother's lies were rooted in fear, shame, and the desperate hope that the abuse would really stop. But it never did.

What Lindsay hadn't understood was why everyone had accepted her mother's lies over and over again. No one had stepped in and no one had cared. And her mother had paid with her own life.

Jennifer appeared, her expression grim and angry. "Room number six looked pissed when she stormed past."

Lindsay straightened her shoulders, clinging to the

hope that kept her going. "Yeah, but she kept my card. I see that as a hopeful good sign."

Jennifer frowned. "Is she going home?"

"That would be my guess. It's human nature to return to places we know best."

"But she's not safe there!"

Lindsay clung to the bright side. "I have to have faith that she'll survive until she finds the courage to call me or someone else for help."

"Damn it! That just doesn't seem good enough. Isn't there anything we can do?"

"Don't underestimate a victim. They know how to survive. They've learned how to walk on eggshells."

"This really sucks, Lindsay."

"Jen, I've been down this road too many times. Just pray that she finds the courage to leave. Or better—that bastard husband of hers drops dead."

The humidity and temperature had risen the heat to an almost unbearable level. Black thunderclouds thickened in the western skies.

Zack and several of the uniforms, including a canine unit, had combed every inch of the shelter's backyard and the surrounding yards for Turner's hand, the murder weapon, or anything that might connect to the murder. They'd found nothing.

Sara had photographed the crime scene from every angle and sketched it. She and her assistant had collected hair and fiber samples from the corpse and then given the go-ahead for the body removal company to take Turner to the medical examiner's office.

Zack and Sara had watched as officers had lifted the dead man into the body bag. After zipping the bag closed, Sara had sealed the zipper with a plastic tie. The seal wouldn't be broken until the corpse arrived downtown at the state medical examiner's office on Jackson Street.

The attendants now placed the body bag on the gurney as Sara glanced at the dark sky. "I'm going to keep working the scene until the weather forces me out."

"Good. You don't have much time." Zack followed the gurney around the side of the house to the hearse waiting in the driveway.

A dozen neighbors, most of them retirees and stay-at-home moms pushing strollers, had gathered near the front yard, which he'd also taped off. Three television news trucks were now parked in the street with reporters lingering close by. Soon the rain would drive them all back inside their homes and vans, but for now he had to contend with an audience.

Zack eyed the crowd, paying close attention to the people's expressions. Killers sometimes returned to the scene to witness the chaos created by their handiwork.

As the body was wheeled through the privacy fence gate, everyone's gaze shifted toward it. Film cameras started taping and following the body. Even some neighbors snapped photos. By this evening, the area would be crawling with curiosity seekers.

Zack had spoken to the police department's public relations officer and told him to ask the press to keep the address and location of Sanctuary a secret. For now, the reporters had agreed. If he could close this case sooner than later, the press would move on to their next story and Sanctuary would be forgotten.

He wanted to protect the shelter. Not only would it be a shame to lose it as a resource, but the place meant so much to Lindsay. When they'd been together, she'd just received the grant application to purchase the property. She had been so excited and had spent long days fixing up the place and transforming it from a run-down rental property into a place that felt like a real home. A month after she'd opened the place, they'd separated and he'd not seen the house since then.

Now, looking at this place, he could see how much work she'd done. She'd had the exterior repainted and she'd replanted the yard, which had been a dust bowl when she'd bought the property. There were traces of her everywhere. The brightly painted walls inside, the potted plants on the porch, the manicured lawn, and a collection of toys in the backyard testified to her commitment.

Too bad she couldn't have invested the same time and energy into their marriage.

An unmarked Crown Vic pulled up in front of the house. In the front seat sat Zack's boss, Captain David Ayden, and Zack's partner, Jacob Warwick.

Annoyed, Zack checked his watch. It had taken Ayden two hours to track Warwick down. Warwick had been on the State Police force for thirteen years, before taking a job with the county's homicide division two years ago. Ayden had paired Zack with Warwick, believing the two would make a good team. Professionally, they did just fine, but personally, they'd not hit it off at all.

Somehow Warwick had found out about Zack's drinking problem and had made it clear he didn't think drunks stayed sober long. Zack could be a hothead who had no trouble sharing his thoughts. But this time he had swallowed his frustration. His drinking had caused a lot of damage, and he knew actions, not words, were going to win his partner over. That had been ten months ago, and so far, he'd not impressed Warwick.

Ayden got out of the car. His muscular build hadn't softened in the last couple of years even though he logged more time behind the desk than he would have liked. His thick hair grayed slightly at the temples and deep frown lines marred his forehead. He was a stubborn guy who had seen his late wife through cancer and now was raising two teenage boys on his own. He had little patience and didn't like being jerked around.

Warwick followed Ayden toward the house. He was built like a wide receiver and carried himself like an athlete. But football hadn't been his sport. Boxing was his specialty. As a teenager, he'd been a Golden Gloves fighter before entering the army, where he'd been in the Special Forces.

Today, Warwick was dressed in jeans and a T-shirt, a sign that Ayden had cut his vacation short. Normally Warwick leaned toward sports jackets and khakis. His hair looked in need of a trim, and though he was clean shaven, he'd have a five o'clock shadow by three.

Warwick nodded to Zack but the men didn't shake hands. "Kier."

"Warwick."

"Can you give us a rundown on the murder?" Ayden said.

"Follow me. I'll walk you through what we know right now."

Zack led the two men to the backyard, pulled a notepad from his breast pocket. Sara was by the back fence shooting more pictures. "The body was discovered over by the trash cans. He was shot point-blank in the chest. A wallet found in the victim's pocket identified him as Harold Turner."

A hiss of air escaped Warwick's lips. "Damn. Are you sure it's him?"

"I don't have a print match yet but it's Harold," Zack said.

Ayden rubbed the back of his neck with his hand. "Any ideas on who might have done this?"

"Nothing solid yet," Zack said. "But there are plenty of leads to run down. It could take weeks to talk to everyone."

"Why didn't you hold the body until we arrived?" Warwick said.

Zack resented Warwick's tone but kept his own tone even. "The skies are about to open up and I didn't want to lose trace evidence."

Warwick frowned. "Why didn't you call me earlier?"

"I didn't know what I had until I got here. When I did, I had Ayden track you down."

Ayden rested his hands on his hips. "What else do you know?"

Zack let his gaze scan the yard. "The backyard looks clean so far. Sara is going over it inch by inch."

Warwick studied the pool of blood caked in the dirt by the tree. "You said his wallet was still in his pocket?"

"Yeah, and it still had a couple hundred dollars in cash and a dozen credit cards in it. His briefcase was set neatly beside him and it also appeared untouched."

"What's the pool of blood from?" Warwick said.

"It's from his left hand. The killer severed the hand at the wrist."

"Shit," Ayden said. "Any sign of it?"

"No."

Warwick's eyes narrowed. "Was Turner left-handed?"

"Don't know," Zack said.

"Do you think this is some kind of ritual thing?" Ayden said.

Zack pointed to the trash cans. "The victim's body was positioned near the cans. His tie was straight and his hair looked as if it had been combed. The killer didn't appear in a rush to leave the body."

Warwick rested his hands on his narrow hips. "Like you said, it'll take weeks to interview everyone who had a beef against Turner."

"My gut tells me that this killing was personal," Zack said.

Ayden shrugged off his coat and loosened his tie. "Turner pissed off a lot of people. But none of them would be likely to stop and fix his tie after they'd shot him."

"No. This murder has a different feel to it," Zack said.

The three were silent for a moment.

"You have anything else?" Warwick said.

"I talked to the shelter staff," Zack said. "Ruby Dillon, an assistant to the director, was on call last night. She didn't see anything until this morning when she found the body." Zack didn't relish what he was about to say. "You might as well hear it from me. The director of Sanctuary is Lindsay O'Neil. She's my wife."

Warwick frowned. "I didn't realize you were married."

"I thought you were divorced," Ayden said.

"Not officially," Zack said.

Warwick's gaze sliced across him. "How long have you two been separated?"

The question reiterated how little the two men knew about each other. "About a year."

"You shouldn't have taken the call," Warwick said.

Zack refused to lock horns with his partner now. It was more important that Ayden keep him on the case. "I want this case, Ayden."

Ayden frowned. "Why?"

Zack couldn't even explain his reasons to himself, let alone his boss. "I just want in on it."

"The last damn thing I need is a conflict-of-interest issue," Ayden said. "A body in the suburbs is going to generate a lot of media coverage. And everyone in the county government is going to be all over this by lunchtime."

"Where was O'Neil last night?" Warwick said.

Zack straightened. "She was home last night."

"Can she prove it?" Ayden said.

"She says she was home alone. No witnesses. She was also late this morning, because a power outage shut off her alarm clock." He knew she hadn't told him everything. There was more going on with her. But still his gut told him she was no killer. One way or another, he'd find out the truth. "There are a lot of people who could have killed Harold."

Warwick exhaled. "You're too close to this case."

Tension rose in Zack's body. He'd had about enough of Warwick's attitude. "Are you questioning my judgment?"

Warwick met his gaze. There was no hint of apology. "Yes."

Ayden raised his hand. His expression allowed for no argument. "Jesus, you two sound like my boys. Cut this crap out." He tightened his jaw and released it. "Fight later. Solve this case now. Turner may have been slime, but he got himself killed in a nice suburban neighborhood. The public is not going to be happy. If you two can't work this case, I'll get Vega and Ricker to handle it."

Zack didn't want to get pulled from the case. "We'll be fine."

Warwick nodded in agreement. This was a case he didn't want to lose either. "We've got it under control, sir."

"You'd better," Ayden warned. "Because if I get even a whiff that you two aren't working well together, you're off this case." Ayden ducked under the tape. "Keep me posted." Without a good-bye to either officer, he disappeared around the side of the house.

"As long as you stay sober, I'll be fine," Warwick said.

"Don't be an ass."

Warwick shrugged and crossed the yard. He crouched in front of the bloodstain and studied it. "Word is Ronnie T. and Turner fought after court yesterday. I heard

Turner presented a plea deal to him. The deal required that he do five years in the state penitentiary."

Zack shifted his gaze to his partner with a measure of respect. "How'd you hear that?"

"I box with guys in the Justice Department. We talk. Harold and Ronnie T.'s argument caused quite a stir yesterday."

"What was said?"

Warwick pulled off his sunglasses and leaned closer to the stain. "Ronnie T. apparently was paying Harold big bucks in exchange for a promise that he wouldn't have to do jail time. Ronnie T. thinks of himself as a family man. He wants to see his three kids grow up."

"The son of a bitch got his start selling drugs to kids and he's worried about being away from his own. Priceless."

A fat rain droplet fell and hit Zack on the shoulder. "Damn." He glared at the sky and then at Sara. She nodded and picked up her pace. "This doesn't look like Ronnie T.'s work."

"I agree. A drive-by is more his style, but he's got to be checked out." Warwick rose. "Do you have Turner's home address?"

Harold's wife was at the top of Zack's list. "Yes. His home is about twenty minutes from here."

More rain droplets started to cut through the leaves above and hit the ground around their feet. "Let's go talk to Mrs. Turner and then we'll have a chat with Ronnie T."

Chapter Seven

Monday, July 7, 12:02 P.M.

Zack took off his suit jacket as he and Warwick moved toward Zack's Impala. Several reporters and cameramen rushed toward them but neither paused before getting into the car. Zack fired up the engine and wove through the neighborhood and out onto the main road that fed into the interstate. He gunned the engine and pulled onto the ramp into traffic.

Scattered rain droplets peppered the windshield. He flipped on the windshield wipers. The rain came down harder.

A hand on the steering wheel, Zack glanced toward Warwick, who was staring out his window. Zack had tried small talk with Warwick when they'd first been partnered up, but the guy simply wasn't interested, so he'd given up.

Craving a cigarette, Zack reached in his pocket and found gum instead. He pulled out the pack, unwrapped a stick, and popped it in his mouth. He offered one to Warwick, who declined.

Ten minutes later, Zack had gotten ahead of the rain, which was moving in from the west. He maneuvered the

Impala off the interstate and down River Road. This was
the high end of town where pedigree was just as important as a fat wallet. Turner hadn't been born into the
right family, but he'd married into one of the oldest in
the state.

Zack pulled onto a tree-lined side street and into
Harold Turner's circular driveway. The enormous brick
Colonial was bordered by manicured beds filled with
boxwoods, daylilies, and a rainbow palette of annuals.
The house, like the man who'd remodeled it, screamed
money.

Warwick whistled as his gaze traveled over the home's
exterior. "Look at this place. It's worth more than I'll
make in five lifetimes. This is a far cry from Harold's sub-
sidized housing days at Randolph Court."

Zack didn't feel envy, just a curiosity for the well-bred
woman who had married a man like Turner.

The fixer-upper he'd just bought could fit in one of
Turner's garages. However, this house was cold. His
house, which Lindsay had spotted shortly after they'd
married, had character and was full of possibilities. Yeah,
it had dents and dings—just like their marriage—but
that's what made it interesting. Or so he kept telling
himself.

He stared at the ivy-covered house willing it to reveal
its secrets. "I called Ricker about an hour ago and had
her do a quick rundown on Mrs. Turner. She's a George-
town grad and in her midthirties. She and Turner married about five years ago. They have no children, but
she's a member of a children's hospital board and a
member of several other children's charities."

Warwick flexed his fingers. "How did those two
hook up?"

"He was her father's attorney."

Warwick raised an eyebrow. "Her old man is not so squeaky clean?"

"He was charged with investment fraud. Turner got him off."

"So he kept the old man out of jail and married the daughter."

"So it seems." It was amazing how much dirt could be hidden behind such regal walls.

Zack opened his door and was struck by the humidity, thick with the promise of rain within minutes. As Warwick got out, Zack pulled on his suit jacket. The worsted wool felt scratchy against his skin. The suit was classified as a "nine months suit," and he'd bought it figuring he'd get the most wear out of it. He now realized July was one of the three months it was not intended to be worn. He straightened his tie.

Warwick studied a large iron planter filled with ivy. "If she's such a class act why marry a shyster like Turner?"

"Love's a fickle thing." Crushed gravel crunched under their feet as they walked up the walkway. Eight months in homicide and he'd not gotten used to the grim task of delivering news of a death.

"Love ain't got nothing to do with this union. It's all about the money." A shadow darkened Warwick's face.

"Are you completely cynical?"

Warwick shrugged. "Just calling 'em as I seem 'em. Women gravitate toward the coin. Saw it a million times when I worked undercover. Go into a club dressed as a bum, and none of the chicks talk to you. Return to the same club dressed as a player, and it's like bees and honey."

Money didn't motivate Lindsay. She had walked away from their marriage without a dime. In fact, she had given the money from their joint savings account to his mother and asked her to put it toward Zack's recovery.

He'd used that money a month ago to put the down payment on that fixer-upper that Lindsay had loved.

"When we get to the door," Warwick said, "let me do most of the talking."

"No problem."

"Don't say we're from homicide. I don't want her shutting down. Once anyone hears homicide, they start gauging their words carefully."

"I know the drill." Irritated, Zack rang the front bell.

Within seconds footsteps sounded on the other side. The door opened to a young Hispanic woman dressed in a maid's uniform. "Yes?"

Warwick held up his police badge. "We're here to see Mrs. Jordan Turner."

The young woman frowned. "Just a moment, please." The front door closed with a soft click.

"Do you think she'll show?" Zack said.

"I don't know."

The door opened a second time. This time a tall slim woman appeared at the threshold. She was dressed in a simple black sheath that accentuated full breasts and a narrow waist. A gold cross dangled from a chain around her neck. Long black hair grazed the top of slender shoulders and framed a lovely oval face that could have been classified as angelic if not for the sharpness behind her violet eyes.

Behind her, polished wood floors gleamed. Walls papered in cream and black stripes served as a backdrop to eighteenth-century portraits. A crystal chandelier hung from the vaulted ceiling, twisting sunlight into rainbows.

"Mrs. Jordan Turner?" Warwick said.

"Yes?" A crease formed between neatly plucked eyebrows as her gaze shifted between the two of men. "I understand you're with the police department."

Both men reached in their pockets and pulled out badges.

"We're with Henrico County Police," Warwick said.

"What can I do for you?" Her tone turned cautious.

"Is there anyone else in the house with you?" They didn't want her alone in case she took the news of her husband's death badly.

She glanced behind her. Feminine laughter sounded from inside the house. "I've a few ladies from the church here. What's this about?"

"Have you seen your husband this morning?" Warwick said.

Answering a question with a question often led to more information.

"Harold and I had dinner together last night. After that we went our separate ways. I had a late church meeting and didn't get home until after eleven. I'm not sure what plans Harold had scheduled on his calendar."

"What time did your husband come in last night?" Warwick said.

She frowned. "What's this about?"

Warwick ignored her question. "I would appreciate it if you would just confirm his arrival for me."

Jordan drew in a breath. "We have separate bedrooms." Color rose in her cheeks as if she was embarrassed by the admission. Appearances were clearly a priority for her. "Harold has terrible back problems and he needs a special mattress."

Zack tucked the badge back in his pocket. "What time did you have dinner with him last night?"

Her lips flattened. "Six. We left *La Mer* at seven. Is Harold in some kind of trouble?"

"May we come inside?" Warwick said.

Jordan stepped out onto the front porch, softly closing the door behind her. "As I said, I've a group of women visiting from the church. Now is not a good time to hear about Harold's latest indiscretion."

"It's more than an indiscretion, ma'am," Zack said.

She fidgeted with her five-carat wedding ring with her thumb. "What has my husband done this time?"

"This time?" Zack said.

"A month ago he was arrested for drunk driving in the city."

Warwick's gaze didn't waver from Jordan's face. "Mr. Turner was found dead this morning behind Sanctuary Women's Shelter."

For a moment, she just stared at them, her eyes blinking slowly as if her brain couldn't process. She raised her hand to her mouth. Finally, she found her voice, which possessed surprising steel. "Are you sure it was Harold?"

"Yes, ma'am," Warwick said. "We found his wallet in his breast pocket."

Sudden tears glistened in her eyes. But Zack couldn't tell if they were born in sadness or relief. "What happened to him? How did he die?"

"He was shot." He wasn't telling her anything that wouldn't appear on the six o'clock news. Details about the mutilation and the caliber of the gun would remain confidential until the case was solved.

She flexed her French-manicured fingers. "Where exactly did you say you found Harold?"

"Behind Sanctuary Women's Shelter," Zack said. Shock was natural, but this calm reaction wasn't. Normally, when a loved one was reported dead, strong emotion followed.

But Jordan Turner didn't show much sign that she was upset. In fact, she looked confused. "This doesn't make any sense. Harold wouldn't ever go to a women's shelter."

"There's no reason Mr. Turner would be at Sanctuary Women's Shelter?" Warwick said.

Amusement softened her features, as if he'd just said something funny. "No, Harold would never go to a place like that."

"Why not?" Warwick said.

"He doesn't support any charity unless it advances his standing with the media. And even if Sanctuary was a media darling, he wouldn't support it. He doesn't like quitters."

"Quitters?" Zack said.

"Women who give up on their marriages."

Zack's temper rose. "They're abused women, Mrs. Turner."

The censure in his voice had her shoulders stiffening. "Until death do we part, detective. Those are the vows we all take when we marry in the church. We may not like the way our marriages turn out but that doesn't mean we abandon our promise before God."

"You don't believe in divorce," Warwick said.

She released the cross she had been holding. He could almost hear her defenses slamming into place. "I don't. I also don't believe in murder."

"No one says that you do," Zack said.

She raised a brow. "Please, I've been married to a defense attorney for five years. I know how it works. The spouse is always at the top of the suspect list when there is a murder."

"No one's a suspect yet," Warwick said. "These questions are standard procedure. Right now we're just trying to establish a time line."

A fat rain droplet leaked through the porch roof and landed on Zack's shoulder. He didn't need to glance up to know the sky was about to open up.

Jordan turned, dismissing them as she reached for the front door handle. "I will contact my attorney and he'll be in touch with you. If you have more questions, you can ask them of me in front of him."

"There a reason you need an attorney?" Zack said. More droplets hit him on his broad shoulders.

She met his gaze head-on. "Harold said you always, always need an attorney when cops are around. Now I must go."

Warwick stopped her retreat by asking, "Know of anybody who would want to kill your husband?"

The question made her smile again. "I'll draw up a list. My attorney will submit it." She opened the door, then closed it in their faces as she went inside.

Warwick planted long hands on his hips. "Smooth, controlled, and not exactly torn up," he said, summing her up.

Zack turned up his collar as raindrops peppered the ground. "I'll subpoena phone records and get a full background check on her."

Rain greeted Lindsay's Jeep as she pulled out of the Mercy Hospital parking garage. She flipped on her headlights and windshield wipers to cut through the river of water falling from the sky. Slowly she merged into traffic and followed the procession of red taillights onto I-64 West. The downpour made drivers hesitant and slow. The trip back to shelter was going to take longer than she'd planned.

Seeing Gail made her think of Jordan. Unable to resist, she picked up her cell and dialed Jordan again. She doubted Jordan would pick up, but she felt as if she had to try although she wasn't sure what she'd say to Jordan when she got her on the phone.

After the third ring, the call connected.

"Jordan?"

"Yes. Why are you calling me, Lindsay?"

"Because we need to talk."

"I've said all I'm willing to say to you."

"Don't hang up. Please, we need to talk about Harold."

"There's nothing to say. The police were just here. They told me about him."

Harold Turner may have abused his wife but that didn't mean Jordan didn't love him or wasn't feeling a great sense of loss. "Are you okay?"

"I'm fine. Now, leave me alone. I can't talk to you anymore." Jordan's voice sounded brittle, more tense than usual.

"We need to talk about Harold."

"I have nothing to say about him."

The questions had to be asked. "Jordan, you said a couple of weeks ago that you could handle him. Did you kill him?"

There was a long pause. "Why would you ask me a question like that? Harold was found behind *your* shelter."

"Because I think whoever put him there was sending me a message. I think you might have been telling me that you'd handle him by killing him."

"He was worth more to me alive than dead. And I was handling him." A heavy silence followed before she added, "Did you kill him?"

Lindsay felt dizzy. "No."

"It makes sense that you would. I saw the way you looked at him at that charity party. You hated him."

"Jordan, I didn't kill Harold."

"Who else would? Harold was right about you. He said you hate men."

"I don't hate men, Jordan. I hate it when men hit the women they say they love."

"Harold did love me."

"Jordan, you told me he held a gun to your head and played Russian roulette."

"I also told you the gun was empty. If he'd wanted to kill me he would have, but he didn't. He said he was just kidding."

Lindsay nearly cried out her frustration. "Jordan, you have to understand that a man shouldn't treat a woman that way."

"Don't tell me any more of your lies. I don't want to hear them. Harold and I would have been fine if you'd just stayed out of our lives."

"Jordan, you're the one who came to me."

"You killed my husband."

"I did not!"

"I'll never forgive you for what you did to me." The line went dead.

Lindsay shoved out a breath and closed the phone. Frustration ate at her. Jordan had decided Lindsay was the cause of her problems.

Lindsay tapped her pinky ring—her mother's high school ring—against the steering wheel. She clicked on the radio, hit "scan," and hoped for some kind of news about Harold. Nothing. Each station played a collection of songs and advertisements, but no news.

Aware that her breathing had grown shallow, she drew in deep breaths. Slowly the muscles in her chest eased.

What had Harold been doing behind the shelter? Sanctuary was the kind of place he despised and he had no reason to be there—unless Jordan really had lured him to the shelter and killed him as some kind of message to Lindsay.

"Jordan, please tell me you didn't do anything stupid," Lindsay whispered to herself.

The deluge of rain slowed. Streets glistened with rain.

Steam rose from the hot pavement. Puddles collected on the shoulders of the road.

Lindsay flipped open her cell phone and redialed Jordan Turner's number. The phone rang once and then went straight to voice mail.

"This is Jordan. Leave me a message and I'll get back to you."

"Jordan, it's Lindsay O'Neil. I need to talk to you again. You've got my number."

Lindsay clipped the phone back into its holster on her waistband. Ten minutes later she parked in front of Sanctuary. The downpour had just stopped but it had chased away the forensics team and the curiosity seekers. A squad car with a lone officer in the front seat remained parked in the driveway and two television news trucks lurked across the street. The reporters huddled inside the front cabs.

A streak of lightning shot across the sky. Lindsay flinched. She counted to five. Thunder boomed. Another storm was close.

Grabbing her purse, she hurried across the muddy front lawn and climbed Sanctuary's front steps. She darted in the front door.

The morning calm had been replaced by a buzz of video games and children's chatter. Jamal and Damien Greenland had arrived home from summer school. Damn. They shouldn't be here. Ruby should have picked them up at school.

"Ruby!" Lindsay shouted. She pushed open the pocket door that portioned off Ruby's small office.

Ruby sat behind her desk, a phone cradled under her chin. When her gaze met Lindsay's she hung up. "How was the hospital?"

Lindsay brushed the rain from her face. "Time will tell. Planted a few seeds. Why are the Greenland boys still here?"

"The school wouldn't release them to me and I couldn't get hold of their mother. I had no choice but to let them ride the bus home. The bus just dropped them off. I decided to plant them in front of a video game until you got back."

Lindsay sighed. "Now that the rain has let up, the cops are going to return soon to salvage what they can from that backyard. I'll run the boys over to Riverside now. I don't want the kids around when they return."

"Are you sure?"

"Yeah, I'll be back in an hour."

Lindsay headed into the front family room, where the boys were playing the video game on the television. Ruby had closed the shades to block all views of the police car and news vans parked out front. "Hey, guys, how's the game going?"

Damien glanced up from the screen. "This game is kinda lame, Lindsay. No guns, no bombs, no fun."

The video game system had been anonymously donated to the shelter two months ago. She was grateful for the donation but had immediately sifted through the stack of games that came with it and tossed the violent ones. The kids who lived there saw enough violence in real life. "That hasn't stopped you fellows from playing it nonstop."

Damien had a concerned look on his face. Usually during the day she was too busy to chat. "Is Mom okay? I saw the cop outside."

She could have sugarcoated the whole issue, but she'd hated it when adults had condescended to her after her mother's death. *It's going to be fine, dear. Don't you worry.* "Your mom is fine but we're going to have to move you, your brother, and your mom to another shelter today."

"Because of *him*." Damien's voice wavered even as he

jutted out his chin. His brother set down his video controller and looked at her.

Him was their father—Marcus Greenland. He'd been a star linebacker in college. During his junior year, he'd gotten involved in drugs and trouble with the local police. He'd been suspended from the team. Then he'd hooked up with another college but hadn't lasted the season. From then on, he had been on a downward spiral. Frustrated by his own failures, Marcus took out his anger on his wife and children.

Lindsay laid her hand on Damien's shoulder. "No, your father has nothing to do with this."

Suspicion narrowed Damien's eyes. "Are you being straight with me?"

"I promise, Damien. I can't give you details but I swear that this has nothing to do with you, your mom, or your dad."

Finally, the anxiety eased from the boy's shoulders. "Thanks, Lindsay."

"No problem, kiddo."

"Can I save the game to the memory card?" Damien said.

"I thought it was lame," she teased.

"Not too lame," he added.

Unless this murder was resolved quickly, the shelter would close, and she had no idea if and when it would open again. "You can take it and the game with you."

He grinned. "For real?"

"Absolutely."

"Thanks!" Jamal exclaimed.

As the boys finished up their game, she grabbed a plastic grocery bag from under the kitchen sink. Jamal pocketed the disc and memory card as Damien unplugged the game and tucked it in the bag. The three headed outside.

"We can really keep this?" Jamal said.

"Until you and your brother get settled in a real home with your mom. When you guys are feeling comfortable in your new place, I'd like it back for the next kid."

Jamal frowned. "Damien and I aren't the last kids?"

Sadly, there would always be a next kid in her line of business. It was the main reason why she was there. But Jamal didn't need statistics or grim predictions of the future. He needed hope that his life would one day be happy and normal. "I sure hope you are."

Lindsay ushered the boys outside to her car. They buckled in and soon were headed across town. Fifteen minutes later, they rolled into the Riverside parking lot. The shelter was also in a residential neighborhood and looked much like the other trilevel houses around it. Toys now damp from the rain littered the front yard. The front door was open. Inside, lights glowed.

Aisha Greenland came outside, her shoulder-length braids brushing her wide shoulders. She grinned when she saw Lindsay and the boys. The boys scrambled out of the backseat and ran up to their mother. She hugged them close.

Lindsay followed with the video game system in hand. "How'd the interview go?"

Aisha grinned. Hazel eyes flashed with genuine happiness. "I got the job."

Lindsay knew Aisha had been terrified of the interview. It had been eight years since she'd worked out of the home. "That's great."

Jamal cupped his mother's face in his hands. "You got a job?"

Aisha kissed her son. "I sure did, baby. I sure did. I'm gonna be working as a cashier at the supermarket." She lifted her gaze to Lindsay. "Thank you."

"Happy to help." Moments like this made all the bad stuff fade.

"I have just a little something for you," Aisha said.

"You don't need to give me anything."

Aisha shook her head and from her pocket pulled out a small wrapped box. "I heard Ruby saying it was your birthday on Wednesday."

Emotion tightened Lindsay's chest as she slowly opened the box. Inside was a plastic butterfly. Clearly it wasn't expensive, but that didn't matter. "You know butterflies mean rebirth."

Aisha shook her head. "I just liked the pretty colors."

Lindsay hugged her. "So do I. Thank you." Unshed tears burned the back of her throat. "Good luck. You guys take care. I've got to get back to Sanctuary."

Inside her car, Lindsay turned on the radio, found a good song, and cranked it. She felt good and wanted to savor this small victory. To celebrate, she went to a drive-thru to treat herself to a milk shake, burger, and fries. The delicious smells made her stomach rumble for she couldn't remember the last time she'd eaten.

Twenty minutes later, when she parked in front of Sanctuary, she'd eaten the fries and drank half the milk shake. A little food on her stomach had settled her nerves and she felt steadier.

The cop car was still parked out front, as well as the forensics van. Only one news van remained. And that was a good thing as far as she was concerned. She prayed the press would lose interest and this whole thing would just go away.

She was halfway up the shelter's front steps when she heard a woman shout, "Lindsay O'Neil!"

Turning, she saw a tall woman with dark hair pulled back into a low, tight ponytail. She was wearing a sleek sapphire silk blouse that accentuated flawless porcelain skin expertly made up and black pants that showed off long legs and a narrow waist. Kendall Shaw, former cover model and now a reporter for Channel 10, was perfectly dressed as always.

One look reminded Lindsay that she'd barely had time to run a brush through her hair this morning. "Hey, Kendall."

Kendall grinned and held out her hand. "It's good to see you again. I guess it's been a couple of months."

Lindsay shifted her fast-food bag and drink to one hand so she could shake Kendall's with the other. "Since you interviewed me a couple of months ago for that free-lance article for *Inside Richmond.*"

Kendall's grin broadened. Her grip was strong and firm. "That article was well received. The paper said that their sell-through for that month was eighty percent. You were a hit."

"It wasn't me. The other gals you profiled were pretty amazing."

Kendall let her gaze travel over the white vinyl siding and the trimmed boxwoods. "So this is Sanctuary. I always wondered what Sanctuary actually looked like. Those couple of times we met at the coffee shop, you never said where it actually was."

"That's the idea. We need to keep our location secret. We still do."

She nodded. "Oh, don't worry about that. I won't talk location. None of the news stations are." She slid manicured hands into her pocket and pulled out a slim notebook. "But I was hoping you could tell me more about what went on here this morning. The cops' public relations guy said Harold Turner was killed here but won't say much else. Any thoughts why?"

That was the million-dollar question. "I don't know anything else. I'm just as much in the dark as you are."

Kendall didn't look convinced. "Oh, come on, you must have an idea." She'd dropped her voice as if they were somehow coconspirators. "Detective Kier was in your office for over a half hour. And he was very tight-lipped when I tried to talk to him. He must have told you something."

Zack hated the press. He never spoke to them unless he absolutely had to. "I really don't know anything, Kendall."

"I thought he was your husband?"

Lindsay didn't ask Kendall how she'd found out about her marriage. No doubt she'd done extra digging while working on the article. "I can't add anything." She inched past Kendall up the stairs toward the door.

Kendall followed. "Harold's death didn't have anything to do with the Pam Rogers case?"

Tension snaked up Lindsay's back as she reached for the doorknob. She'd never considered the two could be linked. But Kendall thought more like a cop.

"Kendall, I'd help you out if I could." Another lie. "But I don't know anything."

Kendall's smile was smooth as she laid her hand on the front rail. "Oh, come on, you must know something that you can share with me. I mean, I figure you owe me."

Lindsay dropped her hand from the doorknob and faced the reporter. Whatever goodwill she'd felt toward Kendall had vanished. "You want to run that one by me again?"

Kendall didn't look intimidated. "You were quite the 'it' girl there for a few weeks after the article came out. I'd heard that donations to the shelter had soared."

Donations had risen for a while but that didn't mean Lindsay liked being pushed. "Right now I can't say a word."

Kendall's eyes hardened but she maintained her trade-mark smile. "But when you can you'll give me a call."

"Don't count on it." Lindsay escaped inside the shelter but the well-being she'd felt on the drive back had evaporated. Kendall Shaw's questions had set her teeth on edge and reminded her that no matter how hard she worked on the pending grant applications, the specter of another shelter-related murder could shut her down permanently.

Lindsay headed to her office. Carefully, she laid the butterfly in the center of her desk as she studied a long white flower box sitting on her chair. It was wrapped with a thick red ribbon. There was a card on the box. It read, "For Lindsay."

No one ever sent her flowers.

"Hey, Ruby," she shouted, "what's with the flowers?"

"They just came." Ruby rounded the corner, a big grin on her face. "They're for you."

"Do you know who sent them?" Had Zack remembered her birthday? Could he have sent the flowers?

Ruby grinned. "Open the card and find out."

Tenderly, she touched the ribbon that seemed to have been wrapped with care. "There must be some kind of mistake. I've never gotten flowers." The truth was she didn't like flowers, because her father always gave her mother flowers after he hit her.

Ruby shrugged. "No mistake. And if you've never gotten flowers, it's high time you did."

Her curiosity rising, Lindsay opened the card. "*Lindsay, you are not alone anymore. The Guardian.*"

Ruby came around behind Lindsay and glanced over her shoulder and read the note. "'Lindsay, you are not alone anymore.' What does that mean? And who is the Guardian?"

Lindsay also was puzzled. "I've no idea."

Ruby cocked an eyebrow. "I hate it when men play games. There a name?"

"No."

"There's no man in your life?"

"No."

"What about your husband?"

"He knows I don't like flowers. Besides, romantic gestures aren't his thing."

Curious, Lindsay untied the crisp bow. She laid it carefully aside before opening the lid to reveal purple irises. They'd been one of her mother's favorite flowers and, consequently, she loved them as well. "They're beautiful."

Ruby leaned over her shoulder, admiring the bouquet. "Maybe it's from that doctor."

"I bet you're right. I saw Sam this morning. He knows I was having a rough day and he's one of the few who knows where the shelter is located."

Sadness coiled inside her chest. It was foolish to want or expect anything from Zack. But for a brief moment she had. "I think we have a vase or a large jar in the kitchen."

"I think it's under the sink. I'll be right back with it." Ruby disappeared down the hallway.

Lindsay lifted the flowers out of the box. As she raised the blooms to her nose she saw a bundle wrapped in green tissue paper. She laid the flowers aside on her desk and opened the second package.

Bile rose in her throat. For a moment she thought she'd throw up as she dropped it and backed away from her desk.

Cradled in the tissue and wrapped in a zip-top bag was a severed hand.

No one noticed delivery people. Some might glance at the name *Joe* embroidered over a breast pocket, but few would gaze under the bill of a hat or look beyond a nondescript magnetic florist sign stuck on a van.

That was the problem with people, the Guardian thought. They were selfish and far too wrapped up in their own lives to notice what didn't directly concern them.

That's why it was easy to feel safe moving past the unmarked police car and the cop now distracted by a well-timed cell phone call from his kid's day care.

And the Guardian smiled at the ambitious reporter as she tamed a strand of hair and practiced smiling as her cameraman began taping her intro for the six o'clock news report.

Like everyone else, the cop and reporter were blind. Blind to the delivery. Blind to the pain and suffering around them. Blind to everything but their needs.

The only one who could truly see was Lindsay.

She reached out to others in need. She put the lives of others in front of her own.

The Guardian closed the door to the van and started the engine and pulled out. She would get the flowers soon. Soon she would know she wasn't alone. "Happy birthday, Lindsay."

Tightening fingers on the steering wheel, the Guardian slowed at an intersection when the light turned yellow. The car in the left lane darted through a red light and he frowned.

"No respect."

Today had been a good day.

The rains had purified the killing ground and signaled the beginning of a long overdue holy cause.

Together, Lindsay and her Guardian would destroy The Evil Ones.

Chapter Eight

Richard pinned Christina's hands down over her head as his heavy body pressed her into the mattress. She could feel his erection pressing against her skin and knew what would come next. His breath smelled of stale cigars and whiskey. She felt dirty and so unclean when he touched her.

She didn't want his idea of lovemaking. She didn't want him.

But she was careful to hide her revulsion and fear. The last time she'd tried to resist him, he'd slapped her hard across the face, and after he'd raped her he'd locked her in a dark closet all night long.

Richard thrust inside her, using as much force as he could. She couldn't suppress a wince.

He smiled and pushed into her again and again until tears spilled down her cheeks and stained the silk pillow under her head.

He slipped his hands under her buttocks and gripped hard. He was enjoying her suffering.

"You love this, don't you?" he whispered against her ear.

Christina swallowed. She couldn't bring herself to respond.

He straightened and slapped her hard against the face. "Say you love this."

She tasted blood. "I do."

Richard smiled, satisfied. He cupped her full breasts with his large hands. "I want us to have a child, Christina. I want a child to bind us together forever."

Fear burned inside her. She begged God not to give her a child.

How had her life gotten so messed up? How had she slid from independence to this?

He moved inside of her, faster and faster. He fisted his fingers in her long dark hair and pressed his cheek to hers. His beard scratched her skin. His breath was hot against her face. Sweat dripped from his body.

"Say you love me," Richard commanded.

She didn't speak. Saying the words always made her ill.

"Say it!" he urged. He tightened his hold on her hair and pulled until sections started to come out.

Pain seared Christina's scalp. She started to weep again. "I love you."

He grunted, satisfied. Even in his own twisted way, he needed assurances. He released her hair and kissed her lips. "I love you, Christina. We'll be together forever. Until death do us part."

The words were heartfelt. He did love her. And at one time she had loved him.

Richard found his release. He collapsed on top of her, his body damp with sweat. Tenderly he stroked her hair.

"We are destined to be together forever."

Nicole Piper awoke with a start. Her mind was still clouded by the dream and for a moment she was confused and afraid.

She didn't know where she was as she swung her legs over the side of the overstuffed couch. A book that had been in her lap fell to the floor. Sweat dampened her brow. Her heart raced.

Drawn window shades bathed the room in near darkness and added to her disorientation. Overwhelmed by the sensation that she wasn't alone, she frantically searched the living room's shadowed corners for any sign of her husband, Richard.

A chill prickled her skin. "Who's there!"

No one answered.

"Richard, are you there?"

Still nothing. And yet the feeling that someone watched lingered.

Seconds passed. No phantoms appeared. Her heart slowed.

Nicole's mind cleared. "He's far away, three thousand miles away. Richard is in San Francisco. Christina is dead. I'm Nicole now." She was in Virginia and living with her friend Lindsay O'Neil.

"I'm safe. It was a dream." Nicole switched on the lamp by the faded floral couch. As she hugged a colorful pillow, her gaze traveled over the living room's hodgepodge of antique and modern furniture. An assortment of clocks ticked and chimed on the mantle. A large area rug warmed the scuffed parquet floor. The room should have looked disjointed, but Lindsay had united the salvaged pieces and given them a new life and purpose.

She'd done the same for Nicole.

Without question, Lindsay had taken in Nicole when she'd fled her abusive marriage. She'd given her safe harbor and was helping her to regain control of her life.

Nicole curled trembling hands into fists and said aloud, "He can't find me. I've covered my tracks well. I'm safe." But the helpless fear still remained.

A clock chimed four times. Other clocks joined in, creating a symphony of sounds. Four o'clock.

It was time to get ready for her evening shift at the studio.

Just a week ago, Nicole had told Lindsay she had to get back to work. Lindsay had tried to convince her to just hang out for a while and give herself time to heal, but Nicole had refused. She needed to work so that she could push the past from her mind. Lindsay had understood and had gotten Nicole a new Social Security number. Nicole wasn't sure how Lindsay had accomplished the feat so quickly but she hadn't asked.

Within two days, Nicole had gotten a job at a mall portrait studio. She'd only been on the job about a week and knew that snapping photos of babies and high school graduates was a far cry from the artistic photography she'd done in San Francisco. But right now she didn't have the luxury of being a snob. This job was about making money, which equaled the means to run if Richard found her.

Nicole moved through the dimly lit apartment to the kitchen and got a soda from the fridge. She popped it open and savored the cool liquid on her dry throat and uneasy stomach.

She was afraid all the time and that made her angry with herself. She'd been a fool to love Richard, a man who had ruined her life.

Richard.

He'd been the man of her dreams and she'd loved him so much in the early days. But behind the kindness and flowers lurked a man who was evil incarnate.

Two years ago when he'd burst through the front door of her San Francisco photography studio, he'd been dodging an onslaught of rain. Dressed in jeans, a white linen shirt, and Gucci loafers, he had immediately captured her attention with his dark good looks. They'd hit it off. He'd been so charming. She'd been enthralled.

They'd married less than two months later in a sunset
ceremony on the beach. Her parents had passed away
by then but she'd had a collection of friends to stand by
her side. She'd worn a silk halter dress that had shim-
mered in the light of a hundred torches. Flowers had
adorned her head. She'd worn no shoes.

Richard had held her hand as they'd stood before the
minister. His hand had been cold and she knew he was
nervous. She'd been charmed that such a sophisticated
man could be nervous. He'd sworn that they'd be together forever.

Forever.

The word haunted her now.

They'd been married less than six months when the
problems started. She'd been late coming home one
night because she'd spent extra time in the darkroom,
burning and edging the print of a mother and child
until it was perfect. When she'd left the studio, she'd felt
so proud of the work. She was finding her voice as an
artist. And commercially, she was on the brink of something big in her career.

When she'd arrived home, Richard had accused her
of seeing someone else. The idea was so ridiculous, she'd
laughed. His temper had snapped. He'd called her a
whore. A cunt. He'd said he despised the sight of her.

The words had cut through her like knives. She'd
started to cry.

Instantly contrite, Richard had begged for her forgiveness and poured her a snifter of brandy to settle her
nerves. He'd sworn he'd never lose his temper again.

Stunned and shaken, she'd allowed him to hug her.
And God help her, she'd clung to him.

Each day for the next month, he'd sent her flowers:
large and lavish displays of roses, tulips, rare orchids.

Slowly, she'd dropped her guard. She'd believed his words of love.

But as her success grew so did Richard's resentment. He didn't like the demands her work made on her time. And like a fool, she'd confused his need to control with love. And so she had tried to appease him. She'd downplayed her successes and awards. And when that didn't work, she'd cut back her hours. Seen her friends less so she could be with him more. Each time she gave up a piece of herself, he seemed to be mollified. But he was never content for long. She realized she could never sacrifice enough to make him truly happy.

Nicole began to despise her marriage. Increasingly, she'd felt trapped. Angry. Alone. She'd even gone to a local community center to hear a woman, Claire Carmichael, speak about abuse. But at the time, Nicole just couldn't believe that her marriage was that bad.

Then, almost three weeks ago, Richard had lost his temper because he'd not liked the dress she'd chosen. It had looked cheap to him and in his eyes a poor reflection of his standing.

She'd tried to explain it was the latest fashion. But she had been silenced by the anger and venom that had erupted from him. He'd beaten her so badly that she couldn't leave the house for days. He'd told her if she ever tried to leave him, he'd kill her. With great relish, he'd spoken of drugs that could keep her alive for days as he'd slice away at her flesh with a knife.

She'd been terrified, knowing he would do exactly what he'd threatened to do.

Confident that he'd totally trampled her spirits, he'd given her a lavish display of roses and then left their San Francisco home for an overnight business trip to New York.

Nicole had known, as she'd stared at the roses, that if

she didn't get out, he would eventually beat her to death. The next flowers she'd receive would be placed on her grave.

Her body still aching, she'd packed what clothes could fit in a large purse. She couldn't leave their home without his driver, Jimmy, who was always there watching. Donning dark sunglasses, she had asked Jimmy to take her across town and drop her near the waterfront. She had vanished into a restaurant bathroom and climbed out the window.

Near the restaurant was Claire Carmichael's small New Age bookstore. She'd raced to Claire's and told her she needed to be hidden. Claire had remembered her and offered her a bed at the local shelter. Nicole had known she had to get farther away from San Francisco than a local shelter. So, Claire had given Nicole $200 cash and the keys to a beat-up Honda. In gratitude, she had given Claire her wedding bands and told her to hawk them.

Grateful and terrified, she'd headed east, not sure at first where she was going. In Denver, she had bought a hat and tucked her hair up inside it. She also had calmed enough to sit and think where she'd go next. She had remembered Lindsay. They had been roommates at the University of Southern California but had lost touch over the years. Nicole had remembered a notation in the USC alumni magazine. Lindsay had returned to her native Virginia. She worked with battered women.

So, Nicole had called information from a pay phone and gotten the number of the abuse hotline in Lindsay's area. She'd begged the counselor to find Lindsay and have her call Nicole at the pay phone. The counselor hadn't made any promises, but five minutes later the pay phone had rung. It was Lindsay.

Lindsay hadn't hesitated. She'd given Nicole directions to her house, and when she'd arrived two days later, Lindsay had opened up her home to Nicole.

Sunlight peeked around the edges of the shaded kitchen window. Nicole set her soda can on the counter and opened the blinds. Afternoon light made her squint, but the sun warmed her face. The rain had stopped.

Men like Richard didn't have the right to walk this earth. They stole dreams and lives. They nurtured humiliation and fear. They all deserved to die.

Somewhere along the way, she'd lost herself. But she'd corrected the mistake. She was in control now.

San Francisco, 1:00 P.M. PST (4:00 P.M. EST)

Jimmy Quinn had endured a lot of pain during his career in the boxing ring, weathering split lips, broken bones, and bruised knots the size of goose eggs. Long after a damaged right hand had forced him from the ring, the boys on the street respectfully called him Iron Jim, because he could take a licking better than anyone. He was the toughest of the tough.

However, never during his sixty-four years had he ever, *ever*, hurt so bad that he wanted to die.

Now, the pain ravaging his body made him wish he were dead.

Someone splashed ice water on his face and his head snapped up. But he couldn't see so well. Both his eyes were swollen shut.

"One last time, Jimmy. Where is Christina Braxton?" The calm, even voice came from the shadows. Jimmy couldn't see the speaker's face anymore, but he knew it was Vincent Malone.

"I don't know," Jimmy whispered.

He tried to flex his swollen fingers, now numb from the too-tight ropes that secured his hands behind his back. Blood caked his well-lined face and stained the white button-down shirt he'd pressed himself this morning. Or was it yesterday? The beatings had robbed him of any sense of time.

His last clear memory was of entering the waterfront warehouse to meet his former boss, Richard Braxton. Only, Mr. Braxton hadn't been there. His right-hand man, Vincent, and a couple of his goons had been waiting for him. There'd been no conversation as the goons had strapped him to a chair. To set the tone, Vincent had taken a billy club and smacked it hard against Jimmy's knuckles. And then the questions about Mrs. Braxton had started.

"Don't make me hurt you, Jimmy. I don't like hurting you," Vincent had said.

"I don't know where she is. I ain't seen her in two weeks." Pain had burned every muscle in Jimmy's body.

Jimmy didn't want to give Vincent Mrs. B. He had liked her from the moment he'd first laid eyes on her. Pretty didn't come near to describing her. She was a stunner. And Mrs. B. was a kind soul. She'd treated him with respect from the get-go, always calling him "*Mr.*" Quinn. No one had called him "*Mr.*" anything in his entire life.

This past year Mrs. B. had been his responsibility. It was his job to drive her where she wanted to go, wait for her until she finished whatever it was she was doing, and then take her home. And it was his job to report to Mr. Braxton every move she made. The boss wanted to know everything his wife did, who she saw and even what she read.

Jimmy hadn't been proud of the work but he'd done his job, figuring it didn't hurt anybody. Who was he to say what went on between a man and his wife?

Two months ago, everything had changed. Mrs. B had gotten into the black Lexus wearing a vicious shiner. She'd said it was an accident. He'd accepted the excuse, because he liked the pay his job brought in and didn't want any trouble. But more bruises followed. He wasn't so punch drunk or stupid to see what was happening. Braxton had started to beat his wife.

Jimmy had begun to hate Mr. Braxton.

Through it all, Mrs. B. had been nice to him, always calling him Mr. Quinn. But he could see the light in her eyes was fading, bit by bit. He'd have quit the job, but Mrs. B. needed him and he needed the money.

"Remember the last time you saw her, Jimmy? You dropped her off somewhere. Where was it?" Vincent now leaned close to his ear. "Tell me, Jimmy, and I'll make the pain stop. She isn't worth this kind of trouble. She's a lying whore."

Rough hands shoved his head back against the chair. A sharp blade pressed against his cheek. It cut into the tender flesh under his eye.

Jimmy screamed. Blood streamed down his face.

"Next come the eyes, Jimmy."

"I dropped her near the water at a restaurant." He gave the address. "I think she slipped out the bathroom window."

"Where'd she go?"

The blade slid over his eyelid. "The restaurant owner said north."

"Did you see anyone else? Did she meet another man?" He jabbed his thumb into the fresh cut under Jimmy's eye.

Jimmy screamed. "I didn't see no one, I swear."

"That's all?"

Jimmy figured he'd burn in hell for what he was about to say. But what could Satan do to him that Mr. Braxton hadn't already done? "He hurt her. Made her cry. She had bruises on her face."

"I believe you, Jimmy." The voice he heard now was Richard Braxton's. Terror flooded his broken body. He tried to open his eyes but couldn't. God, but he hurt. "You got to believe me, Mr. B. I didn't know she was planning to run."

He heard a cigarette lighter snap open, then smelled the scent of a freshly lit cigarette. Braxton liked his smokes when he was tense. "You shouldn't have let her get away."

"I know."

The tip of a gun pressed against his temple and fired.

Chapter Nine

The law offices of Turner and Barlow were located in a suburban office park twenty miles west of Richmond. The five-story building had a shiny, reflective exterior and was nestled next to a large lake surrounded by pristine park benches and tree-lined jog paths. Tall front doors led to a foyer capped with skylights that magnified sunlight down on polished black marble floors.

Zack and Warwick checked the business directory posted on the wall and rode the elevator to the fifth floor. The elevator door dinged opened to muffled shouts. It was impossible to make out what was being said, but the tone was unmistakably angry.

Wordlessly, the detectives bypassed the stunned receptionist and cut around the maze of cubicles toward the corner office on the building's south side. The name on the office door read Quinton Barlow.

"I want to see my damn attorney! Where is he?!" the male voice thundered behind the wood paneled door.

Zack hesitated. "That sounds like Ronnie T."

Warwick nodded. "He's either one damn good liar or he doesn't know what happened to Harold."

"My money's on one damn good liar."

Ronnie T. had built a drug empire that stretched up and down the I-95 corridor. He'd evaded arrest on drug-trafficking charges; however, thanks to Zack's under-cover work, the Feds had been able to make a case for income tax evasion.

Without announcing himself, Zack opened the door and strolled into the plush office. "I thought I heard a familiar voice."

Warwick was a step behind him. "What's got everyone so upset?"

Ronnie T. stood in front of Quinton Barlow's desk, his right hand clenching an ornate walking stick that coor-dinated with his white jumpsuit and custom Nikes. He sported a ball cap cocked at a jaunty angle and wore a thick gold chain worth more than most cops made in a year.

Across the desk, a composed Quinton Barlow faced him. Short and pudgy, he wore a white monogrammed dress shirt, red silk tie, and dark suit pants. Barlow had been practicing criminal defense law for thirty-plus years. Dealing with men like Ronnie T. was standard.

Barlow met Zack's gaze and smiled pleasantly. "Gen-tlemen, what can we do for you?"

Ronnie T.'s eyes narrowed before he smiled at Zack. "Five-O. Shit. Before you ask, I ain't done nothing wrong. My hearing was canceled this morning, because my damn attorney didn't show. I was just asking Quinton here where the hell Harold is hiding."

Zack pulled a slim notebook and pen out of his pocket. "So where is Harold?"

Ronnie T. flashed a signature grin even as his grip tightened on his cane. "Quinton isn't telling."

"Ronnie only just burst into my office," Barlow said.

Zack raised an eyebrow and looked at Barlow, unsure of what he really knew about his law partner. "Do you know where your partner is?"

Barlow didn't flinch. "I've spoken to Jordan. She told me about your visit."

"She didn't waste any time," Zack said.

"She understands even the innocent need an attorney when dealing with the police," Quinton said.

Ronnie T. leaned on his cane. "Someone mind filling me in on what's what?"

Zack studied Barlow's guarded expression before he shifted his gaze back to the dealer. "Harold's body was found this morning behind Sanctuary Women's Shelter. He was shot point-blank in the chest."

Ronnie T.'s eyes widened and his mouth dropped open. "Shit."

Zack wasn't fooled by Ronnie's surprise. "When's the last time you saw your counselor?"

Barlow cleared his throat. "Don't answer any of their questions."

Ronnie T. shrugged. "I don't mind answering, Quinton. I ain't got nothing to hide. I saw Harold yesterday after court."

"Word is you two fought," Zack said. "Fact, I hear it was nearly a knock-down, drag-out fight in the courthouse."

"Ronnie," Barlow warned, "keep your mouth shut."

Ronnie T. waved Barlow off. "Yeah, we mixed it up. He wanted me to take a plea agreement. I told him I was paying him the big bucks to keep me out of jail. The deal was no time spent behind bars."

"What time was that?" Warwick said.

"About three."

"Do you know where Turner was headed?" Zack said.

"Said something about dinner with his old lady."

"And where were you last night, Ronnie T.?" Zack said.

Ronnie T.'s full lips split into a wide grin. "I was at a swim meet. My kid was swimming the butterfly for the first time at the community pool. He's on the Mite team. And he won his heat."

"I'm assuming you have witnesses," Warwick said.

"I do." Ronnie T. sounded amused. "They are some of Richmond's finest—all white folks. I can give you a list of names."

Zack flipped to a clean page in his notebook. "Let's have them."

Ronnie T. rattled off a half dozen names. He looked pleased with himself. Whatever had gone down last night, Ronnie T. had made certain that he was in a very public place.

Barlow picked up a letter printed on the firm's stationary. "I too have an alibi. In this letter is the name and phone number of the manager of my country club. He can verify my alibi for last night. You'll also find Mrs. Turner's alibi contacts on that sheet."

"Can those witnesses vouch for where she might have been at four or five this morning?" Warwick asked.

"As a matter of fact one can vouch for her at that time. Her sister and she were talking on the phone between three A.M. and six A.M. Her sister lives in Australia. There is also a maid who lives in the house who says she heard the women talking until almost five."

Zack took the paper but didn't bother to read it. He'd call all the names on both lists but already knew each contact would verify the stories he'd been given.

Warwick picked up an engraved crystal paperweight off of Barlow's desk. He tossed it between his hands. "How was the Turner marriage overall? Happy? Tense?"

"I wasn't privy to their personal life until just minutes ago," Barlow said, frowning at the paperweight in Warwick's hand. "However, Jordan did tell me that she confided the details of her troubled marriage to Lindsay O'Neil two weeks ago. Jordan said Ms. O'Neil was quite angry and upset when Jordan refused to leave her husband."

Zack bit back an oath. Lindsay had been holding out on him. "Why would Mrs. Turner share that bit of information?"

"She said Harold's body was found behind Sanctuary, which, if I'm not mistaken, is the shelter your wife oversees."

What kind of angle was Jordan Turner working?

"Did O'Neil and Jordan Turner have any other contact after that meeting?" Warwick said.

The question was necessary but nevertheless annoyed Zack.

Barlow shook his head. "Mrs. Turner said that Ms. O'Neil called her this afternoon."

Zack swallowed another oath. "And they talked about?"

"Mrs. Turner was concerned that Ms. O'Neil had killed Harold," Barlow said.

"Did she have proof?" Zack asked.

"No."

Amused, Ronnie T. raised a finger. "What a minute. Lindsay O'Neil was your wife, wasn't she, Detective Kier?"

Zack's jaw tightened. "She still is."

Ronnie T. cackled. "I thought she divorced your sorry ass a year ago."

Warwick set the paperweight down, stepping between the two men. "We'll want to interview Mrs. Turner again."

Barlow moved the paperweight out of Warwick's reach. "We'll be happy to help in the investigation in any way."

"I'd be happy to ask my associates if anyone hated ole Harold enough to kill him," Ronnie T. offered.

"The last thing I want is your help," Zack said. The dealer's favors always had strings attached.

Ronnie T.'s smile didn't fade but his eyes hardened. "Is my help too good for you now that you're sober, Detective Kier?"

Zack got right in Ronnie T.'s face. "Stay out of the investigation."

Ronnie T. laughed. "But I want to help."

Warwick nudged Zack. Zack reined in his temper and backed up. "Neither of you leave town."

When Barlow and Ronnie T. both agreed, the two cops walked out of the office. Zack pushed the elevator button. His temper seethed. The doors opened. They got in. Neither spoke until they were outside by the car.

Warwick glared up at the building. "Ronnie T. really pisses you off."

"I crossed paths with him during several narcotics investigations. That million-dollar smile hides a ruthless heart." He'd tried several times to supply Zack with drugs. Once after Lindsay had moved out, he'd been tempted, but he'd refused, as always.

Zack's cell vibrated. He checked the number. Ayden. He flipped open his phone. "Kier."

"Get over to Sanctuary." Ayden's sharp voice jumped through the phone. "Someone delivered Harold Turner's hand to Lindsay."

The police had ordered Lindsay into the shelter's family room across the hallway from her office. She'd been told to wait for the detectives. She sat on the couch, her arms folded and her stomach knotted. She tapped her foot, believing she was going to jump out of her skin.

A half dozen uniformed officers had taken over Sanctuary. One was posted outside Lindsay's office, two on the front porch, and three in the kitchen. They spoke in hushed tones laced with nervous excitement.

With each flash of a camera bulb, she knew Sara, the forensic tech, was in her office shooting pictures, no doubt from every conceivable angle, of the hand and the boxed flowers. Lindsay lost count how many times the digital camera had flashed.

News vans now from all three local television stations were parked out front. She noticed that Kendall Shaw was talking with her cameraman. A frown furrowed the tall brunette's brow as she jabbed her finger in the air. Kendall was angry that there was no film of Lindsay running hysterically out of the shelter toward the unmarked police car. Too bad for Kendall, Lindsay thought bitterly. That bit of film would have made great news.

This day was churning memories that she'd thought were long buried. Running out of the shelter today reminded her of a similar July day twelve years ago when she'd found her mother. She'd bolted from the house. Screaming, she'd run a half mile to the neighbor's house and pounded on the door until a befuddled Mr. Jenkins had answered. Words had rushed from her mouth. Most had been unintelligible. And she'd nearly hyperventilated. But her neighbor had pieced together enough, figured out what had happened, and called the sheriff. She never went back in her parents' house again.

Lindsay shoved a trembling hand through her hair. Rising from the couch, she moved to the window. She'd been almost as rattled today.

Jesus. Someone had sent her a severed hand.

Ruby came around the corner from the kitchen with a cold soda. She pushed the can into Lindsay's hand. "Why don't you come into the kitchen so I can make you something to eat? I've got turkey and bread."

Food was the last thing on Lindsay's mind. "No thanks, Ruby."

"Milk shakes don't cut it, honey. You're going to get sick. I should make you a turkey sandwich."

Lindsay's argument died on her lips when she saw concern in the older woman's eyes. She knew Ruby wasn't so worried about food, but the entire situation. She needed something to do. "You know what, turkey sounds great to me. Extra mustard?"

Ruby nodded. She was obviously relieved. "I'll have it for you in two shakes. Now, come away from the window and sit down."

"We're going to have to move the shelter," Lindsay said. "I thought this morning that maybe, just maybe, we could dig our way out of this, but not now. The press aren't going to sit on our location much longer."

Ruby planted meaty fists on her wide hips. "Don't borrow trouble, Lindsay. Let's just take it one step at a time."

"We don't have the cash reserves for a move. And Dana is going to be furious." She closed her eyes and pictured her boss's tight angular face. She sensed an invisible tide had turned against her.

Ruby laid a hand on Lindsay's shoulder. "Honey, you're good at what you do. The board knows that. You'll find a way out of this."

One way or another, she would fight for this shelter. But she'd been in enough uphill battles to recognize one. "Thanks for the vote of confidence, but in the meantime, you'd better see if you can pick up extra hours at your other job. I know we've never been able to pay you much, but we may not have much to offer for the near future."

Ruby had a teenage daughter to support. "I hate leaving you."

She didn't want Ruby to worry. "I'm going to be fine."

Frown lines formed around her mouth. "I'll be back as soon as you can have me."

Lindsay squeezed her hand. "I know."

Tears in her eyes, Ruby disappeared into the kitchen as the front door opened.

Zack strode in the foyer, his stern expression sweeping clockwise until it landed on Lindsay. Behind him stood a tall, grim-faced man dressed in jeans and a T-shirt. Even if he'd not been wearing his badge on a chain around his neck, she'd have guessed by his demeanor he was also a cop.

Zack made no move toward Lindsay but stared at her long and hard before he released a deep breath. "Are you all right?"

Unexpected relief flooded Lindsay's body. She wanted to rush to him, let him take her in his arms and assure her everything would be okay. But she didn't run to Zack. She stood her ground, her back stiffer than wood.

"I'm great. Never a dull moment, is there?" She tried to sound glib but instead sounded brittle. So be it.

Zack was deadly serious. "You look pale."

"I'm fine." She put steel behind the words, knowing if he showed her any pity she'd break. "Just figure out who sent me that little present in there and I'll be even better."

His expression reflected his disbelief. He knew stress made her bitchy. Knew this shelter meant everything to her. Knew about her mother's death. Knew *her.*

Tension knotted her lower back. She folded her arms over her chest. This was not the time to have unwanted feelings rolling to the surface.

Zack cleared his throat. "This is my partner, Detective Jacob Warwick. This is Lindsay O'Neil. She's the director of the shelter."

Warwick nodded. "Ma'am."

Lindsay prided herself on reading people, on being

able to size up anyone in a nanosecond. But this guy was a blank slate. Tight, controlled, he reminded her of Zack during his undercover days when life and death depended on cloaking emotions.

"I'll bet you worked undercover at one point," Lindsay said.

Warwick didn't seem to appreciate her hard tone. "That's right. That a problem?"

Shrugging, she feigned disinterest. "Nope. I can just spot you guys a mile off."

"Tell us what happened," Zack interjected.

Lindsay drew in a deep breath. "I had just returned from taking the last of my residents to the Riverside shelter and was headed into my office. Ruby told me someone had sent me flowers. I opened the box and saw the irises."

If Zack had remembered that he'd once sent her irises he gave no indication. "And?"

"And I picked up the flowers. That's when I saw the second package. I opened it and saw the hand. I dropped the package. I ran straight to the police car outside." No need to mention her scream could have shattered glass.

"Do you know who might have sent the flowers to you?" Warwick said.

"If I had an idea I would have shared it with the other six officers who asked me the same question in the last fifteen minutes."

Warwick let his doubt show. "Would you have told the police?"

The challenge caught her off guard and irritated her. She stepped forward. "Yes, I would have. Do you think that this is fun or that I want this kind of drama in my life?"

"That's a good question," Warwick said.

"What about Jordan Turner?" Zack countered.

Her defenses rose. "What about her?"

"Harold Turner was smacking her around. Not only did she run into you at that charity fund-raiser, but apparently you two had a long conversation about Harold's abuse at the party. And you called her today."

"I'm not about to apologize for doing my job. I consider her a client. Our conversations were—are—privileged."

"Not legally," Zack said.

She raised her chin. "Morally."

"Do you think she could have done this?" Warwick asked.

She shifted her gaze from Zack to Warwick. "No."

"But you thought she could have killed her husband," Zack said. "That's why you didn't share the details about your conversation with her two weeks ago. It's why you called her this morning."

No sense denying what Zack already knew. "I wasn't sure what she'd done at first." She sighed. "When I realized it was Harold, I was afraid she'd snapped. But after seeing the hand, I know she didn't do it."

Zack's eyes narrowed. "Why do you say that?"

"Because cutting off Harold's hand was some kind of public declaration. The killer is making some kind of statement."

"And Jordan wouldn't do that?" Warwick said.

"She wouldn't. Above all else, Jordan Turner is a very private woman. Appearances are important and this kind of drama is not her style. She'd find it tacky, for lack of a better word."

Neither cop looked convinced.

"Unless she thinks we'll never catch her," Zack said.

Zack knew Lindsay put her heart and soul into her work. It didn't make sense that she'd trash it all. But he'd come across crimes before that made little or no sense.

He and Warwick walked into Lindsay's cramped office, made more claustrophobic by Sara as she snapped pictures of the scene with her digital camera.

Sara glanced up at them and smiled at Zack. "So we meet again."

Stoic, Zack pulled out his notebook. "Yeah."

She raised the camera to hide her frown.

"What do you have?" Zack asked.

"I've rolled prints from the flower box but have yet to run them through AFIS." AFIS, the Automated Fingerprint Identification System, would compare crime scene fingerprints with millions of others across the country in hours. If the murderer was in the system, they'd find him.

"Anything else?" Warwick said.

"No hair fibers so far, but I've yet to take the hand out of the bag. I'll do that when I get back to the lab."

Zack glanced at the note, now sealed in a plastic evidence bag. He picked it up, holding the bag by the corner. The bold script was large and covered most of the white card with embossed edges.

"*Lindsay, you are not alone anymore,*" he read. Zack handed the note to Warwick.

Warwick glanced at the note and then at Zack. "Who the hell is the Guardian?"

"I have no idea. Lindsay comes in contact with hundreds of different people in a week. Some are pretty rough characters." Zack had never liked the idea of her dealing with thugs. In his mind, she took too many chances. "And then there was that damn newspaper article in May. How many thousands read it?"

"I'm going to need Lindsay's fingerprints," Sara said.

As a husband, Zack wanted to defend his wife and tell everyone she was no killer. As a cop he couldn't rule anyone out as a suspect at this stage of the investigation.

"She had a police background check when she applied for this job. Her prints are on file."

She nodded. "I'll pull them."

Warwick studied the hand positioned neatly in the box. "He wrapped the hand in a plastic bag. That explains why we didn't have a trail of blood leading from the crime scene."

"He's meticulous," Zack said. "The crime scene this morning suggested he's an organized killer."

Warwick stared at the hand's bloated fingers with blackening nail beds. "Why the left hand?"

Zack didn't like the scenario forming in his head. "Turner's wedding band is still on his ring finger. Mrs. Turner was abused. The left hand is supposedly the one that leads to your heart. I'd bet it's symbolic in some way."

"The killer doesn't like abusive husbands," Warwick said.

"Maybe. Or maybe Ronnie T. killed his attorney and set all this up to throw us off the trail. Ronnie T. also knows Lindsay is my wife."

Warwick nodded. "Why go after you?"

"Payback. When I worked narcotics, I put one hell of a dent in his operation."

"Ronnie T. is smart and dangerous, but I don't see him going to this kind of trouble. Like I said, a drive-by is more his style."

"Maybe. But for now it's a theory we've got to consider."

Zack left Warwick and returned to Lindsay, who stood in the family room by the French doors that faced out back. Yellow crime scene tape, pelted by the rain, drooped in mud puddles.

"Who is the Guardian?" Zack said. He watched closely for any reaction.

She looked puzzled. "I don't know."

"Why would he write you a note?"

She hugged her arms around her. "I've no idea."

"Have you received any unusual phone calls lately, notes, contributions, anything out of the ordinary?"

"Nothing that jumps to mind. That May article generated several donations."

Zack could have pressed Lindsay about sharing her case files, but he didn't. He was going to wait for the warrant. The delivery of Harold's hand had officially bumped this case to high priority. From here on out, each step of the investigation could have huge ramifications, so he'd do everything by the book.

Lindsay flexed her fingers as if trying to release the tension knotting her muscles. "I have a grant application due in three days. Can I at least grab that file so I can work at home?"

Stress always did send her running in to work. "Nothing leaves the office for now."

She stabbed long fingers through her hair. "The grant has nothing to do with this. But it means everything to the shelter."

Despite it all, she was still trying to hold on to this place. "It's in the office so it stays."

A helpless sigh shuddered from her. "What about my purse?"

"Nothing leaves the office."

"I need my car keys."

"I'll drive you," Zack said.

"I'm supposed to speak to a local church group tonight."

"Cancel it."

She took a step back. "No, thanks."

"Lindsay, there's a guy running around town who's left a dead body in your backyard and sent you a severed hand. It's not safe for you."

She stiffened. "Bullies don't scare me."

But he saw fear in her eyes. "This one should."

"Is it my safety that you're so worried about or are you afraid I'll skip town because I'm the killer?"

She was going for the jugular, trying to throw him off balance. Two could play that game. "Honestly, I can't rule you out yet."

Her mouth dropped open. "You're kidding."

"I'm not. You have motive and no alibi."

"I didn't do it."

"Prove it."

She paled and turned away.

Satisfied he had the last word for now, Zack left and found Warwick talking to Ruby in the kitchen. The older woman was smiling and stared up at Warwick with a twinkle in her eye. Damn, what had he said to soften her up? When Zack entered the room, Ruby's smile vanished.

Ruby's simmering resentment suggested she knew about his and Lindsay's separation.

"I'm going to run Ms. O'Neil home." Zack had made a statement, not a request.

Warwick's eyes narrowed. "I'll ride along."

"Suit yourself."

"She doesn't need you," Ruby said. "She can drive herself just fine."

Zack dug his keys out of his pocket. "Not with her car keys sealed in a crime scene."

"I'll take her," Ruby said. "She's got enough stress right now without you adding to it."

The older woman had painted him as the bad guy in the marriage. And truthfully, she wasn't off base. "Thanks, but I've got it covered."

Ruby frowned but wasn't in a position to argue.

Zack found Lindsay by the front door. "Do you have spare keys to your house?"

"Yes. Hidden under a pot by the front door."

He'd lectured her enough about safety when they'd been married. He'd always feared his undercover work would spill into his personal life and put her in danger. "That's not too safe."

Her face colored as if she remembered what he'd said. "It's handy."

As soon as they emerged from the house, the reporters who'd been on the front lawn lunged toward them. Zack shielded her from the cameras and hustled her to his car while Warwick ran interference with the press. Zack opened the backseat side door. She was half inside the car when Kendall darted around Warwick and caught up to them.

The reporter shoved a microphone toward Lindsay's face. "Lindsay, can you tell me why you were so upset earlier? Why did the police return? Has someone else been killed?"

Zack waited until Lindsay was fully inside before he closed the car door. "No statements now, Ms. Shaw."

Kendall looked annoyed. "I'm just trying to do my job, detective. Lindsay, tell me what happened."

Warwick moved beside Kendall, using height and size to intimidate her. "Talk to the department's public relations guy."

Kendall didn't look threatened, but annoyed. "When I'm interested in the party line, I will. Right now I'm looking for real answers."

Warwick frowned. Clearly he didn't like the woman. "No comment." He slid in the front passenger seat.

Cameras rolled as Zack got behind the wheel and started the car. In silence, they drove through the neighborhood to the main road.

Lindsay stared out the window. From the rearview mirror, Zack could see her jaw was tight and her body tense. She needed a friend right now.

But Zack couldn't be that for her. Not if he was going to figure out who killed Turner and who now harbored an obsession for her. He merged onto the interstate.

"Tell me about that charity function and the Turners again," Zack said.

She fidgeted with the bracelets on her wrist. "Like I said, I didn't kill Harold. And neither did Jordan."

Warwick stared out the side window as if he were a million miles away, but he wasn't missing a syllable.

Zack couldn't let her off the hook. "There's no need to protect Jordan. She's got an attorney and an alibi for the time her husband was killed."

Her lips flattened. "Like I said, I met them at a charity function two weeks ago. Jordan was on Harold's arm, smiling radiantly. They looked like the perfect couple." She hesitated. "I should have known then that something was up."

"Why?"

"No such thing as a perfect couple." She sighed and recapped the encounter with Jordan. "A half hour later, Harold approached me at the party. He told me to stay away from Jordan. I told him to stop hitting his wife. We got into a big fight. Then I left the party."

"Witnesses?"

"No doubt. I noticed several people were staring, but I couldn't tell you who."

Zack tightened his hands on the wheel. "That's it? You never saw Harold again? You never communicated with him?"

Disgust darkened her face. "Not Harold. But I did call Jordan several times. I hoped I could help her. And I did call her this morning after I saw you."

"To tell her about Harold?"

She hesitated. "To try to figure out if she'd crossed the line." She dug fingers through her hair. "The last time I talked to Jordan, she told me not to worry about Harold. She said she could take care of him."

"And you figured that meant murder."

"Not at the time. A lot of women believe they can handle their abusive husbands. They think that if they always smile, that if the house is immaculate and sex is always available, everything will be fine. But no matter what they do, it's never enough. Sooner or later the guy snaps again and hits her."

They'd only talked about her mother's death once. As a husband he'd let his unanswered questions lie. As a cop he couldn't. "Did your mother think she could handle your father?"

Lindsay flinched, glancing to Warwick. He met her gaze in the rearview mirror. It was one thing for Zack to know about her past; quite another for Warwick. Humiliation washed over her.

"My mother has nothing to do with Harold Turner's murder."

Zack didn't enjoy opening a painful wound. He'd always avoided discussing the subject with her because he knew it bothered her. "Your family life was beyond rough, Lindsay. That changes a person."

Warwick glanced in the rearview mirror at her, as if trying to peer into her mind.

Lindsay lifted her chin. "I went into social work and opened Sanctuary because of Mom. I didn't become a murderer because of her."

Zack shot her a glance in the rearview mirror. "The Commonwealth's attorney could argue that because you couldn't have it out with your old man, you picked the next best target—Harold."

"That's crap. Remember the killer sent *me* Harold's hand."

"You could have sent it to yourself," Warwick said.

She leaned forward, fingers gripping the seat. "And written myself a creepy note?"

Warwick turned toward her. "You wouldn't be the first to try something like that."

"I can't believe we are having this conversation." Her voice sounded loud, angry.

Warwick kept his tone even, calm, but the menace was unmistakable. "Whoever killed Harold did it in anger. He *cut off* Harold's left hand. If that isn't a statement about shattered vows, I don't know what is."

"I didn't kill him."

"You don't have an alibi," Zack said.

"I can't help that. It's not my fault the damn power went out." Arms folded, she dropped back in the seat and turned toward the window. She swiped away a tear.

The only time Zack had seen her cry had been that day in the attorney's office. Tension twisted his gut.

Five minutes later, they reached her town house development. Well-manicured lawns jutted out from near identical row houses that looked as if they'd been stamped from cookie cutters. This kind of development was very un-Lindsay. She'd always leaned more toward the older, quirky homes that needed more attention than a full-time job. Why had she chosen such a place? Zack kept his question to himself as he parked in the numbered spot she directed him to. A sprinkler system whooshed in the background and a dog barked.

"Thanks," she said ironically, opening her car door. She walked to the planter, tipped it back, and retrieved the front door key.

Following, Zack didn't bother to hide the frustration in his voice. "From now on, don't hide the key there."

Lindsay shoved the key in the lock. "I can take care of myself."

He flashed a smile that looked more like a snarl. "Humor me."

A flicker of movement caught his eye. A man dressed in a green maintenance uniform moved toward them. Blond, pudgy, and short, he was smiling as he held hedge clippers in his hand.

Zack moved his right hand to his belt closer to the .22 holstered on his hip.

Warwick got out of the car and leaned against it. His demeanor stated he was ready to intervene if necessary.

"Lindsay," the maintenance man said. "What are you doing home in the middle of the day?"

Zack and Warwick watched the man very closely.

Lindsay seemed to relax around him. "Hey, Steve. How's it going?"

Steve glanced at Zack and Warwick. His eyes narrowed. "You friends of Lindsay's?"

Ole Steve seemed a little territorial when it came to Lindsay. "Detective Zack Kier," Zack said as he flipped open his wallet and showed his police badge. "This is my partner, Detective Warwick."

"Steve Hess. I manage this property. Everything all right?"

Zack watched Lindsay smile at Steve. She had resented his interference about the key but seemed to appreciate Steve's protective tone.

"It's fine, thanks," she said. "Did you want to tell me something?"

Steve was distracted by Zack and Warwick's presence. "Oh, I was just headed into your place to check the AC unit. You said it wasn't working well."

"Did I?"

"You put in a maintenance request about three weeks ago."

She smiled. "Right. Thanks. Do you mind if we do this another time?"

"No problem. Oh, and the cable guy came by to check on your television. Your reception is all cleared up."

"Thanks," she said.

Steve's gaze flickered between the cops. "Why the police escort home?"

Lindsay unlocked her front door. "There was a little trouble at work today. It's nothing to be worried about. Detective Kier is just being extra careful."

Steve's smile turned brittle. He didn't seem to like cops. "Tax dollars at work."

"Something like that," Zack said. "Can you tell me anything about the power outage this morning?"

Steve rubbed the back of his neck with his hand. "It was a real mess. The whole east side of the development was out from about midnight last night to eight this morning."

At least Lindsay hadn't been lying about that. "What happened?"

"Transformer blew late. It took Virginia Power until this morning to get it up and running."

"Does that happen often?"

"Been fifteen years since the last transformer blew and that was in an electrical storm," Steve said. "Must have been some freak power surge."

An outage caused Lindsay to be late to work. Across town Harold was murdered. The two incidents weren't necessarily related, but that didn't mean they weren't.

Zack glanced back at Warwick, still positioned by the car. "I'll be back in a minute."

Warwick pushed away from the car. "No rush. I have a few more questions for Steve."

Zack left the nervous maintenance man with Warwick and followed Lindsay inside her town house. She flipped the lights on. The ticktock of clocks jived with the hum of the AC unit.

He saw far enough into the town house to see a floral couch. The pillows on the couch were straight and neatly fluffed. If the outside was cookie cutter the inside was vintage Lindsay. The clocks, the restored second-hand furniture, and the stacks of books were all her. The place smelled of linseed oil, which, he remembered, she used to dust her furniture.

Standing this close, he caught the soft scent of her soap. He'd forgotten how good she smelled.

Lindsay lifted her gaze and for a moment a connection sparked between them. She sensed it as much as he did. He leaned forward, testing. She drew back.

"Mind if I have a look around?" he said.

She blocked his path. "As a matter of fact I do."

"Why?"

"I don't want you here."

His gaze narrowed. "What are you hiding?"

"Nothing."

He took a step back. "You're hiding something. And I'll figure out what it is."

Chapter Ten

Lindsay was fighting a headache when she arrived at the church just before six. Without car keys, she'd had to borrow a car from her neighbor. The gal had been a little reluctant at first, but Lindsay had promised to drive carefully and have the car back by nine.

She'd considered canceling this speaking engagement to the church's group. Despite the extra sleep last night, she felt wrung out and exhausted after the day she'd had. But Nicole was at work and the idea of staying home alone didn't sit well.

Besides, this church's pastor was one of the shelter's best supporters. He had called her after the *Inside Richmond* article and offered his congregation's support. For several months since then, there'd been a stream of clothes, some money, and food donations.

She didn't want to let him down tonight. So, she made a double espresso and pushed through the fatigue.

The Methodist church was located on Shady Grove Road in an affluent tree-lined section of the city. The church had been constructed less than five years ago. It had a tall A-line roof and tall windows that let the sun shine in. The church also had an education building that was joined to the church by an arched breezeway. This building had a more streamlined look and was suited strictly for function, not worship.

The day's heat hadn't cooled much and the sun was still bright. The large gravel parking lot was nearly deserted. There were only a half dozen cars, including the one that filled the *pastor*'s slot. It looked as if it was going to be a low turnout tonight. Not surprising. Low turnouts weren't uncommon. Few wanted to give up their evening to hear about grim domestic violence stats.

Lindsay grabbed her laptop with her PowerPoint presentation and made her way to the education building. She opened the side door and started down the long red-carpeted hallway to the minister's office.

Halfway down the hall, a man came out of a side parlor. He was tall and thin with dark thinning hair. He looked to be about fifty and was dressed in a golf shirt and khaki pants. He had a "father knows best" way about him that made you glad he was in charge.

He noticed her immediately and smiled warmly. "Ms. O'Neil?"

Lindsay nodded. "Pastor Richards."

"How are you doing?"

The evening news hadn't hit yet so he didn't know about the murder. "Great," she said. She didn't want to discuss the murders. After the evening news, she'd be answering a lot of uncomfortable questions.

Pastor Richards moved toward her and shook her hand. He had an extension cord in the other hand. "Thank you for coming out this evening."

"Happy to. Thank you for having me."

He nodded toward the parlor. "I've got you set up in the green room. In fact, I was just going to see if I could

Mary Burton

find a longer extension cord. You said you needed power for your computer."

"Yes. I've a PowerPoint presentation."

"Go on in and get yourself set up. I'll see if I can't find a longer cord."

"Sure." She moved into the room. It was elegantly decorated with silk swag curtains on the tall windows; a Chippendale sofa and chairs; and, in the corner, a baby grand piano. Pastor Richards had set up a podium and table for her, a white projection screen, and a dozen chairs. In the back of the room was a small round table set up with coffee, lemonade, and cookies.

She removed her computer from the case and set it up just as the pastor returned.

"I can't find the longer cord," he said, scratching the side of his head. "Our church secretary is on vacation and, honestly, she is the brains behind this operation. When she's away, the church and I just stumble along until she returns."

Lindsay smiled. "It's fine. I should have enough battery power to get through the presentation. And if not, I'll do what I do best—talk."

Chuckling, he checked his watch. "Most of the folks should be here any second. They're just wrapping up their Monday night supper down the hall. It's a summer Bible study program and they decided to turn it into a pot luck. They're four weeks into a six-week program."

"Great."

"Help yourself to coffee."

"Thanks."

She moved to the back table and filled a Styrofoam cup with coffee. "So tell me a little more about the group I'm speaking to tonight."

"It's a ladies circle group and their husbands. They're studying references to marriage in the Bible and I thought it would be interesting to discuss a modern take on marriage. Domestic abuse is just one of the topics we're looking at this summer."

"Right." She sipped her coffee. Compared to the espresso, it tasted like water. "I want to thank you again for all the help the church has given Sanctuary. We've really appreciated it."

Pastor Richards's smile was warm and there was a kindness about him. "Oh, we're just happy to help." He shoved his hands into his pockets and looked a tad embarrassed.

"A friend of mine works for the police department," he said. "He told me a body was found behind your shelter."

"Yes. It was Harold Turner." She didn't want to talk about the murder but knew it had to be addressed. "I don't know why he was murdered in our backyard."

The pastor nodded. "I've met his wife. Our church works with hers on several children's charities. Lovely woman."

She remembered her conversation with Jordan this morning. "I hope she has good support around her now."

"Oh, I'm sure she does. I want you to know this doesn't change First Methodist's commitment to the shelter. We believe in what you're doing."

Relief washed through her. "Thanks. That does mean a lot to me."

Within minutes the group of couples gathered in the room. They all looked to be in their fifties and sixties. Each wore a wedding band. The minister made introductions and soon Lindsay stood before the group.

Lindsay had spoken to groups like this many times before. In fact, she had never turned down an opportunity to speak, believing that if she did, she might somehow miss the one person who needed her help.

"I'm not going to give you a bunch of statistics or talk to you about the problem of domestic violence," Lindsay began. She smiled and tried to look relaxed and comfortable. "I'm here to tell you a story."

She didn't like to stand behind podiums. She liked to feel a connection with her audience, no matter how small it was. She clicked on the first slide. A picture of a young, smiling, dark-haired woman appeared on the white projection screen.

"This is Pam when she was a senior in high school in Henderson, North Carolina. Pam was a smart girl. She made all As in high school and she married her high school sweetheart. His name was Matt. Pam got a good job as the executive secretary to an insurance president, and he would later say that Pam was hardworking and diligent and that everyone at the insurance company liked her. Five years ago, Pam and Matt moved to Richmond. She didn't get another job, because Matt wanted her to stay home. They were trying to have a baby. Pam was thirty-five.

"In December of last year, Pam showed up at work wearing dark glasses. And underneath the lenses was bruising. The company president asked Pam about her eyes and she explained that she'd been in a car accident. Two days later, police were called to her residence. The neighbor had heard shouting. But when police arrived Pam assured the officers that she was fine."

Telling the story always made her sad. "Two days later she ended up in the emergency room. I met with her then and was able to convince her to spend a few nights at Sanctuary. I took her to the magistrate's office and walked her through the protective order process. She seemed relieved."

Pastor Richards frowned. "Did I read about this case in the paper?"

Lindsay nodded grimly. "You did. About nine months ago. And, in fact, the husband was just sentenced about a month ago." She sipped her coffee as she searched her notes for the spot where she'd left off.

"We'll say a prayer for them at the end of the meeting," the pastor said.

Lindsay smiled, not sure what to say to that. Maybe wherever Pam was now, the prayers would help. "We can offer board in our shelter for only thirty days. As the thirty days ticked away, Pam began to worry that she wouldn't have a place to live. Her parents were gone, she'd made no friends, and she wasn't close to her brothers, who had never liked her husband. Matt had seen to it that she'd stayed isolated. Anyway, Pam called Matt. And he came to the shelter and picked her up." She paused. "We found her body the next morning. She'd been beaten to death."

A woman with short gray hair folded her arms over her chest. She glanced at her husband, a short, stocky man with a ruddy face. "I can tell you I wouldn't tolerate that kind of behavior from my husband."

Lindsay shrugged. "None of us knows what we'd do."

The woman grinned as if she had all the answers. "I know what I'd do if my husband ever hit me—I'd shoot him."

Nervous giggles rippled through the room.

Lindsay smiled. "Do you know how to boil a frog alive?"

Everyone sobered. "You put it in cold water and then you very slowly start to turn the heat up under the pot. When the frog realizes it's too late and is about to be boiled alive, the heat overcomes the frog and kills it."

Few in the room took the analogy that seriously. But when she raised her gaze, she realized Pastor Richards was staring at her with a renewed intensity that made her uncomfortable.

Zack and Warwick returned to the shelter. It was past six. Ruby had gone home and Sara was still processing the crime scene in Lindsay's office.

The two detectives questioned neighbors but learned little other than Lindsay kept a nice yard. Few knew the house was a shelter, though none worried about the number of cars that came and went during any given day. No one noticed anything unusual around five that morning.

After several hours, Zack and Warwick called it quits with the promise to meet again at headquarters by seven the next morning.

By the time Zack pulled into his driveway, he was bone tired. He turned off the car and just sat. His last encounter with Lindsay played in his head as he stared at the salt-box house he'd just bought. He took in the broken windows, peeling paint, overgrown shrubs and, for the hundredth time, wondered why he'd purchased the damn place. He knew the answer.

Because Lindsay had loved it.

He'd passed the house a dozen times in the last month, each time pausing to see if the FOR SALE sign had been pulled up. It hadn't. In this waning real estate market, the house required more work and attention than most were willing to give. Yet, he still kept coming back, staring past the decay and rot to the possibilities Lindsay had once envisioned.

Zack got out of the car and slung his coat over his shoulder. After climbing the front steps, he unlocked the door. He prayed his beeper wouldn't go off before the morning briefing. He needed downtime and sleep.

Inside the house, plaster walls had trapped the day's heat, leaving the foyer stuffy and humid. The supplies from the hardware superstore had been delivered a couple of days ago, but the job had kept him on the run and he'd barely had enough time to stack the supplies into the empty living room.

Late-afternoon sun streamed through the transom above the front door. His footsteps echoed as he moved over scarred hardwood floors toward the kitchen. The place felt unwelcoming.

He dropped his keys on the gray kitchen counter and laid his coat on a stack of boxes by the back door. From the kitchen window above the sink, he stared at the back-yard. It reminded him of the surface of the moon: barren, lifeless.

Zack went to the new, starkly white refrigerator. When he and Lindsay had been together their refrigerator had been covered with pictures of them, schedules, and drawings from the kids at the shelter.

He opened it. The bright bulb illuminated two boxes of Chinese food, a half-full carton of orange juice, and a couple of cans of soda. He craved a beer right now but tried not to think about it as he snatched a soda and headed back out to the front porch. He sat on the front step, loosened his tie, and popped the soda's tab. Maybe he'd go for a run and then order a pizza.

Zack downed the last of the soda and crushed the can just as a black SUV pulled up in front of the house. The car belonged to his brother, Malcolm.

This wasn't Malcolm's part of town. He must be doing recon for their mother.

Malcolm wore a loose, white T-shirt, faded jeans, and flip-flops. He strolled around the side of his truck, a brown paper bag tucked in close at his side, sunlight bouncing off his chrome aviator glasses. Malcolm was a year younger than Zack and, at six one, a couple of inches shorter.

"Tell Mom I'm fine," Zack called.

Malcolm shook his head. "That won't be good enough. She's going to want details." He stopped in front of the house, pulled off his glasses, and studied the exterior. "Were you sober when you bought this piece-of-crap house, Zack?"

"Sober as a judge."

"Now I'm really worried about you. Do yourself a favor and bulldoze it and start fresh."

That coaxed a grin from Zack. "It's a great investment. The realtor said lots of potential and charm."

Malcolm's gaze scanned the peeling paint on the front porch and the dry rot by the front door. "Lots of work. Lots of money to fix it up."

"Consider it therapy." Zack nodded to the bag. "What's in the bag?"

"Mom sent food." Malcom handed him the bag.

Zack opened the bag and found a large tinfoil container of ziti, cellophane-wrapped bread rolls, two cookies, and a plastic fork. He was starving. "Bless you."

Malcolm sat down on the porch and studied the house. "Why'd you pick this place?"

Because Lindsay had once looked at the house and talked about filling it with babies. Instead he said, "It's an investment. I paid next to nothing for it." He was nostalgic but not stupid.

Sighing, Malcolm glanced down the street at the collection of half-century-old homes. Most had been renovated. "Fixed up, it could be worth a fortune," he said.

"That's my thought. If it doesn't work out I can always flip it for a profit."

He sighed and didn't seem convinced. "Oh, Mom said to remind you about the party."

"Party?"

Malcolm looked at him as if he were dim-witted. "Damn, Zack, Eleanor's birthday party. Saturday. Mom's been planning it for months. Be there or suffer the consequences."

"Oh yeah, right." He opened the tinfoil container and savored the blend of ziti, tomatoes, oregano, and basil. His sister, Ellie, had talked about the party for weeks, and he'd cut off his right arm before he'd disappoint her. "I won't miss it."

"Mom would have come but the restaurant is packed tonight. She couldn't get away."

"No sweat."

"I saw the six o'clock news. I guess you saw Lindsay today." Malcolm didn't hide the fact that he disapproved of Zack's *un*marriage to Lindsay.

"Yep. And I'm in no mood for lectures about Lindsay, our marriage, or unsigned divorce papers."

Malcolm held up his hands. "You'll get none from me today."

"Good."

"Still, this investigation is going to be a hornet's nest. Is Ayden going to let you stay on the case?"

"Yes, but Warwick's taking the lead."

Malcolm frowned. "He eased up on you at all? Or is he still being an ass?"

"Like always, he's expecting me to screw up." Zack bit into a slice of warm, buttery Italian bread. "Warwick will have to wait until hell freezes over before I drink again."

The comment pleased Malcolm. "Any leads on the Turner case?"

"No forensic evidence on the body. Turner's wife has an ironclad alibi, as does his number one drug-dealing client and his law partner."

"What about *your* wife?" Malcolm kept his voice neutral.

"Lindsay doesn't have an alibi. She says she was home alone. Frankly, her alibi is so lame, it could be true. But I need to be sure. The judge should sign my search warrants in the morning, and then I'll work my way through her phone, computer, and office records."

Malcolm traced a callus on the palm of his hand. "Lindsay can be tenacious when it comes to protecting battered women."

"But I'm betting she's no killer. She hates all kinds of violence."

They sat in silence for a moment as Zack ate.

"So what are you two going to do about your marriage?"

Zack jabbed his fork into a cluster of ziti. "We're not talking about that, remember?"

Malcolm stretched out his legs and crossed them at the ankles. "Cut the crap and answer the question."

Zack chewed his ziti slowly. "I'm going to do my best to save our marriage."

"Shit, Zack, have you lost your mind? She left you." Malcolm was a man of strong opinions. During Zack's recovery he'd been a rock. But even though Zack had regained his balance, his brother remained overprotective.

The truth behind his failed marriage shamed Zack. "She had good reason."

"She should have stuck by you when you got sick."

Sick. Zack shook his head. "It's not like I had cancer, Mal. I was a drunk. I let her down."

Malcolm shook his head. "Marriage is for better or worse in my mind. Sickness and health."

"I guess this is the worse part."

"How can it ever get better between the two of you? Lindsay is obsessed with work. She can be abrasive. And she is now a suspect in a murder investigation. No one in their right mind would want her."

Zack grinned. "And your point is?"

Malcolm's eyes darkened. "This isn't funny."

Zack sobered. "No, it's not. My marriage is sloppy. Sucks right now. But once, it was pretty great. I want that back."

Malcolm shook his head. "Will she have you back?"

"I don't know."

The Guardian clicked off the television, irritated by the evening news reports. Harold's name had been released to the press, but the stations had given the murder little airtime. All three stations had screwed up the story, but that dumb bitch reporter from Channel 10, Kendall Shaw, had missed the point completely. She'd prattled on about the county's low murder rate and domestic violence statistics. She seemed more worried about her own image than reporting the story.

That was the problem with people. They were selfish and far too wrapped up in their individual lives to notice what didn't directly concern them.

The only one who could truly *see* was Lindsay.

She reached out to others in need. She put the lives of others in front of her own.

Her warrior spirit should have appreciated Harold's hand nestled in a bed of irises. Like the flowers, which telegraphed Friendship, Hope, Wisdom, and Valor, the hand was rich with symbolism. It not only bore Harold's platinum wedding band, but it was the left hand and it was well known that the attorney was a lefty. It was his dominant hand. His power center. He'd always struck his wife with his left fist.

One click of another remote and a very different image snapped on the TV. This in full color as well, but it was an image of Lindsay's living room.

The cameras had been placed in her apartment thirty days ago. It had been appallingly easy to gain entrance. A work order and a report of fuzzy cable was all it had taken. The cameras had been easy to install. Several weren't bigger than the size of a dime, and the transmitter, which boosted the signal up to seven miles, was easily wired into an outlet behind the AC unit.

The Guardian settled back in a chair and studied the television screen. In the background, Lindsay's favorite Sugarland CD crooned. The country western song was upbeat, fast paced. In the background he heard Lindsay singing.

Seconds later Lindsay emerged from the kitchen. Her hair was damp from a shower and she wore an oversized, well-worn T-shirt that said "USC." She had a large bowl of popcorn and a diet soda. Her favorite evening ritual before bed.

Lindsay's habits were so predictable. Two cups of coffee before work. An hour of yoga in the morning. Glasses only when she read. Weekends when she wasn't on call meant refinishing the chest of drawers that would be a showpiece. Insomnia when she was troubled.

Lindsay sat on her carpeted floor and switched on a cable news station. Silently she watched and ate her popcorn.

Her phone rang and she leaned over and grabbed the receiver off the cradle. "Hello."

Late calls never boded well. They always meant a crisis that pulled her away, and she'd already had a long enough day. She shouldn't have gone to the church. But then she wasn't one to quit on a promise.

A flipped switch and the call broadcasted over the speakers.

"Hey, Aisha," Lindsay said. "Is everything all right?"

Aisha sighed. "The shelter is fine. Everyone is real nice."

"And the boys are settled in?"

"Yes. We're all in the same room. They like that."

"What's wrong?"

"Marcus called me again this evening on my cell phone. He keeps telling me how much he loves me."

Lindsay's expression tightened. "We've been through this before, Aisha. He wants to control you. What he feels for you isn't healthy."

"I know, I know. And I told him I wouldn't be coming back to him no matter what. And I meant that. I really did."

"Good girl."

Lindsay and the Guardian spoke the two words in unison.

"But he wants to see the boys. He says they're his sons and he has a right to them. I don't want to keep Damien and Jamal from their dad."

"The boys are afraid of him."

"He hasn't hit them in a while."

Lindsay gripped the telephone, struggling with her temper. The children always got to her. "He is talking about his rights as a father but you have rights, too, Aisha. You and the boys have the right to a safe home."

"I know, but . . ."

"Have you called my friend at Legal Aid about the divorce and custody?"

"Not yet."

Lindsay pressed fingertips to her temple. "We've been through this before. Call the woman at Legal Aid whom I told you about. She's very nice. She'll tell you about your rights."

"Okay."

"Are you going to call?"

"Yes."

"Good. You're doing a good job, Aisha. I'm proud of you."

A sob escaped Aisha. "Are you really?"

"I really am."

"Thanks."

They talked a few more minutes about the legalities of divorce and custody before Lindsay hung up. The Guardian switched off the phone speaker.

Lindsay turned back toward the television and rubbed her temple. She scooped a handful of popcorn and took a bite. But she no longer seemed to enjoy her snack. Frowning, she tossed what remained in her hand back in the bowl.

Absentmindedly, she pushed away the bowl. She had a tendency not to eat when she was upset. And at the rate she was going, she was going to make herself sick.

Lindsay rose, then began to pace. She moved around her town house like a caged animal.

The Guardian touched the television screen and traced the profile of her face.

Harold's death, the hand, even the note hadn't been enough to assure her that she wasn't alone in her Holy Cause. She needed to know she had an ally. She wasn't alone.

But words didn't matter to Lindsay. Only deeds mattered to her.

The real way to prove to Lindsay that she had a true friend now was to ferret out more Evil Ones. The more men who died now meant that many fewer battered wives whom Lindsay would have to care for.

As the bodies would begin to stack up, she would see the pattern. She would see that she had a true Guardian.

Chapter Eleven

Kendall Shaw was pissed. She stopped the recording of her eleven o'clock news report and climbed down off the elliptical trainer she kept on the sun porch of her mother's house.

The story she'd filed had been nothing short of lame. Murder in the city's west end. Identity of victim. A brief recap of his career and murder stats in the metro area. Domestic violence. *Ya, ya, ya.*

It was all very bland, very ordinary, and not the kind of story that was going to get her to a bigger television market like L.A. or New York.

But her boss had given in to pressure from Dana Miller, the shelter's board chair, and had ordered her not to mention Sanctuary or its location. For now, all stations were protecting the shelter's identity. And unless something broke soon, Dana would see to it that the story faded away.

As Kendall had stood outside Sanctuary today, she had sensed she'd stumbled upon a big story. She'd wanted to linger and remain on hand with her cameraman, Mike.

Something was going to break—she could feel it in her bones.

But the evening news producer had felt otherwise. He'd wanted film of a warehouse fire. She'd argued. He'd denied her request to stay and had pulled her cameraman.

Minutes after Mike had left and Kendall was packing up, Lindsay had run screaming out of the shelter. Her terrified screams had the cop in the patrol car scrambling toward her. Within minutes, the place was swarming with more cops.

Something *big* had happened in the shelter.

And if she'd had film, it was the kind of *something* that would get her a better job.

Mike did return, but by then it was too late. The cops didn't release any details and she'd had to file her original story.

From her briefcase she pulled out a CD of the raw footage from this morning. She swapped it out for the other CD in the tray and hit "play."

She fast-forwarded through the morning interviews with neighbors. The last interview of the morning was with Mrs. Young, the neighbor across the street, who kept going on and on about how nice Lindsay's yard was and how no one knew the house was a women's shelter.

Blah, blah, blah.

Kendall slowed the tape to just before Mike had shut off his camera. This time she didn't focus on Mrs. Young but the background just to the right of the shelter.

A cat chasing a squirrel. Thunder clouds. And then in the bottom-right corner, the bumper of a van pulled into the frame. At the time, her back had been to the shelter and she'd been on the phone with her producer. She'd not noticed the driver. Hell, who ever noticed delivery guys?

Now as she reviewed the footage, she watched closely.

The driver, head tucked low and a box of flowers in hand, got out of the van, ran up to the front porch, rang the bell, and set the box down. As the driver turned, the tape turned to static. Mike had switched off the camera.

"Damn it!" Kendall rewound the tape. She watched the footage again. Lindsay had returned to the shelter around two. She started screaming minutes later. Whatever had freaked Lindsay out had to be the box.

"What the hell was it? What was sent to her?"

Kendall had good instincts and she had learned to listen to them. Whatever had gone on at the shelter today had to do with Lindsay. She couldn't prove it, but she'd bet money that Harold had been killed for Lindsay.

She dashed upstairs to the stack of files in the corner of the living room. She kept all her interview notes filed away in case she ever needed to reference them again. Since she'd moved into the house last December, she'd not taken the time to put the notes away, convinced that she was here only temporarily.

Flipping through the manila folders, she pulled the file containing her article about Lindsay.

Scanning the pages, she read her notes from her late April interview. There seemed nothing out of the ordinary. She had notes on Lindsay's day-to-day routine at the shelter. She had stats on domestic violence in the county and the country. All this was strictly background.

Kendall flipped to her notes on Lindsay's past. She was a graduate of the University of California. She entered school at the age of nineteen and attended on a full scholarship and was an honor student. Lindsay worked for a landscape company to pay for living expenses. And she made it through in three years so that she graduated with her class. Originally she was from Ashland, a town in Hanover County, Virginia.

That notation had Kendall pausing. She'd forgotten Lindsay was a Virginian. Lindsay had only mentioned it in passing and had spoken of herself several times as a California girl.

It wasn't unusual for a kid to go so far from home for school, nor extraordinary to take a year off between high school and college. Still, something nagged at her.

Kendall dug her Blackberry out of her briefcase and looked up the number of the *Herald Progress,* the local paper that covered the town of Ashland and Hanover County.

Last year, she'd done a very nice piece on the *Herald Progress'* anniversary celebration. The paper's assistant editor had always said to call if she needed anything. Well, she needed a favor.

Unmindful of the time, she dialed his number.

The phone rang five times before a groggy male voice answered, "Hello."

"Barry. Kendall Shaw. I need a favor."

"Kendall?" She heard fumbling with what must have been a light switch. "It's midnight. Can't this wait until the morning?"

"Not really. And I'm sorry for the late time, but I'm working on a story. Can you do a search for me?"

"*Now*?" he groaned.

"Yes."

"You are insane. I'm not digging up anything for you at this time of night."

She rushed to say, "You said you owed me big for that piece I did on the paper's anniversary."

Grogginess mingled with irritation. "Kendall, it's midnight."

She twirled her finger in her hair as she paced. "Look, do this search for me and I'll *owe* you."

"What's that mean?"

"Name your price."

He cleared his throat. "Cover my book signing at the Book Nook next week?"

Kendall had received and read his press release on the signing of the self-published book of homespun stories. She'd tossed the release and hadn't given it a second thought. Damn. "Deal. But I need my information now."

"I want to be on the morning news."

"I'll make it happen."

"Swear."

"Swear."

Barry chuckled. "What do you want?"

"Anything and everything you have on Lindsay O'Neil. She would have lived in your area about eleven or twelve years ago."

"O'Neil. That name doesn't ring a bell."

"I wrote an article on her for *Inside Richmond* back in May. She's about thirty. A very pretty blonde."

"Oh yeah, I remember her. That article caused a bit of a buzz up here."

"Why?"

"I don't think her name was O'Neil when she lived up this way. Anyway, a few of the old guys at the paper remember when she was tangled up in some murder."

Kendall straightened. "What murder?"

"I don't remember."

Impatient, she tapped her foot. "You've got to get me more information, Barry."

"I'll see what I can dig up."

Lindsay was the key to this story. "Do that."

Chapter Twelve

Tuesday, July 8, 5:05 A.M.

Jacob Warwick had loved the smell of a boxing gym since he was a kid. The leather. The sweat. The liniment. He also loved the rhythmic sound of gloves hitting the speed bag, the thump against the heavy bag, and the skipping rope scraping the floor.

All conjured feelings of *home.* Not so surprising since he'd grown up in Myers's Gym.

He drove his fists into the punching bag suspended from the ceiling, savoring the burn in his muscles, the rapid pumping of his heart, and the sweat on his body. There wasn't anyone else working out at this early hour. The gym didn't officially open until six, but because Pete had given him a key he could come and go as he pleased. Often he boxed early.

By seven, the place would be full of men training and fighters sparring in the ring.

"Let me adjust those laces for you," Pete Myers's familiar rusty voice said behind him.

Jacob wiped the sweat from his eyes with the back of

his glove. "What are you doing here this early? I'd have figured you wouldn't get here for another hour."

Pete flashed a grin. "Ah, you know me. I'm not much of a sleeper and I like it here better than at home." Barring a few extra gray hairs, the sixty-nine-year-old man looked exactly like he had the first day Jacob had met him twenty years ago. He stood a few inches under six feet, kept his body fit by sparring daily, and always wore a wide grin. "Let me see your glove. The laces look loose."

The tension in Jacob's body eased as he held out his gloved hands. "Thanks."

When Jacob had first found Myers's gym, he'd been twelve and his mother had been on a weeklong drunken binge. Angry and wanting to wreck something, Jacob had stolen a dozen eggs from the market and made a beeline for the gym, which was celebrating its grand opening. Jacob had covered the freshly painted exterior with yolk. It had been a real laugh until a pissed Myers had come looking for him. Jacob hadn't figured the old man could run so damn fast or that he'd chase Jacob two blocks before catching him. The ex-boxer's grip had been like iron.

Myers had dragged Jacob home, taken one look at Jacob's drunken mother, and then called Social Services. Jacob's mother hadn't fought for her son, and within two weeks, Jacob was living in the small apartment above the gym with Pete. The two had clashed a lot in the beginning, but Pete had never given up on Jacob.

That was twenty years ago. And a day never passed when Jacob didn't thank God for Pete. The old boxer had saved his life.

Pete tightened the laces. "So why are you here so early?"

"I needed to break a sweat before work." Jacob hit

the long punching bag hanging from the ceiling, testing the laces.

Pete got behind the bag and steadied it. "Everything all right?"

"Yeah. Kier and I have a homicide."

"Who died?"

"Harold Turner. It was on the news last night."

Pete snorted. "I saw that. Can't say I'm too sorry. A dead attorney ain't gonna make me miss sleep."

Sweat dampened Jacob's T-shirt as he pounded the bag. "Yeah, he wasn't exactly a model citizen."

"You guys got a suspect?"

"Not yet."

"You're a smart kid. You'll figure it out."

Jacob hit the bag again. Normally, he didn't talk about cases but Pete was family. "This case could be a little dicey. Kier's wife is right in the middle of the investigation."

"Not good for Kier."

"Nothing is good when it comes to Kier. The guy is a disaster waiting to happen."

Pete frowned. "Is he drinking again?"

"No, so far I've not gotten a hint that he's had a drop. But once a drunk always a drunk."

"Your partner ain't your mother, kid. From what you've said over the last few months, Kier seems to be getting his shit together."

"We'll see."

Pete's gaze grew serious. "So how long you going to make the guy jump through hoops before you cut him some slack?"

"I'll let you know when he reaches it."

"The department was smart to pair you up with Kier. You'll keep him straight. He might even get you to lighten up."

The old man's confidence meant everything to Jacob.

"I don't want to baby-sit. And I sure as shit don't need a friend. I want a partner I can count on."

Pete nodded thoughtfully. "Until the guy screws up, cut him some slack."

Jacob knew he couldn't do that. "Sure."

Pete understood some of his foster son's scars ran deep. And he knew when to change the subject. "So when are you going to bring Sharon around the gym again? I liked her."

A twinge of regret nagged Jacob. "Sharon and I are history."

Pete shook his head. "Damn. The gal is built like a brick house and can cook. What the hell more do you want from a woman?"

"Sharon was fine. It just didn't work out."

The old man swore. "Bachelorhood ain't what it's cracked up to be. A man should have a wife and children."

Imitating Pete's raspy voice, Jacob said, "Dames are more trouble than they are worth. I do just fine by myself."

Wrinkles deepened in Pete's forehead as he smiled. "Don't you want a family of your own, Mr. Smart-mouth?"

"No." Jacob hit the bag. Truthfully, the idea made him feel backed into a corner. "Besides, you never had a family."

Pete shrugged. "Keeping you out of trouble wore me out."

Jacob frowned. "Did you ever regret taking me in?"

The old man grinned and shook his head. "You drove me to the brink of insanity more times than I could count, but I was never sorry I took you in. I'm only sorry your mother never let me formally adopt you."

Emotion tightened Jacob's chest. He hit the bag harder.

"If you don't ease up on that bag, the bones in your hand are gonna look like Swiss cheese," Pete said.

"I don't want to ease up. It feels good to push myself."

"It's not a matter of what you want, kid; it's a matter of what you need. Lay off for today. You've done enough."

Jacob stopped. His muscles ached with fatigue, just the way he liked it. But he always listened to Pete.

Pete grabbed a clean towel for Jacob and handed it to him.

"Thanks."

Pete started to unlace Jacob's right glove. "So I guess you'll be working this weekend?"

"Depends on the case." Jacob wiped the sweat from his eyes. "What do you have in mind?"

"I'm looking for a sparring partner for a fighter. I want to schedule a few friendly rounds on Saturday."

"I'd love to do it. I should know by late Thursday how the case is going."

Pete nodded, satisfied. "Great. I knew I could count on you."

Whoever said life was supposed to be easy?

The words Lindsay's mother had spoken to her so often played in Lindsay's head as she cradled a cup of coffee in her hands. She sat in an Adirondack chair on the back patio garden of her town house. The sun had crept up high in the sky but the air remained comfortable, thanks to yesterday's storms, which had banished a lot of the humidity.

The rains had been a welcome respite from the July heat for her gardens, which covered most of her ten-by-twelve backyard. Her yard was separated from the others by a tall privacy fence that looked like all the others in the development. However, her yard was completely

I'M WATCHING YOU   141

unlike the others, which were little more than patchy plots of grass.

Her yard was an oasis. She'd only been in this town house eleven months, but already she'd filled the tiny land plot with numerous flower pots overflowing with brightly colored annuals, including marigolds and petunias. There were more pots filled with tomatoes, lettuce, cucumbers, and sweat peas.

Lindsay had learned to garden from her mother, who had always kept a lush garden. Her mother had always taken pride in her tomatoes, which frequently placed in the county fair, and her roses, which were once photographed for the paper. Her mother had spent hours in that garden, tenderly caring for her plants. Lindsay had loved digging alongside her mother in the rich soil. In the garden not only could they create, but they could escape her father's foul moods.

Sipping her coffee, Lindsay wished she had more gardening space and more land. One day, she'd have a real home with property around it to plant bushes and trees, and a vegetable garden. One day.

A flicker of movement caught Lindsay's attention. She turned as Nicole pushed open the sliding glass doors. Her friend wore an oversized T-shirt and long pajama pants that brushed her ankles. Blond hair swept high on her head in a rubber band accented clear green eyes and a high slash of cheekbones.

Nicole surveyed the garden. "You and your garden. I'm starting to think it's an obsession."

Lindsay stretched out her legs. "What can I say? I'm a sucker for greenery."

Nicole sat in a matching Adirondack chair next to Lindsay. She touched a bright yellow marigold blossom in a pot next to her chair. "Remember sophomore year in college when we had the room that overlooked a flat roof?"

"How could I forget? We lived next to that girl who liked to play Broadway tunes at five in the morning. I swear, if I ever hear the theme to *Cats* again I'll go nuts."

Nicole smiled. "I was thinking about your garden."

"I filled the windowsill with pots."

"And when the windowsill filled, you expanded your garden pots onto the roof. Inch by inch you took it over and filled it with every kind of vegetable imaginable. I'm surprised security didn't bust you."

Lindsay sipped her coffee again, hiding a grin. "Actually, they did. Mr. Wheeler, the head of security, found the garden and threatened to tear it down. I gave him a few tomatoes to try and he was hooked. I supplied him with vegetables all spring and he looked the other way."

"Bribery? I'm shocked, Ms. O'Neil."

Lindsay laughed. "I learned early on how to work the system."

Nicole's normally tanned skin looked pale, tired. At first, Lindsay had attributed it to her change in hair color. Lindsay had cut Nicole's dark hair and helped her dye it blond. It was a shame because her black hair had been so beautiful.

"Want some coffee?" Lindsay offered. "I just made a fresh pot."

Nicole held up a hand in surrender. "No, thanks. I'm a little queasy again. I think I've caught another bug from one of the kids I photographed. I had one yesterday sneeze all over me."

"So, how was work last night?"

She tucked her legs underneath her. "Good and bad. I actually got some great shots of the two kids I photographed. Their mother was thrilled and she ended up ordering twice as many prints as she'd planned."

"Good. What was the bad part?"

"My boss, Bill, loves my work too. He keeps raving about it. He keeps wondering how such a talented photographer landed on his doorstep."

"Why is that bad?"

She brushed her bangs out of her face. "He wants to enter some of my photography in a national competition. Says the publicity would be great for his business. I really was flattered. I'd gotten so used to downplaying my work. And it's been too long since someone has praised my photos. I'd forgotten how much I missed that."

Lindsay set her cup down on the arm of the chair. She understood living in secret was hard, but it was necessary right now. "Nicole, you can't enter a national competition."

"I know, I know. I'm not foolish enough to risk national exposure." She drummed her fingers on the chair's arm. "But I really hate living under the radar. I want my life back. And I want a divorce."

"You've only been here a couple of weeks. The bruises have only just faded and you're running on raw emotion. It's very natural that you'd be angry."

"I am angry. In fact, I'm furious. Last night I woke up and was so mad I couldn't get back to sleep."

Lindsay kept her tone even. She remembered how battered Nicole had been when she'd first arrived. And from what little Nicole had shared about her marriage, Lindsay knew Richard was a monster. "And if Richard were to find you, he would force you back to San Francisco. And I'm afraid he would treat you far worse than before."

Nicole picked at a loose chip of paint on the chair arm. "This is the twenty-first century. It shouldn't be this way. I have rights too."

"I know, I know. This isn't fair. But sometimes it's

better to be safe than right. Sometimes the only solution is to just vanish."

A heavy silence settled between them. "I'm starting to feel like Christina Braxton died. She's starting to feel like a distant memory."

"She became Nicole Piper. And Nicole Piper is going to have a wonderful life."

"But I'll always worry. I'll always have to look over my shoulder. Unless I get lucky and Richard drops dead."

Lindsay understood Nicole was in a no-win situation and didn't bother with platitudes. "What time do you work today?"

"Three." Nicole shifted in her seat and looked through the sliding glass doors at the wall clock. "Hey, it's almost eight. You're running late."

Lindsay had been up since six. She'd practiced her yoga for almost ninety minutes, trying to fill her time and to push the murder and Zack from her mind. "I don't have to be in the office until nine."

"Is today a shelter day?"

"No, I'm working out of the Mental Health Services building today." She hesitated. She didn't want to tell Nicole about the murder, because she didn't want her to worry. But better Nicole hear from her about what had happened. "We had some trouble at the shelter yesterday."

A deep crease formed on Nicole's forehead. "What happened?"

Lindsay chose her words carefully. "Ruby, the Sunday night volunteer, found a body behind the shelter near the trash cans."

Nicole lurched forward. "What!"

Lindsay held up her hands. "The cops have identified the guy. He's a local attorney who apparently had lots of enemies." She skipped the details about the flowers, the severed hand, and the Guardian's note. "It's nothing for you to worry about, because it has nothing to do with you or Richard."

Nicole's expression grew more serious. "Lindsay, don't patronize me. A dead body is something to worry about. How did he die?"

Lindsay picked at the chipping paint on her chair arm. "He was shot in the chest."

Nicole blew out a breath. "Who was it?"

"His name was Harold Turner."

"This isn't good."

Lindsay smiled, hoping to lighten Nicole's worries. "It's under control. The police are all over this case. I'm sure they'll figure out who did this. And I want you to know that I haven't told anyone that you're living here."

Nicole relaxed a fraction, as if Lindsay had touched on a secret worry. "Okay."

"This will blow over soon enough."

Nicole looked skeptical. "What can I do to help you?"

"Nothing. Everything is fine. If I need you, I promise to unload my troubles, okay?"

"I'm holding you to that. You've done so much for me." Nicole shifted, pressing her hand into her stomach.

"You aren't feeling well, are you?"

Nicole's skin looked sallow. "No. I can't seem to shake this stupid bug."

Lindsay studied Nicole's tight face. She knew her friend was under a terrible strain, but some topics couldn't be avoided. "I've been tiptoeing around this subject for a couple of days. But there seems to be no getting around it now. When was your last period?"

Nicole shook her head and held up her hands. "Don't even go there. I'm not pregnant."

Lindsay relaxed back in her chair. "So you've had a period recently?"

Slim fingers drew into fists. "No, but I've been under

a lot of stress the last couple of months. Things were getting pretty bad with Richard toward the end."

Lindsay's concern returned threefold. "How long has it been since your period?"

Nicole frowned, closed her eyes as she thought. "Two months."

Lindsay leaned forward and clasped her hands in front of her. "Have you ever gone this long before?"

Hope flickered in Nicole's gaze. "When my mother died, I missed one."

"But not two or three."

"No."

Lindsay blew out a frustrated breath. "You need to take a pregnancy test, Nicole."

"I don't need a test. I'm not pregnant." Anger etched her delicate features. "Richard said he wanted to have a baby. He said a baby would bind us together forever. But I was able to use some kind of protection almost every time."

Lindsay rose, then squatted in front of Nicole's chair and laid her hand on her arms. "I'd love to think this is just the flu. But you've been sleeping a lot and you've been nauseous too often to ignore it any longer. I know you don't like the idea of carrying Richard's child, but the possibility exists, doesn't it?"

Defiance burned in Nicole's blue eyes. "It was only just one time that he completely surprised me and I wasn't able to take precautions."

"When?"

"May."

The timing would be right. "Once is all it takes, honey."

Nicole pressed trembling hands to her cheeks. "I can't have Richard's baby. I *can't.*"

"Hey, hey, don't panic or borrow trouble. Just pick

up a pregnancy test tonight. They have to be taken in the morning. By this time tomorrow, you'll know where you stand."

Nicole's voice was a hoarse whisper. Her gaze reflected fear. "Lindsay, what if I *am* pregnant?"

"Honey, let's just do the test first. Then we'll figure out what the next step is."

Nicole offered a weak smile, but her eyes still looked panicked. "You're right. One step at a time. You've been saying that since I arrived here."

Lindsay admired Nicole's strength. With only the clothes on her back, she had left a very powerful, very vengeful man. "Do yourself a favor and get out of the house today. Go see some of the city. Put that new camera of yours to work." Photography would give Nicole something positive to focus on temporarily.

A sigh shuddered through Nicole's body. "I have been itching to try out the vintage Leica I found at the flea market last week."

"Perfect. This apartment could use some real photographic art on the walls."

A clock in the hallway chimed eight times. "Now, I've got to get my act together. And my car is still at the shelter, so I'll have to call a cab."

"Why is your car at the shelter?"

She shrugged. "Long story."

Nicole rose, shaking her head. "You don't want to tell me."

Lindsay smiled. "Not right now."

"I get that we all have things we don't like to talk about. Okay, I'll drive you. Give me fifteen and I'll be ready to go."

Lindsay touched Nicole's shoulder. "It's going to be okay, baby or no." *It's going to be okay.* She was trying to reassure herself as well.

Nicole straightened her shoulders. "I know."

Both smiled.

But neither believed the other.

Minutes before seven, Zack arrived in the lobby of the Public Safety building. The modern building, located in the west end of the county, housed the homicide division and sat adjacent to the police training facility.

Zack headed past the guard at Reception and, instead of taking the elevator, climbed the steps to his second-floor office. In deference to the heat, he'd skipped the suit today and dressed in khakis and a white collared shirt. The way he figured it, he and Warwick would be doing a lot of legwork on the Turner case.

The homicide division consisted of five small offices, one for each detective, and a conference room with a long table that sat twenty. Fluorescent light made the industrial-blue carpet look gray and the ivory walls washed out.

His eyes itched with fatigue. Dreams of Lindsay had invaded him and kept him awake half the night.

Last night's dreams were different from the others he'd had this past year. They weren't a replay of the fights they'd had during the last days they'd lived together. These dreams had been purely sexual. Until yesterday, he'd almost forgotten how good the sex could be between them. When he'd awoken, a restless energy had been churned up. He'd gone for a long run, taken a cold shower, but neither had been enough to banish Lindsay.

"Damn." He grabbed a cup of coffee from the break room and headed to Warwick's office.

Warwick glanced up from his desk. "You look like shit."

Zack had come to recognize the tone. It meant Warwick was gunning for trouble. Normally, Zack ignored it, but today, he didn't have the patience. "I haven't been drinking, if that's what you're implying."

Warwick looked unrepentant. "This isn't the time to fall apart."

Zack hadn't even had his first cup of coffee and already he was pissed at his partner. "I'm not falling apart and I'm not going to drink again. The sooner you accept that fact the better our partnership will be."

Warwick didn't hide his skepticism. "We'll see."

Zack shook his head. "And I thought I had hang-ups. But I'm begining to believe you've got some real issues of your own."

Warwick rose abruptly. "What's that supposed to mean?"

"Was it your mother or father who was the drunk?"

Tension radiated from Warwick's body. "Don't try to lay your problems on me."

"As long as I'm sober, I don't have a problem. But you, you could be sober as a judge and still have demons chasing you." He sipped his coffee, enjoying the fact that Warwick was the one at a disadvantage. "I'd say it was your mother who was the drinker. Or was she a drug addict?"

Warwick tightened his jaw and released it. "Fuck off."

Zack shrugged.

Warwick snatched up a file from his very orderly desk. "I asked everyone in the division to meet us in the conference room at seven. They should be waiting for us now."

Zack knew he'd just opened a wound. If Warwick hadn't been such a prick these last eight months, he'd have felt bad about it. "Let's do it."

Warwick nodded stiffly. "Right."

The two went into the conference room as Detective Vega offered Detective C.C. Ricker Danish from a bakery bag.

C.C. glowered at Vega. The redhead stood just over five feet and had a compact, lean body. In her late twenties, she had come up through patrol, the domestic violence division, and for the last two years had worked homicide.

Catching sight of Zack and Warwick, Vega wiped his hands clean. Nick Vega was tall, had olive skin, and wore his black hair slicked back. Born in Cuba, he'd immigrated to New York when he was six. He spoke Spanish like a native and English like a New Yorker.

C.C. stood a little straighter. "So I hear you boys snagged yourself a juicy murder."

Warwick's frame dominated the space. "Lucky us."

Vega chuckled. "Tread carefully. C.C.'s on another diet. Low carbs this time. And she's mean as a snake."

Warwick sat down. All traces of the anger toward Zack had vanished. "What's the occasion and how long do we have to suffer before you can have a real meal?"

C.C. frowned. "My sister's wedding." They'd all seen the pictures of C.C. and her three sisters. The other Ricker sisters were tall and blond. C.C. had often joked she was a genetic throwback. "So how's Sharon?"

Warwick's smile didn't waver but his eyes hardened a shade. "No more Sharon. I'm a single man again."

C.C. didn't hide her sadness. "Sorry to hear that. I liked her."

"No biggie," Warwick said.

Zack wouldn't use any more armchair psychology to his partner again. Their exchange a few minutes ago, coupled with the fact that he'd broken up with another good woman, told Zack all he needed to know. His partner had been raised by a drunk and it had left its mark. No matter what he did, no matter how long he stayed sober, Zack would always be a drunk to Warwick.

Add that to the three detectives' camaraderie and Zack wondered if he'd ever live down the days he drank.

Ayden entered the room, silencing any other banter. He had rolled up his sleeves and loosened his tie. Under his arm, he held a stack of files. In his left hand, which still bore his wedding band, he gripped a mug that read "#1 Dad," a gift from one of his sons. He tossed the files on the table.

"Zack and Warwick. Phone records just arrived." He pushed the files toward them. "Harold and Jordan Turner's are included as well as O'Neil's and the shelter's records. There are hundreds of calls to wade through."

Zack thumbed through the records. He remembered the feeling he'd had yesterday that Lindsay was hiding something. God only knew what they'd find.

"Is Sara joining us?" Ayden said.

"I'm here," Sara said, breezing into the room. Her neat ponytail suited her khakis, crisp white shirt, and polished brown flats. "And please tell me no one expects DNA this morning."

They all laughed.

"Let me guess, your crankiness is a sign that you're scheduled to speak at the academy today. Am I right?" C.C. said.

"I was there last Friday. I've heard it said there are no stupid questions, but sometimes I wonder," she said, smiling, then opened her file. "Everyone under twenty-two thinks it takes the press of a button to get DNA results. The *CSI* craze is killing me."

Again everyone laughed.

"What have you found?" Zack said. He didn't mean to sound so abrupt.

Sara straightened. She was all business. "From the crime scene, I didn't learn that much. So let me start with the body. I spoke to the ME this morning. Harold was killed with a .45-caliber shot to the heart. We've got the slug but so far no matches to anything in the ballistic databases. I *can* tell you that Harold was dead before he hit the ground. The bullet shattered his heart. He had no defensive wounds or any other signs of trauma on his body. His hand was removed postmortem with the use of a very sharp object."

"Any theories on the instrument that was used to cut his hand off?" Warwick said.

"Machete or an ax. The ME and I are leaning toward a machete. The cut was narrow and did minimal tissue damage at the wrist. Bone was severed cleanly." She flipped a page over. "We won't have the toxicology screen on him for a couple of weeks, but there were track marks on both arms and behind both knees. This guy was a full-blown drug addict. Just the promise of drugs would be enough to get him to go almost anywhere."

"Which explains why he'd have gotten into a car with his killer," Warwick said.

"Exactly."

"And the crime scene?" Zack said.

"The killer was very careful and very methodical. He left no fingerprints, shell casings, or hair or fabric fibers; however, there was a footprint. I was able to get a very good footprint impression by the back gate. The ground had been softened by a leaking garden hose, so the soft soil created the perfect medium to make a mold." She glanced at her notes. "Men's size twelve running shoe. And I can tell you that his foot turned inward. My guess is that he has an excessively high arch, which can shorten a foot up to an inch. If the print belongs to the killer he has a slight limp. Also, there was an unidentified white powder on the heel. It's definitely not drugs and I'm having it analyzed."

"That's it?" Ayden said. He looked frustrated.

Sara nodded. "As I said, the killer was careful and, unfortunately, I only had a couple of hours to collect data before the rains came and literally obliterated the evidence. We returned after the rain, but the backyard was a mess."

"What about the hand sent to Lindsay O'Neil?" Zack said.

Sara nodded. "It's definitely Harold's. His prints match ones we had on file. I also checked the hand's nails, hoping for a partial print from the killer, but nothing. The flowers are fresh irises. They can be bought in fifty different places in the metro area."

"What about the flower box?" Ayden said.

Sara frowned. "The only prints on the outside and inside of the box were Lindsay's and her assistant's."

C.C. nodded. "I worked with a couple of robbery detectives last night and we called all the florists in the city. None had an order for the shelter address yesterday."

"Did anyone notice who delivered the box?" Ayden said.

Zack shook his head. "The cop parked in the driveway was on the phone with his kid's day care. He'd received a call that his child had been badly injured. Turned out to be bogus. And Ruby Dillon had three calls come in at once to the shelter. She was too distracted to notice the guy."

"You and Sara refer to the Guardian as a male, but do we know for sure that the Guardian is a man?" Ayden said.

Zack frowned. "Not for sure."

"What about the TV news crews?" Ayden said. "Think a camera might have picked up something? Shaw at Channel Ten had her cameras running all morning."

"I'll talk to Shaw," Warwick said.

"Do you think the killer delivered the flowers personally?" Zack said.

Warwick shrugged. "Who knows?"

No one spoke for a moment as the weight of what he'd said sank in. Did the killer return to the shelter to deliver the hand?

"And the note that was attached to the flower box?" Zack said. "What do you know about that?"

Sara glanced at her notes. *Lindsay, you are not alone anymore, The Guardian.* "I've sent it to a handwriting expert. At first glance, he says the Guardian likes control, as exhibited by the note's neat block lettering and the deep indention of the letters. He's going to look at it more and see what he comes up with."

"And the paper?" Zack said.

"The paper is extremely common and can be found in dozens of card stores."

Zack kept his voice neutral, trying not to hint at the fear he felt for Lindsay. "Lindsay's never heard of the Guardian and doesn't know why he's fixated on her."

"What's her connection to Turner?" Ayden said.

Zack recapped the facts as Lindsay had told him.

C.C. looked skeptical. "I saw Lindsay once in court. It was the trial of a woman accused of shooting her husband. Lindsay testified for the defense about battered victim syndrome. She said that a perfectly sane woman who has been badly battered can snap. On cross the Commonwealth attorney tried to get Lindsay to waver but she didn't. Lindsay is one intense woman."

"Lindsay *is* intense." Zack hesitated, dreading what he needed to say next.

"There's something we all should know about Lindsay, isn't there," Warwick said. "You hinted in the car yesterday that there was domestic abuse in her home when she was growing up."

Warwick was right. Everyone did need to know about Lindsay's past.

Zack folded his fingers together. "Lindsay had a complicated childhood." All gazes zeroed in on him. He felt disloyal even though the Department of Social Services had done a background check on her and knew her history. "She's from Ashland, about twenty miles north."

"I thought she came from California," C.C. said. "I remember talking to her about USC at some department Christmas party. She led me to believe she was from California."

Zack nodded. "She did go to school out there but she's from here."

"So why lead everyone to believe she's from the West?" Ayden said.

He drew in a deep breath. "Her mother was abused by her father for years, but it's worse than that. Her mother was murdered by her father. It was twelve years ago. Lindsay was seventeen. And her last name was Hines then." A hush fell over the room.

C.C. and Vega glanced at each other and Warwick sat back in his chair, his shock evident.

Ayden leaned forward. "Shit. I remember that case. The Hanover sheriff was a friend of mine. We talked about it a lot, because the murder scene was so bloody. It really shook him up."

"Lindsay's father beat her mother to death with a hammer," Zack said. "Lindsay found her mother."

No one spoke for several seconds.

"When did Lindsay change her name?" Warwick finally asked.

"When she turned eighteen," Zack said. "O'Neil is her mother's maiden name."

"For those of us who didn't live here then, what else can you tell us about the case?" Vega said.

Zack longed for a cigarette. "I don't know much more than that. I only know what Lindsay told me. I'd like to send a teletype to the Hanover sheriff's office and request the murder file. I don't know if the details are relevant but they could be."

Ayden nodded. "Do it."

"What happened to her after her parents died?" Warwick asked.

"She told me she moved to California. For a while she lived in shelters and in her car. Eventually, a social worker got involved with her and encouraged her to get her high school diploma. This woman also helped her earn a scholarship to the University of California."

Vega frowned. "No disrespect, Zack, but the more I hear about this the more I worry about how impartial you can be. Lindsay is your wife. Are you the guy who should be looking into this murder?"

Ayden tented his fingers. "Vega, we've already taken care of that. Warwick is taking the lead and Kier is backing him up. But I want everyone working this case."

Zack hid his satisfaction.

Warwick didn't miss a beat. "I'd like for C.C. to start going through the phone records. Look for any patterns, connections to the shelter, any unusual calls Mrs. Turner might have made."

C.C. nodded. "Will do."

"Vega, talk to Ruby Dillon, the woman who stayed at the shelter the night of the murder. Kier talked to her but she made it clear she doesn't like him. She might remember something if *you* ask the questions."

"Sure," Vega said.

Zack wasn't about to take a backseat to Warwick. "Also, C.C., once you've gone through the phone records, find out who sells machetes or anything sharp enough to cut bone."

She glanced at Warwick, and when he didn't protest she nodded. "Sure."

Warwick glanced at his watch. "I'll send the teletype to Hanover now and then Zack and I will head up there."

Chapter Thirteen

"We're with Henrico County Police," Warwick said to the clerk at the Hanover sheriff's office. "I'm Detective Jacob Warwick."

Zack showed his badge. "I'm Detective Zackary Kier. We sent a teletype an hour ago about the Hines murders."

The clerk was a short, round woman in her midfifties. She wore her graying hair in a tight perm that drew attention to a strawberry birthmark on her left cheek. "The sheriff and most of his deputies are in a staff meeting this morning, but the deputy who worked the case stuck around so he could talk to you personally. Let me buzz him."

She picked up the phone and told the person on the other end they'd arrived. "Deputy Graves will be right out."

"Thanks," Warwick said.

Zack knew the personnel turnover in this office had to be low. "You been here long?"

The woman nodded with pride. "Thirty years."

"You remember the Hines case?"

Her weathered face twisted into a deep frown. "I sure

do. It was one of the saddest cases I'd ever seen. Just about everyone in Hanover knew someone who knew the Hines family. And when their little girl ran away, it just about broke my heart. We said prayers for her at Sunday service for months."

Zack rattled the change in his pocket and tried not to pace. He thought about Lindsay at seventeen: young, alone, frightened.

The urge to protect her was so strong.

They didn't have to wait long for Graves. He pushed through a side door. He was a tall, stocky man with full, ruddy cheeks and thinning red hair. His protruding belly stretched the fabric of his brown uniform.

He offered his hand to Zack. "Deputy Marty Graves."

Zack shook his hand and discovered the deputy's grip was strong.

"You've come about the Hines murder?" Graves said.

"Yes," Zack said.

"I've got the file on my desk. Come on back."

They followed him through a pair of heavy security doors and down a narrow corridor to his cramped office. Both took a seat in front of his desk.

"Can I get you men coffee?"

Both declined.

Graves sat and put on his reading glasses. "I remember this case. Fact, I knew Frank Hines from Rotary. Nicest guy you'd ever want to meet. And Deb was in my wife's circle group at church. Both would give you the shirts off their backs." He cleared his throat. "We were all shocked at first when Frank did what he did. But then later, as folks started to compare notes, we started to piece together a few things. Life in the Hines house had to have been bad for years."

"What about the daughter? What can you tell me about her?" Zack said.

"Lindsay." A sad smile played at the corners of Graves's mouth. "She was a lifeguard at my grandkids' pool. She saved a child from drowning that summer. The youngest Thompson kid, a four-year-old, had gotten out of the baby pool and fallen into the deep end of the main pool. The *Herald-Progress* did a story on her. Both her folks seemed proud. And all the boys wanted to date her, but she kept them at arm's distance. My grandson, Joel, worked with her as a lifeguard at the pool. He always figured she was playing hard to get. Of course, none of us really knew what was going on at home. Her mother never reported any abuse and Lindsay never said a word."

Zack wondered what kind of hell Lindsay had witnessed in her home.

Warwick tented his fingers. "What happened to Frank Hines?"

Zack knew the short answer to that question but wanted to hear the deputy's version. He realized now how much Lindsay had downplayed the problems in her past.

"After he killed his wife, he fled the scene. Went to a local motel, downed a bottle of Jack Daniels, and then killed himself." Graves flipped through the file. "He left a suicide note for Lindsay. I never showed it to her." He found the note in the file and handed it to Zack.

Zack read it. Typical MO for a wife beater. "Shit."

Graves nodded. "There was no sense dumping that kind of crap on a kid. She had enough to deal with."

Zack handed the note to Warwick. "He blames his wife and Lindsay for his problems. Said if they'd been a better wife and child he'd have been fine."

"What a piece of work," Warwick muttered.

"You think you know a guy," Graves said.

Zack thought about the hell he'd put Lindsay through

when his drinking had gotten so heavy. No wonder she'd tossed him out.

Graves dropped his gaze to the file. "We did receive a 911 call from the Hines' house about three months before Frank and Deb died. Before the caller could speak the line went dead. According to the report, the dispatcher called the house back. Frank answered. He said it was a mistake."

"Only the one call?" Zack asked.

"Yes."

"Anything unusual happen recently to remind you of this case?" Zack said.

"Nope. Of course, I saw that article a couple of months ago about Lindsay. I recognized her the very instant I saw her. She's the spitting image of her mama. It did my heart good to see she's done so well for herself."

"That article didn't prompt any talk about the murders in town?" Warwick asked.

"Well, of course it did. We all remembered it. I talked about it with Joel at Sunday supper after the article came out. But nothing out of the ordinary came up. Why all these questions about a twelve-year-old murder?"

"Just following up on a lead," Zack said. "Lindsay have any relatives?"

"No one came forward after her parents' deaths." Graves shook his head. "There was no one to take custody of her, so the state stepped in. She was sent to a foster home."

"But she ran away," Zack muttered.

"Right," said Graves. "This got something to do with the murder at Sanctuary yesterday?" When they hesitated, he smiled. "I wasn't born yesterday, boys. You think that murder's tied to Lindsay's past?"

"We don't know," Zack said honestly. "Can you tell us where the Hines house was?"

"I can draw you a map to the lot. The house burned to the ground not one month after the murders. Fire department said it was arson, but we never did figure out who set it."

"Was Lindsay a suspect?" Zack said.

"No. She'd run off by then."

"We'll take a look at the lot then."

"Sure." The deputy drew a map, clipped it to a copy of the file, and slid it across the desk.

Five minutes later, Zack and Warwick left the building armed with the hand-drawn map and the Hines file.

Zack tossed his keys to Warwick. "Mind driving? I'd like to look at the file."

"Sure."

They got in the car.

Zack opened the file and studied the color photos of the murder scene. The victim lay on her back, her face discolored and swollen from the brutal beating. Her wide-eyed death stare reflected the panic she had to have felt those last few seconds of her life.

"My God," Zack said.

Warwick glanced at the map. "Never gets easy."

"No, it doesn't." His problems with alcohol abuse this past year had been a bitch, but through it all he'd had a solid family behind him. Lindsay had been alone when she'd lived her nightmare.

"The less personal you make this," Warwick said, "the easier it will be."

His partner's sudden empathy surprised Zack. "Autopsy reports on Lindsay's mother show that she'd suffered multiple factures over the years—nose, right arm, left hand." He flipped over a page and discovered a medical report on Lindsay. "Lindsay's doc reported that she was in a state of shock. He also stated that she'd suffered a spiral fracture of her right wrist."

"Someone twisted her hand so hard her wrist broke."

Zack tamped down his anger. "Yeah. Doctors reported that her and her mother's breaks occurred a couple of years before the murder/suicide."

"What does the report say about Frank Hines?"

"Died of a single gunshot wound to the chest. A forty-five."

"Like Turner," Warwick said.

Turner and Hines shared similar fatal wounds made by the same caliber gun. Another coincidence. Things weren't looking good for Lindsay. "Yeah. Autopsy reports show advanced liver disease, a by-product of excessive drinking."

Warwick shook his head. "Lindsay ever tell you this stuff?"

His wife had hidden her darkest secrets even from him. "Only the barest details. I tried to talk to her about it, but she always changed the subject. She said she'd put her past behind her and didn't want to discuss it."

Warwick tightened his hands on the wheel. "This is the kind of stuff that can really fuck with someone's head."

Zack flipped to a picture taken of Lindsay when she was a junior in high school. Challenge radiated from her eyes. "That doesn't mean she killed Turner."

"Turner smacked around his wife. Lindsay knew it. Maybe she'd had enough of bullies."

Zack stared at the more than decade-old crime scene photos. And then he noticed the date. "*Shit.*"

"What?"

"Yesterday was the twelve-year anniversary of the Hines murder/suicide."

Warwick tightened his jaw and turned down a country road. "This is a little too connected to be a coincidence."

"Yeah."

Another right and another left and they arrived at the Hines' driveway. As Graves's map indicated, it was marked by a tall oak tree that had been split down the center by lightning. The rusty mailbox had long fallen from its post and lay on the side of the road covered in weeds.

They drove down the rutted driveway until they reached the end. Before them stood the charred remains of the home Lindsay had grown up in. The only part of the structure left standing was the brick fireplace and the foundation.

They got out and walked toward the foundation.

"Who owns the land?" Warwick said.

"Lindsay said the county took it for back taxes about eight years ago. They tried to sell it to a developer, but the well water in the area turned up contaminated from one of Hines's underground storage tanks. Remediation was too expensive so the land has just been sitting."

Lindsay had said her mother had loved to garden, but there were only hints of the flower beds she'd told him covered the property. Soil mounds for vegetables cut through a portion of the field behind the house. A flowering vine twisted around a gazebo that had been ravaged by the weather and time. And on the back of the lot, there was a greenhouse.

"Let's have a look."

They walked around the house's foundation toward the greenhouse. Most of the windows had been shattered by vandals' rocks. The door hung on one hinge and it was easy to push open. Inside were rows of long-dead plants and a collection of clay pots. Zack picked up a stack of pots. Lindsay's birthday was tomorrow. If he had time, he'd clean these up for her.

"We'd better get back to town," Warwick said.

"Yeah."

As they turned, Zack spotted words carved over the

doorjamb. The letters were crude and looked as if they'd been carved with a knife.

He reached up and wiped the dirt free. The words read, *L and J forever*. "L and J. What was Graves's grandson's name?"

"Joel Heckman."

"Let's have a chat with Joel."

It wasn't hard to find Joel Heckman. He worked at a bicycle shop in the town of Ashland, the county seat. Zack and Warwick stepped through the shop's doors fifteen minutes later.

A lean man in his early thirties stood behind a glass display case filled with expensive bike accessories. He was holding a bike shoe and trying to fasten a clip to the bottom. "Welcome. Can I help you?"

Both detectives pulled out their badges as they approached the counter.

"Joel Heckman?" Warwick queried.

"Yeah."

"We came to ask you a few questions about Lindsay O'Neil."

He looked puzzled. "O'Neil?"

"You'd know her as Lindsay Hines."

Joel's eyes widened. "Lindsay. God, I haven't seen her in years. What's this all about? Is she okay?"

"She's fine," Zack said. "We're looking into her background."

Joel nodded. "Her mother's murder."

"Yeah," Zack said. "What can you tell us about it?"

He shoved out a breath and set down the shoe. "I wish I'd gone into the house with her that day. I always thought if I'd gone in I might have found her mother first and spared her the sight."

"But you just dropped her off," Zack said.

"Yeah. She was excited to be home early. It was Thursday and her mother's regular afternoon off. Her mom had started working at the diner in town and had to work all the time. They didn't see each other much."

"Know anything about her extended family? She ever talk about anyone?" Warwick said.

"Naw, she never talked about them at all. I think her mom had a falling out with her family. They didn't like Frank, I think."

"She talk about anything?" Zack said.

"She always kept the conversation light. She never brought friends home and spent a lot of time in the library. She could have graduated a year earlier because she had so many credits but she wanted to stay in town. I think now it was to be close to her mom. Maybe she thought she was protecting her."

"What about her father?" Warwick said.

"There's no nice way to say it—he was an asshole. He lost his temper once with her at the pool because she kept him waiting five minutes." Joel shook his head. "Lindsay had been giving a kid a swimming lesson. The kid was terrified of the water and Linz always spent extra time with her."

Linz. Joel's affection for Lindsay was clear. "She was your friend."

"Yeah. She was great. And I can tell you she didn't deserve her father's shit. I can tell you if Frank Hines hadn't killed himself, there were about a half dozen people in town who would have killed him. Myself included."

Chapter Fourteen

Tuesday, July 8, 10:00 A.M.

Vega and Ayden pulled up in front of Ruby Dillon's small brick house, located just a couple of miles east of Richmond International Airport. Crabgrass covered the front lawn, but there was a pile of neatly piled bricks, as if someone was planning to fix the place up. There were three cars parked out front. By the looks of the property, several people lived there.

This was Vega's neck of the woods. He'd grown up in the east end of the county. His old man had worked for one of the airlines and his mom had taught math at Highland Springs High School. His little brother, Michael, was a cornerback on the same school's football team. Both his folks were active in the church.

As Vega and Ayden got out of the car, a jet engine roared over their heads. Vega glanced up at the sky. He'd never gotten used to the noise. His roots were in this part of New Kent County, but he'd chosen to live twenty miles east in a rural section.

They strode to the front porch. Rap music blared

from inside the tiny house. The music was so loud that Vega could feel the bass in his chest.

Ayden rang the bell. "My boys like this crap. I bet they're cranking it just as loud at my house."

"I thought they were going to summer school."

"The oldest is. The younger one works afternoons at a hardware store."

"They doing all right?"

Ayden frowned. "We're all still stumbling through the motions. Carol has been gone a year and a half and we still can't get our shit together." He pounded on the door. This time a dog started to bark.

"At least the dog knows we're here," Vega said.

The sound of locks unlatching followed. Ruby Dillon opened the door. She wore a brown and orange uniform. Vega and Ayden knew that she worked as a nurse's aid at Virginia Commonwealth University Medical Center. They pulled out their shields as she faced them.

Ruby frowned and then turned to shout, "Brianna, turn that music down!" After a second's pause, the music stopped. She didn't open the screen door. "You come about that dead man, I suppose."

Ayden nodded. "Yes, ma'am. We'd like to ask you some questions."

Her jaw set. "I spoke to two other detectives yesterday. I've told them all that I know."

"We've got a few more questions, if you don't mind," Vega said.

Ruby pursed her lips. "I do mind, as a matter of fact. I've got to get to work."

The woman looked familiar to Vega. He'd bet money she knew his mother through the church. His mother knew everyone in this part of the county. "Excuse me for asking, but do you know Rita Vega?"

Ruby eyed him. "Maybe I do."

Vega smiled. He was good at shooting the shit and getting people to warm up. "You go to Third Baptist?"

"I do."

"Thought so. My parents attend. Mom's been a fixture there for twenty years."

Ruby's frown softened. "You're one of Rita's boys?"

"I am."

Her stance relaxed. "I haven't seen Rita in a few weeks. How she doing?"

"Fine. My brother, Michael, is giving her fits. He gets his driver's license in a week and can't wait to drive. Dad swears his heart won't be able to take Michael driving."

Ruby chuckled. "Michael's a good boy. Full of piss and vinegar, but he's good. Rita and George will get a handle on him." She was thoughtful for a moment. "Your mama was one of the few that was nice to me when I got released from jail. She even took Brianna shopping for her prom dress this spring."

Vega and Ayden had discussed Ruby on the way over. She had been hiding cocaine for her boyfriend when the cops busted her. She'd done six months in exchange for testimony against him. He was now doing ten years at Greensville Prison. But they had realized this morning that the boyfriend, as it turns out, worked for Ronnie T.

Ruby pushed open the screen door. "I got a couple of minutes before I got to go. Come on in."

Vega promised himself he owed his mother a big thank-you. If not for her, Ruby Dillon would have shut the door on them now.

Ayden didn't look rushed. He glanced at the surrounding yards before stepping over the threshold into the house. "We'll do our best to hurry things along."

Vega's gaze scanned the living room, which reminded him so much of his parents'. The furniture was old and worn, but the room was neat and organized. Off the living room at the kitchen table sat a teenage girl. She wore shoulder-length braids and an *Usher* T-shirt. No doubt that was Brianna, the one who had been playing the loud music.

Ruby didn't move from the small foyer nor did she offer them a seat.

"Tell me about yesterday," Vega said. "How did you find the body?"

Ruby sighed her impatience. "I told that Detective Kier yesterday that I got the shelter women off to work and the kids off to school. It was a regular day and nothing out of the ordinary. I loaded up the trash like I do each morning I work at the shelter and took it out to the trash cans. That's when I found him."

"You didn't see anyone else in the backyard?" Ayden said.

"Nope. And I didn't hear or smell nothing either."

"What about during the night?" Vega said.

"Quiet. But I did hear a dog barking around five. It woke me up. I got up and looked out the front window but didn't see anything."

"How many nights a week do you stay at the shelter?" Ayden asked.

"Three or four, depending on the schedule. My son stays with Brianna when I'm gone overnight. I generally show up around five and leave by ten. Yesterday was the exception. I stayed late to help Lindsay."

"You were there when the flowers were delivered?"

"I was."

"Did you see who dropped off the flowers?"

"I didn't. Lindsay's office is closer to the front door than mine, so it would be simple for anyone to come in the front door and drop the box on her desk. I thought I heard somebody but figured it was a cop. After I answered all those calls, I went into Lindsay's office, thinking she'd returned. That's when I saw the box."

"Did you open it?" Vega said.

"Well, yeah, I peeked inside. Lindsay never, ever gets flowers and I wanted to see what she'd gotten." She shuddered. "I had no idea what was under those blossoms."

"Did you look at the note?" Ayden asked.

"No. The note was private."

"Did the shelter have any trouble recently? Other than yesterday?" Vega said.

"One of our residents, Aisha Greenland, kept getting calls from her husband, Marcus, on her cell phone. He left her all kinds of nasty messages. Finally, Lindsay had Aisha change the number. And a couple of weeks ago, we had to toss a gal out for drug possession. She was pissed."

"She got a name?"

"Sally somebody. It's in Lindsay's records."

"I didn't see surveillance cameras at the shelter," Ayden said.

"We can't afford them right now."

Vega made a note. "Is there anything else you can tell us?"

Ruby's first response was to shake her head no, but then she stopped. "Well, I'll tell you, last week something did happen, here, at my house. It wasn't much and I didn't bother to tell Lindsay."

"What happened?" Vega said.

"I had a break-in. Someone came inside my home while I was at work and Brianna was at school. Nothing was taken but I knew someone was here."

"Any idea what they were looking for?" Ayden said.

"There was a time when someone might have found *something*, but I did my time and there is no more of that here."

"You report it?" Ayden said.

"No. Like I said, nothing was taken. But someone was in my house."

The detectives asked a couple more follow-up questions

about Ruby's job and Lindsay's work. Nothing out of the ordinary came up and they left.

"So why break into a woman's house and not take anything?" Vega said as they walked to their car.

"I hate coincidences," Ayden answered.

"So do I."

Chapter Fifteen

Tuesday, July 8, 11:00 A.M.

Mental Health Services was in a one-story brick building that was curtained off from the main road by a row of trees. It had tinted windows and nondescript signage. Few noticed it when they drove by.

Lindsay was on staff at Mental Health Services as a full-time counselor. Tuesdays and Wednesdays, she worked eight-hour days. On Thursdays she worked a twenty-four-hour shift, manning the crisis line. The rest of her time was spent at the shelter.

Since the shelter location was a secret, she used this facility to meet with her shelter family members on Mondays and Fridays. The county also allowed her to host her shelter's board of directors' meetings in the main conference room and interview potential shelter staff here on her off days.

Today, like every Tuesday, her morning was insanely busy. She had held her regularly scheduled counseling sessions and had also ended up on the phone with her board director, Dana Miller. The conversation had lasted almost a half hour. Keeping her tone positive, she had filled Dana in on everything about the Turner murder investigation. Dana had reminded her that so far she'd been able to keep the press at bay. Lindsay had thanked her and promised that with luck they'd be back in business by the end of the week.

Dana hadn't sounded happy, but she hadn't complained too much.

Lindsay's last morning appointment was with Howard and Marilyn Jackson. The couple was in their late fifties, came from an affluent background, and split their time between Richmond and Boca Raton. Lindsay had first met the couple when she'd helped their twenty-six-year-old battle alcoholism. Brenda had moved in with the couple a few months ago, and all had seemed well— until last week, when Marilyn had discovered her daughter was using illegal drugs. Marilyn had called Lindsay on Sunday night for help. Lindsay had agreed to a Tuesday appointment.

Marilyn and Howard sat side by side across the conference table from Lindsay. Dark circles marred the white flesh under Howard's eyes. Clearly he'd not been sleeping. And the lines in Marilyn's face looked deeper.

"How long do you think she's been using?" Lindsay said.

Marilyn's large purse sat in her lap as if it were a shield. "I don't know. Years maybe. I'm starting to wonder if we ever knew her."

Howard remained silent, his arms folded over his chest. Deep wrinkles creased his temples and the corners of his mouth.

"Will she come and talk to me?" Lindsay offered. "I've dealt with my share of drug addicts and alcoholics."

Marilyn shook her head. "She refuses to talk to you or attend any AA meetings. She thinks she has all the answers. She thinks she's in control."

"Believe me, she's not in control," Lindsay said.

Howard nodded as if he was relieved to hear someone else say those words.

Lindsay understood firsthand how difficult and persuasive substance abusers could be. "What I'm proposing won't be easy."

Howard shifted forward as if needing a plan of action. "We'll do what it takes."

Lindsay nodded, saying, "Don't underestimate what it takes to help her get clean and sober."

Marilyn lifted her chin. "We're not afraid of hard work."

Hard didn't begin to describe what lay ahead. "You need to tell Brenda that if she doesn't get help there are going to be consequences."

"Such as?" Howard said.

"If she doesn't stop drinking and using, then you will withdraw all financial support. No access to your cash, definitely no use of your car, until she sees me or an AA counselor. And you can always ask her to leave your house."

Marilyn's shoulders slumped. "How can we ever ask her to leave? She depends on us so much. I don't want to see her suffer anymore."

"I understand the rough road you face," Lindsay said softly. "I'm not saying you put her out on the street today. But she needs to understand if she's going to stay in your house, she's expected to be clean and sober. It's your house and your rules." Lindsay kept her tone gentle. "The alcohol and drugs are eating her up. It's only going to get worse."

Tears ran down Marilyn's lined face. "But she needs our help. And I'm afraid if she doesn't have us, she'll go back to her ex-husband."

Lindsay thought back to the hour-long conversation they'd had on Sunday. "Brenda is twenty-six, and she doesn't have a job. She depends on you for cash, which she's using to buy drugs and alcohol. She's stolen from you. Marilyn, it's time to stop making it so easy for her to drink and use."

Marilyn started to weep.

Howard's frown deepened. "Have you ever been through anything like this? And I mean personally, not just professionally."

Lindsay nodded. "As a matter of fact, I have. I've been through the kind of battle you are going to fight."

Marilyn sniffed. "Who did you have this problem with? A brother or a sister?"

Lindsay usually was careful not to reveal too much about herself. It was important to keep barriers between her and her clients. But today her guard was down. Seeing Zack yesterday had brought a lot to the surface. "My husband. I was devastated when I realized he was an alcoholic, like my father had been."

Marilyn stared at her through watery eyes. "What did you do?"

"I begged him to stop drinking. And when he refused, I kicked him out of our house."

Howard stiffened. "That sounds drastic."

"It was. But he is a tough, arrogant man and I wanted to get his attention. I wanted him to understand he had to clean up."

"Did he?" Howard asked.

Her hope had been to save her marriage, not destroy it. "Yes. In the end, he got sober. But it was a very long haul."

Marilyn swiped a tear from her cheek. "Did he ever thank you? Did he ever understand what you really did for him?"

Sadness tightened Lindsay's chest as she remembered the morning after he'd left. She'd been guilt ridden after their fight, so she'd called his cell early the next morning to talk. A woman had answered. *He's in the shower right now. Can I have him call you?*

That's when she'd realized Zack had slept with another woman and their marriage was truly over.

Lindsay swallowed the emotions in her throat. "He's living a happy, productive, and clean life now. That's all I really wanted for him."

"So it was worth it," Howard said.

Lindsay tried to smile. She still loved Zack, but understood it was over for them. "Yes."

Howard and Marilyn thanked her, made promises to consider what she'd said, and left.

Lindsay had spent a long time talking to the couple, and she felt completely drained. Normally, she worked through lunch, but today, she had to escape the building and get fresh air.

She dug in her jeans pocket and counted out the money she'd scrounged this morning from the coin jar on her washer. It was only six dollars and twenty-five cents. Not a fortune, but until she got her purse back, it was enough to buy her lunch.

She pushed through the security doors separating the counselors' offices from the lobby, then swung by the receptionist desk. "Back in a half hour. Need anything, Madge?"

The forty-something woman peered over reading glasses. "A man who cooks."

Lindsay laughed as she signed out. "I'll see what I can do. Any particular type of cook you're looking for?"

"No, baby. Just as long as his food is tasty and hot, I'm good. It doesn't take much to make Madge happy."

As the phone rang, Madge handed Lindsay a stack of pink telephone messages before picking up the line.

Lindsay shuffled through the messages. Dana had called again. Ruby called once. And Zack called at 11:32.

Out of habit she reached for her cell in her purse. But

she had no purse and no cell. Both were in her office. She felt naked without them. "Damn."

She considered returning to the conference room to return the calls, but her stomach grumbled. Eat first, and then tackle the calls, she decided.

Outside, midday heat warmed her skin, which had been chilled by the hours in the air-conditioning. For a moment, she just stood and drank in the warmth. She opened her eyes and stared into the cloudless sky before returning her gaze to the pink message from Zack. The "Please Call" box was checked. A lightning quick image of Zack's piercing, unreadable gray eyes flashed across her mind. Her stomach clenched and her heart quickened. She wondered if his lips still tasted the same.

Not good. She crumpled her messages and shoved them in her pocket.

She started across the parking lot. A quarter mile down the road there was a fast-food joint where she could grab a burger. Not her first choice but it would fit the bill.

Halfway across the parking lot she heard, "Lindsay O'Neil!"

The gruff voice had her turning to find a tall man wearing faded jeans and a Redskins T-shirt. He weighed about 200 pounds and was losing his fine blond hair to age. He quickly closed the dozen feet separating them.

"Yes?" Lindsay said. The sun shone in her eyes, forcing her to squint.

The man's jaw tightened, released. "My name is Burt Saunders." He dug calloused fingers into his jeans pocket and tossed her rumpled business card back at her. It fluttered to the ground and landed near her feet.

Saunders. Gail Saunders. This man was married to the woman she'd seen yesterday at Mercy Hospital. So this was the creep who had beaten the hell out of his wife. Damn, he must outweigh his wife by a hundred pounds.

Bloodshot eyes glared at her as he advanced a step. "Where is my wife?"

She glanced back toward the building and wondered if anyone on the other side of the tinted glass could see her. Wasn't there supposed to be a security guard by the door? "I don't know."

He swayed as if he'd been drinking. And he reeked of beer and vodka. "She moved out last night. All she left me was a goddamned note that said good-bye and not to come looking for her."

Good for her! Lindsay would gladly have gloated over the victory but she wasn't a fool. Burt Saunders was a big man, he was drunk, and he was real pissed. "I don't know anything about your wife's whereabouts, Mr. Saunders."

"You know where she is. She had your card."

She took a step back. "I don't know anything."

He moved with lightning speed, wrapping his hands around her throat. With a violent shove, he ground her back into the hot metal of a parked car, which quickly started to burn through her cotton top. "Bitch, I'll kill you if you don't tell me where my wife is staying."

The pressure on her throat made speaking difficult. She thought about the mace she carried in the purse she didn't have. "Get your hands off me," she managed.

He snarled and put his lips to her ear. "I ought to choke the life out of you."

Lindsay grabbed his hands and tried to pry them from her neck, but his grip tightened. Black spots dotted her vision. She coughed and gasped for air. Soon she'd black out.

Without warning, Saunders released his grip and lifted his weight off of her. She staggered away from the car and fell to her knees. At the same moment, Saunders dropped to the ground with tremendous force. He was clutching his own neck.

Lindsay looked up, squinting into the sun.

Looming over Saunders was Zack, who was already removing cuffs from his waistband and reciting Saunders his Miranda rights.

Warwick was right behind Zack, gun drawn.

Zack didn't take his gaze off Saunders as he shoved the man down on the ground to his belly. Zack then wedged his knee into the man's back and forced his face to the ground. Cuffs clamped on wrists.

Saunders had regained a little of his composure and started to fight the cuffs. "Fuck you!"

Zack pressed his knee deeper into Saunders's back. "Don't you speak one more word." He glanced over at Lindsay. "Are you all right?"

Her throat burned as she straightened and coughed. "Yes. I'm fine."

Warwick didn't lower his weapon. "Do you have him, Kier?"

"Yes."

Warwick called dispatch. "This is Detective Jacob Warwick. I need a patrol car at the county mental health building on Woodman Road." He waited as the dispatcher responded, "Right."

Saunders struggled. "Let me go. That bitch won't tell me where my wife is."

Again Zack dug his knee into Saunders's back. This time the guy flinched. "Don't say another word." The menace in his voice chilled Lindsay and reminded her of a time when he'd been that furious with her.

Still, she'd never been happier to see anyone. "Thanks."

Zack shot her a glance, swiftly assessing her. "Are you sure you're all right?" His voice sounded brittle.

"I'm good."

Warwick moved beside her. "Your neck looks bruised."

The guy almost sounded concerned. "Like I said, I'm fine."

Zack studied her for another beat and then turned his attention back to Saunders. He informed him he was under arrest for assault.

Saunders's wrists strained against the restraints. "The bitch deserved it. She butted into my life."

Zack jerked on the cuffs. "Shut up."

Within seconds two blue-and-white patrol cars, lights flashing, pulled into the parking lot. The uniforms took custody of Saunders and put him in the back of one of the squad cars.

The reality of how close she'd come to a bad beating or worse sank in.

Zack rested his hands on his hips and stared at her. He kept his voice low but she heard the tension. "What happened?"

"The guy's name is Saunders. His wife was taken to Mercy Hospital yesterday. She had injuries consistent with a beating, so the doctor on call asked me to visit with her."

"That's the appointment at the hospital you had."

"Yes. I spoke to Gail, this guy's wife, and gave her my business card, but I didn't think she cared about what I was saying." She nodded to the car where Burt sat in the backseat. He was glaring at her. "Ole Burt said she moved out last night. He found my card and figured I knew where to find her. And for the record, I don't know where she is." She frowned. "She could have called me. But if she had, she couldn't have gotten me at Sanctuary or on my cell, which is in my purse in my office."

Zack tightened his jaw. "I'll get your purse back today."

"Thanks." Lindsay watched with satisfaction as Saunders struggled against his cuffs in the squad car's backseat.

"Gail might not have been willing to file assault charges against him, but I have no problem with it."

Zack moved away and spoke to Warwick. After several minutes of discussion, Warwick got in the front seat of the patrol car holding Saunders, and the car drove off.

The shrill of an ambulance siren had her cringing. The flash of red lights got closer and the ambulance turned into the parking lot. "Please tell me that ambulance isn't for me."

"It sure is," Zack said.

She dragged a shaky hand through her hair. "I'm fine."

He towered over her. "Easier to get an ambulance here than you to the hospital."

His proximity made her uneasy. She'd always had trouble thinking when he was close. "I'll go see my family doctor."

Even, white teeth flashed. "Time has not made you a better liar."

She tried to sound offended. "What's that supposed to mean?"

"I know you. You're not going to see a doctor. You'll retreat back to your office, maybe eat a pack of Nabs, and drown yourself in work."

Uncomfortable, she shifted. He'd hit the nail on the head. Still, pride had her denying it. "You're wrong."

The paramedics got out and shook hands with Zack. "Bill, good to see you."

Bill was medium height, muscular, with ink black hair and a Cary Grant cleft in his chin. "You too, Zack. So what's going on?"

Zack took Lindsay by the arm. His touch was gentle but unbreakable as he pulled her toward Bill. "Have a look at her. I just pulled a creep off her. He was trying to strangle her."

Strangle. It sounded more frightening when Zack recapped the incident. Adrenaline fading, she felt her knees weaken.

Bill lifted his sunglasses. His green eyes were sharp as he leaned forward to look at Lindsay's neck. "Some red marks that will likely lead to bruises. Come over to the back of the truck and sit down, so I can have a closer look."

Lindsay didn't argue. Saunders could have done real damage and she'd be a fool at this point to pass up a quick once-over from the paramedic.

Zack walked with her to the ambulance.

Bill opened the back of the truck and his partner climbed inside and removed a tackle box filled with medical supplies. With Zack behind her watching, Lindsay climbed inside and sat on the cot.

After donning rubber gloves, Bill turned her head from side to side studying her battered skin. "You've got some scratches and you'll have a couple of fingerprint-size bruises in a few days. Can you swallow?"

Lindsay nodded. "Yes. My throat is fine."

Bill pulled an alcohol swab packet from the tackle box and tore it open. "This might sting but I want to get those scratches cleaned."

She winced when the alcohol made contact with her raw skin.

"He grab you anywhere else?" Bill asked.

"No. Just the throat," Lindsay said.

"Who did this to you?" Bill asked.

"Some guy who took exception to the fact that I encouraged his battered wife to leave him."

Bill's lips flattened into a grim line. "I thought I recognized you. I've seen you over at Mercy Hospital in the emergency room. It was a couple of months ago. You showed up to talk to a woman who had been beaten."

"Good memory." Lindsay held out her hand. "Lindsay O'Neil."

Bill took her hand and grinned. The smile was warm, genuine, and she found her foul mood lifting. "Bill Kline." He wiped her neck a second time, his hand lingering close. "I work out of the station house down the road."

The guy was flirting with her. And she felt flattered.

Zack pulled off his sunglasses. Dark eyes flashed annoyance. "Does she need to see a doctor?"

Bill's gaze skipped between Lindsay and Zack. Realization that Zack wanted Lindsay to himself had Bill easing back a fraction from her. "A throat X-ray wouldn't hurt."

"No," Lindsay said. "I'm fine."

Bill took a last look at her neck. "If you have any trouble swallowing, get to a doctor immediately. Otherwise, aspirin and rest are the best medicine."

"Thanks," Lindsay said.

Zack nodded. "I'll keep an eye on her."

She scooted off the cot and hopped down onto the asphalt. "Thanks, fellows, I'm fine." As the paramedics packed up, she painfully started walking the quarter-mile toward the fast-food joint. She needed to sit down before her knees gave way.

Zack followed Lindsay as she made her way across the parking lot. She needed a cold soda and a couple of aspirin.

"I don't need a babysitter," Lindsay said.

Zack wasn't put off. He fell into step beside her. "When's the last time you ate?"

She faced him. "I was on my way to lunch when what's-his-name decided to turn my neck into hamburger."

Zack glanced down the road. "The closest place is a burger shop."

"Walkers can't be choosers."

"You need a real meal—the kind with plates, a table with a cloth, and napkins."

"I don't have time or a car for that kind of stuff."

"You can spare an hour. I'll drive."

He was right. She was hungry, shaken, and needed to collect her thoughts. "Fine."

Zack guided her to his car, opened the door, then closed it after she got in. He slid behind the wheel, put the car into gear, and pulled onto Woodman Road.

In the confined space, Lindsay was aware of his hands on the wheel, the width of his shoulders, the way he clenched and unclenched his jaw as he drove. Suddenly, she wasn't so sure this was a good idea.

"So where are we headed?" she said.

"An Italian place close by."

She tried to relax back into the seat. She needed to loosen the reins for a little while but feared if she did the energy would completely drain from her body.

Zack soon pulled into the parking lot of a small eatery, put the car in park, and turned off the engine. She had climbed out and was halfway around the car before she really looked at the restaurant. *Zola's.* The restaurant owned by his parents. "Aw crap, Zack. Not here. It's your parents' restaurant."

He had the nerve to look shocked. "Why not? It's the best food in town."

She shot him a frustrated look. "Zack, I'm not exactly on your parents' favorite person list. I haven't seen them in a year."

That seemed to surprise him. "They've nothing against you."

She blew out a breath. "Please, Zack."

He stood so close to her she could see he wore the shirt she'd given him. "They like you, Lindsay. It will be fine. Besides, they're not even here today. Mom's got Dad helping her with Eleanor's birthday party. It's Saturday."

His explanation didn't dispel her unease. "Eleanor must be excited."

"Mom's turning the party into a big thing. Dad is going along without a fight, which tells me he's having fun. They've invited half of Richmond."

Lindsay's heart clenched. When she'd eloped with Zack the Kier family had welcomed her with open arms. She'd fallen for the entire clan as hard as she'd fallen for Zack. And when she'd kicked him out, she'd desperately wanted to explain to his parents why. But they'd never called her and she hadn't felt right about calling them. As fast as she'd made a family, she'd lost one.

Lindsay managed a smile. "I'm glad for them. Don't they have an anniversary coming up soon?"

"Next month. Thirty-five years."

"Wow."

Zack stared at her as if trying to read her mind and then, placing his hand in the small of her back, guided her into the restaurant. Immediately they were hit with a blast of cold air. The interior was dark and it took a moment for their eyes to adjust. The place was deserted.

"Where is everyone?" she said.

"We don't open until four on Tuesdays."

"If they aren't open, why are we here? I don't want to put anyone out."

"You're not. And they've always got pots on the stove simmering for dinner. I know we can scrounge a decent meal."

The familiar smells of marinara and freshly baked bread swirled around her, and for a moment she was transported back to those few months when everything had been good between them. "The place is just as I remembered it."

"Mom wants to redecorate—she's even called in a few

contractors for bids. But Dad refuses. He says people like tradition, places that don't change."

Her gaze skimmed the small square tables covered with crisp white linens. Even the napkins were cloth, pressed neatly into rectangles. On each table was a small hurricane lamp with an unlit candle.

Oddly, the restaurant had always made her feel at home. "Your dad is right. I always liked the place just like it is."

"Don't let Mom hear you say that."

Audrey Kier was a force to be reckoned with. A former stage actress, she had a flare for drama, which was accentuated by her short silver hair and still-trim body. She was outspoken, generous, and fiercely loyal to her family. Cross one of hers and you crossed her.

Lindsay's unease returned. "Maybe this isn't such a good idea."

Zack grabbed his sunglasses and tucked them in his breast pocket, "You're not afraid are you?"

Challenge punctuated each word. "No."

He smiled. "Then stay and have lunch."

He was daring her. "Fine."

Zack's brother, Malcolm, pushed through the kitchen door. Dressed in black, Malcolm possessed the same gray eyes as his brother, but his build was more muscular. Zack was the runner; Malcolm, the bodybuilder.

Malcolm frowned, clearly not happy to see Lindsay. "Zack. Lindsay. What's up?"

Zack grinned. "Looking for some lunch."

Malcolm glared at Zack as if to say: *We'll talk later.* "There are a few things brewing on the stove."

If Zack noticed his brother's dissatisfaction, he ignored it. "Great. We'll have two plates of whatever you've got. What are you doing here today?"

"Mom's got Dad wrapped around the axle about the party. I had a few days off so I offered to fill in today."

Zack grinned. "You swore after high school you'd never work in the restaurant again."

Malcolm shrugged. "Never say never, right? Go ahead and pick a table and I'll send Eleanor out with bread. Pasta and marinara sound good?"

Zack looked at Lindsay, his eyebrow lifted. "Work for you?"

Malcolm could have offered rusty nails on a plate and she'd not have argued. She smiled. "Sure."

Zack guided Lindsay to a back table tucked in a corner. He pulled out a chair for her, waited while she sat, then took the seat nearest to the wall—he always liked his back to the wall, eyes facing the door. This quirk was a holdover from his undercover days.

"Well, that's a first," she said as she sat.

"What?"

This close she could smell his soap. She loved the simple, masculine scent. "You held out a chair for me."

He opened a napkin. "Even an old dog can learn a new trick." Extra meaning punctuated the comment, and she didn't know how to respond. An uneasy silence settled between them before he broke it. "How secure is your apartment?

She opened a pack of crackers. "K-bar in the sliding glass door. Dead bolts on front and back doors. Extra long screws in the doorjambs. Not real high tech but effective."

"Lose the key under the flower pot yet?"

Lindsay nodded. "I'm willing to admit it was stupid to keep the key under the pot. It is now gone."

Zack seemed satisfied. "Ever had any trouble with anyone connected to the shelter? Anyone ever follow you home?"

"No. That hasn't been an issue. But I've been called every name in the book by enraged husbands and boyfriends. Even the victims can get nasty when I push them to testify against their abusers. But that's all par for the course. Nothing new."

"What about the woman who was killed by her husband about nine months ago? What was her name? Rogers?"

"Pam Rogers. And I blame myself for that one."

He frowned. "Why?"

"I should have seen it coming. Pam was extremely codependent and terrified of living without her husband. I told her time and again not to call her husband, but she couldn't let it go. Thirty minutes after I left for the day, she called him. A half hour after that he picked her up. He was hitting her before they were in the car. The volunteer on call telephoned me. We called the police."

"She was found dead the next morning," Zack said.

"Yes. I went to her funeral. One of her brothers approached me. He was angry and blamed me for what had happened. I remember someone from the crowd dragging him away."

"She was an adult, Lindsay. You couldn't have stopped her."

"But if I'd been there I could have talked her out of calling." The *but-ifs* stalked her.

His voice softened. "You can't be there twenty-four/seven."

She shook her head. "I still remember the pain in her brother's eyes."

"What was his name?"

"Simon Palmer."

"Where does this guy live?"

"Richmond. Southside, I think. He's an accountant."

"You had any contact with him since his sister's funeral?"

"None."

The doors to the kitchen swung open and a young

waitress with honey blond hair swept into the room with a tray of water glasses, bread sticks, and plates of pasta. Lindsay recognized Zack's older sister, Eleanor, immediately. Eleanor was thirty-three years old, vivacious, and had Down syndrome. She had as much pride as the other Kiers and was determined to be as independent as possible.

Lindsay beamed. "Eleanor!"

"Hi, Lindsay," she said, grinning.

When Lindsay had met Eleanor, Eleanor had been living in her parents' house but had wanted a place of her own. Her fiercely protective family had vetoed the idea. It had been Lindsay who'd suggested that the room over the Kier family garage be converted into an apartment. The idea had been a hit, and within months the room had been turned into a fully functioning apartment. Eleanor had been thrilled. So had her parents.

Eleanor set her tray on a stand and served them.

Lindsay then stood and hugged Eleanor. "You look wonderful."

Eleanor grinned broadly and hugged Lindsay back. "You look skinny."

Lindsay laughed. Eleanor had no pretense and always said what was on her mind. The honesty was refreshing. "So everyone keeps telling me. I guess I'd better eat."

Zack stood. There was softness in his gaze when he looked at his sister. He was a year younger than her, but he'd always been her protector. He'd once told Lindsay that Ellie was the reason he'd become a cop.

"So what are you doing here this afternoon, Ellie? I figured you'd be helping Mom and Dad with the party."

Eleanor made a face. "No way. Mom is driving us all crazy. She wants the party to be perfect. And Dad is mumbling a lot under his breath."

Zack smiled. "What else is new?"

"Nothing." Eleanor waved for Lindsay and Zack to sit. "Can I get you anything else?"

Lindsay smiled. "No, this is great."

Zack nodded. "We're good."

Eleanor leaned close to Lindsay and said in a stage whisper, "Zack is real sorry about your big fight."

Zack coughed. "Would you beat it, Ellie? Lindsay and I have business to discuss."

"Marriage business?" Eleanor said, hopeful.

Heat rose in Lindsay's face. She didn't dare look at Zack, but she could feel his gaze on her. "Just business."

"Zack, you need to fix this marriage," Eleanor said.

Zack cleared his throat and glared at her. "*Ellie.*"

She matched his glare. "What?"

"Butt out."

She grinned. "No way, José."

"*Ellie,*" he warned.

"Okay, okay, I'm going. But I'm going to be listening at the door."

When Eleanor vanished into the kitchen, Zack said, "She can be a little outspoken."

Lindsay broke a breadstick in two. "I always liked that about her."

He laughed. "I do too, most times."

She took a bite of pasta. It tasted like heaven. She didn't realize how hungry she was. Before she knew it, she'd eaten half of the pasta on her plate.

Zack set down his fork. "Ellie's right, you know."

"About what?"

"Sooner or later, we're going to have to settle this marriage business."

Chapter Sixteen

Tuesday, July 8, 2:00 P.M.

These days it was the little things that reminded Nicole of how much she'd lost during her marriage and was only now regaining in increments. Walking through the park. Ordering an ice cream cone. Having money that she'd earned in her pocket.

She still felt shaky about life in general, but she was discovering how much she'd forgotten how good it felt to make decisions and to be independent.

She strolled down the Carytown district sidewalk. This was her favorite section of town. She loved the early nineteenth-century row houses that were painted bright colors and housed ethnic restaurants and curio shops as eclectic as their patrons.

Nicole moved past the smoothie store, the chocolate shop and into her favorite French bakery. She purchased a croissant and a café au lait and savored both before wandering back outside. Down here, she could almost pretend her life was normal.

Her gaze drifted to a familiar FOR RENT sign posted above a Pilates studio that was sandwiched between a jewelry store and a restaurant. Again, she imagined reopening her photography business.

Giving rein to impulse, she climbed the narrow steps of the building to the second floor. She followed a RENTERS INQUIRE HERE sign to a half-open green door. She knocked.

"Come in!"

Nicole pushed open the door and found a tall woman dressed in a loose-fitting pants-and-shirt ensemble. She had long black hair and dark brown eyes that reminded Nicole of a cat.

"Can I help you?" the woman said.

"I saw your FOR RENT sign."

The woman smiled and extended her hand. "That's wonderful. My name is Fiona Moore. I own the building."

"Nicole Piper." She shook Fiona's hand, grateful she hadn't stumbled with her new name.

"Would you like to see the space?"

Her throat felt dry. It really was madness to entertain owning a business. "Yes."

The woman grabbed keys from the desk drawer. "Follow me."

Nervous, Nicole tightened her fingers around the strap of her bag. "Great."

Fiona moved with the grace of a dancer as she walked down the hallway. She unlocked a door, pushed it open, and flipped on the lights. "So what kind of business do you have?"

"I'd like to open a photography studio." Soft scents of lavender and fresh paint swirled as she stepped into the all-white room distinguished by high ceilings, chair molding, hardwood floors, and a bay window that over-looked Cary Street. The space was small but the southern exposure lighting was exquisite. Immediately, she imagined furnishing the room with simple pieces that she could use as props for her portraits. The place had so many possibilities.

"The space is only about three hundred square feet," Fiona said. "But there is a kitchenette with a large sink that could be converted into a darkroom. That is, if you need a darkroom. So much photography is digital."

Nicole strolled into the center of the room. She pictured cameras on tripods, lights, and backdrops. "I can take digital, but I prefer film. There's a richness that comes through when I develop the photos individually."

Fiona smiled. "You're an artist."

At one time art was all she was about. Now it was a luxury she couldn't afford. These last two months she'd learned to be brutally practical and ruthless. "How much is the rent?"

"Seven hundred plus utilities."

Nicole tried not to wince. Once she could have afforded the price. "I'm just getting started and poverty is a fact of life right now."

Fiona wasn't put off by her honesty. "Do you have a portfolio?"

Nicole moved out of the room. No sense dreaming about what wasn't to be now. "I've a collection of recent work I've done since I came to Richmond. All portrait work."

"I'm looking for a photographer to take pictures of me and the studio. Big marketing push for the studio in the fall. I'd love to see your work."

Excitement rose inside her. "Sure."

"I can't pay much." Smiling, Fiona locked the door behind them. "You're not the only one on a tight budget."

Nicole mentally leafed through her pictures. Already she'd taken several dozen portraits. What she had to show didn't measure up to the caliber of her old stuff, but it was still good. "Might take me a couple of days. I could come by next Monday."

Fiona brightened. "Ten?"

She thought about her work schedule. "I can make that."

Fiona held out her hand. "See you on Monday at ten, Nicole Piper."

A wide grin tugged at Nicole's lips. "Great."

The thought of freelance work filled her with hope for the future. She didn't have the money to open a business now, but she'd taken the first step toward it.

Nicole hurried down the stairs but was so distracted she nearly bumped into a man. He had dark hair slicked back off his face and Rayban sunglasses.

For just a split second, she thought the stranger was her husband, Richard.

Heat from the sidewalk shot upward, and sweat began to trickle down her bare legs. "Excuse me." Her voice cracked.

The man nodded. "No problem." He kept walking.

She stared after him. He wasn't Richard. Richard was 3,000 miles away. Yet, her heart hammered in her chest. She started walking, but her gait wasn't as confident. The ease she'd felt just seconds ago had vanished.

She'd not seen Richard in nearly three months, but that didn't mean she was safe. She *knew* her husband. He was out there looking for her, and if she wasn't very, very careful he'd find her. She glanced back at the FOR RENT sign. What had she been thinking? A business was just too risky.

She opened the cell phone Lindsay had given her and turned it on. She usually kept the phone off because Richard had used her old cell to keep tabs on her.

Her hands trembling, she dialed the number of the woman who'd helped her escape Richard: Claire

Carmichael. As the phone rang, she wasn't sure what Claire could tell her. Maybe that Richard was still in San Francisco . . . that he'd forgotten about her.

Claire's voice mail picked up. When the beep sounded, Nicole panicked and couldn't speak. Lindsay had warned her about any contact with people from her old life. She closed the phone.

Let sleeping dogs lie.

Better to be safe.

For the millionth time, she wished Richard was dead.

San Francisco, 11:15 A.M. PST

Richard Braxton had chosen his home because of the stunning view of San Francisco Bay. The original house on the lot had been old, filled with "charm," according to the historical society, but it hadn't suited his vision of the home he deserved. So he'd had the house razed. There'd been an outcry, protests, lawsuits even, but he'd maneuvered through it all.

The showpiece house he'd created, with its steel and sleek modern lines, didn't suit the narrow-minded tastes of his neighbors, who preferred brick and boxwoods. But that didn't concern him. Richard Braxton did what *he* wanted, *when* he wanted.

Richard understood his greatest skill was his ability to see the potential; to know when a house, a market, or a woman was worth his attention.

Potential had been the reason he'd been drawn to the lot and it had been the reason he'd been attracted to Christina, his wife. Christina was a beauty, a stunner, and he had known from the moment he'd first seen her in that rundown photography studio that he could make her into something special.

Training her had not been easy. She had a fierce and spirited nature, and it had taken so many lessons to mold her into the vision he'd had for her. In the last few months they'd been together, he'd begun to believe that he had nearly succeeded. She no longer argued with him. She dressed perfectly in the tasteful Chanels and de la Rentas. She'd learned to be punctual, to keep her makeup perfect, and had tamed that thick mane of black hair.

Perfection had been in his grasp.

And then she'd vanished. That fool chauffer had let her slip away.

How long had she been planning to run from him?

The thought tormented him daily. He replayed every moment they'd shared those last couple of months. He thought about the books she'd read, the movies she'd seen, and the people she'd spoken to, looking for clues. He'd been insanely busy with work during that time and had been distracted. But he'd thought she'd been transformed and there was nothing to worry about.

For her to run, there had to be someone else. She had to have taken a lover.

A soft knock on his study door had him turning to find Vincent Malone standing at the threshold. Vincent wasn't a tall man, but his wiry body was compacted muscle. His Italian double-breasted suit complemented his frame, and his ice blond hair, pulled back in a pony-tail, accentuated vivid green eyes. He was Richard's right-hand man. He knew all his dirty secrets. For the last two weeks, he'd done nothing but search for Christina.

"Anything come of that lead Jimmy gave us?" Richard said.

Vincent closed the study door behind him. "I've had men canvassing the area and showing her picture around. No one has seen her."

Richard moved to his large mahogany desk that he'd had specially made in Spain. "So that's it? She just vanished?"

Vincent smiled. Like Richard, he savored a good hunt. "Everyone leaves a trail, Mr. Braxton. The trick is being able to find it."

"Has there been activity on a credit card or cell phone?"

"No. There's been no activity on her cards, phones, or Social Security number. And I've had computer experts check every chip in her computer. Nothing. I've still got men looking in every airport, bus and train station, and car rental place. But there's been no sign of her."

Anger was nearly driving him insane. Killing Jimmy had made him feel good for a while. But his well-being hadn't lasted long. "So we've got shit."

"Not exactly."

Richard flexed his fingers. "So you've found something?"

"Claire Carmichael."

His patience wore thin. "I don't know her."

"She owns the New Age bookstore about five blocks from the restaurant where Jimmy lost Christina."

"Why do I care about her?"

"She's part of this network of people who help abused women disappear. She speaks regularly at community centers in your area."

Months of pent-up rage burned in Richard. "Abused women. Christina wasn't abused. I gave her everything. I love her."

Vincent nodded his head in deference. "I didn't mean to suggest she was."

Richard drew in a deep breath. "So you think this Carmichael woman helped Christina?"

"Yes. Your wife's driver remembered taking her to a

Bay Area church several weeks in a row. I checked. It was a support group run by Claire Carmichael. I want to talk to her."

Richard shook his head. "The bitch interfered with my marriage. Give me her address."

Vincent looked doubtful. "Wouldn't you rather I take care of it? Better to let me do the dirty work."

"I like the dirty work."

Richard downshifted the gears of his BMW and pulled into a parking spot in front of the New Age bookstore located near San Francisco Bay. The store was housed in an old row house that had survived the big earthquake a hundred years ago. Tall with a sharp roof, square bay windows, and lots of gingerbread trim, the building was considered a treasure, but by his way of thinking it was an old pile of junk.

He'd never have given the place a second glance if not for Claire Carmichael.

He shut off the car engine and got out. Inside the store, he spotted Claire. She was about thirty, olive skin, not tall. She wore a frumpy, flowing dress that hid her curves, and she had pulled back curly hair into a high ponytail that highlighted sharp cheekbones and bright eyes. Not his type, but loosen the hair and ditch the dress and she might be worth a spin.

Richard grew hard.

He imagined her eyes lighting with desire as he shoved inside her. And then he pictured the passion shifting to fear as he wrapped his hands around her neck and squeezed the life out of her. She'd fight to breathe. She'd kick, try to scream. But in the end, the life would fade from her body.

It was almost closing time and it didn't take long before the store emptied of customers.

Richard had all night to chat with Little Miss New Age about Christina.

When she disappeared behind a curtain into the back room of the store, he went inside, careful to keep the bells on the door from jingling. Softly he shut the door, locked it, and flipped the OPEN sign to CLOSED.

Richard moved behind the counter and unplugged the phone.

"Hello, is someone out there?" Claire called.

He reached into his pocket and let his fingers slide over the cold steel of his knife.

Claire heard the creak of footsteps in the store. The hair on the back of her neck rose. She'd had trouble with shoplifters in the last few months and didn't like to leave the store unattended.

She took off her glasses and laid them on the ledger on her desk. She stood and crossed to the curtain separating the back room from the retail portion of the store. She pushed through the curtain. "Can I help you?"

The man standing by the display of healing crystals wasn't what she'd expected. He was hardly a teen thug looking to grab up what he could. And he wasn't remotely like her regular patrons.

He was smartly dressed in a stylish suit that looked handmade. His white open-neck shirt was made of crisp linen. His nails were buffed and his short black hair was brushed off his face. Strong jaw. Tanned skin. Nice to look at.

The man raised his head and met her gaze. His eyes were so dark that the pupils all but disappeared. She'd never glimpsed the face of Evil but now she sensed she was looking right at it.

The man tossed her a quick smile. "I hope you can help me."

A lump formed in the pit of her stomach. "What do you want?" Her tone had grown hard, losing all hint of welcome.

He set down the expensive crystal he'd been cradling. "My wife. Christina Braxton."

Claire remembered the woman vividly. The bruises on her arms and neck testified to the trauma she'd suffered at the hands of her husband. Claire had sensed the fear and the goodness in Christina. It had been an easy choice to give her cash and the keys to the secondhand car. "I don't know what you're talking about."

Richard nodded almost as if he were pleased by her answer. He pulled the switchblade from his pocket and he flicked the blade open. "I was hoping you wouldn't talk too quickly."

Panic exploded inside Claire. She snatched up the phone and discovered the line was dead. She bolted to the back of the shop to the back alley exit.

Richard moved quicker than a cat. He reached her just as she made it to the door. He grabbed a handful of her hair and jerked her head back. He drew the knife blade along her cheek, slicing flesh as he went. Pain burned her face as warm blood oozed down her cheek.

"Where is my wife?" he whispered against her ear.

"I don't know."

Claire wasn't going to tell him where Christina was hiding. And she knew the cost of her silence was going to be her life.

Chapter Seventeen

Tuesday, July 8, 3:20 P.M.

Kendall was very pleased with herself. She and Mike had shot her evening report and it had gone better than good. Lindsay's past made great television. This newscast was going to get Kendall noticed.

Her phone rang. Without taking her eyes off the road, she pulled the phone from her purse and flipped it open. "Kendall Shaw."

"You're a hard woman to find." The deep male voice sounded smooth, confident, but she didn't recognize it.

"Who's this?"

"Detective Jacob Warwick, Henrico County Police. Your phone has been busy all morning."

Damn. She thought about the film footage of the delivery truck at the shelter. That was the kind of information she should have shared with the cops first thing this morning. An obstruction of justice charge would not help her career.

Kendall kept her voice smooth. "Sorry. Running down leads on a story. What can I do for you?"

"I'd like to chat with you about the shelter murder and review your tape from yesterday."

She kept her voice cheerful. "Sure. What time works for you?"

"Now would be nice."

The steel behind the words left little room for argument. And she wasn't about to piss anyone off at this point. "I can swing by the station and get a copy of the footage." No need to mention she had one at home. "It will take me at least a half hour to get the tape and meet you at my office."

"I'll meet you at the at station office."

Her mind turned. Maybe she could even score a quote or two from Warwick. "See you in a half hour."

Kendall arrived at the television station fifteen minutes late. When she rushed into the lobby, she spotted the detective immediately. He was staring into one of the station's trophy cases, his hands clasped behind his back. He had a relaxed way that she suspected was deceptive. "Detective Warwick?"

His smile didn't reach his piercing eyes. "Kendall Shaw."

Kendall crossed the lobby and accepted Warwick's hand. His grip was powerful. "Good to meet you."

"I appreciate the help."

"If you will follow me, I'll take you upstairs. I can burn a copy of that footage onto a CD for you." The west wing of the Deco-style building was littered with ladders and plastic tarps. "Excuse our mess. We're undergoing a huge renovation."

"No problem."

They wound down the narrow corridors. "Would you like a tour of our newsroom?"

"No thanks." He flashed even, white teeth. "Maybe another time."

"Sure." Under his easygoing demeanor was steel. "When the renovation is done, all this is going to be gone. From what I hear, it will all be very sleek."

"Really?"

So much for small talk. She led him to a news edit bay, a small glassed-in room off the hallway furnished with a computer station. She sat down on the swivel chair in front of the computer. "The station's new P2 cameras are equipped with hard drives, so there's rarely a tape anymore. With luck we still have the footage. Generally, when we've filed the story, we dump the raw stuff to clear space on the computer."

Warwick frowned. "Let's hope it's still here. The other stations didn't have anything."

Kendall punched a few buttons and opened a file. "You're in luck. The footage is here." She burned a CD and handed it to him.

"Thanks."

She rose and had to look up to meet his gaze. "No problem."

When he nodded and started to turn, she said, "I hear Lindsay had a rough past. Think there is any connection between this murder and her mother's death?"

The comment surprised Warwick. "You've been doing some homework."

"That's my job. Do you think the two killings are linked?"

His expression was unreadable. "We don't discuss the details of an active case."

"Just seems odd. Her mother is the casualty of a domestic murder and this latest body is dumped behind a women's shelter."

"Can't help you."

She'd have better luck getting blood from a stone than information from Warwick. "Thanks."

Chapter Eighteen

Tuesday, July 8, 4:25 P.M.

Lindsay stood behind Zack as she watched the uniformed officer crate up her office files. Impotent rage roiled inside her. She'd worked for a year to make this shelter into something worthwhile, and in twenty-four hours it had fallen apart.

"Do the cops have to mess everything up?" Lindsay asked, unable to remain silent.

Zack turned. "Lindsay, wait in the kitchen. When Warwick returns, we'll all talk."

Frustration ate at her. A few hours ago, they'd shared a meal. She'd laughed with his sister. Now, he was all cop again. "Can I have my purse? I'd rather go back to Mental Health Services. At least there I can be productive."

"I'll bring it out to you," Zack said.

The wall was back between them. "Great."

She went into the kitchen. This time of day the kitchen should have been teeming with activity. Kids would be running around, residents would be talking, and the phones would be ringing off the hook. Now it was dead silence.

Needing something to do, she went on the back deck to the potting table. There were four six-packs of marigolds, a pot, and soil. All the supplies were still damp from yesterday's rain. Careful to keep her back to the murder scene, she opened the bag of soil and poured rich, dark dirt into the pot. It felt good to have her hands in the soil. She gingerly removed a marigold from the plastic container and pushed it into the soil. She was reaching for the flower pack to get another when the back door opened.

"Ms. O'Neil," Warwick said, "could we talk?"

She shoved out a breath, wondering when he'd returned. "Sure." She headed back into the kitchen and washed her hands. Zack came into the room and the three sat at the kitchen table.

Warwick opened his notebook to a clean page. "We've got our warrant, which gives us open access to your files. You can help us by telling us those that should be red flagged."

Lindsay had thought about that a lot last night. "It's hard to say."

"We'll get the names with or without your help. But your help will make the investigation go faster."

She sighed. The sooner Harold's killer was caught the sooner the shelter would reopen. "We've had some rough cases the last few months. Give me your notebook and I'll write the top ten."

Warwick pushed the notebook and a pen toward her. She scratched out the worst of the abusive spouses she'd dealt with.

Once she'd finished, Warwick studied the names. "Do you think any of these men could be the Guardian?"

"I don't know. But they're all violent men. And none of them would want to help me."

Zack leaned forward but remained silent. Clearly this was Warwick's show.

"When is the last time you saw Turner?" Warwick asked.

She didn't like his tone. "I told Detective Kier all this."

Warwick flashed white teeth. "Again, please, for my benefit."

She reviewed the details of her encounter with Turner.

"And you confronted him at the party?" Warwick said.

She felt that evening's anger returning. "It wasn't my intention, but, yes, I did have words with him."

"Remind you of your old man?" Warwick said.

Angered that Zack must have discussed her past, she straightened. "Yeah, in a lot of ways Turner did remind me of him."

Warwick tapped his index finger on the table. "It's clear you love this place. The toys, the warm colors, and the flowers—they were all done by you, weren't they?"

"Sure."

"And you care about the women and children. I've leafed through a few files. Your notes suggest you really do want these women to succeed."

She sensed a setup. "Cut the compliments. What's your point?"

Warwick's expression hardened a fraction and she had a sense he'd mentally taken off the gloves. "I went to your folks's place in Hanover. It looked as if it had been a nice place at one time."

A sudden weight pressed against her chest. "You were there?"

"Kier and I read your mother's murder file. We see how rough you had it."

"Why are you telling me this?" Her voice was just above a whisper.

"You grew up with an abusive man and then you run into someone like Harold, who reminds you of your father." He met her gaze head-on. "He gets in your face and in essence threatens to close the place you love. It would be reason enough to kill him."

Zack said nothing, nor did he show any emotion. She'd never felt more alone.

"I didn't kill Harold," Lindsay said, teeth clenched.

"You have no alibi, Ms. O'Neil."

"I told you that I was home asleep."

"A fact you can't prove."

Jordan Turner may not have wanted her help but Nicole Piper did, and Lindsay wouldn't tell the cops about her. Richard had contacts in the San Francisco Police Department, and she couldn't risk inquiries from the guys on this end. She'd find a way out of this mess somehow. "No, I can't."

Warwick closed his notebook. "I suggest you get an attorney, Ms. O'Neil."

She glanced at Zack, expecting some kind of support. "I need an attorney?"

Zack showed no hint of emotion. "It wouldn't hurt."

Abruptly she rose. "I can't believe this," she said. "I've got some nutcase out there sending me body parts and now the cops are breathing down *my* throat. I didn't kill Harold. But I'm the first to admit I hated the guy and I won't lose any sleep over the fact that he's dead."

Zack stood but said nothing. He shoved his hands in his pockets and rattled change.

Warwick was unfazed by her outburst. "Get a lawyer."

"Are you going to charge me?" she demanded.

"Not yet."

Lindsay couldn't believe this. All she'd done was stand up for herself when Turner had tried to browbeat her and now she was a murder suspect. "Can I have my purse?"

Warwick slowly rose. "Yes. It's on the banister by the front door."

"Thanks." She started down the hallway.

"Don't leave town without calling me, Ms. O'Neil," Warwick said.

She didn't glance back. "Right."

She snatched up her purse and dug out her keys. She didn't bother with a sideways glance into her office at the jumble the cops had made of her files as she pushed through the front door.

Once in her Jeep, she cranked the engine and backed out. As she drove home the surge of adrenaline from her interview began to fade.

Lindsay felt weary and so alone. She couldn't tell the cops about Nicole. The woman was just getting her life back. She prayed the real killer would be found soon so the spotlight would leave her.

Fifteen minutes later, she pulled in front of her town house. She moved up her walkway and shoved her key in the lock. God, all she wanted now was a hot bath and a cup of tea.

"Lindsay!"

Sam's cheerful voice had Lindsay turning. He wore khakis, a white button-down shirt, and loafers without socks. The late afternoon light pulled red highlights in his thick sandy blond hair.

In a flash she remembered her promise to have dinner with him tonight. "Sam."

"Sorry I'm late," he said.

She glanced forlornly at her home. God, but she wanted to get into bed and pull the covers over her head. "Oh, no problem."

Creases formed around his blue eyes. "You forgot, didn't you?"

She glanced down at her keys in the door and

grinned. "Or maybe I saw you drive up and was headed out to meet you?"

He laughed. "We can go with that story, if you like."

She could feel her blood pressure dropping. "Works for me."

Sam's eyes grew serious. "If you want to bag tonight, it's fine. You look like you've had a tough day."

Her hand went to her ponytail, which had sunk low on her head. "I'm good. I need a night out or I'll sit at home and stew."

He grinned. "Good. There's a new French restaurant out on Patterson."

"I should change."

"Naw, you look good. Besides, it's casual."

She wasn't hungry. Lunch had been filling. Still, an evening out that wasn't emotionally draining would be welcome.

Sam guided her to a sleek Audi and opened the door for her.

Lindsay couldn't help but smile. "You're spoiling me."

"You could use that once in a while." He closed her door and came around the front. The car's interior smelled new.

He slid behind the wheel and started the engine. The soft scent of his aftershave reminded her that this was a *date*.

Crap. Didn't she have enough on her plate?

They'd not driven a block when his cell rang. He glanced down at the number and sent the call to voice mail.

"Why don't you answer that?" Lindsay said. Zack always took his calls.

"It's not important. You are."

Not all men were like Zack.

And that was a good thing. Right?

Alone in the car, this close to Sam, she felt a bit awkward. If he'd been Sam the *friend,* she'd have had no trouble talking to him. But Sam the *date* felt like an entirely different person. Suddenly pressure existed where there'd been none before.

"So how was the hospital today?" she said.

He kept his gaze on the road. "Same old, same old."

Normally, Sam had half a dozen stories to tell about his day in the ER. And his unexpected silence had her scraping for something else to say that would keep the conversation going. "No war stories?"

"None. Ever notice we always talk about work?"

"Yeah."

His expression turned serious. "Let's do our best not to talk shop tonight."

Suddenly she was tongue-tied. What would they talk about? First Zack and now Sam. Why couldn't she carry on a conversation with an adult male? "That doesn't leave much."

He grinned. "There's the weather."

She laughed but realized seeing Sam like this felt dishonest somehow. She was legally separated from Zack and a signature away from finalizing the divorce. She was rebuilding her life without him. Dating was *okay.*

Sam pulled into the restaurant's parking lot and parked in a spot close to the door. She got out and met him at the front of the car. He placed his hand into the small of her back and guided her into the restaurant.

It was a quiet, small bistro that had only opened a couple of months ago. Most weekends the place attracted large crowds. Tuesdays offered a slower pace.

The hostess led them to an intimate table in the back near a fireplace filled with votive candles that flickered in the dimly lit room. "Stop indulging me."

He chuckled and took his seat. "You deserve to be spoiled once in a while."

Lindsay spread her napkin over her lap. "I'm so used to taking care of everything. Being spoiled makes me feel uncomfortable."

The waitress arrived and Sam ordered a bottle of wine as well as a sampling of appetizers. Within minutes they arrived. The wine was excellent, as was the display of cheeses.

As he swirled the Merlot in a glass, his gold signet ring winked in the candlelight. "So why are you so used to taking care of yourself?"

She shrugged. "Long, long story, Sam."

Sam laid his hand on hers. It was warm, soft. "Is there anything I can do to make this day better?"

Her hand felt steadier as she raised her glass to her lips. "Know any good defense lawyers?"

The Guardian watched a drunken Burt Saunders stagger out of the bar on Third Street. In less than twelve hours the bastard had made bail. No wonder people said the American justice system was in the toilet.

Anger roiled inside the Guardian as Saunders lumbered down the sidewalk toward a red Lincoln with a white convertible top. A pink parking ticket lay flat under the windshield wiper. Saunders tossed the ticket in the gutter and fumbled in his pockets for his keys.

He didn't realize that Death stalked him.

Saunders dropped his keys on the street by his car door. He wobbled forward and patted the ground for the set. He lost his balance and hit his shoulder hard against the car door. He swore.

The Guardian moved closer until inches separated them. "Looks like you're having a bit of trouble tonight."

Saunders's bloodshot eyes narrowed. "Fuck off."

No manners. Typical. "You look like you could use a score."

Saunders found his keys and snatched them up. "Like I said, fuck off, bitch."

Killing this fool was going to be a true pleasure, one destined to be savored. "I've got some coke if you're interested. It would go a long way to taking the edge off."

Licking his lips, Saunders glanced around to make sure no one watched. "I don't know what you're talking about."

The fish had taken the bait. "I can make all the pain go away."

"You look like a cop."

"Follow me and I'll show you what I've got."

"I don't need you." To punctuate his statement, he tried to put his key in the car door lock. His hands trembled so badly that he couldn't manage the task.

"Suit yourself." To be too eager would spook the prey. Saunders was a mean son of a bitch but he wasn't stupid.

The Guardian started to walk back toward an alley.

Saunders hesitated and then staggered forward. "How much?"

"Fifty."

"Thirty is all I've got."

"Make it forty."

Saunders considered the counteroffer and then nodded. "Fine."

Gotcha. "In the van in the alley over there."

The drunk nodded and followed. In the moonlight the shadows were long and narrow, shrouding the alley in the darkness. The scent of garbage and urine clung to humid air.

Saunders's large feet shuffled as he moved away from the street. He pulled two crumpled twenties out of his pocket.

The Guardian thought about Saunders's wife, Gail. The woman had been broken and afraid when she'd run from the hospital yesterday. She'd tried so hard not to cry when she'd fumbled with her keys in the hospital parking lot. So brave. So much like Debra. "In the van."

Saunders climbed in, the hunger bright in his eyes.

From a jacket pocket, the Guardian pulled out a baggy filled halfway with white powder. Saunders tossed his money on the seat and snatched the bag.

As he turned to leave the van, the Guardian pressed a Taser to Saunders's neck. The tall man's body jerked and convulsed and he fell back against the seat.

Fear sharpened the haze in Saunders's eyes. "What the fuck?"

The Guardian jabbed the Taser to the soft flesh of Saunders's neck again. The man convulsed painfully. His eyes rolled back in his head and his chest rose and fell as he struggled to suck air into his lungs.

"Retribution is mine," the Guardian whispered, uncapping a syringe and shoving it into Saunders's arm.

Within seconds Saunders's eyes glazed over. The Guardian started the van and eased into the street. There was no hurry tonight. No nervous fear either, like the other night with Turner.

Lindsay couldn't fall asleep. Today had started off as a good day. She had finished her first week in kindergarten and was excited about the day she'd just spent in school. Her teacher had shown the class how to make paper butterflies. Lindsay had loved the colors and the way the crepe paper folded and made delicate wings.

But the joy she'd felt at school had quickly faded when she'd returned home. Her mother had been edgy and worried. When Lindsay's father came home the tension had gotten worse. Her father didn't like the dinner her mother had prepared and he seemed determined to find fault with everything.

Now Lindsay lay curled on her side in her bed with the covers pulled over her head. Her father was shouting at her mother and her mother was crying.

"Who gives you the damn right to talk to him about our problems? I'm your family."

"He's my brother."

"A brother who's not been around for years. I've been here all along. I've been the one putting food in your mouth and clothes on your back. He hasn't."

"He was just worried about me. And I missed seeing him."

"Well, if you think he's so damn great, you go and live with him. But Lindsay stays with me."

"I'll never leave her."

"She's mine. Just like everything else in this house. So if you want to leave, you leave with the shirt on your back."

Footsteps sounded down the hallway toward Lindsay's room. Her mother was crying louder and her father was shouting more. Lindsay's door opened and light from the hallway shone into her room.

"Don't touch my daughter!" her mother shouted.

Flesh smacked against flesh and someone stumbled back. Lindsay peeked out from under the covers and saw her mother fall.

Lindsay started to cry.

Lindsay's cell phone, perched on her nightstand, rang just after midnight and jerked her awake. Accustomed to being awakened in the middle of the night, she sat up and answered it. "Hello?"

No answer.

She shoved back her hair and glanced at the clock on

the bedside table. Sam had dropped her off over three hours ago and she'd fallen into bed exhausted. "Hello?"

There was breathing on the other end. Normally, when she got late-night calls, it was a frightened woman hiding out from her abuser, too afraid to talk. Often she had to coax the woman into speaking.

But tonight, she didn't sense someone in trouble. She sensed danger. Her voice harsh, she demanded, "Who is this?"

There was a moment's pause. And then the line went dead.

Lindsay checked the incoming number and discovered it was blocked. She closed the phone. Fully awake, she swung her legs over the side of the bed and clicked on the bedside lamp.

A chill slithered through her.

It wasn't like her to be so easily spooked. She got out of bed, clad only in an oversized T-shirt. The air-conditioning chilled her skin.

Careful not to wake Nicole, Lindsay hurried past her roommate's closed door and went down the carpeted stairs to check the lock on the front door. She peered out the peephole. Nothing. Then she went to the back sliding glass door. Locked. She moved from window to window checking them. All locked.

She flipped on the floodlight and it shone over her backyard garden. She stared into the yard looking for any sign of movement.

Nothing moved.

And yet she had the feeling that someone was watching. Hugging her arms, she stared into the darkness inside her home. There was no one there.

She shoved stiff fingers through her hair. This was insane. She was driving herself nuts over what was likely a wrong number. She shut off the backyard light. "Too much caffeine."

She opened the refrigerator and peered inside at the carton full of leftovers from the bistro. She opened the container of chocolate cake and sampled a piece. It melted in her mouth. After closing the door, she moved into the living room, switched on a light, and sat down. In the silence, she ate the cake, savoring every bite.

As she rose to pitch the takeout container in the the kitchen trash bin, she spotted the door under the stairs. Behind it was a small storage place where she kept a box of old pictures. She tossed the carton, wiped her hands, opened the door, and removed the worn box. She carried it to the couch, sat, and dug among the photos, careful to avoid the ones with Zack. She'd never organized or put the photos in an album, but she'd written dates and notes on the back of each.

There were pictures of Lindsay with her friend Joel. They were at the pool, smiling. Joel had his arm wrapped casually around her shoulder. She smiled as she traced Joel's face. Joel and his dad had been the ones who'd gone back to the house after her mom died and gotten these photos and her clothes.

Going deeper in the photo box, she found a picture of herself as a baby. Other pictures of herself at swim and tennis meets with her father and mother smiling proudly behind her. They looked so happy. Picture perfect.

And yet, behind the smiles, there was tension in her parents' eyes. Most wouldn't have noticed it, but she did.

She found deeper in the box black and whites of her mother as a young girl before she'd married her father. Her mother had had a bright smile, dark wavy hair that set off her hazel eyes and peaches-and-cream complexion. In one photo, Lindsay's mother stood with her older brother, who was fifteen years older than her mother. He looked to be about twenty-five in this photo. His arm was slung casually around her mother's shoulders, and he wore a sailor's uniform that accentuated his trim waist and broad shoulders. She had no memories of her uncle except for the rare story her mother told.

Buried at the bottom of the box were pictures of three-year-old Lindsay holding a baby boy. The child had been her younger brother; he had died of crib death when he was just seven months old. Her mother had rarely spoken about her brother, Bobby, but Lindsay knew the boy's death had left a hole in both her parents' hearts that had never healed.

Maybe if Bobby hadn't died. Maybe if . . .

These stupid mind games weren't going to change her past. It was what it was. A mess.

She dropped the pictures back in the box, unable to bear the sadness. She replaced the lid and put the box back in the closet under the stairs.

Suddenly very tired, she climbed the stairs and got into bed. The sheets felt cold against her skin. Despite her fatigue, her mind was restless.

She reached for the light. She'd searched the house and assured herself that she and Nicole were alone. And yet, she still felt as if someone stood over her.

Watching.

The Guardian checked Saunders's bindings. Secure. The man lay unconscious, his arms and legs stretched wide and tied to stakes driven in the concrete floor.

After turning on the three TVs, the Guardian flipped on the evening news reports. He wanted to see what the press was saying about him.

The first two stations had nothing to report beyond police

were still trying to unravel the murder of a local attorney. He flipped to Channel 10 to see Kendall Shaw reporting.

. . . a troubled past marred by the violent murder of her mother. When I spoke with Lindsay O'Neil earlier this spring, she talked about her passion for saving women in abusive relationships. But Lindsay O'Neil harbored a dark secret. Her father, Frank Hines, a garage owner in Hanover, a church leader and well known in his community, routinely beat his wife—Lindsay's mother.

Two days before Lindsay's seventeenth birthday, Hines killed his wife and then shot himself.

Now exactly twelve years after the Hines murder/suicide, the body of a murdered man has been found behind the women's shelter O'Neil created. The victim, Harold Turner, a local attorney, was seen just weeks ago arguing with O'Neil at a local fund-raiser.

Tension rippled through the Guardian's body.

Kendall Shaw's news report bordered on hateful. She'd all but called Lindsay a murderer.

Facts could suggest that O'Neil could have embarked on her own plan of revenge.

Kendall Shaw's raw ambition had driven her too far. She was twisting facts to suit her own purposes. She was a liar and a manipulator and very much like the men who abused their wives. She abused the public trust with her half-truths and innuendo.

The Guardian turned back toward Saunders. He was out cold. No good. He needed to be awake.

He needed to feel pain.

A broken ammonia capsule waved under his nose woke Saunders instantly. Wide-eyed, the man stared around the room, trying to take in his surroundings. He muttered several foul words through his gag and tested the ropes that held him.

"We're in a basement, Mr. Saunders. It's very secluded. Very private."

Bloodshot eyes focused on the Guardian. Confusion gave way to anger. Saunders jerked at his restraints.

The Guardian was pleased. "You're not going anywhere. Not until you've learned a few lessons."

Saunders kicked his legs, trying to loosen the ropes. They didn't budge. He screamed into his gag.

"You're a fighter. I like that." The Guardian grabbed a black bag. "Harold Turner caved when I cornered him. He cried like a baby. You aren't going to cry are you, Mr. Saunders?"

Saunders's eyes narrowed.

"Good. I don't like criers."

From the black bag came the machete. The shiny blade reflected the dim lamplight. "You know what this is? It's the blade I used to cut Harold's hand off."

Saunders swallowed. His fingers clenched into tight fists.

The Guardian traced the flat side of the blade over the man's left wrist. "Are you afraid?"

Defiant, Saunders clamped down on his gag. But the Guardian saw the sweat beading on his upper lip.

"Fear is an uncomfortable feeling, isn't it, Mr. Saunders?"

When he didn't budge, the Guardian traced the sharp blade over Saunders's wrist. This time bravado gave way to terror.

"Fear is what Gail lives with every day. You put that fear inside her. Didn't you?"

Saunders stared, his eyes wide as he shook his head "no."

"You enjoyed seeing her afraid. You enjoyed knowing you had total power over her life." When Saunders didn't answer, the Guardian drew the blade over the inside of his arm, splitting the skin and spilling blood.

Saunders groaned as the pain burned.

"Did you enjoy hurting your wife?"

He nodded.

"And now you will be punished."

Saunders strained at his bindings. He screamed, the sound swallowed by the gag.

"I shot Harold first and then took my trophy. But this time . . ."

Saunders's muffled screams filled the room as the Guardian raised the machete high. In one clean chop, he brought it down and severed Saunders's left hand from his wrist. Blood splattered.

Saunders's eyes rolled back in his head and he pissed on himself. He screamed through the gag. The thick scent of urine filled the air as the coppery blood drained out of the stump on his left arm and pooled on the basement floor.

Energy surged through the Guardian as life seeped from Saunders's body. Nothing had ever felt sweeter.

"You should be feeling some relief now. Your sins have been cleansed with your own blood."

Saunders's body began to shake. He was going into shock.

The Guardian watched, anticipating a river of blood. He expected Saunders to bleed out in minutes, but as the minutes ticked by, the blood flow began to slow. Ten minutes later the blood flow was little more than a trickle. Saunders was still breathing.

"Damn." The arteries had sealed. "You're a tough old bastard. Foolish to think I could destroy evil so easily."

Undeterred, the Guardian grabbed a knife from the workbench and sliced through the femoral artery in Saunders's leg. Saunders screamed. And this time the blood did flow. Saunders was dead in five minutes.

The Guardian hovered, mesmerized by the sight of Death, and with trembling hands combed Saunders's hair until it was smooth. "There are so many more to kill."

Chapter Nineteen

Lindsay woke with a stiff neck and a dull headache throbbing behind her eyes. She'd spent the better part of the night tossing, turning, until finally around three A.M. she'd fallen into a fitful sleep. She dreamt of eyes watching her.

She swung her legs over the side of the bed, shoved her hands through her tangled hair, and glanced at the clock. With a groan, she pushed out of bed and walked to the pile of running clothes by her door. Most mornings, she ran or did yoga. Physical exertion had a way of resetting the barometer in her body no matter how messed up life felt.

Today, she didn't need quiet meditation. She needed to sweat, to push her muscles until they burned, and to have endorphins flooding her brain.

She dressed in jogging shorts and a tank and slipped on running shoes. Combing her fingers through her hair, she swept her thick blond strands into a high ponytail and moved quietly into the kitchen. She didn't want to wake Nicole, who was an extremely light sleeper.

The coffeepot, always set for 5:45 A.M., was full of hot coffee. She poured a cup and sipped as she moved to the small table by the bed, where she kept her cell phone on a charger next to her house key. She glanced out the front window and searched for the morning paper. It hadn't arrived. Frustrated, she took a few more sips of coffee and then hooked the phone to her waistband. She did a few stretches to loosen up her muscles.

Lindsay had a running buddy, Tasha Winters, and the two met near the University of Richmond on Wednesdays at Bandy Field, a small park inside the city limits. They started their workout with a few laps around the park's large open sports field, and then they cut through either surrounding neighborhoods or the university campus.

She arrived at the park a couple of minutes past six and found Tasha stretching. Tasha was in her late twenties, petite, and had a tight muscular build. She reminded Lindsay of a pixie—a term Tasha hated. Too many people underestimated Tasha because of her small size, and all were surprised to learn she was a cop and a member of Henrico County's canine unit.

Rex, Tasha's Belgian shepherd, sat next to her, quietly waiting, watching, and ready to spring if she gave the command. The two had passed their twelve-week training course just six months ago and already they were inseparable. Rex was trained to find explosives.

Tasha saw Lindsay and waved. "Happy birthday."

She'd forgotten her own birthday. "Thanks."

"You look like hell."

Lindsay shrugged. "It's been one of those years."

"Tell me on the trail. We've got to get cracking. I've got to be at headquarters by nine."

"Right." The two started off at a slow jog moving around the dirt path that circled the mile-long trail that cut through the park. Even after a mile Lindsay's muscles didn't relax. Normally during a run, this was when she hit her stride.

Tasha picked up her pace a notch, knowing Rex liked the workout. "So, what's up?"

Lindsay struggled to match Tasha's gait. "Do you want the long version or the short?"

"We've got five miles to go. How about the long?"

"Zack."

"Ah." Tasha had worked with both Lindsay and Zack and knew their history. "Is he investigating the homicide at the shelter?"

"He's one of the detectives on the case."

"So how did it go seeing him?"

"Very weird. I don't see him for a year and now he's everywhere I turn."

Tasha frowned. "This can't be good."

"We went out to lunch yesterday. He took me to his parents' restaurant."

"And?" Tasha didn't sound happy. She'd consoled Lindsay after the separation. She'd watched Lindsay cry until she was nearly sick.

"It felt very odd."

"Sounds like you're having doubts about the divorce. *Again.*"

"No, I'm not. I need to finalize this."

"Then why haven't you?" The tension in her voice had Rex perking up his ears. Tasha smiled at the dog to reassure him.

"I don't know." She was having trouble finding a comfortable rhythm today.

Tasha wiped sweat from her brow, jumped over a pothole. "You know his work always—*always*—comes first. And don't forget that little thing called his drinking problem. Or the little detour into that little cheesecake's bed."

The recap of Zack's faults made Lindsay cringe. "I haven't forgotten any of it. There were times I wished I could forget, but I haven't forgotten."

"Good."

Too many nights she longed for the old Zack. He'd been strong. With him she'd felt safe, a feeling she'd not had in more years than she cared to count. "He seemed different yesterday."

Tasha shot her a you've-got-to-be-kidding look. "Different how?"

Her heart raced and she found it harder to breathe evenly. "Different in the way he used to be, before the drinking."

Tasha stopped and Rex halted. "You're joking."

Lindsay stopped. Sweat dripped from her forehead, stung her eyes. "What? I'm just saying he seems different."

Tasha placed her hands on her hips. Her blue eyes looked as if they could breathe fire. "Do you know what you sound like?"

Lindsay wiped her brow. "I know, I know. One of my clients."

"That's right. You sound like every woman whom you've ever counseled. How many times have you wanted to pull your hair out because one of *your* clients couldn't see the bad in the man in her life?"

Lindsay's defenses went up. "Zack is far from perfect, but he *is* a good man. He's not like the others."

"Hey, don't get me wrong. Zack isn't a bad man. He's flawed but he's good at heart. And I like Zack. He's one of the best cops on the force and I wish him the best. But he's not husband material."

Unshed tears stung Lindsay's throat, forcing her to swallow hard. "I know."

"Look," Tasha said more softly, "my job here is not to rip out your heart, stomp on it, and make you suffer. But

I don't want you to forget that you and Zack separated for very good reasons."

"You're right. You're right." Maybe if she said it over and over it would sink into her own brain.

Tasha patted Lindsay on the shoulder. "There are a lot of really nice fish in the sea, kiddo. And a lot of them don't come with the kind of baggage Detective Kier has. Don't you have that nice doctor who's interested?"

"Yes."

"Well?"

"Got it." Only she wasn't interested in the other fish. She wanted Zack. Wanted what they'd had in the beginning.

They finished their loop around the park and it came time to cross Three Chopt Road and extend their run through the neighborhoods. Tasha went first and as Lindsay followed a van unexpectedly rounded the sharp curve. The driver hit the brakes and blared the horn.

Lindsay bolted the rest of the distance but paused on the side of the road, her heart pounding in her chest. "Damn."

Tasha stopped. "Are you all right?"

Lindsay glanced at the van as it sped through the light a block away. "Yes."

They started running through the neighborhood. The houses were small, one story, and most were built in the 1940s. The lots were large and most of the lawns were well manicured. Lindsay had always liked this neighborhood. She loved the feeling she got when she drove through. If she lived in this area, she could walk to get coffee or jog over to the university.

There was a house on Morgan Street that she had always loved. It was one of the simpler houses and needed a lot of work. But there was a large bay window in the front, and the backyard was huge and got at least five hours of sun a day. She'd always been able to imagine herself filling the barren yard with loads of flowers.

"Let's go by my house and see if it's still for sale." She'd been ecstatic to learn that last month it had gone on the market. She'd thought maybe she could put together some kind of creative financing plan and swing the asking price—that is, until she pulled the listing up on the Realtor's Web site and saw the actual cost.

Tasha grimaced. "Why do you torture yourself? It's too expensive."

"A girl can dream." She grinned. "Besides, it's my birthday, remember? You have to humor me."

"I'm going to humor you *only* because it's your birthday."

They rounded the corner and turned down her street. She'd loved this street since the first time she'd jogged down here with Tasha a couple of years ago. They came almost weekly, though in the last few weeks, she'd been so absorbed with work that they'd had to cut their runs short before they reached this neighborhood.

As Lindsay approached her house, she noticed the FOR SALE sign was gone. For a moment she stopped. Her house had been sold. She didn't realize until this moment how many dreams she'd pinned on this house. "Somebody bought my house."

Tasha jogged in place. "Maybe it's for the best."

It didn't feel like it was for the best. "I guess."

Lindsay started to turn but spotted a Jeep in the driveway. The vehicle was black, had a soft top and a dented back right fender. It looked like Zack's Jeep. And then she noticed the unmarked police Impala parked in front of it.

Zack.

"What the devil are Zack's cars doing in the driveway of *my* house?" Lindsay said.

Tasha groaned when she saw the cars. "It's not your house, Lindsay."

Angrily, she swiped sweat from her brow. "Yeah, I know, but it's not *his* either."

"He could be the person who bought it."

Lindsay couldn't imagine why Zack would have bought the house. He'd never really liked it. When they'd driven by it a few times, he'd always complained that the place would be a money pit for whoever bought it.

She clenched her fists. "He can't buy *my* house. He knows how much I love this place."

"Lindsay, you're sounding a little crazed and you're getting worked up over a house that never belonged to you. Who cares what house Zack buys?"

"Logically, I understand that what he chooses to do with his life now is none of my business. I should just walk away." Instead she marched up the driveway.

"Where are you going?" Tasha demanded.

"To find out why Zack bought my house." Lindsay stomped up the front steps and knocked on the door. When there was no answer, she pounded on it.

Tasha hovered in the driveway, not sure if she should run or drag Lindsay off the porch. "This is insane. We don't even know if that's Zack's car."

"It's Zack's." Footsteps sounded in the hallway inside. Just to irritate him more, she banged on the door again.

"I'm coming!" Zack's voice boomed through the closed door. There was no mistaking that he was pissed. Good. She could use a good fight now.

The front door swung open. Zack wore suit pants, a dress shirt, and a tie not yet knotted. His shirt cuffs were rolled midway up his forearms and his gun holster and cuffs hung from his belt. He smelled faintly of soap and aftershave. He held a cup of coffee in his hand.

Zack's gaze initially reflected annoyance, then confusion and then understanding. "What are you doing here, Lindsay?"

The softness in his voice caught her by surprise and for a moment she hesitated. God, she had lost her mind. Quickly, she regrouped. "Why did you buy my house?"

He didn't smile, but his eyes sparked with amusement. "It wasn't your house."

She planted her hands on her hips. "But you know I wanted to buy it."

He sipped his coffee as if savoring this moment. "As I remember, there were no other bidders on the house." He sounded so damn reasonable.

Sweat dripped into her eyes. She swiped it away. "But you knew I loved this house."

His shoulders filled the doorjamb. "What do you want me to say, Lindsay?"

She was acting like a lunatic. Unreasonable. And she didn't care. "Damn it, Zack. This is my house. You know how much it means to me. Of all the houses in Richmond, why would you buy this one?"

Her tirade didn't affect him in the least. "Care to have a look around?"

The abrupt shift caught her off guard. "What?"

"Care to look around? I'd be happy to give you a tour." And without taking his gaze off Lindsay, Zack added, "Tasha, you and Rex are welcome to come in and look around as well."

Tasha chuckled. "Front row seats to World War III? No thank you. Lindsay, let's just get going. The house is gone."

A bit of the fight drained from her. Tasha was right. The house and her dreams were gone.

Zack seemed to sense her shift in mood, but instead of encouraging her to leave, he challenged her with his darkened gaze. "Are you leaving or staying, Lindsay?"

Lindsay fumed. He knew she'd always wanted to look inside the house. He was using the house to get to her. Well, he was mistaken if he thought he could get under her skin again. "Tasha, I'm going to have a look around."

Tasha shook her head. "Why?"

"I want to see the place," Lindsay said defensively.

Zack sipped his coffee as if to hide a smile.

Tasha shook her head. "Well, I'll take a pass. I'll call you later."

"Thanks." She watched as Tasha and Rex jogged down the street back toward her parked car, just a few blocks away.

"Are you coming in? I've got to be at work in an hour," Zack said.

Now very aware that she and Zack were alone and that she wore only her jogging top, thin shorts, and running shoes, Lindsay felt her resolve fade a fraction. But pride goaded her forward as she moved around him, careful not to touch him.

The house was a disaster. Piles of construction supplies were stacked high in the living room alongside unpacked moving boxes. Dust covered scuffed hardwood floors and the paint on the walls was an obnoxious shade of avocado green. She doubted the interior had been updated since the sixties.

But Lindsay could see beyond all that. The bones of this house were excellent. Plaster walls under the green paint were sure and strong, the doors were solid wood, and the hardwood floors would glisten once they were sanded and refinished. The large bay window in the living room looked even better from the inside and once it was cleaned would allow sunlight to fill the room.

She moved down the center hallway to a kitchen in the back. Zack had furnished the room with a retro Formica kitchen table that had a funky appealing style to it. Knowing Zack, he'd chosen it more for utility than style, but it fit the kitchen perfectly. On the kitchen counter, a modern coffeepot simmered fresh coffee.

Except for the refrigerator, which she'd bet was empty, the appliances were outdated and would need replacing sooner than later, but morning sunlight streamed into the room through the large picture window. It would be a bright cheery room once it was updated.

Seeing this place stirred dreams of children and laughter. For a moment, emotion tightened her throat. "You've got yourself a winner here."

"That's what I thought." The deep timber of his voice sunk into her bones. "By the way, happy birthday."

It surprised her he'd remembered. "Thanks."

"Are you doing anything special?"

"No. This week's a little out of control."

"An understatement."

She moved to the window over the sink and studied the backyard. It was a patch of weeds, and the oak tree way in the back needed serious trimming, but already she could picture marigolds and geraniums brightening up the darkness.

"Any suggestions for remodeling?" He stood so close she could smell the scent of his soap.

She had tons. Mentally, she'd already painted the living room a pale yellow and arranged her furniture to catch the light. She stopped her train of thought.

This house and the dreams that came with it were from a life she'd had to let go. "No, this is your gig. I'm going to have to find another dream house." And that thought triggered a swell of emotion. She hadn't realized how often she'd dreamed about this house—about turning it into a real home. *With Zack.*

He brushed against her as he reached around her and set his coffee cup on the counter. The electricity from his touch startled her. It had been so long since he'd touched her and she felt half starved for contact. Sexual energy burned inside her.

"Part of the reason I bought this house was that you loved it so much. I remember how you used to talk about the yard, the gardens."

"I'm not sure what to make of that comment, Zack." Her voice sounded husky. And she wanted to touch him.

"I've dreamed of us living in this house too." His voice was raspy with emotion.

She met his gaze and, in a rare moment, saw the strong emotions he held on to so tightly. She nearly went to him.

And then she caught herself.

Tasha was right. This was a mistake. "I'd better go."

Lindsay pushed past Zack and headed toward the front door. She had her hand on the doorknob.

"Lindsay, don't go."

She hesitated, realizing how much she wanted to stay. She turned and took a step toward him.

He moved with purposeful steps down the hallway, closing the distance between them. Their faces were only inches apart.

Her heart pounded hard against her chest, its beat filling her ears. She was certain he could hear it.

As their gazes held, she felt a change in the atmosphere. He wanted to kiss her. And she wanted to kiss him.

This is stupid, she thought, yet she didn't move away.

Leaning forward, he kissed her. The kiss was soft, gentle, a testing of the waters, but it was enough to set her on fire. She wrapped her arms around his neck and kissed him back. Warm lips molded against hers.

Zack pressed her back against the door, deepening the kiss. A calloused hand slid up under her tank top and cupped her breast and teased her nipple into a hard peak. Sexual desire exploded. She moaned her pleasure and pushed her tongue into his mouth.

This doesn't mean anything. This isn't reconciliation. This is purely about sexual release.

And the need for sexual fulfillment overrode everything. Lindsay refused to think about tomorrow, this damn house, or her messed-up childhood. She just wanted sex and the temporary ecstasy it promised.

Zack moved his mouth to the base of her neck as he pressed his body against her. His hand slid from her breast down to her flat stomach. His fingers moved under the waistband of her shorts to the nest of hair. He explored her moist, tender flesh and she thought she'd explode.

She cupped his buttocks with her hands and then slid her hands over his hard, flat stomach. It felt so good to touch him, as if she had come home.

She reached for the buckle of his belt and unfastened it, then unhooked the button on his pants. She pushed the fabric away and wrapped her hands around the smooth hardness of his erection.

Zack kissed her harder, driving his tongue deep into her mouth. A deep primal groan rumbled in his throat. "I've dreamed about this," he murmured.

So had she but she couldn't speak the words out loud. Her hesitation had him pulling back to study her face. Rigid control held his lovemaking at bay. "Do you want this, Lindsay?"

She didn't want to think. She just wanted to feel.

But he seemed to need to hear the words. "Do you want this?"

She moistened her lips, which now tasted of him. "Yes. I want this."

Those words were all Zack needed to hear. He yanked her shorts and panties down, exposing her. She was moist, ready. He pressed his erection against her and kissed her on the lips. His kisses trailed down her neck to her cleavage. He licked the top of her breasts. This was strictly about sexual need, she told herself.

"God, I've missed you." His warm breath brushed against her cheek as he spoke.

The need in her had built to a fever pitch. The pulse in her loins had robbed her of everything other than the desire for fulfillment. She stepped out of her shorts and panties and pressed her body against his. "Don't make me wait any more."

His kiss devoured her lips, and then in one swift move he lifted her off the floor as if she weighed nothing. He pressed her back against the door and she wrapped her legs around his waist and guided his erection to her. He drove into her. For a moment, she was overwhelmed by the sensation of him stretching inside her. Seeming to sense this, he went still and waited for her to become accustomed to him.

She dug her fingers into his back as he started to slowly move inside her.

Desire built and then she dropped her head against the door as the first spasms rolled over her and rocketed through her body. Within seconds a violent orgasm washed over her.

Zack pushed harder into her. Faster and faster. Tension racked every muscle in his body and he pushed in to the hilt. And then he stiffened and came inside her.

He collapsed against her and rested his face in the crook of her neck. Neither moved. Their hearts hammered in their chests. His breath felt warm and soothing against her skin.

For a brief moment, she felt at peace, as if everything in the world made sense.

But as the seconds clicked away, the passion faded.

And as quickly as it had risen, it vanished. Even with him close against her, she felt a chill as the full emotional impact of what they'd done sank in. They'd had sex.

Unprotected sex. No birth control. Jesus, she'd lost her mind.

Lindsay shifted under his weight. "Zack."

His breathing had slowed to a lazy pace. "Yes."

She tried to wriggle out from under his weight. "This was a mistake, Zack. It shouldn't have happened."

He nuzzled her neck. "It didn't feel like a mistake. It felt pretty damn incredible."

God, she'd been so stupid. Tasha had just warned her not to come into the house but she didn't listen. "Zack, I need to go."

He raised his head and held her gaze. He looked confused. "Why?"

"I just need to go."

"Stay."

She pushed him away and yanked up her panties and shorts. "I've got to go."

He stepped back and jerked up his undershorts and trousers. "Don't just run away, Lindsay. I want to talk about this. There's too much between us that needs to be dealt with."

Panic rumbled inside her. "I don't want to talk."

"We have to talk."

"I can't. I can't love you again. I can't."

"Lindsay, please stay."

"No." She fumbled for the doorknob, turned it, and rushed outside. The heat and humidity had already burned through the crisp morning air.

She hurried down the three steps. Her legs felt like rubber, and she needed to keep her gaze trained ahead. And still, she turned to look at him again.

Zack stood in the doorway. His shirt was untucked as

he ran fingers through his dark hair. He expression looked stricken.

"Let me drive you to your car," Zack said.

She needed to get as far away from Zack as she could. She would not allow herself to trust him again. He would never hurt her again. "No. Thanks."

He came out onto the front porch and halfway across the yard. "Lindsay, use some common sense."

Hysterical laughter bubbled in her chest. She'd lost all her common sense. She felt like she was losing her mind.

She turned and started to run, picking up her pace as if her life depended on it.

God help her.

She still loved Zack.

But this time, she didn't look back.

Chapter Twenty

As Zack drove in to work, he was in a foul mood when his cell phone rang. Sex with Lindsay had been better than he could have imagined. And for a moment he'd thought their troubles were behind them and they would find a way back together. And then she'd panicked and bolted.

He took the Parham North exit off I-64 toward police headquarters. He unhooked the phone from his belt and snapped, "Detective Kier."

"It's Warwick. We've got another mutilated body."

Zack's fingers tightened on the steering wheel. "Where?"

"At Meadow Farm Park."

Zack glanced at the dashboard clock. "I'll be there in fifteen minutes."

He did a U-turn at the intersection, merged onto I-64 east, and followed the interstate to the Mountain Road exit. He pulled into the graveled parking lot. A dozen cruisers, blue lights flashing, filled the lot. It looked like a three-ring circus.

Zack got out of the car. Already the heat of the day was oppressive. Sweat trickled down his back. He removed his coat, tossed it in the backseat, and rolled up his sleeves. He headed toward Warwick, who stood outside the yellow tape that roped off a colorful playground play set. "What do we have?"

Warwick wore khakis and a black T-shirt. His gold badge hung around his neck. "The call came in about a half hour ago. A jogger found the body."

Both donned rubber gloves and put paper booties on their shoes.

"Ayden will be along soon," Warwick said. "The chief is chewing his ass out. The county manager is going nuts. The area hasn't seen a stranger murder in years and now we've had two in three days. It looks like no one is sleeping until this guy is caught."

Zack followed Warwick under the yellow tape into the wooded area. The body was propped against a thick oak tree. The victim was a white male in his midforties with a shock of black hair on his head and dark stubble covering his square jaw. His jeans and burgundy sports shirt were covered in dirt, blood, and the thick scent of urine. His left hand had been cut off.

"I know this guy," Zack said.

"Burt Saunders," Warwick said. "He attacked Lindsay yesterday as she left work for lunch."

Zack shoved out a breath. He hoped Lindsay had an alibi.

"He wasn't shot," Warwick said. His expression was grim. "It looks like Saunders bled out from his wrist and a sliced femoral."

"Jesus," Zack said.

Warwick pointed to the body. "He has pronounced bruising on his right hand and around his ankles. He fought against his restraints."

Zack squatted, studied the body. "There's not much blood here. He was killed somewhere else."

"Wherever he died has to be soaked in blood."

Humid heat clung to Zack's skin as he stared at the stump that had been Saunders's left hand. "Look at the cuts. The killer wasn't in a rush. He worked the guy over pretty well."

Warwick frowned. "And the victim is another connection to Lindsay."

Zack was loyal to his wife. "Lindsay is no murderer."

Warwick's silence telegraphed his uncertainty. "Do you know where she was last night?"

"No." He sighed. "Where is the guy's wife?"

Warwick checked his notebook. "His wife, Gail, has a sister in Blacksburg. I called there a half hour ago and spoke to Gail. And her sister will verify that Gail hasn't left her sight since she arrived thirty-six hours ago."

Two men who both were accused of beating their wives were dead. Both wives had an alibi. Jesus. He didn't want to consider that they had a serial killer on their hands.

"Is there a note?"

"No."

"Any sign of the hand?"

"Not yet." Warwick shoved the notebook in his back pocket. "I reviewed the Channel 10 news tape from Monday. The cameraman caught the edge of a vehicle arriving at Sanctuary and a delivery man sprinting to the door with a flower box. The tape shuts off before he turns. I can't tell what kind of vehicle it was and the driver is unrecognizable."

"You think it was the Guardian?"

Warwick nodded as he stared at Saunders's body.

The rumble of a truck had them both turning. The Channel 10 news van rolled to a stop.

Kendall Shaw got out. She looked cool and sophisticated as her gaze scanned the scene. A faint smile danced behind her eyes.

"Speak of the devil," Warwick said, staring at her. "She's eating this up with a spoon."

"This story will be national by tomorrow."

Zack watched the reporter approach the yellow tape. The uniforms blocked her advance. The patrolman would keep her out of their hair for the time being.

"Where is Lindsay now?" Warwick said.

The image of her fleeing his house an hour ago dug at him. "I'm guessing she's at home."

"We'd better head over there."

"You're right. If the Guardian repeats his last performance, she's going to get another hand."

"She also has questions to answer," Warwick said.

"Let's go."

The forensics van arrived. Sara got out and Kendall Shaw was forgotten. The tedious process of data collection began.

As Kendall Shaw watched Kier and Warwick leave the murder scene, she tapped a manicured finger against the side of her microphone. "Now why are they leaving?"

Her cameraman, Mike, a tall burly man with a walrus mustache, hoisted a camera on his shoulder. "Is it important?"

"He's investigating a murder and he leaves five minutes after arriving with the other lead detective. You know he's married to Lindsay O'Neil?"

"No shit?"

"Yeah. I searched her name at the Department of Vital Statistics. Their marriage license popped up."

"They don't act like they're married."

"Separated."

Where was Lindsay's husband going? She'd bet money that he was headed out to find Lindsay.

"Hurry up and shoot as much as you can."

"I'm not going to get much. The cops have us too far back and they've parked their vans right in front of the body."

"Can we get enough if I need to fall back and write a report?"

"Give me twenty minutes."

"Good. After you're finished we're leaving."

"Where, dare I ask?"

"I want to go to Lindsay O'Neil's town house."

Mike lowered the camera, giving her a "you're a diva" look. "And why is that?"

God, he could be so shortsighted. "Because," she said, lowering her voice, "Lindsay O'Neil's husband just left the crime scene and he'd only do that if it were really important. He's worried about his wife."

Mike shrugged. "Okay. Whatever."

"Let's shoot those scenes and get over to Lindsay's."

Lindsay lingered in the shower longer than she should have. But the hot water felt good against her skin. And she hoped if she stayed under the cleansing spray long enough she'd erase the memory of this morning from her mind. She had soaped up her entire body and washed and applied conditioner to her hair. Now, as she rinsed the conditioner from her hair, the hot water started to cool. She'd drained the hot water heater.

After shutting off the water spray, she toweled off. Through the fog on the bathroom mirror she stared at herself. "What insanity possessed you today?"

She turned away, then dressed in a simple black skirt and a white collared shirt. Normally, she didn't wear a skirt to work, but normally she didn't have to cancel morning appointments to make time for a meeting with Dana. She dried her hair and put on lipstick and mascara before sweeping her hair into a ponytail, then headed downstairs.

Lindsay made a fresh pot of coffee. As the machine spit and hissed, she stared out the back window into her garden. Normally, just staring at the lush plants calmed her. But not today. Today she was filled with a restlessness that made her feel as if she could jump out of her skin.

Sex with Zack. It was the dumbest thing she could have done.

Lindsay had sworn she'd never be like her mother. In college she'd been labeled "ice queen" by the men she'd dated on campus. She'd refused to get close to anyone, because no man was going to ruin her life. Or make her repeat her mother's mistakes.

But the moment she'd met Zack, all her vows to keep men at arm's distance had vanished. When she'd met him, he'd had long hair and worn a small gold hoop in his left ear. He'd had a two-day growth of beard on his chin and he'd reminded her of a pirate.

From the very beginning, she'd been drawn to him. She hated the terms *soul mates* and *We were meant to be,* but both described how she'd felt about Zack in the early days. The ice had melted, and for the first time life was filled with brilliant color and hope.

He was dedicated to his work. He loved catching the bad guys, as he liked to say. In her mind, he was the warrior-protector. With him, she felt safe.

Their third date had been a charity fund-raiser for the yet to be opened Sanctuary. It was a pancake breakfast and she'd vowed to make and sell a thousand hotcakes to raise money for the shelter. She'd had five volunteers on board to help, and when two hadn't shown up, she'd panicked. Zack had chosen that moment to stop by, and when she'd told him of her dilemma, he'd rolled up his sleeves and started making pancakes. He'd dazzled the crowds and was a better cook than she was.

They'd made love for the first time that night. And Zack had been touched and humbled when she'd shyly confessed that she was a virgin.

After that their courtship had been quick, hot, and intense. They'd met in March and by mid-April they were on a plane bound for Las Vegas. They'd driven straight from the airport in a rented Jeep with the top down. The sky had been a brilliant blue and the air warm.

Lindsay had been nervous but Zack had been steady as a rock. They'd bypassed the hotel and gone to the Little White Chapel, ending up in the Chapel of Promises in front of a justice of the peace. They'd both worn jeans and she'd carried a bouquet of white roses that Zack had purchased at the chapel. They'd exchanged traditional vows and in that moment Lindsay had believed in happy endings.

But once they had returned home the tide had quickly turned against them. Lindsay had thrown herself into the creation of Sanctuary and Zack had returned to undercover work almost immediately. His case, which had involved child trafficking, had required that he be gone for days at a time. When he had been home, he had drank more than she had thought was good for him. When she'd mentioned his drinking to him, he'd told her to back off. His anger had felt like a betrayal and she'd fallen into her old habit—she'd retreated into herself.

Zack had apologized. She'd accepted his apology. He'd confessed that the case wasn't going well—that he'd seen things that could never be erased from his mind. She'd tried to understand. They'd made love and she'd thought that was the end of it. But within days he had been drinking again and they had been fighting again.

As quickly as they'd fallen in love, they'd seemed to have fallen out of love. The wall that had risen between them felt unbreakable.

And then this morning Zack had touched her, and her vows to guard her heart had evaporated. In those explosive moments, there'd only been the heat of his touch and the pulse of desire in her body.

"Stupid, stupid, stupid."

Yesterday, she'd spoken to Nicole about options regarding pregnancy. She'd sounded so reasonable and so calm. But now that she faced the same problem, black and white faded to gray. Her hands slid protectively to her stomach. What if she was pregnant?

Lindsay halted her dangerous train of thought. "Don't borrow trouble."

After clicking off the coffee machine, she got her purse. She had no time to spare if she was going to get downtown for her nine o'clock meeting with Dana.

She headed outside, closed the door behind her, and clicked the dead bolt into place. This time she pocketed the key, instead of putting it under the flower pot.

Dashing down the walk, she spotted the morning paper. "Finally." She reached down and scooped it up.

The instant she touched the newsprint, she knew something was terribly wrong. The paper was too heavy and bulky, and it was wet.

She glanced down and saw the red stain of blood seeping through the newsprint and onto her hand. Terrified, she screamed and dropped the paper.

Her hand was covered in blood.

And at her feet lay a severed hand.

* * *

Warwick's cell phone rang as Zack pulled the Impala into Lindsay's neighborhood. "Warwick."

The cop's face tightened as he listened. "Right. We're minutes away."

Zack sensed the shift in Warwick's tone instantly. Warwick hung up. "What happened?"

"You were right. Lindsay O'Neil just got another delivery. A hand wrapped in her morning newspaper."

A protective urge exploded in Zack. "Is she all right?"

"Yeah, she's fine, but the patrolman says she looks like she's about to freak."

Zack maneuvered the Impala down the side streets. As he rounded the final corner to Lindsay's cul-de-sac, he saw the blue and white patrol cars and their flashing blue lights. He parked the car and he and Warwick got out.

Yellow tape looped around bushes and a light post and blocked the sidewalk leading to Lindsay's town house. A crowd had gathered.

Lindsay sat in the backseat of a patrol car. The door was open and her head rested in her hands. Even from fifty feet away, she looked rattled.

He strode to Lindsay and crouched by the open door. He wanted to touch her but was careful not to. He was mindful that Warwick's gaze was trained on him. "Are you all right?"

Lindsay lifted her head. Her eyes were red as if she'd been crying. "No, I'm *not* all right. I'm completely freaked out."

"What happened?"

"I was on my way to a meeting with my boss. I spotted the paper and picked it up. Immediately, it felt wrong. Then I saw the blood. I dropped it, and then I saw the hand and screamed. The maintenance man heard me and called the police."

"Did you notice anyone different standing around?"

The question came from Warwick, who now stood behind Zack.

"No. But I was running late and I was distracted. And then after I saw the hand, I didn't see anything else."

"When's the last time you saw Burt Saunders?" Warwick asked.

Her lips flattened. "You were there yesterday. He attacked me in the parking lot at Mental Health Services."

"You haven't seen him since?" Warwick said.

She glared up at him. "No." She paled. "Is that his hand?"

Zack rose and faced Warwick. "Did anyone call the EMTs? Lindsay should be checked out."

Warwick frowned. "She looks fine to me."

Lindsay got out of the car. "I *am* fine. Do you know whom that hand belongs to?"

"Do you have an alibi for last night?" Warwick said.

"I was out with a friend." She sighed. "Dr. Sam Begley."

Zack frowned but said nothing.

"He's at Mercy Hospital?" Warwick said.

"Yes." She kept her gaze on Warwick. "He's the one who called me about Gail Saunders. We went out for dinner."

"He's also the doctor who treated Jordan Turner and Gail Saunders," Zack said.

"He didn't have anything to do with this," Lindsay said.

Zack's brow lifted, surprised by her defense of the man.

She shook her head. "I know how cops think. Everyone is a suspect."

Warwick studied her. "The doctor has a connection to both victims."

"Dr. Begley is one of the good guys."

"How long have you known him?" Zack said.

"Seven months."

"Are you dating?" Zack challenged.

"That's my business."

Zack muttered an oath as the forensics van arrived. Warwick excused himself and went over to the technician as he unpacked his equipment. Zack caught Lindsay glancing toward her town house. "Is something wrong?"

"No."

"Is someone in the town house? Maybe your Dr. Begley?"

She met his gaze. "Sam is not in my town house."

Two hours ago, Zack had been inside her. In those moments they'd been so close, the world had felt right, balanced. Now, she was doing her best to keep space between them. They were back to being near strangers. "Is there anything else I should know?"

She shook her head. "You have all my shelter records. I don't have any more secrets to hide."

"You're protecting someone. I know it. Is it Dr. Begley?" Zack challenged.

Her face flushed. "I told you, Sam has nothing to do with this."

He lowered his voice so that only she could hear him. "You're holding back on me."

"I've done nothing wrong."

"Warwick is running this investigation now. He's got a reputation for being tenacious as hell. He won't give up until he has answers. Tell me what you're hiding."

The slight shift in her gaze spoke volumes. "I'm not hiding anything."

He'd felt nothing but frustration from the moment he'd laid eyes on her two days ago. "Don't make this harder than it has to be."

She almost smiled. "It was never easy for us, Zack. So why start now?"

Zack cursed and strode away.

* * *

Vega and Ricker pulled into the parking lot in front of the church. Vega shut off the engine. His phone rang and it was Warwick who updated him on the latest murder.

"Thanks," Vega said. He gave Ricker the rundown.

She shoved out a breath. "This gets nastier by the minute."

"Yeah."

Ricker checked her notes. "Pam Rogers has a brother and a half brother. She and the accountant shared both parents. She and the minister share only a mother. The accountant checked out, so now let's have a chat with the minister."

They got out of the car and crossed the graveled lot toward the modern church. "The church was built last year," Ricker said. "It already boasts three hundred families on its Web site."

Vega shrugged. "Business is booming."

They entered the side door and followed the signs to the office. At this early hour, the place was quiet. It felt deserted and kind of creepy as far as Vega was concerned. And the new-carpet smell didn't sit well with him either.

There was no one sitting at the reception area, so Ricker pushed past it to the door to an inner office. She knocked on the door.

"Yes?" The voice was male, cultured, and sounded a little annoyed.

Ricker pushed open the door. "Pastor Richards?"

The young minister looked up from his computer. He sat behind a large modern desk. Behind him were rows of shelves filled with books. A large wooden cross hung on the wall across from him. "Yes?"

"We're detectives with Henrico police. We have a few questions."

The minister was dressed in a golf shirt and light-colored pants. He rose. "What is this about?"

"Lindsay O'Neil," Vega said.

Recognition flashed in the minister's eyes. "Come in and have a seat."

They each took one of the seats in front of the desk.

Vega didn't feel like beating around the bush. "You know Ms. O'Neil?"

"I do. Our church has kind of adopted her shelter in the last couple of months."

Vega didn't like the guy. He was too polished. "Does she know that your sister was a resident at Sanctuary?"

The minister's brows knitted. "No. I never told her that Pam was my sister."

"Why not?"

He steepled his fingers. "I've wanted to. In fact, I almost did the other night. She was here speaking to a group of parishioners about domestic violence and she used Pam's story as a case study. It nearly broke my heart."

"Why didn't you tell her?"

"I like her. I know Pam's death hurt her. I didn't want to cause Lindsay any more pain. The woman is practically a saint."

"How did you two hook up?" Ricker said.

"A couple of months ago, I was looking for an outreach project for the church and I saw the article about her in *Inside Richmond*. It felt like a sign from God, so I called Lindsay."

Ricker's eyes narrowed. "*Lindsay*. You've called her Lindsay twice."

"That a problem?" Richards asked.

"It's the way you say her name. You really like Ms. O'Neil, don't you?"

He swallowed. "There's a lot to admire about her."

Vega picked up Ricker's vibe. "Feels like a little more than admiration."

Richards stiffened as if he'd been caught doing something illicit. "Does this have to do with the murder at the shelter? Because if it does, I can tell you I had nothing to do with it."

Rickard leaned forward. "Where were you early Monday morning and early this morning?"

"Here, working at the church on sermons and budgets."

"Any witnesses?" Vega asked.

The minister shrugged. "No."

Chapter Twenty-One

Wednesday, July 9, 10:10 A.M.

Lindsay worried about Nicole as she numbly sat in the back of the police car watching the forensics team do its job of collecting evidence. Warwick interviewed the complex's worried-looking maintenance man, Steve, while Zack talked to neighbors. No doubt they'd check Steve's past and also look into Sam's background. Everyone she knew was being pulled into this mess.

One killing had been sensational enough. Two equated a pattern—and major headlines, a fact that was driven home to her when Kendall Shaw arrived with her cameraman.

The last thing Nicole needed was for Lindsay to be the center of a major news story.

Across the street, a black Mercedes pulled up and Dana Miller got out. She was dressed in white Armani and carried a thick, efficiently designed purse. She frowned as she surveyed the scene from behind large white-framed sunglasses.

Lindsay rose and moved toward her boss. "Dana."

Dana offered a curt smile. Her expensive perfume

swirled around her. "I got your voice mail. When you said there was trouble I decided to see what was happening for myself. What's going on?"

The story was so outlandish, she felt foolish telling it. "Another man was murdered. And another hand was sent to me."

Dana's rouge-painted lips flattened. She reached in her purse and pulled out a long, slim cigarette case. "Is the murder victim connected to the shelter?"

"Not to the shelter, but to me. I think the victim's name is—was—Burt Saunders." She recapped the highlights of the last few days.

Dana removed a cigarette from the case and lit it with a monogrammed lighter. She inhaled deeply and exhaled slowly. "This is not good, Lindsay."

Lindsay's worried expression reflected in Dana's sunglasses. "I know."

Dana glanced toward the camera crews. "Do you have any idea who's behind this?"

The question almost made her laugh. "If I knew I'd be sharing it with the cops."

Dana studied the scene. Her frown deepened when Kendall Shaw started her report. Neither could hear what the reporter was saying, but they got the gist of it. "Lindsay, I've always believed you were Sanctuary's best asset. You're a big part of our success. You have a passion for your work that few possess."

Her boss rarely tossed out compliments. "But . . ."

"But right now, you are our biggest liability. The press is on your doorstep because some crazy person is fixated on you. By tomorrow, you won't be able to move without someone spotting you."

"Dana, I've worked under pressure before. I can handle the media."

"That's yet to be proven."

An uneasy helplessness tightened Lindsay's belly. "Then let me prove myself. I don't want to abandon Sanctuary."

Dana puffed on her cigarette. "I'd like to. I really would. But none of us can afford the bad press."

Us. Dana didn't want the bad press.

"I've called in every favor to keep this story as quiet as possible, but nothing is going to keep the media away from this."

"Dana, let's just give this another day or two. The police might find the killer and then all the questions will be answered."

Dana dropped her half-smoked cigarette to the concrete sidewalk and ground it with the tip of her high heel. "I wish it were that easy, but it's not. I've no choice but to suspend you."

Lindsay couldn't swallow her outrage. "You're firing me?"

Dana looked away. "Not firing, but suspending you until this mess is cleared up. I don't want you associated with the shelter."

Lindsay curled her fingers into fists at her sides. "I didn't do anything wrong."

Dana lifted her chin. "No one said you did. You're a victim."

"I am not a *victim*." How many times had the social workers said that Lindsay was a *victim*? A *victim* of a bad family. A victim of domestic violence. A victim of fate. "I can overcome this."

The force behind Lindsay's tone had Dana softening. "I've no doubt that in time you will. You're smart and bright. However, in the short term you are a liability to the shelter and me. Don't take it personally, Lindsay. This is business."

Aware that Kendall was watching, Lindsay kept her

voice low. "Dana, how can I not take it *personally*? You're canning me."

"I'm not firing you. This is a paid leave."

"Sanctuary is more than a business to me. It's more than a paycheck."

Dana pulled her Blackberry out of her slim purse. Consciously or not, Dana was shifting her mind to the day's next problem. "I've got to go."

Lindsay once again clenched her fists at her sides. "That's it? I'm out?"

Dana checked her watch. "Call my secretary. We'll set up a meeting. Hopefully, this will all be behind us in a week or so." She hurried toward her car and vanished behind tinted windows.

Lindsay had the sick feeling that *this* was going to be with them for a long, long time.

She stood alone, her fists still clenched, her stomach churning.

Zack walked up to her as Dana drove off. "What was that all about?"

Unshed tears tightened her throat. She wanted to bury her face in his chest. "I've just been canned."

His hands slid to his waist below the black handle of his shoulder holster. "She fired you?"

"I'm on 'paid leave.' But I know that look. I'm done with Sanctuary." A wave of helplessness washed over her, reminding her of the months following her mother's death. No matter what she'd done then, she hadn't been able to regain control of her life.

Zack frowned. "Your boss is an idiot."

She was grateful he didn't toss any pity her way. That would have been her undoing. "She's very savvy. And very image conscious. I'm now a liability."

"Like I said, an idiot."

Silver bracelets jangled as she ran her hands through her hair. "I want this guy caught, Zack."

His eyes narrowed. "We all do."

"I'll do whatever I can to help."

He lifted a brow. "That's a change."

"This guy, the Guardian, is tearing at my life. I won't be able to help anyone if he keeps at it. I want him stopped. I want my life back."

"The detective going through your shelter records would appreciate your help. She was having trouble deciphering your handwriting in some of the files."

She was eager to get started. "I can go by headquarters now."

"First, I want you to see something."

The delay frustrated Lindsay and it showed in her voice. "What?"

Zack disregarded the snap in her tone. "The Guardian left another note."

"Where?"

"It was wrapped in the newspaper."

"What does it say?"

"I'll let Warwick tell you." Tension laced the words but she was too worried to question them.

Zack guided Lindsay over to the edge of the yellow tape roping off the front of her town house. She'd been shut out of Sanctuary and wondered now if she would be barred from her home.

Warwick approached her. "Ms. O'Neil."

Lindsay braced. "Detective. What does the note say?"

Warwick glanced at his notebook. "'*One less demon to battle, Lindsay. P.S. Be careful of cars when you jog. The Guardian.*'"

Despite the heat, a chill shot down her back. "He's watching me."

"When's the last time you went running?" Warwick said.

"This morning. I ran near Bandy Field. I was nearly hit by a van when I crossed Three Chopt." Anger rose up in her. "The bastard is watching me."

Zack's jaw tightened. "Did you see anyone this morning?"

She couldn't look at him as the memories of this morning returned. "No. But I wasn't running alone. I was with my friend Tasha Winters. She works with the canine unit. I can call her. She might have seen something."

Warwick shook his head. "I'll take care of it. What time were you running?"

"Between six and seven."

"Winters was with you the whole way?" Warwick said.

Color flooded her cheeks. "No. She had to get to work. I ran longer."

Zack straightened at the simple lie that masked their complicated meeting. "You might as well hear this from me, Warwick. Lindsay was at my house this morning."

Warwick lifted a brow. "Your house?"

Lindsay wanted to melt into the ground. "That has nothing to do with *this*."

Zack held up his hand to silence her. "When Lindsay and I were together, she admired a house near her jogging route. I recently bought the house. She asked for a tour."

Warwick frowned. "How long was she at your house?"

Zack didn't flinch. "About a half hour."

A half hour? Is that all it had been?

"What did you two talk about?" Warwick said.

"Personal things," Lindsay interjected.

"Nothing related to the murders," Zack said.

Warwick didn't look pleased. "All right."

"Lindsay privately offered to go through her case files with Ricker and see if any suspects come to mind."

Warwick nodded. "All right."

"Hey, Lindsay, what was that in the newspaper? It looked like a severed hand." The voice belonged to Kendall Shaw. She stood at the edge of the yellow tape with her cameraman. "Your friend sending you tokens of his affection?" Lindsay ignored the question and turned from the camera. Zack and Warwick refused to comment.

Kendall was patient as she watched the maintenance man move away from the cops. The guy looked pale and upset. He'd seen something. She turned to Mike. "Stay put. I want to talk to the maintenance man."

"Whatever."

Kendall cut through the growing crowd of curiosity seekers and made her way up to the guy. She thought about tossing him one of her smiles but decided she needed to be more subtle with this guy. She'd play it concerned. "Hey, are you all right?"

"Not by a long shot." With a shaky hand, the guy reached into his breast pocket and pulled out a pack of Camels. He pulled one out and lit the tip. Smoke billowed around his lean face as he puffed.

"What's got you so spooked?"

His eyes narrowed as he stared at her through the haze. "You're a reporter."

She smiled. "Yeah."

"You're with Channel Ten?"

"I am." She moved closer to him and gently laid her hand on his shoulder. "Can I get you anything?"

"A six-pack of beer?"

She lifted a brow. "It can be arranged."

He shook his head as he took anther drag. "God knows I deserve a drink. But the property management firm will fire my ass if I drink on the job."

She held out her hand. "I'm Kendall Shaw."

He took her hand and held it gently. "I know. And I'm Steve Hess."

"Nice to meet you, Steve."

He moistened his lips. "I watch you on TV a lot. You're good."

"Thanks."

"Every time I see you, I wonder why you're not in a bigger city."

She grinned. "From your lips to God's ears."

He chuckled, and with a hand that still shook a little, he took another drag off his cigarette.

"You see my piece last night?"

"Naw. I ended up working overtime in a flooded unit. Fucking pipes burst."

If he was a Lindsay devotee it was better he hadn't seen the piece. It had stirred quite a buzz. And she'd gotten just as many negative e-mails as positive. "I hear you're the one who called the police for Lindsay."

"I was in my truck across the street when I heard her scream. She was so freaked out."

Kendall decided to play a hunch. "It was bad for you too, wasn't it?"

"Yeah."

"I still think you could use a drink. After what you saw, I can't imagine any boss would deny you a stiff one. They don't pay you enough to see what you saw."

A sigh shuddered through him. "Jesus, it was a mess."

He was a volcano ready to erupt. He just needed a nudge and someone to listen.

"I saw the body at the park."

Steve looked at her, his eyes alit as if he'd found someone who understood. "Was he missing a hand?"

That caught her up short. "Yes," she lied.

"Jesus, whoever this nutcase is, he's sending the hands

of his victims to Lindsay. She said he sent her a hand on Monday as well."

Kendall hid her smile. "Does she know who's doing this?"

"She doesn't have a clue. But it's starting to mess with her."

She leaned forward, and in a low tone said, "I can't imagine what she's going through."

Chapter Twenty-Two

Detectives Dominic Rio and Monica Perry arrived at the burned-out New Age bookstore, which was still hissing with charred timbers. Lights on three fire trucks flashed as firemen sprayed a stream of water on the coals. A collection of people stood behind the barriers looking stunned and frightened.

Rio put the car in park and set the emergency brake. Perry grabbed her notebook. Perry was in her early thirties, divorced, and originally from Minnesota. She was brutally efficient, detail oriented, and cool to most. Rio was a bachelor, a Texan by birth, dark skinned, and had hair so black it looked blue in sharp sunlight. At first glance, he seemed outgoing and laid-back but he was just as detached as Perry.

The two had worked together for two years. They'd fallen into an easy relationship, each able to anticipate the other's thoughts. Other cops in the division jokingly called them an old married couple, though romance had never sparked between the two.

A lazy mist had settled over the city, sending temps

into the sixties. Rio got out of the car and pulled off his sunglasses. He paused at the front of the car and waited for Perry. She wasn't fond of the chivalry but had long ago accepted that it came with his Southern roots.

They walked side by side up to Fire Battalion Chief Stanley. Stanley had thick silver hair and mustache and a booming voice that could be heard over any siren.

Rio stuck out his hand. "Stanley."

Stanley shook both their hands. "Thanks for coming."

"You have a body?" Perry asked.

Soot deepened the lines on Stanley's face, making his grim face sterner than usual. "Yeah. She wasn't killed by the fire. She was murdered."

Rio hooked his thumb in his belt loop. "You know this how?"

"The fire was pretty hot and would've completely obliterated the body if a metal shelf hadn't fallen on it. It acted as a shield against the flames." He released a breath. "Her body was in the back, out of sight of the street."

Perry scratched down a few notes. "Is it safe for us to take a look?"

"Yeah, but I've got helmets for you both, just to play it safe." Stanley handed each a helmet and glanced at Perry's steel-tipped boots and Rio's loafers. "Rio, your shoes are pretty but not practical. Take a page from your partner's book and wear a more substantial shoe."

Rio raised an eyebrow as he stared at her practical, but ugly boots. "Naw."

Perry smiled crookedly at her partner. "Rio's got a thing about his image. Likes to look good."

Rio shrugged. "And you're a Girl Scout."

They made their way into the charred building. The smell of smoke blended with the scent of Perry's perfume. Carefully, the trio picked their way through the rubble of incinerated books and collapsed shelves and beams toward the back of the shop.

Perry's stomach tumbled when she saw the body. The dead woman lay on her back, her hands stretched out in a T-shape. The heat of the flames had all but incinerated or melted the bottom half of her body. But her torso and head had remained untouched by the flames. "Jesus."

The victim's face had been systematically cut with diamond-shaped patterns. By the looks of it, the killer had used a scalpel.

Stanley's jaw tightened. "Like I said, that metal shelf shielded her face from the worst of the blaze; otherwise, there wouldn't be anything left of her."

Perry leaned forward and studied the position of the shoulders. "This some kind of ritual killing?"

Rio squatted down, his long tanned hands draped over his knees. "The guy who did this enjoyed himself."

Perry checked the name of the store owner in her notes. "If this is the store owner, then her name is Claire Carmichael. She's clean, just a speeding ticket in ninety-nine."

Rio rubbed his chin. "Let's have a look at the crowd. Maybe someone saw something. Stanley, the forensics van should be here any minute."

Stanley spoke matter-of-factly. "What the fire didn't destroy, we did when we put it out."

Rio scowled. "Something our killer was banking on."

Richmond, Virginia, 11:00 A.M. EST

Nicole couldn't take it any longer. She had stayed inside, out of sight of the police, because Lindsay had asked her to. Lindsay was trying to protect her. But Nicole had had enough of running scared. And hiding.

Richard be damned.

She'd not cower anymore. Especially now that Lindsay needed her.

Nerves jumping, she opened the back patio door, cut through the backyard garden, and pushed open the privacy fence door. She moved around the side of the town house to the edge of the yellow tape. Reporters started to swarm toward Lindsay.

Two men already stood beside Lindsay. The first had his hand raised to block a cameraman's lens. He was dark. Brooding. Zack, she guessed. Lindsay had only spoken about him a little.

The second man was just as tall as Zack but he had hard eyes, a nose that looked as if it had been broken once. This man caught sight of Nicole almost immediately. His gaze bore into her with an intensity that made her want to run.

Nicole held her ground as he excused himself and moved toward her. He moved like an athlete, sleek and graceful, yet powerful. He stopped just feet from her. "Where did you come from?"

The suspicion in his raspy voice had her straightening. "I'm Nicole. I'm Lindsay's roommate."

Warwick frowned. "She never said anything about a roommate."

"She's trying to protect me."

"From whom?"

"My husband."

Warwick signaled for Zack and Lindsay to come over. When Lindsay saw Nicole, she immediately glanced behind her to make sure the camera crews weren't filming. "Zack, can we have this conversation inside?"

Zack nodded toward the door. "Sure."

The four stepped into Lindsay's town house.

Lindsay closed the door. "Nicole, you should have stayed inside."

Nicole shook her head, aware of Warwick's gaze. "No more hiding, Lindsay."

"I could have handled this."

"Thanks, but I don't want you to protect me anymore."

Zack pulled a piece of gum from his coat pocket and popped it into his mouth. "Mind introducing us, Lindsay?"

Lindsay glared at him and then at Nicole. "I wanted to tell you."

Zack folded his arms over his chest. "I'm all ears now."

"This is Nicole Piper," Lindsay said.

Nicole felt awkward but held her ground. "I've been living with Lindsay. She's been helping me hide from my husband. He could be quite violent."

"Who is your husband?" Zack said.

She hated thinking about him, let alone saying his name. "Richard Braxton. He's a businessman based in San Francisco."

"Did you ever file charges against him?" Warwick asked.

A sad smile lifted the corner of her mouth. "No. I was too afraid of him. Two and a half months ago, while he was on a business trip, I fled with the clothes on my back and two hundred dollars cash. If not for Lindsay, I don't know what I would've done."

"How do you know Lindsay?" Doubt clouded Zack's eyes.

Lindsay cleared her throat. "We went to college together at USC."

"Were you here on the night Harold Turner died?" Zack asked.

"Yes," Nicole said.

"Can you verify Lindsay was here?" Warwick said.

Nicole glanced at Lindsay. "I wish that I could. But

we both slept very hard that night, as if we were drugged."

"Why do you say drugged?" Warwick said.

"Every night since I left my husband, I've had nightmares. I didn't dream at all that night."

"Would you be willing to submit to a drug test?" Zack asked.

"Certainly."

"Do you think there'd be any traces left in our systems?" Lindsay said. "It's been forty-eight hours."

Nicole shrugged. "We can try."

Warwick looked around the apartment. "Have you noticed anyone strange around here lately?"

"No. But I started working at a photography studio last week, so I've stayed busy."

"A job? A job would expose you to your husband," Warwick said. "Your Social Security number can be traced."

Lindsay cleared her throat. "She's changed her name. Her real name is Christina Braxton. And I encouraged the name change and a new hair color and cut. I also got her a new Social Security number."

"How?" Zack challenged.

Lindsay wasn't apologetic. "I have contacts."

Zack muttered an oath. "There are legal channels she could've gone through. Social Security can change numbers in domestic-abuse cases."

"I was afraid Richard would find out," Nicole said.

Zack kept his gaze on Lindsay. "Have you gotten new IDs for others before?"

"Sometimes the only solution is to vanish and then create a new identity."

Zack stared at her long and hard. "That's what you did after your mother died."

Lindsay swallowed. "Yes. Look, if you need to file

charges against me for buying the ID of a dead person, go ahead. But Nicole had nothing to do with it."

Nicole shook her head. "I knew what I was doing, Lindsay. I take full responsibility." Nicole felt sick. "What do we do now?"

"First things first," Warwick said. "Let's get those blood tests."

"And after that, where does Nicole go?" Lindsay said. "She can't stay here. It's only a matter of time before the press will spot her and word will get back to her husband."

"I know a place," Zack said.

"Where?" Lindsay said.

"My folks' house."

Lindsay could see that Sam was upset as he drew her blood. Outside the curtained examination room Zack stood like a modern-day centurion. "I've never seen you frown so much."

Sam took the vial of blood and laid it on the metal tray by the exam table. "Lindsay, the cops want me to do a full toxicology screen. What happened?"

The concern in his eyes touched her heart. "They think that whoever killed Harold on early Monday morning might also have drugged Nicole and me. My sleeping in put me about three hours behind; otherwise I'd have been at the shelter at the same time the murderer was."

His jaw tightened. "I don't like this. I'm worried about you."

"Hey, I'm okay. I'm always okay."

He shook his head. "Don't kid yourself. I saw the news reports. All this has to have churned up stuff from your past."

"I'll muscle through it, just like always." That was a lie. She honestly didn't know how she was going to see her way clear of this mess. "Look, I've got to go. I need to get Nicole settled."

"Right."

"Make sure you also run a pregnancy test on her." In two weeks Lindsay could very well be doing the same for herself.

"Sure."

Lindsay kissed him on the lips. Unexpectedly, he wrapped his arm around her waist and pulled her close. The move was possessive, as if he was staking a claim. She let him hold her until she ended the kiss.

"See you soon." She pushed back the curtain.

Zack shot Sam a hard glance and then escorted her to the elevators, where Warwick and Nicole waited. Next to the cop, her friend looked so pale and fragile. And if not for Nicole, she'd never had agreed to go to the Kiers' house.

As Zack began the drive to Hanover, Lindsay stared out the backseat window, knowing she was about to face her in laws after nearly a year of silence. She felt as if she were venturing into a lion's den.

Zack slowed the car and pulled into a gravel driveway. The Kiers' farm was located off a rural road in Hanover County about thirty minutes north of the city. Dust kicked up around the car and gravel popped under the tires as Zack continued down the driveway. At the end stood an old white farmhouse that her in-laws had purchased about ten years ago and were still renovating. Audrey had often joked that she'd be in her nineties before her husband would be finished working on all his projects.

Zack parked the car in front of the wide front porch and got out. He opened the door for Lindsay. Under better circumstances, she'd have kidded him about such chivalry. Today she wasn't interested in any sort of humor.

Warwick opened Nicole's door. She looked so small

and delicate next to the detective, who stood a good ten inches taller. Nicole held her shoulders back. If she was afraid, she was doing her best to hide it.

The screened door opened and out stepped Mr. and Mrs. Kier. They were smiling, but Lindsay saw the strain in their eyes.

Audrey Kier was a tall woman with silver hair, which she'd swept into a ponytail. Mr. Kier's dark hair had turned salt and pepper and the sun had left deep wrinkles around his blue eyes.

Audrey came straight up to Lindsay and gave her a hug. "It's so good to see you, dear."

Lindsay tried to relax but the unexpected contact felt awkward. "Thank you for having us, Audrey. I really do appreciate it."

The older woman stepped away and let her gaze drift over Lindsay. "Ellie said you were too thin."

Lindsay pretended she didn't hear the comment or the genuine concern in Audrey's voice. The less attached she remained, the better.

Audrey's vivid gray eyes, so like her son's, shifted to Nicole. Her assessing gaze took in a dozen different details in a split second. "Welcome."

Nicole seemed stiff and nervous. "Thank you for having us, Mrs. Kier."

Audrey smiled. "Please call me Audrey. Mrs. Kier always sounded so formal to me."

Mr. Kier cleared his throat. He was as tall as Zack and his shoulders as broad. His body remained fit. Only the deep wrinkles around his eyes and the calloused palms from working his hands gave his age away. "She's been Mrs. Kier for almost forty years and she's never gotten used to it."

Audrey tossed her husband a bemused look. "Why

don't you girls come inside and I'll make you something to eat."

Lindsay's mother-in-law had always fretted over Lindsay's eating habits. "Thanks, Audrey. It's very generous of you to open your home."

"Nonsense, honey. You're family."

Family. Lindsay's throat tightened. Fearful her voice would crack, she simply nodded.

The older woman hooked her arm around Nicole's shoulder and led her into the house.

Warwick looked to Mr. Kier. "I've numbers for you in case of an emergency."

Mr. Kier tossed a curious look at Lindsay and Zack. "Come inside. I'll write them down."

Warwick nodded. "Sure." Mr. Kier and the detective disappeared inside the house.

Lindsay hesitated on the second step. For better or worse she owed Zack. "I'd forgotten how nice your mom is."

He stopped at the bottom stair. They were almost eye to eye. "She was glad to do it."

It was hard to hold his piercing gaze. "I know I'm not her favorite person these days."

He took her hand in his. "Lindsay . . ."

She pulled away. "Please, don't."

Zack shoved his hands in his pockets. "She loves you, Lindsay, like a daughter. Nothing has changed that."

The loss of the Kier family stung. "She's a nice woman. It's in her DNA to be kind."

"Oh, Mom has her dark side. She's let me have it more than a few times this past year. She knows why we split up."

Zack's infidelity and drinking had humiliated her. And now his mother, a woman she'd always respected and liked, knew. "Why did you tell her?"

He didn't look away. "I wanted her to understand why you were so angry."

Frustration spilled from her. "What I don't understand is why you did it. I know that that last night we fought bitterly, but to just run to another woman's bed?"

His face was rock hard, expressionless. "The booze was a big part of it. It clouded my mind. You'd tossed me out. That hurt like hell. You were the savior for so many wounded souls and when I hit trouble you ditched me."

Guilt mingled with anger. "You were addicted to alcohol. Throwing you out was the only thing I could think of to get your attention."

His jaw tightened and released. "I see that now. Hell, I'd have done the same thing to me if I were you. But then I was angry as hell. And I wanted to hurt you back."

Tears burned the back of her eyes. "You couldn't have done a better job if you'd planned it."

He sighed. "I know and for that I will always be sorry. I'd never cheat on you again, Lindsay."

As much as she wanted to believe, she refused to allow herself. "I know you believe that."

Zack raked his hands through his hair. "I've waited a year to talk to you, for us to be clearheaded enough so we could say what needed to be said. I want to fix this."

Pain pierced her heart. "Some things can't be put back the way they were."

He spoke slowly, patiently, as if he'd practiced a thousand times. "So we build something different and stronger this time. Different doesn't mean it won't be better. We're stronger together."

His words tempted. She wanted to give herself to Zack and love him like she once had. "Forgiveness leads to terrible things."

"I'm not your father, Lindsay. We're not like your parents."

Lindsay shook her head. "I saw my mother return to him too many times. Each time he hurt her. I can't do it."

"Lindsay, we can work through this."

Her chest tightened and her breathing felt labored. "I've got to get out of here."

"You don't have a car and you have nowhere to go. Your apartment isn't safe. The Guardian knows where you live."

She couldn't stay here. This place reminded her of what she wanted most and what she'd never have again—a family. "I work the hotline tonight at Mental Health Services. It's not my regular night but they always can use the help. I'll be in a lockdown facility with security guards."

"Lindsay, stay with my folks." He enunciated each word carefully.

"I need to work."

"You need to worry about yourself. The world can survive a night without you working."

Lindsay felt anxious. "I don't know how to be still."

Zack laid his hand on her shoulder. "For your own well-being, figure it out. You need the night off."

The front door opened and Warwick appeared. He glanced between the two and then said, "I just got a call from Ayden. We need to head back to the office."

Lindsay looked at Warwick. "Can I snag a ride back? I've got to get my car."

Warwick lifted a brow. "Sure."

Zack glared at him. "She's staying put. End of story. Call the office and tell them to get someone else."

"But . . ."

"No," Zack said. "It's too dangerous now."

They left Lindsay standing in the front drive, looking as if she could kill.

Chapter Twenty-Three

Wednesday, July 9, 3:00 P.M.

When Zack arrived at headquarters, the rest of the homicide division was in the conference room. Ricker, Warwick, Vega, and Ayden had the television on and were watching Kendall Shaw's latest report.

According to my contacts on the scene, the killer is mutilating his victims by cutting off their left hands and delivering the hands to Lindsay O'Neil. Police won't confirm these reports but . . .

Shaw's report continued.

Zack turned away, disgusted. "Jesus, that woman is determined to blow our case."

"How did she find out about the hands?" Ayden asked. His words were laced with restrained fury.

A headache pounded behind Zack's eyes. "Shaw arrived at Lindsay's just after I did. She might have caught a glimpse of the hand on the sidewalk before I covered it. And I saw her talking to the maintenance man."

Grim faced, Ayden sat across from Zack. Vega sat down on Zack's right and Warwick on his left. Ricker took a seat next to Ayden.

"So what do we have?" Ayden said. "And tell me we have something. Two murders in three days and the chief and county manager are breathing down my neck. Ricker, you lead off."

"I've been through Turner's phone records," C.C. said. "All his calls pan out expect one. The questionable call was placed at one A.M. Monday morning to Turner's cell. The call came from a prepaid phone purchased at a local store. I'm trying to trace the phone to the store. Once I have the store, I'll start sifting through register receipts and if we're lucky surveillance cameras."

A long and tedious process that was necessary. "Okay," Ayden said. "What about Turner's car?"

"Found at the mall near the shelter. Forensics is going over it now, but so far it looks clean," Vega said.

Ricker shifted the papers in front of her. "Lindsay and I spoke a half hour ago. She did help me with deciphering her files. We discussed her twelve hottest cases. Six of the abusers are in prison now, five have rock-solid alibis, and one is unaccounted for. We're looking for him now. But it's not likely he'd go to Lindsay's aid. She has a restraining order against him."

"What about Sam Begley?" Zack asked.

C.C. checked her notes. "Been at Mercy about eight months. No record. Liked by his coworkers. Last random drug test at Mercy was negative." She flipped a page and lifted a brow. "I did discover the guy likes to gamble. He owes over ten grand to a local bookie."

Ayden rubbed the back of his neck. "That doesn't make him a killer."

Zack was sorry they couldn't pin more on the guy. He didn't like or trust him. "I'd still like to talk to him."

Warwick's cell vibrated. He checked the number and rose to take the call in the hallway.

Ayden shifted his gaze to Warwick. "Neighbors? Her assistant, Ruby?"

Vega shook his head. "Ruby and the neighbors have nothing new to offer." He flipped through his notes. "Also, Saunders was last seen in Byrd's Bar. The bartender stopped serving the guy around eleven and sent him on his way. No one saw him after that and he didn't appear at work in the morning." He raised an eyebrow. "Here's an interesting note. Remember Pam Rogers? She has two brothers and one is a minister close to Sanctuary. And his church has taken the shelter under its wing."

Warwick returned to the room. "That was the medical examiner. It appears Saunders's hand was cut off before he died. But the veins and arteries collapsed and blood flow slowed to a trickle. That explains why the killer cut the femoral artery. He wanted his victim to bleed to death."

A heavy silence settled in the room.

"The killer is getting more violent," Zack said.

Ayden pinched the bridge of his nose. "Let's dig a little deeper into the minister's comings and goings. What do we have on Lindsay's roommate?"

Vega scanned his notes. "Nicole Piper's prints do match Christina Braxton's, which were on file, because she was arrested at an animal rights rally when she was in college. No missing person reports have been filed on Ms. Braxton. However, the phone number for her photography studio has been disconnected and her Web site is off-line. She was building quite a name for herself on the West Coast as a photographer. But she stopped taking clients and showing her work about a year ago."

"That fits with a domestic-abuse situation," Ayden said. "Her husband was isolating her."

Vega nodded. "She appeared out here as Nicole Piper two weeks ago and started working at a mall portrait studio ten days ago. I spoke to her current boss. Nicole is already very popular with his customers. Basically, her story checks out."

"Still," Ayden said, "she came out of nowhere, moved in with Lindsay just two weeks before the Guardian started killing people."

Warwick shook his head. "She's just over five feet and weighs a hundred and ten pounds soaking wet. Maybe she could have gotten the jump on Turner, but there's no way she could have subdued a man like Saunders. The guy outweighs her by a hundred pounds."

"She could have drugged him," Ricker offered. "Just because she's small doesn't mean she's not cunning. Do we have the toxicology reports on Lindsay and Nicole?"

"They were negative," Zack replied.

Vega said, "I spoke to Sara. She has nothing to report on the second note. It's as clean as the first. No prints. No hair fibers. Standard paper. Standard printer."

Ayden again rubbed the back of his neck with his hand. He looked like he hadn't slept last night. "So the only link we have to this guy is Lindsay O'Neil. '*Be careful of cars when you jog.*' The tone of the note sounds paternal. It's something I'd say to my own boys. He was worried about her." His gaze flicked to the television screen. "Shaw could be right. This killer could be from her past."

"What do you know about her extended family?" Vega asked Zack.

"When her folks died she ran away. She was seventeen and Social Services didn't make an effort to track her down. She said something about family in California. I'll ask."

Ayden nodded. "Every family tree has its nuts. Let's shake hers and see what falls out."

* * *

"Gin!" Eleanor laid down her cards on the kitchen table.

Lindsay laid down hers. She'd not been able to make a single match or straight during this round. "You got me again."

Eleanor frowned. "You used to play better, Lindsay. Today you're awful."

Audrey, who stood at the kitchen sink, frowned. "Eleanor."

Eleanor shrugged. "Sorry, but she *is* an awful player today."

Lindsay rose and watched Eleanor gather the cards to shuffle again. "My mind is distracted. I'm just worried about work."

Eleanor started to deal the cards. "It's okay, Lindsay. We can try another game."

Lindsay thought she was going to go mad. She'd had to call in and get a replacement for tonight. Her boss had been happy to accommodate her and, in fact, had sounded a little relieved. But she felt as if she was letting everyone down.

Still, Lindsay smiled. "Eleanor, let's take a break. I'd like to go outside for a minute."

Eleanor rolled her eyes. "It's a thousand degrees out there."

"I love the heat," she lied. "I'll be back."

Before anyone could disagree, she bolted outside. The afternoon sun bore through the trees and the humidity hit her like a brick. Sweat started to bead on her forehead. At least outside, she could breathe.

She stared at the line of trees wondering why the Guardian had chosen her. Had they randomly crossed paths? Had she done something inadvertently to trigger this chain of events? She dug her hands through her hair and paced back and forth.

The screened door squeaked open. Lindsay turned and saw Audrey standing outside with a pitcher of iced tea and a plate with a sandwich. Nervously, Lindsay rubbed damp palms on her skirt.

"You've got to be thirsty and hungry," Audrey said.

Lindsay folded her arms over her chest. "You don't have to worry over me."

Audrey frowned as she set down her tray on a small table. "Of course I do."

Lindsay didn't want the Kiers to be kind. She'd bonded with them once and she'd lost them once. She couldn't go through that a second time. "Thanks, but I've been thinking that I'll call a cab and head back to town."

Audrey didn't hide her shock and disappointment. "A cab? You can't leave now. It's not safe."

"I'll go straight to the Mental Health Services building. It's got locks and guards and I have tons of work."

Challenge had Audrey's back stiffening a little. "I'm not going to argue with you, Lindsay. If you want to call a cab, then call one. But for just five minutes, sit, relax, and eat something. At the rate you're going you're going to collapse."

To appease Audrey, Lindsay took half the sandwich. She bit into it and discovered it tasted good. "Thanks."

Audrey looked satisfied. "I saw the noon news report."

She felt so weary. "I missed it. What did it say?"

Disgust darkened her eyes. "Kendall Shaw talked about your past."

An odd sense of acceptance rolled over her. How the reporter had found out didn't matter at this point. "It was inevitable that it would all come out. Frankly, I'm even a little relieved."

Audrey hesitated as if she wasn't sure she should speak. "I knew you'd lost your parents, honey, but I had no idea that you'd suffered such a tragedy. Zack never told me."

"I asked him not to tell you."

"Why?"

"I guess I was embarrassed. My home life wasn't exactly *Leave It to Beaver*. And your family life just seemed so perfect." Her reasons for keeping silent sounded silly when she voiced them. "I didn't want you to think less of me."

Audrey shook her head. "Perfect families don't exist, Lindsay."

She pinched a corner of the sandwich off. "Yours seems pretty close to perfect."

A sad smile tipped the edge of Audrey's lips. "Don't be fooled. Robert and I have had our share of hard times. Things were particularly bad after Eleanor was born. She was our first child and we had such hopes. And then the doctor's told us she had Down's."

That surprised Lindsay. "You all adore her."

"Of course we do. But in the beginning, it was so hard to deal with the fact that our firstborn wasn't perfect. All those dreams we'd harbored when I was expecting her vanished. It was especially hard on Robert." She slid her hands into the pockets of her khaki pants as if the memory made her uncomfortable. "She was so sick in the beginning. Not only did she have Down's but her heart was defective. A couple of times we almost lost her. Robert and I were so tired, so scared, and we fought a lot then. We even separated for a few months, because he simply couldn't handle the stress."

"From what Zack said, Robert is Eleanor's staunchest ally. He lobbied the schools, Girl Scouts, and the local soccer teams to make sure she'd have a chance to do everything she wanted to do."

"Yes, he's great. But after Ellie was born, it was just too

hard for him. So he left." A shadow crossed her face as the memories returned, and then she caught herself. "He learned that living without us was unbearable. So he asked for a second chance. I wasn't going to give it to him. I remember telling my mom we weren't meant to be. Boy, did that ruffle Mom's feathers. She said, 'Love may happen by chance but a good marriage is just plain hard work.' I gave him—us—that second chance. And I thank God every day I did."

Lindsay had fallen in love with Zack because he'd seemed so strong. She'd felt safe with him. And when he'd failed to measure up and showed weakness, she'd been devastated. And she'd run.

Now he wanted a second chance.

Was she ready to give him one?

Lindsay pinched a piece of crust off her sandwich. The question was too huge for her to consider right now. "The gardens look great."

Audrey accepted the change in topic with grace. "It's finally coming back after the hurricane last year."

The place looked perfect. "You had a lot of damage?"

"Thirty-three trees down. And we lost all the azaleas. But on the bright side, the house didn't see any damage."

"That's good." She shoved her hands in her pockets. "My mother used to take such pride in her gardens."

"I've never heard you talk about your mother."

Lindsay set her sandwich down. "I guess it just hurts too much."

Audrey folded her arms and stared at her with interest. "What was she like? What did she enjoy?"

The questions surprised Lindsay. No one had ever asked them before. The people had always focused on the pain and sadness. Normally, she kept her emotions bottled tight, but sometimes, they bubbled over, and now hot tears burned her eyes. She swallowed. "She loved her gardens. And she loved music."

Audrey moved beside her. "What's your favorite memory of her?"

Lindsay cleared her throat. "There are a lot. She was at every one of my swim meets cheering me on. She baked the best chocolate cakes for my birthday. And she gardened for hours. When I was ten she won a blue ribbon for her tomatoes at some fair."

Audrey touched Lindsay's shoulder. "I'm sorry you lost her. I know she'd be very proud of you."

Stunned, Lindsay's hands hung stiffly by her side. "Thanks."

Audrey squeezed Lindsay's arm. "I'd love to see a picture of her."

"I have a box at home."

"Sometime you'll show it to me?"

"Sure." It was a promise Lindsay doubted she'd ever keep.

Talking about her mother stirred a deep restlessness inside her. Work usually kept the old issue at bay, but without it she felt backed into a corner.

She needed space. She needed time alone. "Audrey, can I borrow your car? I'd like to go visit my mother's grave. It's only about five miles from here."

Audrey planted a hand on her hip. "I will if you stay in Hanover and promise not to go home until Zack gives the all clear."

The mother was as shrewd as the son. "Deal."

"Promise?"

"I swear."

"All right."

Ten minutes later, Lindsay was headed north into Hanover County. After several miles she turned off of Route 360 and headed down a smaller road that cut through rolling cornfields. A few more twists and turns of the road and she arrived at the quiet cemetery where her mother was buried.

She passed through the twin brick pillars at the entrance; waved to the groundskeeper, who smiled back at her; and drove to her mother's grave. Located in a treeless grassy part of the park, the grave site was set apart from the others. She parked Audrey's car on the access road and walked through the wet grass to the grave site.

She'd come empty-handed. No flowers, no greens to fill the urn that was usually set upside down and empty. Guilt washed over her. She'd not done such a good job of tending her mother's grave in the last year.

Thick, hot air and afternoon sun made her sweat, but she savored the gentle sound of the leaves being rustled by the breeze. She'd forgotten how quiet the country could be.

When she reached her mother's spot, she was surprised to discover that the brass urn was turned rightside up and filled with freshly cut white roses.

Lindsay knelt by the bronze plate, unable to take her eyes off the roses. Gingerly, she touched a silky petal. "Who put the roses here?"

She glanced around at the headstones, still decorated with Independence Day reds, whites, and blues.

There was no one around.

She frowned. "Roses were your favorite."

It touched her heart that someone had remembered her mother.

She picked up a stray leaf and tossed it aside. "I saw Zack. He looked good and had clear eyes and a steady hand. It's as if he never drank." She shook her head. "All the crap that guy put me through and he still makes me weak in the knees."

Until this week, she'd thought her feelings for Zack were dead and buried. But after seeing him again, she realized he was still under her skin.

"I have no idea what I'm going to do about him."

Closing her eyes, she tried to imagine her mother's bright smile and the advice that would follow. But in the silence, there were no answers.

She dusted the dirt from her palms. Sweat damped her shirt and plastered her bangs to her head.

The crunch of gravel had her turning. A tall, lean man stood ten feet from her. The sun behind his back shadowed his face. "Afternoon."

Rising, she shadowed her eyes with her hand. She recognized the cemetery caretaker. They'd never spoken before but she'd seen him out here before. "Hey, how's it going?"

The caretaker smiled. He had rawboned features, tanned skin, and rough hands that looked used to manual labor. "Going well, thanks." He glanced at the headstone. "Who are you here to visit today?"

"My mom."

"I've never seen you here before."

The simple comment stirred guilt. "Yeah, I've been busy. I haven't been such a good daughter. But I was here at Easter. I think I saw you then."

He nodded. "Sorry, don't remember."

"I was leaving and you were coming."

He glanced at the headstone. "You couldn't have been more than a kid when she died."

"Yeah."

"I bet you were a fine daughter when she was alive."

"I always felt like I should have done more."

"We all do the best we can at any given time."

Emotion tightened her throat. "Sure is a hot day, isn't it?"

He stared at her for a long moment and then pulled the bill of his hat forward. "Supposed to top a hundred, I hear."

"I can believe it. Hey, do you know who put these flowers in this urn?"

He frowned. "No, don't believe I do. Are they a problem?"

She squinted into the sun. "No. No. I just thought it might be some mistake. Mom didn't have many relatives except me."

"Well, the ladies at the church down the road put flowers on graves from time to time. Especially around a holiday."

"That's kind. Is there anyone at the church I can thank?"

"Oh, they're not looking for thanks. Just happy to do it." He touched the bill of his hat. "Well, I've leaves to rake and flowers to plant. You have a good day. I've got to get back to work."

"Thanks."

He turned and walked back to his pickup truck. Lindsay captured another petal between her fingertips. Soft. Delicate. As she pulled her hand away, she saw a white slip of paper. She removed it from the tangle of stems and unfolded it. Written in bold Times Roman print was the statement, *You are stronger than her.*

The Guardian. For a moment she felt dizzy as she stared at the words. She glanced around the cemetery. The caretaker was gone.

Her hands trembled as she laid the note on the grass. He'd been *here.* He'd left flowers at her mother's grave. She dug her cell out of her purse and dialed Zack's number.

Zack answered on the second ring. "Hello."

"Zack, it's Lindsay. He was here. The Guardian was here." She couldn't hide the fear in her voice.

"Where are you?" His voice was razor sharp.

"I'm at my mother's grave." She gave him the directions.

He swore. "I'll be there in twenty minutes. Get in your car and lock the doors."

Lindsay hugged her arms around her chest. She didn't want to be afraid. She didn't want to be intimidated. But she was. She went to Audrey's car, got in, and locked the doors. Despite the heat of the day, she felt cold.

Less than five minutes later two Hanover deputies appeared. They inspected the flowers, careful not to touch the note or the urn. They searched for the caretaker but couldn't find him. All three waited until Zack and Warwick arrived fifteen minutes later, lights flashing. Lindsay got out of her car as Zack got out of his. He strode toward her, closing the gap in seconds. He laid a hand on her shoulder. "Are you all right?"

She wanted him to hold her. "Yes."

"Where's the note?" The question came from Warwick.

She didn't pull away from Zack's touch. "I left it by the grave."

Warwick snapped on rubber gloves. "What did it say?"

"*You are stronger than her.*' I think he's talking about my mother." When Warwick only stared, she added, "She forgave my father over and over again. She was too afraid or too in love to ever stay away from him too long."

Warwick's gaze darted between Lindsay and Zack. "Is he referring to your relationship with Zack?"

Zack stood stock straight, his jaw tight. "I think so."

Lindsay pushed her hand through her hair. "It's no secret that I haven't signed the divorce papers. And if he was watching me this morning he knew we visited."

"Visited," Warwick said. The word had a volume of meaning.

"Was anyone else out here?" Zack said.

"Just the caretaker."

"Where is he now?" Zack asked, glancing around.

"I don't know. He walked away before I found the note."

"How do you know he's the caretaker?" By the brick front gate, Zack spotted a set of surveillance cameras. He pulled out his notebook and made a notation.

Lindsay thought Zack was being overly paranoid. "I've seen him here before."

"When did you first notice him?"

"Easter. He was headed toward this direction with a rake as I was pulling out of the cemetery. I caught a glimpse of him in the rearview mirror."

"Have you two spoken before?"

"Not before today."

Zack's expression was grim. "Did he see *you* at Easter?"

"No."

His jaw tightened as he surveyed the deserted grounds. "You shouldn't have been out here alone."

"I never figured that the Guardian would know about this place."

"I don't think it's a coincidence that Harold was killed on Monday, which was the anniversary of your mother's death, and Saunders was killed on your birthday."

"The Guardian is from my past?"

"I think so."

"Well, it can't be the caretaker. I've never seen him before."

He tried to smile but failed. "Don't worry. We'll figure this out."

"Sure." Her knees felt weak. She watched as Warwick

and Zack strode toward the headstone. They knelt by the grave, studied the flowers and the note.

Another deputy's car arrived as Warwick pulled a pen from his pocket and gingerly lifted the flap of the note. He read it. His frown deepened. He spoke to Zack but she couldn't hear what was said. They both glanced toward the front gate and the cameras.

Zack rose and approached her. "Is that Mom's car?"

"She let me borrow it."

His annoyance seemed to be growing. "I'm taking you back to my parents' house. And as soon as I can get a sketch artist scheduled you'll talk to her."

She shook her head. "I didn't see his face. The sun was to his back."

"Can't hurt to try."

Unconvinced, she got into Audrey's car and, with Zack following, drove the five miles back to the Kiers'.

When she parked the car, Zack was waiting. He placed his hand in the small of her back. "Do you remember the first time we met?"

Confused, she tried to follow his train of thought. "It was at the triathlon in Charlottesville. The awards ceremony."

"I saw you before that. I was on my second loop of the bike portion of the race when I came around a corner. You were about a hundred yards ahead of me. On the side of the road there was a kid, not more than fifteen. He'd dropped his bike and was holding his stomach. Five racers in front of you had just passed the kid. You stopped."

She'd never noticed Zack. "He had stomach cramps."

"I rode ahead to the aid station and sent back a medic."

"What does this have to do with us and now?"

"I fell in love with you that day, L. I knew you were the one for me. The problem is I forgot that along the way. I blew it. But I'm going to fix this between us."

"You can't fix what I don't want fixed."

He didn't move toward her. "It took me months to screw things up between us. It'll take at least that long to fix it, but I will." He moved toward the front door. So arrogant.

She stood her ground. "Let it go, Zack. Let *us* go."

He opened the front door. "No."

He strode inside.

Numb, she followed and found him lecturing his mother about lending out her car. Audrey got the message loud and clear. Lindsay was to stay put.

Zack kissed his mother. "I'll be back later tonight."

"Don't strand me here," Lindsay said.

"You're safe with my folks."

Eleanor came around the corner with the games *Operation* and *Monopoly* in hand. "Lindsay, don't be worried. Nicole's awake and ready to play a game. This is going to be fun family time."

There was no escaping the Kiers.

Richard Braxton sat in the back of his Gulf Stream plane. The pilot he'd hired was waiting for clearance from the San Francisco tower.

He picked up the morning edition of the *San Francisco Chronicler* and reread the article on page A3. He smiled. According to the article, the fire had destroyed most of the evidence and the lone victim's identity had yet to be confirmed.

He licked his bottom lip, remembering the way the woman had whimpered as he'd sliced the flesh on her face. The killing had been thrilling, more exciting than anything he'd ever done. Already he wanted to kill again.

Beyond the pure entertainment value, though, torturing the woman had not gotten him what he'd wanted.

She had been a stubborn bitch and had refused to tell him anything about Christina.

However, Carmichael's cell phone had told him quite a bit. Her "address book" hadn't panned out, nor had "recent calls." But under "missed calls," there had been a call from a number in Richmond, Virginia.

Richard had been unable to resist and had called the number as a dying Claire had watched. There had been no answer. He'd then called Vincent and had given him the number. Twenty minutes later, Vincent had a name. The number, along with another number, belonged to Lindsay O'Neil. Richard had called her, half expecting to hear Christina's voice. When he hadn't recognized the voice, he'd hung up.

Three hours later, Vincent had called him with a great deal of information about Lindsay O'Neil, including the fact that she'd gone to USC with Christina and was now the suspect in two local murders. Vincent believed Christina was staying with Lindsay.

Richard tapped his finger on the morning paper. Soon he'd be in Richmond. Soon he'd find Lindsay O'Neil and his wife. Soon both women would curse the day they'd crossed him.

Chapter Twenty-Four

Wednesday, July 9, 8:15 P.M.

Marcus Greenland came out of the convenience store with a six-pack of beer and a bag of chips tucked under his arm. He had seen the evening news. That reporter had talked about that bitch O'Neil — the one who had hid his wife and kids from him. It figured the cunt had some kind of screwed-up past that made her hate men. *Bitch.*

But he'd be damned if he'd end up one of her victims. She'd not get her hooks into him.

"Hey, are you looking to make some money?" The raspy voice had Greenland whirling around. An old white guy stood directly behind him. The stranger had come up behind him without making a sound.

Shit. There was a time when no one snuck up on Marcus Greenland. His heart hammering, he said, "What the hell do you want?"

The guy flashed a lopsided grin that was almost apologetic. "I'm looking for a strong man who can do some heavy lifting. I've got a piano to move."

Greenland glared at the old man. He had stooped

shoulders, gray hair, and horn-rimmed glasses. The son of a bitch didn't look like he could lift a bag of sugar. "It's after eight o'clock at night. Who the hell moves a piano late at night?"

The old man shrugged and smiled sheepishly as if he was embarrassed. "Hey, it's not me. It's my wife. She wants the damn thing moved before a party she's having this weekend. Personally, I think it looks fine where it is, but she wants it moved. Just between you and me, my wife can be a pain in the ass when she doesn't get what she wants, so I'm not arguing with her."

"Can't live with 'em, can't shoot 'em." Greenland laughed at his own joke.

The stranger hesitated before he laughed. He reached in his pocket and pulled out a hundred-dollar bill. "It won't take more than an hour of your time."

Greenland relaxed when he saw the bill. He sure as hell could use the money. "Sure, why not?"

Behind the horn-rimmed glasses, blue eyes glistened. "Great. My van is over here."

Greenland snagged a beer from the six-pack and popped it open. He took a long drink, savoring the cool liquid on his throat. It would take at least the six-pack to get even a mild buzz. "You'll bring me back to my car?"

"Absolutely. I'll have you back in less than an hour."

Greenland followed the man to a simple white van. The vehicle looked nicked up and well used. "I figured you for a Volvo or a minivan kind of guy."

The man pulled keys from his pocket. "This is a rental. The trunk of my Audi is big but not big enough for a piano."

Greenland was impressed. He liked nice cars. "An Audi. A-6?"

"Yeah."

"Good car. It hugs the corners real well." He sipped his beer. "I used to sell cars."

"That so? What kind?"

They'd been used cars. "Lexuses mostly."

"Nice."

The stranger slid behind the wheel as Greenland climbed in the passenger side. With a hundred bucks, he could buy his boys that new video game and maybe a nice bottle of bourbon.

Thinking about the boys made him sad. The last time he'd seen the kids, he'd hit Jamal, because the kid wouldn't stop talking. The boy had fallen to the ground hard. Damien had cried and cowered. He had tried to console Damien, but the child had only wailed. That had pissed Greenland off. He'd smacked the kid until he'd shut up.

Now, guilt gnawed at him. As their father, he wanted the boys to respect him, but he also wanted them to love him. That video game would make it up to them.

The stranger fired the ignition. Greenland settled back in his seat. "Want a beer?"

"No thanks. The wife doesn't like it when I drink."

No matter how rich you were a wife could bring you down. "Is she a real ballbuster?"

The stranger's hands tightened on the steering wheel as he smiled. "You could say that." He pulled out onto the main road and quickly merged onto the interstate. They headed west toward farmland bathed in the setting sun's amber light.

Greenland took a long draft from the beer. The alcohol loosened him up. "My old lady busted my chops every time I had a drink too many." Just thinking about Aisha pissed him off. He killed the first beer and opened a second. "My wife is a bitch. And full of lip. And now she's taken my kids—*my sons*—and run off. It isn't right that a man can't see his own flesh and blood. I have a right to them."

The man frowned. "Family is about the most important thing there is."

"Damn straight. Once I get me a real job, I intend on getting mine back."

"You said you sold cars?"

"Did. Now it's construction mostly. I'm also licensed to drive trucks."

"Well, then you should have no trouble getting work. Construction is booming."

He couldn't seem to hold a job. "Not so easy. All the outfits are run by pricks. That's what I say."

The stranger kept his gaze on the road. "Hey, don't I know you from somewhere?" He snapped his fingers. "You played college football for Tech."

Greenland grinned. "That's right."

"Heard you went to the pros."

"Did for a while. Then I busted my right knee."

"Damn."

Greenland took a long drink of beer. It still pissed him off the way that coach had cut him loose as if he were nothing.

"That was one hell of a catch in the Sugar Bowl."

"Yeah." The memory of that one night made him proud. "I was a damn superstar that night."

"And rightly so."

The stranger pulled off the highway and skirted down a rural road. Soon the lights of the interstate vanished. Only the headlights of the van lit the way.

"Is it going to be much farther?" Greenland asked. He had to pee.

"Just another mile or two."

"Okay." Greenland didn't like the country. Full of wild animals, snakes and shit.

They pulled off the side road down a gravel driveway. Tall trees hovered over the road. Gravel popped under the tires. It felt as if they'd driven off the face of the earth.

At the end of the road was a clearing. No house.

Greenland leaned forward. "Where the hell are we?"

The stranger put the car in park and shut off the engine. He pulled out a gun and pointed it at Greenland's head. "The end of the line. Get out."

"Hey, man, if this is about robbery, then you've got the wrong guy. I don't have two damn nickels to rub together."

He cocked the gun. "Get out."

"Like hell I will."

Behind the horn-rims, the eyes that had looked old and weary hardened. The stranger fired past Greenland's head and the cab exploded with sound as the bullet shattered the passenger window. Broken glass nicked the back of Greenland's skull. He dropped his beer on the floor. "Shit!"

Fumbling for the handle, Greenland opened the door and lunged toward the ground. He didn't know who the hell this freak was, but he wasn't going to stick around and find out.

The hard rains from Monday had left the normally marshy ground even softer and he slipped in the mud. He struggled to stand. He slipped again. The freak got out and walked around the side of the van.

Greenland pulled himself upright. He held up his hands in defense. "Hey, man, I don't want no damn trouble. Just let me go and we'll call it even."

The stranger looked taller, stronger now that he held his shoulders upright. "We are far from even."

Panic knifed Greenland. "Who the hell are you?"

"The Guardian." He said it with pride.

"What the fuck does that mean?"

"It means, I kill men like you."

Greenland felt sick. "Hey, man, I ain't never done anything to you."

Moonlight glinted on the gun barrel. "You should have treated your wife with more respect." He fired. The bullet sliced into Greenland's left knee. Pain scorched through his body and he dropped to the cold, soft ground. He clutched his knee.

"What the fuck!" Greenland howled. Blood oozed out from under his fingers. "Did that bitch wife of mine send you to kill me?"

The Guardian loomed over him. "Don't talk about the mother of your children like that."

Greenland's entire body burned. He tried to breathe through the pain like his coaches had taught him in college. *Suck it up.* But this pain was worse than any lineman's tackle. He could barely think as he rolled on his side into a fetal position.

The Guardian stepped closer. Greenland's hands were inches from his feet. This son of a bitch was going down. Moving quickly, he grabbed the Guardian's ankle and yanked as hard as he could. The Guardian fell backward and hit the ground hard, grunting in pain as his ribs connected with a stump. The gun flew off into the darkness.

The Guardian's pain gave Greenland satisfaction and hope. He started to crawl away. If he could get to the thick of the woods around them, he could hide.

The Guardian wrestled his body to a sitting position. His breathing was ragged and labored. With a grunt, he started to crawl around and look for the gun. He couldn't find it.

Greenland clawed at the dirt and dragged his useless leg behind him. "Jesus, save me."

Get to the woods. Get to the woods.

Greenland looked back and saw the Guardian chasing him. Determination had hardened the set of his jaw.

"Oh, Jesus," Greenland muttered. His knee burned. His lungs ached with the effort of breathing.

The Guardian's gait was uneven, but his two good legs easily overtook Greenland.

The Guardian kicked Greenland in the head. The blow cracked teeth and robbed him of the air in his lungs. Greenland rolled on his back. He tasted blood and spit out a tooth.

Every nerve in his body screamed.

"You're not getting away from me," the Guardian growled. He went back to the van, retrieved a machete, then hurried back to again kick Greenland, this time in the side. Ribs shattered. Greenland was near passing out when the Guardian planted his booted foot on his left forearm.

The Guardian ground the bottom of his boot into the tender flesh of Greenland's arm. "Retribution is mine."

"Why?!" Greenland shouted.

The Guardian didn't answer. Instead, he raised the machete high over his head. The blade caught the moonlight before it came down and sliced through the wrist's flesh and narrow bone.

Greenland screamed until his throat felt raw. He pissed on himself. His own blood pooled around his body, dampening the ground under him.

The Guardian held up the severed hand and howled with satisfaction.

That was Greenland's last image before he passed out.

Chapter Twenty-Five

Thursday, July 10, 5:30 A.M.

Warwick was operating on next to no sleep. Zack had been up half the night running down leads on the Turner/Saunders murders. He'd been going over Saunders's phone record and studying Kendall Shaw's news tape from Monday. So far, he'd come up empty-handed. And the brass was getting very antsy. If an arrest wasn't made soon, jobs were going to be lost.

They'd left the office at four A.M. Warwick had headed to the gym for a quick forty-five-minute workout that he hoped would at least get his blood flowing and sustain him through the day.

The gym had been dark when he had arrived, so he had used his key and let himself in. Now he pounded the punching bag, driving the full weight of his frustration into it. Kendall Shaw had called him four times yesterday, trying to get a quote for her next report. He had refused her once and had told her not to call again. But she had.

The woman didn't understand the word *no.* She was a pain in the ass. And still he'd imagined Kendall Shaw walking toward him with her hair flowing around her shoulders and wearing only a red silk robe. He'd pictured her dropping the robe in a puddle around her feet and in the soft moonlight lying down for him and opening her legs. Moaning with pleasure, he had straddled her and cupped her full white breasts. She had smiled up at him, begged him to take her, and he'd driven his hard cock into her.

The fantasy had left him hard and restless.

"Shit," Warwick grumbled before he smacked the bag one last time.

He finished his workout and hit the showers. After a quick shower, he dressed in jeans and a T-shirt and slicked back his still-wet hair. Gym bag in hand, he headed into Pete's office. He'd promised to spar with one of Pete's fighters on Saturday, but at the rate things were going, he wasn't going to make it. Everyone would be living at the station until the killer was found.

He moved down the dim hallway past the dozens of black-and-white photos that spanned two decades. The images were of Pete's fighters. Some were taken during fight matches, others were publicity head shots, but all of Pete's fighters were on the wall. Pete took pride in his fighters—his family, as he'd often called them. Warwick glanced at his own picture taken when he was eighteen. He grimaced, amazed he'd ever been that young.

He knocked on the office door, which was ajar, thinking maybe Pete had slipped in while he was working out. "Pete?"

The door swung open. The lights were off in the office. Warwick flipped them on.

Like always, Pete's dark wooden swivel chair sat in front of a large desk that butted against the wall. The desk was a mess, covered with papers, newspapers, books, and, in the center, a state-of-the-art computer, his only concession to the modern world. Pete updated his computer every year and had the latest software on it. Above the desk on the wall hung a bulletin board covered with news clips covering the charity events Pete had hosted in the last few years. And there were more photos.

Warwick found a pencil and a Post-it pad. Quickly he scratched out a note begging out of the bout scheduled for Saturday. As he pressed the note to the computer screen, he caught sight of a framed picture nestled on the far-right corner of the desk. He never remembered seeing the picture before. Curious, he picked it up.

Unlike the others, this picture was of a twentysomething Pete holding a young girl not more than five. She had yellow hair, fair eyes, and a big gap-toothed grin. Pete stared down at the girl, his gaze tender and full of love.

Did Pete have a kid? In all the years Warwick had known Pete, he'd never talked about having any other family. He'd always said Warwick was all the family he'd needed.

But who was Warwick to criticize the old guy for having a few secrets.

God knows, Warwick had his share.

Richard Braxton arrived at the posh Richmond Hotel suite just after seven. His back was stiff and his head pounded as he watched the bellboy set his overnight bag on a luggage rack at the foot of the bed. Richard set his computer bag on the bed, pulled a fifty from his pocket, and handed it to the bellboy. "Thanks."

The kid glanced at the fifty and his eyes brightened. "Anything else I can do for you?"

"Where can I set my computer up?"

The bellboy pointed to a table by the large window that looked out toward the river. "Just call down to the front desk and they'll give you the password for the wireless hookup."

Richard handed the kid another twenty. "Do me a favor and get the password for me. There should also be a package for me at the front desk. Deliver both back to my room in thirty minutes along with an egg-white omelet, orange juice, and whole-wheat toast dry.

The bellboy pocketed the bill. "The package arrived before you did." He walked into the sitting room. "Here it is."

Richard took the twelve-by-twelve-inch box. "Thanks."

"I'll take care of the password and omelet right away."

"Good."

The kid was annoyingly bright eyed but useful. "Is this your first time in Richmond?"

Richard managed a smile. "Yes."

"Business or pleasure?"

"A little of both." He hated travel. It threw off his routine and generally put him in a foul mood.

"If there is anything else I can do for you, just ring. Ask for Johnny."

"Thanks, Johnny. I'll do that."

When Johnny closed the door behind him, Richard turned to the window and loosened his tie. This city was as hot as blazes and the humidity was so thick he could cut it with a knife. He missed California, his views of the Pacific Ocean, and he couldn't wait to return.

But he was willing to put up with all the inconveniences if it meant finding his Christina. His home hadn't felt right without her.

He opened the box. Inside was a strand of nylon rope, a .38 pistol, a switchblade, vials of sedatives, and syringes. Lessons would have to be taught to Christina. She would have to understand that running from him was wrong.

"Soon, Christina, soon I will find you and soon you will come home with me, where you belong."

Greenland's body, now wrapped in tarp, was heavier than the Guardian had anticipated. Add to that the pain of his cracked rib and it was a struggle to haul the body out of the white van as the sun rose.

The Guardian grabbed the rope around the tarp and jerked hard. Pain scorched through his midsection and shot up and down his spine. For a moment he had to pause and catch his breath.

Sweat beaded on his forehead. He'd gotten sloppy last night. He'd underestimated his enemy and he'd nearly screwed everything up. He rubbed the sweat from his brow. He'd not slept in four or five days and his reflexes were off. But to sleep would mean a break from the killing and he wouldn't stop. *Couldn't* stop.

He could have left the body in the woods but it was important to display his work. People needed to know that monsters like Greenland weren't safe from *him.*

After wiping more sweat from his forehead, he gritted his teeth and pulled the body to the ground. He dragged it across the dry earth toward a tall oak by the mountain biker's trail in Deep Run Park. Few traveled the path this early, but by midday it would see enough traffic that someone would find the body.

With a grunt he pulled the body upright. Quickly, he unwrapped the tarp, uncovering Greenland's head and torso. He'd position the body and then deliver the hand—the trophy—to Lindsay.

The cracking of twigs had him stiffening. Damn. Who the hell was out this early?

"Holy shit!"

The strained voice had the Guardian whirling around.

Two teenage mountain bikers paused on the trail as they straddled their bikes. The taller one was a male, no more than seventeen. Long stringy hair accentuated oily skin and acne. The shorter one, also male, had blond hair and a KISS T-shirt. Each wore bike helmets and gloves.

The Guardian's heart hammered. Jesus, why did they have to find him? He released Greenland's body and reached for the gun tucked in his belt at the small of his back. "Hey, guys, it's not what it looks like. I'm a cop." To prove his claim, he flashed a badge.

The taller teen's eyes narrowed. "What the hell is that?"

"A dead body." There was no hiding what they'd seen and there was no disguising his own face as he tucked the badge back in his pocket. They had seen him. Damage control was his sole option. He didn't want to sacrifice them. Shit. They didn't deserve to die. But the Greater Good was at stake here. Hadn't God tested Abraham by asking him to kill his only son?

He smiled. "I've just called for backup. More cops are going to be here soon."

The shorter teen laid his bike down and took a step closer. "What happened to that guy?"

"Shot, by the looks of it. We won't know until the medical examiner gets here." Hand still behind his back, he pulled the hammer back on the gun.

"Damn," the teen said. "I've never seen a dead body before."

"It's rough."

The other teen had made no move toward him. "Hey, Mark, come on back. You shouldn't get that close."

Mark shrugged. "He's dead, Jeff. He can't hurt me."

The Guardian smiled. "Naw, he can't hurt you. Have a good long look." As Mark moved even closer, the

Guardian jerked the gun free but his ribs pinched hard and slowed what should have been a fluid motion.

Mark saw the gun and immediately started running toward his friend.

He fired. The first bullet went wide and missed Mark. He fired again and this time hit him in the leg. Mark fell to the ground, screamed, and clawed at the dirt. He cried for his mother.

For a split second, the Guardian froze like a deer caught in the beam of headlights. "Jesus, please forgive me. Forgive my sins."

Jeff stared in horror at the Guardian and his wounded friend. Fear turned to shock and then anger. He dropped his bike and scooped up a branch. Screaming, he rushed toward the Guardian.

The branch tip caught the Guardian on the shoulder and drew blood. Pain jerked him out of his own funk. Instinct took over and he fired.

The bullet hit Jeff in the chest. He stood stunned for a moment as if not quite sure what had happened. And then a plume of blood began to stain his shirt and he dropped to his knees. Air gurgled from the hole in his chest.

The Guardian's ribs ached and his shoulder burned as he staggered over to Mark, who was crying and calling even louder for his mother.

The Guardian stared at him. "Damn it, kid. Why did you have to be here?"

Tears streaked Mark's freckled face. "Why are you doing this to me? Me and Jeff never would have told."

"I'm sorry. I couldn't take that chance." Tears filled the Guardian's eyes. "Dumb, damn kids. You shouldn't have been here."

He raised his gun and shot Mark in the head.

* * *

Frank Hines's angry voice echoed through the house. His wife, Deb, was crying. He'd been drinking again, and judging by the sounds, he'd been hitting Deb again.

"I told you I don't want that worthless brother of yours coming around here!" Frank said.

"Why, Frank? He's my brother. He's family."

"I am your only family!"

Lindsay was ten. And she was hiding in the darkened closet of her bedroom. She was too old for teddy bears and yet she clutched the threadbare one she'd had since she was a baby.

Her father began to yell again. She had grown to hate her father, and though her mother had told her to hide, she could no longer stay cowered in the dark closet in her room. The shouting and the crying was driving her insane.

She wiped the tears from her face and stood. Slowly she opened the closet door and moved through her room down the hallway to her parents' bedroom. She opened the door and peered inside. Her father stood over her mother, his arm raised in the air. He brought the back of his hand down. The blow connected with her mother's jaw and it sounded as if it had shattered some of her mother's teeth. Her mother cried and ducked her head low.

Rage filled Lindsay. She pushed open the door and ran toward her father. She wanted to make him stop. "Leave her alone!"

He turned and glared down at her. "Brat!"

The ferocity in his gaze made her hesitate with fear. He was so tall.

Her mother raised her head. "Lindsay, go away. Run."

She fisted her fingers. "Leave my mother alone!"

Her father grabbed her and twisted her arm so hard she felt flesh and bone tear and break. She dropped to her knees. Anger collided with a deep feeling of helplessness that seared her soul.

Lindsay awoke with a start. Her body was covered in sweat and she could barely breathe. She glanced around the dark room trying to get her bearings. For several seconds she didn't know where she was. And then she saw the sewing machine in the corner, the flowered wallpaper, and the chair with her purse slung across it. She was at the Kiers' house.

"I can't hide. I've got to get out of here."

Zack walked into Warwick's office just after seven. Warwick gently set the telephone down in its cradle. He wore a deep, pensive frown.

"What's happening?" Zack asked.

"That was a Detective Rio from the San Francisco Police Department. I was returning a call in response to a teletype he sent me late last night."

"About?"

"Your wife."

Zack tensed. "What does San Francisco PD have to do with Lindsay?"

"Rio is investigating the death of a Claire Carmichael. She was killed two days ago in San Francisco. She owned a New Age bookstore. The murder was grisly and the killer burned her place to the ground."

"I don't see the connection."

"Claire placed a phone call from her store to Lindsay the night she was murdered. The call was logged in at eleven P.M. pacific coast time, or two A.M. eastern standard."

Zack's mind turned. "Lindsay knows a lot of women in high-risk relationships."

"Claire wasn't involved with anyone. And witnesses report that she closed her shop early on Tuesday. Around lunch. Friends say Claire never closed early. And she also volunteered at a local women's shelter from time to time."

Zack's stomach clenched. "Richard Braxton is from San Francisco."

"Yeah."

Warwick's phone rang and he snapped up the receiver. Immediately he cradled the phone under his chin and started to write notes on a pad. "We'll be right there. And keep a tight clamp on the entire area. I don't want the media to even get a whiff of this."

"What is it?"

Warwick hung up and grabbed his coat off the back of his chair. "Marcus Greenland's body was found in Deep Run Park. He was at the top of that list Lindsay reviewed with C.C. He's one violent SOB."

"Lindsay was at my folks' place last night."

"There's no pinning this one on her."

"Why?"

"Two teenagers came upon the killer as he was dumping the body. He shot them both."

Zack felt sick. Damn it. "How are they?"

"One is dead and the other is in critical condition at Mercy Hospital. He's the one who called in the shooting from his cell phone."

"Can he give us a description?"

Warwick shook his head. "He's in surgery right now. It'll be a couple of hours."

Tension tightened the muscles in Zack's back. "I'll drive us to the park."

"Fine."

Zack tried to call Lindsay several times on her cell but she didn't pick up. He called his parents' house and got Eleanor, who told him Lindsay had just left in a cab. "Damn it. Can't the woman listen just once?" he muttered.

He covered the ten-plus miles to Deep Run Park in rush-hour traffic in less than twenty minutes. He wove in and out of traffic, one hand on the steering wheel and a cell under his ear as he called Ayden.

He pulled into the park entrance and rolled down the hill to the back parking lot near the soccer fields, where ten police cruisers were parked.

Zack got out of the car. He shrugged off his jacket and tossed it on the front seat. Rolling up his sleeves, he moved toward Sara, who was squatting by Greenland's body as she photographed it. She stood and moved to the edge of the yellow crime scene tape.

Sara looked pale and grim. Any death involving a kid shook everyone to the core. She pulled rubber gloves and booties from the pocket of her white jumpsuit and handed them to Zack and Warwick. They put them on and ducked under the yellow tape.

Zack yanked off his sunglasses and squatted by Greenland's body. Greenland's dark skin had turned a pasty gray and his lips blue. His eyes were half open. The tarp had been partially removed and he could see that Greenland's right hand had been chopped off.

"He didn't finish his job," Zack said.

"The boys interrupted him." Warwick muttered an oath as he glanced at the covered body of the teenager. "Sara, did he leave anything else behind?"

Sara pointed to an orange flag sticking from the ground. "A forty-five shell casing. And I found traces of blood on the tip of a stick the dead boy was holding. I've already bagged it and sent it to the lab."

Zack rubbed the back of his neck with his hand. "Let's hope he's in our DNA database."

"Any sign of the hand?" Zack said.

"None."

Zack glanced at Warwick. "The last two hands were delivered to Lindsay. We need to find her."

Warwick nodded. "Right."

* * *

Dressed in yoga pants and a tank top, Kendall had been up half the night listening to the police scanners. There'd been nothing out of the ordinary. The piece she'd done on the killer had been priceless. The fact that he was mutilating his victims and sending the hands to Lindsay was more than she could have hoped for.

She'd received five times the usual number of e-mails from viewers. But there'd been no response from the killer or the network producers to whom she'd overnighted tapes.

Exhausted and hungry, she'd reached her limit of listening to the routine police calls: loud music, drunk teenagers, an overdose in a convenience store parking lot, and a speeder on the interstate.

She rose from the varnished kitchen table and opened the refrigerator. Eggs, a half carton of milk, and a salad left over from the salad bar at the grocery store. When she'd been a kid, her mother had kept this refrigerator stocked.

Crap. She needed to get out of this house and start fresh away from Richmond.

She set a pan on the stove, clicked the burner dial to medium high, and cracked a couple of eggs in the pan. *Eat first and then catch an hour or two of sleep.* She and Mike needed to be at the station by noon.

"Dispatch, this is 8021."

Kendall was only half listening now. "Dispatch, over."

"Dispatch, the mutilated body found in Deep Run Park—"

"8021, Homicide has requested this communication be handled on a secure channel. Switch to . . ."

"Shit." Kendall's mind reeled. Mutilated body. The eighties were the western end of the county, which was near her and the shelter. She ran to the avocado green wall phone and dialed her cameraman's phone number.

On the fourth ring, a gravelly voice heavy with sleep answered. "What?"

"How soon can you pick me up?" She paced the kitchen, frustrated that a phone cord tethered her to the wall.

"Kendall?" He swore. "Why?"

"Body at Deep Run Park. I think it's our guy."

He cleared his throat. "Give me twenty minutes."

"Make it fifteen and I'll be out front waiting."

"Right."

Fourteen minutes later, she stood outside, briefcase in hand. She didn't have the time to shower, so she'd swept her hair up with a French twist comb, quickly applied her makeup, and slipped on a simple blue sheath and heeled sandals.

"So where we going?" Mike said when he pulled up. Thick stubble covered his square jaw, and his thinning shoulder-length black hair was loosely bound at the nape of his neck. His Hawaiian shirt flapped in the air from the AC vent.

She flipped through her notes. "To Lindsay O'Neil's house."

Mike sipped the last of yesterday's Big Gulp as he put the van in reverse and backed out of the driveway. The faint smell of cigarette smoke hung in the air. "I thought the body was at some park. I know the other news teams will be there."

"And I know the cops are going to have the area locked up tight."

"So why Lindsay's again?"

"Because after the last two murders, there was a disturbance just a few hours later near Lindsay. If our friend Steve is correct, the killer is sending hands to Lindsay. My guess is, the killer is going to send her something now and I want to be there when he does."

"Why send her a hand?"

"Who knows? Who cares really? He's like a cat that dumps a mouse at its master's feet."

He considered what she'd said. "The killer thinks of Lindsay as his master?"

"Maybe. Or maybe he's fixated on her. Whatever his motivations, we've got three murders now. Richmond has a serial killer." She tapped her foot. "If I could find a way to draw this guy out, I could write my own ticket."

Mike looked at Kendall as if she'd lost her mind. "You want to draw out a serial killer."

"I sure do."

"How are you going to do that?"

"Go after Lindsay. If I can make her miserable enough, hound her with the cameras, I'm willing to bet our guy gets pissed and shows himself."

"Or he just kills you."

The thought didn't frighten her enough to change her mind. "I'll be fine."

This story was going to take her places. She dug her cell out of her purse and punched in her news director's number. She relayed the information and told him to call the network. This was the stuff of national news.

Mike drove by Lindsay's town house. "I don't see her Jeep."

"Park the van down the street out of sight."

"And?"

"Get your camera and come with me. We'll wait out of sight. Five'll get you ten the fireworks explode sooner than later."

Lindsay wasn't going to hide anymore, from anyone. She needed to reclaim her home, her life, and she needed to prove that she was in control.

It had been easy to be brave on the cab ride over. But now as she stood alone and stared at the yellow crime scene tape by her front door, she found herself searching the bushes and the surrounding terrain. He could be out there watching her.

No one lurked nearby and there were no grisly packages waiting for her. And still her nerves danced with tension. She had hoped the worry that had kept her up most of the night would vanish once she was back at her own place. But it didn't.

Digging her keys out of her purse, she moved up the sidewalk, careful to step around the spot where she'd dropped the bloody hand wrapped in the newspaper. Sucking in a breath, she moved toward the front door. As she shoved her key in the lock, she realized the door wasn't locked.

Immediately, she backed away, leaving her keys to dangle in the lock. Heart hammering, she dug in her purse for her cell phone.

Her hands trembled as she punched in Zack's cell phone number. Her front door opened.

Steve, her maintenance man, came out. He was frowning.

Her thumb on the "send" buttons, she paused. "Steve, what's going on?"

He held a screwdriver in his hand. "I thought I'd check the place out for you. After what that creep left you yesterday, I wanted to make sure your place was secure. And then I figured I'd go ahead and fix your AC."

She noticed his white van across the street and felt foolish. She closed her phone and dropped it in her purse. "Oh. Sorry, I'm just a little on edge."

"Understandable." He smiled. "I was just on my way to the van to get a different screwdriver."

"Right." Lindsay waited as he retrieved a large flathead screwdriver. "What do you think caused the AC to go?"

He shrugged. "Part blew. Looked like an overload. And the power outage the other day sure couldn't have helped."

She followed him inside to the living room. The house was quiet and the drawn shades blocked out almost all of the morning sun. She moved into the kitchen to brew a pot of coffee. She'd left so early from the Kiers' that she'd not had any. And now she felt so exhausted. She needed something to get her moving.

Steve went to the AC utility closet sandwiched between the living room and the kitchen. "Sorry it's taken me so long to get to this."

"Believe me, I've got bigger problems than no AC."

Steve unscrewed the front panel of the unit and then pulled out the filter. He clicked on his flashlight and stared into the comb of wires. He frowned. "Have a look at this."

"What?"

He reached inside the air conditioner and pulled out an electronic box with an antenna on top. "I didn't see it before because it was tucked in the back."

She frowned. "It looks like a transmitter."

"Why would there be a transmitter in your place?"

"I've seen pieces like that before, at a security conference I attended last year. It can be used to boost the signal of a camera."

He looked puzzled. "I service every unit in this complex and I've never seen this."

"Is there a wire attached to it?"

"Yeah."

"Where does it go?"

He shined the flashlight into the unit. "The wire

snakes out a small hole in the back of the unit and crosses to another hole drilled in the wall."

Lindsay glanced behind the unit and saw the wire. "It vanishes into the wall between the closet and living room."

Steve shined the flashlight into the hole in the wall. The wire rose up and vanished into the darkness. He moved out of the utility closet and into the living room. Above their heads was a grate. "That's odd."

Lindsay didn't like the concern in his voice. "What?"

"That grate on your living room ceiling shouldn't be there."

She stared at it. She'd never noticed it before.

"Let me get a ladder."

Lindsay folded her arms around her chest. "Sure."

He was back in less than a minute and on the ladder. He undid the screws and popped off the grate. Drywall and paint tore. He peered into the hole.

Lindsay stood on tiptoe. "What do you see?"

He removed a small electronic device. "A camera."

She felt sick inside. She'd heard about cameras like this. They were easily found on the Internet and were used by people to spy on other people.

Someone was spying on her.

Someone was watching her.

Steve climbed down from the ladder. He handed her the camera. It was small, compact, and state-of-the-art. She knew this model could send a signal up to seven miles away.

Lindsay rolled the device between her fingers as she glanced behind her trying to imagine the angle of the camera. "It would have recorded everything happening in the living room."

The Guardian. He'd been watching her.

Steve shook his head. He looked worried. He had full

access to the units and he'd be the first questioned by the police.

A deep sense of shame washed over her. She felt violated. The Guardian had been spying on her during her most private moments. She remembered the other night when she'd been awakened by the phone. She'd had the creeps then and sensed she was being watched. Had he been watching her then? Had he been the one to call her?

Lindsay dug her cell out of her purse and dialed Zack's number. He answered on the first ring. "Where are you?" He sounded terse, and in the background she thought she heard tense voices.

Her hand shook as she shoved it through her hair. "I'm okay. I'm at my town house. My maintenance man found a camera in my AC vent."

A heavy silence followed. "Don't move, I'm only five minutes out."

"Thanks." She wanted him close, wanted his protection. She could have listed seven reasons off the top of her head why it was wrong to depend on him, but right now she didn't care about reason. She needed Zack. And she knew he would be there for her.

Steve held the screwdriver in his hand in a tight grip. "I didn't have anything to do with this."

"It's going to be okay," she told Steve. "The police are coming."

Steve looked worried and he started to pace. "I didn't do this."

His agitation caught her off guard. He'd always been so easygoing and quick with a joke. "No one said you did."

He shook his head. "They might think I'm guilty when they discover that I have a police record."

Lindsay stared at him and her concern grew. Truthfully,

she knew nothing about him. Steve could be the Guardian. "What were you in jail for?"

He shoved out a breath. "It doesn't matter. I have a record."

Lindsay glanced toward the open door of the town house. "I'm going to wait outside."

He nodded. "Me too."

Hugging her arms, she ran out into the sunshine and moved away from Steve.

Instead of waiting with her, he moved quickly toward his van.

"Where are you going?!" she shouted.

"Away. I've seen those tabloid news shows. I'll be tried and convicted on the news before I even get to court."

"The police are coming to talk to you."

"Screw the police." He got in the van and fired it up. Gravel kicked up as he punched the gas and drove off.

Lindsay stood on the corner, counting the seconds until Zack arrived.

Minutes later, the white Impala pulled around her street corner. The wheels had barely came to a stop when Zack hopped out of the vehicle. He strode directly toward her. He stared at her for a long moment before asking, "What did you find?"

"My maintenance man found a camera in an AC vent. He swears he didn't put it there."

"Where is he?"

"He drove off. Said he had a police record."

Zack's jaw tensed. Warwick got out of the police car as Zack moved toward him. He relayed what she'd said and Warwick grabbed the radio. He called in a description of the van and Steve.

The sound of sirens echoed in the distance. More cops were coming.

Zack moved toward her. "Lindsay, there's been another murder. Marcus Greenland."

Her brows knitted as she stared back at her house. "I was on the phone with Aisha Greenland the other night. I sat right in my living room and talked to her about her divorce. She was scared. The Guardian must have been watching and listening." She felt sick. "He calls himself the Guardian. Does he think he's helping me?"

"In his mind, it might have started out that way, but its grown way beyond that."

"What's happened?"

"While the Guardian was dumping Greenland's body early this morning, two teenagers came upon him. He shot at them. One is dead and the other is at Mercy undergoing surgery."

"My God." Her voice hitched with sadness and tears pooled in her eyes.

Zack worked his jaw. "He's not helping anyone."

Two teenagers—*children*—shot.

"Did you find any other cameras?" Zack asked.

"We haven't looked yet."

Warwick strode up to them. "I've called for the cavalry. They'll be here in the next few minutes to sweep the place. With any luck, we can link this system to the guy who installed it."

Her skin felt clammy. "The Guardian is taking over my life."

"Who's the Guardian?" Kendall Shaw's voice caught them all off guard.

They turned, stunned.

"Where did you come from?" Zack demanded.

Kendall ignored him. The light on the cameraman's camera clicked on, and like a lioness looking for prey, Kendall shoved a microphone toward Lindsay's face. "Is the Guardian the guy who's been killing those men? Has he been secretly videotaping you as well?"

Lindsay stared, stunned. Warwick frowned.

Zack raised his hand and blocked the lens of the camera. "This is not the time or place for this."

Kendall didn't flinch. "Come on, Lindsay, Detective Kier. I know this killer has been on a rampage since Monday. And it's the anniversary week of Lindsay's mother's death. Lindsay lost her job because of him. He's killed four, maybe five people."

"No comment," Zack said.

But Lindsay's temper roiled. Not at the reporter, but at the Guardian. He had invaded her life, ruined her job, and watched her while she moved around her home. She'd promised herself this morning she'd not hide anymore. If the Guardian wanted her, he could come and get her.

Lindsay said in a loud voice, "I don't know who the Guardian is."

"Lindsay," Zack warned.

Mike stepped sideways so that he had a clear shot of Lindsay. Kendall moved closer. Her eyes gleamed with hunger.

"I can tell you this," Lindsay said. Zack grabbed her arm, squeezing a gentle warning for her to be silent. But she wouldn't stay silent. This creep wasn't going to hurt anyone else if she could stop him. "I've grown to hate and resent whoever is doing this to me."

"Why is he sending you the severed hands of his victims?" Kendall asked.

"I don't know. He's got a twisted form of justice that I want no part of. If the Guardian is watching, back off. Leave me alone. I don't want your help or anything else to do with you."

Zack slapped his palm over the camera lens. "Enough."

Kendall smiled. "That was excellent, Lindsay. Really excellent." She'd gotten the quote she wanted. "We're going. I've got to hurry if we're going to get this edited for the noon news."

Zack's expression was harsh as he watched Kendall and Mike leave. "Get them out of here." He shook his head. "You could very well have turned yourself into a target, Lindsay."

She dug her hands through her hair. For the first time since she was a child she felt oddly in control. "Good. Better me than another child."

Richard Braxton sat in his rented Mercedes down the street from Lindsay O'Neil's town house. The place was swarming with cops. There was no sign of Christina, but in the center of the cops stood two women. He glanced at the photo of Lindsay O'Neil and then back at the two women. The shorter one was O'Neil.

He twisted his wedding band around his finger. "Where are you hiding my wife, Ms. O'Neil?"

The cops wouldn't surround her forever. Soon there'd be an opportunity to get her alone. And when he did, he would make her regret that she'd ever interfered with his marriage.

Patience.

Chapter Twenty-Six

Lindsay felt dirty and violated as she watched the cops go through her house searching for electronic bugs. So far they'd found five: one in the kitchen, one in the back patio, one in the front entryway, and two in the living room.

Zack came down the stairs and moved within inches of her. "We didn't find any bugs in your bedroom or the bathrooms upstairs."

She didn't feel any relief. "I guess that's the Guardian's way of protecting my privacy."

Zack nodded. "I think you're right. In his own way, he seems to be looking out for you."

She glanced around the room at each of the vents. She hugged her body, warding off a sudden chill. "Nicole said this place gave her the creeps. I even felt it once or twice. But I shrugged it off to fatigue. Do you have any idea how long the bugs have been there?"

"No. But if I had to guess I'd say all this started around the time that article came out in the paper about you."

"I agreed to that damn piece because Dana had said it

would boost fund-raising. Now I wish I'd never met Kendall Shaw."

"That article landed you on someone's radar," Zack said. "Anyone different you've noticed lurking around lately?"

She lifted an amused brow. "Zack, you know me. I'm so busy on any given day I couldn't tell you if it's raining or not."

Zack offered her a half smile as if a memory played in his head. "Can you think of anyone who might have come into your home?"

"Just Steve the maintenance guy as far as I know. But I don't own this place. The property management firm has the right to send in anyone they want if there are maintenance problems."

"What about Nicole? Did she bring anyone in here?"

"No. She's barely getting used to the place herself."

He considered what she'd said. "Does the property manager have to notify you when they come in?"

"They're supposed to. But the girls in the rental office are young and not so focused on their jobs."

Zack's face looked as if it had been carved from stone. "I'll talk to the rental office. How many people know you legally changed your name when you turned eighteen?"

"Since I returned to Richmond, I've told no one about my past except you. But I grew up in Ashland, and any one of the people there could have seen the article and recognized me."

"Have you had contact with anyone from the old days? Like Joel, maybe?"

"How do you know about him?"

"Warwick and I spoke to him the other day."

She couldn't be angry. He was being thorough. "I haven't seen him since high school."

"He was worried about you."

"He was a good guy."

He didn't confirm or dispute the comment. "What about family?"

"There wasn't much family. My dad was an only child and his parents were gone by the time I was born. My mom's parents were dead too. And her brother only saw her rarely." She stopped, remembering the dream she'd had last night. "I remember my uncle called my mom when I was about ten. Mom had lunch with him. My father was furious."

"Any pictures of your uncle or your parents?"

"As a matter of fact, I found a few pictures the other night." She went to the closet below the stairs and pulled out the box of photos. She had to dig deep to find what she wanted. She handed Zack the grainy color photo. "It was taken on my parents' back porch. That's my mom and dad, me in the center, and my uncle on the end."

Zack studied the picture. "He's in a Navy uniform."

"Yes. That's why he was away so much."

"What was your uncle's name?"

"Henry is all I remember."

"O'Neil?"

"No. He and Mom were half brother and sister. They had different fathers. There was a fifteen-year age difference between them. I don't remember his last name."

"Which would make him how old?"

"Sixty-nine. Mom would have been fifty-four this year."

As thirty loomed for her, she realized just how young her mother had been when she'd died.

He tucked the photo in his pocket. "Who is Claire Carmichael?"

The out-of-the-blue comment stunned her. "Claire? She runs a bookstore in San Francisco but also does a lot of volunteer work with battered women. She gave Nicole money so she could leave the city. Why?"

"She was murdered on Tuesday."

Grief washed over her. Claire and she had been good friends. They'd lost touch but she'd liked the woman immensely. "My God."

"Someone placed a call from her cell to your phone on the night she died. Tuesday night."

"I got a late-night call on Tuesday on my cell phone. It woke me out of a sound sleep. It really rattled me. The call came from outside the calling area, so I just figured it was a misdial. Was it Claire who called me?"

"We don't know."

An unthinkable thought crossed her mind. "Richard Braxton got to her."

"Whoever killed Claire was a sadist."

"Nicole said Richard could be quite violent. We've got to warn her."

"I'll have a sheriff's deputy posted outside my folks' place so we can keep an eye on her. I want you back there."

"No." When he frowned she added, "I appreciate what you're doing, Zack, but I can't let the Guardian or Richard ruin my life."

"You can't stay here."

"I know. I'll bunk with Ruby. No one will ever find me there."

The elevator doors opened to Mercy Hospital's fifth floor and out stepped a grim-faced Captain Ayden. Anger overrode fatigue and fueled him as he approached the intercom by the locked metal doors of the surgical recovery floor. He'd not slept in forty-eight hours. He had arranged for his boys to stay with the neighbors and had called them a couple of times just to hear the sound of their voices. He missed them now more than ever.

This latest shooting of the teenage boys had hit too close to home for him. His own sons, fourteen-year-old Zane and sixteen-year-old Caleb, were athletic and active in local mountain bike clubs. Each could have been on that trail this morning and stumbled upon the Guardian.

Ayden pressed the buzzer that sounded at the ICU nurses station.

"Yes," a woman said.

"I'm Captain Ayden and I'm here to see Dr. Moore."

"Sure, just a moment." Another buzzer sounded and this time a lock on the door clicked and the doors swung open.

Ayden strode into the ICU ward toward the nurses station, where a woman stood reading a chart. She was in her early fifties and wore her shoulder-length dark hair tied back with a rubber band. Wisps of hair stuck out, framing her angled face. Dark shadows hung under vivid blue eyes.

He pulled out his badge. "I'm Captain Ayden."

The woman closed the chart and set it down. "My name is Dr. Moore. I'm Mr. Langford's surgeon."

"*Mr.* Langford." Ayden swallowed an oath. He was doing his best to keep his voice calm. "The kid isn't old enough to shave and we're talking about him like he's an adult."

Dr. Moore kept her expression neutral, unapologetic. "The less attached I am the better, detective. I can't do my job if I'm emotionally involved. A cop should understand that."

Ayden frowned. "I understand but I still don't like it." He turned his back to the curtain separating them from patients. Unseen monitors beeped. "How's the kid doing?"

"The bullet tore into his chest."

"But he will live," Ayden said.

Dr. Moore met his direct gaze head-on. "I'm going to do everything I can to save him. Either way he's got a long road ahead of him."

He shoved out a breath. "Does he know his friend died?"

"No."

"Can I talk to him?"

"You can only if you promise to keep your conversation very short. The boy's only been out of surgery for an hour."

"Understood," Ayden said. "I won't do anything to jeopardize his health."

Dr. Moore led Ayden to a corner cubical curtained off from the rest of the floor. She pushed back the curtain. The boy in the bed was deathly pale and shirtless. IVs stuck in each arm. Sensors were pasted to his bare chest. Blood dripped from a bag into his arm.

"Mr. Langford," Dr. Moore said.

The boy laid open-mouthed, his eyes shut.

Ayden shifted. "What does his mom call him?"

Dr. Moore checked her chart. "Jeff."

Ayden leaned close to the bed, careful not to disrupt the wires. "Jeff."

The boy's eyelids fluttered.

"Jeff," Ayden said louder.

A monitor indicated that the boy's heart rate rose from sixty beats a minute to seventy. He was waking up.

"Jeff, I'm a cop. I'm trying to figure out who shot you. Can you tell me anything about the person who did this to you?"

Jeff moistened his dry lips. In a bare whisper, he said, "Never saw him before."

"What did he look like?"

"Gray hair." He ran his tongue over his dry lips again.

Ayden laid his hand gently on Jeff's. It felt cold. "Can you tell me anything else, Jeff?"

"He limped, like he'd been hurt." The boy shut his eyes.

Dr. Moore glanced at the monitors. The boys heart rate was dropping again. "He's not going to be able to give you much more. Not until tomorrow."

"Where's Mark?" the boy whispered.

Ayden squeezed the boy's hand. "Don't worry about him now."

Jeff's eyes fluttered closed.

Frustration dogged Ayden. This boy was the key to catching the psycho. "I have just one more question."

The doctor looked annoyed. "You can ask all the questions you want but the boy isn't going to talk. He's heavily sedated and his mind isn't going to clear for at least twenty-four hours."

Ayden handed his card to the doctor. "Call me when he can talk again. I don't care if it's day or night."

She tucked the card in her white coat pocket. "I'll do that."

He was grateful to leave the room and the hospital with its antiseptic smells and dull green colors. It was time to turn his attention to what he did best—catching killers.

Kendall Shaw had filed an updated news report on the Guardian just barely in time for the news at noon. It was a good piece. No, it was a *great* piece. Her best.

She'd known when she'd stuck the microphone in Lindsay's face that she was going to get a hell of a quote. Lindsay was a powder keg. And it hadn't taken much to set her off and get her talking.

And then Kendall had looked directly into the camera

and challenged the Guardian. She'd called him a coward who hid behind Lindsay O'Neil.

If this wasn't going to be *the* tape that got her noticed she'd be shocked. Success was so close she could almost taste it.

Kendall's heels clicked on pavement as she crossed Channel 10's small city parking lot to the side street where she'd parked her car. The sun was low in the sky and the day's heat waning. She was headed to her hair dresser to treat herself to a wash and blow-dry. There hadn't been much time to doll up before the noon news report, but when she rebroadcast at six she wanted to look her best.

Kendall reached her red sports car and clicked the lock open with the keyless remote.

"Ms. Shaw?"

The raspy voice had Kendall turning toward a pleasant looking man dressed in khakis and a white collared polo shirt. His graying hair was brushed off his face. Deep lines around his eyes made him looked distinguished more than old.

"Yes?"

"I saw your news report today. It was something else."

She opened her car door, aware she had no time to spare if she was going to get her hair done and be back at the station in forty-five minutes. "Thank you for noticing."

A smile tipped the edge of his mouth. "You're one great reporter. Not many would have the spine to call this killer out."

She was accustomed to being recognized. It was part of the job. She'd learned long ago to be nice to viewers while not getting pulled into lengthy conversations. Still, the clock was ticking. "Thanks. I'd chat but I'm really late for an appointment."

He held up calloused hands. "Oh, no problem."

She tossed her purse in the car, grateful that this guy, whoever he was, wasn't going to ask a thousand questions. "You have a good afternoon."

"You too."

Kendall had all but put the man out of her mind when she felt the first sharp electric bolt rip through her body. Every one of her muscles convulsed and gave way. Her knees buckled. She'd have hit the ground hard if the guy hadn't grabbed her.

He smiled down at her, no hint of surprise in his warm brown eyes. "You all right there, Ms. Shaw?"

She couldn't speak.

"Cat got your tongue?" He pulled her up and half walked, half carried her toward a van parked next to her car.

Oh, God. Oh, God.

"I wasn't real happy about your report today. You baited Lindsay and made her say things she wouldn't normally have said. You called me a coward. I didn't like that either."

Her blurred senses started to scream. This man was the Guardian.

A deep moan formed in her chest. She wanted to scream, to run, but her body refused to work. As if he read her thoughts, the Guardian touched her with the Taser again. Her knees buckled and he now supported her weight completely. He had surprising strength.

The Guardian opened the back door to the van. He laid her on the metal bed of the van, climbing in, and closed the doors behind them. He clicked on a dome light, whose light was contained by the blackened windows.

Kendall knew the grim statistics. Once a victim was trapped in a vehicle her chances of survival drastically diminished.

Her left hand twitched. If her body would start working, she could ball her fingers into a fist and punch him. She could still get away.

The Guardian put his lips close to her ear. "I know what you're thinking. But you're not going anywhere." He raised the Taser close to her face. The electrical current snapped and popped just inches from her eye.

He jabbed the Taser into her side. Her head jerked back as she convulsed and a silent scream clogged her throat. "You're not going anywhere. Not until you've paid like all the other abusers."

He grabbed a length of rope and tied her wrists together and then her ankles. Her fingers tingled as her too tight bindings constricted the blood flow. She forced herself to meet his gaze. She wanted to memorize every detail so that she could tell the police what this bastard looked like.

He wadded up a cloth, shoved it in her mouth, and secured it with a piece of duct tape.

She struggled to breathe and her bravado waned. Tears welled in her eyes and she hated her weakness. She needed to stay calm. If she was going to get out of this alive, she needed to think. Her cell was in her purse in her car. She had a meeting with Mike soon. Would he see her car in the side street and launch a search for her?

The Guardian stroked her hair back off her face. "So soft and so pretty. But you have a heart of stone." He sighed. "You know what I do to my victims, don't you?"

She winced as he jabbed a needle into her arm and emptied the syringe.

"I cut their left hands off," he said quietly. He ran his hand lightly down the length of her arm to the hands tied behind her back. His fingers encircled her wrists. "What you may not know is that they're alive when I take my trophy."

The matter-of-fact tone made the statement all the more frightening. Panic could easily have tipped to hysteria, but the drugs he'd put into her system had started to take effect. Her mind grew foggy.

The Guardian cupped her chin in his calloused hands and moved his lips up to her ear. "I won't have any trouble snapping your delicate wrist in two with my machete blade."

Tears ran down Kendall's face. She shook her head. This couldn't be happening.

The Guardian got behind the wheel of the van and fired up the engine. He calmly merged into traffic as if he had all the time in the world. "I never thought I'd kill a woman. It just seemed wrong in so many ways. But then I saw that broadcast of yours today and I knew you would be the exception to the rule." He chuckled. "I never have liked you. And you know, from the moment you started covering this story, I knew we'd clash. I just knew it."

Her mind tumbled and her muscles went slack.

"Look at the bright side, Kendall. You'll be headline news tomorrow when they find your body."

Lindsay sat in her car, a suitcase packed and sitting on the passenger seat. Zack was wrapping up details at the town house, and then he was going to escort her to Ruby's. She'd agreed that she couldn't stay in the town house. In fact, she doubted she could ever live there again. And Zack had understood that she felt uncomfortable at his folks' place. They'd compromised. She was staying at Ruby's.

Before she headed out she wanted to touch base with Nicole. She called her at the Kiers', and spoke to Eleanor briefly before Nicole picked up. "Nicole?"

"Hey, how are you doing?" Nicole's voice sounded stronger, as if she'd gotten some sleep.

"Been better. But I'm hanging tough. I wanted to let you know that I'm staying at Ruby's tonight. I'll drive out to see you in the morning."

"Sounds good."

"Hey, have you run that test yet?"

"No. I'll do it first thing in the morning." She sighed. "Pregnancy is a problem I don't want right now."

"One step at a time."

Nicole hesitated. "I dreamt about Richard again. I can't help but think that he's close."

Lindsay thought about Claire. She chose not to tell Nicole. "Stay close to the Kiers. They'll keep you safe."

"Thanks."

"I'll call you in the morning."

"Good."

Lindsay rung off and dialed Sam's number. He'd have the results of the bloodwork by now. His phone rang five times and then went to voice mail: "This is Dr. Sam Begley. Leave me a message unless this is an emergency. If it is, hang up and call 911."

"Sam, this is Lindsay. Where are you? Call me. I need to talk to you."

"Detective Warwick, this is Rio from San Francisco." Warwick glanced at the clock on his desk. It was ten here so it was seven in the evening on the West Coast.

"Were you able to find Braxton?"

"My partner and I went to his house. He's gone. According to his secretary, he filed a flight plan to Vancouver. He has businesses up there. Airport records show that he did file the flight plan."

Warwick closed his eyes and pinched the edge of his nose. He was bone tired. "Did you find him in Vancouver?"

"Not yet. But we're in contact with Canadian authorities. I'll let you know as soon as we find him."

"If you even get a whiff that he's headed east call me. Anytime."

"Consider it done."

"I don't know anything about Braxton. What's your gut reaction on this one?"

Rio sighed. "He's a tricky bastard. Looks clean and acts clean but it didn't take much digging to find out he came up hard. When he was seventeen he killed a man. Because he was under eighteen, he got off with time in juvenile hall. He was linked to other violent crimes but nothing ever stuck. I wouldn't put anything past him."

Chapter Twenty-Seven

Friday, July 11, 6:00 A.M.

Richard Braxton sat on the edge of his bed. The whore who'd showed up in his room late last night lay under the rumpled sheets. Her dark hair swept over her face. He imagined that in the right light, she could look like Christina.

He rose and pulled on his trousers. He handed her several hundred-dollar bills.

A sly smile lifted her lips. Now that his desire had cooled, he could see that the woman had coarse features made worse by layers of makeup. She swung her legs over the side of the bed. Her naked breasts bobbed and she pulled a tight T-shirt over them. She wriggled into her skirt and slipped manicured feet into four-inch heels. "It was fun. You in town long?"

Richard slipped on his shirt and buttoned it. "Long enough."

She slid her hands seductively down her thighs. "If you want another romp, call me."

Now that his desire had been satisfied, the whore

disgusted him. Like yesterday's trash, she needed to be dealt with. "I need for you to make a phone call."

She traced a long finger down his chest and looked directly into his eyes. "Sure, baby. You want Mama to talk dirty again?"

"No." Richard handed her a disposable cell phone and a piece of paper with a number and a message on it. "This is what I want you to say."

The whore shrugged and sat on the edge of the bed. She crossed her legs and dialed. She grinned up at him and ran her tongue over her lips suggestively. One ring. Two rings. "It's going to voice mail."

Damn. "Go ahead and leave the message."

She nodded and he heard a distant message: "*I can't take your call right now . . .*"

The whore sat straighter. She followed the script. She'd said she'd wanted to be an actress.

Richard moved to the other side of the bed and pulled a length of rope out of his back pocket. He leaned over the bed and kissed the back of her neck as she closed the phone. "That was nice."

"You want me to be anyone else? I could be her again. What was her name? Christina?"

Hearing his wife's name made him cringe. "I'd like that," he said silkily.

She started to turn, but he stopped her as he leaned forward and kissed her neck again. She tipped her head back, her long black hair falling over his hands. He fisted his fingers in the hair. He'd chosen her because of her hair.

As he continued to kiss her neck, he freed his hand from her hair and he carefully wound the ends of the rope around both hands and fisted his fingers around it.

In one swift move, he raised the rope over her head and wrapped it around her neck. He jerked hard, forcing her back. Immediately, she started to gag and her hands went up to his. She scratched his skin.

Her cheap perfume swirled around him as he tightened the noose. She tried to wriggle free as she thrashed her arms backward toward his face. Her fist connected with the side of his cheek. The pain pissed him off and he squeezed even harder. He could feel the vein in her neck pulsing wildly against his hand. Her body screamed for oxygen. His erection returned.

"Christina," he whispered in her ear. "You said you wanted to be Christina."

The fight slowly drained from her as her face turned bluer and bluer. Her hands dropped to her side, limp and lifeless, and finally her body slumped back against his.

To be extra careful, he held the rope in place several extra minutes until he was certain she was dead. Finally, he released her and she dropped to the carpeted floor in a heap.

Richard flexed his fingers. Now it was time to go to the hospital and wait.

Lindsay woke to the sound of her cell phone ringing. She sat up in bed, confused and disoriented. Her head throbbed and her body ached. She glanced at the phone number and didn't recognize it. Assuming it was another reporter, she let her voice mail take it.

She swung her legs over the side of the twin bed. Brianna Dillon slept in the other bed. Lindsay had called Ruby late yesterday and her friend had welcomed her into her home without question.

Rising, she pulled her jeans on beneath the T-shirt she'd worn last night. She combed her fingers through her hair and pulled it up with the rubber band she'd tucked in her jeans pocket.

Quietly, she slipped out of the room. A light in the kitchen and the smell of coffee lured her down the hallway.

In the kitchen, she found Ruby standing next to the gas stove scrambling eggs.

Lindsay stifled a yawn. "Good morning."

Ruby's green housecoat skimmed her dimpled knees. Pink slippers warmed her feet. "Come in and have some coffee, baby."

Her head felt like it was filled with cotton. "Bless you."

Ruby poured a cup and handed it to Lindsay. "You look exhausted."

"I didn't sleep well." She sipped the rich brew. It tasted so good. "Too many dreams."

Ruby planted a hand on her hip. "You dreaming about that crazy man or that husband of yours?"

"My husband."

"Was it a bad dream?"

"Not really. It was nice." The coffee warmed her chilled fingers.

Ruby pulled a cigarette out of her pocket, placed it between her lips, and lit it. "There have been a couple of men in my life that weren't good for me, but that didn't stop me from loving them. And I've got to say, your detective ain't so bad. I saw the way he looked at you yesterday. He really does care about you."

"I know."

Lindsay's phone beeped, reminding her of the voice mail message. She set her cup down and played back the call. She sighed. "It's a nurse at Mercy. There's a battered woman in the emergency room. Domestic."

Ruby shook her head. "Do you have to be the one to take it?"

"Yes."

"I promised Detective Kier—your husband—I'd keep

an eye on you after he told me that that Richard Braxton guy might have killed that poor Carmichael woman in San Francisco. There's no telling where he is. He could be in Richmond now."

"Last word on the street was he was in Canada. And I won't be afraid."

"If you had a lick of sense you'd be terrified."

"Don't look so worried. I'll be at the hospital. It's safe there."

Kendall Shaw woke and realized she was on a cold, damp floor. She shifted her weight and found that her hands were bound over her head and tied to a chain that linked to the wall. The rope around her wrists was so tight her fingers felt numb. How long had she been there? All night?

The gag in her mouth had left her mouth and throat dry. She could moan but not scream loud enough for anyone to hear.

Think. Think. Don't freak out. She twisted her hands against her restraints and discovered there was enough slack in the chain for her to move. Her body was stiff and weak but she managed to roll on her side and up into a sitting position. She tugged at the rope and chain. Neither budged.

She looked around the small, dimly lighted room that smelled of mold and rust. As her eyes adjusted she looked through an open door into a larger room. To the left, a rickety staircase led up to a closed door. On the far side, a workbench with multiple television screens.

Where was she? A basement? A root cellar? In a darkened corner a rat squeaked and scratched against the floor. She drew her feet up.

She wasn't sure how long she sat in the darkness, but

her mind became clear as the drugs dwindled from her system. Her back started to ache from sitting up, but she didn't dare sit close to the wall for fear of the rat.

And then she heard the steady thud of shoes on the floor above. Someone upstairs was pacing. The footsteps sounded as if they were getting closer, and then she heard what sounded like a dead bolt scraping free of a lock.

Her heart pounded in her chest. The door at the top of the stairs swung open. Light rushed down to the room. She blinked, her eyes unaccustomed to any light. At the top of the staircase a man's silhouetted figure appeared. He flipped on the overhead lights.

Immediately, she winced against the brightness and ducked her head. The footsteps moved closer to her as she opened her eyes slowly and allowed them to adjust.

She realized the dampness wasn't water. It was blood. She struggled to move free of it and couldn't.

"Good, you're awake." The familiar rusty voice had her straightening. He took a few more steps and stood over her. Then he crouched and pulled the duct tape off her mouth. She spit out the gag.

"Who are you?" she whispered. Her tongue was swollen and it was difficult to talk.

"I thought you'd figured it all out."

The man before her looked so ordinary, so regular. Kind even. "The Guardian?"

"Very good." The man seemed pleased she was awake and alert. "I've been waiting for you to wake up. I was afraid that I'd overdosed you last night in the van."

She remembered the needle pricking her arm. "What are you going to do with me?"

"You have to die, Kendall. You crossed the line."

A sob burned in her throat. But she kept her chin high. "What line?"

"You didn't know when to quit. Your reports were hurting Lindsay."

"I was just following the trail of evidence." She moistened her lips. If she could keep him talking, maybe she could delay or change what was to come. "Tell me what I did wrong."

He rose, wincing. He was injured. "There's no time for that."

It had been her experience that ego drove everyone. People loved to talk about themselves. "But I want to get the story right. Don't you want the world to know the truth?"

"They will soon enough." He moved to the workbench and studied the monitors.

Only two screens were on. They televised images of a living room. "You've been watching her."

"Watching over her. Protecting her." From the bench he lifted up a machete. The blade glinted in the light.

Half his face was in shadows, but she could see the intensity behind his gaze. He was going to kill her. The realization was so clear. She didn't want to be chopped into bits and watch the blood drain from her body, but she'd not lie there passively. She struggled against her binds.

Don't panic. Don't panic. "Why are you watching Lindsay?"

"I'm her only family. And family takes care of family."

"Who are you?"

He smiled. "It doesn't matter."

Keep him talking. "It does. I can set the record straight."

His face crinkled in disgust. "You've done enough damage."

Keep him talking. "Why did you kill the others?"

"They were evil."

The brick wall now dug into her spine. "What were their crimes?"

"They hurt the innocent." He ran his thumb along the edge of the machete blade. Blood appeared.

"How did you choose your victims?"

"They hurt Lindsay."

She pulled against her restraints. They didn't budge. "Lindsay doesn't appreciate what you're doing. She hates violence."

His face hardened. "You don't know her."

"I know her better than you think. We spent long hours talking when I interviewed her. I'll bet I've spent more time with her than you have."

A pained look darkened his eyes. "You talk too much."

Kendall had only just begun to talk. "Does it bother you to know she doesn't approve of what you do?"

"She's glad those men are off the street."

Kendall knew she was playing with fire but the longer she strung him along the better her chances of getting out of this. "You killed two boys. *Children.* She hated that."

Guilt shadowed his stony features. "Every war has collateral damage."

"Lindsay will never forgive you for hurting those boys."

He jerked a gun from his waistband and pointed it directly at her. "Shut up!"

She stared into the barrel. All she could seem to think about was that no one was going to miss her when she died. She struggled to keep her voice even and soothing. "Lindsay would hate this. She would want you to let me go."

"Liar. Lindsay despises you. Your lies and half-truths have ruined Sanctuary."

He cocked the gun.

"No!" she shouted.

He fired.

The bullet struck her in the shoulder and she fell back

against the hard floor. Pain seared through her body. Her vision blurred and for a moment she couldn't breathe. She'd prayed the bullet would kill her outright but realized now death would not come quickly to her.

The Guardian moved toward her. He grabbed a handful of her hair and jerked her head back. "Take back all you said about Lindsay."

The pain dulled her mind. He had the machete in his hand. "Monster."

The Guardian raised the machete over his head. Through the pain she heard the phone ring. She nearly wept with relief as he released her and backed away toward the workbench. He snapped up the phone.

"It took you long enough to call me back," the Guardian growled. "Now, who is the woman Lindsay is going to see at Mercy?"

A slight tense pause had Kendall struggling to stay conscious.

"I don't care if you've lost your stomach for helping me. And I don't care about your gaming debts anymore. You're in too deep. Now tell me what you know."

The Guardian listened, his body tensing as he gripped the receiver tighter. "I'll be there in ten minutes. Be waiting for me in the garage at the regular place."

The Guardian slammed the phone down and whirled toward Kendall, the only one to absorb his rage. He grabbed a handful of her hair. His eyes were as black as Satan's.

Pain from her shoulder overwhelmed her. Her world went blank.

Lindsay swung her car around and brought it to a stop in a space close to the elevator. She took a moment to scan the deck to make sure there were no press or shadowy figures. Satisfied that the area was clear, she got out of the car and locked it with her keyless remote. She crossed quickly to the elevator, punched the button, and tapped her toe as she waited.

Thoughts tumbled through her mind. The Guardian. Richard. Nicole. The abused woman she was about to meet. And even Sam. Where was Sam? He hadn't called her and that wasn't like him. She was beginning to think that all this trouble with the Guardian might have scared him off.

There was a time his possible rejection might have hurt her feelings. But not now. If he couldn't accept her for who she was—the good and the bad—then so be it. She had to give Zack credit. He'd seen the dark side of her past and he hadn't been scared away.

Lindsay leaned forward to push the already lit elevator button again when she heard footsteps behind her. The sound had her nerves tightening like a bowstring. Her heart pounded wildly in her chest. She jabbed the elevator button again before she turned.

A man appeared from the shadows. He was dressed in a green jumpsuit and was pushing a canvas laundry cart. He touched the bill of his *Minton's Laundry* hat and nodded. "Morning."

Lindsay nodded stiffly, her nerves on alert. With the Guardian's identity still unknown, she wasn't taking any chances. The elevator dinged and the doors slid open.

She stepped back. "You first."

The guy shrugged. "There's room for us both."

"Thanks. I think I forgot something in my car." She backed away from the elevator.

"Suit yourself." He started inside the car and she immediately relaxed, chiding herself for being so sensitive. But still, she was going to play it safe.

She decided to get back in her car and drive around

to the front entrance of the hospital. She'd pay for parking on the street.

Lindsay had taken five steps when a damp cloth clamped over her face. The sick, sweet scent of chloroform invaded her senses. Her hands rose up to the ones clamped over her mouth and nose and she tried to pry them away.

She struggled to hold her breath, and when she couldn't any longer, she inhaled a lungful of the chloroform. The drug invaded her system. She couldn't move. Was helpless to scream or fight.

She heard the rumble of male laughter. It was a frightening sound. Evil. Malevolent. He was enjoying her helplessness.

Her brain spun. Her knees buckled.

As she began to lose consciousness, she was aware that the man scooped her up and dumped her into the laundry basket.

He dropped her purse beside her and covered her with a handful of towels. "Now the fun begins, Lindsay."

She passed out completely.

Chapter Twenty-Eight

Friday, July 11, 10:30 A.M.

The cemetery's surveillance tapes for the past year had arrived around eight last night and Zack had reviewed them most of the night. Slowly he'd been able to piece together a chain of events. He rewound the footage and stopped the tape on February eleventh. The landscape on the screen was covered in a dusting of snow. Icicles hung from the trees. The sky was as dull and gray as the headstones.

The homicide team assembled in the conference room. Zack stood and ran his hand over his head.

The entire division had worked all night. No one was going to sleep until this guy had been caught. Detectives from other divisions and uniforms were now helping them run down leads.

Ayden, Ricker, and Vega sat down. "So what do you have? You said it was important."

"I spoke with the cemetery director yesterday because I noticed cameras posted in several of the trees and by the front entrance. It seems he installed surveillance equipment right after Christmas last year. He'd had trouble with someone spray painting satanic symbols on some of the headstones. His graffiti artists haven't reappeared or been caught on tape. But, he did catch us another fish," Zack said.

Ayden frowned. "Where's Warwick? I want him to see this."

"He's at the Department of Motor Vehicles," Zack said. "He'll be here soon." He hit "play." On the television screen a grainy image showed a white van rolling down a distant snowy road into the cemetery. "Pay attention to the vehicle entering the back entrance of the cemetery. As you can see, this segment was recorded on February eleventh. The vehicle enters but stops at the crest of the hill." He touched the screen where the vehicle stopped. "The driver doesn't pull up far enough for us to get a shot at the plates or a look at his face. But if you look closely, you can see that the driver is carrying roses, which he leaves on Deb Hines's grave. Lindsay O'Neil's mother's grave." Everyone in the room leaned forward and watched the driver. "He keeps his head low as he lays the flowers on the grave. He pauses for a moment of prayer and then leaves through the back entrance."

Ayden leaned forward. "He's paying his respects."

Vega folded his arms over his broad chest. "What time is this?"

"Eleven fifty-eight A.M." Zack hit the fast-forward button. "March sixth. The van appears again. It's about noontime. The driver again is careful to keep his face from the camera and the van out of close view. He leaves flowers and again leaves by the back entrance. The Guardian has already proven he's savvy with surveillance equipment, so he must realize the front entrance is covered by a camera."

Ayden muttered an oath. "How the hell are we going to catch this guy?"

Zack grinned. "Stay with me. Now we're coming to April second. Lindsay arrives at the grave. She leaves flowers and stays twenty minutes. She begins to leave. The van arrives. They almost meet this time. But she exits via the front entrance. She said she'd seen a van that day and had thought it was the caretaker."

"She never noticed the flowers before?" Ricker said.

"The cemetery has a policy stating that all live flowers are to be removed every Saturday. Cemetery maintenance always cleared away the old flowers before she arrived."

He hit the fast-forward button again. "It's May third. Again he leaves flowers."

Ricker cocked her head. Her curly hair was twisted up into a high ponytail and her face pale from too little sleep. "May third is the day the article on Lindsay appeared in the paper."

Zack nodded. "Yes. And on this day our mystery man lingers at the Hines grave for over an hour. He seems to be talking to the headstone. His body language suggests that he's agitated. He doesn't show his face, but this time he starts to leave through the front entrance. He catches himself and backs up. But before he does, he gets close enough for us to pull a partial on the plates. That's why Warwick is at the DMV."

Warwick came into the room. He had a file tucked under his arm and was breathless, as if he'd sprinted across the parking lot and up the stairs to the second floor. "Did I miss anything?"

Zack nodded. "Right on time."

Ayden didn't look amused. "What do you have?"

"The DMV ran the stats Kier supplied them. They had fifty-two possible matches. They'd printed out five copies of the list by the time I arrived. I haven't had a chance to look at them."

Ayden shoved out a sigh. "Great work."

Warwick handed copies of the list to the detectives. They each scanned it.

"This could take days to track all these down," Zack said.

C.C. sighed. "I can get the guys from robbery to help."

Warwick frowned as he glared down at the list. The deep tan of his face paled. He blinked and reread the list. "That's odd."

"What do you mean?" Ayden said.

"I recognize one of the names." He swallowed as if he were struggling now. "Pete Myers. He runs the gym where I work out." He shook his head. "This has to be a coincidence. Pete's a great guy."

Ayden frowned. "I just got a report back from Sara. Remember that white powder found at the Turner murder scene embedded in the footprint? She's identified the powder as talc."

Warwick shook his head. "It's not Pete. I know this guy. He'd give you the shirt off his back."

Zack understood Warwick's worry. He'd lived with it when Lindsay had appeared to be the killer. "Let's check him out first. We clear him and you'll concentrate better."

Warwick nodded, grateful. "Thanks. I'd appreciate that."

"C.C., divide the list between you and Vega and robbery. When Kier and Warwick return from Myers's gym give them some of the names," Ayden ordered. "I want this guy found."

The team disbanded. Within ten minutes Zack and Warwick were in Zack's car headed east. "So how long have you known Pete?"

Warwick's trademark confidence had vanished. He looked worried. "Since I was a kid. I still work out at his gym, but it's more than that. He raised me. I was a handful. He kept me in line, gave me direction."

"Do you know anything about him?"

Warwick tapped long fingers on his thigh. "Pete isn't the Guardian. This is just one of those damn coincidences."

No point in arguing. Evidence, not words, would sway Warwick. "I get it. But I still need to ask. What can you tell me about him?"

Warwick understood questions had to be asked even if he didn't like them. "He opened his boxing gym in town twenty years ago. I know because I slathered his grand-opening sign with eggs. He could've called the cops. Instead he gave me a job."

Zack merged onto I-95 south and headed downtown. "Do you have any background on him?"

"He did some time in the military police. Retired in his late forties and came back here to open his gym."

"So he's from Richmond."

Warwick frowned. "I don't know. I do know he has supported dozens of children's charities over the years. Last year he hosted a party at the gym for a bunch of kids whose folks were in prison. He even dressed up as Santa and handed out gifts."

"What do you know about his past?"

"Not much. I do know his name isn't Henry. He never talked about a sister named Debra or a niece named Lindsay."

"Names can be changed. And he plays his cards close to his vest."

Warwick looked troubled but seemed to shake the dark thoughts away. "Maybe."

"Anything else you can tell me about him?"

"He never talks about himself much. He talks about his fighters. He talks about the gym. He talks a little bit about when he boxed in the military." Warwick frowned. "This is bullshit. Let's get to the gym and clear this shit up so we can catch the real killer."

Zack took the Franklin Street exit. "Sure."

"Right." Warwick didn't like this.

Zack maneuvered a few corners and a side alley before he came up behind the gym. There were no cars in the lot.

"The place is usually deserted?"

Warwick got out of the car. "Not usually. But it's not unheard of for him to take off during the middle of the day if business is slow."

"Is summer a slow time?"

"It can be. The weather is warm and people want to get outside."

Zack quietly closed the car door behind him. They moved across the gritty alley to the front door. There was a CLOSED sign on the door.

Warwick tried the door. Locked.

Zack had a bad feeling about this. Warwick was praying Pete wasn't involved. But the whole situation didn't smell right. "Does he still train fighters?"

"He was training a couple last year but he cut them loose a few months ago. Hooked them up with a couple of good trainers. Said he was ready to slow down."

Zack peeked in the front window. The interior was dark. "That seem odd to you?"

"At first, but then I figured he was just getting old."

Zack wasn't leaving this place until he got a look inside. "Any other way inside?"

"There's a door in the back. I have a key." They moved around the side of the building down the chipped sidewalk. The area smelled of garbage. Warwick moved ahead of Zack toward a small metal door, shoved his key in the lock, and unlocked it. "I have a standing invitation to come into the gym. He knows my schedule is squirrelly."

"Myers sounds like a good guy."

Warwick pushed open the door. "He is."

The gym was dark. The only sound came from the drip-drip of a faucet in the men's bathroom.

"Pete!" Warwick shouted.

His voice echoed on the walls. No answer.

Warwick flipped on the lights. He moved down a dark hallway toward Pete's office. The desk was a disheveled mess. "Pete usually keeps his desk neat. Lately, he's let it go. I figured it was just because he's getting old."

Zack jabbed his thumb toward a door. "What's this?"

"Basement access."

"Anything down there?"

"Old equipment mostly."

Zack sighed. Something didn't feel right. He glanced around the office a second time. Myers's desk was covered with stacks of papers, a torn boxing glove, half-eaten food, forms. Being a slob wasn't a crime. And then he saw the black-and-white photo tucked in the corner of a bulletin board on his desk. It was the image of a twentysomething man and a young girl. "This Pete?"

"Yeah. I don't know who the kid is."

The five-year-old girl looked familiar. "Damn. This kid looks like Lindsay."

"Can't be. Look at the clothes. It's early nineteen sixties."

Zack flipped the picture over. Someone had scribbled *Deb and Pete, 1963* in bold handwriting. "You're right." Still, he flicked the edge of the photo with his thumb. "Lindsay showed me a picture of herself as a kid. She looked just like this child."

"I don't know who it is. I figured it was a sister or a cousin."

"A sister." Zack exhaled a breath. "This is a picture of Lindsay's mother."

Warwick's mouth hardened as the implications sunk in. "It can't be."

"Lindsay had a couple of photos in a box when we were married. I only saw them once. But hold up Lindsay's kindergarten picture next to this one and you'd see that she and this kid are the spitting image of each other."

"Oh, Jesus."

Zack scanned the row of shelves above the desk. "We know the Guardian has some connection to Lindsay."

"That doesn't mean Pete does. Likeness or not, this kid could be anyone."

Zack glared at Warwick. "For now we have to assume that that child pictured with Pete is Lindsay's mother."

"Pete can't be her uncle." He sounded as if he were grasping at straws.

"He sure as hell can be." There was a small television set on the file cabinet behind Pete's desk. Built into the set was a VCR. "What did Pete do in the military?"

"Something with radios and the military police."

"Electronics?"

Tension radiated from Warwick. "Maybe."

"The Guardian has been watching Lindsay. And the cameras were positioned in the living room and kitchen. Nothing in the bathrooms or the bedrooms. Private places where a good uncle wouldn't venture." Zack pushed back the VCR tape flap on the television. Inside was a tape dated *July 11*. He turned on the television and hit "Play." Instantly, a black-and-white image of Lindsay appeared. She was standing in Ruby's living room. The time stamp was less than an hour ago.

"Shit," Zack said. "She spent last night with Ruby."

Warwick paled. "Jesus."

"Vega said Ruby had a break-in last week. But nothing was taken. Something was added, though." Zack flipped open his cell and called Ayden. "We have a hit." He explained what they'd found. "Send backup."

Warwick shoved out a breath. He was struggling to hold it together. And if they'd had time, Zack would have pulled him out of there immediately. But he sensed that time was running out.

"I want a look in that basement but I don't want a defense attorney crapping on my case because I don't have a warrant."

Warwick dug in his pocket and pulled out a set of keys. "I have access to the gym with no restrictions." He rubbed the back of his neck with his hand. "If I needed a new set of gloves and couldn't find them upstairs, I'd look in the basement. It's where Pete kept extra equipment when I was here last year."

Zack smiled but there was no pleasure. "I was hoping you'd say something like that."

Warwick opened the basement door lock and flipped the light switch at the top of the stairs. Both cops drew their guns. Slowly they made their way down the rickety steps, their bodies crouched.

Halfway down, Zack moved past Warwick and peered around a blind corner. He saw the computer table. The monitors. And the rows and rows of tapes, each meticulously dated and arranged in chronological order.

Warwick stared at the room in horror and disbelief. His world was shattering. But he was holding it together. Later the problems would come as the enormity of it all hit him.

The heavy coppery scent of blood rose up as they moved toward the computer. Zack glanced toward a second door. He motioned to Warwick.

Warwick nodded. Guns raised, they moved to either side of the door. Zack counted to three. On three he shoved open the door. "Police, come out with your hands up."

A faint moan echoed from the corner. It sounded as if someone was injured. Still, he didn't rush the room.

Careful to keep his body out of a shooter's line of fire, Zack slid his hand into the room and felt around for a light switch. He found one and clicked it on.

The first thing they saw was the blood. The entire floor was covered with it. This had been the Guardian's killing room. No doubt Saunders's DNA would be all over the place.

Warwick's gaze settled in a shadowed corner. "Oh my God."

Zack tightened his grip on his gun. "What?"

"Kendall Shaw."

While Zack covered him, Warwick holstered his gun and hurried toward the reporter. She lay on the floor curled in a fetal position. Fresh blood pooled around her and stained her clothes.

Zack still didn't trust that this wasn't some kind of trap. "Is she alive?"

Warwick touched his fingers to her neck. "A faint pulse. She's been shot in the shoulder." He flipped open his cell phone and dialed Dispatch. "All this blood. It's a miracle she's alive."

"Check her hands. Does she have both her hands?"

The doors to the hospital's garage elevator opened and Dr. Sam Begley walked out. The Guardian got out of the van and glanced at the clock above the elevator. "About damn time."

The doctor frowned and kept moving toward his shiny BMW. "I couldn't get away. We had an emergency."

"I have an emergency. I need to know where Lindsay is."

"She's not in the hospital. I looked everywhere."

"Who was the battered woman brought in? You know never to call Lindsay without calling me first."

Sam's forehead perspired. "I didn't treat a battered woman today. No one from the hospital called Lindsay."

"Damn it."

"The cops were here. They brought Lindsay and her roommate in for blood tests Wednesday. Did you drug them?"

The Guardian was running over an image of Lindsay standing in Ruby's kitchen. She'd been called by the hospital. He was certain. "Yes. It was the only way to keep them safe while I worked."

"Jesus. You never said anything about hurting Lindsay."

He didn't like the doctor's tone. "I would never hurt her."

Begley shook his head. "You shot those kids today. Christ, one is dead and the other is fighting to stay alive."

Guilt gnawed at him. "They could ID me. They had to go."

"This has gone too far. I'm out. It's just a matter of time before the cops connect us."

The doctor didn't have the conviction to honor agreements. Spoiled rich boy had had everything handed to him on a silver platter. He didn't understand commitment. "You promised me you'd help whenever I asked."

Begley lowered his voice. "I'd never have gotten into this if not for my debts. I've more than satisfied my gambling debts to you. I never want to see you again."

The Guardian slid his hand into his pocket. His fingers brushed the cool metal of his gun and silencer. "You're done when I say you're done."

Begley pulled off his glasses and cleaned the lenses on his shirt. The man actually looked defiant. "I'm finished."

The shrill tone in the doctor's voice grated. The Guardian could see the man was nervous. It wouldn't take much squeezing from the cops to make him talk. He'd like to use the doctor longer, but now he realized the time had come for them to part ways. "If that's the way you want it."

"Good."

The Guardian pulled the gun and silencer from his pocket and before the doctor realized what was happening, he fired three times. Each bullet struck Begley in the heart. For just a split second, surprise marred the doctor's face as he glanced down at the plume of blood growing on his chest. He staggered and would have fallen if the Guardian hadn't caught him.

The thrill of taking life sent a tingle through the Guardian's body. "You were part of a noble cause and I won't forget what you did for me."

Begley's eyes rolled back in his head. He was dead.

The Guardian opened the back of his van and dumped Begley's body in. He'd deal with him later. Now, he needed to find Lindsay.

He got in the front seat of the van and turned on a GPS system. The system tracked a bug he'd put under the back bumper of Lindsay's car. Since he'd seen the article about her in May and realized who she was he'd been determined never to lose sight of her again. At any given moment, he could find her.

The GPS beeped and at first he thought it was broken. Then he realized she was parked in the hospital deck. He turned on the engine and started to patrol the decks.

He found her car on the bottom level. With the van still running, he got out and checked her car. It was locked. He scanned the deck but there was no sign of her.

Something was wrong.

The feeling was as intense as it had been those years Debra had lived with her husband. He'd known she was in danger then but he'd bowed to her will and left them alone as she'd begged him to.

He got back in the van and pulled a disposable cell from his pocket and he dialed Lindsay's number. It rang six times and then went to voice mail. Something was very wrong. She always answered her cell.

He closed his eyes. *Think. Where could she be? Think.*

The Guardian's mind raced. This morning when Lindsay had been in Ruby's kitchen, Ruby had spoken of the San Francisco murder. The Carmichael woman. She'd also mentioned that Nicole's husband, Richard Braxton, was from San Francisco.

It made sense that Richard would eventually find Nicole. But he hadn't thought it would be so soon. If Richard was in the area, he'd not likely find her, because she was safely hidden at the Kiers'. But Lindsay was an open target. He'd go after Lindsay first and use her to get to Nicole.

How could he have been such a fool?

He'd been so consumed with Kendall that he'd ignored a critical danger. He'd made the same mistake he'd made with Debra all those years ago, when he'd underestimated his brother-in-law's rage.

The Guardian felt a rush of panic as he tightened his hands on the steering wheel. He had to think. Think like a hunter. What would he do with Lindsay if he were Richard?

He might kill her in front of Nicole as some sort of lesson. Richard would need a secluded place. The scenarios made the Guardian sick but also gave him hope. There might still be time.

Nicole was at the Kiers' and there was the possibility he could beat Braxton there. He dialed the Kiers' home number.

"Hello."

He suspected the young voice belonged to Zack's sister, Eleanor. She was a sweet kid and Lindsay had great affection for her. "This is Dr. Begley at the hospital. I'm calling to speak to Lindsay."

"Lindsay's not here."

"Is her friend Nicole there?"

"She's in the bathroom."

Good. She was still there. "Don't bother her. I'll just call back."

"Okay."

He hung up and threw the car in drive. He still had time, but how much he didn't know. He raced out of the parking deck and cut through city traffic and onto I-95 north.

His heart pounded as he wove in and out of the traffic. He couldn't screw this one up. He couldn't.

Twenty minutes later, he pulled onto the rural road leading to the Kiers' and slowly drove past their house. He parked in a driveway down the street, climbed out of the van, and hurried through the woods that separated the houses. Staying low, he moved toward the house. At first he saw only Mrs. Kier, who was at the kitchen sink washing dishes. He needed to move closer to get a better look but feared being detected.

His pulse raced. "Get out of the way," he whispered.

And then she stepped aside and he was able to see into the kitchen. Nicole was at the table playing cards with anther woman and an older man.

He breathed a sigh of relief. There was still time. He

hurried back to his van and prayed Braxton hadn't hurt Lindsay.

The drugs in Lindsay's system made it hard for her to concentrate. She was aware of strong hands supporting her as she stumbled forward. She couldn't seem to lift her feet or keep her balance.

The area around them was quiet. Wherever they were was far from the main road. She opened her eyes and saw she was being taken toward an old barn.

The air was thick with humidity and sweat had dampened the back of her shirt. "Where are we?" she muttered.

The man holding her laughed. "We are in a very private place. Where no one will bother us. Where no one will hear you scream."

Lindsay swallowed her rising terror. "Why are you doing this? Who are you?"

"I'm someone who doesn't appreciate you sticking your nose where it doesn't belong."

"Who are you?"

"Christina's husband."

Christina. Nicole. "Richard Braxton."

"So she's talked about me?" Hate and resentment laced the words.

"Yes."

Braxton kicked open the rickety barn door and pulled her inside across the dirt floor. When they were in the center, he let go of her. She crumpled face-first into a heap. She tasted dirt and tried to spit it out of her mouth as she rolled onto her back. Above, she saw sunshine peeking through the slats of a room. In the distance she heard birds.

Lindsay moistened her lips. She felt so dry. There was little doubt that Richard planned an awful death for her.

She remembered what Zack had told her he'd done to Claire.

She opened her eyes. Her vision was blurred but she could make out dark hair and a square face. She tried to sit up but he roughly pushed her against the hard ground. He straddled her body. She felt his erection press against her belly and she thought he was going to rape her.

She wanted to fight but found her body drifting as if she were on a raft floating out to sea.

Instead, he pounded two stakes into the ground above her head and then roughly grabbed her hands and lashed them tightly to the stakes. His weight lifted and he moved to her legs. He yanked her legs open wide and tied them to more stakes, then hammered them into the ground.

She tried to pull her hands free of the stakes, but they didn't budge. The hemp cut into the tender flesh of her wrist.

Through the haze, Lindsay understood that she needed to do something to save herself. She drew in a lungful of air and screamed as loud as she could.

Richard cursed, drew back, and slapped her hard across the face. "Shut up, bitch. I don't have time for this."

Pain rattled through her head.

He slid his hand to the flat of her belly and up under her shirt. He squeezed her breast painfully. She struggled in vain against her restraints as her stomach heaved at the thought of what was to come.

Richard put his lips next to her ear. "I don't have time for you right now. I have to go get Christina. I want her to watch what I'm going to do."

Abruptly he got up and left the barn. She heard the engine of his car fire up and gravel kick up under the tires as he drove off.

Tears burned in her eyes.

She was not going to die like this. She started to work on the restraints on her hands and ignored the way the rope sliced into her wrists.

Nicole was lost in thought as she sat at the kitchen table across from Eleanor and Mr. Kier. The pregnancy test she'd taken this morning had been positive. She was carrying Richard's baby.

At first she'd been so numb that she'd not been able to leave the bathroom. She'd sat on the floor and cried.

And then Eleanor had called out to her. So she'd dried her tears and come downstairs.

She laid down her hand of cards on the kitchen table. "Gin."

Eleanor frowned and leaned forward to study the hand. "You don't have gin."

Absentmindedly, Nicole glanced down. "I don't?"

"No. You can't have a straight with mismatched suits."

"Oh."

"Geez Can't anyone play a decent game?"

The phone rang and Audrey came into the kitchen and answered it. "Sure, just a minute. Nicole, the phone is for you."

Grateful for the distraction, she left her cards and moved to the wall phone.

Audrey smiled as she handed her the receiver. "It's a policeman."

Tension rose. "Thanks. Hello?"

"Christina."

Richard's smooth voice raked down her spine. Her grip tightened around the receiver. "What do you want?"

"I'm outside, parked at the edge of the driveway. I want you to smile to the nice people and then walk out the front door, come down the drive, and get into my car. If you don't, I'll be forced to do some very nasty things to your friend, Ms. O'Neil."

Nicole glanced over at Eleanor, who laughed as her father came into the room and tickled her. Audrey stood at the stove working on a pot of sauce.

"Don't keep me waiting, Nicole," Richard urged.

Steel cut through the silk. She *knew* Richard. He would do exactly what he said. "I'll be right there."

She hung up and managed a smile. "I think I need to get a bit of fresh air."

Audrey frowned. "You look pale, Nicole. Are you all right?"

"I'm fine. Just need some fresh air."

Kier lifted a brow. "Who was that on the phone?"

"Detective Warwick," she lied. "He wants to interview me again."

"I'll go outside with you," he said.

"No, no. Challenge Eleanor to a game of gin. I've been a bad opponent so far. I'm going outside for just a few minutes." The lies tumbled off her tongue so easily.

Mr. Kier studied her. "All right."

She turned and stiffly walked out the door. Before she went outside, she stopped at the entryway table, where she'd left her purse. She grabbed her cell phone and a vial of mace and put them in her pocket. Richard wouldn't expect too much resistance from her. And hopefully she could use that to her advantage.

As she reached the country road just out of sight of the house, she saw a dark Mercedes. Black and sleek, it looked out of place.

The tinted passenger window rolled down. Richard sat behind the wheel looking so calm and relaxed. "Good to see you, Christina. If you're thinking about running, I thought I should tell you that I have your friend Lindsay stashed in a very unpleasant place. If anything happens to me, she'll be long dead before anyone ever finds her."

Nicole opened the door and slid into the front passenger seat. "Let her go, Richard. You have me. Just let her go."

His eyes darkened. "Close the door, Christina. *Now.*"

Woodenly, Nicole closed it. If she made a move for the mace and did subdue him, what would happen to Lindsay? She had to wait for the right moment.

The doors locked immediately. He started to drive. "You've cut your hair. I don't like it."

She didn't know what to say to that and decided to stay quiet.

"But hair grows, doesn't it?" He frowned. "Put your seat belt on, Christina. I don't want you getting hurt."

She swallowed and tried not to let her fear show. "Where are we going?"

"Home, eventually. But first we have a stop to make."

"Where?" she demanded.

White teeth flashed. "You'll see."

Lindsay had trouble shaking the effects of the drug. Her mind wanted to drift and her eyes to close. She wanted to float and let the drug take her.

But as seductive as the drug was she knew if she gave in to it she would die.

She had to keep her thoughts focused. To get free of the ropes binding her was a challenge. To keep herself awake, she started to talk.

"Mom, if you're up there, I could use some help. Zack's a great cop, but I don't think he's going to figure this one out."

She'd managed to loosen the binding around her right hand, though she'd not freed her hand completely.

Her wrist was raw from the constant rubbing and pulling against the rope. She focused on the pain in her wrist and the stones on the ground that now dug into her back.

It was hard to judge how much time had passed. But she knew she had to hurry. Time was running out. She moistened her dry lips and opened her eyes. She shook her head from side to side.

"Remember how we dreamed of driving to California?" She kept twisting her right wrist, ignoring the pain. Blood ran down the wrist. "Remember how we'd pore over the maps and imagine every step of the route?"

The silence was her only answer, and it was a stark reminder that her mother was gone and that she was so very alone. Terror burned inside her. "Help! Help!" She screamed until her voice was hoarse.

The odds were stacked against her and it would be so easy to give up.

Above, blue sky peeked through the slats of the roof. For just a moment, Lindsay felt as if something touched her hair. Like a caress.

"Mom . . ." The word felt wrenched from her.

There was no answer. Whether it was her mother or just a trick of her imagination, she didn't know. But the sensation was enough to calm her a little.

She drew in a deep breath as she had done so many times in yoga when she felt overwhelmed and scared. She kept breathing deeply. Her mind started to calm and refocus. "Don't panic. Don't panic. I can do this."

She swallowed and started back on the binding. "Where has Richard taken me?" She sucked in a deep breath and released it as she shook her head. "The sun is high above, so it can't be much past noon. He couldn't have taken me far. Mercy is in the center of the city." She was willing to bet he'd taken her east.

The heavy scent of dirt, cow dung, and hay mingled with the heat. In the shadowed corners mice squeaked.

"I'm in a barn. East of the city. Farmland east of the city. It's abandoned."

She thought about the new mall that was going to be constructed soon in the far eastern end of the county. The farmland had been purchased and the owners had left months ago. Now the land waited for the bulldozers. It would be a perfect place to take her.

Just imagining where she was gave her a sense of control. She tried to pull her right hand free. It slipped a little in the binding but she couldn't quite free it.

She wasn't sure how much more time she had, but she knew if she didn't get her hand free before Richard returned he would kill her.

Richard had brought her here because he wanted to make sure that no one interrupted him when he returned. She guessed he was going to bring Nicole back so that she could watch what he did to her. Her death would be the death he would use to terrify Nicole into submission.

Ignoring the pain in her raw wrist, Lindsay started to jerk harder on the rope. "That son of a bitch is not going to win."

Somehow she had to get herself and Nicole out of this.

The Guardian stayed several car lengths behind as Richard moved onto the four-lane highway. When Richard reached the interstate, he headed east toward the airport. It made sense that the bastard would take his wife back to San Francisco. Familiar territory.

Once Richard left Richmond, finding Lindsay would be almost impossible. He couldn't let that happen.

Tightening his hands on the wheel, he considered ramming Richard's car. But even if he got his hands on the bastard there was no guarantee that he'd say where Lindsay was.

There were so many variables. He had to stay the course and keep his cool. "Stay close and he will lead you to her."

Then Richard made an unexpected move. He drove past the airport exit and continued on until he reached the off-ramp for Route 33. The rural route cut through the town of West Point and then snaked into the countryside. Where the hell was Richard headed?

The fear and exhilaration had made the Guardian forget the pain of his cracked ribs. This was his moment to redeem himself. He would save the child when he hadn't saved the mother.

"God has brought me to this moment. This is my test."

When Richard pulled down a gravel driveway, the Guardian continued on past until he reached another driveway a quarter mile down the road. He turned the van around, and when he reached the driveway where Richard had turned, he stopped.

He glanced down the long driveway. He didn't know what awaited him. Richard very well could have marshaled an army. And as much as he wanted to kill Richard all by himself, he didn't want to risk Lindsay's life. He dialed Warwick's number.

Warwick answered it on the second ring. "Warwick."

"Jacob."

A tense silence followed. "Pete, we need to talk."

Jacob was upset. It took a lot to rattle that kid. "You've found the basement."

"Yes."

Pride mingled with sadness. He'd never wanted to hurt Jacob. He didn't need to share DNA to know the boy was his son. "You were always a smart one. I'm not surprised you figured things out. In fact, I'm glad it was you. The collar will look good on your record."

"Jesus, Pete, where are you?"

Pain and sadness resonated from Jacob's words, but he didn't dwell on the whys. He understood that questions like "Why?" didn't matter until the quarry was caught. Smart kid.

"I need you. And I need all the firepower you can put together."

"What are you talking about? We're after you."

"I don't matter anymore. Richard Braxton is in the city and he has his wife and Lindsay." He gave Jacob directions. "Just come. I'm going to try to catch him alive but I don't know if I'll be able to do it. It's more important to save Lindsay and Nicole."

Pete hung up. He checked his watch. There wasn't time to wait for Jacob and Zack. Richard wouldn't waste time. Pete got out of the van.

A small plane buzzed over and circled to land. There had to be a private airstrip close by. It made sense that Richard would have his own plane.

His ribs tightened around him like a vice. It hurt to walk, to breathe. But he wasn't going to let Lindsay or Debra down. *Not this time.*

He hurried down the long gravel driveway that disappeared into a grove of trees. The heat of the day made him sweat, and soon his shirt was soaked through. When he spotted the Mercedes parked under an oak, he slowed and moved behind a bush.

On the property was an old farmhouse. At one time it had been painted white, but the elements had long ago stripped the paint. Now it was a faded gray. The wide front porch had collapsed in on itself. The windows on the first and second floors were broken.

The house was too dilapidated to hide anyone. But as Pete stared at the house, a deep sadness caught him by the throat. The place looked like the home where Debra and Lindsay had lived with that bastard Hines.

The first time he'd stood on Debra's porch it had been twenty-seven years ago. Lindsay had been two and she had hugged her mother's leg and stared up at him as he'd argued with Debra. He had seen the problems in his sister's marriage then and had begged her to leave. She had defended her husband and had ordered Pete to leave and never come back. A few years later he'd tried to help her a second time, but she wouldn't leave her husband.

And, God help him, he'd given up on her and her daughter.

The last time he'd returned to Debra's house, his sister was dead. Lindsay had run away from her foster care home. That bastard Hines had shot and killed himself in a hotel room.

Pete had been so full of rage and anger. He had burned that house to the ground, believing the flames would singe the sadness from his soul. He'd tried to track Lindsay down but hadn't been able to find her. She'd been lost to him.

And then this past May he'd seen the article on Lindsay in the magazine. He had stared at her blond hair and blue eyes and immediately had pictured Debra. All the memories had roared to life. And he knew God had given him a second chance to set things right.

"You are not alone, Lindsay," he said. He frantically began to search the grounds.

Nicole stumbled when Richard jabbed the gun in her back. "Move."

Nicole had been afraid enough times in her life. Richard had seen to that. But this time the fear cut bone deep. Today wasn't about saving only herself. It was about saving her baby. And Lindsay.

"Open the barn door," Richard ordered.

Nicole refused to make this easy for him. "Where is Lindsay?"

Richard's eyes narrowed. Nicole braced, ready for the hard slap that usually came when she questioned him. However, this time he smiled. He reached around her and pulled the door open. "She's inside."

His acquiescence was more frightening than his ranting. Still, she didn't advance. She thought about the mace in her pocket. If Lindsay was here, she could save her. Her hand slid into her pocket.

Richard was too fast. He grabbed her hand and jerked it back, twisting painfully until she dropped the mace. "You've learned a few nasty habits that I'll have to break you of, Christina. Now, get inside or I'll blow your friend's kneecap off," Richard said.

Nicole knew he'd do exactly that. She had to swallow the rage and play along until she thought of something else. She reached for the rusted lock and pushed it up. The door swung open slightly farther. Hinges squeaked as she pulled the rotting door open.

The large room was lit only by the sunshine peeking in through the rafters, which stretched high up to a peak above them. The floor was compacted dirt. A rusted sickle and an old harness hung from a peg on a post. Mice squeaked in a dark corner. The room had a foul smell, as if something had recently died there.

"Lindsay!" Nicole shouted.

There was no answer.

"Where is she?"

Richard pointed the tip of his gun to the northwest

corner. In the shadows, she saw Lindsay. She lay on her back, her hands and feet tied to stakes on the floor. She moaned, a sign she was still alive.

Nicole met Richard's gaze. "What are you going to do with us?"

Richard closed the barn door behind them as if he had all the time in the world. "Lindsay has caused me almost as much trouble as you have, Christina. And now it's time she learned a lesson, like the one I taught Claire."

"Claire? What did you do to her?"

He laughed. "We had quite a bit of time to chat. She's a strong woman. Or rather, *was* a strong woman. She had a high threshold for pain."

Nicole felt sick. Poor Claire. She'd been so kind and had given her hope when she'd been so afraid. "Richard, spare Lindsay, and I'll go home with you. I'll be a good wife again. You don't need to hurt anyone else."

Richard pulled a set of handcuffs from his back pocket and clicked the first cuff on her wrist. He dragged her to the north side of the barn and clicked the other manacle to a wooden workbench. Driven into the center of the bench was a newly purchased machete.

Tears burned in Nicole's eyes. "Let her go, Richard. *Please.* I'll never run from you again."

"I wish it were that easy, Christina. I really do. But you brought all this on yourself. I want to be gentle and kind but you keep pushing me." His face hardened. "You need to be taught a lesson."

"Richard, please don't hurt anyone else. I'm the one that you're angry with."

"You drove me to this, my dear. You have only yourself to blame."

"I won't ever leave you again. I'll be a good wife."

A smile tipped the edge of his lips as he pried the machete free of the workbench. "I've spent the last weeks covering for you and telling everyone you were in Europe. Do you have any idea how humiliated I was for having to spin those lies knowing my wife had abandoned me?" His eyes glittered as he tested the tip of the machete blade with his thumb. The sharp edge sliced his skin and the tiny wound began to bleed. He smiled. "I did everything for you. I treated you like a princess. And you left me."

Richard was a monster. He was truly insane. Nicole had to keep talking to him so he'd believe she'd surrendered. "I understand now how much I hurt you, Richard. I shouldn't have run. That was so wrong of me. But I was afraid."

Richard stared at her. Sadness darkened his eyes. "Why were you afraid? I rubbed salve into your muscles. I bandaged your cuts."

That had been a truly horrible time. She'd laid battered and bruised on her bed and he'd tended to her injuries. She remembered how good the salve had felt. And how much she had loathed his touch. "You were good to me."

He nodded. "I gave you everything. I molded you into the woman you are today."

If she could just connect with him, perhaps she could spare Lindsay. There was no hope for herself. She would have to return with him. But if she could just save Lindsay . . . "I didn't see that at the time. I should have."

Lindsay groaned as if she were protesting, but she made no attempt to rise.

Tears spilled down Nicole's cheek. "I love you, Richard."

He closed his eyes for a split second as if he were overcome with emotion. "I've waited a month for you to say that."

Her knees wobbled but she faced her husband. *"Please* forgive me." The words tasted bitter.

For a moment his features softened. He looked at her tenderly. She thought she had him. She was going to find a way out of this mess.

And then a switch inside him flipped. His gaze hardened to ice. He advanced on Nicole in two steps and hit her hard across the face. She dropped to her knees. Tasted blood. The handcuffs cut into her wrist.

"You are a lying bitch," he spat. "You need to learn a lesson."

She cupped her stinging face with her hand. "What are you going to do?"

With the machete in one hand, he moved toward Lindsay. "I think the world needs to know that Lindsay's precious protector turned on her and cut off her hand."

Nicole screamed and scrambled to her feet. "Richard, leave her alone. *Please,* I beg you. I'll do whatever you want."

"Oh, you'll do whatever I want. But first you need to learn a lesson."

Lindsay's mind had been crystal clear as she had lain on the hard earth and had listened to Richard rant and Nicole cry. Anger had roiled inside her as ants had crawled up under her shirt and started to bite her but she'd kept her eyes closed. She hadn't made a coherent sound or moved as Richard had badgered and threatened Nicole. It had taken Lindsay all that was in her to keep her temper under control as Nicole had begged Richard to spare Lindsay's life.

Just before Richard and Nicole had arrived, she'd been able to work the binding on her right hand loose so that she could slip her hand free. But she'd not had the time to loosen the ones on her other hand or her feet.

As Nicole had pushed open the barn door, Lindsay had had only had moments to scoop dirt up in her fist. Now, she needed Richard to get close so she could throw the dirt into his eyes.

Richard knelt beside Lindsay and ran the cold steel of the machete blade over her narrow wrist. "I wonder how many chops it will take to remove her hand? I'm willing to bet it hurts like a bitch."

Nicole wept. "Don't do this, Richard. *Please*, have pity."

"I have no pity for traitors. And that's what you are, Christina. You're a traitor."

Lindsay peeked through the slits of her eyelids. Richard had turned to face Nicole. This was her chance.

She drew in a deep breath and in one violent jerk pulled her arm free and threw the dirt into his eyes. The dirt caught him directly in the face. He yelped, dropped the machete, and staggered back. He rubbed his face and hollered like a banshee.

Lindsay quickly grabbed the machete and cut the binding on her other hand. Her heart hammered in her chest as she sat up and sliced through the bindings of her ankles.

Nicole yanked on the handcuffs as if she were possessed. "Lindsay, run. Get away from him."

Lindsay scrambled to her feet and ran to Nicole. "We're both getting out of here. Now stretch out your arm so I can cut the chain."

Nicole's hand trembled as she pulled the chain taut.

Richard fumbled for the gun in his waistband and swiped the dirt from his eyes. "Bitch!" He pointed the gun at Nicole and Lindsay. He cocked it and fired. The bullet whizzed past Lindsay's head and cut through the side of the barn. Sunlight shone through the hole.

Lindsay froze. Her fingers gripped the machete handle.

Richard pointed the gun at Nicole. "Drop the blade or I'll shoot Nicole in the head."

Lindsay stared at Nicole. Tears streamed down Nicole's face and her eyes pleaded for Lindsay not to give up.

Richard jabbed the gun in the air. *"Now."*

Lindsay laid down the machete on the workbench.

"Clever," Richard said. "Toss the machete over in that corner. I don't want you to be temped to try something again."

Lindsay threw the machete in the corner.

Richard laughed. "You couldn't save Mommy and now you won't be able to save Nicole."

Years of buried fury rose up in Lindsay. "You don't know anything about my mother."

He moved closer to Nicole. "I know a lot. Your friend Claire Carmichael had a lot to say as I sliced the flesh from her face."

Sweat trickled down Lindsay's back. "Screw you."

Enraged, Richard fired the gun. The bullet bit into the dirt by Nicole's feet, barely missing her. "If you refuse to accept your lesson, Lindsay, I'll kill Christina."

Nicole shook her head. "Don't do it, Lindsay. Don't make it easy for him. I'd rather die than let him hurt you."

"Shut up!" Richard shouted. He fired again.

This time the bullet nicked Nicole in the arm. He wasn't toying with them. She screamed in pain and grabbed her arm. She stumbled back but managed to stay on her feet.

Richard's face twisted with fury. He raised the gun to Nicole's head. He was going to kill her.

"Richard!" Lindsay shouted. "I'll get down on the ground. Just leave her alone."

Richard's hand shook as he held the pistol at Nicole's head.

"What do you want me to do?" Lindsay asked.

Richard didn't take his gaze off Nicole. "Go over by the machete and lie down on your belly. Stretch out your arms."

"Okay, just don't hurt her."

Blood seeped from the wound in Nicole's arm. "Don't do it, Lindsay."

"Shut up!" Richard shouted. He held the gun steady. "Hurry up. Lie on your stomach and stretch out your arms in front of you."

Lindsay moved across the barn and knelt down. She stretched out trembling arms. She thought about Zack. He'd wanted a second chance and she'd been too afraid to give him one. God, if only she had a second chance.

Richard walked toward the machete and picked it up, then moved beside Lindsay. Glancing at Nicole, he steadied his grip on the machete handle. "This is what happens to bad girls, Christina."

"Don't do this Richard, *please*," Nicole said. "If not for my sake, then the baby's."

His gaze didn't waver. "What baby?"

Nicole swiped a tear from her face. "Your baby. Our baby."

Richard's gaze narrowed. "You're lying."

"I'm not. I just found out."

Lindsay drew in a breath. Maybe they could use the baby to connect with him. "It's true." She started to spin lies. "It's a boy. The ultrasound just confirmed it."

"A son?"

Tears streamed down Nicole's face as she slid her hand protectively to her belly. "Yes. A son. Yours and mine."

"A simple test will prove if you're lying."

Nicole lifted her chin. "I'm not lying, Richard."

Richard's gaze glistened with pride. "All the more reason to get rid of her."

Pete knew he had to act now. There was no telling when the cops would arrive. He had to save Lindsay. She had to know that she wasn't alone.

Swallowing the pain, he held his gun straight. In a split second he took in the scene. Richard had grabbed Lindsay's hair, yanked her head back, and was pressing the machete blade to her neck.

In that moment, Pete pictured Debra's last moments. She'd been alone. Afraid. He raised his gun. This was his moment of redemption. "Let her go."

Richard's gaze snapped up. "Back the fuck off or I'll kill her." He pushed the blade against Lindsay's neck, slicing her skin. Blood trickled.

"Kill her and I'll kill you and your wife," Pete said. He moved into the room so that the wall, not the door, was to his back. He didn't want to kill Nicole but he would.

"No!" Lindsay struggled to get free.

Pete didn't take his eyes off Lindsay. "You come first, Lindsay. If she has to die, then so be it. I came to save *you*."

Richard heard the sincerity in Pete's voice. He hesitated, understanding that Pete would kill his wife and child. "Who the hell are you?"

"I'm Lindsay's Guardian." Pride welled inside him. He'd waited so long to say those words.

Outside, police tires screeched to a halt. Footsteps raced toward the barn.

Richard sneered and lowered his gaze to the blade. He was going to kill Lindsay.

The Guardian fired.

* * *

Guns drawn, Zack and Warwick burst into the barn as Pete's bullet whirled past Lindsay's head and struck Richard in the face. Blood and brains splattered Lindsay's face and body. She screamed.

Warwick's face twisted with anguish. "Pete!"

Pete backed up, his gun still drawn.

"Drop your weapon!" Zack ordered.

Lindsay turned away from Richard's body. She didn't chance a glance down at his body. Instead, she looked at Pete. "You're my Guardian?"

Pete's gun didn't waver. "Yes."

Understanding dawned in Lindsay's eyes. "My mother's brother."

Pete nodded. "I wasn't there for you when you needed me then. But I'm here now."

Zack inched closer. "Pete, drop the gun. Give Lindsay a chance to get to know her uncle. It doesn't have to end for you."

Warwick's face looked carved from stone. "Please, Pete. Don't do this."

For an instant, Pete's stance relaxed a fraction and it looked like he might give up. Then he shook his head. "This is the end of the line." He raised the gun at Nicole, ready to fire.

Warwick hesitated.

Zack didn't. He fired. His bullet hit Pete in the chest. Pete dropped to his knees, the gun still in his hand. He turned his face toward Warwick. "You're a good kid."

Warwick froze, his weapon pointed forward.

Pete raised his gun a second time.

Zack fired again. This time the bullet struck Pete in the head, killing him instantly.

Adrenaline pumped through Zack's veins. For several

seconds he didn't move. He wanted to run to Lindsay to take her in his arms, but he resisted the urge. He swept the room with his gaze. There didn't appear to be anyone else there.

"Lindsay, is anyone else here?" Zack asked.

She shoved her hands through her bloody hair. "I don't think so."

Zack looked at Nicole. Her skin was as pale as porcelain. "Anyone else?"

Nicole shook her head. "Richard said he'd come alone. He didn't want anyone to know where I was."

Outside the distant sound of sirens began to grow louder. Backup would soon arrive. Still, Zack let his gaze roam over the rafters and in the shadowed corners.

Warwick cleared his throat. "I'll cover you."

"You can handle this?"

Warwick looked like he'd aged a decade. "Yes."

Zack searched the room, and only when he was satisfied that the danger had passed did he holster his weapon and go to Lindsay.

She was covered in so much blood that he was afraid he might hurt her if he touched her. "Lindsay, are you all right?"

Green eyes locked on his. Tears filled her eyes and streamed down her face. "Yes." She wrapped her arms around him. "I thought I'd never see you again."

Zack held Lindsay tight. "It's okay, baby. I'm here."

Warwick, careful not to look at Pete, moved to Richard's body and searched his pockets for the key to the handcuffs that held Nicole. Finding it, he moved to her and unlocked them. He had a white-knuckle hold on his control and he wouldn't be able to hold it forever. He guided Nicole out of the barn.

Lindsay stared at Pete's body. "How did he know we were here?"

"He's the one who had been watching you on the cameras. There are cameras at Ruby's house too."

"My God."

Zack wrapped his arm around Lindsay and held her tight. Her heart beat rapidly against his chest. "Let's get out of here."

"Yes." In the harsh sunlight, Lindsay squinted and tucked her head against his chest.

As the backup cops arrived and fanned into a tight perimeter, he kissed her. "Lindsay, I love you."

She clung to him. "I love you too, Zack."

Chapter Twenty-Nine

Saturday, September 20, 1:05 P.M.

"That's the last of it," Zack said as he kicked the front door of the saltbox house closed with his foot.

"Still glad I'm moving in?" Lindsay said as she eyed the stack of boxes and furniture in the living room.

Zack set the box down and pulled her into his arms. Light from the transom above him shone into the hallway, giving the house a bright, cheery feel. He kissed her long and hard. "Absolutely. You're exactly where you belong."

Lindsay snuggled close to him. In his arms everything felt so *right*. After her nightmare experience in July with Richard Braxton and her uncle, Pete Myers, she'd realized just how much she loved Zack. No matter what their problems had been, she'd known she'd work with him to solve them.

Together, they'd gone into marriage counseling and had started to work on the issues that had kept them apart. The sessions weren't always easy. There were tears and some anger, but through it all they kept communicating and trying to find their way back to each other. And they had. Their relationship wasn't perfect, but then no relationship was. They both still had busy, demanding work schedules but they both understood that no matter what, they belonged together. Their love would carry them through anything.

Lindsay laid her head against Zack's chest. She savored the steady thud of his strong heartbeat against her ear.

So much had happened in the last couple of months. Kendall had survived her injuries. For reasons no one understood, the Guardian, Pete, had not cut off her hand. He'd left her to die, expecting her to bleed out. But because Zack and Warwick had found her in time, she'd survived the gunshot wound to her shoulder. She had lost a great deal of blood and was near death when they'd found her. It had had been touch-and-go for Kendall for a couple of days. Lindsay had visited her daily, feeling an odd connection to the woman who'd nearly been killed by Lindsay's own flesh and blood. When Kendall had awakened for the first time, she had been surprised to see Lindsay. She had been even more shocked by Lindsay's concern. However, as the days had turned into weeks and Lindsay had continued to return to the hospital, Kendall and Lindsay had forged the beginnings of a friendship.

The news media had swarmed all over the story. Their coverage had been relentless. Kendall was used to covering events herself and had hated being the center of attention. Ironically, Lindsay was one of the few people who understood how wrenching such coverage could be.

"I don't like this," Kendall said as she laid in her hospital bed, her right arm in a gray sling. She was pale and drawn, fragile even, but still held her chin up as if she were queen of the world. Lindsay had to give the woman credit. She was a survivor.

"Another story will come along," Lindsay said. "You'll be forgotten soon enough."

Kendall's face tightened as she absently plucked at a loose thread on her blanket. Tears welled in her eyes. "I'm sorry."

Lindsay frowned. "For what?"

"I wasn't fair to you when I was covering the Guardian story." She smoothed long fingers over her thigh. "But I've had a taste of what I put you through. I've been *the* story for the last month and it's not been pleasant. I was willing to sacrifice you for my career. I'm sorry."

"You were doing your job. I understand that it wasn't personal." Lindsay was trying her best to let go of her anger.

Kendall shook her head. "I was doing my job a little too well. And no, it wasn't personal, but that kind of media coverage can be hurtful. I see that now." An awkward silence settled between them.

That one apology had banished a good bit of her resentment. She managed a soft smile. "How's the shoulder?"

"Stiff and it really throbs at night. I'll be in rehab for months." Kendall wiggled all ten fingers. "But I'm very grateful to have both my hands."

"When does rehab start?"

"Two weeks. The doctors are pretty sure I'll regain full range of motion." She smiled. "I've heard my physical therapist is the best, but other patients say she can be a bit of a sadist."

Lindsay nodded grimly. "It's going to be her job to make your arm move in directions it doesn't want to go. I'm sorry it's going to be so painful."

She shrugged. "The pain doesn't bother me. It will just feel good to have my life back."

"Are you going to take that job at the New York television station?"

Kendall shook her head. "I don't know. I don't have to make a decision for a few weeks. By the way, how's Nicole? I hear she's back in Richmond."

Lindsay gave her the recap. Nicole was also moving on with her life. Her bullet wound had been superficial and had not impacted the baby. She'd chosen to carry the child to term but hadn't ruled out adoption. Her biggest fear was that she could never love Richard's child.

Nicole had flown back to San Francisco to reclaim her life. With Richard gone she was free to reclaim her old studio and the bank accounts she'd not been able to access. But she'd quickly discovered that the city no longer felt like home. There were simply too many bad memories. So, she had returned to Virginia within weeks and had announced she was reopening her business on the East Coast.

Kendall nodded. "She's welcome to stay with me. I've got a huge house to myself."

"Thanks, I'll tell her."

Later, Nicole had agreed to room with Kendall, knowing she'd not be able to make any firm living arrangements until she decided about the baby.

When Lindsay thought back on all that had happened she still felt overwhelmed. But what always brought her down to earth was Zack. "I love you, Zack Kier."

"I love you, Lindsay O'Neil." He kissed her on the forehead. "I have something for you in the kitchen."

"Please tell me it's lunch," she said, teasing. The appetite that had eluded her this past year was returning. "I'm starving."

He grinned. "I'll grill us some hamburgers in a minute but first I want to give you this." He guided her into the kitchen. He reached in the drawer beside the sink and pulled out a small black box.

Her heart thumped wildly in her chest as she accepted the box and cracked it open. Inside was a ring. It was a thick gold band with three small sapphires and two diamonds embedded in it. "Wow."

Zack took the ring from the box and slipped it on her ring finger. It fit perfectly. "When we got married, we never bought rings. I thought it was time I gave you a proper wedding band."

Tears glistened in her eyes. For so many years, she'd felt an emptiness that had cut to her bone. Now, her life and heart felt so full. "It's stunning."

"You really like it?"

"Yes."

"I knew you wouldn't want anything fussy, but I wanted the ring to have some sparkle."

Emotion tightened her throat. "It's gorgeous."

He pulled a second ring out of his jeans pocket. "I picked up one for me as well."

Grinning through tears, she took the ring from him and slipped it on his ring finger. His hands were warm, calloused, and already she was imagining them on her naked body. "I guess this makes us official."

He laughed. "I want the world to know we're married."

She had come so far. There'd been a time when she had feared marriage, even love. And now she embraced them both.

Lindsay's counseling sessions with her therapist had focused not only on her relationship with Zack but with her uncle, Pete Myers. Police investigations had revealed that Pete had retired from the military twenty years ago and had settled in Richmond. He'd opened his gym and had become a foster father to Jacob Warwick. By all accounts, he had been a model citizen and father to Jacob. What no one realized was that Pete had harbored bitter disappointment and guilt over his estrangement from his sister, Deb, Lindsay's mother. When Deb had been brutally murdered twelve years ago, Pete's mental health had suffered a severe blow. Jacob was in the army and there'd been no one to ground Pete.

Pete had traveled to Hanover searching for Lindsay. When he'd discovered she'd run away he'd gone to the Hines house and burned it to the ground. From then on, Pete's mental health never fully recovered. All outward appearances suggested he was fine, but video journals found by the police revealed that he had a very troubled mind.

In the video diaries, Pete had ranted about his dead brother-in-law, about his own rage and his need for revenge. In fact, arson investigators were able to link several unsolved fires to Pete.

Seeing Lindsay's picture in the May article in *Inside Richmond* had snapped Pete's hold on reality. He had believed the article had been a sign from God for him to become Lindsay's Guardian. He had planted the cameras in Lindsay's town house and had obsessively followed her. His surveillance had alerted him to Sam Begley. Pete had surreptitiously known of Sam's obsession with gambling and it had been easy to lure him into a couple of bets on boxing fights. Pete had seen to it that Sam had lost. And then he'd used the doctor's debts to force him to supply confidential information about patients. Police later found Sam's body in the back of Pete's van.

In the end, Pete's obsession with Lindsay had destroyed Sanctuary Women's Shelter, the haven Lindsay had created as a tribute to her mother. But ironically, she'd not have been alive today to rebuild another shelter if not for Pete's fixation on her. If he had not been following her that hot day in July and figured out where Richard had taken her and called Jacob, Zack would never have found her alive. Richard would have brutally killed her, as he'd killed Claire, and Nicole and her baby would be back in California suffering under Richard's iron hand.

Even the loss of Sanctuary was only temporary. A month ago, Dana and Sanctuary's board of directors had given Lindsay the go-ahead to find a new location for another women's shelter.

Lindsay stared down at her ring, and despite her best efforts to remain positive, thoughts of the teenage boy who had died because of Pete haunted her.

Zack detected her shift in mood. "What's bothering you? Is it the ring?"

"No, it's perfect." She blew out a breath. "I still think of those boys my uncle shot." One had survived his wounds but the other had been buried. The wrenching funeral had attracted more than 500 mourners including Lindsay, Zack, and Jacob. "I just wish I could have stopped Pete from going over the edge."

He tucked a stray strand of her hair behind her ear. "You hadn't seen the guy in over twenty years. How could you be responsible?"

"Intellectually, I get that. Emotionally, I feel awful about what happened." When she was close to Zack, she felt as if she could get through anything. "I saw Jacob yesterday. He opened up a little about his feelings, but I can see the guy is a wreck."

"I'm glad he at least talked to you. He's gone to the department shrink but I don't think he's saying anything more than he has to. He needs someone to trust."

"Trust is a tall order for him to fill right now. His mother left him scarred and Pete shattered what little trust he'd regained." She shook her head. "It's odd. If my uncle had found me right after Mom's death, Jacob would have been a kind of foster brother to me."

Zack laid his hands on her shoulders. "You're good at getting people to open up. Keep talking to him. He's going to need you."

"We've pieced together some of his life but not all of it. Peter Henry Myers was a complicated man."

"He cared about you both."

"Yeah." Lindsay felt the need to talk about something cheerier. "Enough sadness. Today is a happy day. Let's get those burgers on the grill. I'm starving."

He smiled warmly. "And after that, I vote we bag the boxes for today and try out that new bed."

She glanced out the kitchen window onto the deck to the only splash of color in the backyard. He mother's clay planters that Zack had rescued were filled with pansies and ivy. "Sounds good."

Zack collected the burgers from the refrigerator. "Mom called this morning."

Lindsay grabbed the hamburger buns from the bread basket. She and Audrey had shared a pleasant lunch last week. It felt good to be back in the Kier fold. Even Malcolm was warming to her. "And?"

"She'd like to throw us a wedding." He shrugged. "She doesn't want to put any pressure on us, but she'd like to see us married in a real church. She even wants to throw a reception at Zola's."

"That's very generous. I'd love to renew our vows, Zack, but finding the time to plan a big event is going to be kind of hard now. We have the house and we're both busy with work."

"Mom wants to do the whole thing for us. It's her gift to us. She'd wanted to do it after we first eloped but . . ."

"We didn't last long enough." Lindsay felt touched by her mother-in-law's offer. "That's really sweet of her."

Zack grinned. The smile softened his normally serious features and gave them a boyish quality that had her heart skipping. "So that's a yes?"

A soft breeze blew through the kitchen window and cooled her skin. "To remarrying you in front of all our friends and family?" She nodded. "That's a definite yes."

"And the party?"

"It sounds fabulous. I'm ready for a whole new start."

The terror continues as a serial killer murders his way closer to the one he most longs for— and to the Richmond, Virginia, homicide detective who'll risk everything to stop him . . .

Beside each body, he leaves a simple charm bearing a woman's name. *Ruth, Judith, Rachel.* The victims were strangers to each other, but they have been chosen with the utmost care. Each bears a striking resemblance to Kendall Shaw, a local anchorwoman . . . each brutally strangled by a madman whose obsession will never end . . .

In front of the cameras, Kendall exudes confidence. But at night she's haunted by nightmares in which she is young, alone, and filled with fear. Are these memories—or omens? Despite warnings from Detective Jacob Warwick, Kendall can't stop investigating the recent murders. She knows she holds the key to catching a psychopath—if he doesn't get to her first. But as Kendall and Jacob dig into the victims' backgrounds, from the shadows of the past a legacy of evil resurfaces. Every murder, every moment has been leading to Kendall. And this time, nothing will stop the killer from making her his final victim . . .

Please turn the page for an exciting sneak peek of Mary Burton's DEAD RINGER, coming in July 2012!

Prologue

Sunday, January 6, sunset

"It's time, Ruth."

A cheerless finality hardened the man's softly spoken words. His heart truly felt heavy as he stared out the frost-streaked window. Outside, pine trees bowed under the ice's extra weight as arctic gusts rushed over the fields, swirling around, creating minitwisters in the snow.

"I don't want you to go," he said, turning toward Ruth.

The woman sat in a wooden chair, her head bent forward. Dark hair cascaded over her tear-streaked face. "Please," she said.

The room was decorated with rose wallpaper, white iolite curtains, and a large braided rug with interwoven strands of yellow, pink, and blue. A white four-poster canopy bed covered with a cherry comforter and dozens of stuffed animals dominated the space. He'd built this room for her and the others.

"Shh. I have to let you go. We both knew this time would come." Sadness tightened his throat.

Ruth raised her head a fraction. She glanced down at

her wrists, lashed tightly to chair arms. "No. No. I don't want to go. I want to stay with you."

The hoarse whisper was a lie. Instinctively, she understood what leaving truly meant. Dying.

He crossed the room, hoping to reassure her. "You don't need to be afraid." He knelt beside her and laid his hand on the ropes lashed to her pale wrists, now raw and bleeding after days of struggling. "It's okay, Ruth. It's all for the best. You'll see," he said tenderly.

Tears rolled down her face. "No. Let me stay." Desperation sparked in her eyes. "We can still be a family."

"You have to trust me, Ruth. I know what's best." He touched her cheek.

She flinched and then offered a faltering smile as she raised her pale green eyes to meet his. "Allen, please."

He liked it when she said his name. "I can't. You know that."

Lovingly he touched her chin and tipped her face back so he could look into her eyes. Fresh tears fell and dampened his calloused hand. For a moment, his resolve wavered. He really didn't want to send her away. He wanted to keep her here forever.

But he couldn't.

Wouldn't.

He rose and moved behind her. Gently he stroked her hair, which no longer smelled of coconuts and summer, but of fear and sweat. "I've really enjoyed our time as well. I've been alone for so long. But you must join the Family now."

She shook her head but was unable to lift it. She whimpered, "Please. Don't."

Allen pushed her hair away from her slender neck. "You will be grateful in the end."

He'd been searching for her for years, knowing that one day he'd find her and they'd be together again. And then he'd found her and he'd nearly cried out in joy. For weeks, he watched her attend church, drive to her secretarial job at the engineering firm, and go to the grocery store. He stood in the shadows as she'd wept at her parents' graveside. He'd scrutinized. Admired. Waited for the perfect opportunity to bring her to this special place that he'd created.

He slipped his hands under Ruth's thick mane of hair and brushed the soft skin of her neck. It felt cold. Her faint heartbeat drummed under his fingers. The drugs that had made her sleepy, almost nonresponsive, were wearing off. Soon she'd be struggling again, screaming until her voice grew hoarse.

He'd not wanted to use the drugs, but she'd been so defiant and unwilling to talk to him. She'd fought, called him names, and rejected him. The drugs had calmed her, made her see the good in him.

"I wish we had more time," he said.

She craned her head to the side and looked up at him. Desperation made her eyes spark. "We can still be a family."

A smile twitched at the edge of his lips. "Not in the way that it matters. There is too much that can come between us."

"It could be different this time. You'll see. I promise I will love you."

Love. For a moment he closed his eyes and let the word roll through his mind. No one had loved him in so long. "You can't really love me until you join the Family."

"I can."

He didn't blame her for the lie. He knew she was afraid of the transition. Crossing over always triggered fear in his girls. She'd say anything at this point. He understood and wasn't mad.

"Shh. It's going to be okay, Ruth."

A sob rose in her throat. "I'm not Ruth. I'm not Ruth."

He drew circles on her neck with his thumbs and then slid long fingers around her neck. Her pulse throbbed faster now. "Don't fight it. It's so much easier when you don't fight what is best for you."

"No." She jerked against her bindings and started to thrash her head. "I don't want to go!"

He tightened his hold and began to squeeze.

Initially, she thrashed harder. A muffled cry escaped her lips. But the pressure on her neck quickly robbed her of air, sound, and energy. Soon, she choked and gasped for air. She pulled against the bindings and balled her slender fingers into fists.

"Ruth, you were always the strong, brave one."

He tightened his hold, savoring the rush of power and excitement coursing through his body. His body warmed, despite the chill in the room. In this moment he felt connected, *alive.*

For so long he'd been alone, lost and wondering. Now, Ruth was about to join his Family. She would be with him forever.

"Family. It is everything. Without family life isn't worth much. People today don't get that. They are so busy rushing around they don't take the time to be with each other."

She strained her neck and twisted her head, gagging, trying to break free.

His arms and hands ached but his grip remained tight. Her pulse drummed frantically, proof her lungs struggled for air. And then the *thump, thump, thump* skipped several beats. His heart raced faster. A few more erratic pulses followed and then stillness.

Life ebbed from Ruth's body, like water down a drain. She slumped forward. A tranquility only death could create washed over her.

Lovingly, he rested his palm on the top of her head. "It's better now, isn't it? You are finally at peace. You are free of all your worries and pain."

She didn't move. There were no more uneven protests. No pleas for freedom.

"Praise be," he whispered.

From his pocket he pulled a gold chain with an oval charm. Inscribed on the charm was the name *Ruth*. He slipped the chain around her neck. The clasp was small, delicate, and his large hands fumbled with the fastener until finally he hooked it.

He moved around the chair and knelt in front of her. The charm lay in the hollow of her neck just above her breasts. The pendant was a fine piece of jewelry that had taken him weeks to make. But it was worth it. He touched the shiny gold.

Ruth deserved the best.

He untied her wrists and took her hands in his. He kissed her cold fingers and then pressed them to his cheek. "I love you so much."

He put his hand under her chin and tipped her face back. Under partially open lids, green eyes stared sightlessly at him. He imagined he saw laughter in their glassy depths.

"You won't be alone much longer, Ruth." He laid her hands in her lap, crossing them demurely over each other. "Soon, I will find the Others and I will send them to you."

Allen smiled at the thought of the Others. Joy burned inside him. "Soon, we all will be together as the Family was meant to be."

Chapter One

Tuesday, January 8, 8:10 A.M.

Homicide detective Jacob Warwick flexed his right hand, working the stiffness from his joints as he strode over the frozen land toward the flashing police car lights. The five patrol cars were parked on the rural patch of land near the James River's banks. Friday's snowstorm had whitewashed the landscape, robbing it of color and life. A morning haze obscured the southern bank of the river and most of the river's smooth waters.

The temperature hovered around thirty degrees, but the breeze made it feel like twenty below zero and cut through his jacket as if it were thin cotton.

The cold irritated his bruised knuckles and he regretted leaving his gloves at his apartment. He turned up the collar of his worn leather jacket and shoved his fists into the pockets. A skullcap covered his military short hair and a black scarf warmed his neck.

An hour ago, Jacob had been at the gym, enjoying his day off by giving what he had to a punching bag. Breaking a sweat sent endorphins rushing through his brain and for a little while eased the tension that stalked him.

His cell had rung midswing. He'd steadied the swaying punching bag, muttered a foul oath before wiping the sweat from his eyes, and dug his cell out of his gym bag.

His partner, Detective Zack Kier, had recited the bare facts. Female murdered. Midthirties. Caucasian. The body had been dumped on the banks of the James River at the Alderson construction site, located in the east end of the county a dozen miles past the airport. Jacob had showered, burying his face under the hot spray and regretting that he couldn't linger.

Another gusty breeze off the river sent Jacob deeper into his coat. This parcel of land was all raw fields and spindly cedar trees, but if the sales sign he'd passed on the way in was correct, Alderson Development Company would transform all this into a lush golf course surrounded by brick houses with perfectly placed trees and flower beds. The proposed clubhouse would offer tennis courts and a heated swimming pool.

Starting in the $900,000s. The slick marketing signs implied that the riverfront houses, with their top-of-the-line amenities, also supplied the right brand of status and a *Father Knows Best* kind of happiness. Life had taught him there were no guarantees. And thirteen years on the force had shown him misery could be found in high-dollar homes as well as low-income ones.

Jacob spotted a group of ragged-looking men standing by a muddy black Suburban. They wore jumpsuits and camouflage jackets. They were the Alderson Development's survey crew. This was their job site. They'd arrived just after sunrise to survey the north bank of the James River. They'd been the ones who'd found the body.

"Hey, when are you gonna let us get back to work or let us go home?" The shouted complaint came from one of the surveyors. Steam rose from the coffee cup in his hand.

"Can't say," Jacob said. "But stay put."

Jacob moved toward an older officer with a buzz cut and a perpetual frown. The other officer stamped his feet and rubbed his gloved hands together. "Cold enough for you? My bones can't take too much more of this frosty shit."

Jacob's body still ached from a boxing match last week. "I hear ya."

"What are you complaining about? I've been here for an hour already."

Jacob smiled. "You're tougher than I am."

"My ass." Watson's gaze narrowed as he glanced at Jacob's face. "That the remnants of a shiner?"

"Yeah. The other guy had a mean right hook." But that hadn't stopped Jacob from winning the charity boxing match.

Watson's gaze narrowed. "How old are you now? Thirty-four, thirty-five?"

"Give or take."

Watson shook his head. "You're getting too old for those kind of antics. You're not eighteen. You should stop now while you still have all your parts."

Thirty-six wasn't old in the big scheme but for a boxer it was ancient. In the army he'd been Golden Gloves. Since he'd left, he'd remained a strictly amateur boxer. Boxing gave him a thrill, reminded him he still had it. Whatever the hell *it* was.

But the sport was taking a toll. He didn't rebound like he used to. He'd taken on so many bouts these last few months there was rarely a day when his body didn't ache. Watson was right. He didn't recover as he had in his twenties. "I'll keep that in mind."

Watson eyed him. "Bullshit. You ain't gonna stop."

That coaxed a guilty grin.

Most outsiders—noncops—didn't understand how they could chat about everyday things or be so casual in the face of death. But this kind of banter, even humor, was a way of blowing off steam and cutting the tension so they didn't go insane.

Jacob pulled rubber gloves from his jacket pocket. "Forensics isn't here yet?"

"Tied up at another scene. Will be here any minute."

"Good." He ducked under the yellow tape and strode toward his partner, Detective Zack Kier.

Zack Kier faced the icy river. Tall, broad shouldered, he possessed a lean build suited so well for the triathlons he enjoyed. His unseasonably tanned skin was a souvenir from a Caribbean second honeymoon with his wife, Lindsay. A black overcoat brushed his knees and plastic gloves covered his dark winter gloves.

"So what do we have?" Jacob asked. He yanked on his gloves.

Zack turned at the sound of his voice and nodded toward the river's edge. "See for yourself."

Jacob followed Zack down the embankment toward the frozen riverbank. Where water met land lay a woman on her stomach. She wore a camel overcoat, gloves, scarf, navy pants, and flat shoes, all soaked with water. Her gloved hands were outstretched in a T fashion. One hand lay in the water and the other on land. Her face was turned toward the river and her long dark brown hair streamed over her cheek in a gloomy curtain. Small waves lapped against her body.

Jacob moved toward the body but stopped ten feet short. He didn't want to contaminate the scene any more than he had to before forensics got there. His heavy sigh froze on contact with the air. "Do we know who she is?"

Zack shook his head. "Not yet. There was no ID in any of her pockets. And no purse to be found."

Jacob squatted. He stared at her face, mostly hidden by her thick brown hair. How did a neatly dressed middle-income woman end up here? "There are a few bridges downstream and dozens of docks. Suicide?"

Zack's expression was grim. "That's what the responding uniform thought at first."

Jacob frowned. "And?"

"He felt for a pulse on her neck when he arrived. He had to push back her hair to make contact with her skin." Zack tightened and released his jaw. "He found black-and-blue finger marks around her neck."

"Strangled."

"He also spotted marks on her wrists. Looked like rope burns."

Jacob shifted his gaze to the edge of her coat sleeve. He wanted to push up the wet fabric and see the marks for himself but he would wait for forensics. "Did the responding officer touch the body anywhere else?"

"No. Only on the neck and wrist to check for a pulse."

Forensics needed a complete record of everyone who touched the body. "Good."

Jacob's gaze settled on the victim's wrist. "Whoever did this held her captive before he killed her."

"That's what I'm thinking."

The victim was fully dressed, down to scarf and gloves. But that didn't mean she hadn't been stripped and sexually assaulted. Some killers, especially novices, often suffered remorse for their victims. In the killer's mind, redressing her would have been a way of safeguarding her dignity. "We need to make sure the coroner checks for signs of rape."

"Already noted."

Jacob flexed his right hand, trying to work the stiffness from it. He studied the partially exposed side of the victim's face. Determining time of death would be tricky. The freezing temps would have slowed down the decomposition process. "Any missing persons reports?"

A cold gust of air made Zack drop his head. "I put a call in about fifteen minutes ago. No one fitting her description has been reported missing, but that could change."

There could be a hundred reasons no one had called in a report. The victim had been traveling. She'd had a fight with her spouse. She lived alone and had few friends. Sooner or later, though, most people were missed by someone.

A glance upriver revealed no signs of a dock, boat, or landing where she might have been dumped. "She's soaked but her skin isn't discolored like it would be if she'd been in the water. And there'd be weeds or grass over her if she'd been in the river."

"The freezing rain yesterday would have drenched anyone to the skin."

Jacob could think of a dozen reasons how a middle-income woman could end up like this. Secret life of drug addiction. Domestic abuse. At this point all would be guesses.

Jacob stared at her body. "Why leave her here?"

Zack scribbled in his notebook. "Whoever did this might have thought she wouldn't be found for a while."

"Or he figured she'd be found quickly. Construction crews have been all over this place for weeks."

"That brings up a whole new set of problems."

Most killers didn't want anyone to know they'd murdered. If this killer dumped the woman intentionally, Zack was right. It opened the door to a darker scenario.

The rumble of a vehicle engine had them both glancing back up the hill. The forensics van had arrived. White with blue lettering, the side read *Henrico County Forensics.*

A young dark-haired woman slid out from behind the driver's seat of the van. Tess Kier, Zack's sister. Tess had been with forensics three years. She was meticulous and one of the best in the country.

Tall for a woman, she had sharp features and a lean body. Jacob had thought more than once about hooking up with her, but he had never made a move. Not only was she his partner's baby sister, but they interfaced on crime scenes often. *Keep your dick out of the company payroll.* It had been a favorite phrase of his army sergeant's. Sage words he was careful to live by.

Zack's grim features softened a fraction and he headed up the hill toward Tess.

Jacob remained by the river's edge, close to the victim. He turned and stared out over the river, not sure what he was looking for. This was a sad, desolate place. "No one deserves this."

Tess came down the hill in her jumpsuit, booties, and gloves. A digital camera hung from a strap around her neck and she held a clipboard in her hand. A pencil stuck out from the ponytail holding up her ebony hair. As Tess approached she glanced down at Jacob's hands.

Jacob read her mind as if it were a book. He wiggled his fingers. "I've got my gloves on like a good boy."

"Good." Tess's pale, smooth skin accentuated sharp, blue eyes. "I don't need anyone contaminating my crime scene." She cast a pointed gaze at her brother. "I know I don't have to tell you about the right gear."

Zack looked bored, as if he'd heard this speech a thousand times. "Anybody ever tell you that you're mean in the morning?"

"My ex-boyfriend." Tess tucked the clipboard under her arm and started to snap pictures with the digital camera.

In the dim morning light the camera's flash illuminated the victim with a brutal clarity. All chatter ceased and a grave silence settled on the scene.

Tess documented the body from every conceivable

angle. She stood on the bank and then moved into the shallow, frigid waters and snapped more pictures. She drew sketches and took notes.

Jacob studied the victim as the camera flash exploded. He tried to put himself in her head. To think as she had.

Her shoes and clothes were sensible. Almost prudish. Her hair was loose now, but he guessed that she normally wore it tied back in a tight ponytail. That practical style would have matched her short, neat, unpolished nails. The scarf around her neck was tied in a square knot.

She looked like a librarian. A churchgoer. Someone who walked on the correct side of the road. She was the type of person who would be noticed if she went missing.

The cold seeped into Jacob's bones and he grew restless. He shifted his weight from one foot to the other, trying to get the circulation moving. Blazing heat and humidity didn't bother him, but the cold pissed him off.

Jacob swung his gaze to the huddle of surveyors. "I'm going to talk to the crew."

Zack nodded. "Right."

The frozen ground crunched under his foot as he made his way up the embankment. He stopped in front of the men who stood in front of the black Suburban.

A tall man standing in the center of the group nodded. He weighed at least two hundred pounds, sported a thick black beard, and had a tattoo of a fallen angel on his neck. The other crewmen looked younger, maybe mid-twenties, and their bloodshot eyes suggested they'd done some heavy drinking last night.

"Which one of you found the body?" Jacob asked.

The tall one answered. "I did. I'm the party chief."

"Your name?"

"Frank Burrows." A deep southern drawl drew out the last name and suggested he was a transplant from the southwestern part of the state.

"Walk me through what you saw," Jacob said.

Tension deepened the furrows on the man's brow. His gaze darted toward the river before settling on Jacob. "I was setting up the survey equipment along the river. Rob here," he said, jabbing his thumb toward the man to his right, "was a few paces behind."

Rob shifted his stance. "I had to take a leak."

Burrows rolled his eyes. "I'd just placed the tripod when I spotted the woman's coat. I thought it was debris from the storm. We're always finding stuff in the water. Tires, shoes, clothes, furniture. I walked over to get a closer look. When I realized it was a woman, I called nine-one-one."

"Did you touch her?"

Burrows folded his arms over his large chest. "Hell no. She didn't look like she was breathing and I didn't want to get too close."

"You didn't check for a pulse?"

He sniffed, his air now defensive. "No."

"Any of your men touch her?"

"No."

Jacob glanced at the crew. "See anyone around here who didn't belong?"

They all shook their heads no.

Burrows spoke up. "This isn't the kind of place people come to for fun in the winter. There's an old deer stand in one of the trees, so hunters have been through here at one point. But that was before Alderson bought the place. We've got a few illegal trash-dump sights but most of those are a few months old."

"No one lurking around?"

"The road you drove in on is the only way in by car. It ends about a hundred yards past the turnoff."

"How about tire tracks on the road? See anything different, suspicious?"

"Hard to tell what tracks are ours or someone else's. And the snow last night would have covered up anything new."

"What about river access to the site?"

"A flat-bottomed boat could navigate the area but we haven't seen one." Burrows nervously tugged at a string dangling from the edge of his coat.

"Something wrong?" Jacob asked.

A half laugh, half curse burst out of Burrows. "What do you think? I found a dead woman at my job site. All I want right now is to sit in a warm bar and drink a cold beer."

"Warwick," Zack called up from the river's edge. "Tess has found something."

Jacob turned from the surveyors. "Be right there."

Burrows shoved out a breath. "Can I let my men go now? They didn't see nothing and we have another survey job that we can jump on so this entire day isn't a waste."

Jacob shook his head. "Hang around just a little longer."

The party chief swore. "If I'd known this was going to tie us up so long I'd have called the cops after we'd finished our work. A few hours don't matter to her either way."

Jacob glared at him until the man had the sense to drop eye contact. Irritated, Jacob made his way back down to the riverbank and discovered Tess had turned the victim on her back.

The woman's cheek was turned to the side but he could see she had a wide face; high cheekbones; and pale, white skin. Her eyes were closed. The bruising on Jane Doe's neck was very visible now, as were the marks on her wrists. In the gray morning light, her frozen features made her look more like a mannequin than a human. Yet, there was something familiar about her.

Jacob swallowed. Personalizing the body could rob him of objectivity. He'd do a better job in the end if he thought of the body as just a piece of evidence and nothing more.

"Look at her necklace," Tess said.

Jacob leaned closer. A gold charm hung from a chain around her neck. The scripted engraving read *Ruth*. "Her name is Ruth?"

Zack jotted a note in his spiral notebook. "The necklace looks nice."

Tess nodded as she snapped pictures of the body and got close-ups of the neck and charm. "It's very nice. I'd say it cost good money."

"She doesn't look like one to wear expensive jewelry," Jacob noted. "She's all about practicality."

"Maybe it was a gift," Tess offered.

"Maybe." Sometimes the odd detail in a case could bother him for days or weeks. He'd had an apparent suicide last year. The man appeared to have shot himself. The house was clean, everything in its place. Only the man's tie and suit jacket were dumped in a sloppy heap on the floor. No big deal. But the detail just hadn't fit the picture. Jacob had sat at that crime scene a long time before he reasoned the man had dumped the clothes in a final act of rebellion.

And now he had an expensive charm around the neck of a woman who looked like she shopped at discount stores. It could be nothing, like the discarded clothes. But it still bothered him.

"I'll check on the charm," Zack said.

Jacob nodded as he stared at the woman. Despite the ravages of death and the elements, he still felt as if he'd seen Jane Doe before. "She looks familiar to me."

Tess nodded. "I thought the same thing. Been trying to place her since I first got a look at her face."

How did he know her?

Tess gently placed her fingertips under the woman's chin and turned her face toward them.

The full-on view of her face startled him. Recognition dawned.

Jane Doe . . . Ruth.

She looked like the news anchorwoman on Channel 10 News. Kendall Shaw.

HE IS THEIR JUDGE . . .

In death, they are purified.
Holding his victims under water, he washes away
their sins as they struggle for their last breath.
Then he stakes their bodies to the ground,
exposing them for what they really are.
Witches, sent to tempt and to corrupt . . .

JURY . . .

No one knows about defense attorney Charlotte
Wellington's murdered sister, or about her childhood
spent with the carnival that's just arrived in town.
For Charlotte, what's past is past. But others don't
agree. And as a madman's body count rises, she
and Detective Daniel Rokov are drawn into a mission
that's become terrifyingly personal . . .

AND EXECUTIONER

At last, she is within his reach. All his victims
deserve their fate, but her guilt is greatest.
And with every scream, he will make her see
what it means to suffer and repent—
before she dies . . .

**Please turn the page for an exciting sneak peek of
Mary Burton's
BEFORE SHE DIES,
now on sale at bookstores everywhere!**

Prologue

He could pinpoint the day, the hour, even the second when he'd chosen his first kill. In that sacred moment, fear, rules, and consequences ceased to matter and long-nurtured fantasies elbowed aside judgment. The switch had been flipped. And a line would be crossed.

He raised his gaze to the blindfolded young girl tethered to the wooden chair. She was slumped forward, unconscious from the drugs he'd administered. A curtain of lush dark hair covered her pale oval face, cascaded over tight full breasts, and grazed a full waist and gently rounded hips. Not more than seventeen or eighteen, the girl worked at the carnival. She was the psychic. The seer. The seducer. For the average person she was a delightful diversion or a harmless amusement. But he was a rare breed, empowered with gifts that allowed him to see beyond her youth and beauty to the timeless evil.

The decision to kill her had come seven days ago when he'd visited her carnival tent. On that night, he'd patiently waited in the line that trailed outside her tent.

He'd been nervous, edgy, and still clueless that his life was about to change.

When he'd finally entered her domain, candles flickered in shadowed corners, soft music drained from unseen speakers, and the heavy scent of incense clung to the air. She'd been sitting behind a gilt desk and had worn a bright red flowing gypsy costume. A dark wig framed a lovely face half hidden by a black domino mask. He'd felt the rush of excitement as he'd stared at her and sat across the table from her.

"Madame Divine," he'd said.

Nodding, she turned his hand over and exposed his palm. "Yes."

"You look so young."

"Do not be fooled by my youth." Confidence dripped from each word as she traced his jagged lifeline.

He wasn't deceived. "I saw the line. You are quite popular."

Green eyes bore into him. "What is your question?"

Her abruptness stoked his anger but he was careful to keep it checked. "Did she love me?"

Nodding, Madame Divine traced another line on his palm. "I can answer that question for twenty dollars."

His skin tingled as he pulled his hand free, dug a rumpled twenty-dollar bill from his jeans pocket, and laid it on the velvet-draped table. She set the timer at her side before she again cradled his hand. Her skin was soft and warm. Sweet, subtle perfume drifted around her and mingled with the heavy stench of scented candles. She closed her eyes and asked the spirits for guidance.

As he stared at the delicate frown that creased her forehead, he imagined what it would be like to strip the clothes from her body and beat her until she wept. How would her voice sound when she begged? He imagined she'd beg, cry, and plead. And when he wrapped his fingers around her neck, how long would it take for the life and warmth to drain from her body? He wondered all these things as she traced the lifeline on his palm and spoke of prosperity and good fortune.

And then suddenly she straightened as if she'd been kicked by the Devil. Tension rippled through her fingers and her breathing grew shallow. She released his hand as if it had burned her flesh. She stared at him, fear glimmering in the green depths.

In this panicked moment, he *knew* that she saw his true intent.

The realization rattled him. No one had ever seen beyond his veneer. She was a true seer. A witch.

She was The One that God wanted him to kill.

"Are you okay?" he said.

"Yes. Yes. I'm fine." She moistened her lips. "Tell me about this woman you love."

He smiled, knowing he could be charming when it suited him. "We met at the university. We're in the same class."

"What's her name?"

"Carrie. I loved her very much. Why didn't she love me back?"

The predictable question coaxed some of the tension from her shoulders, and she eased forward a fraction. She smiled but he knew her fear, as visible as the sweat on her brow, lingered. "Carrie loves you, but she is afraid of . . . her emotions."

Despite his resolve to be strong, her soft voice speaking Carrie's name drew him in closer. He wanted to believe the woman had loved him. "She said she hated me."

"She doesn't hate you. She loves you. You must go to her and tell her that you care."

She spouted more nonsense about good fortunes and happiness, but when the timer buzzed, she immediately released his hand.

His open palm lingered. He yearned for her touch.

Emotions demanded he take her now. *Kill. Kill. Kill.* But logic kept him on a tight leash. *Wait. Prepare.*

And so he quietly left the tent and used the next week to prepare this room for her. She was his first kill and he wanted the details to be perfect.

On the seventh night after his reading, he'd waited in the shadows. When she returned from her whoring in town and ventured to the carnival bathroom by the wood's edge, he grabbed her and covered her mouth with his gloved hand. An injection in her arm had immediately rendered her silent and compliant. He easily dumped her in the trunk of his car and brought her to this hunter's cabin, nestled in the hollow of the Virginia woods.

Now moonlight streamed through the small windows and mingled with the glow of three lanterns. The only concession to luxury in the rough cabin was a water pump, which fed into a deep basin. Furnishings were limited to a long wooden table and a few straight-back chairs by an old soot-stained hearth. Those who inhabited this place were prepared for a monk's life, an idea that appealed to him.

Eagerness churned inside him. Too many years of fantasizing and dreaming were about to become reality, and it was hard to maintain control. His skin tingled. His stomach clenched. If he didn't soon unleash the raw energy brimming inside him, he'd go insane.

Unable to wait for her to awaken, he grabbed a bucket of cold water and poured it on her face. She awoke cussing, screaming, and sputtering. The hint of panic behind her screams enhanced his excitement. He stared at her silk blouse, now wet and plastered to full, full breasts.

Breathless, his own muscles aching with want, he retreated to the cabin's corner and sat down. He'd not expected so much desire. He'd always considered himself a chaste and prudent man, but she made him crave dark, evil passions.

Anticipation burned through his body, and he knew if he didn't rein in his desires, he'd break his covenant with God.

She must confess and be purified first.

As she coughed, he muttered a prayer for patience. Retrieving the small Bible from his pocket, he gently kissed the gold cross embossed into the well-worn black leather. The Bible had been a gift from his mother on his tenth birthday. Though not fancy or substantial in size, the book provided him with answers, insights, and in times of stress, it was a guiding force.

With trembling fingers, he flipped through the pages, scanning and rereading passages. As he focused on the words, he suddenly felt her gaze through the blindfold. Her head was tipped back and cocked in his direction. Water dripped from her hair and face over a gold chain and down between the cleavage of her breasts.

Tied up, cold and wet, she should have been contrite and scared, but instead she possessed a dark, brooding bearing that unsettled him. He didn't like her absence of fear.

"Don't stare at me," he said.

She shook her head. "I'm blindfolded. I can't see anything."

"You are looking at me."

"So what if I am?" Her voice was rusty, seductive.

"You are Satan's child."

She actually smiled. "So I've been told."

Fury scraped at his nerves. He crossed the room and grabbed a fistful of her hair. He pulled a knife from his back pocket and pressed it to her neck so she could feel the sharp tip. Her jugular pulsed under the blade.

He was a half second from slicing her throat when reason shoved its way to the front of his mind. "I need you to confess your sins to God so you can be released from this earth clean and pure."

A defiant set to her jaw said as much as her words. "The clean and pure days are long gone for me." The girl's tone resonated a lifetime of experience.

"I need your confession. I need to send you to God pure."

"Then I guess it's your bad day." She cocked her head. "I know you."

This close, he could smell the hint of a spicy, no longer sweet perfume mingling with the stale scent of the threadbare gypsy costume. He turned her face roughly to the side so the lantern light caught the high slash of cheekbones. She was pretty, but she possessed a callous aura that would grow more insensitive with time. By thirty, she'd be washed up and spent.

Why had she seemed so different a week ago?

"It's just you and me, baby," she whispered. "Why don't we play instead of fight? Some boys like to play rough but I promise gentle is better."

The grip in her hair tightened. "Don't call me baby."

She reminded him of a cat toying with a mouse. "Why not? I'm good and you'll like what I can do for you."

Tempted by her honeyed words, he dropped his gaze to her breasts, so round and full. He ached to touch and suckle them. The balance of power was shifting. "Shut up."

"Be my baby, and then I promise you'll forget all about this cabin."

He pulled her hair until she cried out. "Whore. Harlot."

Tears of pain, not fear, ran down under the blindfold's creases over her cheeks. "Baby, just take me. You know I'll be good. I'm always good." She had enough range of motion in her bound hand to brush his jean-clad thigh with her fingertips.

The faint touch sent an explosion of sensation through him and immediately he grew hard. Honeyed words, as sweet as a siren's call, tested his resolve and summoned him to temptation's edge. Though he was the one with power over life and death, she'd somehow mesmerized him with her soul-stealing features and a simple touch.

"You don't have to hurt me, baby," she said. "We can be good together. Untie me and you'll see."

"Do you think I'm stupid?"

"No." Her supple lips belied the word. "But we better get busy before someone catches us."

It was his turn to smile. "No one is going to bust in on us. Only a handful know about this cabin, and those that do wouldn't bother with a visit until deer season." He stroked her hair. "And that is still weeks away."

She moistened cracked, dried lips and this time a faint tremor rippled under her words. "Kiss me. I know you want to kiss me."

And God help him but he did. He'd dreamed about taking her since he'd first seen her seven nights ago. It had taken repeated razor cuts to his thighs and belly to keep himself chaste and controlled until the right moment.

He leaned forward and tasted her rosy lips. They were soft, salty, and before he thought, he greedily cupped her full breast in his smooth palm. He squeezed her nipple until she wimpered. He grew harder and fantasized about releasing her bindings and taking her. Perhaps he could keep her a few weeks in the special box under the floorboards where he hid his toys. There she'd be safe, secured, and always at the ready to play. Maybe given more time, this Delilah could be cleansed and sent to God pure and clean.

And then in the distance he heard the Voice, summoning him back to his path.

"She is a witch. She will steal your soul if you give yourself to the temptations of the flesh."

He jerked back and stepped away from her. He swiped his mouth with the back of his hand.

She must have sensed his panic because her smile radiated arrogance. "It's okay, baby. You can love me. Let me free, and I'll show you what real fun can be."

He'd dreamed and fantasized about killing. He'd chosen his victim. He'd planned. And now, when he should follow through, he was faltering. What was wrong with him? He backed away from her, snatched up his Bible, muttered random prayers, and reminded himself that he was a soldier of God. "I am not weak. I am stronger than your temptations."

She moistened cracked, dried lips. "Let me love you, baby. Let me love you. You don't even have to take the blindfold off."

He set down the Bible. "'Thou shalt not suffer a witch to live.'"

Scorn pulsed from her. "I love you, baby. I just need you to unchain me so I can show you."

"You are a sinner. You need to confess." His voice, roughened by desire, was unrecognizable.

"I have nothing to confess."

"We are all sinners, baby." She again moistened her lips, and shifted her body so her breasts gently bounced.

His erection throbbed.

He pressed his hands to the fresh cuts he'd made to his chest that morning. Pain seared his senses, and for a moment he struggled with his breath as the desire leaked from his body. "'Thou shalt not suffer a witch to live. Thou shalt not suffer a witch to live.'"

The words from Exodus rolled off his tongue, again and again, half statement and half prayer. He'd been born to destroy the wicked, not be drawn in by their earthly temptations.

His own blood dampened the front of his white shirt and his hands now. In the moonlight, the blood had darkened from red to black. He smeared it on the woman's forehead, mingling his blood with her own. The scent and smell of their blood was sweet, indeed.

He turned and moved to the pump and bucket in the corner. He cranked the pump's lever until the water spat and then flowed free.

She turned her head toward the water. "What are you doing, baby?"

He filled the bucket and transported it to a long metal tub near the woman. He repeated this process until the tub was full and brimming with water.

His fingers fumbled at her wrists. "It's time to play."

"Good," she said. "You'll be glad. We'll be good together."

Hefting her slight form, he carried her toward the tub and forced her to her knees. He grabbed a shock of her hair and dangled her face above the water's rippling surface.

"What are you doing?" Bravado could no longer hide her terror.

"Confess and be free of your sins."

"Confess what?"

He shoved her face into the cold water, savoring the way her body flailed and squirmed. Only when he saw bubbles rise to the surface did he draw her head back. She coughed and sputtered and gripped the edge of the tub with trembling fingers.

"Are you ready to confess?"

Wet strands of black hair draped her face as she coughed, sputtered, and tried to pull free.

She screamed.

The sound ricocheted off the log walls and swirled in the air above his head. "No one can hear."

Her cries slowed and stopped. "Why are you doing this? I've done nothing wrong."

He shoved her face so close to the water's edge the tip of her nose touched it. "You know why, *Witch*."

She yanked at her bindings and shook her head. "Why do you keep calling me a witch? I'm not a witch!"

He shoved her face in the water, counted to thirty, and then lifted it. She coughed and gagged. "I saw you coming out of the sorceress's tent tonight at the carnival. You held my hand a week ago and spouted your evil."

She jerked her head and tried to break his hold. "We're just stupid carnies. The fortune-telling is just for fun."

"You read palms. You do the devil's work."

Her black, thick hair clung to her face like a spider's web. "You know it's all bullshit. None of that stuff is real. It's all a show. An act."

He loomed over her. "You were right about too many things."

"I'm good at the game. One of the best. But there's no magic." She shook her head. "People pay us a few bucks and we tell you a little about yourself. No magic. It's bull-shit."

This time he held her face under water for the count of forty-five. "Liar. Heretic."

She gagged and rolled her head to the side, frantically coughing and expelling the water from her mouth and lungs. "You want me," she said. "I feel it. Let me make you feel better."

"I don't want you anymore."

"You do!" Bitterness tangled around the words.

Defiance still lingered in her rusty voice as her face loomed over the water's edge. It made sense that she would be strong. She'd been raised among the carnival people, traveling demons that moved from town to town.

This time when he shoved her head under the water, he held it there until her body stopped flailing and went limp. When all the fight had leeched from her body, he jerked her free and turned her on her side to allow the water to drain free. He checked her pulse, and when he felt that it had stopped, he panicked. "She needs to confess."

He tipped her head back and started mouth to mouth. After several chest compressions, she inhaled sharply. She vomited water from her lungs.

He ripped off her blindfold. He wanted to see her eyes. He wanted her to see his face.

Contrition. It was the first step toward salvation.

"Why are you doing this to me? Please." Her voice sounded hoarse and raw.

He leaned forward and brushed the wet hair off her face. Her skin felt cold, clammy. "What are you sorry for?"

Vibrant green eyes bore into him. "Whatever I did, I'm sorry. Just don't punish me anymore."

Again, her gaze caught him off guard. It lured him in as it had before and made him want to forget about crusades and righteousness. He simply wanted to sink inside her warmth. As he'd dreamed of so many times, he kissed her gently on the lips and smoothed hair from her eyes. "If you don't know what you did, then how can you be sorry?"

Renewed panic replaced the silent pleas. "You called me a witch."

He'd never deny that she was a smart, clever girl. "I did."

She licked her lips. "You're not the first. Other men have said I bewitched them."

He traced his hand over her flat belly. The idea of other men staring and leering at her troubled him. She was his and his alone. "So you admit you are a witch, a sorceress, a stealer of souls? I wouldn't be driven to this if it weren't for your magic."

Her gaze remained locked on his as she laid her hand on his. "Yes. I'm a witch and whatever else you said."

He tightened his fingers on her breast and squeezed. She winced but continued to smile. This one understood the powers of her body and how best to wield them. "And you repent? You swear that you are evil?"

"Yes."

For a moment he laid his head between her breasts and listened to the rapid thump, thump of her heart. "Praise be."

"Let me go," she said. "I won't tell. I won't. And I can still make you feel real good. I swear."

He closed his eyes. "After what I just did to you, you still want me?"

"Yes. I want you. Just us, baby, no one else."

He still longed to suckle her breasts and shove inside her softness. As he lifted his eyes and prayed for strength, his gaze settled on the cracked mortar sandwiched between the logs of the cabin's wall. He likened the mortar to his own soul. Flawed and damaged, it was still strong enough to carry the burden. With trembling fingers, he combed her hair back. She stared up at him, vulnerable, scared, and ready.

Before he could surrender to temptation, he shoved her head under the water. She fought him, straining and twisting her body as her fists flailed. She tried to kick him with her feet, but he used his weight to render her immobile. Slowly, he counted away the seconds until her struggles lessened and she stopped fighting. Bubbles gurgled to the surface and still he held her face firmly under the water until the three-minute mark.

This time when he released her, her body slumped to the dirty floor, pale, cold, and dead. "Go with God, Grace."